the ONION®

AD NAUSEAM

COMPLETE NEWS ARCHIVES • VOLUME 13

the ONION®
AD NAUSEAM

COMPLETE NEWS ARCHIVES • VOLUME 13

EDITED BY
Robert Siegel

WRITTEN BY
Robert Siegel, Carol Kolb, Todd Hanson,
John Krewson, Maria Schneider, Tim Harrod,
Mike Loew, Joe Garden, Chris Karwowski, Rich Dahm

GRAPHICS BY
Mike Loew, Chad Nackers

DESIGNED BY
David Garcia, Paul Bonifacic

ADDITIONAL MATERIAL BY
Dave Sherman, Peter Koechley, Ben Wikler,
Josh Greenman, Dan Guterman, Barry Julien,
Ian Dallas, Kurt Luchs, Tom Scharpling, Stu Wade

COPY EDITOR
Stephen Thompson

MADE POSSIBLE BY
Peter Haise

SPECIAL THANKS
Ken Artis, Brian Belfiglio, Christine Carlson,
Chris Cranmer, Scott Dikkers, Dan Friel, Daniel Greenberg,
Annik LaFarge, Lindsay Mergens, David Miner, Michael O'Brien,
Philip Patrick, Keith Phipps, Nathan Rabin, Tasha Robinson,
Steve Ross, Dorianne Steele, Scott Templeton, Andrew Welyczko

THREE RIVERS PRESS • NEW YORK

PHOTO CREDITS

p. 1, Doorway, Hodgkin's; p. 4, Ass; p. 5, Richardson; p. 7, Bread, School; p. 8, Girl; p. 10, Chicken; p. 13, Voter, Magazine, Grave; p. 15, Bratzke, Turpin; p. 16, Girlfriend, Group; p. 25, Rabbit, Teen, Parents; p. 28, Bus, Door; p. 31, Dogs; p. 32, Cellini; p. 43, Diorama, Krueger, Bergkamp; p. 46, Family; p. 49, Bucket, Linder; p. 53, Aufiero; p. 55, Winner, TV, Employee; p. 56, Employees; p. 59, Gund; p. 61, Germs, Register; p. 62, Award; p. 67, Signs; p. 69, Christians, College; p. 73, Tissue; p. 77, Harroway; p. 79, Man, Guy; p. 85, Blaine; p. 86, Sharpe; p. 91, Twister, Turnbee; p. 93, Ketchup; p. 97, Toe, Starbucks; p. 98, Watch; p. 103, Letter, Truck, Cereal; p. 105, Cord; p. 109, Phone Book; p. 115, Action Figures; p. 121, Grill, Guy, Accountants; p. 139, Plate, Broskowski; p. 141, Friends; p. 145, Site; p. 148, McIntosh; p. 153, Mom; p. 154, Kaner; p. 157, Jacket, Laid-off, Friends; p. 158, Todd; p. 163, Pistone; p. 165, Slacks; p. 166, Streeter; p. 169, Protesters, Metzler; p. 175, Bottle Cap; p. 181, Ganser, Exposer; p. 182, Olson; p. 187, Gum; p. 193, Cashier; p. 195, God; p. 196, Chalkboard; p. 201, Branch; p. 205, Realtor; p. 206, Krouse; p. 208, Parker; p. 211, Cat; p. 212, Hobish; p. 217, Shirtless, Dittman, Store; p. 219, Hutchins; p. 223, Cheer, Door, Melchner; p. 227, Grocks; p. 229, *Guys Gone Wild*; p. 231, Lovers; p. 243, Pivarniks, McClary; p. 244, Coke; p. 245, Paul; p. 247, Browsing, Livorno; p. 249, Link; p. 250, Lisowitz; p. 253, Toastables, Buttons, Dansby, Moreland; p. 257, Green; p. 259, Plant, Kaminowitz; p. 260, McDonald's; p. 261, Groznic: Chad Nackers/Onion Photos. p. 1, Playboy Mansion: AFP. p. 1, Kissinger: Jason Kirk/Getty. p. 2, Schwantes; p. 9, Nisley; p. 25, Shoes; p. 26, Renfro; p. 38, Kempner; p. 53, Bingham; p. 60, Bag; p. 61, Paschal; p. 90, Sake; p. 224, Britt and Kass; p. 230, Leff: Mike Loew/Onion Photos. p. 6, Brooks; p. 241, Employee; p. 264, Shirts: Tim Boyle/Getty. p. 7, Korman: Jonathan Alcorn/Zuma Press. p.7, p. 11, Stern; p. 12, McMahon; p. 36, Scooters; p. 137, Carty: Ezio Peterson/UPI. p. 13, Bush: Kevin Coombs/Reuters. p. 13, Gore; p. 258, Billboard: Lucy Nicholson/AFP. p. 18, Wal-Mart: Billy Suratt/Getty. p. 19, Police: Mike Nelson/AFP. Explosion: HO/Reuters. p. 23, Bush; p. 259, Bush: Paul J. Richards/AFP. p. 25, p. 30, Grinch: R. Batzdorff/Universal Studios/Zuma. p.47, Enthusiasts: Robert Padgett/Reuters. p. 48, Madonna; p. 163, Ben Stiller; p. 247, Diesel: Chris Weeks/Getty. p. 50, Soldiers: Sean Cayton/Getty. p. 55, Cabinet: Archive Photos. p. 57, Party; p. 109, Prairie Dogs; p. 244, Boone: Carol Kolb/Onion Photos. p. 61, Manson: Margaret Grey. p. 63, Manson: Chris Martinez/Reuters. p. 66, McCartney: Peter Kramer/UPI. p. 71, Lava Lamp: David Harrison/Index Stock Imagery. p. 67, Clinton: David Scull/Getty. Assassination Attempt: Regan Library/Reuters. p. 72, Dion: Darrin Bush/UPI. p. 75, Homicide: Mark Milstein/Zuma Press. p. 76-77, Valentines; p. 148-149, Victorian Greeting Cards; p. 199, Popeye; p. 209, Sleepyland; p. 221, How To Tell If You Were Adopted: Maria Schneider/Onion Graphics. p. 79, Pitt: Chris Delmas/Zuma. p. 84, McVeigh: Bob Daemmerich/AFP. p. 85, Bush: Paul J. Richards/AFP. p. 87, Deforestation: Steven Holt/Picture Desk Photos. p. 90, FBI: Alex Wong/Getty. p. 91, McMahon: Tom Hauk/Allsport Photos. p. 97, p. 98, p. 102, Lopez: Scott Gries/Notimex. p. 103, De Niro: Javier Echezarreta/AFP. p. 109, Miners: STR/Reuters. p. 115, Elfman: Laura Farr/Getty. p. 115, Recovery Unit: Mike Segar/ Reuters. p. 116, Dashboard: William Jordan/Zuma. p. 118, Kennedy: Bob Strong/AFP. p. 120, Mickey Mouse; p. 133, Gays; p. 134, Leatherdaddies; p. 144, Strike; p. 183, Pump; p. 210, CNN: David McNew/Getty. p. 121, Teacher: Paul Harris/Getty. p. 122, Jeff Haynes/AFP. p. 127, Dinner: Peter Muhly/AFP. p. 129, Iggy Pop: Bob Foy/Getty. p. 132, Lambs: Vincent Boon/Reuters. p. 133, Crash: Rex B. Cordell/KRT. p. 133, Zemin: STR/Reuters. p. 142, Baucus: Business Wire. p. 145, Bush: Jana Birchum/GAMMA/Zuma. p. 145, Jameson/Nancy Kaszerman/Zuma. p. 151, Amway: Alexander Fedorets/AFP. p. 151, Ashcroft; p. 190, Jordan: William Philpott/Reuters. p. 151, Allen: Andy Hayt/NBA Photos. p. 151, SUV: KRT. p. 156, Olympics; p. 205, Yacht: Frederic M. Brown/AFP. p. 157, Destiny's Child: Big Pictures/Zuma. p. 157, Bush: Eric Draper/UPI. p. 159, Wal-Mart: David Perry/KRT. p. 162, *Pearl Harbor*: KRT. p. 169, Chili's; p. 199, The Weebles: Scott Templeton/Onion Photos. p. 171, Asses: Richard B. Levine. p. 175, Jenna Bush: Larry Downing/Reuters. p. 176, Protest: Oka Budhi/AFP. p. 176, Shooting: Laszlo Balogh/Reuters. p. 180, Princess Diana: Jamal A. Wilson/Getty. p. 181, Carey: Archive Photos. p. 184, *Planet Of The Apes*: Sam Emerson/20th Century Fox/Zuma. p. 187, Protest: Kim Kulish/AFP. p. 190, Reparations: Jon Levy/AFP. p. 193, Allen: Steve W. Grayson/Getty. p. 196, Jackson: Arnaldo Maganani/Liaison/Getty. p. 199, Arby's: Robert King/Getty. p. 202, Brokaw; p. 204, Clinton: Spencer Platt/Getty. p. 205, Mathers: Franklin Berger/Zuma. p. 205, Manatee: Frank Staub/Index Stock Imagery. p. 205, Laura Bush: Reuters. p. 207. Mathers and Dow: Archive Photos. p. 211, Bush: Alissa Kempler/UPI. p. 213, Pharmacy: Rebecca Cook/Reuters. p. 215, Chimp: William West/AFP. p. 215, Hawking: AFP. p. 217, Ashcroft: Chris Corder/UPI. p. 222, Helms: Ian Wagreich/UPI. p. 223, Rappers: Contographer/Big PicturesUSA/Photographer Showcase. p. 225, Trekkies: EFE. p. 228, Euro: Sean Gallup/Getty. p. 235, Hugging: Joe Raedle/Getty. p. 235, WTC: STR/Reuters. p. 235, Bush: Getty. p. 235, Falwell: Richard Ellis/Getty. p. 240, Security: Alex Wong/Getty. p. 241, Library: Chris Martinez/La Opinion Photos. p. 241, Spears: Timothy A. Clary/AFP. p. 241, Cruise and Cruz: Fred Prouser/Reuters. p. 241, Condit: Mark Wilson/Getty. p. 241, Jackson and Taylor: Star Max. p. 242, Lopez: Laura Cavanaugh/UPI. p. 246, Jordan: Mario Tama/AFP. Fleischer: Roger L. Wollenberg/UPI. p. 248, Goldberg: Icon Sports Photos. p. 248, Goldberg: Mary Ann Owen/Zuma. p. 252, *Enterprise*: Paramount. p. 253, Hope: David Keeler/Online USA, Inc./Getty. p. 253, Limbaugh: Getty. p. 259, Osama bin Laden: AFP. p. 261, Paul Drinkwater/NBC/Zuma. p. 262, Oil Rig: Greg Locke/Picture Desk Photos

This book uses invented names in all stories, except notable public figures who are the subjects of satire. Any other use of real names is accidental and coincidental.

Published by Three Rivers Press, New York, New York.
Member of the Crown Publishing Group, a division of Random House, Inc.
www.randomhouse.com

Three Rivers Press and the Tugboat design are registered trademarks of Random House, Inc.

Printed in the United States of America

Design by The Onion

Library of Congress Cataloging-in-Publication Data is available upon request.

ISBN 1-4000-4724-2

10 9 8 7 6 5 4

First Edition

AREA MAN AT DAWN WITH AX

Area Man woke one night to the sound of thunder. How far off, he sat and wondered. He rose from his bed and turned his clock around—before he lay down every night he aimed its rear speaker at his sleeping ear, to increase the odds it might shake him—and found the time: 4:30. Only an hour earlier than he usually got up, so, he thought, he might as well get a few things done. He descended the carpeted and stained stairs of his home, shared with his housemate Jeff, and opened the back door. He stepped onto the porch, its square posts rounded from paint applied in coats and without care, and found it wasn't raining. There was only the thunder without its truant sister lightning, the humidity of late July, and a sky like charred meat.

In the kitchen, he pulled his boots over his fraying longjohns and grabbed his jacket, denim with wool lining, and his work gloves, and left the house. His backyard needed its grass cut, and the long blades, a foot tall and soaked with dew, blackened his blond boots as he strode toward the hill. A frog leaped out of his way and shook the weeds to his right and continued leaping until a splash signaled its entry into the small pond dug by his father, twenty years ago, to approximate a swimming pool. Area Man came upon the shed to find its door ajar, indicating that Steve had borrowed something, probably the chain saw, and had neglected to lock up. He pulled the beaded line, the light sprung into the tiny room. The ax stood ready, upright and gleaming, and he wrapped his hand around its neck and pulled it up and free.

Area Man tugged the chain and returned the shed to darkness, locked its door, and continued around the path. He came upon the back gate, separating his property from the land owned by the city and zoned for new homes, lifted its latch, and passed through. The highway beyond the hill groaned and the thunder came again, still without rain or illumination.

Area Man had a lot on his mind and had been reading Camus; this combination had proven problematic. *If the only significant history of human thought were to be written, it would have to be the history of its successive regrets and impotences.* Myth of Sisyphus. How true was this? He wasn't sure. He knew only that his eyes had passed over those words at a point in his life when he was too susceptible to suggestion, to this kind of summary and aphorism. This sentence, amid the book's first section, about absurdity and suicide, was sticking to him like something tarry but alive. It articulated a malaise that now he wished had gone unspoken.

Tramping up the path and over the hill, he could now see the highway, busy with trucks, full of purpose—at the end of a run, at the beginning of a run, in the middle of a task that had to be completed. Area Man lacked this kind of mission. Descending the hill toward the meadow below, he framed his own life within the statement—*history of its successive regrets and impotences*—and almost nothing he could conjure contradicted its conclusion, its dim implications. Yes, he had had his triumphs, small victories. He had, one cool March day last year, actually eaten all he could eat at that steakhouse with the onomatopoeic name. He'd gotten his money's worth that night, and that granted him a satisfaction that lasted days. But when else had he been given, or brought to himself, that kind of contentedness? He could go farther into the past to find bright spots, but why bother? Recent history was more important, and recent history seemed crowded with moments of impotence, when success or joy or moments of even small and temporary glory seemed attainable—but then he'd failed to grasp them. Another moment came to him. At work he'd been given a new mop-head, and this had sent his heart galloping, so strong was his pleasure at seeing it, snow-white and virginal. He'd been asking for a new mop-head for so long, being unable to truly clean any surface with tendrils so brown and rank, and finally it had come. "Merry Christmas," his boss had said, and he did, strangely, feel that kind of elation. But then, just as quickly, came shame: Who was Area Man, to feel joy at the sight of a new mop-head? What kind of fool was he?

Ax in hand, he came upon the Morris home, the first house built in this new subdivision, replacing the meadow that stood here, for about half a mile, throughout Area Man's childhood. As befitting a neat and tidy family, the Morris home was sturdy and of a size that spoke of great comfort without the sin of pride. The path wound close to the home, and Area Man peered into the window, seeing the darkened living room, with its television, ensconced in a large oak cabinet and its perfectly wired stereo below, surrounded by discs and books. The coffee table with magazines, stacked with crisp corners, and the colorful building blocks of the Morris kids, Andrew and Molly, six and eight. Who the hell were the Morrises? New people. Familiar people, but new people. The Morrises knew who they were. Their certainty was never questioned. Everything they did and owned spoke of confidence. But yet—did they know their own hearts? Surely they knew, or perhaps knew only that they would never know... or, more likely, never wondered in the first place. This, above all, separated Area Man from these people, with their gleaming chandeliers and plates, Dutch and immaculate, arranged above the mantle. His grip on the ax, which he realized was tight and desperate, loosened with his sigh, and he walked on.

I can sketch one by one all the aspects it is able to assume, all those likewise that have been attributed to it, this up-

bringing, this origin, this ardor or these silences, this nobility or vileness. But aspects cannot be added up. This very heart which is mine will forever remain indefinable to me. What did Area Man know about himself? He knew he grew up here, in this brown brick town, twenty-six minutes from the city around which all of this had been built and was being built, each town different only in name—and even then, each title an uninspired combination of River, Glen, Oak, Elm, Field, Ford, Hurst, and Burg. He knew his father and mother watch over him from their new home in Florida and have granted him this, the right to watch over the house he grew up in and to take in boarders for extra money. He knew his job, four days a week cleaning at Hamilton's, a midscale eatery on the highway, keeps him interested enough—the camaraderie there seems real—but, then again, leaves him feeling undernourished.

Area Man came to the clearing in the meadow where the developers had been stacking the trees chainsawed to make way for the new homes. Area Man had made an arrangement with the builders, that if they sawed the logs into two-foot segments, he'd make them into firewood, and they'd split the money. He'd been doing this for months, and the work was lucrative enough and brought air into his lungs. This day, there was plenty to be done. At least four great maples had been felled, and they lay before him, strewn out on the dirt, ready to be quartered.

And here are trees, and I know their gnarled surface, water and I feel its taste. These scents of grass and stars at night, certain evenings when the heart relaxes—how shall I negate this world whose power and strength I feel? He felt it only when he raised his ax above the round tree segments and divided them. He swung the ax over his head, as he'd done so many thousands of times before, and let it drop, guiding it and tugging it earthward, until it struck the middle of the log, momentarily pausing but then cleaving it, like a wave pauses on the shore before spreading itself over it.

Yes, he had moments when he thought beyond this land, the mile or so around his bed, where he spent most of his time, most of his life. He had flashes, bizarre and galloping visions of himself as something more, as someone whose daily activities would mean something to someone else. What if someone, somewhere, cared about, could read about, his encounter with his new mop-head? Would this give meaning to his own world, or further prove its lack thereof? He chose to believe that it would bring not only clarity to his own minutes, but—he let his head babble on with possibility—there could be thousands or even millions who would read about the things he'd done, however trivial, and would take from them some kind of meaning. His movements would inspire others! Why not meaning, for example from his mop-head? In his existence others might see elements of their own! Perhaps his work, making Hamilton's gleam, and perhaps his home, shared with Jeff, whose room had a smell that was only Jeff's, would become, in the eyes of others, heroic. Others, from Phoenix to Crystal Lake, would look to him for hope, a kind of leadership, and in his example guide their own lives. They would watch him, read about him—him, Area Man!—and perhaps in their collective watching, in their interest in the small and smallest moments of his life, he might achieve a kind of definition—that is, the space between them and him, between his life and their eyes, might define him, as water fills the space between and everywhere defines the borders of continents.

Area Man paused, his ax resting on his shoulder, and listened to his breathing, even and strong. Finally there was light, a thin blue shoelace laid across the horizon. It would be morning soon, and he, Area Man, thank the Lord for him, had work to do.

Dave Eggers
St. Petersburg, Russia
June 2002

'Decision 2000' Actually Made In Smoke-Filled Room In 1997

see NATION page 3A

Local Man's Body A Really Big Temple

see LOCAL page 10C

Anna Nicole Smith Awarded $450 Million In Nonagenarian-Fucking Fees

see PEOPLE page 2D

STATshot

A look at the numbers that shape your world.

What Is Our Favorite New CBS Show?

0%	Yes, Dear
0%	Welcome To New York
0%	That's Life
0%	CSI: Crime Scene Investigation
0%	Bette
0.001%	The Fugitive
0%	The District

0 74470 94595 6
38

---

the ONION®

VOLUME 36 ISSUE 38   AMERICA'S FINEST NEWS SOURCE™   26 OCTOBER–1 NOVEMBER 2000

Half-Naked Kissinger Thrown Out Of *U.S. News & World Report* Mansion

Left: Kissinger socializes with a trio of *U.S. News & World Report* Copy Girls hours before the outburst. Above: The fabled mansion.

WASHINGTON, DC—Another chapter was added to the infamous history of the *U.S. News & World Report* Mansion Saturday, when celebrity politico Henry Kissinger, former Secretary of State and long-time fixture at the journalism and pleasure palace, was forcibly removed from the premises after removing his pants and drunkenly plummeting from a second-story balcony into a pool.

"Hank is a longtime friend of the mansion, and the events of last weekend won't change that," said *U.S. News & World Report* editor-in-chief Mort Zuckerman, speaking to reporters in the mansion's jungle-themed Southeast Asian Correspondent Room. "He just had a few too many Harvey Wallbangers, and we had to send him home. Nobody knows how to go off the deep end like the Kiss-Man."

see MANSION page 4

School 'Fine,' U.S. Teens Report

WASHINGTON, DC—According to results of a survey released Monday by the Department Of Education, most U.S. teenagers characterize their education as "fine."

The survey, conducted by the Office of Educational Research and Improvement (OERI), polled more than 2,000 public-school atten-

EDUCATION WATCH

dees between the ages of 14 and 18. The students were asked a wide variety of questions about their educational experience, ranging from the subjects they were studying to their feelings about homework, to what they had for lunch that day.

To the question, "How was

see SCHOOL page 5

Man With Hodgkin's Disease Way Over Sick-Day Limit

PULASKI, TN—Atco Tool & Design machinist Richie Loftus, diagnosed four months ago with Hodgkin's Disease, has already exceeded his allotted number of sick days for the year, his employers warned Monday.

"It's unfortunate, what's happening with Richie, but company policy clearly states that employees are permitted 15 sick days per year," Atco Tool & Design office manager Mike Phelan said. "Richie's already missed a month and a half of work since June. You just can't run a business that way."

Loftus, 32, admitted that his constant fever, crippling fatigue, and malignant splenomegaly has affected his job performance.

"I've definitely missed my share

of days," said Loftus, diagnosed with Stage III Hodgkin's lymphoma on June 20 after a steady decline in health prompted a biopsy. "I've tried to keep my chemotherapy sessions down to just one a week so I don't have to drop down to part-time at Atco and lose my health coverage, but it's been tough."

Though Loftus used a majority of his sick days after the diagnosis, Phelan noted that he had not been a paragon of regular attendance beforehand.

"By the time Richie went in for his tests in late June, he had already missed a heck of a lot of work," said Phelan, leafing through Loftus' personal file. "In fact, the week before the disease even start-

Above: Loftus rests at home after radiation therapy, putting him even further over the sick-day limit.

ed, he was out for three days because of headaches, nausea, and vomiting."

"And even when he was here,"

see HODGKIN'S page 4

1

U.S. Leads World In Mexican-Food Availability

UNITED NATIONS—According to a U.N. report released Monday, for the 16th straight year, the U.S. ranks first in the world in Mexican-food availability. "America boasts an unrivaled abundance of Mexican food, producing 23 billion pounds of tacos, enchiladas, and burritos in 1999," the report read. "No other nation on Earth can claim such plenty with regard to beans-and-rice-based Mexican fare." Japan ranked second, with the top five rounded out by Canada, Mexico, and the United Kingdom.

Congressman Picked Last For Committee On Youth Fitness

WASHINGTON, DC—U.S. Rep. David Bonior (D-MI), an awkward, unpopular legislator from Michigan's 10th District, was picked last for the new House Committee On Youth Fitness Monday. "I didn't even want to be on that dumb committee," said Bonior after being made the final pick by Rep. J.C. Watts Jr. (R-OK), the committee's athletic, well-liked chairman. "I'm only doing it because I have to be on one more committee to get full credit for this term." Bonior reportedly stood at the front of the House floor during the selection process, trying to be noticed.

Filmmakers Call Vincent Canby's Life Overlong, Poorly Paced

NEW YORK—The life of Vincent Canby, the longtime *New York Times* senior film critic who died last week at 76, is being called "an overlong, poorly paced mess" by filmmakers. "Mr. Canby's life builds glacially, taking an excruciating 21,549,600 minutes to reach the part in which he finally begins writing for the *Times*," said director Roland Joffé, whose 1986 film *The Mission* was panned by Canby as "a singularly lumpy sort of movie." "The life then completely falls apart in its final third, with Canby retiring in the most anticlimactic manner possible before an inevitable death scene as awash in bathos as any you're likely to see."

Woman Feels Guilty After Switching Brands

RUTLAND, VT—Area resident Teresa Grant was plagued by feelings of guilt Monday after buying a box of Snuggle fabric softener, ending years of unswerving brand loyalty to Downy. "I remember my mother using Downy when I was a toddler," a distraught Grant said. "It's just that I got a trial size of Snuggle in the mail and, well, I kind of preferred the smell." Grant added that, while taking the Snuggle box from the supermarket shelf, she strove not to make eye contact with the baby on the Downy bottle.

Retiree Purchases Recliner He'll Eventually Die In

DADE CITY, FL—Retiree Chuck Leyner, 66, treated himself Monday to a La-Z-Boy Cardinal Reclina-Rocker chair, in which he will die of heart failure approximately eight years from now. "Oh, this is gonna be so great to watch football in," Leyner said of the attractive, comfortable death recliner, boasting five leg settings and a luxuriously padded back which will absorb the shock of his final death throes. "This thing is gonna last for the rest of my life."

Sharon Stone To Star In Major Backstage Drama

HOLLYWOOD, CA—*Daily Variety* reported Monday that Sharon Stone will star in a major backstage drama on the set of the upcoming Barry Levinson film *This Charming Man*. "Look for Ms. Stone to electrify onlookers throughout the Paramount Pictures lot with her gripping performance as a star outraged that some wardrobe-department nobody keeps knocking on her trailer when she's trying to get into character," *Daily Variety*'s Peter Bart wrote in his Back Lot column. The Stone scene is expected to generate major buzz in Paramount studio head Sherry Lansing's office. ∅

My Brother Is Going To Love This Forwarded List Of Lawyer Jokes

I've got a question for you: How do you tell when a lawyer is lying? His lips are moving!

That's just one of the countless great zingers on this list of lawyer jokes my wife's friend Kate forwarded to me yesterday. Luckily, I'm on Kate's e-mail forward list, so whenever she gets something funny, I'm sure to get it, along with the 30 or so other people on her list. In turn, I always make sure to forward the stuff I get to people I think would appreciate it—like my brother Jim!

By Steve Schwantes

There are about 200 lawyer jokes on this latest list. I haven't actually read them all; I just scrolled down a few pages. I did, however, make sure to forward them to my brother, because I figured he'd enjoy spending 30 to 40 minutes going through it. Same thing goes for the long list of golf jokes I forwarded him last week and the list of blonde jokes the week before.

> I haven't actually read them all. I did, however, make sure to forward them to my brother, because I figured he'd enjoy spending 30 to 40 minutes going through them.

Now, my brother isn't actually a lawyer. And I don't think he has any lawyer friends. And, as far as I know, he doesn't specifically have anything against lawyers. But who doesn't enjoy a few hundred good-natured jabs at lawyers every now and then? I mean, lawyers are like vultures. In fact, do you know the difference between a lawyer and a vulture? The lawyer gets frequent-flyer miles. Boy, my brother is going to love that one!

You know what? Something strange just occurred to me. Even though, for the past two years, I've faithfully forwarded stuff to Jim three or four times a week, he's never sent anything to me. Never. Not so much as one Lewinsky joke. Not one "You Know You're A Redneck If..." list. Not one "Wassssup!" parody. (Not even the one where the rabbis say "Shalom!" instead of "Wassssup!" Have you seen that one? It's hysterical!)

Jim e-mails me occasionally with a friendly message or to ask me a question, so I know his outgoing mail works. I guess his coworkers at the university are so out of the loop that no one sends them any funny stuff. Just between you and me, I once met some of them, and they did seem a little—how can I put this nicely?—brainy.

I've really worked up a good forwarding list of my own, about 25 people in all. Besides my brother and some other relatives, the list includes my wife, a bunch of her coworkers at the pet clinic, the people in my department at J&H Marketing, some of my old high-school buddies, my podiatrist, my insurance agent, and a few folks I met last year on a vacation to Yellowstone. There are also a few addresses on the list, like 753bc@globonet.com and mmbtinfo@yahoo.com, where I can't remember to whom they belong. Oh, well: Whoever they are, I'm sure they love constantly getting e-mailed funny stuff, like this latest list. Speaking of which, why won't sharks attack lawyers? Professional courtesy.

When you forward a mass-for-

see E-MAIL page 5

Around The World In One Paragraph

photo circa 1911

By T. Herman Zweibel
Publisher Emeritus

Yesterday in my bed-chamber, Nurse Pin-head opened the glass-doors to my private balcony to release the fetid cloud of odors, miasmas, and sour regrets which had built up over the past several weeks. But as soon as this poisonous atmosphere was expelled, my bed-chamber became contaminated with the cacophony of the out-side world. I could hear the milk-maids' buckets clatter, the cows lowing in the dell, and the indentured servant boy's tor-tured cries as he was being flogged. But punctuating this din was a sort of inane chattering, occasionally interrupted by a shrill cackle.

"What in thunder is all that whinnying?" I asked Pin-head.

"The Baintons are making last-minute preparations for their world-tour," she replied in her disquieting baritone.

The Baintons are my blue-blooded, old-money next-door neighbors. Their cretinous noises can be heard in Timbuctoo, so I should not have even posed such a stupid question. In fact, some days ago, Chauncey Bainton had burst into my bed-chamber uninvited to announce the news.

"What ho, Zweibel, old corpse!" he said. "Come Monday dawn, we set sail on our capital voyage across this scrumptious orb of ours! The old girl and I can't wait to sample the exotic fruits of the Orient, the Byzantine intrigues of Constantinople, the bazaars of Morocco, the splendor of the Siamese court, the wonders of..." The dolt continued on for seemingly an eternity, oblivious to the fact that I was trying to asphyxiate my-self with my own hands.

My only consolation is that the Baintons have finally vacated the area for a few months, leaving me some measure of peace. Now that they are gone, I must confess I could have saved them time and considerable expense, for in my youth I visited most of the nations of the world and quickly concluded that they are all pretty much the same, save for the color of their inhabitants' skin and the amount of hostility these inhabitants harbored toward me.

The following is all you need to know about the world: Africa is filled with Hottentots, and the services of an entire village are required just to raise one child, which is highly inefficient. The yellow hordes of the Far East may initially seem obsequious, but they would sooner bake you in a pie than submit to your authority. What the French lack in reason they make up for in sheer gall. I could go on, but I think you get the picture. The only thing breaking up the monotony is the odd volcano, and those don't erupt nearly as often as they should. ∅

Area Man Experimenting With Homosexuality For Past Eight Years

Above: Self-described "open-minded" heterosexual Michael Litwin.

LOUISVILLE, KY—Describing himself as "going through a little phase," 26-year-old heterosexual Michael Litwin has been experimenting with homosexuality for the past eight years.

"I'm a very open, curious person, and right now I'm in a bit of an exploratory phase, sexually," Litwin said. "The woman I marry will definitely have to be okay with my past."

Since first deciding to "open up and try new things" in 1992, the "99 percent straight" Litwin has had 23 male sexual partners and one female partner. And, though he said that "having a wife and kids and the house out in the suburbs with the white picket fence" is his eventual goal, Litwin is currently dating "a real mix of people."

"Before I do settle down with one woman for the rest of my life, it's important for me to 'do a little exploring,' so to speak," Litwin said. "And part of that process, for me, involves trying out some new things. Again, though, I must stress that it's temporary: Dating people of my own gender is not something I see myself doing in the long run."

Though Litwin has many gay friends and possesses "a certain appreciation for gay culture," he can't see himself in a permanent same-sex relationship.

"I just can't get used to the idea of only having sex with men," Litwin said. "The truth is, I simply adore women." As evidence of his attraction to women, Litwin pointed to the copy of the Madonna book *Sex* on his coffee table and a framed poster of Audrey Hepburn on the wall.

"I have absolutely nothing against homosexuality," Litwin added. "Some of my best friends are gay."

Of these friends, Litwin has had at least limited sexual contact with nearly all. Among them is Peter Skye.

"I met Michael at an art opening a few years back and, boy, did we hit it off," said Skye, 27, a waiter and part-time actor. "It's too bad he's not gay, because he was incredible in bed."

After dating Skye for seven months, Litwin ended the brief flirtation with homosexuality in favor of a period of experimentation with restaurateur Tyler Randolph. According to Litwin, he "sort of saw" Randolph on a strict "no promises" basis for two years.

"I was living in Chicago when Michael and I met at a party," Randolph said. "Right from the start, there was amazing chemistry between us. We started seeing each other every weekend. But eventually, the strain of the long-distance thing got to be too much. That's why we broke up. That and Michael's inability to keep his cock out of my roommate Bruce's mouth."

According to Litwin, he has only had one serious relationship in his life: a three-year romance with high-school sweetheart Jenny Tankart that ended during the pair's sophomore year of college.

"I simply haven't had enough experience to really know what I want yet," Litwin said. "What I do know is that I don't need to be seriously involved with anyone right now. I've really enjoyed being single all these years. I like having my own place, with my own TV and my own leather five-piece sectional. Things were just way too claustrophobic with Jenny."

Now married with children, Tankart looks back fondly on her relationship with Litwin.

"Michael was a really nice guy— and a real gentleman, too," Tankart said. "He was always very supportive about my wanting to wait until marriage. So many of the guys I used to date just wanted one thing. Not Michael."

Litwin said he has been searching for the right woman for years, but every time he thinks he has found "the one," something goes wrong.

"My first few dates with Rachel went great, but then I found out she has a dog," Litwin said. "Then there was Annette a few years later, but there was just something about the way she dressed that turned me off. And Julie was terrific, but she lived all the way over in the next town. I

see HOMOSEXUALITY page 6

Above: A passed-out Kissinger is sprawled across a mansion bathroom floor after vomiting. He would later awaken to stir up more trouble.

Sporting his trademark purple velvet smoking jacket and pipe, the smiling Zuckerman stressed that there were "no hard feelings" about the incident and joked that Kissinger was welcome back to his regular guest room at the mansion any time, "as long as the old boy can keep it in his pants next time."

The *U.S. News & World Report* Mansion has long been notorious for its wild parties. However, Saturday's gathering exceeded even its usual standards for debauchery. Former Clinton aide George Stephanopoulos was spotted poolside debating Social Security restructuring with leggy Fact-Checker Of The Month Caryn Alderson. Nearby, leather-clad Senate Republican Policy Committee chair Larry Craig (R-ID) stood atop the pool bar, challenging all comers to "try and beat me in arm-wrestling." An all-nude romp in the mansion's legendary Domestic Affairs Grotto included such journalistic luminaries as CBS anchor Dan Rather, *Weekly Standard* publisher William Kristol, and sultry, neoconservative MSNBC political analyst Laura Ingraham.

"It was like the fall of Rome," said historian and presidential biographer David Halberstam, who attended the party on the arm of former Clinton press secretary DeeDee Myers. "At one point, while everybody was circling the solid gold Party Globe in the Grand Newsroom in a conga line, poor Kissinger wiped out on a huge pile of AP-wire printouts that had col-

> ## "It was like the fall of Rome," said historian and presidential biographer David Halberstam, who attended the party on the arm of former Clinton press secretary DeeDee Myers.

lected in the sunken-fireplace pit by the gold statue of [*U.S. News & World Report* founder] David Lawrence. We thought he'd broken his neck, but in a flash, he was back on his feet and calling for 'more wine, more wine' in his unmistakable, German-accented, *basso profundo* voice. Then he shouted that he was 'more bombed than Cambodia in '73.'"

A short time later, a group of *U.S. News & World Report* Copy Girls, renowned for keeping the magazine free of errors and for their trademark skimpy outfits, formed a kickline as

former CIA director John Deutch treated the crowd to an improvisational blues jam paying tribute to the evening's guest of honor, former president George Bush. The jam was cut short when a pantless Kissinger burst through the kickline in full stride, diving through a large balcony window into a pool two stories below.

Bush, who at one point disappeared for a half-hour into the mansion's Velvet Typesetting Room with wife Barbara and CNN *Crossfire* co-host Mary Matalin, defended Kissinger's behavior.

"Kissinger—disco king, no doubt, no doubt. Did he do anything the rest of us wouldn't? I'd say not. Good man, the Kisser—knows how to get down," Bush told reporters from his guest room at the mansion, where he is recuperating from a "heckuva hangover." "Loves the wine? Sure, sure. Women? Song? No question there. But a good egg, and I'll stand by him."

Zuckerman defended his mansion and its parties, which have come under renewed fire in the wake of the latest incident.

"Some people may say that *U.S.*

News & World Report's commitment to incisive, cutting-edge news reportage, and all the fun that entails, is excessive or immoral," the 72-year-old Zuckerman said. "In fact, Calvin Trillin wrote a very critical piece in last week's *Time* about us—probably because he was mad he wasn't invited—but condemnations of the news-gathering lifestyle are both hypocritical and unenlightened. There's no reason reporting the news can't retain the fantasy element it had when we were in our teens and 20s. News should be informative, but also sexy and fun. That's always been my magazine's approach, and it's the only way to get unbiased, comprehensive coverage while remaining young at heart."

"Of course, a solid supply of Viagra and dating the Weinbaum triplets doesn't hurt," added Zuckerman, referring to Mindy, Cindy, and Windy Weinbaum, the three 22-year-old interns he has been dating since divorcing 1991 Copy Girl Of The Year Bobbi Brandt in April. "And now, if you'll excuse me, there's an 'event' that needs 'covering' in the Business & Technology Bungalow." ◢

Phelan continued, "he wasn't anywhere near as productive as we'd have liked, always needing to lay down in the breakroom. So we're not exactly talking about the most reliable employee to begin with."

Loftus said he has tried to make adjustments in his approach to the job, but it has been difficult.

"I've tried to find a way to get around this whole illness thing," said Loftus, resting on his living-room couch after a morning of radiation therapy. "Unfortunately, I don't have the kind of job where I can work from home, even if I had the energy and lucidity to do so. And even when I can make it into the shop, it's tough to work the machines, because these club fingers I've developed are just as ridden with subdural hemophilia as the rest of me. I feel terrible about being such a drain on AT&D."

Nearly broke, Loftus recently asked Atco Tool & Design management if he could take some of the 22 paid personal days and 31 vacation days he has accumulated during his six years with the company and use them as sick days. The request was denied.

"They said I couldn't do that, because that would open up a whole can of worms, with employees messing around and mixing up the different types of paid leave," Loftus said. "They did say, though, that I should feel free to use my vacation days and take a nice trip to Hawaii or somewhere—so long as I don't get any treatment while I'm there."

Added Loftus: "Hawaii probably wouldn't be much fun, anyway, what with this explosive diarrhea."

Loftus' expensive treatment is 80 percent covered by his employee health plan, a benefit that is costing Atco Tool & Design a significant amount of money.

"Richie's type of extended-illness coverage costs this company an extra $22 per employee

> ## "I feel for Richie, but I don't think anyone would hold him up as a model employee," Phelan said.

per month. That adds up. Not only that, but he goes through Cisplatin, Cytarabine, and Dexamethasone like they were going out of style," said Atco Tool & Design general manager Mel Huffinger. "And those drugs are not cheap, that's for sure. Richie would have to work here another 45 years without a single major illness for us to break even on him. And we all know that ain't gonna happen."

"I feel for Richie, obviously, but I don't think anyone would hold him up as a model employee," Phelan said. "He's a decent guy, and I hope he gets through this and becomes a healthy, productive worker again as soon as he can. But right now, he's hardly giving us incentive to hire Hodgkin's Disease sufferers in the future." ◢

My Baby Don't Want No Medicine

By Amber Richardson

I hate them doctors. They always talking a bunch of shit like they know so much, always trying to act all big and important, like they a movie star or something. That bitch Dr. Ennis be telling me I got to give Rywanda some stupid medicine when she ain't even sick. Fuck that shit. My baby don't want no medicine.

That pink shit nasty. I tried pouring it over Rywanda's lunch, but it just made the Fruit Loops all soggy, and she wouldn't eat it. Me and my baby got a trustful relationship, so when she tell me she don't want no medicine, I trust her that she got her reason.

I told Dr. Ennis that Rywanda don't wanna take that medicine, but she don't listen to me. She say I supposed to give it to her anyway. Dr. Ennis say Rywanda supposed to swallow a spoonful of that stank-ass shit every six hours.

That means I'm supposed to wake her up at night after she already sleeping. Hell, no.

Dr. Ennis don't know my baby. My baby smart, and when she don't wanna eat something, she tell you. And once she make up her mind that she don't wanna eat something, ain't no making her eat it. If you try, she just scream and cry and go all buckwild on your ass. She ain't gonna take no shit from nobody. I know she got that from me, 'cause I the same way.

That's why I hate it when them fuckin' punk-ass doctors try to tell me how to raise my baby. I don't go to they house and tell them how to raise they baby, do I? No, I don't.

I think I'm gonna call up and get a different doctor, one at the eastside clinic. At least that way, if I gotta take the bus over there, I'll be near the mall. But whichever clinic I go to, I gotta get rid of Dr. Ennis. I think she might be some kinda pervert, after some of the shit she wanna know about Rywanda. Like how many times Rywanda took a shit last week. Why she gotta know that? That's just nasty.

The only reason I went to see a doctor in the first place is because Debra, that fat old social-worker bitch, got all up in my grill about getting Rywanda some shots. Then, when I go in, they say Rywanda got something in her intestines and that's why her stomach so big. I'm like, her stomach so big 'cause she always eat like a pig! She always crawling up to the refrigerator and sitting there, waiting for me to open it up. Or when I'm drinking a can of Coke, she always grabbing at it until I put some in her bottle for her.

Now, don't you start gettin' all on me like everybody else do. I know babies ain't supposed to drink Coke 'cause it's bad for them. They got to have Kool-Aid or Hi-C or something that ain't got bubbles in it. Anyway, I only give

Dr. Ennis don't know my baby.

my baby Coke when I run out of the cans of shit I get from Debra. I finally got Debra to stop ridin' my ass about not breast-feeding Rywanda. That's just fucked-up, and I ain't even gonna talk about it.

I don't even know where Dr. Ennis get off saying Rywanda sick. She sleeping real good lately. Instead of being all, "Mama, mama," she actually sleep when she supposed to. And Rywanda used to just crawl around in front of the TV and not even look at it. But now that she getting older, she smart enough to sit down and watch talk shows with me. Rywanda's over a year old now. Her birthday was in September. I think the 14th.

A couple days ago, I ask my friend Erin if Rywanda look sick to her. Erin's baby was in the hospital last month, so she would know. Erin said, 'Fuck, no. Rywanda fine.' She said doctors just wanna take your money. She say it's even worse when you got a Medicaid card, 'cause then they treat you like shit and think they can tell you what to do even more. You know what I say? Fuck that. ∅

SCHOOL from page 1

Above: Edina, MN, high-school junior Megan Brodhagen, one of the millions of U.S. teens who praise their educational experience as "good."

school today?" 68 percent of participants responded "fine," while 18 percent answered "good" and 10 percent "okay." The remaining 4 percent replied with a shrug.

"This is the highest 'fine' response we've gotten since these surveys were first conducted in the 1960s," said Jeanette Franks, an OERI researcher who supervised the survey. "By comparison, in last year's survey, just 44 percent said school was 'fine' today, while 41 percent said 'ehh,' and 15 percent said 'I 'unno.' This year, the 'I 'unnos' didn't even rank."

"The findings of this survey should be heartening to parents and educators nationwide," Education Secretary Richard Riley said. "Children are our greatest natural resource, and for a majority of them to feel that they are receiving a fine education is wonderful news."

U.S. students also expressed optimism about their ability to succeed in school. Asked if they expect to do well on upcoming algebra tests, 87 percent said, "Sure." Asked if they were prepared for English exams, 51 percent responded "Yeah" and 40 percent "I guess."

Students were even more enthusiastic about America's hard-working educators, with 71 percent characterizing their social-studies teachers as "incredibly fascinating" and earth-science teachers as "not at all boring." A full 82 percent said that their civics class is "so important, I don't want to miss a second of it."

According to Franks, America's teens have an unusually strong sense of the importance of their education and the vital role it plays in becoming productive members of society.

"We asked our survey participants if what they were learning in school was helping them become better people and giving them a sense of values and concern for the community," Franks said. "A whopping 89 percent answered, 'Sure,' with the remaining 11 percent split among 'Yeah, sure,' 'Sure, I guess,' and, 'Sure. Whatever.'"

Despite the welcome results, the Department Of Education is refusing to rest on its laurels.

"Yes, my department is extremely pleased by the poll's results, but we still have a long way to go," Riley said. "I, for one, will not rest until every child in America feels that school is 'fine.' In this, the richest and most powerful nation on the planet, no child should receive an education that is merely 'ehh.' Our kids deserve better." ∅

E-MAIL from page 2

warded e-mail, you get a good feeling inside. As nice as it is to receive a 10-page list of mommy-mommy jokes, it's even nicer to send that list along to dozens of other people you think would enjoy it, too. Like my brother Jim. Jim is just the sort of

To give you an idea of his crazy sense of humor, he once replied to a list of "25 Reasons I'm Late For Work" that I forwarded him. His reply read, "Stop sending me all this crap." Isn't that hilarious?

guy who appreciates funny stuff like that. To give you an idea of his crazy sense of humor, he once replied to a list of "25 Reasons I'm Late For Work" that I forwarded him. His reply read, "Stop sending me all this crap." Isn't that hilarious? That's exactly why I know he'll love these lawyer jokes! ∅

5

The Subway Series

For the first time in 44 years, baseball's World Series is a Subway Series, with the New York Mets and New York Yankees squaring off. What do *you* think of the all-Big Apple Fall Classic?

"At long last, the eyes of the nation are finally on New York."

Danielle Coomes
Graduate Student

"It'll be exciting to see which team's fans get to trash Times Square in victory rioting."

Maryellen Janus
Linguist

"As an Upper East Side Yankee fan, I prefer to think of this as a Door-To-Door Car-Service Series."

Bill Anderson
Stock Broker

"Know what would make this perfect? If there were some sort of hat or shirt that people excited about the series could buy and wear. Wait, wait—hear me out on this."

Ray Loney
File Clerk

"This is just the sort of thing that leads to epic, era-defining novels of the American experience by Don DeLillo."

Larry Boone
Systems Analyst

"I've been waiting years for this glorious event. What? No, I'm not a Met or Yankee fan. I'm a terrorist with a relatively small amount of plutonium."

Victor Kritikos
Trader

The Brooks Break-Up

After 14 years of marriage, country superstar Garth Brooks and his wife Sandy are divorcing. What are the terms of the split?

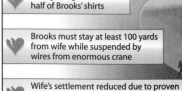

- Wife gets lighter-colored half of Brooks' shirts
- Brooks must stay at least 100 yards from wife while suspended by wires from enormous crane
- Wife's settlement reduced due to proven extramarital relationship with Australian pop star Chris Gaines
- As per terms of precedent-setting Jerry Reed divorce settlement, wife to get gold mine, Brooks to retain shaft
- Wife to receive 50 percent of royalties on any hit ballads inspired by the divorce
- Brooks forbidden from startling wife with spectacular, show-stopping fireworks
- Wife assumes half of responsibility for ruination of country music

the ONION
America's Finest News Source

Herman Ulysses Zweibel *Founder*

T. Herman Zweibel *Publisher Emeritus*
J. Phineas Zweibel *Publisher*
Maxwell Prescott Zweibel *Editor-In-Chief*

FOUNDED 1871 • "TU STULTUS ES"

By Lloyd Schumner Sr.
Retired Machinist and
A.A.P.B.-Certified Astrologer

Aries: (March 21–April 19)
You will find yourself feeling strangely disappointed after a night of fairly amazing sex with the 11th most beautiful woman in the world.

Taurus: (April 20–May 20)
Though it seems to make sense, there's just something you don't trust about this newfangled "eat right and exercise" weight-loss plan.

Gemini: (May 21–June 21)
You will earn the gratitude of *The New York Times* for your unusually humorous contribution to the paper's obituary section.

Cancer: (June 22–July 22)
Don't worry: Men won't realize it's a prosthesis at first, and by the time they do, they'll have paid and gone.

Leo: (July 23–Aug. 22)
Your lifelong fear of caramel apples will finally prove useful, albeit a little too late.

Virgo: (Aug. 23–Sept. 22)
You will spend two years in prison for sodomy, though you were sentenced for embezzling.

Libra: (Sept. 23–Oct. 23)
You will shock the nation when, due to an amazing set of circumstances, you accidentally pass for 347 yards and two touchdowns against the Redskins.

Scorpio: (Oct. 24–Nov. 21)
You will find yourself on the wrong side of Loretta Lynn this weekend when you foolishly come home a-drinkin' with lovin' on your mind.

Sagittarius: (Nov. 22–Dec. 21)
There is nothing you can do to avert what fate holds in store for you this week, mostly because there is nothing you can do at all.

Capricorn: (Dec. 22–Jan. 19)
Though *People* mentioned your satisfying family life and hobbies, you still think you were put in the magazine because of your fame and good looks.

Aquarius: (Jan. 20–Feb. 18)
You've been on hold for three years now and are beginning to suspect that your call isn't important to them, after all.

Pisces: (Feb. 19–March 20)
You are mystified that, after all these years, people still ask you to explain your constant nudity.

HOMOSEXUALITY from page 3

wonder if I'll ever find true love."

While no woman has yet won Litwin's heart, women have taken an interest in him.

"When Michael started working

"It's too bad Michael's not gay, because he was incredible in bed," said Peter Skye, a waiter and part-time actor.

here, I thought he was really cute," said Samantha Ringley, a coworker of Litwin's at Yellow Moon Graphic Design. "I didn't want to be wasting my time, so I asked him outright if he was gay. He started laughing and said, 'No, no, no!' After laughing for a long time, he said, 'I guess you could say I'm straight but not narrow.'"

STUBBY from page 2

were amazed by the unusually large amounts of blood. Passersby were amazed by the unusually large amounts of blood. Passersby were amazed by the unusually large amounts of blood. Passersby were amazed by the unusually large amounts of blood. Passersby were amazed by the unusually large amounts of blood. Passersby were

I'll do anything easy to lose weight.

amazed by the unusually large amounts of blood. Passersby were amazed by the unusually large amounts of blood. Passersby were amazed by the unusually large amounts of blood. Passersby were amazed by the unusually large amounts of blood. Passersby were amazed by the unusually large amounts of blood. Passersby were amazed by the unusually large amounts of blood. Passersby were amazed by the unusually large amounts of blood. Passersby were amazed by the unusually large amounts of blood. Passersby were amazed by the unusually large

see STUBBY page 44

Harvey Korman Cracks Up Denny's Waitress

see PEOPLE page 11D

Clinton Goes Back In Time, Teams Up With Golden-Age Clinton

see NATION page 4A

Man Accidentally Ends Business Call With 'I Love You'

see PEOPLE page 11D

the ONION®

VOLUME 36 ISSUE 39   AMERICA'S FINEST NEWS SOURCE™   2–8 NOVEMBER 2000

Howard Stern Organizes Women's Health Symposium

NEW YORK—Citing his "responsibility as a public figure to the betterment of the community" and his "longstanding commitment to issues of concern to women," talk-radio personality Howard Stern announced Tuesday the First Annual Howard Stern Women's Health Symposium.

A free community event to be held over the next five days in Central Park, the symposium will feature more than 30 women's-health-related lectures and workshops, including "Maximizing The Female Ejaculation," "Six Safe Ways To Wax The Bikini Area: A Demonstration," "Combating Small-Breast Syndrome (SBS)," and "Lesbians: Miracles Of Nature." The symposium will con-

see STERN page 11

Right: Howard Stern at the kick-off to the First Annual Howard Stern Women's Health Symposium.

Nation Fills Up On Bread

WASHINGTON, DC—Despite repeated warnings from federal officials not to eat too much before their entree arrives, an alarming 89 percent of U.S. citizens filled up on bread Monday, leaving them too full to enjoy the rest of their meal.

"Paying little heed to the many cautionary announcements we have issued, the American people have stuffed themselves with dinner rolls and, as a result, have no room for their soup or salad, much less their main course," said U.S. Secretary of Health and Human Services Donna Shalala. "America, look at your plates: They've hardly even been touched."

According to a Health and Human Services report, an unprecedented two billion pounds of uneaten sides were trucked away from U.S. dinner tables, including

Left: In a scene familiar across America, a Scotch Plains, NJ, bread basket sits empty.

see BREAD page 10

Something Weird Going On In That Montessori School, Neighbor Reports

ALLEGHENY CITY, PA—According to retired steelworker Martin Kramarczyk, 67, something weird is definitely going on inside that Montessori school across the street from his house.

"I've been keeping an eye on that place for a while now, and I'm telling you, something just ain't right about it," said Kramarczyk, peering at the Allegheny Montessori Learning Center through his living-room window. "I wouldn't be surprised if one of these days the FBI came down and busted it for some sort of kinky, perverted stuff."

Though Kramarczyk has no hard evidence of improprieties at the school, he said he has "some pretty strong suspicions" about its internal activities.

"Everything about it seems a little off. I mean, they got kids playing out on the playground at all times of the day. And scraping away on those weird Mexican gourds. What kind of school is that?" Kramarczyk said. "And the teachers have al-

Above: The suspicion-arousing Montessori school.

ways got the kids doing these weird little puppet shows. That's gotta tell you something right there."

One of almost 4,000 such schools in the U.S., the Allegheny Montessori Learning Center was founded in 1978 and employs educational methods pioneered in 1912 by Italian physician and educator Maria Montessori. The school's 47 students, all of whom are under 10, are encouraged to learn at their own pace through activities designed to engage their intellect.

"We provide a stimulating and inspiring classroom environment that empowers children to de-

see MONTESSORI page 10

Candidate Delighted To Be In Chair Factory

LAUREL, NE—During a campaign stop Monday, Republican U.S. Senate candidate and former Nebraska attorney general Don Stenberg expressed great pleasure to be at a chair factory. "I can't tell you how thrilled I am to be with the fine men and women of the Laurel Chair Works on this beautiful day," Stenberg told the crowd of 200 employees, donning a Laurel Chair Works baseball hat given to him by factory owner Darrell Widcock. "Just as you have done for so many satisfied customers throughout Nebraska, it is my hope that you can provide me with a 'seat' in Congress." Earlier in the day, Stenberg was overjoyed to be at an elementary school, a mall, a senior-citizen community center, and an Episcopal Church.

Man Breaks Out Dating Boxers

SUFFOLK, VA—Having secured a date for the first time in seven months, area resident Andrew Agee removed his dating boxers from the bottom of his dresser. "No tighty-whities for me tonight," said Agee, taking off a pair of dingy Fruit Of The Loom briefs and slipping on the blue Calvin Klein boxers with a small, understated white "CK" logo near the bottom of the right leg. "A girl might actually see me in my underwear." Agee added that if the date goes well and future encounters with the woman seem likely, he will purchase a three-pack of boxers.

Captain Kirk's Life Flashes Before Dying Trekkie's Eyes

MILFORD, CT—Moments before dying, car-accident victim and hardcore *Star Trek* fan Glenn Schaefer saw Captain James T. Kirk's life flash before his eyes. "It's all coming back to me," said Schaefer, bleeding profusely and fading from massive head trauma. "The Salt Vampires of M-113, assisting Spock through the Pon Farr, outmaneuvering Khan Singh in the Mutara Nebula, the dilithium mines of Rura Penthe. I'm even seeing portions of the animated series and the *Lost Years* novels." Before taking his final breath, Schaefer turned to attending medical personnel and said, "It was... fun."

You The Newest Subsidiary Of Kraft Foods

NORTHFIELD, IL—In the company's latest acquisition, Kraft Foods announced Monday that it has gained a controlling interest in you for an estimated $11,000, nearly 20 percent less than the amount forecast by *Forbes Magazine's* market analysts earlier this year. "We are pleased to bring you under the umbrella of fine Kraft products and individuals," Kraft CEO Betsy Holden said. "After some retooling and repackaging, expect to be on store shelves sometime in early spring."

No Clear Winner In Feces-Throwing Conflict

TABORA, TANZANIA—After several hours of fierce feces-slinging from both sides, no clear winner emerged Tuesday in the conflict between Tabora-area male silverback gorillas Lugo and Kamala. "While Lugo looked strong early on, heaving large quantities of his own dung at his opponent, Kamala came back with an equally impressive volley of his own," primatologist Dr. Donald Schayes said. "We might not have a clear handle on the outcome until mating season." The animals have tentatively scheduled an additional series of fecal flings over the next three weeks.

Awful Show A Repeat Again

PRESCOTT, AZ—According to local TV viewer Randy Bolz, Monday's episode of the "absolutely awful" CBS show *The King Of Queens* was a repeat yet again. "*King Of Queens* is bad enough when it's a new episode," Bolz said, "but this is the third time I've seen that stupid one where Doug buys the really expensive car against Carrie's wishes, then his company goes on strike. Even if I actually did like this show, I certainly wouldn't after seeing the same damn episode three times in less than a year. Christ." ∅

Mall Security All Up In Girl's Face

FORT WAYNE, IN—In spite of the fact that she wasn't doing nothing wrong, Northwood Mall security got all up in local 16-year-old Katrina Cuellar's face Monday.

"So I'm, like, hanging out on the benches with Jill [Nichols] and Amanda [Beresford] and Alicia [Hackett], and this security guy gets all up in my face and is like, 'Hey, you—you're being too loud! And clean up that mess you made!'" Cuellar said. "That's total bullshit."

The confrontation with mall security guard Eric Boyd occurred at approximately 8 p.m. on the benches in front of Hot Topic.

"Yeah, we were hanging out, but we weren't causing no problems," said Cuellar, who has related the injustice to nearly 30 friends throughout the Fort Wayne area. "Then that mall cop comes up and gets all Nazi Russia on us."

Boyd disagreed with Cuellar's account of the incident.

"That pack of girls was up to no good," said Boyd, 44, a Northwood Mall employee since February 1999. "I had a report from Patricia at the Original Cookie Company that they had been yelling inappropriate remarks at other mall patrons, so I went up to the girls to tell them to keep it down. That's when I noticed the napkins and empty Burger King cups in the potted plants adjacent to them."

Boyd said he politely asked the girls to deposit their trash in an appropriate waste receptacle. Cuellar responded that the garbage did not belong to them.

"The girls were holding Burger King bags, and there were a number of corresponding Burger King cups and napkins in the nearby plant," Boyd said. "Do you mean to tell me it was merely a coincidence that these girls were eating Burger King food, and just a few feet away in the plant were Burger King items that belonged to somebody else? That seems unlikely."

Boyd informed the group that he didn't care to whom the garbage belonged, saying that Cuellar and her friends "had better hop to it" and pick up the refuse if they wished to remain at the mall.

"That cop didn't have no right to get all up in my face," Cuellar said. "I'm supposed to clean up trash like I work there or something? I don't work there."

Added Cuellar: "I got a right to go where I want. I ain't in jail or nothing."

Dorothea Lurman, a noted teens'-rights activist, expressed outrage over the incident.

"I am deeply saddened to hear that this sort of injustice is still going on in this supposedly free country," Lurman said. "Can't nobody just go shopping without getting hassled by some fat old mall cop?"

Lurman called America's malls the "final frontier in the fight to eliminate teenist discrimination in our society."

"Where, if not the mall, can youths

Above: Cuellar stands outside Northwood Mall shortly after her clash with Boyd (inset).

go to find a safe space in which to express their individuality free from the disapproving glare of society as a whole?" asked Lurman, author of the 1997 book *Everybody Ridin' My Ass: The Youth Experience In The American Mallscape*. "Our young people desperately need a place where they can just chill and do they thing in peace."

Northwood Mall has refused to issue Cuellar and her friends an apology.

"While we are disappointed that this unfortunate incident had to happen, we stand by the actions of Mr. Boyd," Northwood Mall general manager Ted Parrott said. "For the safety of all of our patrons, we must strictly enforce certain rules of conduct."

According to Cuellar, this is not the first time mall authority figures have unfairly gotten up in her face. On Oct. 19, employees at Northwood Mall video arcade The Game Den reportedly jumped on Cuellar about spilling soda on a Tekken III machine. While the sign

see GIRL page 10

8

The Peace Of The Womb

By T. Herman Zweibel
Publisher Emeritus

photo circa 1911

As the publisher of the greatest news-paper the Republic has ever known, I have not had a peace-ful existence. My thousand daily cares are like great chains of iron on my spirit, and my soul shrivels inside me as if weeping heart's-blood from a thousand cuts. And being an ulcerated, leprous 132-year-old man with cast-iron dentures and prosthetic ears doesn't help one God-damned bit.

The one consolation I have in my advanced state of decline is my dear, dear son, N. Aeschylus, whose tread upon the stair is that of a joyous bull-dozer, whose metallic shriek of laughter wakes me with a start every 10 minutes.

Indeed, N. Aeschylus' antics recently provided me, albeit inadvertently, with my only moment of true peace in more than 75 years. As he sported playfully around my bed-chamber, amusing me as I lay helplessly in my iron-lung, he happened to brush against the iron-lung's padded head-piece. Quicker than it takes to tell, the collar which held me fast in the mechanism's cold embrace popped open. The force of N. Aeschylus' gallivant thrust my head inside like a musket-ball up a consti-pated Hessian. Just as quickly, the brass sea-hatch on the outside clanged shut, sealing me inside my iron-lung!

I opened my mouth to cry out in the darkness, but it quickly filled with the warm, briny solution in which my carcass is suspended. Panicked, I added a good deal of my own body's effluvia to the mixture. I flailed meekly about in the viscous fluid for several minutes before realizing that, for the first time in living memory, I was actually quite comfortable!

The darkness, warmth, and total absence of sound I experienced as I floated in the iron-lung were much like that of the womb. Like many people, I have always wanted to re-turn to the womb. But in my early days, I was discouraged by my dear mother, and I later became engrossed in business. But my time in the iron-lung was peaceful, indeed, although it stank. And, unlike the time I spend in the uncertain realm of sleep, I was not haunted by hundreds of betrayed and uneasy ghosts.

Unfortunately, I was removed by my steam-fitters before I drowned inside. What's worse, I cannot repeat the experience, as I suffered a horrible case of the bends. So my pain in life is doubled again, but it was worth the five or so minutes of Elysian respite I experienced. Dear N. Aeschylus! He may cause all the accidents he wants if they are all so blessed! ∅

I Must Take Issue With *Entertainment Weekly's* C-Plus Grade For The DVD Release Of *The Patriot*

By Ronald Nisley

I usually enjoy *Entertainment Weekly* a great deal, devouring everything from Jim Mullen's Hot Sheet to the Gimme Shelter profiles of on-the-market celebrity homes to the always-cheeky CyberDigest column. And, as a rule, I trust the magazine's reviews, confident that if Ken Tucker says the new CBS show *The Fugitive* is an A-minus, it's an A-minus. I must, however, take strong issue with the C-plus grade for the DVD release of *The Patriot*.

While I concede that *The Patriot* had its flaws, it hardly deserves the pitiful C-plus rating the usually reliable Ty Burr mystifyingly chose to bestow upon it. In dismissing *The Patriot* as a "revolutionary ruckus," Burr willfully ignores all that was worthwhile about this Revolutionary War epic, including the kinetic, vibrantly directed battle scenes that put moviegoers mere inches from the Redcoats. And Aussie heartthrob Heath Ledger's (*10 Things I Hate About You*) star-making performance as Mel Gibson's (*Braveheart*) eager-to-fight teenage son. And the numerous extra goodies on the DVD, including director Roland Emmerich's (*Independence Day*) surprisingly illuminating commentary track.

I'm not saying the movie deserved an A. Or even a B-plus, for that matter. *The Patriot* is rife with historical inaccuracies, and the German-born

> ## While I concede that *The Patriot* had its flaws, it hardly deserves the pitiful C-plus rating the usually reliable Ty Burr mystifyingly chose to bestow upon it.

Emmerich's grasp of the colonial political climate of 1776 is tenuous at best. But don't you think at least a B would have been in order? Is this really the sort of movie that would cause one to muse that "the narrative breakthroughs of *Saving Private Ryan*... have been swallowed by the mainstream and digested into pap"? Apparently so, provided your name is Ty Burr.

I don't know what was going on over there at the *EW* offices this week, but something was definitely off. I mean, rating Fatboy Slim's new single "Ya Mama" a C? Giving a B to the WB fansite www.charmed.org? Doling out a C-minus for Keri Russell's delightful new hairdo? None of these, however, got my goat quite like the C-plus for *The Patriot*.

Then there's the not-so-small matter of the title of the review. "Soldier Ploy"? Upon what, pray tell, is that supposed to be a pun? When *The Patriot* first hit theaters, *EW* cleverly titled its review "Revolution-ary Bore." You may have disagreed with that assessment (I certainly did), but there's no denying that it's a clear, direct play on "Revolutionary War." But "Soldier Ploy"? What's that? My only guess is that it's a play on "Soldier Boy." Should that be the case, such punnery would have to be regarded as a stretch, to be kind.

The only aspect of *The Patriot* review that was dead-on was the caption accompanying the photo of Gibson as lead character Benjamin Martin. The movie is, indeed, "all about the Benjamin." Gibson is in top form throughout, virtually exploding off the screen with brooding, musket-wielding bravado. But one good photo caption is not much to recommend about an entire review.

To prove that injustice was, indeed, served by Mr. Burr, we need only look at the "What We Said Then" addendum which follows "Soldier Ploy." The addendum, a paragraph-long distillation of Owen Gleiberman's June 30 review of *The Patriot*, concludes with his original grade for the film: B-minus. The grade is a far more accurate appraisal of the movie's worth. For some reason, though, four months later, the magazine's editors made a cowardly retreat from Gliebermann's more *Patriot*-friendly stance, docking the film a notch. They say hindsight is 20/20, but in *Entertainment Weekly's* case, it seems to be more like 20/80.

I'd give Ty Burr's review a C-minus. No, make that a D-plus. ∅

BLUDGEONER from page 2 ━━━

the unusually large amounts of blood. Passersby were amazed by the unusually large amounts of blood. Passersby were amazed by the unusually large amounts of blood. Passersby

> ## All the good priests are either seeing married women or gay.

were amazed by the unusually large amounts of blood. Passersby were amazed by the unusually large amounts of blood. Passersby were amazed by the unusually large amounts of blood. Passersby were amazed by the unusually large amounts of blood. Passersby were amazed by the unusually large

see BLUDGEONER page 37

9

velop their personalities and become strong, independent-minded individuals," AMLC instructor Ellen Driscoll said. "The Montessori method rejects the traditional teacher-student relationship, in which the teacher is in control and the student passively accepts knowledge. Instead, the teacher serves as a guide who enhances children's learning ability by appealing to their creativity and recognizing their individual talents. The child learns by doing things herself."

"Today, some of the older students are learning how to make rock candy," Driscoll continued. "Then we're going to learn a traditional folk song from the French province of Picardy!"

"Look, I was taught by the nuns and, sure, they could go a little overboard with the switch sometimes, but it was a good, thorough education, with none of this weirdo stuff," Kramarczyk said. "I had to drop out of the ninth grade to support the family, but I knew the three Rs up and down. All these kids know how to do is play autoharps and grow bean plants. That ain't education to me. I don't know what it is, but it ain't education."

Kramarczyk said that in the past few months, he has observed numerous strange goings-on at the school, including children fanning out across the neighborhood, armed only with hand-drawn maps and compasses; teachers pretending to be students and vice-versa; and energetic sing-alongs in observance of Learn Three New Things Day.

Most disturbing of all, Kramarczyk said, was a May occurrence he calls "The Egg Incident."

"A truck pulled up to the school one afternoon and a couple men got out," Kramarczyk recalled. "They were carrying in boxes. A day later, I could see a bunch of egg incubators on the windowsills of one of the classrooms. Then, a couple weeks later, as I was walking the dog near the school, I heard peeping noises. Why'd those kids need to hatch eggs? Aren't there farms that do that sort of thing? It just don't add up."

Kramarczyk said he has had direct contact with school personnel just once, and the meeting only confirmed his suspicion.

"A few months back, I was trimming the hedges, and a ball came flying over their fence and into my front yard," Kramarczyk said. "I looked down at it and noticed it was a multi-colored, knitted-fabric kind of ball I've only seen at the Montessori school. That type of ball doesn't even bounce. That's another queer thing. Montessori balls never bounce."

Continued Kramarczyk: "Next thing you know, standing in front of me is a Montessori teacher with one of the kids, who's probably about 7. So I toss the kid back his strange little ball, and the teacher says to him, 'What do you say to the man, Jeffrey?' The kid looks up at me and says, 'Merci beaucoup.' Then the teacher says, 'Or...' and the kid says, 'Danke schoen.' Then the teacher says, 'Or...' again, and the kid says, 'Domo arigato.' Then they walk off."

AMLC director Roberta King insisted that Kramarczyk misunderstands the school's curricula and teaching methods.

"We are aware of Mr. Kramarczyk's fears about our school, and the various theories he has circulated at civic-association meetings," King said. "I'd like to take this opportunity to say that, although the Montessori method is of Italian origin, we are not affiliated with the Mafia in any way. Nor is the school a sweatshop that forces the children to produce black-market finger paintings. And not one toddler who is enrolled in our daycare program has ever been boiled in a broth."

To help Kramarczyk better understand Montessori education, King offered to take him on a personal guided tour of the school. Kramarczyk rejected the offer.

"Oh, no, forget it," Kramarczyk said. "There's no telling what would happen to me in that place. They'd probably strap me to their big abacus and pelt me with Montessori balls. Or cover me with plaster of Paris and leave me there to harden into a life-size statue for use in some kind of educational display about retired steelworkers. No way, folks. I wasn't born yesterday." ∅

Above: A perfectly good meal going to waste, having been thrown into an Athens, GA, trash bin.

150 million pounds of mashed potatoes, 200 million pounds of stuffing, and 450 million pounds of steamed carrots. What's worse, HHS officials said, Americans discarded nearly 300 million choice cuts of meat—which is the most expensive part and has all the protein—without taking much more than a bite.

"America must learn that filling up on bread beforehand is just foolish, because then you can't enjoy your meal," the report read. "Sure, they give you plenty of bread. But then you can't eat the food you paid good money for. That's how they get you."

The HHS report has provoked strong reaction from appetite-conservation activists nationwide.

"For decades, excessive and unregulated pre-meal bread consumption has been the number-one threat to the U.S. appetite," said Hannah Dowling, author of the best-selling *Saving Some Room For Later*. "Despite decades of awareness-raising efforts on the part of appetite conservationists, filling up on bread remains the leading cause of leaving the dinner table early for Americans in the 7- to 64-year-old age

ers can pose a threat to Americans' hunger.

"Many people, conditioned to expect instant satisfaction in our convenience-obsessed society, lack even the simplest mealtime gratification-delay skills—skills which, in generations past, children were expected to have mastered by age 5 or 6," Dowling said. "As a result, presented with unlimited access to fresh bread, bread sticks, and crackers—not to mention the ubiquitous packets of butter and alliterative butter substitutes such as Country Crock and Shedd's Spread—the American eater is like the proverbial horse that, left unsupervised, will gorge itself until it dies."

"Remember," Dowling added, "bread expands once it gets in your stomach, and then you feel full even when you're not."

In a recent U.N. study, the U.S. ranked last in the world in appetite-preservation skills. The average American, the study found, was only able to maintain an empty stomach for three minutes before sating his or her hunger. Standing in sharp contrast is Botswana, whose citizenry ranked first, able to preserve their appetites for an average of more than seven months.

"The problem of appetite spoilage has reached epidemic proportions here in America," Shalala said. "No other country is as bad at staying hungry as we are."

Shalala said major changes are in order in the wake of the report.

"If we can't control ourselves with the bread, we'll have to face hard facts and accept that we're just not going to have any room for pie later," Shalala said. "And nobody, regardless of our political differences, wants a tragedy like that." ∅

In a recent U.N. study, the U.S. ranked last in the world in appetite-preservation skills.

group, and the second-leading cause for citizens over 65."

According to Dowling, even the seemingly harmless dinner-table presence of such food-service hospitality items as individually wrapped breadsticks and Saltine-brand crack-

at The Game Den's entrance clearly prohibits the drinking of soda on arcade premises, Cuellar insisted that she wasn't drinking soda, but merely carrying it in her hand.

On Oct. 24, the iron fist of mall au-

On Oct. 24, the iron fist of mall authority struck again—this time in the form of Gadzooks assistant manager Naomi Gronson.

thority struck again—this time in the form of Gadzooks assistant manager Naomi Gronson. According to Cuellar, Gronson began bitching out Cuellar and Beresford for trying on clothing. Gronson claimed that the girls tied up one of the store's two fitting rooms for more than an hour, leaving as many as 25 items on the re-hang rack without purchasing a single item.

"[Gronson] went all psycho on us, just because we didn't buy anything at her store," Cuellar said. "Well, just because all her clothes are gay-ass, that don't make it my fault."

So disgusted is Cuellar with her mistreatment at the hands of Northwood personnel that she is considering a boycott of the mall.

"If I want to deal with some retard who wants to ride my ass for no reason, I'll just take the bus," Cuellar said. "That fuckin' driver on the E-line is almost as bad as Mr. Big Shot Mall Cop." ∅

clude Sunday with an attempt to break the Guinness World Record for largest group mammogram.

"Today's woman faces a multitude of specialized health concerns that may go ignored if awareness is not raised. Like, for example, she could

> **Day one of the symposium will feature Stern's keynote speech, "Implants: Silicone Or Saline?" and free breast-cancer screenings by Hank The Angry Drunken Dwarf.**

get a real bad yeast infection," said Stern, broadcasting live from the event. "Believe me, I oughta know, because I saw plenty of them on [estranged wife] Alison, and they can get real nasty. Isn't that right, Robin?"

Upon receiving acknowledgement from on-air partner Robin Quivers that this was, in fact, true, Stern added: "Robin's probably never had one herself, because she's got class. She knows how to wash down there. But some of these chicks out there, we're talking cottage-cheese discharge, the works."

Day one of the symposium, Stern said, will feature a number of events of interest to women. These include

Stern's keynote speech, "Implants: Silicone Or Saline?"; free breast-cancer screenings by Hank The Angry Drunken Dwarf; complimentary testing of women's buttocks for lunchmeat adhesiveness; and a roundtable discussion of issues facing uninsured women of color, presided over by Wack Pack members Big Black, Angry Black, and King Of All Blacks.

"This is racist!" Angry Black told reporters. "Black women can't get no insurance in the white man's world!" He then lapsed into a string of profanities.

Subsequent events include free body appraisals by Stern's friend Ralph Cirella and Gary The Retard, as well as a Shaving Cream Battle Royal illustrating the importance of proper lubrication in pubic-hair removal. Stern will himself quiz three *Penthouse* centerfolds on reproductive-health issues.

"A lot of women don't know that a diet rich in folic acid is essential during pregnancy," Stern said. "Also, we're going to have a gal on who has huge labia. Huge. I mean, they hang off her like drapes."

On Friday, activities will focus on cosmetic surgery, culminating in a panel discussion mediated by Stern, porn star Houston, and *Howard Stern Show* head writer Jackie "The Joke Man" Martling.

"Guy tells his wife, 'Honey, you got some saggy goddamn breasts,'" Martling said. "She says, 'Don't complain, it's cheaper than plastic surgery, 'cause at least they drag some of the wrinkles out of my fuckin' face!'"

Stern stressed that the event is a non-profit public-health initiative. "As we learn how to better meet the needs of the public, our event should only continue to get better in the coming years," Stern told *New York Times* reporter Samantha Matheson.

"You know, for a woman in your 30s, you're not half bad. Turn around. Yeah, you've got a nice little ass on you, honey."

Added Stern: "God, I'd love to bang you."

Pausing a moment to transfer Matheson to his lap, Stern continued: "We hope in time to establish the Howard Stern Women's Health Foundation as the nation's leading organ of women's health awareness." Upon hearing Stern use the word "organ," longtime sound-effects man Fred Norris activated a pre-recorded comic "sproing" sound.

Stern explained that his creation of the symposium was largely motivated by the recent breakup of his marriage.

"Alison was a hell of a gal, and sometimes I think that if I'd been more knowledgeable and attentive to her various female-specific problems—of which there were, Christ, maybe 10 million?—perhaps we could have worked it out," Stern said. "Plus, I'm dating again, and there'll be a lot of broads there with huge cans." ∅

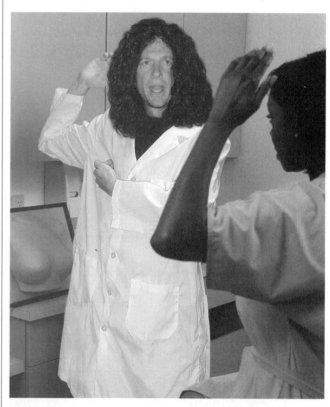

Above: Stern demonstrates the proper procedure for a monthly breast self-examination.

This Casino Is So Glamorous!

Oh! Oh, my goodness! When Helen and Patty said they were going to take me to a casino, I thought it would be nice, but this is something else! I had no idea the casino would be so glamorous!

When we first drove up to the Mishwauketomee Casino, I really didn't think it looked like much. From the

By Rosemary Potter

outside, it just looked like a big windowless building out in the woods. Boy, was I in for a shock! The moment we got out of the car, the glamour began. There was a man out front in a black tuxedo who wel-

comed us and gave us a "Golden Goodie Bag" with a complimentary two-dollar chip inside!

Ritzy as that was, it was nothing compared to what met my eyes when I walked in the door. (Which, by the way, was opened for me by another young man in a tuxedo.) Talk about fancy! Through the entire room, the floor was covered with acres of red-and-black, Hollywood-style carpet with fruit and flowers and birds of paradise woven into it. There were glittering lights everywhere and chandeliers hanging from the ceiling with the fancy light bulbs that look like flames. And there were mirrors everywhere, some of them tinted gold! And there were big draperies and gorgeous red velvet ropes to help you around. It

was so beautiful, I couldn't believe it—it was like being inside the Taj Mahal!

Nothing in the Mishwauketomee Casino was tacky. There were no clocks on the wall to break up the elegance of the decor. There weren't even any windows, so you didn't have to look at the ugly outside world and spoil the fantasy. I'm telling you, these folks thought of everything!

And talk about service: I was waited on hand and foot! There was always a man willing to show you how to play blackjack or poker, or to get you more of those chips you use instead of money. (Which is classy and relaxing because it helps you stop worrying about the expense.) A beautiful lady brings you free drinks

as long as you're playing something, even the slot machines. There's also a buffet you can visit any time, with people who serve you prime rib and cheese spread, not to mention fancy shrimp with the thickest breading I've ever seen! Why, they even have ladies who hand you towels when you use the restroom! And all of these people are in tuxedoes, too. I was happy to see the signs saying "NO TIPPING," because I certainly couldn't have afforded all that service if I had to pay for it.

Did I mention the entertainment? That place just has one famous soap-opera star after another coming by to mingle with us regular people. Just last week, Tristan Rogers, who used to play hunky Robert

see CASINO page 12

Into The Home Stretch

The presidential election is less than a week away, with polls indicating a virtual dead heat between Bush and Gore. What do *you* think?

"I'm not voting. Clinton has been doing a great job, so why bring in some new guy?"

Glen Eyers
Engineer

"I was going to vote for Gore until I found out he was losing."

Neil Kuberra
Cook

"My vote for Ralph Nader will send this country a powerful message: Bush is a bad president."

Paula Buechner
EMT

"I'm sorry. I don't mean to be so emotional. It's just that, well, this time of year I really miss John Chancellor."

Lena Levenhagen
Florist

"Which candidate is going to tax soda? Neither? Looks like I'm back to square one."

Cory Morrow
Usher

"Everyone's making such a fuss about it being the closest election in years, but what did they expect from the closest candidates in years?"

Christopher Rich
Systems Analyst

The XFL

Last weekend, the inaugural player draft was held for the XFL, the new World Wrestling Federation-backed pro-football league. What are some of the league's features?

- Opening kickoff fired from Howitzer
- Teams embody character archetypes: all-hillbilly team, all-sumo-wrestler team, all-evil-clown team
- Instead of Vince Lombardi Trophy, teams will compete for the hand of the lovely Elizabeth
- Players will be allowed to return from the grave to avenge an injured teammate
- Futuristically armored James Caan will lead New York team while being pulled behind streamlined motorcycle
- Using folding chairs on opposing players a five-yard penalty
- Players to have colorful names like "Razor," "The Mortician," and "Former Denver Broncos Third-Stringer Tommy Maddox"

the ONION

America's Finest News Source

Herman Ulysses Zweibel *Founder*

T. Herman Zweibel *Publisher Emeritus*
J. Phineas Zweibel *Publisher*
Maxwell Prescott Zweibel *Editor-In-Chief*

FOUNDED 1871 • "TU STULTUS ES"

By Lloyd Schumner Sr.
Retired Machinist and
A.A.P.B.-Certified Astrologer

Aries: (March 21–April 19)
No change for Aries this week, except for those who may be affected by bursting Brooklyn gas mains.

Taurus: (April 20–May 20)
You will occupy the national spotlight and win the hearts of Americans for reasons no one will be able to remember in six months.

Gemini: (May 21–June 21)
Your inability to grasp contemporary world events will be cleared up this week when you realize you've confused *CBS Evening News* with *Cleopatra 2525*.

Cancer: (June 22–July 22)
You will meet the girl of your dreams after a week of recurring nightmares about manipulation, betrayal, and fire.

Leo: (July 23–Aug. 22)
Your carefully considered, issues-based presidential vote will be negated by a hairdresser who likes the other guy's ties.

Virgo: (Aug. 23–Sept. 22)
You will be the toast of Napoleon's Paris for your airy yet visceral performance of *The Little Minuet.*

Libra: (Sept. 23–Oct. 23)
Remember: There is nothing wrong with a vigorous and athletic display of sexuality, so long as you have the money.

Scorpio: (Oct. 24–Nov. 21)
Give in to your rebellious impulses at work this week: Disobey your boss by letting the door hit you on the ass on the way out.

Sagittarius: (Nov. 22–Dec. 21)
Though the stars know exactly what will happen in your life, this doesn't mean that astrology is consistent with the Christian tenet of predestination.

Capricorn: (Dec. 22–Jan. 19)
A dangerous but comical event will occur every time you ask the rhetorical question, "What next?"

Aquarius: (Jan. 20–Feb. 18)
If a really good roast-beef melt isn't the best sandwich in the world, Aquarius would like to know what is.

Pisces: (Feb. 19–March 20)
From this moment forth, you will be elected treasurer of every organization you join.

CASINO from page 11

Scorpio on *General Hospital*, was there. I saw the list of recent appearances, and some of those actors hadn't been on a soap for 10 years! Mishwauketomee must be a pretty fancy place to get all those famous actors to come out of retirement and visit us up in Minnesota.

Well, I was a bit intimidated by all the high-society trimmings, so I decided to lay low and just play the slot machines. But you know what? They're fancy, too! All brassy and silvery, with big, important-looking arms that make you feel important when you pull them. And those red leather stools! They were so comfy, I must have parked my tush on one for about six hours! (Who knew how long it really was, though. I certainly wasn't in any rush to return to the real world.)

I wasn't very good at the slot machines and the gambling, but I certainly had a wonderful time. It was worth every cent of the $340 I spent to be part of high society for an afternoon. I even got to keep the special Mishwauketomee Casino coin bucket I was using. Talk about being queen for a day! Ø

PRONGS from page 9

were amazed by the unusually large amounts of blood. Passersby were amazed by the unusually large amounts of blood. Passersby were amazed by the unusually large amounts of blood. Passersby were amazed by the unusually large amounts of blood. Passersby were amazed by the unusually large amounts of blood. Passersby were amazed by the unusually large amounts of blood. Passersby were amazed by the unusually large

I think I'll wear the exact same thing everyone else will be wearing.

amounts of blood. Passersby were amazed by the unusually large amounts of blood. Passersby were amazed by the unusually large amounts of blood. Passersby were amazed by the unusually large amounts of blood. Passersby were amazed by the unusually large amounts of blood. Passersby were amazed by the unusually large amounts of blood. Passersby were amazed by the unusually large amounts of blood. Passersby were amazed by the unusually large amounts of blood. Passersby were amazed by the unusually large amounts of blood. Passersby were

see PRONGS page 42

Vote, Voter Wasted

see NATION page 3A

Magazine Correctly Judged By Its Cover

see MEDIA page 3C

Office Casual-Day Policy Hastily Rewritten To Exclude Unitards

see OFFICE LIFE page 4E

Sex Had

see LOCAL page 11D

A look at the numbers that shape your world.

Top Write-In Candidates

36%	Lee Marvin
21%	Heywood Jablomi
16%	That guy on that one show
14%	Pat Boocannon
9%	George Washington Jr. The XXVth
3%	Ralph Nader
1%	My big black ass

74470 94595 6

---

the ONION®

VOLUME 36 ISSUE 40   AMERICA'S FINEST NEWS SOURCE™   9–15 NOVEMBER 2000

DECISION 2000

Bush Or Gore: 'A New Era Dawns'

AUSTIN, TX, OR NASHVILLE, TN—In one of the narrowest presidential votes in U.S. history, either George W. Bush or Al Gore was elected the 43rd president of the United States Tuesday, proclaiming the win "a victory for the American

Above: Bush and Gore, one of whom called the election "a victory for America."

people and the dawn of a bold new era in this great nation."

"My fellow Americans," a triumphant Bush or Gore told throngs

of jubilant, flag-waving supporters at his campaign headquarters, "tonight, we as a nation stand on the brink of many exciting new challenges. And I stand here before you

see ELECTION page 17

Neighborhood Children Gear Up For Hotly Anticipated 'Opening Of The Gerbil's Tomb'

COVINGTON, KY—In what promises to be the biggest neighborhood event since July's golf-ball dismantling, Andy Mefford, 9, announced plans Monday to exhume Marshall, his sister's deceased pet gerbil.

"Guys," said Mefford, addressing fellow fourth-graders from the jungle gym during recess, "this Saturday morning, right after *Batman Beyond*, I'm gonna dig up Marshall to see what he looks like now."

Marshall, who died June 24 of complications from an eye infection, was laid to rest the following day beneath the large oak tree in the Meffords' backyard. The gerbil was entombed in a styrofoam hamburger container, along with a daisy and a poem written by its devoted owner, 7-year-old Kimberly Mefford.

Andy Mefford's decision to exhume the rodent, made partly in response to a recent Learning Channel

Secrets Of The Pyramids documentary, has sparked excitement among children throughout the Reardon Street area.

"That's gonna be so cool," said classmate Danny Stossel. "I bet it's all gross, with worms crawling out of his eyes and stuff."

"My brother once dug up a parakeet after it was buried for, like, three weeks, and it was all black and hard," next-door neighbor Douglas Beane, 10, said. "This'll probably be even better."

Added Beane: "I wonder if the tail will still be there."

Despite such enthusiasm, not all neighborhood children support the gerbil exhumation.

"You can't dig somebody up after you bury them," said Amy Coryell, 7, who will not attend the dig. "That disturbs their spirit, and then you can get haunted by the dead ghost, I bet."

Speculation regarding the con-

Above: The soon-to-be-disturbed burial site.

tents of the Marshall gravesite is running high, with guesses ranging from a gerbil skeleton to a gerbil zombie. The latter theory was posited by Bradley Dorner, 9, who has been fix-

see GERBIL page 16

13

NS/ND/C/DWF Wondering Why She Can't Find Someone

MINNEAPOLIS—Susan Stenerud, a divorced, white, non-smoking, non-drinking Christian who has placed "countless" personals ads over the years, wondered aloud Monday why she can't find someone special. "All I want is to find a D/D-free NS/ND/C/SWM who shares my strong morals and doesn't waste his time going to bars and parties," the 32-year-old said. "For some reason, no men seem to respond to that description."

Report: TV Teens 15 Times More Likely To Crack Wise Than Real Teens

NEW YORK—According to a report released Tuesday by the Center For Media Studies, TV teens out-wisecrack real-life teens by a 15-to-1 margin. Said researcher Dr. Andrea Brewer: "Our study found that, when told by a parent, 'You know, son, when I was a kid, I didn't have my own TV in my room,' actual teens were far less likely to respond, 'Yeah, that's 'cause they hadn't been invented yet!' than their fictional counterparts." Brewer noted that the handful of real-life teens who make such smart-alecky retorts have a mere 2 percent chance of being met with laughter and applause.

Mozambique Out Of Toilet Paper

MAPUTO, MOZAMBIQUE—Mozambican officials declared a state of emergency Monday following the depletion of the nation's bathroom-tissue supply. "We are imploring Zimbabwe and Tanzania, please look into your hearts and think about loaning our nation just a few million rolls until we can go shopping again," President Joaquim Chissano said. "We are just sitting here." Chissano said citizens of the African nation are making do with napkins and paper towels until reinforcements arrive.

Man Builds House He Designed When He Was Eight Years Old

LODI, CA—A lifelong dream was realized Monday following the completion of "Fort Awesome," the high-tech home of the future Lodi architect Don Reese designed as an 8-year-old boy. "My dream is at last a reality," said the 36-year-old Reese, cutting the ribbon on the 10-room, 16-story mansion, which boasts a rooftop trampoline, seven free soda machines, and a McDonald's. "From this day forth, let Fort Awesome serve as a citadel of fun and excitement for all to enjoy. Except Dougie Wendell." A $5 million laser-guided trap-door system was installed to protect the home from infiltration by Wendell, a onetime Reese playmate who is now an actuary in Danbury, CT.

Kinko's Patron Pulls The Old Copy-Key Switcheroo

LAWRENCE, KS—Kinko's patron Matt Morrow, 21, saved $9.23 Tuesday by pulling the old copy-key switcheroo. "After making 200 copies of a flier for my band's upcoming gig, I put back the copy key and took a fresh one. I then used the new key to make 11 decoy copies, which I paid for." Morrow, a self-described "broke-ass bassist," called the five cents Kinko's charges per photocopy "a total rip."

Half-Empty Bottle Of Malibu Found In Woods Behind School

JASPER, GA—A half-empty bottle of Malibu rum was discovered Monday in the woods behind Jasper Junior High School by a trio of eighth-graders. "We have located alcohol," said Mason Tomlinson, 14, upon making the coconut-flavored find. "Repeat: We have alcohol." Following their one-capful-at-a-time consumption of the bottle's contents, Tomlinson and drinking partners Jake Seidel and Jesse Kite took turns insisting that they felt drunk. ∅

Access Hollywood Producer Would Never Work For Entertainment Tonight

HOLLYWOOD, CA—Danielle Pierce, 33, an assistant producer at *Access Hollywood*, told a friend Monday that she "could never and would never" work for *Entertainment Tonight*.

"Work for *ET*? No way. Never," Pierce told Liz Sharkey, a production assistant at Castle Rock Entertainment, over drinks at a Melrose Avenue bar. "Have you seen that show lately? They're so derivative over there. And slow. They didn't show a first look at the *Charlie's Angels* trailer until a week before the premiere. We hit air with it—and a bumper piece on Cameron's comic roles—10 days after ShoWest."

Scanning the bar in search of what she called "Extra Terrestrials," Pierce continued: "*ET* has no voice of its own. One minute, they're doing an E!-style fashion bit. The next, they're trying to be *Extra*. Our press kit says we're brash, up-to-the-minute, and wholly unique—and it's true. We lead, *ET* follows. It shows in everything we do, from the exclusive on-set peek at M. Night Shyamalan's latest thriller to the report on Angelina Jolie's controversial Oscar dress, to our coverage of more difficult subjects like the ru-

mored friction on the *Friends* set."

"Sure, *Access* doesn't pay as much as *ET*. But we don't have to," said Pierce, squeezing a lime slice into her margarita. "People know they've stalled and that the culture just isn't the same. I met an *ET* researcher at a party last month—slightly phony guy—and, anyway, it was clear he didn't believe in the job. It's much more of an assembly-line mentality over there: Just churn it out. And that's really not helped by having [Bob] Goen and [Mary] Hart at the desk. Bob's a poor man's John Tesh, and Mary, she couldn't say her name without a cue card. [*Access Hollywood* anchor] Pat [O'Brien] is trusted and really knows his stuff. We could go live if we had to."

Pierce offered a specific example of what she believes to be *Entertainment Tonight*'s lack of "freshness, savvy, and insight."

"I was watching their show last night, and they were doing a spot on the breakout new shows of the fall season—almost all of them were Paramount shows, of course. Shameless corporate tie-in. Okay, we do it sometimes, too, but not that bad. Anyway, at the start of this thing, they had a 'pro-

duced by' line, and there were three names. How can it take three people to produce this one segment unless you're really overstaffed and stifling people's creativity?"

As a result of the shows' radically divergent philosophies, Pierce said that *Access Hollywood* and *Entertainment Tonight* draw different types of viewers.

"They're half a ratings point above us in the average week, unless we land some kind of Tom Cruise exclusive or something. *Survivor* helped them, too, since they've got so many CBS carriers," Pierce said. "But their demos are for shit. I mean, we absolutely cream

them among 18-to-35s. The only ones *ET* scores big with are people too old to know or care what's truly going on in Hollywood."

Added Pierce: "The difference is apparent in the names of the shows. They're all about the surface aspect of entertainment. We've got a deeper, far more insider angle, yet are still accessible to the casual fan."

"No, Liz, I could never, ever work there," Pierce said. "Not unless they changed their entire way of doing things. Why? Have you heard anything about that executive-producer position? Not that I'd be interested or anything." ∅

Above: *Access Hollywood* assistant producer Danielle Pierce.

Dungeon Master

By T. Herman Zweibel
Publisher Emeritus

photo circa 1911

With the feast of the Thanks-giving nigh upon us, I thought it only proper that I graciously liberate a number of individuals currently chained in my estate's dungeon. Those who have earned pardons this year are:

Mr. Roger Upshaw, who I am certain has by now been cured of his delusional notion that he is a Census Bureau employee.

Mr. Kenneth Phelps, photo-play critic of *The Onion*, who in 1926 called into question the acting skills of my favorite male performer of the moving-daguerreo-types, Adolphe Menjou. Mr. Phelps has been hanging upside-down in shackles ever since.

Mr. and Mrs. William and Kristin Kronauer, tourists who took a wrong turn. Also, their children Tiffany and Jason, as well as their unborn baby. (At least it was unborn at the time.)

The remains of Isabel C. Quinn, who I hear was actually named a martyr by the Roman Catholic Church due to her pious sufferings in my dungeon. Well, if she hadn't gone delinquent on her *Onion* subscription, she could have avoided this mess.

Mr. Woodrow Wood-pecker, whose well-documented history of uncouth behavior was for decades the Republic's greatest shame. What he did to that walrus gentleman was inexcusable. After years of trying, my Swiss Guard finally snared him in a tiger trap, into which 10,000 gallons of quick-drying cement was poured. I am willing to excavate him, but only in exchange for those two back-sassing crows.

The long-missing crew of a merchant-marine sloop that was wrecked on the rocks below my estate. I was going to keep them for ransom at one point, but I forgot to get around to it. Just call me Mr. Procrastination, I suppose.

(I was only jesting just now. You may only address me as Mr. Zweibel. Any other appellation will be dealt with in the harshest manner possible. Do I make myself clear?)

Sherman Willetts, an editorialist for *The Daily Worker*, who once accused me of oiling my wheelchair with the blood of laborers. While I appreciated the sentiment, I felt the premise unforgivably weak, as blood is an extremely poor lubricant. It dries much too quickly. Better to use pus.

Mr. Oscar Zzunivich, the last person listed in the local telephone-directory. Such ostentation is extremely off-putting in a democratic society, but I feel confident that Mr. Zzunivich has learned his lesson, and that in the future he will abstain from owning a telephone. *Ø*

OPINION

Point-Counterpoint: Bears

Whoooooo! Bears!

By Bob Bratzke
Bears fan

Man, what a beautiful day for football. I cannot wait to see those Bears do their thing. Today's the day they're finally gonna win one at home.

All right! The Bears! They're taking the field! Whoooo, Bears! Go, Bears, go! Whoooo! All right! Whoooo! Who let the dogs out? Who! Who! The Bears, that's who!

Yo, Henry! Grab a beer and a burger and get ready for a real battle! Get in here! The Bears are gonna go right through the Vikes like they're not even there!

What? Jesus Christ! Yes! It's McNown! He's not even supposed to play today! I guess the shoulder's not as bad as they thought! All right! Go get 'em, Cade! Whoooo!

All right, Bears! We gotta take it to the house!

Come on, Allen, run! Run, for chrissakes! No! No, they're gonna get him from behind! Wait—yes! Yes! Beautiful! Give him a few more carries, baby, and we got a chance! That's the way.

And they said we shouldn't have taken that kid in the draft. Whoooo!

Jesus, that Urlacher is huge! The way he took Smith down with one arm? God almighty! We'll see that over and over on *SportsCenter* tonight, I bet. And I'm never gonna get sick of it.

Run, baby, run! Dammit, Bears! Why did you have to roll over and go to sleep like that? They're gonna beat themselves, the way they keep relaxing out there.

Aww, no! No! Stupid fucking Villarrial! You gotta make that block! Stupid bastard! Work out there, will you?

Oh, my God! Hail Mary! The whole game comes down to this.

Yes! That's the way! Yes, yes, yes! Robinson's at the 20! The 15! The 10! The 5! He's got it! He's got it! Thank you, Jesus! Time's run out and it's all over! It's all over!

WHOOOOOO! *Ø*

Aaaaaggh! Bears!

By Dan Turpin
Bears victim

Man, what a beautiful day for a camping trip. I cannot wait to get down to the lake. Today's a perfect day to get away from home.

Oh my God! Bears! They're coming across the field! Aaaaggh! Bears! Aaaaggh! Go, kids! Go! Run! Leave the dog! Aaaaggh! Bears!

No, honey! Leave the beer and the burgers and just run! Run! Get out of here! The bears are going right through the tent like it's not even there!

What? Jesus Christ! No! Not Connie! She's not supposed to go this way! No! Don't let 'em get you, Connie! No! Aaaaggh!

Aaaaggh! Bears! We've got to try and make it to the car!

Come on, Bernie, run! Run, for chrissakes! It's gonna get you from behind! Go! Oh, God, no! NO! God, it's too horrible! He never had a chance carrying that baby.

We never should've taken the kids here! Aaaaggh!

Jesus, that motherfucker is huge! The way he dragged Connie down by her arm? God almighty! I'll never forget that. I'll see that over and over again for the rest of my life. I think I'm gonna be sick.

Run, baby, run! Damn you, bears! Why can't you just go away and leave us alone? Why don't you go off and eat each other? We just wanted to relax out here!

Aaaaggh, no! No! Stupid fucking car keys! Open the goddamn lock! Stupid bastard! Work, goddamn you! Work!

Oh my God! Hail Mary, full of grace! My whole life has come down to this.

No! Not this way! No, no, no! The bear is within 20! 15! 10! 5! He's got me! He's got me! Aaaaggh! Time's up! Oh, Jesus! Aaaaggh! It's all over! It's all over!

AAAAAGGH! *Ø*

New Girlfriend Tests Poorly With Peer Focus Group

RALEIGH, NC—Preliminary data collected Monday from a focus group of friends indicates that new girlfriend Christine Carr is an unsuitable mate for Evan Lindblad.

"I was really excited for everyone to meet Christine," said Lindblad, 25, a graduate student in clinical psychology at North Carolina State University. "I was sure everyone would like her. But now that the numbers are in, I guess I really dropped the ball on this one."

After three weeks of dating, Lindblad held a small party at his home to introduce Carr to a random sampling of his closest friends, ages 22 to 27. Over the course of the evening, Lindblad presented the focus group with a variety of Carr-related queries, ranging from "What do you think of Christine?" to "Is she or isn't she everything I said?"

Lindblad also silently observed focus-group members, making careful note of their spontaneous reactions to Carr.

"At first, everyone was a little shy about speaking up," Lindblad said. "But sometime around 10:45 p.m., when a majority of the focus group was in the kitchen getting beer and Christine was in the other room, everyone really started voicing their opinions. I was right there with the clipboard, taking it all down."

According to Lindblad, Carr scored highest with his five friends from college, with 60 percent of them saying that they "strongly agreed" or "somewhat agreed" with the statement that "Christine seems pretty nice." Carr also fared better with male constituents of the focus group,

Above: Members of the focus group discuss Carr (inset).

who were three times less likely to respond disparagingly to the question, "Did you see what she's wearing?"

After tallying Carr's score in the areas of likability, originality, and believability, Lindblad found that his new girlfriend had garnered a meager 25 percent overall approval rating from the group.

"It was clear that they simply were not enamored with Christine," Lindblad said. "I'm definitely pulling the brakes on bringing her to Eric Barrowman's Christmas party until I can fully assess this data."

In addition to the low approval rating, 11 focus-group members reported feeling "uninterested" or "bored" when speaking to Carr. Further, while in the kitchen, members compiled a list of her negative qualities they would like to see addressed.

"I did not respond well to that laugh," Lindblad friend and coworker Toni Evers said. "It was way too high. And I would've liked to have seen a little more knowledge about Evan's field of work."

Carr even scored poorly in areas in which Lindblad expected her to fare well.

"Christine is beautiful, no one can deny that. But feedback indicated that the group wanted to see someone with a 'more mature look,'" Lindblad said. "The midriff-baring shirt actually worked against her there. Who would have guessed? Well, that's why we do these tests."

By evening's end, a full 85 percent of Lindblad's friends said they agreed with the statement, "Evan can do a lot better."

"I've been close with Evan for several years, and I respect him very much," Evers said. "But if he goes ahead with this relationship, my approval rating of him could drop significantly."

Surprised by Carr's poor showing, Lindblad turned to best friend Jake Hadler for his take on the results. Hadler told Lindblad that his pre-party hyping of Carr, in which he described her as "really funny and incredibly smart," may have backfired.

"I'd heard so many times from Evan how funny Christine was," Hadler said. "It was all, 'Christine said this' and 'Christine did that.' Well, at the party, I had a six-minute exchange with her to ascertain her wit quotient, and during that entire time, she didn't make one joke."

Had expectations not been so high, Carr may have fared better, focus-group participants conceded.

"After the huge build-up, we went in there expecting not merely to be pleased, but blown away," said Lindblad's coworker, Glen Delk. "Had Lindblad simply billed Christine as 'great' or 'a really cool girl,' we'd have approached it differently. But he kept saying, 'This girl may be the one,' forcing us to evaluate her potential as a major love interest instead of a minor fling."

Despite the negative reviews, Lindblad is not yet ready to end the relationship.

"I'd hate to kill this so quickly after just one focus group," Lindblad said. "Maybe she can learn a little more about what I'm studying in school. And work on the laugh. That could get the numbers up." ∅

GERBIL from page 13

ated by death and zombification since a Sept. 15 viewing of *Return Of The Living Dead* on cable TV while his parents were out at a play.

"Seriously, there are these zombies, and they're dead bodies, and they come back to life and try to eat

Basic precautions against the undead will be taken.

your brains," an agitated Dorner told Mefford upon learning of the plan. "Including animals. I saw it."

Unbowed by the prospect of attacks by the undead, Mefford reiterated his intention to open the styrofoam crypt. As a concession to those concerned about zombies, however, basic precautions against the undead will be taken, including the presence

of garlic, a cross, and a Bible. In addition, a large shovel will be kept nearby for the purpose of hitting Marshall if he moves posthumously in any way.

As an added measure, all children who plan to attend the ceremony have been sworn to strict secrecy by Mefford.

"My mom is gonna take my sister to dance lessons at 11, and my dad never gets up before noon on Saturdays, so we have to do it between 11 and 12," Mefford told his jungle-gym audience. "But nobody tell anybody, or we'll get busted, okay?"

Mefford warned potential security threats that compromising the secrecy of the event by tipping off neighborhood adults or engaging in any other form of "telling" would result in their being barred from all future Mefford-sponsored events, including street-hockey games and secret-fort meetings. In addition, tattle-tales would be subject to revocation of treehouse-hideout privileges for one year. ∅

Above: Mefford (center) and some of the children who plan to attend Saturday's gerbil exhumation.

A Year Without Movie Magic? Say It Ain't So, Hollywood!

**The Outside Scoop
By Jackie Harvey**

Item! Are you sitting down? I've just received some very, very bad news. A reliable source tells me that **Hollywood's actors and writers** are preparing to strike, meaning no movie magic in 2001! At first, I thought this was a sick joke, but apparently it's true. Come on, Tinseltown, surely there must be some way for you to settle your differences without resorting to measures that would devastate the rest of us. I was all set to spend next year at my local dodecaplex, enjoying the big-screen thrills of **Josie And The Pussycats**, **The General's Daughter II**, and whatever **Jerry Bruckheimer** had in store. Now what will I do?

Item! Model-actress **Anna Nicole Smith**, star of **The Hudsucker Proxy**, is now millionaire-millionaire Anna Nicole Smith! For those of you Harveyheads who haven't been following the story of this buxom blonde bombshell as closely as I have, let me fill you in. Smith was a stripper, and then she changed her name and posed naked in **Playboy**. Then she married a **really old Texas multi-millionaire** (the real kind, not the TV kind) who died, and he didn't leave her anything! Then she sued the dead millionaire's son and got $500 million.

It's like a Hollywood fairy tale come to life! You go, girl!

I've got a bottle of orange marinade that's been in my refrigerator for almost a year. Do you suppose it's still good?

Item! I just saw **Charlie's Angels** last night, and all I can say is, "Wow!" Actually, that's not all I can say. I can also say, "Talk about your slam-bang action!" Don't let anyone say that **Drew Barrymore** can't act, because she was dead on the money as The Red-Haired Angel. And lovely **Lisa Ling**? She was every bit as good in her role as The Asian Angel. But do you know who the real star was? **Cameron Diaz** as the Blonde Angel. Of all the sexy angels, she was the sexiest. Talk about your all-around star power: Diaz, Ling, Barrymore, **Murray**... If this movie were a weapon, it'd be **a giant bazooka**!

There's a lot of craziness going on in the Middle East right now.

Item! The new TV season is here, so it's time for Jackie Harvey's New Season Scorecard! I was a little hesitant about **The Fugitive**, since TV shows adapted from movies are never that good. (**Bill And Ted's Excellent Adventure**, anyone?) But this really delivers the thrills. So does **Deadline**, the show about the hard-boiled New York reporter who doesn't just write the stories, he makes them. The jury's out, though, on **Normal, Ohio**. I love **John Goodman**, and there were plenty of laughs, but I didn't think the premise was very realistic. Also

boasting star power and laughs is **The Geena Davis Show**. Geena plays a woman named Geena, but not Geena Davis, and she has some sort of job and is married to a single dad after only two dates! You can see the comic potential there. There are plenty more that I haven't seen yet, but I'll try to catch them. My verdict? You

At first, I thought this was a sick joke.

Bette-r believe, the new television **CSI**-son is a **Titans**-ic hit!

I have a little time on my hands, so I've decided to look for a hobby. I've got it narrowed down to two choices: collecting postcards or photography.

Item! A few months back, I broke the story that **Welcome! You've Got Mail** star **Meg Ryan** and **former SNL funnyman Randy Quaid** were calling it splits. Well, I just caught wind of the reason behind the breakup. My sources tell me that Ryan has been playing footsie with Australian superstar **Crocodile Dundee**! Now, while I am 1,000 percent behind the institution of marriage, part of me is hoping that this new romance will add some zest to the forthcoming **Crocodile Dundee III: THIS Is A Knife**. Here's to hope!

You know what's coming up in just

a few weeks? **The Grinch**! Now, at first I had my doubts. I grew up loving the book and the faithful cartoon rendition. The more I thought about it, the better I felt. After all, how can you go wrong with **Ron Howard** at the helm?

Did you know that 90 percent of all dust is really **dead skin**? That rates pretty high on the Jackie Harvey Ick-O-Meter.

In the spirit of the movie **Pay It Forward** (which I haven't seen yet, but I'm dying to!), I am going to help three people, who will help three people, who will help three people so we can live in a better world. So, if you need help moving or want a ride somewhere, let me know. I'd be happy to pay it forward.

Hey, whatever happened to **alternative music**? It used to be the hugest thing, but I haven't heard anyone mention it in a long time. I guess everybody's too busy listening to all that terrific music being made by **black people** and **children**.

Well, I'm out of space for right now, but I've got some stuff up my sleeve next week. Since you asked, here's a little teaser: Wedding bells for **Madonna**? Wedding bells for **Kevin Spacey**? Wedding bells for **Samuel L. Jackson**? Plus, in the where-are-they-now file, **former Today show co-anchor J. Fred Muggs**. All that and plenty more! In the meantime, pop yourself a bowl of popcorn, wrap that blanket around yourself, and soak in the Hollywood magic! ∅

ELECTION from page 13

to say that I am ready to meet those challenges."

"The people have spoken," Bush or Gore continued, "and with their vote they have sent the message, loud and clear, that we are the true party of the people."

With these words, the crowd of Republicans or Democrats erupted.

Bush or Gore attributed his victory to his commitment to the issues that matter to ordinary, hardworking Americans. Throughout the campaign, the Republican or Democrat spoke out in favor of improving educational standards, protecting the environment, reducing crime, strengthening the military, cutting taxes, and reforming Social Security. He also took a strong pro-middle-class stand, praising America's working families as "the backbone of this great nation."

"During this campaign, I had the good fortune to meet so many of you. And I listened to your concerns," Bush or Gore said. "And do you know what I found? That your concerns are the same as mine. Like 64-year-old Rosemary Cullums of Wheeling, WV. She said to me, '[Mr. Bush or Mr. Gore], we need to restore a sense of values and

decency to this country. I have three young grandchildren, and I worry about the filth they're exposed to on a daily basis from TV and the movies. We need Hollywood to take responsibility for its actions and stop peddling sex and violence to our young people.' I told Rosemary I agreed wholeheartedly and gave her my word that when I became president, I would demand accountability on the part of the entertainment industry. Would my [Democratic or Republican] opponent have said the same?"

"The greatest thing a president can do is set an example for the people," Bush or Gore continued. "And as a devoted family man with a wonderful wife and [two or four] wonderful children, I promise to make the White House a place Americans can feel good about."

The crowd erupted again, with thousands of delirious Republicans or Democrats waving signs reading, "America's Families For [Bush or Gore]" as a blizzard of red, white, and blue confetti fell from the ceiling.

During his 30-minute victory speech, the president-elect also praised his campaign manager, Joe

Allbaugh or Donna Brazile, for refusing to resort to the "negative smear tactics of my opponent."

"Unlike my [Democratic or Republican] counterpart, my staff and I in-

Waving to acknowledge his supporters, the Ivy League graduate and scion of a political dynasty called for "a time of renewal and rebirth in America."

sisted that this election be about the issues," Bush or Gore said. "We refused to take the low road and stoop to dirty tricks in order to get elected. While [Mr. Gore or Mr. Bush] was

busy with cheap innuendo and unfounded accusations, we were out there taking our message to the American people. And, judging from what happened today at the ballot box, you heard that message loud and clear. And I thank you."

More confetti rained down from the ceiling, this time accompanied by balloons.

Waving to acknowledge his supporters, the Ivy League graduate and scion of a political dynasty called for "a time of renewal and rebirth in America."

"America has always been the land of promise and possibility," Bush or Gore said. "And never has that been more true than today. The opportunities that stand before us are great. The challenges are many. But I am energized by what lies ahead. Make no mistake, there is much work to be done. But we are more than up to the task. Remember that I am here to work for you, the people. Because you are the people who put me here. This is a fresh start. Our children are the future. America is ready for change. And new ideas. And a fresh start." ∅

The Low Voter Turnout

Despite being one of the closest presidential races in decades, the 2000 election drew a disappointingly low turnout. What do *you* think?

Dina Ackles
Student

"Well, I, for one, knew it was going to be close, and I didn't want to, you know, influence it one way or the other."

Dianne Hoppe
Dentist

"I blame MTV for failing to rock the vote to a sufficient degree."

Mitchell Blake
Systems Analyst

"I was just acting in accordance with the Voter Apathy Act of 1989."

Fred Runnels
Waiter

"I'd have voted if my local races were cooler. Like in Missouri: They had a dead guy on the ballot there, man."

Matt Slocombe
Shipping Clerk

"Not voting is one of the perks of being a convicted felon."

Larry Buckley
Office Manager

"What do you mean? I've done nothing but vote all year—for my favorite song, for most exciting NFL touchdown, for whether the rabbit gets his Trix. I'm fuckin' exhausted."

Wal-Mart In Cyberspace

Amid much hype, Wal-Mart, the world's largest retailer, launched Walmart.com earlier this month. What are some of the features of the online store?

- ↗ Virtual 90-year-old greets visitors at home page
- ↗ Live streaming video of white-trash mother screaming at children to "get down outta that cart"
- ↗ Site causes computer monitor to emit 900-watt fluorescent light
- ↗ Electronics section features Java applet of 50 televisions blaring Disney's *Tarzan*
- ↗ Search option includes RealAudio file of adolescent stockboy saying, "Uhhhhhhh..."
- ↗ McDonald's web site conveniently built into site
- ↗ Four-pack of Maidenform cotton ladies' briefs just $3.96
- ↗ Special viral marketing software erases all other online stores from local servers
- ↗ Shop-at-home convenience enables visitors to shop in underwear, just like in real Wal-Mart

WE SELL FOR LESS

WAL·MART

the ONION

America's Finest News Source

Herman Ulysses Zweibel *Founder*

T. Herman Zweibel *Publisher Emeritus*
J. Phineas Zweibel *Publisher*
Maxwell Prescott Zweibel *Editor-In-Chief*

FOUNDED 1871 • "TU STULTUS ES"

By Lloyd Schumner Sr.
Retired Machinist and
A.A.P.B.-Certified Astrologer

Aries: (March 21–April 19)
As an alternative to cancellation, the stars have decided to cut costs by presenting your future in black-and-white.

Taurus: (April 20–May 20)
You can't shake the feeling that your friends and coworkers discuss your misshapen hump and antlers when you're not around.

Gemini: (May 21–June 21)
True inner peace eludes you when you eat seven chorizo-guacamole tacos with extra hot sauce.

Cancer: (June 22–July 22)
The nation's top onomatopoeia experts will be summoned to describe the wet, cracking, splattery sound you made when you finally hit the pavement.

Leo: (July 23–Aug. 22)
You're not just "big-boned." And it's not glandular. And you *can* help it. Also, that's not just a cold sore.

Virgo: (Aug. 23–Sept. 22)
It's not true that nobody understands your pain. After all, you've been telling people about it for years.

Libra: (Sept. 23–Oct. 23)
Your Thanksgiving plans are dashed when you learn that there has already been a "Libra killer."

Scorpio: (Oct. 24–Nov. 21)
You will spend this weekend trying to come to grips with the awful fact that the American people could elect such a loser on your birthday.

Sagittarius: (Nov. 22–Dec. 21)
You are blessed with great luck to live in a society that feels obligated to try and save your incompetent, drunk ass from its own failings.

Capricorn: (Dec. 22–Jan. 19)
Things may look bad, but this is no time for Cancer to panic. Just put the gun down and trust the officer with the megaphone. He wants to help you.

Aquarius: (Jan. 20–Feb. 18)
You're beginning to realize that, even though your telemarketing job is a good start, it's not as ghoulishly evil as you'd like.

Pisces: (Feb. 19–March 20)
After 20 years of searching, you are forced to admit that there just isn't anything good on TV.

PARTY-PAK from page 11

by the unusually large amounts of blood. Passersby were amazed by the unusually large amounts of blood. Passersby were amazed by the unusually large amounts of blood. Passersby were amazed by the unusually large amounts of blood. Passersby were amazed by the unusually large amounts of blood. Passersby were amazed by the unusually large amounts of blood. Passersby were amazed by the unusually large amounts of blood. Passersby were amazed by the unusually large amounts of blood. Passersby were amazed by the unusually large amounts of blood. Passersby were amazed by the unusually large amounts of blood. Passersby were amazed by the unusually large amounts of blood. Passersby were amazed by the unusually large amounts of blood. Passersby were amazed by the unusually large amounts of blood. Passersby were amazed by the unusually large amounts of blood. Passersby were amazed by the unusually large amounts of blood. Passersby were amazed by the unusually large amounts of blood. Passersby were amazed by the unusually large amounts of blood. Passersby were amazed by the

unusually large amounts of blood. Passersby were amazed by the unusually large amounts of blood. Passersby were amazed by the unusually large amounts of blood. Passersby were amazed by the unusually large amounts of blood.

Those Thai child slaves are really slacking off, if these uneven stitches on my Air Pegasus 2000s are any indication.

Passersby were amazed by the unusually large amounts of blood. Passersby were amazed by the unusually large amounts of blood. Passersby were amazed by the unusually large amounts of blood. Passersby were amazed by the unusually large amounts of blood. Passersby were amazed by the unusually large amounts of blood. Passersby were amazed by the unusually large amounts of blood. Passersby were amazed by the unusually large amounts of blood. Passersby were amazed by the

see PARTY-PAK page 37

Tipper's Thumb Delivered To Gore Campaign Headquarters

see ELECTION page 2A

Naderite Loyalists Nuke Dam

see ELECTION page 4A

Bob Dole: 'Bob Dole's Been Shot'

see ELECTION page 7A

McVeigh Urges Calm

see ELECTION page 8A

0 74470 94595 6

41

the ONION®

VOLUME 36 ISSUE 41   AMERICA'S FINEST NEWS SOURCE™   16–22 NOVEMBER 2000

Nation Plunges Into Chaos

Pro-Bush Rebels Seize Power In West; D.C. In Flames

Above: Riot police advance through downtown Miami, where clashes between Gore and Bush factions left 23 dead Monday night. see COVER STORY page 20

Clinton Declares Self President For Life

WASHINGTON, DC—Denouncing the American electoral process as "immoral and corrupt," President Clinton announced Tuesday that he will not step down on Jan. 20, 2001, instead declaring himself "President For Life."

Proclaiming Nov. 14 a new na-

see CLINTON page 22

Right: Clinton greets his subjects from a White House balcony.

NBC News Reverses Earlier Report Of Gore's Death

NEW YORK—Three hours after placing Al Gore in the "dead" column, NBC News retracted its projection early Tuesday, changing the vice-president's status to "too close to call."

"I'm sorry, but it now appears that we reported Mr. Gore's death prematurely," NBC News anchor Tom Brokaw announced on air at approximately 2:15 a.m. EST. "The latest read-

see NBC page 24

Communication With Florida Cut Off

TALLAHASSEE, FL—Federal officials confirmed Tuesday that all forms of communication with Florida, the bloody battleground for 25 electoral votes, have been cut off.

Across the state, Atlantic Bell phone lines and relays have been severed. The efforts of Georgia-based emergency crews hoping to reconnect lines have been hampered by piles of burning vehicles

see FLORIDA page 21

Bush Executes 253 New Mexico Democrats

Retakes State's Five Electoral Votes

ALBUQUERQUE, NM—New Mexico's five electoral votes swung back into the Bush column Monday when George W. Bush executed 253 Las Cruces-area Democrats. With their deaths, the Al Gore-backing Democrats were declared ineligible, wiping out the Democratic candidate's narrow 252-vote victory margin in New Mexico and giving Bush the state by just one vote.

"We express great sorrow for the families of the condemned," said Karl Rove, Bush's senior strate-

gist. "We must keep in mind, however, that these are not innocent people we're talking about here. These individuals were guilty of a variety of crimes, from vagrancy to jaywalking to reckless endangerment of pedestrians' lives through inappropriate use of rollerblades. And for these crimes, they paid a fair price."

Continued Rove: "The fact that their deaths deliver the state of New Mexico to George W. Bush, well, that's merely a happy coincidence."

The New Mexico De-

Above: The bodies of Democrats are taken by Bush 2000 coroners.

mocrats, all of whom lived less than 20 miles from the Texas border city of El Paso, were arrested last Friday during a day-long law-enforcement sweep by

Texas state troopers. A majority of the arrests were made in El Paso, where many of the New Mexicans were visiting

see NEW MEXICO page 23

Recount Reveals Nader Defeated

TALLAHASSEE, FL—A third recount by Florida election officials has "definitively determined" that Green Party candidate Ralph Nader was defeated in the state. "There was a very significant 25,603-vote discrepancy between the first two counts, with Nader losing by respective margins of 2,812,339 and 2,837,942, so we decided to conduct a hand recount," Florida Attorney General Jim Smith said. "We now know that Nader lost by precisely 2,821,278 votes." It is not yet known whether Nader lost to Gore or Bush.

Strom Thurmond Begins Preparing Cabinet

WASHINGTON, DC—With the presidential-succession crisis threatening to drag on for months, U.S. Sen. Strom Thurmond (R-SC) began the process of assembling his Cabinet Monday. "See here, I believe I'll take Lester Maddox as my Secretary of War," said the 97-year-old Thurmond, who, as president pro tempore of the Senate, is second in line for the White House if the president-elect is not determined by Inauguration Day. "And that Orval Faubus would do a fine job as Secretary of Slaves, he surely would." Thurmond said he has not yet decided who would head the Department of Cows and Chickens.

Child Subjected To Elaborate Hairdo

GRAND RAPIDS, MI—Renée Wilkins, 4, was subjected to a painful, elaborate hairdo at the hands of her mother Monday. "Look how pretty my baby looks," said Chanté Wilkins, 31, after spending three hours meticulously braiding her daughter's hair and stringing 250 multicolored plastic beads onto the braids. "Doesn't she look just like Venus Williams?" Ever since the completion of the elaborate procedure, the child has worn a stocking cap to muffle the beads' ceaseless clacking sound.

Government-Publications Enthusiast Makes Pilgrimage To Pueblo, CO

PUEBLO, CO—Fulfilling a lifelong dream, Kim Cheever of Ames, IA, made a pilgrimage Tuesday to Pueblo's Federal Consumer Information Center. "This is the happiest moment of my life," said Cheever, touring the center that has produced informative government leaflets for the past 30 years. "To think that pamphlets like 'Making The Updated Tax Code Work For You' were dreamed up right here." Cheever ended her visit with a stop at the gift shop, where she purchased a copy of the classic 1972 brochure "Preparing For The Metric Conversion" and a rare misprint edition of "Raising Poultry For Meat And Eggs."

Area Man A Walking Encyclopedia Of Everything Except Leading A Normal Life

ODESSA, TX—Gene Weldon, 34, was praised by friends and family Monday for his expertise on dog breeding, spelunking, and countless other subjects except leading a normal life. "One time, I asked Gene what he thought about the recent market fluctuations, and he gives this long lecture on the history of the Nikkei Index," friend Mindy Becker said. "With a body of knowledge like that, you'd think he'd at least own a car." Cousin Mike Framisch agreed, saying, "For a guy with no regular full-time job, he knows an awful lot about the ecosystem of the Marianas Trench."

Hypothetical Question Clearly Not Hypothetical

YUMA, AZ—Brad Thorstadt was rattled Monday, when hiking partner and longtime friend Ken Daniels asked him a hypothetical question that clearly was not hypothetical. "What the hell did he mean by, 'Hypothetically speaking, if you and Cheryl were into threesomes, would you consider me?'" Thorstadt asked. "That's not the kind of thing you just ask hypothetically." Thorstadt added that he likes Daniels and everything, but damn. ∅

A Nation Is Engulfed In Violence And Darkness

WASHINGTON, DC—Presidential-election-related violence continued to spread across the nation Tuesday, with Day Seven of the battle for the White House claiming another 1,200 lives.

In Bush-controlled Tennessee, news of Gore's call for a sixth recount in the disputed territory of Florida sparked full-scale rioting, with Republican militiamen setting fire to Gore's heavily fortified Nashville compound. It is believed Gore running mate Joseph Lieberman was trapped in the blaze, though his whereabouts and status were unknown as of press time.

In Austin, Democrats continued to clash with armed Bush troops outside the Texas capitol building. Inside, the Bush family waited for news on the welfare and whereabouts of Dick Cheney, who was carried off by a band of NARAL Reproductive-Freedom Fighters.

Washington sources reported via short-wave radio that the city is littered with burning and abandoned National Guard tanks. The last D.C. television transmissions, which were broadcast at 11:22 p.m. EST Monday, showed the drowned bodies of more than 200 Young Republicans in the National Mall's cyanide-laced reflect-

Washington sources reported via short-wave radio that the city is littered with overturned and abandoned National Guard tanks.

ing pool. It is unknown whether the deaths are a mass suicide or the work of a Democratic guerrilla group operating out of the Gore-controlled territory of Maryland.

Since declaring himself President For Life, President Clinton has remained sealed inside a subterranean White House bunker with a cadre of Secret Service personnel and a stock-

pile of canned goods. Like the many state governors who declared themselves regional warlords over the weekend, Clinton said he plans to wait out the fighting in the streets.

Meanwhile, Bush and Gore steadfastly maintained their claims to the presidency after respectively declaring Austin and Nashville the provisional national capitals. While Gore controls much of the nation's Northeast and Upper Midwest, Bush currently holds all territory west of the

Mississippi River except California and Washington. Each man has issued commands to the American people to cease rioting and acknowledge him as president, and has ordered the armed forces to salute him as the next Commander In Chief.

Borders between Gore states and Bush states have been witness to some of the fiercest fighting of the past week. Along the Illinois-Indiana border, an estimated 240 people have

see CHAOS page 22

A Portentous Estate Sale

photo circa 1911

By T. Herman Zweibel
Publisher Emeritus

Several months ago, I informed *The Onion*'s Middle-western readers of their impending sale as part of an offering of this news-paper's mid-continental distribution district. This transaction was conceived as a way to shore-up the paper's dwindling cash reserves. I still believe my asking price of $20 million and the marriage-hand of Lillian Gish was more than fair, but to date I have received no letters of inquiry. God damn my fellow plutocrats for the weak-willed, lily-livered cheap-skates that they are!

So, in lieu of this transaction, I was forced to sift through my mansion to look for any salable items I might have laying about the place that would be suitable for the auction-block. I charged this important task to several servants, most of whom soon became unaccounted for, presumably either making mad-dashes for freedom or being consumed by the Mor-locks who reside in the base-ment.

A few managed to crawl back to the main foyer with some objects, of which I was able to select a catalogue that I fully believe will bring a good price and keep me in disposable diaper-maids for another quarter.

For sale on offer, certain items formerly attached to the Zweibel Estate:

- Busts of Mother Zweibel, lot of 44, some tear-staining.
- An oaken credenza, five feet high by four feet deep by 86 feet long. Suitable for royalty. Plenty of space for china and silver-ware. Was once HMS Redoubtable, now decommissioned.
- The Stone Of Scone.
- One fine German-made Zeppelin, confiscated for religious reasons by T. Herman Zweibel's Swiss Guard. Warranty expired. No guarantee expressed or implied. Sporting shade of grey. Smells somewhat of mildew.
- A medium-sized casque of bright and shining jewels roughly the size of hen's eggs.
- Several bright-eyed buck Irish-men.
- The Type-setter's Stone, a mystical tailing of basalt which transforms gold into the purest lead.
- Several absconded ballot-boxes from the election of 1912.
- 12,044 quarts of billionaire's urine, in jars.

What a plethora of munificence! What glorious crap! I hate to part with it. But I have no doubt that it shall all be sold by the time you read this, and I shall be rolling in filthy lucre once more. ∅

I'm Like A Chocoholic, But For Booze

By Ralph Chadwick

Did you ever know a "chocoholic"? One of those folks who just can't get enough chocolate? I bet there's at least one in your home or workplace. At my house, it's my wife Emily. She's got to have her little bowl of Hershey's Kisses in the living room. She can't go shopping without bringing home some chocolate ice cream or a chocolate-cake mix. She's even got a funny little sweatshirt that says, "My Name Is Emily, And I'm A Chocoholic."

To be honest, I'm a bit of a chocoholic myself. Except for one small detail. You see, instead of being addicted to chocolate, I'm addicted to booze. Yep, from dawn to dusk, there's one thing on my mind: booze! Beer, liquor, wine, all that stuff!

When my wife gets one of her cravings, she reaches for a Baby Ruth or Mars bar. With me, it's Icehouse beer. My refrigerator is always stocked with plenty of it. I also have a little flask of whiskey in my desk drawer at work. In fact, if you can keep a secret, I even keep some booze in my car in case of traffic jams. I just can't stand to be without booze for too long!

I'm a lot like that Cookie Monster on Sesame Street. Only it's more like the *Booze* Monster. When I walk into a party and see that they have booze of any kind, it's like, "Whoa-hoa! All bets are off! Lemme at that booze!"

I remember this one time when there was no chocolate in the house. Emily was going out of her mind, trying to scrape up some sort of chocolate fix. In the end, she resorted to drinking a cup of hot cocoa. It was so cute! Sort of like the time I drank all her hairspray because there was no booze in the house. Or that other time with the rubbing alcohol. Or the Nyquil. Or the Aqua-Velva.

Another time, I was completely out of booze, and all the stores and bars were closed, so I drove 45 minutes to find a place that would sell me some beer or something. I was kind of embarrassed, because here it was late Monday night, I had to work the next day, and I'm driving around looking for booze. But, hey, that's just how things are when you're a "booze-oholic" like me! I finally found a huge all-night liquor store. You should have seen how I loaded up! Cases of this, fifths of that. It was 5 a.m. when I finally got home, so I just said, "To heck with work!" and had my own little improvised holiday. I called it Booze Day! I'd been working hard, getting to work on time almost every day for two weeks, so I figured I'd earned what wound up being the rest of the week off.

Sometimes Emily and I think we should cut down a little—you know, health concerns and all. But there's always some special occasion that gives us an excuse to go off our "diets." Halloween was Emily's last big bender. We only got three trick-or-treaters the entire night, so the whole big bowl of Reese's Peanut Butter Cups went straight to her. (Or straight to her thighs, as she said!)

My most recent bender was today. There was a good movie on TV, and I figured, hey, I'll need steady hands to change the volume. Of course, it all went straight to my liver, but what are you gonna do?

For my birthday, Emily gave me the funniest coffee mug, perfect for Irish coffee. It has a little teddy bear on it with a "don't mess with me" look on his face, and it says, "Hand Over The Booze And Nobody Gets Hurt." I laughed so hard! That bear was just like me when I robbed the party store earlier this year! Also, the mug is really big, so it can hold a lot of booze... another plus!

Yes, those chocoholics are a funny sort. But they won't hurt you—as long as they have their chocolate, that is. Or, in my case, booze! ∅

FLORIDA from page 19

choking all roads leading into the state.

In addition to the loss of phone contact, Internet, television, and radio communications have been lost to the surging violence plaguing the most bitterly contested state in the nation.

"We are attempting to bring swift and fair closure to these elections," said Florida Gov. Jeb Bush during a statewide televised message at 7:35 p.m. EST Monday, the last known transmission from the Sunshine State. "We ask that Gore and his followers concede gracefully and allow a dignified end to this long—what the...? No! Back! Back!"The screen then went black.

Though technicians stationed along the Georgia border have reported receiving faint, garbled radio signals from walkie-talkies and ham radios, the content of these transmissions is unclear. Through the heavy static, the technicians have reportedly heard a variety of unconfirmed sounds, including screams for help, the toneless recitation of random strings of numbers, and harshly barked combat orders.

The technicians could also make out certain specific words and phrases, including "Bush by three," "rerererererecount," and *"Oy gevalt."* Several heavily accented female voices could also be heard wailing, "Elián."

According to reconnaissance photos taken by Russian military aircraft, the entire southeast portion of the state, including Miami and Ft. Lauderdale, is obscured by thick smoke. In a recent photo of Biscayne Bay, the water has a distinct crimson tint. Another photo shows a flotilla of commercial fishing boats, overloaded with refugees and sailing in the direction of Cuba.

"We have no idea what's going on down there," said Captain Matt Tunney of the Georgia National Guard, one of the few reserve units available to respond to the Florida crisis. "There are 15 million people trapped in that boiling cauldron, everyone from Boca Raton retirees to Jacksonville rednecks to Miami Beach fashion models. To be honest, I don't think I want to know what's going on." ∅

21

Serbia Deploys Peacekeeping Forces To U.S.

BELGRADE—Serbian president Vojislav Kostunica deployed more than 30,000 peacekeeping troops to the U.S. Monday, pledging full support to the troubled North American nation as it struggles to establish democracy.

"We must do all we can to support free elections in America and allow democracy to gain a foothold there," Kostunica said. "The U.S. is a major player in the Western Hemisphere and its continued stability is vital to Serbian interests in that region."

Kostunica urged Al Gore, the U.S. opposition-party leader who is refusing to recognize the nation's Nov. 7 election results, to "let the democratic process take its course."

"Mr. Gore needs to acknowledge

Above: Serbian peacekeeping troops patrol Washington, D.C.

the will of the people and concede that he has lost this election," Kos-

tunica said. "Until America's political figures learn to respect the in-

stitutions that have been put in place, the nation will never be a true democracy."

Serbian forces have been stationed throughout the U.S., with an emphasis on certain trouble zones. Among them are Oregon, Florida, and eastern Tennessee, where Gore set up headquarters in Bush territory. An additional 10,000 troops are expected to arrive in the capital city of Washington, D.C., by Friday.

Though Kostunica has pledged to work with U.S. leaders, he did not rule out the possibility of economic sanctions if the crisis is not resolved soon.

"For democracy to take root and flourish, it must be planted in the rich soil of liberty. And the cornerstone of liberty is elections free of tampering or corruption," Kostunica said. "Should America prove itself incapable of learning this lesson on its own, the international community may be forced to take stronger measures." ∅

CLINTON from page 19

tional holiday as "Day One of Americlintonian Year Zero," Clinton issued a directive of total martial law over "all territories formerly known as these United States, from now on to be called the Holy United Imperial Americlintonian Demopublic (HUIAD)." He added that all election results are "hereby invalidated under Demopublican pro-

visional law."

"The American people have spoken," Clinton said. "By failing to generate a 51 percent majority for either candidate, they have shown their inability to muster the drive to collective action. The time has come for a new America, a strong Americlintonian Empire, capable of providing the indecisive electorate with direction through one man's sheer force of will."

Dressed in full military regalia and flanked by members of his elite Demopublican Guard, Clinton told reporters, "Let all peoples of the land know this: The era of bipartisan inaction and paralysis has ended. The Age of the Great Cleansing Fire begins today."

A significant portion of the U.S. Armed Forces has sworn loyalty to the Imperial Demopublic Council of Generals, the new military wing of the Clinton regime. But in spite of such support, many political observers question the constitutionality of Clinton's actions, which in-

clude the burning of the Constitution, the dissolution of Congress, and the establishment of "re-education camps" in suburban D.C.

At a sparsely attended press conference, U.S. Attorney General Janet Reno raised the prospect of a Justice Department investigation of "possible illegal activities" on the part of Clinton. Most observers, however, believe that such a probe is unlikely: Less than an hour after Reno spoke, her battered and broken body was publicly fed to Clinton's dogs.

"Let them bring their pitiful reprisals to the impotent courts. Their lawyers and lawsuits shall face the wrath of a people united by the almighty fist," said Clinton, whose divinity as HUIAD's first Emperor-God was ratified late Tuesday night by the Americlintonic High Priest Council. "Let them recount their puny paper ballots. They shall wither, as will the bankers, lawyers, and lobbyists all, before the Holy Cause of Americlintonia's glorious, righteous might."

Defiant in the face of objections from the Bush and Gore camps, Clinton has consolidated his power over the last several days, ordering armed takeovers of major federal buildings and the systematic collection and display of his enemies' heads on iron pikes.

In a test of the new regime's power outside the nation's capital, Senator-Elect Hillary Clinton, rechristened "Bride of the Lord Clinton on Earth," summarily ordered HUIAD troops to fire on

Manhattan crowds, leaving more than 2,500 dead on Wall Street and quickly dispersing protesters loyal to defeated Republican challenger Rick Lazio.

Resistance movements are already forming. The new Legion of Californians has sworn to defeat HUIAD in the west, and anti-Clinton groups have been reported across the U.S., including Naderist factions in Washington State and Maine.

Clinton has publicly dismissed such insurrections as "pathetic," confident that nothing will stem his authority over "the former U.S."

"The rebels are but mewling kittens who shall taste blood instead of milk," said Clinton, threatening to deploy HUIAD-controlled nuclear weapons against members of resistance movements. "The holy power of the atom shall, if it must, cleanse this nation of all infidels." ∅

CHAOS from page 20

died in skirmishes, including 47 Danville, IL, residents in a midnight Hoosier raid on the Gore-controlled state. On Sunday, police at the Arizona-California border turned away more than 40,000 Golden State Republicans seeking to cross into Bush-controlled Arizona. Democratic refugees attempting to cross in the opposite direction were similarly rebuffed.

News of other presidential candidates is sketchy at best. On Monday, National Public Radio reported that a man "strongly resembling" Ralph Nader was crucified at the hands of angry New Hampshire Democrats.

Pat Buchanan is believed to have entered Florida with several hundred Jewish followers shortly before communications with the state were lost. Libertarian Party candidate Harry Browne is believed to be mounting a challenge to election results in Suffolk County, NY, where Constitution Party candidate Howard Phillips edged him out for fifth place by just two votes.

Alan Greenspan, who established the Fed-In-Exile in Paris last Friday, has announced a freeze on the markets until order can be restored. He has temporarily fixed the value of the U.S. dollar at $15 Canadian.

Citizens have been urged to stay in their homes and keep their lights off until further notice. ∅

FOOSBALL from page 2

were amazed by the unusually large amounts of blood. Passersby were amazed by the unusually large amounts of blood. Passersby were amazed by the unusually large

Can we discuss this after I pee?

amounts of blood. Passersby were amazed by the unusually large amounts of blood. Passersby were amazed by the unusually large amounts of blood. Passersby were amazed by the unusually large amounts of blood. Passersby were amazed by the unusually large amounts of blood. Passersby were amazed by the unusually large amounts of blood. Passersby were see FOOSBALL page 34

friends or relatives over the weekend.

Asked if the executions were in any way motivated by his narrow deficit in New Mexico, Bush said, "They most certainly were not."

"All 253 individuals were found

Above: Bush gives the go-ahead sign to executioners at the El Paso Correctional Facility.

guilty in a court of law," Bush said. "They were given a fair, 30-minute trial and handed a punishment commensurate with their misdeeds. Blatant disregard for the law may be tolerated elsewhere, but not in the great state of Texas. Or states close to Texas."

The New Mexico Democrats were administered lethal injection and pronounced dead shortly after 3 p.m. in the El Paso Correctional Facility, making them the 36th through 288th persons to be put to death in Texas this year. Immediately afterward, their ballots were nullified in their home voting district of Dona Ana County.

> "All 253 individuals were found guilty in a court of law," Bush said.

According to Texas Department of Corrections spokesman Martin Cobb, 27 of the executed Democrats were employees of a Las Cruces software company. They had crossed the Texas border to attend the weekend-long Southwest Computer Expo at the El Paso Convention Center.

"All of the information we gathered on the Las Cruces 27 indicated that they were questionable characters," Cobb said. "Some had subscrip-

tions to The New Yorker. A few were confirmed members of the Sierra Club. One even participated in a union-led teachers' strike a few years ago."

Despite cries of protest from families of the deceased, both the Texas Board of Pardons and Paroles and the Texas Court Of Criminal Appeals refused to stay the executions. Rove, however, is confident that they received a fair trial.

"It was presided over by the Honorable Jacob T. Hayes, one of the most respected and experienced judges in the state," Rove said. "You're talking about a man who is a close personal friend of such esteemed figures as the governor of Florida and a former president of the United States."

Bush, who personally presided over the mass lethal injection, expressed sorrow for those executed.

"It is a tragedy that these people chose to take their lives down such a destructive path," Bush said. "Fortunately, they did not die in vain, for their deaths will serve as a deterrent to other New Mexico Democrats who are considering a similar life of crime." ∅

OPINION

Ask A Man Getting Yelled At By His Wife Over The Phone At Work

By Doug Bauer

Dear Man Getting Yelled At By His Wife Over The Phone At Work,

My friend is going all-out for her upcoming wedding—400 guests, tons of flowers, the works. As her maid of honor, I'm spending every minute of my free time driving her from one store to another. I'm honored she wants me at her side on her big day, but does that mean I need to be her personal chauffeur for the three months leading up to it?

—Worn Out In Wilmington

Dear Worn Out,

Doug Bauer, purchasing. Hi, Anne. I really can't talk right this—what's wrong? Well, no, not exactly. Honey, I really can't talk right now. I'm right in the middle of something. No, I didn't forget. I just didn't have time. Yes, I know. Yes. Honey, I really can't—I know. I know. Hold on. I know. Honey, hold on a sec. What do you need, Ben? The Datech order? I'm just finishing it up. Five minutes, I'll bring it down. Anne? I'm sorry. Ben. Ben Upchurch. Yes, the one with the BMW. I'm sorry, sweetie, but I have to go now, okay? I know, but I didn't mean to. I didn't—I'll do it as soon as I get home, I promise. I'm writing it down right now: deck... furniture. I will. No, I won't forget.

Because I said I wouldn't. That really isn't necessary, is it? Why? All right, fine: I promise I'll do it as soon as I get home. Yes, dear. Yes, dear. Yes, dear.

Dear Man Getting Yelled At By His Wife Over The Phone At Work,

Now that I've moved to a small apartment in a retirement center, the last thing I need is clutter. Next month, I'm having my 70th birthday party, which leads to my problem. At previous parties, I've asked that no one bring a gift, but many just dismissed my request as modesty. How do I make it clear that I'm serious about my guests showing up empty-handed?

—Cramped In Cranston

Dear Cramped,

Doug Bauer, purchasing. Anne, I can't talk. Yes, I'm aware what day it is. Of course I did. The what? Aw, Christ. Do we have to? It's just that it's been a hell of a day here. Can't we just skip it? Of course I care about your sister. Of course. Yes, *of course.* I just don't think I... Do you have to bring that up? You said you forgave me for that. I know. I know. Honey, this has nothing to do with that. I know. An ice-cream cake?

Where am I supposed to get an ice-cream cake? Honey, I have a call on the other line. What's Bambi's? Bambi's Bakery? Where is it? Fine, I'll look it up. Sweetie, I really have to get that call. Chocolate? I'll do my best. Marbled? Okay. I've got to go. I understand. Of course I love you. Because I'm very busy, that's why. I'm sorry. I'm sorry. Yes, I love you. Of course I meant it. No, of course not. If I sound busy, it's because I am. Why? Okay, *I love you,* Anne.

Dear Man Getting Yelled At By His Wife Over The Phone At Work,

My boyfriend has the worst taste in clothing. Not only that, he only has about three shirts he actually wears, and they're all worn out and faded. Now he's in line for a possible promotion at work, and I think it's time to whip his wardrobe into shape. I don't expect him to become a fashion plate, but I do think having a neat and professional appearance counts in the eyes of an employer. Don't you agree?

—Exasperated In El Paso

Dear Exasperated,

Doug Bauer, purchasing. Honey, I can't even understand you. Slow down. A phone call? No. No, I wasn't.

Can we talk about this when I get home? I really don't have time right now. Honey, I need to get... Honey, please... Honey, I... Hon—what do you mean? Who? Sarah who? If you don't, how should I? This really isn't a good time for this sort of thing. Because I'm sitting at my desk. I'm in my cubicle and everyone is—I know. It's just that there are a lot of people hovering around nearby, and I'd really rather not—I know. Can't we just talk about this when I get home? When I get home, I promise I'll... I swear, I don't know anyone named Sarah. No. What? Why didn't you say she was calling from Dr. Silver's office? I thought you knew that. Hiding what? Cavities? Anne, I can't sit here and—that was different. It just was. I know. I know. I'm honestly not sure. That's true. Yes, I do appreciate it. Of course. I'm very sorry about that. I have to go, though. We will. Yes. As soon as I get home. In four hours, I promise. I will. Yes, absolutely. Okay, I'll skip the gym. In three hours.

Doug Bauer is a syndicated columnist whose advice column, Ask A Man Getting Yelled At By His Wife Over The Phone At Work, *appears in more than 250 newspapers nationwide.* ∅

Election Madness

With Florida's results in doubt, several other states mulling recounts, and both Bush and Gore threatening legal action, the winner of the Nov. 7 presidential election has yet to be determined. What do *you* think?

"Gore should concede and let Bush have the presidency. After all, he's truly earned it."

Len Ruffin
Meat Packer

"I just hope they do a revote in my district. I'm pretty sure I accidentally voted for Leo Koepke for county clerk instead of Barb Shultz."

Elaine Pasqua
Homemaker

"The only clear mandate I see emerging from this election is that elderly Palm Beach Jews want an end to abortion and affirmative action."

Bethany Aldrete
Teacher

"Man, that Doris Kearns Goodwin must be wetting her pants over this."

Donald Youmans
Chiropractor

"This has been an incredibly difficult time for me, not knowing whether to invest in Solarcorp or GloboPetrochemical."

Andrew Deshaies
Systems Analyst

"See, now this is why I don't vote."

Patrick Bosio
Auto Mechanic

Celebrity Children's Books

From John Lithgow to Katie Couric, celebrities are taking up the pen to author children's books. What are some of the other big-name offerings?

'A' Is For Rechargeable Drill	Larry King
The Prettiest Actress	Jennifer Aniston
Bunny With Honor	Chow Yun-Fat
The Boy Who Was Out Of His Freakin' Mind, Man	Dennis Hopper
Mr. Crazy Shoe-Face Guy Buys A Pie	Adam Sandler
Where The Wild Things Are 2K	Will Smith
The Innocent Lamb	Christopher Walken
You *Will* Be Perfect	Kathie Lee Gifford
The Little Fourth-Quarter Earnings Index That Could	Alan Greenspan
How Would You Like It If Someone Took A Picture Of You When You Didn't Want It?	George Clooney
L'il Lyssa And Her Very Good Publicist	Alyssa Milano
It's Okay To Be "Dehydrated"	Brandy
The Unicorn That Shat Out Rainbows	Jewel
The Boy Who Never Got Picked On Ever	Charlton Heston

 **the ONION**
America's Finest News Source

Herman Ulysses Zweibel *Founder*
T. Herman Zweibel *Publisher Emeritus*
J. Phineas Zweibel *Publisher*
Maxwell Prescott Zweibel *Editor-In-Chief*

FOUNDED 1871 • "TU STULTUS ES"

By Lloyd Schumner Sr.
Retired Machinist and
A.A.P.B.-Certified Astrologer

Aries: (March 21–April 19)
When all is said and done, and your time on Earth is finished, you will just barely have made it to the end of this sentence.

Taurus: (April 20–May 20)
Everything will go smoothly this week, except for the part with the monkeys and the cream pies.

Gemini: (May 21–June 21)
Nothing can stop you now that you have reached light speed and your mass has become almost infinite.

Cancer: (June 22–July 22)
You will survive the upcoming bloody purge at your workplace, only to discover that you're the only one left to pay for all the coffins.

Leo: (July 23–Aug. 22)
Relax, one more little deviled egg won't hurt. You already weigh 435 pounds.

Virgo: (Aug. 23–Sept. 22)
You will regret your vote in the recent presidential election when a pack of Corvairs storms your house and kills your entire family.

Libra: (Sept. 23–Oct. 23)
Stop worrying: It's impossible to be perfect, and people enjoy almost everything about you. It's not your fault that your gizzard is tough, stringy, and tasteless.

Scorpio: (Oct. 24–Nov. 21)
After years of resistance, you will be forced to admit that a strong centralized government that relies on popular hatred of a common enemy is a flawed concept that can't work in the long run.

Sagittarius: (Nov. 22–Dec. 21)
Scientists at the Metropolis Institute of Applied Geology will be happy to loan you the kryptonite—until they discover what you want it for.

Capricorn: (Dec. 22–Jan. 19)
Things being the way they are, you might want to hold off on further pyramid construction until science can prove the designer's far-fetched claims.

Aquarius: (Jan. 20–Feb. 18)
You will learn through harsh experience that you would, in fact, not rather push a Ford than drive a Chevy.

Pisces: (Feb. 19–March 20)
Come on, those first six seals were fun to open! Why not go for the seventh?

NBC from page 19

ings show his red-blood count down to 3.1. At this point, it could go either way."

Gore, shot Monday by a Republican sniper during a foray into the Bush-controlled territory of New Hampshire, has been clinging to life in a hospital just across the Vermont border.

According to NBC News correspondent Tim Russert, nurses and anesthesiologists leaving the operating room at various points during a 14-hour operation on Gore were exit-polled regarding his chances of survival.

"When several sources reported a direct hit to the spinal cord, everyone thought it was all over," Russert said. "It turns out that report was erroneous. The shot missed the spinal cord by a hair's width."

Early in the evening, NBC's on-

NBC was not alone in prematurely calling Gore's death.

screen outline of Gore was colored blue, signifying life. At 11:17 p.m. EST, it turned red, indicating death. When word arrived that Gore had a pulse but no signs of brain activity, the outline reverted to its original uncolored state, meaning "unconfirmed."

In the hours following the erroneous report, NBC was more cautious about making projections, posting the latest readings from Gore's blood-pressure monitor but refraining from speculating about his overall status.

Democratic Party chairman Ed Rendell expressed anger over what he called NBC's "shoddy, irresponsible journalism."

"Who knows how this could affect how Gore is perceived when he attempts to gather military support in disputed states?" Rendell said. "NBC should know better than to call the outcome of an operation before the body is even closed."

NBC was not alone in prematurely calling Gore's death. CBS, ABC, and CNN all made the same mistake.

"In our efforts to bring Americans the most up-to-the-minute news on the war for the White House, we made some hasty decisions," CBS anchor Dan Rather said. "I'd like to apologize to all of our viewers, as well as to the entire Gore junta." Ø

Running Shoes Used Mainly For Computer Programming

see LOCAL page 4C

Another Fond Childhood Memory Destroyed

see ENTERTAINMENT page 11B

Parkay Container Suffers Debilitating Stroke; Now Speaks With Difficulty Out Of One Side Of Lid

see PRODUCTS page 2D

STATshot

A look at the numbers that shape your world.

Top Obsessive-Compulsive Disorders

- **36%** Having sex with exactly eight women on way home from supermarket
- **25%** Stabbing potato three times before buttering
- **16%** Researching OCDs
- **14%** Keeping careful track of usage of the word "the" while reading (2)
- **9%** Always scrubbing hands before performing surgery

0 74470 94595 6   43

the ONION®

VOLUME 36 ISSUE 43   AMERICA'S FINEST NEWS SOURCE™   30 NOVEMBER–6 DECEMBER 2000

Lab Rabbit Strongly Recommends Cover Girl Waterproof Mascara For Sensitive Eyes

CINCINNATI—LR-4427, a two-year-old laboratory rabbit at Procter & Gamble's cosmetics testing facility, Monday gave his full endorsement to Cover Girl Long & Luscious waterproof mascara for sensitive eyes.

"Cover Girl Long & Luscious waterproof mascara will dramatically magnify your lashes for a look that's glamorous and natural," LR-4427 said. "And the great part is, they won't irritate your eyes, even if you accidentally smear some over your clamped-open eyeballs

see RABBIT page 29

Right: Lab rabbit LR-4427 enjoys all-day glamour with Cover Girl Long & Luscious mascara.

Teen Exposed To Violence, Profanity, Adult Situations By Family

BROWNSVILLE, TX—According to the conservative watchdog group Family Research Council, the home of 15-year-old Beth Arnott contains violence, profanity, adult situations, and other material "wholly unsuitable" for those 16 and under.

"That house is filled with inappropriate material that sets a poor example for the impressionable youths living there," said Family Research Council president Kenneth Connor, citing 44 instances of domestic violence, adult language, nudity, and graphic sexual content in the Brownsville

see TEEN page 28

Report: 98 Percent Of U.S. Commuters Favor Public Transportation For Others

WASHINGTON, DC—A study released Monday by the American Public Transportation Association reveals that 98 percent of Americans support the use of mass transit by others.

"With traffic congestion, pollution, and oil shortages all getting worse, now is the time to shift to affordable, efficient public transportation," APTA director Howard Collier said. "Fortunately, as this report shows, Americans have finally recognized the need for everyone else to do exactly that."

Of the study's 5,200 participants, 44 percent cited faster commutes as the primary reason to expand public transportation, followed closely by shorter lines at the gas station. Environmental and energy concerns ranked a distant third and fourth, respectively.

Anaheim, CA, resident Lance Holland, who drives 80 miles a day to his job in downtown Los Angeles, was among the proponents of public transit.

"Expanding mass transit isn't just a good idea, it's a necessity," Holland said. "My drive to work is unbelievable. I spend more than two hours stuck in 12 lanes of traffic. It's about time somebody did something to get some of these other cars off the road."

Public support for mass transit will naturally lead to its expansion

Above: Traffic moves slowly near Seattle, WA, where a majority of drivers say they support other people using mass transit.

and improvement, Los Angeles County Metropolitan Transportation Authority officials said.

"With everyone behind it, we'll be able to expand bus routes, create park-and-ride programs, and

see COMMUTERS page 28

Man Who Threatened To Move To Canada Before Election Still Here

CEDAR FALLS, IA—Despite repeated pre-election threats of expatriation, area resident Ron Glick remains a U.S. citizen, acquaintances of the 43-year-old reported Monday. "For weeks leading up to the election, Ron kept saying, 'I swear, if that clown wins, I am moving to Canada,'" coworker Paula Vogel said. "Well, he's been at work every day since, so unless he's commuting from Winnipeg, he's still here." Glick has threatened to renounce his citizenship every four years since 1980, when Reagan's victory was supposed to have precipitated his emigration to Spain.

Hollywood Diet Secrets Fall Into Non-Celebrity Hands

HOLLYWOOD—In a major Hollywood security leak, an Encino, CA, company has made "Weight-Loss Secrets Of The Stars" available to the non-famous. Direct Sales International made the offer through ads last week in *The National Enquirer* and *Weekly World News.* "Learn how the rich and famous take unwanted pounds off FAST—and KEEP them off!" the ad read. "I am horrified by the implications of this," Julia Roberts said. "The institution of celebrityhood could crumble, with our thigh-trimming and belly-banishing secrets now public. The global balance of beauty has been tipped forever. God help us all."

Employee Worries Coworker's Computer Screen May Be Larger

DALLAS—Dan Pulsipher, a Java engineer with software developer Razornet Technologies, fretted Monday that the computer monitor of coworker Allen Walls may be larger than his own. "I've got a 17-incher," Pulsipher said. "But I'm almost positive that Allen's is a 19. What gives?" Pulsipher, who has been with Razornet three and a half years to his counterpart's six months, also fears that Walls' monitor may have a .26mm dot pitch.

Food Critic's Wife Makes The Best Lasagna She Possibly Can

CHARLOTTE, NC—Fran Greaves, wife of *Charlotte Observer* restaurant critic Paul Greaves, said Monday that she tries to make the best lasagna she possibly can. "I made this gourmet lasagna completely by the book," Greaves said. "I bought fresh ingredients from the farmer's market, I made the pasta from scratch with semolina flour. But I just can't shake the feeling that it still won't be good enough for Paul." Greaves' husband has previously been disappointed in his wife's chicken marsala, veal schnitzel, and lemon chiffon cake.

Death Results In Great Deal Of Paperwork

FLAGSTAFF, AZ—The death of 88-year-old Bea Wexler resulted in a mountain of funeral, burial, and estate-settlement paperwork Monday. "Why now? We just finished the paperwork on our new mortgage," sobbed Peggy Addison, Wexler's daughter. "Why in Arizona, where the probate process can take months?" Addison's husband Bryan hugged her before bearing down on the preliminary death-certificate forms.

Arsenio Hall Writers Still Keeping In Touch

LOS ANGELES—According to former *Arsenio Hall Show* head writer Garry Schenk, the writing staff of the 1989-94 late-night talk show still keeps in touch. "Yeah, I still see Tony [Andruss] every now and then," Schenk said Monday. "And I just ran into Ed [Canzona] a few days ago. He's over at *Kilborn* now and also does some freelance monologue stuff for *Politically Incorrect*. And Fred [Moffatt] e-mailed me maybe a month or two ago. He's working for some radio syndicate that does song parodies and some other bits for morning-DJ shows." Added Schenk: "Man, I can't believe it's been six years." ✐

I Am Refreshingly Open About My Personal Life

By Jason Renfro

Some people never let you know the "real" them. They keep their deepest thoughts and emotions tucked away from the rest of the world. Why they would want to, I'll never know. I, for one, am refreshingly open about my personal life.

Would you like to know about the problems I'm having with my wife? No need to ask. If you are vaguely acquainted with me, you doubtless already know about the miscarriage, the affair, the second miscarriage, the man from Oklahoma City, and the fact that Gloria's allergy-relief medication has a dehydrating effect, which necessitates our use of lubricants during sex. (Chances are pretty good you also know that we prefer WET-brand lubricants over Astroglide.)

Did I tell you about the recent fight with Gloria when I knocked over the Christmas tree? No? I'd be happy to go into all the sordid details. Some people would probably be too closed and repressed to share something like that, but not me.

You see, unlike some people, I'm honest enough with myself to admit that I have problems. And, as part of my healthy attitude, I'm comfortable letting everyone in on them. Sometimes, it takes hours of explanation to really get to the heart of things, but my friends, coworkers, and fellow Food Lion shoppers are worth it.

Just like anyone, I sometimes experience feelings of worthlessness, hopelessness, and doubts about where my life is headed. So when somebody at work asks me, "How's it going?" I take the time to answer truthfully, unafraid to let my true emotions out. If there isn't enough time over lunch in the break room, I'll catch the person as he or she is leaving work and finish up what I was saying. I know exactly what they're thinking when I stop them from climbing into their car. They're thinking, "Thank goodness someone in this world has the courage to cut through all the lies and superficiality and bare his soul. Thank goodness there's at least one person out there who isn't hiding behind a mask."

I'm not just refreshingly open about my emotions, but my desires and interests, as well.

Take, for example, anal sex. I really enjoy it, giving and receiving it. Now, I know I'm hardly alone in this, but for some reason a lot of people consider this classified information. But why should it be? Do we really have to bury our feelings all the time? If my dentist asks me how my weekend went, I'd be a liar if I didn't admit that the highlight was all that great anal sex. Well, I'm no liar. And I refuse to put up walls between myself and those around me.

I like to share with people. It brings us all closer together. That's why, if you know me, you know I like masturbating to women's tennis magazines. Of course, I like masturbating to plain old porn, too, but how many times can I mention that before I feel like I'm intentionally trying to hide my enjoyment of tennis magazines out of some societally imposed notion of shame?

That reminds me of the time I caught pubic lice from a woman I met in a bar. Most people would have been all guarded about it, spending the day at work scratching behind closed doors. Not me. I let everyone know what I was going through, and

that the reason I had to take a longer-than-normal lunch was that I had to run to Walgreens and get some Rid. I wasn't about to sidestep the issue. We all need to share what's really going on in our lives.

Then there's my family history. Some people save so-called "deep, dark secrets" for their closest friends. Why they do this, I'll never know. My mother's addiction to painkillers, my father's cross-dressing, the beatings, and what my childhood babysitter did to me—ask me where I grew up, and I'll tell you all this and more.

All this talk of family brings me to my brother. He's in jail for carjacking an SUV. The whole thing went awry, and he accidentally wound up killing the owner. If I'm with someone who has an SUV, I'm not afraid to say, "Hey, my brother is in jail for killing someone over a car like this." If they express shock over my brother's fate, I just tell them, "Oh, being in jail can't be too bad. You get a lot of anal sex there. I love anal sex." Though they usually have to rush off and attend to their busy lives, I get the satisfaction of knowing that I reached out and connected with a fellow human being, no matter how briefly. ✐

Mockery

photo circa 1911

By T. Herman Zweibel
Publisher Emeritus

Hi, everybody! I'm T. Herman Zweibel! I'm old and stupid! I wet myself a lot! I live in a big, stupid mansion! Listen to me talk about a lot of old stuff! I think it's actually 1907! Blah, blah, blah, blah, blah!

Hey, you damned kids, what are you doing in my study? Get away from that linotype-machine! How the devil did these juveniles breach the walls of my estate and elude my Swiss Guard? Go on, clear out, you gutter-snipes! Hey, I told you to keep away from that linotype-machine!

I am T. Herman Zweibel, the world's most boring person! I am older than Jesus! Remember the War Of 1812? I do, because I'm so old! Hey, Standish, give me an enema!

What? Why, you rat bastards! You churlish reprobates, you ought to be soundly thrashed with a length of barbed-wire! Ah, Standish, there you are! Get these unsanitary adolescents out of here! No, I don't want an enema! Those cocky little street-arabs were merely impersonating me!

I have hundreds of diseases! I yell at people a lot! I hyphenate compound words for no reason! Blah, blah, blah, blah!

Stop it! Stop it! You're wearing out the italics! Standish, look what these youths are doing! Oh! They just spilled India ink all over my precious codicils! And look at that one over there, wearing that beautiful waste-paper basket on his head like a *pickelhaube*! This is all so humiliating! What's that, Standish? You say I should read aloud from this piece of paper? Drat it, man, I don't want to read these brats a bed-time story! You say it may get them out of here? Well, I do not have my lorgnette on me, but I will try any-way:

"Hey, you teen-agers! You are all a bunch of faggots, and I question your sexuality! You wear the same stupid sweat-shirts every day, and no-one will ever have sex with you, ever! Your faces are clotted with pimples, and your hair is oily, and you cannot control your erections! You are all worth-less, ugly, and stupid!"

Look, Standish, they're running away, weeping! Huzzah! I forgot how emotionally vulnerable adolescents are, and that even the most callow insult is their Achilles' heel! A brilliant idea, Standish, turning the tables like that! Quick, alert the Swiss Guard to intercept them as they approach the front gate, and yank their under-trousers up into the chasm 'twixt their buttocks!

No, let's keep the column transcribed as is. I want all teen-agers to see this, and know that they cannot get the best of T. Herman Zweibel, no matter how they try! ∅

EDUCATION

Third-Grader Awaits Lesson For Cursive G

GRAND RAPIDS, MI—Area third-grader Abigail Werner is anxiously awaiting the lesson for the cursive letter G, George Washington Carver Elementary School sources revealed Monday.

"Abigail has come up to my desk five times in the past three days asking when we would be learning G," teacher Ellen Honig said. "I told her we'd probably get to it sometime next week, but that I couldn't make any promises."

Honig began a cursive unit on Nov. 10 as part of her class' regular language-arts instruction. After teaching her students the five vowels, enabling them to "jump right into" writing full words, Honig moved to the beginning of the alphabet, focusing on one letter per session. The most recent letter taught was D.

Werner has paid careful attention to each lesson, practicing the letters at home, on the bus, and at the lunch table. Last Friday, Werner chose to spend recess inside to practice the letter B. In the first week of cursive instruction, Werner went through an entire 50-sheet pack of penmanship paper.

"I know the A and the B and the C and the D and the E and the I and the O and the U," said Werner, holding up a sheet of paper bearing meticulously rendered, cursive versions of such words as "Cab," "Cub," "Abe," and "Ace." "But I can't wait until we learn the G."

With cursive lessons on Mondays, Wednesdays, and Fridays only, Werner may have to wait at least a week to

Above: Anxiously awaiting further lessons, Abigail Werner practices the cursive letter D (right).

learn the seventh letter of the alphabet.

"We should get to G very soon, but you never know," Honig said. "We could have a fire drill, or the multiplication-filmstrip series I ordered might finally come in. I also have to consider that the capital F usually gives students a fair amount of trouble. That may take a whole day in and of itself, separate from the lowercase F."

Until G is taught, Werner will continue to practice the letters she has learned thus far in the "Puppies And Kittens" Trapper Keeper she keeps in her tote tray at school.

"I'm glad we're learning our cursive letters now, because Mom said she's going to let me write my own name on the Christmas cards this year," Werner said. "I want to write my name like a grown-up. And when you draw a picture, you're supposed to sign your name in cursive."

For the past week, Werner has been writing "Abbie" in cursive at the top of her papers. Though she had long spurned "Abbie" as too childish for a third-grader, preferring the more mature "Abigail," the name does not re-

quire any letters she does not know.

Werner stressed that her motives in learning cursive G are not entirely selfish.

"There are lots of people that start with the letter G," Werner said. "My dad's name is Gary, and our dog's name is Grady. And Grandma. Mrs. Honig has a G in her name. And Grand Rapids. And George Washington Carver Elementary. The Powerpuff Girls have a big G. And God, too."

Karen Werner, 38, has been supportive in her daughter's quest for cursive knowledge.

"Abigail's really excited about that G," Werner said. "She had to go to the dentist last week but refused to until I called Mrs. Honig to make sure the class wouldn't be learning G that day. They were only reviewing the vowels, thank goodness."

"I'd teach Abigail the rest of the letters myself, but, to be honest, I don't even remember how a lot of them look anymore," Werner added. "I couldn't make a capital Q to save my life."

Werner said this is not the first time her daughter has become fixated on a

school subject. In May, she developed a three-week obsession with woolly mammoths. During summer vacation, she made 28 baskets using a paper-weaving technique she learned at a library recreation program. And just last month, the 9-year-old became so interested in her classroom's hermit crabs, she requested to be permanently placed on the cage-cleaning duty chart.

"When Abigail is curious about something, she really goes all out," Honig said. "Whether it's the four food groups, pilgrims, rocks and minerals, or penguins, she really throws herself into it."

According to child psychologist Dr. Alexandra Levens, Werner's obsession with the cursive G is perfectly healthy.

"Abigail is an eager, precocious child who wants to do things adults can do, like sign their names," Levens said. "This shows intelligence and maturity on her part. Nevertheless, I'm glad I won't be around when Mrs. Honig tells her she has to wait another three weeks to learn the lower-case L she needs to write 'Abigail.'" ∅

COMMUTERS from page 25

Above: Morning rush hour on one of Los Angeles' economical, environmentally friendly buses.

build entire new Metrolink commuter-rail lines," LACMTA president Howard Sager said. "It's almost a shame I don't know anyone who will be using these new services."

Sager said he expects wide-scale expansion of safe, efficient, and economical mass-transit systems to reduce traffic congestion in all major metropolitan areas in the coming decades.

"Improving public transportation will do a great deal of good, creating jobs, revitalizing downtown areas, and reducing pollution," Sager said. "It also means a lot to me personally, as it should cut 20 to 25 minutes off my morning drive."

The APTA study also noted that of the 98 percent of Americans who drive to work, 94 percent are the sole occupant of their automobile.

"When public transportation is not practical, commuters should at least be carpooling," Collier said. "Most people, unlike me, probably work near someone they know and don't need to be driving alone."

Collier said he hopes the study serves as a wake-up call to Americans. In conjunction with its release, the APTA is kicking off a campaign to promote mass transit with the slogan, "Take The Bus... I'll Be Glad You Did."

The campaign is intended to de-emphasize the inconvenience and social stigma associated with using

public transportation, focusing instead on the positives. Among these positives: the health benefits of getting fresh air while waiting at the bus stop, the chance to meet interesting people from a diverse array of low-paying service-sector jobs,

Collier hopes the study serves as a wake-up call.

and the opportunity to learn new languages by reading subway ads written in Spanish.

"People need to realize that public transportation isn't just for some poor sucker to take to work," Collier said. "He should also be taking it to the shopping mall, the supermarket, and the Laundromat." ∅

TEEN from page 25

Above: A parental-advisory sticker warns of a family not recommended for children 16 and under.

home in the past month alone. "This is hardly the sort of family we should be exposing our nation's children to."

Connor noted that Beth's stepfather, 43-year-old Randy Skowron, frequently walks around the house in an open bathrobe, inadvertently

exposing his genitalia to Beth. He also cited numerous incidents of Skowron hitting Beth's brother Ronnie with an open hand for being "all mouthy and disrespectful." Beth herself was subjected to a similar act of violence when she was caught shoplifting a Victoria's

Secret bra at Valle Vista Mall.

Other inappropriate material to which Beth has been exposed includes frequent use of the term "skank-ass bitch," nightly binges of Mad Dog 20/20, and an incident in which she inadvertently stumbled across Skowron and her mother in coitus just minutes after the pair had been throwing kitchen appliances at each other.

"The family is the most important factor when it comes to promoting family-friendly themes," Connor said. "The Arnotts may pay lip service to being a pro-family family, but their actions speak otherwise."

Author and critic Michael Medved, a leading proponent of stricter moral standards, agreed.

"These are graphic sexual themes which could take a girl, just coming into an understanding of her own sexuality, and twist her around until she doesn't know right from wrong," said Medved, co-author of Saving Childhood: Protecting Our Children From The National Assault On Innocence. "I feel sorry for Beth, for her childhood has been lost and her innocence assaulted."

"We challenge the Arnotts to get serious about the vital role they play in shaping America's culture," said U.S. Rep. Steve Largent (R-OK), who has proposed legislation requiring warning labels on non-family-friendly families. "Look at the Petersons right next door. With their regular attendance at church, frequent family outings to Chuck E. Cheese's, and weekly Sunday-night Scrabble games, the Petersons are the sort of wholesome, socially redemptive family this country needs more of. Why must we put up with this vile Arnott filth when there are such wonderful alternatives literal-

ly right next door?"

Following Largent's lead, concerned Brownsville residents are calling for the placement of a parental-advisory sticker on the Arnotts' front door which warns that interaction with the family is not recommended for children 16 or younger. In addition, locals have petitioned Cat Marine Machine Tooling, Skowron's employer, to fire the man, threatening to withdraw their patronage if the shop continues to "endorse the de-

"This is hardly the sort of family we should be exposing our children to," Connor said.

plorable actions in Beth's home by keeping Mr. Skowron on the payroll."

One neighbor, wishing to remain anonymous, said: "We don't want to censor anybody, but we have an obligation to the community and to our children. We can monitor our kids within our own home, but we can't protect them when they go out into the world every day and are exposed to sex, violence, and drug use by families like that."

For all the controversy her family has stirred, Beth remains indifferent.

"It's not a big deal," said Beth, smoking a Kool cigarette stolen from her mother's purse. "Just because I see Mom giving Randy blow jobs and Ronnie huffing paint don't mean I'm gonna do that shit. I can think for myself." ∅

It'll Be A Blue Christmas Without Stuff

You know that old Christmas carol that goes, "Christmas is coming, the goose is getting fat, please put a penny in the old man's hat"? Well, might I suggest a slight lyric change

**A Room Of Jean's Own
By Jean Teasdale**

to "please put a penny in Jean Teasdale's hat"? And, instead of "a penny," make it "$2,756.29"? Because that's how much my Visa bill is right now, and I'm afraid that Christmas at the Teasdales is not going to be too merry this year if I don't find a way to pay this thing off pronto!

It's not like I haven't been trying to pay it off. I mean, I've been working my tail off at Fashion Bug. (I'm up to 30 hours a week!) I'd work even more if my boss, Roz, would let me, but she hired a new girl, Ellen, who wanted extra hours, too. That irked me a little. After all, it's not like we get a huge amount of business anyway, especially on weekdays, and having an extra person around seems kind of unnecessary. But Ellen is a friend of Roz's, so that got her an automatic in at the Bug. Plus, she's always going off about how she's a single mom with two kids and is strapped for cash. Don't get me wrong: I love kids to pieces and hope to have some of my own someday. (Can't you hear those loud ticks coming from my biological clock?) But just because Ellen is a mom, that doesn't make her better than me. We all have crosses to bear. I mean, I've got a police record now, but you don't hear me trying to get sympathy or favoritism from it.

It's a shame that I'm in such debt, because my own X-mas wish list is about a mile long this year. And, after the Year From Hell that I had, I deserve a little something nice! Of course, I've got one thing going for me: the fact that my family is no longer speaking to me due to that little born-again Christian fiasco of mine. So at least I'll save a few hundred bucks not buying presents for them!

Also on the plus side, hubby Rick agreed to pay the entire amount of rent until I have my debts paid off! The only catch is, he made me promise to pay for the groceries, utilities, car insurance, and cable, not to mention settle at least half my credit-card debt before I even thought of splurging on myself at the mall. The fact that I couldn't get more hours at Fashion Bug didn't soften him a bit. "Just get a second job," he snorted. (Sheesh! Heil Hubby!)

Still, I can't stop dreaming about the stuff I'd love to buy myself this X-mas. For example, I just know there's a DVD player out there with my name on it. Have you seen these things? They're amazing! They can squeeze an entire movie onto a single CD! I swear, after seeing one at Best Buy the other day, I wanted to go straight home and throw our VCR in the garbage! The only thing

> It's a shame that I'm in such debt, because my own X-mas wish list is about a mile long this year. And after the Year From Hell that I had, I deserve a little something nice!

better than a DVD player would be a DVD player with a Patrick Swayze movie in it all cued up and ready to go! (Rowrr, rowrr!)

There's also a great T-shirt I saw at Spencer Gifts. It says, "I'm A Shopaholic In A 12-Step Program. Steps 1 Through 11: Shop. Step 12: Get Drunk After You See Your Credit-Card Bill." My God, whoever came up with that shirt must be a regular reader of my column! Anyway, I've just got to have that thing!

Now, you Jeanketeers out there know that I have a terminal case of Precious Momentsitis, and there's a figurine I'm just dying for. It's a little girl who's about to set a dessert in her heart-shaped cupboard, only to find a darling kitten in it! It's called—what else?—"You Have A Special Place In My Heart." Well, that figurine sure has a special place in mine! (Only problem is, it would also have a special place in my wallet... to the tune of $55!)

I'm also constantly seeing things I want in the dozens of catalogs I get in the mail each month. I really like those miniature indoor water fountains they sell now. They're supposed to alleviate stress and relax you. And, seeing how hectic my life has been lately, I could really use one! I was trying to persuade hubby Rick to buy one since he's always so

uptight, but he just said, "They look Oriental. They're probably Chinese water-torture machines designed to drive Americans insane." (Boy, way to prove my point, Rick!)

Okay, okay, I admit it. I have champagne tastes. Jean Teasdale always wants nothing but the best. As my mother, from whom I am now estranged, likes to say, "The moment Jean has a dollar in her pocket, she'll find a way to spend it." Well, I may have had a lot of Grinches to contend with this year, but that doesn't mean I've lost my belief in Santa Claus!

I don't often admit this to people, but I still believe in Santa Claus. Not in him literally existing, but in the belief that the holidays are a time for magic, and that people will get rewarded for trying their best. Call me an incurable optimist, but it does happen. In fact, it just happened to me. This morning, I was taking my winter coat out of storage and, upon reaching into the pocket, I pulled out a real sight for sore eyes: a $20 bill! And this is one $20 bill that Grinch Rick and his austerity plan will never get, because I'm going out right now and buying one of those hilarious singing bass. They've been out for months now and, darn it, I deserve one!

Oh, don't worry: Rick is on my shopping list, too. After all, 'tis better to give than to receive, right? Only, I don't think he should get one of those inflatable NFL chairs he wants so much. No, I think a gift-wrapped cinnabar candle from Fashion Bug will do just fine. They're 50 percent off right now, and with my employee discount, it'll cost practically nothing. Rick will be proud of my frugality, I'm sure!

(Ain't I a stinker?!?) ✍

RABBIT from page 25

with a Q-tip and can't flush it out for 48 hours."

LR-4427 said he also likes the fact that the Cover Girl product stays on, rain or shine.

"No matter what the weather, you're guaranteed gorgeous lashes with Long & Luscious mascara," LR-4427 said. "And they'll stay that way all day long, in 10 hours of 200-degree heat from a hair dryer or icy blasts from a shower head."

In the past six months, LR-4427 said he has tried "literally hundreds" of different mascaras. Of these, he said, Cover Girl Long & Luscious offers the best combination of good looks, durability, and non-corrosiveness.

"The Cover Girl mascara they ground into my right eye is 10 times better than the Max Factor Midnight Thicklash that was ground into my left," said LR-4427, speak-

ing from immobilization cage 39B. "The Max Factor stuff is greasy and cheap-looking, not satiny and sophisticated like Cover Girl. And, unlike Cover Girl, Max Factor doesn't wash away easily—not even with industrial soap and steel-wool scouring pads."

According to LR-4427, eyes are the first thing you notice about a person. And nothing is more important to the look of a woman's eyes than mascara.

"If you're anything like me, you hate it when the look you spent all day perfecting is ruined by your mascara running or dripping," said LR-4427, cocking his head as much as possible inside his plastic holdfast collar. "Well, your worries are over, because Cover Girl Long & Luscious stays on your eyes right where the injectors put it. With Long & Luscious, there's no need to

cauterize your tear ducts shut, unlike some mascaras I could mention."

LR-4427 added that clinical tests have proven that Cover Girl Long

> According to LR-4427, eyes are the first thing you notice about a person.

& Luscious will leave your lashes 40 percent thicker than Elizabeth Arden mascara. In addition, Long & Luscious will feel 50 percent less like your eyes are melting down your cheeks after being

pierced with red-hot fireplace pokers.

"The last thing you want right before a big date is to lose confidence in your mascara," LR-4427 said. "You need to know that his eyes will be on yours—not on any chemical scarring."

"And if you have a long day... or night," continued LR-4427, attempting a saucy wink in spite of his surgically excised eyelids, "touch-up's a breeze. Just pack more Long & Luscious into your orbital sockets, your nostrils, your anus—any of the delicate tissues that get stressed by your busy lifestyle—and you're ready to go."

LR-4427 then returned to work, where he is finishing up testing a new aloe-scented exfoliating scrub before being reassigned to Procter & Gamble's small-arms ammunition division. ✍

Abolish The Electoral College?

In light of the havoc it has wreaked this presidential election, many Americans are calling for an end to the electoral college. What do *you* think?

"No, we should not stop using the electoral college. We also should not stop spinning our own flax."

Irene Costa
Reference Librarian

"We must keep the electoral college. Without it, last night's *Nightline* probably would have been about the war on cholesterol."

Reggie Ennis
Cashier

"The electoral-college system was designed to protect our nation from the ignorance of its people. And, based on the 2000 vote, it's still dearly needed."

Manny Blake
Systems Analyst

"I'm all for getting rid of the electoral college, but wouldn't that mean we'd have to dig up Samuel J. Tilden and make him president retroactively?"

Tom Kallen
Optometrist

"This election mess confirms what I've been saying for years: Our nation should be split into warring factions, each ruled by a warlord who receives messages from God."

Matt Funk
Cab Dispatcher

"The presidency should go to the candidate who earns the larger minority of the popular vote."

Liz Lowery
Sales Clerk

Seussmania

This year has witnessed the opening of a Dr. Seuss theme park in Florida, the debut of a Dr. Seuss Broadway musical, and the release of a movie version of *How The Grinch Stole Christmas*. Why is the popular children's author suddenly everywhere?

23% Collective desire to reclaim *Cat In The Hat* iconography from hippies

19% Are of South-Going Zax descent; appreciate Seuss' compassionate depiction of their race's plight

14% Identify with Horton's not being believed when he says little invisible people talk to him

10% It was raining, so there was nothing to do but see Jim Carrey movie

22% Appreciate timeless human drama of taking off hat after hat, only to find more florid hat waiting underneath

12% Theodor Geisel dead and can't complain

the ONION

America's Finest News Source

Herman Ulysses Zweibel *Founder*

T. Herman Zweibel *Publisher Emeritus*
J. Phineas Zweibel *Publisher*
Maxwell Prescott Zweibel *Editor-In-Chief*

FOUNDED 1871 • "TU STULTUS ES"

By Lloyd Schumner Sr.
Retired Machinist and
A.A.P.B.-Certified Astrologer

Aries: (March 21–April 19)
Be on your guard this Tuesday: It will feel suspiciously like a Thursday.

Taurus: (April 20–May 20)
Your plan to cash in by pretending to be the long-lost offspring of a celebrity fails when a jury notices you look nothing like Bigmouth Billy Bass.

Gemini: (May 21–June 21)
You find yourself with a career in academia when a banana peel puts you in the physics, comedy, and medical textbooks.

Cancer: (June 22–July 22)
A longstanding neurosis will disappear this week when, during pillow talk, your mother assures you that your Oedipal complex is imaginary.

Leo: (July 23–Aug. 22)
You will lose the respect of your fellow wizards when your "Magic Pancakes" turn out to be normal pancakes made with sour cream instead of buttermilk.

Virgo: (Aug. 23–Sept. 22)
The stars indicate through subtle, non-verbal cues that you have the worst breath they've ever encountered.

Libra: (Sept. 23–Oct. 23)
The "arrogance and hubris" you display by choosing a cabinet is noted to the press by your spouse, who has not yet decided if the two of you are getting a new kitchen.

Scorpio: (Oct. 24–Nov. 21)
Ballistics tests conducted by top experts in the field will reveal that you throw like a goddamn girl.

Sagittarius: (Nov. 22–Dec. 21)
Your refusal to become a team player is a disappointment to the others in your sign. Remember, it's not Sagittari-*you*.

Capricorn: (Dec. 22–Jan. 19)
Your growing paranoia is all in your mind—just ask the KGB field operative who turned you into a top double agent.

Aquarius: (Jan. 20–Feb. 18)
It's time to start acting your age: When most people turn 87, they've been dead a couple years.

Pisces: (Feb. 19–March 20)
You are mystified by everyone's ability to deduce your musical tastes, political beliefs, and sexual habits from your sweater-vests.

WAXY from page 19

Passersby were amazed by the unusually large amounts of blood. Passersby were amazed by the unusually large amounts of blood. Passersby were amazed by the unusually large amounts of blood. Passersby were amazed by the unusually large amounts of blood. Passersby were amazed by the unusually large amounts of blood. Passersby were

How come I never get any credit for all the times I *didn't* run anyone over?

amazed by the unusually large amounts of blood. Passersby were amazed by the unusually large amounts of blood. Passersby were amazed by the unusually large amounts of blood. Passersby were amazed by the unusually large amounts of blood. Passersby were amazed by the unusually large amounts of blood. Passersby were amazed by the unusually large amounts of blood. Passersby were

amazed by the unusually large amounts of blood. Passersby were amazed by the unusually large amounts of blood. Passersby were amazed by the unusually large amounts of blood. Passersby were amazed by the unusually large amounts of blood. Passersby were amazed by the unusually large amounts of blood. Passersby were amazed by the unusually large amounts of blood. Passersby were amazed by the unusually large amounts of blood. Passersby were amazed by the unusually large amounts of blood. Passersby were amazed by the unusually large amounts of blood. Passersby were amazed by the unusually large amounts of blood. Passersby were amazed by the unusually large amounts of blood. Passersby were amazed by the unusually large amounts of blood. Passersby were amazed by the unusually large amounts of blood. Passersby were amazed by the unusually large amounts of blood. Passersby were amazed by the unusually large amounts of blood. Passersby were amazed by the unusually large amounts of blood. Passersby were amazed by the unusually large amounts of blood. Passersby were

see WAXY page 31

Area Senior Up For Some Boggle

see ELDERBEAT page 8D

Personals Ad Omits Goiter

see PEOPLE page 7C

KFC Manager Robbed At Sporkpoint

see LOCAL page 4C

$175 Appliance Makes One Kind Of Food

see PRODUCTS page 11D

STATshot

A look at the numbers that shape your world.

Least-Safe Airlines
1. Amtrak Air
2. Usually Transatlantic
3. Shur-Fine Airlines
4. Air Reparations To Loved Ones
5. Stygian Air
6. Airline '77
7. Macomb County Community College Airlines
8. Bubba And The Plane He Done Builted

---

the ONION®

VOLUME 36 ISSUE 44   AMERICA'S FINEST NEWS SOURCE™   7–13 DECEMBER 2000

Above: National Doggy Appreciation Society president June Erhardt.

Nation's Dog Owners Demand To Know Who's A Good Boy

WASHINGTON, DC—Bearing facial expressions ranging from goofy to adoring, dog owners from across the U.S. gathered in the nation's capital Monday, demanding to know who's a good boy.

"Who's a good boy?" asked Na-tional Doggy Appreciation Society president June Erhardt, speaking before an estimated 300 canines ranging from border collie to schnauser. "Who? Who?"

Added Erhardt: "Is it you? Is it

see OWNERS page 34

Black Guy Photoshopped In

Above left: The original, black-guyless photo. Above right: The Iowa State course catalog, featuring digitally added black guy Marcus Jamison.

AMES, IA—In the spirit of celebrating diversity at Iowa State University, a black guy was digitally added to the cover of the school's 2001 spring-semester course catalog, school officials announced Monday.

"Here at Iowa State, we have a remarkably diverse student body, with literally dozens of non-whites," Iowa State director of student affairs Andrea Driessen said.

"We thought a picture with at least one non-white happily interacting with whites would be a great way to show off this fact. Unfortunately, we didn't have any pictures of whites and non-whites actually interacting, so we had to make one up."

Said chancellor Dr. Michael Arbus: "An unaltered, or 'real,' cover photo would not have adequately

see BLACK GUY page 35

Vatican Warns Against Increasingly Healthy Attitudes Toward Sex

VATICAN CITY—Alarmed by rising rates of pleasurable, mutually fulfilling acts of physical love among Catholics, the Vatican issued a statement Monday warning

Above: Pope John Paul II warns against the dangers of mutually fulfilling acts of love.

against healthy attitudes toward sex.

"The practice of so-called 'healthy sexuality,' with its emphasis on the spiritual and physical nourishment of consenting partners in a relationship built on mutual respect, has no place in the Holy Roman Catholic Church," the 200-page document read. "Those who have derived pleasure from such non-shame-based practices are not living according to God's law."

The Vatican statement cited 183 different "wholly sinful" sexual acts, including the discreet, occasional manipulation of one's own genitals for pleasure, intercourse positions designed to heighten sensations of ecstasy, and intimate, post-coital cuddling and conversation with a loved one outside the bounds of the marital bed.

The statement also listed 244 phrases which are regarded as blasphemous when uttered in a non-procreative context. Among them: "God, your breasts are beautiful," "I feel so complete when you're inside me," and "I love to watch your belly rise and fall after we make love."

Church officials were quick to

see VATICAN page 34

Recount Demanded In 4-4 Supreme Court Decision

WASHINGTON, DC—Insisting that a vote was lost or failed to register, lawyers for George W. Bush are demanding a recount of Monday's 4-4 Supreme Court decision in the case *Bush v. Palm Beach County Canvassing Board.* "With nine justices on the bench and only eight votes accounted for, something clearly went wrong during the vote-tallying process," Bush lawyer Theodore Olson said. "Either that, or one of the justices' ballots was filled out improperly. You must remember that most of these individuals are extremely old and, as such, are easily confused by the complicated butterfly ballots used in Supreme Court cases." Olson said he believes the missing vote belongs to John Paul Stevens, an 80-year-old Gerald Ford appointee whose eyesight is failing and suffers periodic spells of senility.

Shingles Sufferer Sick Of Explaining What Shingles Is

NEWPORT NEWS, VA—Meredith Burr, a Newport News human-resources administrator who contracted shingles three weeks ago, announced Tuesday that she is "completely fed up" with explaining what the illness is. "For the last time, shingles is a viral infection that causes a painful rash similar to chicken pox," Burr said. "The medical term is herpes zoster, and it usually lasts from two to five weeks. Now, will you leave me alone? My skin is burning." Burr added that shingles should not be confused with piles, rickets, scurvy, or the gout.

Freddie Prinze Jr. Fan's Favorite Color Also Green

BURBANK, CA—Reading a profile of teen heart-throb Freddie Prinze Jr. in the December issue of *Tiger Beat*, 15-year-old Caitlin Rasmussen was thrilled to discover that both she and her favorite actor cite green as their favorite color. "That is so unbelievable," Rassmussen said. "Freddie likes green, and I like green. We have so much in common." As further evidence that the pair are soul-mates, Rasmussen noted that she and Prinze share a fondness for ice cream.

Driver Rattled By Brush With Death For Nearly 10 Seconds

DOUGLAS, WY—Following a narrowly averted fatal collision with a weaving semi truck on Interstate 25, motorist Kent Withers was badly shaken for nearly 10 seconds Monday. "My God," said Withers, momentarily pondering the frailty of human life. "I could have been killed." Added Withers: "I could go for a bacon cheeseburger."

Hard Day's Work Fails To Yield Sense Of Job Well Done

EVANSVILLE, IN—After a hard day's work Monday, Cahill Financial Group administrative assistant Janice Croyer mysteriously lacked a deep sense of pride and satisfaction in a job well done. "I don't know what it is," said Croyer, punching out. "I should feel great about the work I did today, but I'm not on any sort of high." It was the 2,076th consecutive work day to produce vocational indifference in Croyer.

Man Can't Decide Whether To Give Sandwich To Homeless Or Ducks

ST. PAUL, MN—While eating lunch in Como Park Monday, Justin Winningham, 34, struggled to decide whether to give his extra smoked-turkey sandwich to a homeless man or a group of ducks. "The homeless guy seemed pretty hungry and probably would have appreciated it," Winningham said. "But those ducks just looked so darn cute, and I knew they'd get all excited and flap their wings if I fed them." After noticing a slight paunch on the homeless man, Winningham decided the ducks needed the food more and lovingly hand-fed them. ∅

48-Year-Old Still Unsure What He Wants To Do With His Life

NORTH BELLMORE, NY—Bob Cellini, a 48-year-old North Bellmore postal supervisor, informed coworkers Tuesday that he is still trying to figure out what he wants to do with his life.

"Working for the post office is okay for some people," said Cellini, addressing a trio of letter carriers in the Newbridge Road Postal Station break room. "But I feel like I've got a lot more to offer the world. I just need to find my true calling, so to speak."

Cellini, who has worked at the Newbridge Road branch for seven years, has held 14 jobs since graduating from Nassau Community College in 1974. Among them: a three-year stint at the Farmingdale Post Office, six years as a UPS delivery driver, two years as a teller at Anchor Bank, and 18 months as an office-furniture salesman with Workplace Solutions.

"At Workplace Solutions, I sold a lot of chairs to Davis-Gennaro Advertising, one of Long Island's biggest ad agencies," Cellini said. "I always did well selling to them. I think that's because, just like them, I'm one of those people who's able to think along creative lines. I think I'd do well in advertising. Maybe I could fill out an application next time I'm in the neighborhood."

Other careers Cellini has consid-

> **Other careers Cellini has considered include lawyer, private detective, special-effects artist, used-bookstore owner, pastry chef, sitcom writer, and paramedic.**

Above: Postal supervisor Bob Cellini.

ered include lawyer, private detective, special-effects artist, used-bookstore owner, pastry chef, sitcom writer, and paramedic.

Cellini said that whatever he winds up doing with his life will undoubtedly incorporate one of his many interests.

"I like tons of different things, and I think one of them will eventually lead to my career," the unmarried Cellini said. "Like, I recently made a spice rack for my kitchen, which got me thinking, 'Hey, and I should start my own woodworking shop!' Other people probably just would have made the spice rack without it ever occurring to them that it could be something more than just a hobby. And these are people who probably have boring jobs they hate. I guess I've just always believed you should follow your passion."

Cellini admitted that his ascent from mail sorter to mailroom supervisor has temporarily sidetracked his search for his ideal career.

"As long as I've been a postal worker, I've been keeping an eye out for something that's more 'me,'" Cellini said. "But I kept getting promotions and raises, which makes this job harder to walk away from. Just as soon as I know what I really want to do, though, I'm definitely out of here." ∅

All's Right With The World

By T. Herman Zweibel
Publisher Emeritus

photo circa 1911

Huzzah and greetings to the fine *Onion* reader-ship! All is well with you, I hope! You have a crust to gnaw upon and whale-oil aplenty, I trust? No more boils than usual? Excellent! Now, be not misled by my unaccustomed cheer. My concern for your welfare is genuine, I assure you, for everything is splendid to-day.

Yes, that's right, I am full of good-will this morning for reasons upon which I cannot put my finger. No, it is not the tincture of laudanum I placed in my thin gruel. If anything, I took less than usual. It is not the ceaseless flow of money into my coffers, for I have yet to affect the sale of the Type-setter's Stone, let alone that of the Middle-West, and I am currently rather light in the pockets for a multi-millionaire.

And, no, it is not my physical well-being that prompts this unusual display of glee. In fact, my iron dentures rusted shut under a cascade of vinegarish drool last night and had to be unseized by black-smith's torches just minutes ago—they are cooling to a dull cherry-red even as I dictate this—and I bloodily shat some vaguely spleen-like organelle into my bed-pan during break-fast. Physically, I feel as miserable as ever.

But if my heart is light within its sheath of crackling gray fat, who am I to question it? All is right with the world. The birds sing and the fawn frolics. Cherubs sing and play upon airy spinets. And God is in his counting-house, counting out his money. I haven't felt this good since just before the influenza outbreak of 1918, when I myself contracted the disease.

And before that, I had not felt light-hearted since the Great Black Season of 1894, when many ill events coincided across the Republic. That was the year Red Indians ate every man, woman, and child in Weehawken, NJ, the year Mother Zweibel died of hysterical lycanthropy, the year base-ball gained wide-spread acceptance. Come to think of it, I only experience times of buoyant mood when disaster is about to bring the shit-hammer down upon my head.

Menstruating Christ! Does this magnanimity of soul fore-shadow some horrible disaster awaiting me, perhaps before the New Year? Should I take this lightness of heart as a sign to post my Swiss Guard six deep around my death-bed, to summon my food-tasters three?

Ah, bull-shit! What could go wrong? After all, I have my millions, my news-paper, my 632-room estate, and my strapping young son N. Aeschylus by my side.

What could possibly go wrong? *Ø*

There's No 'My Kid Has Cancer' In Team

By Jake Dobbins
Sales Manager

All right, team! Look alive! This is the big one. This is the week we finally pull into the sales lead, and that means total focus.

Now, as you no doubt know, the free trip to Vegas for the year's highest-selling office is within our reach. If we can keep the momentum of the past week going, we can pass the Denver office and take this thing. But that means we must all work together as a team. Every one of you is a cog in a well-oiled sales machine.

And I don't want to hear any excuses. That means no more 45-minute lunches. No more lingering around the break room. And, most of all, no more of this "But my daughter is going in for chemotherapy tomorrow" business. From anybody. I'm not going to name any names, but I've heard that one a couple of times this week, and that's a couple times too many. I hope I only have to say this once: There is no "My kid has cancer" in "Team."

I know, I know. Cancer sucks. Hey, I'm not happy your kid has it, either. But the way I look at it, cancer's not a reason to get slacking, it's a reason to get cracking! You think your kid's chemo is gonna be free? You gonna say to the doctor, "Hey, I decided not to go to work this week because I'm too upset about my kid's cancer, so how about you give me that chemo for free?" See how far that'll get you! (It certainly won't get you to Vegas!) As we say in the business, no COM-mission, no RE-mission.

I've seen too many salespeople take a nosedive in this business because they let their terminally ill kid hold them back. They start visiting the kid in the hospital, their cold calls drop off, and their sales numbers suffer. Next thing you know, it's not just the kid who's dying, but the hopes of an entire sales team that wants to win a Vegas trip!

You hear what I'm saying? You're part of a team, here. If you miss a pitch, you might miss a sale, and if you miss a sale, we all might miss winning that trip! Believe you me, we've all got plenty of problems we could use as excuses to miss work, but we don't want to let our team down! Do you see Jerry staying home because of his trial separation? Or Brian because of his car trouble?

What do we sing "The Team Song" at the start of every day for? You think it's just so we can hear Glen howling off-key? (Ha ha, I'm just pulling your leg there, Glen.) What it comes down to is, we're Teamers, not Tumors!

And, while I'm on the subject, what about that trip a certain someone took to Disneyworld recently? You think the rest of us wouldn't love to spend five days whirling around on teacups? You can go to Disneyworld next year, two years from now, ten years from now! I realize the Make-A-Wish Foundation paid for the trip, but that's not reason enough. Hell, I've got tons of frequent-flyer miles piled up, but you don't see me taking off for Bora Bora smack-dab in the middle of our final sales drive, do you?

Did you even try to give the sales pitch to your kid's doctors? The nurses? The Make-A-Wish guys? See, that's what I'm talking about. You're letting opportunities slip through your fingers, and that hurts the team! We'd be the leaders for that Vegas trip if not for your lollygagging. Team has four letters. T-E-A-M. Here's an easy way to remember: Take Every Avenue Manageable. Do you see the letters "T-H-E D-O-C-T-O-R-S S-A-Y T-H-E C-A-N-C-E-R H-A-S S-P-R-E-A-D T-O H-E-R B-R-A-I-N" somewhere in there? I don't.

This job is about one thing: moving vacuum cleaners. Everything else is a blind alley, kiddo. *Ø*

SLURPIN' USA from page 2

Passersby were amazed by the unusually large amounts of blood. Passersby were amazed by the unusually large amounts of blood. Passersby were amazed by the unusually large amounts of blood. Passersby were amazed by the unusually large amounts of blood. Passersby were amazed by the unusually large amounts of blood. Passersby were amazed by the unusually large amounts of blood. Passersby were amazed by the unusually large amounts of blood. Passersby were amazed by the unusually large

amounts of blood. Passersby were amazed by the unusually large

Are there any stores around that offer name-brand prices for less?

amounts of blood. Passersby were amazed by the unusually large

amounts of blood. Passersby were amazed by the unusually large amounts of blood. Passersby were amazed by the unusually large amounts of blood. Passersby were amazed by the unusually large amounts of blood. Passersby were amazed by the unusually large amounts of blood. Passersby were amazed by the unusually large amounts of blood. Passersby were amazed by the unusually large amounts of blood. Passersby were amazed by the unusually large amounts of blood. Passersby were amazed by the unusually large amounts of blood. Passersby were

amazed by the unusually large amounts of blood. Passersby were amazed by the unusually large amounts of blood. Passersby were amazed by the unusually large amounts of blood. Passersby were amazed by the unusually large amounts of blood. Passersby were amazed by the unusually large amounts of blood. Passersby were amazed by the unusually large amounts of blood. Passersby were amazed by the unusually large amounts of blood. Passersby were amazed by the unusually large amounts of blood. Passersby were

see SLURPIN' USA page 43

Left: A Catholic couple sins.

praise the Vatican's denouncement of "the brutal transgression against God that is the enjoyment of sex for its own sake."

"In recent years, Catholics the world over have been exposed to a multitude of sexual practices that, if not resisted, could enrich their lives and deepen their enjoyment of their partners," said Cardinal Joaquin Navarro Valls, speaking on behalf of the Pope. "As Catholics, we must remain vigilant, doing everything in our power to resist such urges. Only the Lord's divine redemption can transform sex into a force for goodness by limiting it to the joyless context of married couples who wish to procreate."

"The position of the Church is absolute: If two people who are not a married couple endeavoring to have children engage in tension-relieving, life-affirming sex, they are committing a grave sin," Archbishop Edward Egan of New York said. "There is nothing holy about people feeling good about their bodies and themselves."

Catholics are taking the condemnation of modern sexual mores to heart.

"In the seven years we've been married, my wife and I have probably had sex about 1,500 times," said Lowell, MA, resident Bill Metz, 36. "We're extremely attracted to each other, and satisfying each other physically is something we've always enjoyed. Until now, that is. I finally see that what we thought was a fun way to celebrate our love was really an expression of hostility and disrespect toward Jesus."

Metz added that he and his wife plan to have at least 15 children as penance for their physical indulgences.

"This is a major step forward for the church," said Father Thomas Mallory, Deacon of Boston's Our Lady Queen of Peace. "We've seen too much healthy sexuality among Catholics in recent years, which has inevitably led to an unholy sense of well-being and contentment. Hopefully, this papal condemnation will put a stop to that." ∅

you?"

Despite its consensus on overall dog adorableness, the dog-loving community remains sharply divided on the question of who is a good boy. Some say the answer is "Such a good boy, yes." Others contend

With canine-cuddliness levels at an all-time high and adorability-boosting ribbons and chew toys plentiful at pet stores across the nation, no resolution to the good-boy-identity issue appears to be on the horizon.

Above: Lebanon, PA, dog Sneakers, who is believed to be a very good boy.

that the good boy "needs his belly rubbed, yes, oh yes." Still other factions maintain that the only good boy is "my special little snuffy-snuffers, the bestest of all the best boys there is."

"The dog owners of this country still have a great many questions that require answers," said Indianapolis NDAS delegate Janine Mulhern. "Who is, in fact, my favorite little guy? Who, for that mat-

ter, has a fuzzy little tummy-wummy? And, perhaps most importantly, who wants to go outside?"

"Outside? Outside?" continued Mulhern, rattling a leash in her outstretched hand. "These are issues that must be addressed. Our high-pitched, cutesy-wutesy voices will not be silenced."

According to the results of a recent NDAS "Who's A Good Boy?" survey, dog owners are split rough-

Still other factions maintain that the only good boy is "my special little snuffy-snuffers, the bestest of all the best boys there is."

ly into three camps, with 40 percent favoring "What a pretty, pretty, pretty boy" and 31 percent holding that "You're such a puppy!" The final 29 percent argued that the correct answer is, "You are such a stinker, a stinker, a stinky-dinky-dinker!" The NDAS survey did not, however, include members of The Pat-Pat League, an extremist group that wants entirely non-verbal resolutions to the issue, including play-wrestling, head-rubbing, fur-tousling, chin-scritching, and even

great big hugs.

"The question of precisely who is a good boy is of fundamental importance to millions of Americans, many of whom pose this query to their loved ones several times a day," said Marvin Sidowsky, an Atlanta-area veterinarian. "In fact, they may even find themselves asking it several times in quick succession while dangling a rawhide chew stick in the air. Clearly, it's high time we had an answer."

"Right, Bogey? Right, Bogey?" said Sidowsky, rubbing noses with his Yorkshire terrier. "Oh, no... oh, no... No, no, no, no, no. No no no no no no no no no. Nonononononono-nononono."

"Awwwwww," concluded Sidowsky, wrapping Bogey in a baby-blue terrycloth towel and cradling him like an infant.

Despite the differences of opinion, dog owners remain optimistic that the good-boy question can be resolved.

"Don't worry, it's okay," said Anita Perlich, Columbia, SC, NDAS chapter president and owner of four Irish setters. "There's nothing to be scared of."

Addressing reporters from a dog-hair-covered couch in her D.C. townhouse, Erhardt stressed the need for calm. "Nothing to worry about... Uncle Joe always does that. Uncle Joe! Down, boy! Down, boy! Down!"

"He's just excited," continued Erhardt, stressing the need for a positive outlook. "He's not used to new people, that's all. Uncle Joe! Get off the nice man!" ∅

H-Dog Jr.

By Herbert Kornfeld
Accounts Receivable

Yo, check it out, Gs: Last week, that freaky ho Judy from tha wack-ass Accountz Payabo krew steps to mah fly cubicle, all smilin' an' shit. I thought she wuz straight trippin'.

"Bitch, flag yo' ass back to tha A.P. before I go buckwild on yo' ass," I say. "I gots a variance here what needs reconcilin', an' I gots no time foe distractions from some A.P. ho."

No diggity, mah homeys. There wuz a negative $194.07 balance in tha subsidiary accountz-reeceevable ledga, an' it needed to be balanced wit' a quickness, lest tha controlling account look all fucked up. Tha Code O'The H-Dog say, shit gots to be balanced before tha end o' tha bidness day. It a matter of HONOR.

"Herbert," Judy say. "Guess what... Agnes from the Cash Room had her baby last night! It's a boy!"

Damn. I be attendin' to bidness 24/7, and I almost forgot about Agnes an' tha shortie. Agnes tell me tha shortie be mine, 'cuz we be knockin' mad bootz in tha Cash Room afta hours. She say I tha only man she be hittin' skinz wit' lately, but then I gets word from my homey Jerry Tha Sharpie Head that tha freaky chicken-head bitch be givin' it up to all tha Accountz-Receeevable highrollas. So I may not even be tha biological.

But at tha same time, when I hears tha shortie be a boy, I be mad proud, word is bond. I always wanted a Baby H. Jr. to carry on tha family trade of accountz reeceevin.' It just a damn shame that his mama be a lowdown, two-timin' beeyotch.

Judy say that ova tha lunch hour, tha whole Midstate Office Supply krew be goin' down to tha hospital to check out

> ## "Hell, yeah, that gotta be my shortie," I say. "Mad propz to tha shortie. He don't take no shit from nobody, just like his daddy."

Agnes an' tha shortie. I mad hyped to peep mah son foe tha first time, but I just acts all hard an' tell Judy, "Whut about it, bitch?" 'Cuz tha bitch don't needs to know about mah bidness wit' Agnes and tha shortie. But even though I gots this fuckin' variance to contend with, I resolve that I must attend to tha shortie wit' a quickness, lest his mama school him in tha ways o' bein a no-skeelz-havin' Cash Room sucka what be backin' azz up foe all tha Midstate Big Willies.

But, damn, afta I finally lose that fool Judy, I remembers that mah hoopty, Tha Nite Rida, be in tha shop. Mah mechanic homey Kurt, he be installin' one a them dope-ass GPS DVD Navigation Systems. Plus, he be throwin' it in, free o' charge, a pair of them phat bead seat covas that supposed to be good for yo' posture an' a fly vanilla air freshener shaped like a crown. So tha H-Dog be without his ride, an' it look like he gots to take tha bus. Unless you wants every hole in yo' body stapled shut, y'all best not make no wisecracks.

Nite Rida or no Nite Rida, H-Dog don't ride no bus, so I decide to call in a fava from a coworka who owed me bigtime. Namely, that wack bastard Dave from Inventory, whose sorry ass I saved when he OD'd on Liquid Paypa during tha Midstate office picnic last summer. I dialed his extension an' told tha mutha-fucka that he best give me a ride to tha hospital if he didn't want a swift beatdown.

Problem is, Dave still ain't got no clue about tha H-Dog protocol. When he be drivin' me to tha hospital, he be tellin' jokes like he Bernie Mac at tha mutha-fuckin' Apollo.

"Hey, Herbert," Dave say. "What's a shy and retiring accountant?"

"How tha fuck should I know, you corny-ass muthafucka?" I reply.

"It's an accountant who's half a million shy, and that's why he's retiring! Get it?"

Damn. If there ever a time to go balls-out Jeet Kune Do on that stupid fool, it wuz then. Huh. He crackin' wise when that missin' $194.07 wuz hangin' ova my head like a muthafuckin' Sword of Damocles. Not to mention them deep thoughtz I be havin' about seein' mah newborn shortie. But I decided to chill an' put tha muthafucka's demise on hold, 'cause we wuz at tha hospital by then. Besides, this a day foe life, not death.

I gets to Agnes' room, an' I spots her sittin' wit' this old, flabby-ass ho I later learn be her mama. Man, she wuz tha oldest bitch I seen since fuckin' Myron Schabe, an' I could tell right off she wuz a stone-col' playa hata. She give me tha evil eye, an' I gives it back, because I don't take no shit from nobody. An' check it out: I don't see no shortie nowheres, but there be all these flowers,

an' them shiny mylar balloons you can see yo'face in, an'some stuffed bearz, an' all this otha plush shiznit tha Midstate krew musta left behind foe tha shortie.

"Damn, I glad I bring this box o' thumbtackz," I say. "How tha shortie gonna be raised proper if he don't got no officin' supplies?"

Agnes' mama say some straight-trippin' bullshit about tha shortie bein' too young foe officin.' Man, you GOTS to start them YOUNG. What tha fuck would she know 'bout officin', anyway? Man, them fuckin' new-jack amateurs wuz really fuckin' wit' mah flow.

Agnes say that tha shortie, who ain't even got no name yet, be off gettin' his picture taken. A coupla minutes later, tha nurse carry him in. But he don't look like no shortie I ever seen. He all red an' shit, an' his face be all pinched up. He don't even look like no boy.

"Yo, thas one sorry-lookin' li'l punk you gots there, Agnes," I say. "How you know it mine? Maybe it Jerry Tha Sharpie Head's. Or Sir Casio KL7000's. Or AirGoNomic's. Or any o' tha otha A.R. bruthahs you be ballin' on tha second-floor copier. Shit, bitch, you think you can keep yo' two-timin' ways from me? Fuck all y'all!"

Agnes' mama grab tha shortie away from me. She tell me she know about my rep foe bein' hard an' that I ain't welcome around her grandson, 'cause she don't want him to turn out to be no "two-bit mid-level office drone." DAMN. Tha saggy-titted pigeon actually had tha balls to disrespect tha H-Dog to his face. Man, I wuz about to lose tha storied H-Kool. I gots this $194.07 variance, this damn fool Dave thinkin' we tight, an' Agnes' mama be ridin' mah jock. Under mah Members Only gear, I wuz fingerin' tha Letta Opener, ready to go 187 on these

see H-DOG page 36

BLACK GUY from page 31

captured the glorious rainbow of multiculturalism that is ISU. We thought it best to take a more illusory, 'less-actual' approach in depicting this school's racial demographic."

The black guy, added using Adobe Photoshop, has been identified as Marcus Jamison. A Shreveport, LA, native, Jamison attended Iowa State for one semester in 1996 before transferring to Grambling University. His face was lifted from a photo of him attending a racial-sensitivity seminar during his freshman orientation and digitally added to the course-catalog cover by graphic designer Brian Tompkins.

"Believe me, this was not an easy task. We combed through hundreds of school-newspaper and yearbook file photos before we found a picture of a black guy," Tompkins said. "Even then, we had to keep searching, because we felt it was important that the black guy be smiling."

> ## "Each black guy you see in this catalog was, in fact, photographed at one point."

Added Tompkins: "If you think it's hard to find a picture of a black guy, try finding a smiling black guy!"

In addition to the black guy on its cover, the course catalog features several inside photos of black guys, though only in single-person shots. University authorities stressed that all of those images are actual photos of actual minorities printed on actual paper.

"Each black guy you see in this catalog was, in fact, photographed at one point," Arbus said. "This booklet is our way of letting people know the importance of including black guys in official school publications. That's the Iowa State promise."

Arbus noted that the school's football team also includes "a whole lot" of black guys not pictured.

"We have nothing against black guys at this school, as evidenced by our dedication to adding them to images of campus life," Arbus said. "That shows just how serious we are about our commitment to diversity."

Spokespersons for Iowa State, which added Jamison to the course-catalog cover with neither his knowledge or permission, expressed confidence that he would be pleased.

"I'm sure Mr. Jamison, wherever he is, would be thrilled to see his

image used in the service of uplifting the black community and promoting friendship between the races," Iowa State director of communications Bryce Jennings said. "In fact, I bet if he knew about this, he'd even thank us. You're welcome, Marcus!"

Iowa State's use of Photoshop has proven so successful, it is quickly becoming a model for other universities across the nation seeking to improve their schools' veneer of diversity.

"Photoshop opens up an exciting new realm of possibilities for America's institutions of higher learning," University of Montana president Karl Watson said. "Here at Montana, we plan to Photoshop up to 10 percent more Latinos into orientation brochures. If we can get funding, we may also Photoshop handicap-accessible ramps onto exterior shots of campus buildings." ∅

Youth Sports, Adult Violence

The past year has seen a surge in adult violence at youth sporting events, including the beating death of a hockey coach by a player's father. What do *you* think?

"Why are these grown men hitting each other? They should be hitting the kid who blew the game."

Marty Behr
Systems Analyst

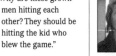

"This parental aggression is spreading into other youth activities, as well. I took a knee to the kidney when my daughter forgot her Christmas-pageant lines."

Joan Weitz
Homemaker

"Hey, if you'd seen that ref's call, we'd have been fighting over the shotgun."

Damian Thomas
Forklift Operator

"Ask me that question again. Go ahead. I fuckin' dare you, you fucking piece of shit."

Bob Bryson
Sales Coordinator

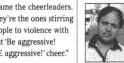

"I blame the cheerleaders. They're the ones stirring people to violence with that 'Be aggressive! B-E aggressive!' cheer."

Dina Sargento
Social Worker

"What better way to impart to our children the important life lesson, 'Do as I say, not as I do'?"

Omar Husserl
Glazier

The Scooter Craze

Across America, millions of kids are cruising around on aluminum Razor scooters. Why are they so popular?

- Reduces number of legs needed for locomotion by 50 percent
- Enables children to establish class distinctions just like adults
- Only vehicle judge said would be okay
- Folds up into convenient blunt object
- Slightly faster mode of transport than walking, without that messy "dignity"

America's Finest News Source

Herman Ulysses Zweibel *Founder*

T. Herman Zweibel *Publisher Emeritus*
J. Phineas Zweibel *Publisher*
Maxwell Prescott Zweibel *Editor-In-Chief*

FOUNDED 1871 • "TU STULTUS ES"

36

By Lloyd Schumner Sr.
Retired Machinist and
A.A.P.B.-Certified Astrologer

Aries: (March 21–April 19)
Your week will be full of success, tempered by depression over the fact that your future can be boiled down to single sentences.

Taurus: (April 20–May 20)
You're starting to suspect that the makers of heroin are trying to turn it into a whole way of life instead of just a drug.

Gemini: (May 21–June 21)
Your view of yourself as the victim in every situation will earn you your own cable talk show.

Cancer: (June 22–July 22)
A published collection of your letters will achieve success not for its literary merit, but because you always chose such neat postcards.

Leo: (July 23–Aug. 22)
It's okay: You're just big-boned, which, along with your anorexia, makes you look like an inflatable skeleton.

Virgo: (Aug. 23–Sept. 22)
You will receive a lifetime achievement award from the National Association for the Advancement of Lifetimes.

Libra: (Sept. 23–Oct. 23)
You will contract a dangerous virus that will target both your brain and the 18- to 26-year-old male demographic.

Scorpio: (Oct. 24–Nov. 21)
As a poet once said, "All who ever lived have died / But not one died of love, nay, nor of a broken heart." Consequently, you're going to need a gun.

Sagittarius: (Nov. 22–Dec. 21)
You will be shocked to learn that your Las Vegas wedding, performed by a transvestite Elvis impersonator, is neither legal nor binding.

Capricorn: (Dec. 22–Jan. 19)
Don't just demand the best from yourself and those around you. Demand coffee from yourself and those around you.

Aquarius: (Jan. 20–Feb. 18)
You will develop a cosmology rooted in the notion that holy vessels containing God's divine light were shattered to create the universe, only to realize that you're about the two billionth person to do so.

Pisces: (Feb. 19–March 20)
Admit it: Things just haven't been the same for you since you gave in and started wearing pants again.

H-DOG from page 35

foolz.

Then, just as I about to start some mad drama, tha shortie goes an' pukes up a bunch of Gerba baby food on his old-ass grandma. Man, that was so off tha hook, I fo-get my rage an' start laughin' my ass off.

"Hell, yeah, that gotta be my shortie," I say. "Mad propz to tha shortie. He don't take no shit from nobody, just like his daddy."

Agnes' mama say shorties do that all the time after they get they eat on, but she just heated 'cause tha shortie show her up, know what I'm sayin'? I wuz startin' to feel mad luv foe tha kid. Suddenly, he didn't look like some Yoda-lookin' freak, but a true son an' worthy heir of tha H-Dog.

I say tha kid's name gonna be Baby Prince H. Tha Stone Col' Dopest Bizookkizeepin' Muthafukkin' Badass Supastar Kornfeld Tha Second. Agnes' mama be sayin' she want tha name to be Andrew Michael, but I be ignorin' her ass, 'cause it suddenly occur to me the source of tha $194.07 variance.

"Yo, I out," I say. "Shortie or no shortie, I gots A.R. bidness to attend to, know what I'm sayin'?"

Check it out, Gs: Back during tha commencement o' tha fiscal year, I recalls getting a check foe $215.63 from this customer what be behind in his bill payments. Shit, I almost had to fade his late-payin' ass, but he got all paid up wit' a quickness once he realize he in tha H-Dog's crosshairs. Anyhow, I couldn't remember no $215.63 check on tha A.R. ledga, but there be one for $21.56. Tha muthafuckin' check had been recorded wrong! Sho' 'nuf, there wuz tha difference, $194.07. An' accordin' to Midstate accountin' guidelines, tha company can eat tha rest o' the cost as long as it under $10.

Mah phat skeelz as a stone col' troubleshoota who saves tha company mad benjamins already be legendary. But, shit, I fuckin' outdid myself this time. An' it all 'cause o' tha shortie. Times were tough foe Daddy H., but tha luv foe mah shortie helped me once again get mah roll on.

Right now, I be sexin' that ova-tha-hill Eloise from the cafeteria, but I gonna get me some of them freaky Marketing hos. An' if I eva accidentally knock one of them bitchez up, I get to decide what the shortie's name be. Thas 'cause it turn out that fuckin' Agnes name tha shortie Tanner behind my back. What tha fuck kinda pussy name is that, Tanner? Shit. Ø

Consumer Confidence Verging On Cockiness

see NATION page 4A

Lab Partner Wants To Be Sex Partner

see LOCAL page 11D

Wildlife Threatened With Broom

see ENVIRONMENT page 2B

Don McLean Decides To Close With 'American Pie'

see MUSIC page 8E

STATshot

A look at the numbers that shape your world.

New Stereotypes For 2001

1. Blacks love taffy
2. Gays tend to shift their weight to their right leg while standing
3. Romanians are Tom Clancy apologists
4. Germans make really good mix tapes
5. Italians can read
6. Chinese prefer walking backwards
7. Puerto Ricans are good at creating and marketing new breakfast cereals
8. Jews can go two months without water

the ONION®

VOLUME 36 ISSUE 45   AMERICA'S FINEST NEWS SOURCE™   14–20 DECEMBER 2000

Scrappy Band Of Lovable Misfits No Match For Rich Kids

WINNEPESAUKEE, NY—A plucky band of colorful misfits from Camp Winnepesaukee proved no match for their spoiled rich-kid rivals Monday, when superior finances and connections

thwarted the underdogs' efforts to stand up in the face of arrogant elitism.

The conflict, characterized by some as a "slobs vs. snobs" scenario, ended in disaster for Camp

see MISFITS page 40

Above: Rich-kids-camp leader J. Jordan Buckminster III.

Joe Eszterhas Brought In To Punch Up Senate Bill

Above: The conference room where S. 1792 was first pitched by Sen. Paul Wellstone (D-MN).

WASHINGTON, DC—Concerned that the bill is too dry to connect with mainstream taxpayers, the U.S. Senate has brought in high-profile Hollywood screenwriter Joe Eszterhas to punch up Internal Revenue Code Amendment Act S. 1792.

Joe Eszterhas

"We're extremely pleased to have Joe working on this project with us," said Sen. Paul Wellstone (D-MN), addressing reporters at a press conference Mon-

see ESZTERHAS page 40

Web-Browser History A Chronicle Of Couple's Unspoken Desires

VALLEJO, CA—The web-browser history on Allen and Christine Pollard's home iMac computer provides a comprehensive chronicle of the couple's deepest frustrations and desires, sources reported Monday.

"By simply opening Allen and Christine's Internet Explorer history folder, we find their innermost longings laid bare," said Dr. Terrence Kimble, dean of psychology at the University of California at Berkeley. "From emotionally stunted, sexually frustrated Allen's frequent visits to porn and Camaro sites to childless Christine's frequent visits to baby-clothes sites, it's all right there."

According to Kimble, the Pollards' browser history, which logs the 200 most recent hits by users of the computer, "offers a glimpse into an entire universe of unvoiced pain and disap-

The Pollards' browser history "offers a glimpse into an entire universe of unvoiced pain."

pointment."

"As the Pollards enter their late 30s, all the dissatisfaction they hide from the world and, in most cases, each other can be easily found under the menu heading 'Go,'" Kimble said. "Because he knows Christine loves living in suburbia, Allen never talks

Above: Allen and Christine Pollard's recent hits.

to her about his dream of roughing it in a cabin in the Rockies. He just spends hours surfing the REI and Patagonia sites, filling his virtual shopping cart with lanterns and sleeping bags, then logs out without

see BROWSER page 41

Make-A-Wish Foundation Criticized After Dying 14-Year-Old Crashes Jet

PASCAGOULA, MS—The Make-A-Wish Foundation is under fire following the deaths of 39 people Monday, when a Harrier jet piloted by terminally ill 14-year-old Joshua Hewitt crashed into an apartment complex near Pascagoula. "We wish to point out that the training and licensing required to fly an AV-8B Harrier ordinarily takes two years—two years Joshua unfortunately did not have," Make-A-Wish spokeswoman Patti Darby said. "Joshua died living his dream, and that's what matters." The foundation has offered wishes to seven children currently in critical condition at Pascagoula Memorial Hospital as a result of the disaster.

Plastic Bag Still Up In Tree

BOISE, ID—Employees at Boise Mutual Insurance reported Monday that the red plastic shopping bag they first noticed Dec. 8 is still ensnared in the upper branches of a tree outside their workplace. "Well I'll be—the darn thing is still up there," payroll secretary Barb Weicherle said. "I really thought this weekend's gusts would have blown it out." Office manager Paul Probert was equally surprised, saying, "Son of a gun. It's still there."

Naïve Detective Suspects Fair Play

CHICAGO—Phil Kelly, a naïve detective with Chicago's 15th Precinct, suspected fair play Monday in the shooting death of local businessman Arnold Haver. "The shocked expression on the victim's face leads me to believe that he received some tragic news and subsequently committed suicide," Kelly said. "The fact that the bullet entered through his back shows just how determined he was to kill himself." Kelly also cited the misspelling of Haver's name in the suicide note and the fact that the left-handed victim was found with the gun in his right hand as evidence of the incredible stress he was under before taking his own life.

Unkempt Japanese Man Must Be Some Sort Of Artist Or Something

PITTSBURGH—After passing a haggard-looking Japanese man on the street Monday, area resident Gary Webber concluded that the guy must be some sort of artist or poet or something. "Normally, you see a guy dressed in a dirty, ripped coat with his hair all scruffed up, you figure he's just poor. But this guy was Japanese," Webber said. "I bet he's in town to do some kind of art opening. Or maybe a book signing. Whoever he is, he's got to be somebody."

Area Man Glad His Brother Is Giving Mom Grandkids

ROME, GA—Area resident Larry Spoerl was thrilled to learn Monday that his brother's wife is pregnant, temporarily relieving him of the pressure to produce grandchildren for his mother. "That's the most wonderful news I've heard in ages," the 31-year-old Spoerl told brother Marc. "Now I can get through Christmas without the whole so-are-you-dating-anyone-how-serious-is-it-does-she-want-a-family interrogation." In spite of his momentary elation, Spoerl said his brother's expected child "only buys me a year or two at best."

Direct Marketer Offended By Term 'Junk Mail'

SPOKANE, WA—Dan Spengler, CEO of the direct-mail-marketing firm Mailbox Of Savings, took umbrage Monday at the use of the term "junk mail." "I'm sorry, but we didn't earn receipts in excess of $8 million last year by filling people's mailboxes with 'junk,'" Spengler told the offending party. "How else will potential customers know about bargains like 500 mailing labels for $8.95 or 10 percent off framing at The Great Frame-Up if not by direct mail?" Added Spengler: "It's not like my company calls people at home like telemarketers. Everyone hates that." ✐

Man Feels Brief Sense Of Triumph After Completing Free-Frozen-Yogurt Punchcard

Above: Roy Kempner proudly displays his fully punched Creamy Pete's Preferred Customer Card.

TRAVERSE CITY, MI—After nearly four months of dedicated frozen-yogurt consumption, Roy Kempner, 47, finally earned the 10th and final punch on his Creamy Pete's Preferred Customer Card Monday, giving him a faint sense of accomplishment.

"Well, I guess I did it," said Kempner, holding aloft the completed punch card. "That'll be one free yogurt for me next time."

Kempner, a Traverse City-area substitute teacher, was offered the card following an Aug. 19 purchase of a medium chocolate-vanilla swirl cone at the yogurt franchise. "When the lady asked if I wanted to join the Preferred Customer Club, I thought it might be some sort of racket with a sign-up fee, like they have at Waldenbooks," Kempner said. "But she assured me it was free and said I'd already earned my first punch for the yogurt I'd just ordered, so I thought, what the heck."

During the next several weeks, Kempner made no additional frozen-yogurt purchases, and the punchcard was soon forgotten in the recesses of

his wallet. On Sept. 12, however, the card returned to the forefront of Kempner's mind when he pulled out his Visa card to pay for dinner at a local Outback Steakhouse.

"I just happened to notice the punchcard there in my wallet," he said. "Then I realized that the yogurt place was just a couple blocks away. It seemed like fate."

According to Kempner, that evening's purchase of a second frozen yogurt, a medium butterscotch with crushed Heath bars, put the punchcard-completion project into high gear. "I was enjoying the yogurt, and I started thinking, hey, I'm already 20 percent there. I could easily eat eight more of these and actually get that free one," Kempner said. "I'd just need to adjust my travel and dining habits to get to Creamy Pete's more often."

Over the next two months, he made four more trips to Creamy Pete's, enjoying such flavors as peanut butter, raspberry silk, and French vanilla, as well as such exotic toppings as Oreo cookie dough and Sour Patch Kids.

Kempner faced his first setback in

mid-November, when he brought his friend Matt into Creamy Pete's. "I thought I could buy a yogurt for myself and one for Matt and get credit for two yogurts," Kempner said. "Matt didn't have a card, so he said I could have his punch. But the girl behind the counter pointed to the rules on the back of the card, which clearly state that credit can only be given for frozen-yogurt items consumed by the card's bearer. Then I asked her if I could get an extra punch if I ate a little bit of Matt's yogurt before he ate it, but she said no."

Embarrassed by his clumsy, ham-fisted attempts to circumvent the

rules of the giveaway, Kempner tossed an extra dollar into the Creamy Pete's tip jar.

Upon reaching the six-punch mark, Kempner's free-frozen-yogurt quest stalled, his interest in frozen yogurt waning with the onset of winter. The quest suffered another setback when the card was misplaced during the transfer of materials to a new wallet.

"I forgot about the card until it somehow turned up in the sock drawer of my dresser," Kempner said. "I usually only eat frozen treats in the summer, so I thought about saving it

see YOGURT page 39

A Walk In The Woods

By T. Herman Zweibel
Publisher Emeritus

photo circa 1911

Well, I must say, this is a surprise! My darling son N. Aeschylus has gently lifted me out of my death-bed and begun carrying me down-stairs and across the main foyer. This is the season of the Yule-tide, is it not? Perhaps he is taking me to the parlor so that we may open our gifts. I do hope I finally got the shawl I always ask for but never seem to get...

N. Aeschylus, is it just me, or is the mansion in flames? And why did you just incinerate Nurse Pin-head with your eye-balls? My goodness, I haven't seen so many dead bodies since the Galveston Hurricane. Did you do this, N. Aeschylus? Far be it from me to put a damper on a young boy's spirited antics, but the laws of our Republic tend to frown upon arson and the murder of human beings, even if they are just servants.

You are taking me into the woods? Look how the snow-flakes are swirling! The whole estate has been blanketed in a peaceful white. Everything is still as a tomb. Well, if you don't count the shrieks emanating from the burning mansion.

What is this? We have reached a clearing in the woods where a giant metal obelisk points its needle-nose to the heavens. This must be the device N. Aeschylus has been working on in the nursery recently. Very impressive, dear boy! Is this your coy way of telling me you wish to join the Masons? You only needed to ask! I'm sure I can secure you a summer internship.

Thank you for setting me down on this stone slab, boy. I must admit, I feel a bit tuckered-out from our constitutional. But are the leather straps really necessary? And what is that whirling metal wheel extruding from your arm? N. Aeschylus? N. Aeschylus?

What's this? An army of black-clad, sword-wielding men are springing from the trees! It's... I can't believe it... The Society Of 800 Avenging Fists! They are the Chinee assassins dispatched by Li Ming, my rival for the title of World's Oldest Man, to avenge my own attempt on his life! Help! Police! Murder! Poison! Save me, N. Aeschylus, save me! Train your fiery eye-beams on them! Slice them limb from limb! Oh, dear: They're swarming all over him! Courage, N. Aeschylus!

Standish! What are you doing here? Quick, untie me from this slab! There's no time to lose! What? You say there's an opening to the metal obelisk? Let's hide in there before the sinister yellow-men see us! Oh, this is terrible! I'm quite sure I just shat out my rib-cage from fear! ∅

I Think I Would Make A Good Member Of A Large Crowd

By Les McCutcheon

I'm not a loner, one of those people who prefers solitude and time to oneself. On the other hand, I really don't do well when I'm part of a group, as interacting with others tends to make me feel self-conscious and uncomfortable. All things considered, I really think I'm best suited to being a member of a large crowd.

You see, I'm not really a people person. I'm what you might call a populace person. I think of humanity as an amorphous, undifferentiated mass with no discernible goals or reasons for existence. And it is there among the faceless masses, blending in and exerting no will of my own, that I feel most at home. I've never been much for

self-determination, so following along with a crowd is something I really think I'd be good at.

To be honest, it doesn't matter how big the crowd is. Times

> ## I'm what you might call a populace person.

Square at rush hour would be fine. So would a packed football stadium. Or a standing-room-only bus. I also think I'd do well in a crowded suburban mall during the height of the holiday season, buffeted about by the frantic swarm of last-minute gift buyers. Basically, as long as I can blend in and float along with the current, I'm

happy.

Don't get me wrong: There are some large groups I would not want to be a part of. Like a mob. A mob is very different from a crowd. Mobs have agendas. Whether it's to protest a piece of controversial legislation or kill the inhuman monster in the castle, a mob has a shared, clearly defined goal. And that is not something that interests me. I just want to be a person who happens to be in the same place as a fairly large number of other people. I want to be surrounded by many different people with whom I share nothing more than the bond of temporarily occupying the same physical space. That is something I would very much enjoy being involved with.

If I ever got the chance to join a large crowd, I would take my responsibilities seriously. I'm not the type of crowd member who

would engage others in even the most fleeting of interpersonal interactions. As a crowd member, I would take pains to avoid coming into contact with any other member. But, if I ever accidentally bumped into someone, I would not make it worse by saying "Sorry" or "Excuse me." I would instead look off in the other direction, maintaining not only the distance between us but also the illusion that no contact had ever taken place.

Like many people, I am happiest when I am an insignificant part of a larger, purposeless whole. I thrive when given the opportunity to be swallowed up by the teeming hordes. It is only when I am not lost in the crowd that I feel truly lost. If you just give me a chance and let me join your crowd, I promise to be the most passive non-entity you've ever met and instantly forgotten. ∅

YOGURT from page 38

for next year. But then I noticed it was stamped with a Dec. 31 expiration date. I was like, uh-oh."

Faced with the choice of abandoning the quest or forcing down cold yogurt in 30-degree weather, Kempner opted for the latter. On Dec. 1, he gained his seventh punch, ordering a large coffee yogurt with Butterfinger topping. Two days later, a medium vanilla with crumbled Cap'n Crunch bits brought him into the home stretch.

With just two punches to go,

> ## The project was nearly derailed when frozen-yogurt fatigue set in.

when frozen-yogurt fatigue set in. "After the eighth punch, I was

the project was nearly derailed

really getting sick of yogurt," Kempner said. "On the other hand, I was only two away. So after digging deep and doing some serious soul-searching, I decided I'd gone too far to turn back."

Forcing himself to make two more trips to Creamy Pete's before the clock ran out, Kempner gamely choked down a medium banana with crushed nuts on Dec. 6. Finally, at 5:13 p.m. Monday, Kempner ordered a small, toppingless vanilla, earning his tenth punch and with it, a dim,

momentary sense of triumph.

Reflecting on his accomplishment, Kempner said: "Well, it was a long journey, but I did it. I ate 10 yogurts."

Gazing at the well-worn punch-card in his hand, Kempner spoke of the future. "As good as I feel now, it doesn't compare to how I'll feel when I get that free yogurt. I will have enjoyed $33 worth of yogurt, and paid only $30 for the privilege—a reward lavished only on the brave." ∅

day. "As the man behind *Basic Instinct* and *Flashdance*, as well as countless other sexy box-office sizzlers, we felt he was the ideal guy to give this bill the jolt of electricity it needs."

S. 1792, which would amend the Internal Revenue Code of 1986 to extend expiring provisions and fully allow nonrefundable personal credits against regular tax liability, has already been through six rewrites, worked over by such Washington heavy hitters as Sen. Fred Thompson (R-TN) and Sen. Joseph Biden (D-DE). But after the sixth rewrite tested poorly in subcommittee, the Senate decided to bring in an outsider.

"We originally envisioned S. 1792 as a small, independent bill," said Wellstone, taking off his yellow-tinted, horn-rimmed glasses. "But after a couple of drafts, we realized that this thing had the potential to be something much bigger. We felt like somewhere in those 120 pages was a major hit just waiting to get out—if only we could find that perfect person to sculpt it and make it shine. That's when my co-writer Barbara Boxer turned to me and said just one word: 'Eszterhas.'"

The bill was immediately sent to Eszterhas, who "really responded to the material."

"I read the bill and thought, this is an amazing piece of work. But it lacks a third act and a compelling villain," said Eszterhas from his Malibu beach house. "Still, I showed it to [director] Paul Verhoeven, and he flipped out. He said I'd be a schmuck if I didn't do it."

After a brief period of negotiations with the screenwriter's agent over points and backend, Wellstone and Boxer got Eszterhas on board.

"We were clear that we wanted Joe to 'dial up' the bill, make it bigger, funnier—really make it pop—but still preserve the soul and integrity of the original," Boxer said.

The first rewrite was satisfactory for both sides, with Eszterhas

Above: A page from Eszterhas' revised draft of S. 1792.

adding sections that would provide tax breaks for Asian hookers, Colombian drug smugglers, and voyeurs with ties to the S&M underworld. With his next rewrite, Eszterhas continued to "add more heat to the bill," shifting its focus from tax credits for working parents earning less than $20,000 annually to increased penalties for stalkers of catfighting exotic dancers. It was also during this rewrite that the bill's name was changed to *S. 1792: Maximum Liability*.

"The buzz on this bill is incredible," said James Swendeman, editor of *CQ Weekly*. "This is going to be the sleeper hit of the 107th Congress, and it hasn't even been formally submitted yet. Representa-

tives will be lining up around the block to vote for it. There hasn't been anything like this since Reagan's Star Wars defense proposal."

The hype generated by *S. 1792: Maximum Liability* has many senators scrambling to inject some of its "over-the-top" feel into their own bill-writing.

"A lot of folks on Capitol Hill are going around saying, 'We need our own S. 1792, something sexy with major crossover appeal,'" said Sen. Tom Harkin (D-IA). "For years, I've wanted to write a bill that would raise the minimum shower time for female prison inmates to 30 minutes, but I felt it would have been too exploitative. Now, I see that's just what Congress wants."

Some Beltway insiders remain cautious about the bill, noting that many previous attempts by Hollywood writers to punch up federal legislation have met with failure.

"When John Sayles worked on the bill for increased health benefits for Alaskan fishermen, it was a beautiful, poignant bill," said Sen. Ernest Hollings (D-SC). "It only got 11 votes in the House, but those congressmen who supported it were deeply moved. Not at all like that $220 billion asteroid-defense-system bill Jerry Bruckheimer put out a few years ago. It was a soulless piece of crap, but everyone showed up for that vote."

In spite of the buzz S. 1792 is generating, some cracks have begun to show in the working relationship between Eszterhas and the Wellstone/Boxer team. In a Monday conference call, the two senators clashed sharply with Eszterhas over the screenwriter's proposed changes to the story arc involving families with two or more dependents.

"We hope to keep the bill out of turnaround, but if pressured, we will put a pin in the project," Boxer said. "According to the contract, we can keep asking for rewrites, but Eszterhas has the power of final draft. Still, if we don't like what we see, we can always take our names off S. 1792 and replace them with the pseudonym Sen. Alan Smithee (I-CA)."

If the bill dies in the Senate, Eszterhas said he plans to shop it around Washington to find a new legislator to submit the bill.

"I see this bill as *Showgirls* meets HR 2859," Eszterhas said. "I'm getting Sharon Stone, Michael Douglas, and Linda Fiorentino to help lobby for it. If Boxer and Wellstone don't have the vision to see that this bill is going to be bigger than 'Don't Ask, Don't Tell,' I'll go over their heads."

Eszterhas has also demanded an executive-producer credit on any sequel bills. ∅

Winnepesaukee, which was unceremoniously bulldozed for absorption into Breckenridge Estates, the well-funded enemy camp across the lake.

The bulldozing brought an end to more than 20 years of conflict between the two camps, which had been locked in an ongoing struggle for control of Camp Winnepesaukee's 57-acre property.

At a Monday press conference, Brian "Wing Nut" Winger, 16, unofficial ringleader of the Camp Winnepesaukee gang, accepted full responsibility for the camp's defeat at the hands of the Breckenridge snobs.

"Since we're just a bunch of lovable losers from the wrong side of the tracks, I figured we could band together and help [Camp Winnepesaukee owner and director] Old Man Guffy save the camp," said

Wing Nut, clad in mismatched red and blue Converse sneakers, a Hawaiian shirt, and dark sunglasses. "Well, we couldn't."

Along with Wing Nut, the motley crew of Camp Winnepesaukee outcasts included his nerdy bunkmate Percy "Doofus" Dufhauser, African-American computer expert Malcolm "Hackmeister" LaVont, undersized-but-feisty Harry "Half-Pint" O'Bannon, and an overweight, long-haired heavy-metal enthusiast known only as "The Heap."

The Camp Winnepesaukee plan was hatched two weeks ago, when Wing Nut, while attempting to peek into the girls' showers, overheard Old Man Guffy talking to a group of Breckenridge "stuffed shirts" about selling them the nearly bankrupt Camp Winnepesaukee. In an inspiring display of moxie and spunk, the

misfits convinced Old Man Guffy to wager the camp's fate on a bet with Breckenridge: Whichever camp could win the annual Summer Splash-Off competition would get the deeds to both camps. In spite of Breckenridge's superior equipment, training, and funding—and Camp Winnepesaukee's 23-year losing streak against their cross-lake rivals—Old Man Guffy reluctantly agreed.

"What a big, dumb idiot I was," said a distraught Guffy after the rout. "They had an army of rich, well-trained prep-schoolers on their side, and all we had was our determination to triumph against impossible odds. Now I don't have jacksquat."

The spirited Camp Winnepesaukee assault included Wing Nut's rigging of Breckenridge canoes to

spring leaks, a midnight panty raid on the Breckenridge girls' dorm, and a heroic effort by The Heap to devour 34 pies in the pie-eating contest. By all accounts, the misfits' efforts went above and beyond what anyone expected. In the end, however, it was not nearly enough.

"We stole a bunch of the girls' panties—so what?" Doofus said. "Did we think the symbolic humiliation of losing their underwear would make them forget they have a crack team of lawyers and powerful family connections in New York law-enforcement circles? Sure, we put a lot of effort into that panty raid, but all it got us was a sexual-harassment suit and $17,000 in fines for breaking and entering."

An effort to use Hackmeister's computer skills to place the mes-

see MISFITS page 42

Above: Christine and Allen Pollard.

school cheerleading days far behind her, Christine has yet to find a new identity with which she is comfortable."

By carefully examining the history log, it's even possible to reconstruct

"We both really enjoy going online," Allen said.

Allen and Christine's respective thought processes.

"Let's look at Christine's time online last night," said Kimble, pointing to an opened history folder on the computer screen. "She starts at the Godiva gourmet chocolates online gift catalog at 7:35 p.m. Then it's on to eDiets.com at 7:43 p.m. and the Nordic Track web site at 7:45. I'm guessing she clicked on a banner ad at eDiets to get there. Then it's on to 'Liposuction FAQs' at 7:52. Next is a page titled 'Sexy Swimwear Sale: Dare To Be Bare.' Then, at 8:06 p.m., it's back to the Godiva chocolates secure-server online order form."

Christine admitted she keeps the details of her Internet surfing from her spouse.

"I don't mention this to Allen, because he would just say I'm being too self-critical, but I wish my nose weren't so big," Christine said. "I tried some of the de-emphasizing makeup tricks on the Maybelline site, but it's clear that what I really need to do is see a professional. Plastic-surgery.com says the procedure only takes six hours and is totally safe."

While Christine's browser history exposes her insecurities about her appearance, Allen's web-surfing patterns reveal his career dissatisfaction.

"It's obvious that Allen wants to quit his dead-end job at the bank and become an author," said Kimble, pointing to a list of Allen's web links to iUniverse.com and NextGreatAmericanNovel.com. "An author who works out of his cabin in the mountains, that is."

Despite doing so on a daily basis, the Pollards are oblivious to the fact that they pour their innermost frustrations into their blueberry iMac.

"We both really enjoy going online," Allen said. "It's just a great way to waste time and have a little fun." ⌀

purchasing anything."

"Likewise," Kimble continued, "although Christine tells her friends that she and Allen have decided they aren't ready to have children, her www.babynames.com bookmark tells a different story."

The unfulfilled desire to procreate is by no means Christine's only source of unhappiness, Kimble said.

"While she maintains a cheery and fun-loving front, it is obvious that Christine has deep-seated self-esteem issues," Kimble said. "She is all but addicted to online quizzes like Redbook's 'Does Your Wardrobe Give Away Your Age?' and Cosmo's 'Are You A Bore In Bed?' With her high-

the ONION presents

Etiquette Tips

In this modern world, good manners have become a lost art. Here are some tips to help you make the right impression in polite society:

- When attending superficial, high-society dinner parties, always stab people in the back with the third fork from the left.

- If you accidentally pass gas at a posh country-club golf course, look around bug-eyed and loudly exclaim, "Did somebody step on a duck?"

- It is not considered necessary to send a formal thank-you letter upon receiving a wedding gift from anyone who makes less than $70,000 a year.

- When fucking your hostess doggy-style, make sure you are not forcing her face into the boeuf au poivre.

- At formal functions, it is customary to pass the dutchie from the left-hand side.

- Avoid talking politics in mixed company. You never know who might be a bleeding-heart Jew liberal.

- If introduced to Her Majesty, the Queen Mother of England, make every effort not to appear repulsed by the musky, overpowering stench that comes off her in palpable waves.

- It is permissible to include sporks in table settings at formal dinners. Curvy straws, however, are unacceptable.

- An invitation for a young debutante to sit down should never be accompanied by face-wiping motions and the words, "Let me clear off a place."

- Do not say "ain't." Say "ai not."

- At a formal dance or cotillion, asking a woman to dance should be followed by marriage and the purchase of a home.

- When laying off more than 500 laborers from a manufacturing plant, it is considered proper to make a perfunctory expression of regret to the press.

- For a black-tie event, dress casually but bring an African-American friend. Explain that you thought the invitation said "black-guy" event.

- Though it has become common practice, it is impolite to wear a Walkman while wolfing pussy.

- Always remember to serve from the left and clear from the right, or you're fired and goodbye green card. Comprende, Paco?

Is Oral Sex Sex?

According to a recent *USA Today* cover story, oral sex is sharply on the rise among teenagers, many of whom do not consider it a form of sex. What do *you* think?

"That's a relief. Turns out I haven't been sexually abusing my son, after all."

Bernie Porter
Locksmith

"I was shocked to find that cunnilingus accounted for a full 1.3 percent of these oral-sex cases."

Nina Hahn
Occupational Therapist

"This is just more of the usual conservative-Christian hysteria over teenagers swallowing miles of cock."

Roger Blauvelt
Systems Analyst

"So is it wrong when I tell my students, 'Make love to me with your mouth'?"

Robert Hastings
Teacher

"These teens will believe anything the president goes on TV and says."

Bernice Cole
Medical Assistant

"As a teen math whiz, I can't say I've heard or seen anything about this."

Leonard Doby
Student

Police-Recruitment Woes

Across the nation, police departments are struggling to fill their ranks. What is being done to attract new recruits?

- Free mustache trimmer
- '10 Percent Off Fridays' at evidence room
- Guaranteed pairing with hard-boiled but lovable father figure
- Tipping now allowed
- Guns: guns guns guns guns guns guns!
- Chance to induce fear in civilians with rhetorical questions such as, "How are you folks this evening?"
- Can use lights and siren whenever Aerosmith is on the radio
- Pays more than jobs where you don't get shot at

America's Finest News Source

Herman Ulysses Zweibel *Founder*

T. Herman Zweibel *Publisher Emeritus*
J. Phineas Zweibel *Publisher*
Maxwell Prescott Zweibel *Editor-In-Chief*

FOUNDED 1871 • "TU STULTUS ES"

By Lloyd Schumner Sr.
Retired Machinist and
A.A.P.B.-Certified Astrologer

Aries: (March 21–April 19)
You will be crushed to learn that the Black Sabbath song is titled "Fairies Wear Boots," not "Aries" as you had long thought. Return all your boots.

Taurus: (April 20–May 20)
The dog next door will speak to you with the voice of Satan, commanding you to bring it the unclean meat which masquerades as bacon but is not bacon.

Gemini: (May 21–June 21)
Tell those smartalecks at work that if they think your job is so easy, they should try inheriting the nation's third-largest paper-goods manufacturing firm.

Cancer: (June 22–July 22)
Federal investigators sent to the disaster site will find it hard to discount your standing there with a bloody tire iron.

Leo: (July 23–Aug. 22)
You will not be sure how to take it after you're described as "the Sherwood Anderson of *Sailor Moon* fan fiction."

Virgo: (Aug. 23–Sept. 22)
It's not that you're in a no-win situation; it's just that *you* can't win.

Libra: (Sept. 23–Oct. 23)
Everyone will be talking about your wonderful personality and kind nature next week, which is customary at funerals.

Scorpio: (Oct. 24–Nov. 21)
Your cat does nothing all day but wash itself and play with a sparkly ball, so it seems you'll have to solve the vicar's murder all by yourself.

Sagittarius: (Nov. 22–Dec. 21)
This birthday may mark the halfway point of your life, but look on the bright side: You're finally old enough to drive.

Capricorn: (Dec. 22–Jan. 19)
Your field research disproves conventional wisdom, demonstrating that pimping is, in fact, extremely easy.

Aquarius: (Jan. 20–Feb. 18)
You will be recognized as the voice of small-town America after getting drunk and singing George Jones songs in the street all night.

Pisces: (Feb. 19–March 20)
You will meet a tall, dark Aquarius who is compatible with you in every way, right down to the unhealthy fixation with Mary Todd Lincoln.

MISFITS from page 40

sage "Breckenridge Blows" on every screen at the rival camp's computer lab also met with failure.

"We were all laughing and giving each other high-fives, like we actually accomplished something," said Hackmeister, currently being held in federal prison for multiple violations of state and federal anti-hacking statutes. "The feds showed up at my cabin the very next morning with, like, 12 subpoenas."

Despite fully expecting to defeat the rich kids and learn something about themselves in the process, the only thing the Camp Winnepesaukee underdogs learned was that they were too poor and outmanned ever to stand a chance.

"When Breckenridge's blue-blood camp director Mr. Harding—who we all called 'Mr. Hard-On'—came running out with the eviction papers, we set off a carefully orchestrated booby trap that sent him tumbling into the lake," Half-Pint said. "Then we all laughed and cheered and partied, like we'd somehow defeated him. Meanwhile, Harding just drove back to his lawyer's office and got new copies of the papers. Duh. You obviously can't nullify litigation just by getting somebody wet."

The night before the final obstacle-course race, Wing Nut attempted to rally the troops with a stirring speech. "I told the gang that if we stuck together and reached for our dreams, we could beat those rich kids," he said. "But I couldn't even finish my speech, because I was pelted with stale hot dogs."

Seated in a high-back leather chair, Breckenridge alumnus J. Jordan Buckminster II told reporters he was not surprised the gang from Camp Winnepesaukee lost.

"Those Winnepesaukee boys have no breeding," Buckminster said. "The sooner they accept their fate as losers in life, the better." He then punctuated his remarks by clenching a pipe in his teeth and taking a long sip of vintage Cognac.

When asked by reporters what lesson they learned, the misfits unanimously agreed.

"The lesson is simple: Give up," Wing Nut said. "If there are any scrappy underdogs out there who hope to gain inspiration from our determination to win in the face of impossible odds, my advice to you is this: Don't. You're doomed to fail."

Diorama Of Rome Built In A Day

see EDUCATION page 7C

Dorito-Factory Employee Can't Get Cool-Ranch Smell Out Of Clothes

see WORKPLACE page 10B

Ghost Of Joe C. Teaches Kid Rock Valuable Christmas Lesson

see PEOPLE page 5E

STATshot

A look at the numbers that shape your world.

What Are Our New Year's Resolutions?

→ Lose 25 pounds before due date
→ Advance to front register
→ Test bus' crumple zone
→ Break it off with altar boy
→ Finally get rid of all those boxes of uncounted ballots in garage
→ Change CD in player

0 74470 94595 6   46

the ONION ®

VOLUME 36 ISSUE 46   AMERICA'S FINEST NEWS SOURCE™   21 DEC. 2000–17 JAN. 2001

National Machete Association Speaks Out Against Machete-Control Legislation

Above: National Machete Association director Wayne Manning addresses the group's annual convention.

WASHINGTON, DC—Vowing to "vigilantly defend the Second Amendment and preserve our most basic civil liberties," the National Machete Association denounced congressional efforts to enact machete-control legislation Monday.

"The U.S. Constitution gives Americans the right to bear machetes, be it for recreational or self-defense purposes," said NMA executive director Wayne Manning, speaking at the organization's annual national convention. "For Big Brother in Washington to deny Americans this right is a rejection of the very principles upon which this great nation was founded."

see MACHETE page 47

Religious Cousin Ruins Family's Christmas

MONTOURSVILLE, PA—The arrival of devout Christian cousin Barb Krueger has "for all practical purposes ruined" the Langan family's chances of having an enjoyable holiday season, sources reported Monday.

Barb Krueger

"Christmas Day is something our whole family greatly looks forward to, drinking egg nog, opening presents, sitting around the family room in our pajamas and robes, and sipping hot cocoa throughout the day," said Marv Langan, 51. "Well, you can forget about that this year, with Barb hovering over us with her Bible."

The Langans have for years treasured Christmas as a time for family bonding and good cheer. But all that is likely to change this year due to the presence of Krueger, 30, who de-

see COUSIN page 46

Ping-Pong Somehow Elicits Macho Posturing

'Boo-Ya! How You Like Me Now?' Says Ping-Pong Playing Man

APPLETON, WI—The non-macho game of table tennis, popularly known as "ping-pong" for the bouncy little sound the ball makes, has somehow elicited tough-guy posturing and braggadocio from Appleton resident Tim Bergkamp, sources close to the 27-year-old revealed Monday.

"I don't know what the deal is," said Marty Zielke, a coworker of Bergkamp's at an Appleton-area Target, "but ever since we got that ping-pong table in the break room, Tim's been acting like he's Macho Man Randy Savage or something."

The table, brought in by fellow Target sales associate Jason Hersh after he decided to remove it from his basement rec room, has "brought out the competitive animal" in the mild-mannered Bergkamp.

"You should see him when he gets going. You'd think ping-pong was some kind of ESPN2 extreme sport," Hersh said. "He's all like, 'Time for a serious ass-kicking, Jason. Think you can take it when I bring the hammer down on you? Think you can handle the humiliation of another devastating defeat at the hands of the master?' Then, whenever he scores a point, he shouts, 'Boo-Ya!' and does this gloating victory dance, strutting back and forth and waving his arms in the air. I mean, it's ping-pong, for Christ's sake."

"No one can withstand the awesome

Above: Self-described "ping-pong ninja" Tim Bergkamp taunts his opponent during a match at Appleton-area fun center B.Z. Bonkers.

might of the Ponginator's vaunted 'OverThruster' serve," Bergkamp told coworker Rebecca Stairs during a re-

see PING PONG page 47

Bush Calls For End To 'Era Of Political Argument'

AUSTIN, TX—In a televised speech to the nation Monday, president-elect George W. Bush called for "an end to the era of political argument." "My fellow Americans," Bush said, "after a difficult period of partisan debate, the time has come for unanimity. We have seen how destructive it is when political rivals disagree, and we as a nation can no longer afford such ideological division." Bush said he is committed to making his presidency "The Age Of Assent."

Letter From Employer Thankfully Omits Balls-Copying Incident

SAN FRANCISCO—Randall Konerko, a 39-year-old database administrator looking for a new job in the field, was relieved to learn Monday that a letter of recommendation from his former employer makes no reference to the Dec. 11 balls-copying incident that led to his dismissal. "Whew, that's a relief," said Konerko after an interview with Luminant Worldwide. "I was sure Mr. Alland would mention that whole thing, but, mercifully, he didn't." Konerko has made a promise to himself never to engage in testicular Xeroxing, even if it's 2 a.m. and the office seems empty.

Broke Dad Makes Son PlayStation 2 For Christmas

DAYTON, OH—Determined to make his son's Christmas dreams come true in spite of financial woes, David McManus spent three hours in his garage Monday constructing a PlayStation 2 from scrap lumber and transistor-radio components. "I can't wait to see the look on Andy's face when he unwraps this," said McManus, lovingly painting a "2" onto the front of the handmade video-game console. "I didn't get to sand the controllers as smoothly as I'd have liked, but still." McManus added that he hopes he can make a "Tony Hawk's Pro Skater 2" CD in time for Andy's birthday in March.

Communists Now Least Threatening Group In U.S.

WASHINGTON, DC—According to a report released Tuesday by the Pentagon, Communists rank last on a list of 238 threats to national security. "Communists may now safely be ignored," Secretary of Defense William Cohen said. "The Red Menace has been surpassed by militia groups, religious extremists, ecoterrorists, cybercriminals, Hollywood producers, and angry drivers." Other groups deemed more threatening than Communists include rap-metal bands (#96), escaped zoo animals (#202), and Belgians (#237).

Man Reading Pynchon On Bus Takes Pains To Make Cover Visible

PHILADELPHIA—According to riders on the northbound C bus, John Bolen, 23, made a conscious effort Monday to make the cover of Thomas Pynchon's *The Crying Of Lot 49* visible to all on board. "Instead of resting the book on his lap or on the seat in front of him, he was holding it up in this really awkward, uncomfortable-looking way," rider Caryn Little said. "Then, every so often, he'd glance around to see if anyone was noticing what he was reading." Bolen vehemently denied the Pynchon-flaunting charges, insisting that "the light was bad" on the bus.

Real-Life Grinch Celebrates 'Hanukkah'

FREDONIA, KS—A real-life Grinch was found Monday in Fredonia, where, unlike his fellow residents, Josh Baum refuses to celebrate Christmas. "I'm looking forward to a nice Hanukkah," the Yuletide-shunning misanthrope said. "We'll be lighting the same menorah that's been in my family for generations." Baum would not comment on the possibility that spontaneous Christmas caroling would cause his small heart to grow three sizes. ∅

Critics Hail Porn Director's Debut As 'Shamelessly Masturbatory Male-Empowerment Fantasy'

LOS ANGELES—Across the nation, critics are unanimous in their praise of *Brenda In The Ass 2: Butt Reams May Come*, hailing the debut of porn director Ricky D'Alessandro as "the most exploitative, shamelessly masturbatory male-empowerment fantasy ever committed to video."

"I've never seen such utterly depraved filmmaking," raved Kenneth Turan, film critic for the *Los Angeles Times*. "D'Alessandro portrays women as little more than sexual receptacles. What little dialogue and plot he provides are flimsy excuses to undress starlets Brandi Reardon, Rebekka Rivers, and Jizzelle."

Turan's colleagues were quick to heap further laurels on the film. "*Brenda 2* is a pandering, lowest-common-denominator wank-fest," CNN reviewer Paul Clinton said. "Perverted beyond belief."

"D'Alessandro plumbs the depths of sexual abomination, then goes one nauseating fathom deeper," said Peter Howell of *The Toronto Star*. "I never imagined a film could be this sick."

"*Brenda 2* is disgusting and demoralizing," said *Entertainment Weekly*'s Lisa Schwarzbaum, who said she "would not be a bit surprised" if D'Alessandro were nominated for Best New Director at this year's Adult Video News Awards. "This is nothing but gratuitous, non-stop flesh with zero redeeming artistic value."

According to Entertainment Productions, D'Alessandro's Burbank-based production company, the film took less than a week to shoot in D'Alessandro's living room, jacuzzi-equipped bathroom, and van.

"No dark impulse is left unexplored," *New Yorker* critic Anthony Lane breathlessly gushed. "If sickening close-ups of Rebekka Rivers' super-stretched anus is your idea of entertainment, by all means rush to your video store. Not even the repetitious, saxophone-laden soundtrack, sloppy editing, and total lack of filmcraft can detract from the aura of sleazy, shamefully adolescent puerility in which D'Alessandro soaks the entire film.'"

D'Alessandro, already at work on his next feature, said he is "stunned" by the positive response to *Brenda 2*.

"Who would've thought a regular

Above: Acclaimed newcomer Ricky D'Alessandro.

guy like me could make 'the most obscene, corrupt pornographic filth ever committed to high-definition video'?" said D'Alessandro, speaking from the Van Nuys Motor Lodge, where he is scouting locations for his next film. "Look out, San Fernando Valley—I'm the porn king of the world!" ∅

44

The Final Frontier

photo circa 1911

By T. Herman Zweibel
Publisher Emeritus

Well, I hate to be the bearer of bad news, but Standish and I are currently hurtling away from the Earth in a giant metal rocket-ship. It turns out that the obelisk in which we were hiding as the murderous Society Of 800 Avenging Fists attacked my poor son N. Aeschylus was not an immobile object at all, but a powerful mortar-shell timed to automatically propel it-self from the Earth's grip.

Standish tells me we are approaching the speed of light, and that N. Aeschylus, my son and creator of the device, set the vessel's coordinates to a place called the Andromeda Galaxy. In fact, Standish is transmitting this column to Earth on a ship-board wireless-radio. He says we are quickly losing contact with Earth, so I should make haste.

Standish also claims that N. Aeschylus designed the rocket-ship so he could flee Earth after destroying my estate and slaying me in a bizarre ritual, but that he was thwarted by the surprise attack. Standish has always had some-thing against that sweet tot, and I don't know why. I would have Standish stoned to death if I were able-bodied.

What-ever happens to us, I want the citizenry of the Republic to know that *The Onion* will always be in good hands. Should it turn out that my beloved heir N. Aeschylus succumbed to the ambush or to the intense heat-blast of the rocket-ship's engines, control of this newspaper must be granted to a joint directorship composed of Bernard Baruch and Aunt Jemima. I am confident that these two titans of American states-manship will adroitly guide *The Onion* into the 20th century.

As for my readers, I will always look upon them with a combination of unconditional love and bottomless hatred. All I ask is that you continue to solemnly observe Zweibelmas every Sept. 21. A few grief-crazed suicides in my name would-

n't hurt, either.

For my part, I am already finding the rocket-ship's accommodations ingenious and pleasing. Standish has discovered some-thing called a "replicator," which can produce anything from enema-bulbs to cozy shawls, seemingly out of thin air. And, most wondrous of all, we found my old iron lung, with which the evil Mr. Tin absconded several years ago! It's in pristine condition, just as I remember it! A final gift from my ingenious and beloved son. I wonder how he knew.

Come, Standish, come away from that wireless-radio and seal me into it.

Yes, I think every-thing will be just dandy from here on in.

Huzzah! ∅

I Can't Believe You Blew My Perfect Feedback Rating

By droogie73 (210)

Ever since I placed that very first "LOGAN'S RUN ORIGINAL JAPANESE MOVIE POSTER ***MINT***" for sale on eBay two and a half years ago, I've prided myself on being the best seller I can possibly be. I always reply promptly to e-mail inquiries. I include sharp, clear pics with item descriptions but limit their size to 50 KB for quick page downloads. I never fail to contact the high bidder within the required three days. In fact, I usually do so within hours of the end of an auction.

And, for my two and a half years of dedicated eBay salesmanship, I have been duly rewarded with a perfect feedback rating. That's right: 211 positive comments with not so much as a single neutral. To preserve that perfect record, I've consistently gone the extra mile, purchasing bubble wrap when another seller would make do with balled-up newspaper, making special trips to the post office to get packages in the mail before 5 p.m., and attaching cheerful Post-It notes to sold items with messages like, "Hope you enjoy the Rutles CD!"

If you don't believe me, just look at my profile feedback. In it, buyer after satisfied buyer heaps accolades upon me: "Praise: Great transaction! Friendly Emails." "Praise: TAHNKYOU." "Praise: Great Auction!!!" "Praise: Great packaging job! GOOD SELLER." "Praise: Definitely reccomended.

A++++!" "Praise: Arived lightening fast!!"

The testimonials to my professionalism are overwhelming. Baldeagle1965 (41), high bidder for Item #513921485 "SPUMCO JOHN K. ORIGINAL ANIMATION CEL—NO RESERVE!," said I am "a pleasure to do business with!" Kewlgal (25) was so happy with her *Iron Gi-*

> ### As for the statement, "Bad picture quality," I scarcely know how to respond.

ant collectible bank that she said, "Excellent Mdse at an excellent price!!!" As you can see, I earned that turquoise star icon next to my name. Yes, my rating, like my reputation within the eBay community, was flawless.

Until Monday, that is.

For me, Dec. 18, 2000, will forever be known as Black Monday, the day I received a stinging slap to the face in the form of a negative feedback comment. Bananaman (37), how could you?

When I placed Item #538328761 "SUPERSTAR—RARE TODD HAYNES FILM—VHS" up for bid, I did so expecting that whoever was named the High Bidder at 12:44:54 PST would recognize and praise my top-notch service, just as 211 previous auction winners did. But, to my shock and dismay, Bananaman (37) blindsided me with the negative feedback comment, "Bad

picture quality. Came too slow."

Though you do not deserve it, Bananaman (37), I will now deign to respond to your groundless complaints. As for the charge, "Came too slow," I am flabbergasted. I explicitly informed you that should you choose to pay with a personal check instead of a money order, I would have to hold that check up to 10 days until it cleared. It was your choice to do so. As for any further delays, it appears I must point out the obvious fact that UPS is greatly overtaxed this time of year.

As for the statement, "Bad picture quality," I scarcely know how to respond. I invite you to re-examine the item description: "Film by director of *Safe* and *Velvet Goldmine*. Story of life and death of Karen Carpenter, as told with dolls. VHS. Good transfer. Super-rare. A must-have for any film buff!"

As you see, I stated that the tape was a "good transfer," and I stand firm on this assertion. I did not say it was an "excellent transfer" or a "perfect transfer." I promised a "good transfer," and I delivered.

I cannot help but direct you to the bid history, which shows that no less than seven other bidders were interested in this item. No doubt, any of them would have cherished it, not to mention been better equipped to judge the picture quality. Do you even realize what it is you now have in your possession? *Superstar*, Haynes' 43-minute 1987 film debut, the story of Carpenter's battle with anorexia as told with Barbie dolls, was never released because the Carpenter estate refused to grant music rights. Perhaps I should have added in the

item description that the film is a "CULT CLASSIC" and "NEARLY IMPOSSIBLE TO FIND."

Bananaman (37), do you think I even need the $32.50, plus $4.50 for shipping, that I received from you for this film? I am making copies of *Superstar* and selling them as a service to film connoisseurs everywhere who otherwise might not have access to this little-seen, underground masterwork.

Here is my question to you, Bananaman (37): If you were dissatisfied, why didn't you contact me and give me the chance to make amends before going public with your dissatisfaction, besmirching my good eBay name? After all, that is the procedure suggested on the eBay user help page titled "The Feedback Forum: One Of Your Most Valuable Tools."

Had I known you were dissatisfied, I would have happily refunded your money, no questions asked. I could have rushed you reimbursement the same day via PayPal. But for some reason, you chose to remain unapproachable in your fortress on high in "Location: Waterville, MD," stabbing me in the back without even giving me a chance to redress your grievance, unfounded as it may have been.

No, instead you chose to soil my reputation with a negative feedback comment. It is a scarlet letter I must carry for a full six months, visible for all the world to see on my eBay ID card. I could strike back with a negative comment on your profile, but I refuse to stoop to your level, Bananaman (37). Let me just say that we will not be doing business again. ∅

scribes herself as having "a deeply committed personal relationship with my Lord and Savior, Jesus Christ."

"Jesus is the reason for the season," Krueger said.

The trouble began for the Langans in early December, when the family was contacted by Krueger, who explained that she was in the Montoursville area for a six-week Bible-study program and looking for a place to spend the holidays. The Langans, who readily welcomed the visiting cousin into their home, were unaware that she had spent a majority of her adult life attending various "personal enrichment programs," converting to a conservative synod of the Lutheran church and gradually alienating all non-Christian members of her social circle.

"The first thing she did when she got here was explain that our Christmas tree was a pagan tradition Jesus never would have approved of," said mother Janet Langan, 49. "Not long after, she nearly fainted when she discovered we didn't have an Advent calendar in the house, so Marv had to run out and buy one."

With Krueger's arrival came other changes, as well. The Langans, who belong to Montoursville's Holy Christ Almighty Church but attend services just a few times a year, soon found themselves roped into twice-weekly visits.

"Last Thursday night, I'd just baked a pie, and the whole gang was getting ready to go sledding together," Janet said. "Next thing you know, Barb is asking about Advent services. I'd forgotten that there was such a thing. Well, there was no sledding that night, let me tell you."

Other holiday-cheer-killing activities foisted upon the family include daily "devotionals" involving candle-lighting and scripture readings, formal prayers before all meals, and longwinded harangues explaining why Jesus wants the Langans to reject such "blasphemously secular" holiday TV specials as *Frosty The Snowman* and *Rudolph The Red-Nosed Reindeer.*

"Caroling is usually my favorite thing," 8-year-old Justin Langan said. "But Cousin Barb says we shouldn't sing Santa songs. All she likes is stupid, hard-to-sing, religious stuff about Good King Wenceslaus and Feast of Stephen—crap like that."

According to daughter Brianna Langan, 17, the family's annual trip to see Santa Claus at the local mall was "a complete wash-out" because of Krueger.

"It totally sucked this year," Brianna said. "The whole time, everybody just stood there all quiet, glancing back at Cousin Barb, worried about what she would think." Brianna added that while waiting in line to see Santa, her visiting cousin told her she shouldn't be wearing makeup at her age.

"I didn't talk to one boy the whole time we were at the mall," said Michelle Langan, Brianna's 15-year-old sister. "Every time I saw somebody

Above: Members of the Langan family struggle to enjoy the holiday season in spite of their guest.

I knew from school, Cousin Barb just glared at them and scared them off. She says Jesus teaches us to love the sinner and condemn the sin, but I hate her."

"I hope she never comes back here again," Michelle continued. "I hope she gets run over by a bus and goes to Heaven. That way, she could spend the holidays with her best friend Jesus." ✐

Jim's Got A Big Wish List This Year

Hola, amigos. I know it's been a long time since I rapped at ya, but I've had my hands fuller than John Holmes' shorts. Between my car

**The Cruise
By Jim Anchower**

catching fire, getting sacked for showing up to work late, and making all those waffles, I ain't had time to lay back and just be me. Now, I know you're thinking: "Back up there, hombre. What's this about waffles? I'm sure there's some story there." Well, there is, but I don't wanna get into it right now. Let's just say I got tired of drinking syrup straight out of the bottle.

See, I got important business to take care of in this column. Namely, letting people know what's on my wish list for Christmas. It's not like I believe in Santa. And even if I did, I wouldn't be getting anything from him but a lump of coal in my stocking, because Jim Anchower's been plenty naughty this year. But I figure

it can't hurt to let the people know what I'm hoping for, just in case any of my faithful readers feel like surprising me with a little something, if you catch my drift.

> **A decent Camaro would do the trick. Hell, it don't even have to have a stereo. I can just rip the one out of my burned car and drop it in.**

Anyway, what do I want? Let's see. Well, I'll start big. I want a car. Nothing too fancy. A decent Camaro would do the trick. Hell, it don't even have to have a stereo. I can just rip the one out of my burned car and drop it in. Of course, some of the wires got roasted in the fire, but that's no big thing. And it should be red or black. Don't get me nothing

green or yellow. All over the road, I see these new green VW Bugs that look like globs of snot that just flew out of somebody's nose. If that's your idea of a good color, maybe you should be reading somebody else's wish list.

What else? Oh, yeah, my Super Nintendo kind of got beat up in the apartment flood, so I could use a new system. Like a PlayStation 2. I need something to occupy my mind, otherwise my thoughts start running away with me and I get into trouble. A PlayStation 2 would keep me out of trouble for the next few years. Oh, and throw in some kind of fight game while you're at it. Robots, ninjas—I don't give a rat's ass what kind it is, so long as there's one thing beating the crap out of another thing.

I'd also like the Led Zep box set, to replace the one that got swiped from my car last year. I never got around to replacing it, and 75 mph just ain't 75 mph unless you got the windows down and "Black Dog" cranked. If you want to throw in some other CDs, that'd be cool, too, so long as they rock. I don't mean alternative rock, either. The last thing I wanna hear

while I'm cruising is some overgrown nerd yelling about how he got picked on in high school.

I hate to waste a Christmas list on stupid shit, but I could use some dishes. No gravy boats or other wedding-registry crap like that, just the basics. Ron was knocking around my cupboard a couple months ago, looking for a mouse he swore he saw, and broke most of my plates and glasses. All I got left is one plate and a "Lordy, Lordy, Look Who's 40!" mug I snagged from a free box at a rummage sale.

I know that all this is pretty expensive, so if any of you want to get Jim Anchower something that ain't going to break the bank, here are some ideas. Get me a video of *Detroit Rock City,* 'cause I know what that's all about. Or the Jenny McCarthy issue of *Playboy,* 'cause I lost mine. Or you can get me a joint, 'cause, well, just because.

Well, that's about it. There's a bunch more stuff I could use, but I don't want to get greedy. I suppose I should wish for something like world peace, but until I get myself a piece, the rest of the world can go to hell. ✐

cent match. "Pretenders to the throne, beware!"

Stairs said she is mystified by Bergkamp's ping-pong bravado.

"How anyone could associate such alpha-male chest-thumping with a polite pastime like ping-pong is beyond me," Stairs said. "It's baffling. Speaking of which, one of his many nicknames for himself is 'The Baffler.' He says that's because no one ever knows where the next shot is coming from."

Bergkamp has given himself numerous other monikers, including The Human Wall, because no opponent can get the ball past him; the Harlem Pongtrotter, employed when he whistles "Sweet Georgia Brown" to psyche out opponents; and the aliases Cobra Verde, Cobra Rosa, and Cobra Negro, which vary according to his paddle's color.

"I like to start out slowly, lulling my prey into a false sense of security," Bergkamp recently confided to Stairs. "Then I turn up the heat with a little smack-talkin', which throws off their game. Then, once they're dazed and confused from the psychological warfare, I lock on the target and fire off a vicious volley of spin shots, from which

> ## "I deliver my enemies into the arms of their maker with neither remorse nor regret," Bergkamp said.

my hapless victim can find no shelter."

"They've learned to expect no quarter, and none is given," Bergkamp said. "I deliver my enemies into the arms of their maker with neither remorse nor regret."

Bergkamp's obsessive drive to dominate the ping-pong table is not limited to the Target breakroom. On weekends, he frequents Appleton-area amusement center B.Z. Bonkers, challenging unwitting newcomers to "a lesson in ping-pong pain [they] will never forget." In addition, he recently acquired a table for his own apartment, inviting opponents to "experience the thrashing of your soon-to-be-over life."

Last week, Bergkamp also began construction on "Solo Pong Station 3000," a makeshift half-table placed against a rebounding wall in his garage. When completed, the structure will enable him to play ping-pong even when alone.

"When I'm *mano a mano* on Pong Station 3000, that's when I'll face my worthiest adversary of all: me," Bergkamp said. "It's the proverbial irresistible force going head-to-head with the immovable object."

Though sometimes irritated, coworkers say Bergkamp's ping-pong-fueled bravado is mostly harmless.

"I'd never get that excited about ping-pong, but if that's what gets his rocks off, more power to him, I guess," said Karl Hiestand, Bergkamp's immediate supervisor. "I'll play him every now and again, usually when he asks if I'm 'recovered enough from [my] last beatdown for a rematch.' In a way, it's kind of cute how he talks all tough about it. It doesn't make sense, but it's sort of funny, I suppose."

When told of his supervisor's remarks, Bergkamp lifted his ping-pong paddle over his head in a two-fisted stance and said, "None, not even the Karl-Tron himself, can withstand the terrifying fury unleashed by Tim Bergkamp, a.k.a. King Pong."

Added Bergkamp: "There can be only one."

Manning then hoisted a 22-inch machete over his head and exclaimed, "Out of my cold, dead hands."

According to NMA members, the government does not understand the important role machete ownership plays in their lives.

"I need my machete—and not just for play," said Delmore Taggart of Coffeyville, KS. "Sure, I enjoy taking it out to the barn and having a little fun with the animals. But it's also vitally useful. How else am I supposed to, say, slash my way through dense jungle vines? Or harvest a sugar-cane crop, if there were any around here?"

Bud Hastings, president of the Sweetwater, TX, NMA chapter, agreed.

"Them East Coast types just don't get it," said a shirtless Hastings, brandishing a silver 14-inch model he bought at a recent machete show. "They may not have much use for machetes in their big cities, but out here in the country, they're a necessity. If I were to somehow get my hands on a coconut, what do you suppose I'd slash it open with—a knife and fork?"

"The day I turned 10, my daddy took me out to the woods and showed me how to handle a machete," said Sparta, TN, NMA member Earl Slocum. "And the day my boy turns 10, I'm gonna do the same with him."

The push for machete-control legislation gained momentum in April when a Chicago man hacked his wife to pieces with a machete during a domestic dispute. Machete violence made national headlines again in September, when a 6-year-old Casper, WY, girl accidentally killed her infant sister while playing with her father's machete.

Slocum rejected the notion that machetes should be banned or restricted for safety reasons.

"That's a load of bunk," Slocum said. "When handled properly, machetes ain't dangerous. If other people are getting hurt by machetes or letting them near children without proper supervision, that ain't my fault. I shouldn't have

Above: Machete enthusiasts examine new models at the Southwest Machete Expo in Tucson, AZ.

my machete taken away from me, just because somebody else is careless with theirs."

The NMA strongly opposes all federal regulation of machete use, including seven-day waiting periods for machete purchases, background checks on potential buyers, and mandatory use of safety sheaths. Manning said he is committed to keeping the pressure on Congress to keep machetes free.

"If restrictions are passed, how is that hardworking Nebraska farmer going to harvest cocoa-bean pods? How will he divide his breadfruit in equal shares among members of his clan?" Manning asked. "If you take away his machete, how will he defend his family from savage criminals who may burst into his home at any moment, armed to the teeth with huge machetes with massive slashing power? Legal or illegal, criminals will always manage to get their hands on them. It's the honest, law-abiding machete owner who will suffer if they're banned."

Said Slocum: "There's nothing more American than a Chevy pick-up with a machete rack on the back. And I'll be damned if some pansy in Washington who's never held a blade in his life is going to tell me what I can and can't do with mine."

Darling, Will You Spend The Next Six To Ten Years With Me?

By Jon McNally

Darling. We've known each other for more than a year now. During that time, we've shared so much—our hopes, our dreams, our fears. I know when I met you I wasn't thinking of starting up a serious relationship, but my admiration and respect for you quickly blossomed into love. You're my best friend and my confidant, and I can't imagine spending the better part of the next decade without you.

I know I've been vague about taking "the next step," but all that has changed. Your patience, loyalty, and love have made me see the world in an entirely new light. It's a place where true love can exist. So I ask you, Julie Bramhall... Will you spend the next six to ten years with me?

I realize it's sudden. We just moved in together three months ago, and I'm still looking for a better-paying job. But when I look into your eyes, I see all the things I never used to want. A big wedding. Kids. A house with a white picket fence that I'll have to move out of in about seven years when you discover I'm sleeping with my secretary. I never thought I'd say this to anyone, but you're the only one I want to wake up next to for the rest of my 30s.

I remember telling you early in our relationship that I never wanted to get married. But sometimes, I stay awake after you've fallen asleep and just look at you and stroke your hair. I can't believe what a lucky man I am. When the moonlight hits your delicate features just right, I see an angel. An angel who will turn cold and indifferent to me in five years because of festering resentment over my drinking. But if I could only capture how you look on film during those moments, I swear we could make a million dollars. God, you're so beautiful at this stage of your life.

Did you know that most of my friends are amazed that a woman of your caliber would even be going out with me, much less be interested in marrying me? They're always talking about how smart, funny, and drop-dead gorgeous you are. I have no choice but to agree. When I take a step back and look at things, there's no reason someone so luminous should be interested in a guy like me. Of course, I always point out to them that your looks will be pretty well faded by 2008. But when I think how stunning you are now, I can only shake my head in disbelief.

Marriage is a big step to make, I

see DARLING page 48

OPINION

The $252,000,000 Man

Last week, free-agent shortstop Alex Rodriguez signed the richest contract in sports history, a 10-year, $252 million deal with the Texas Rangers. What do *you* think?

Eleanor Jeffries
Reference Librarian

"Boy, when that state isn't busy putting Hispanics to death, it's paying them ridiculous sums to run around a baseball field. Is there no in-between?"

Brandon Wiley
Security Guard

"It's outrageous that the Rangers signed this guy for $252 million. Only the Yankees should get to do that."

Bruce Dickerson
Baseball Executive

"As a Texas Rangers front-office official, I'm extremely excited to have Rodriguez on board—in a nauseous, tight-chested kind of way."

Vanessa Simon
Teacher

"Sure, a quarter of a billion dollars is a lot of money, but we are talking about a guy with a career .374 on-base percentage here."

Dan Agarawal
Bricklayer

"I'm so psyched to see A-Rod play for my beloved Rangers, I've already started saving up for a $135 bleacher seat."

Randall Keith
Systems Analyst

"Just think: He makes more than all the other Rodriguezes in Texas combined."

Madonna's Wedding

Later this month, Madonna and director Guy Ritchie will marry at a Scottish castle. Among the known details:

- ♥ Madonna to walk down aisle to remix of "The Wedding March" by DJ Jellybean Benitez
- ♥ Ritchie gets to invite 3 percent of the guests
- ♥ Ceremony to reflect Madonna's "total respect for Buddhism and yoga and the Kabbalah and stuff"
- ♥ Wedding photographer expressly instructed only to take pictures of bride
- ♥ Madonna to wear tank top her mother wore on her wedding day
- ♥ Receiving line to consist of 25 lithe, shirtless, gay black men writhing to electronic breakbeats
- ♥ Kurt Loder to cry eyes out in back pew
- ♥ Upon completion of vows, son Rocco Ritchie will no longer be bastard; daughter Lourdes Leon, however, will remain bastard
- ♥ Madonna to brilliantly reinvent self as aging, strident, twice-married martinet

the ONION

America's Finest News Source

Herman Ulysses Zweibel *Founder*

T. Herman Zweibel *Publisher Emeritus*
J. Phineas Zweibel *Publisher*
Maxwell Prescott Zweibel *Editor-In-Chief*

FOUNDED 1871 • "TU STULTUS ES"

HOROSCOPES

By Lloyd Schumner Sr.
Retired Machinist and
A.A.P.B.-Certified Astrologer

Aries: (March 21–April 19)
The courts deny your request to change your name, forcing you to remain John Jacob Jingleheimer Schmidt for life.

Taurus: (April 20–May 20)
You will be disappointed when no one is surprised to hear that you attended a science-fiction convention.

Gemini: (May 21–June 21)
You will discover a new miracle weight-loss plan that will enable you to lose weight and get in shape. Then you won't follow it.

Cancer: (June 22–July 22)
Love alone will fail to see you through the hard times. It's a good thing you're also incredibly rich.

Leo: (July 23–Aug. 22)
Next time, ask yourself: How would I feel if *I* were a nurse and someone murdered *me* that way?

Virgo: (Aug. 23–Sept. 22)
You will be mortified to realize that you misspelled the words "fiery," "dynamite," and "vengeance" in your letter to the president.

Libra: (Sept. 23–Oct. 23)
You used to think that it would be cool to have a computer implanted in your skull, but it turns out it's not.

Scorpio: (Oct. 24–Nov. 21)
When offered potato salad, decline politely, saying that you'd take some if you liked it, but you don't. Unless you do like it. In that case, by all means, have some potato salad.

Sagittarius: (Nov. 22–Dec. 21)
You will feel both alienated and betrayed when you realize that your town's beloved teen center will not mature along with you.

Capricorn: (Dec. 22–Jan. 19)
On second thought, maybe the idea of an Irish-themed rap group was kind of silly, after all.

Aquarius: (Jan. 20–Feb. 18)
Put it back. Don't look at Aquarius like you don't know what it's talking about. Put it back. Now!

Pisces: (Feb. 19–March 20)
You will learn the hard way that cryogenically freezing yourself until a cure for cancer is found is not something you just do at home.

DARLING from page 47

know. But when I think of all the memories we've shared together, it makes me want a medium amount more. Do you remember that time we stumbled onto the bridge in Georgia overlooking a moonlit river, and we just held each other close, watching the waves gently

> ## When I think of all the memories we've shared together, it makes me want a medium amount more.

lap on the shore? What about all the Sundays we lay in bed together until early afternoon? I cherish these memories, and I want to share more until our relationship is reduced to screaming fights, endless hours of legal battles, and an

attempt on your part to stab me with a potato peeler.

If you asked me two years ago if I was ever going to want kids, I would have looked at you like you were crazy. But sometimes, when I'm walking with you hand in hand, I imagine us pushing a stroller. And I like that image. I see us with two kids, a boy and a girl. That would be perfect. They could hold each other up after I'm gone.

I really think you'd make an incredible mother, Julie. And I think you'll eventually make a great single mother, too. You've got that inner strength.

You don't have to answer right away if you don't want to. It's a big decision, and I wouldn't want you to take it lightly. Think it over. Talk to your friends and family. I already asked your father for your hand in marriage, and he gave his blessing. But before you answer, you should know that I truly do love you and want to spend nearly a decade with you. Without you, my life is incomplete. At least, until I meet our daughter's dance instructor.

So, please, Julie Bramhall... Say you'll grow early middle-aged with me. ∅

NEWS

Ø **the ONION** ®

| VOLUME 37 ISSUE 01 | AMERICA'S FINEST NEWS SOURCE™ | 18-24 JANUARY 2001 |

Chinese Guy Still Insisting It Was Him In Front Of That Tank

see WORLD page 4A

Denny's Introduces 'Just A Humongous Bucket Of Eggs And Meat'

see FOOD page 3C

Date With Proctologist Ends Predictably

see LOCAL page 10D

STATshot

A look at the numbers that shape your world.

How Did We Celebrate MLK Day?

36% Let freedom ring in lieu of alarm clock

21% Re-waterproofed deck

16% Drove down Martin Luther King Jr. Blvd.

11% Realized that *Card Sharks* was a pretty good game show

9% Wondered why bank was closed on a Monday

7% Gestured emptily

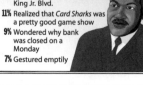

THE ONION
VOLUME 37
ISSUE 01

$2.00 US
$3.00 CAN

Bush: 'Our Long National Nightmare Of Peace And Prosperity Is Finally Over'

Above: President-elect Bush vows that "together, we can put the triumphs of the recent past behind us."

WASHINGTON, DC—Mere days from assuming the presidency and closing the door on eight years of Bill Clinton, president-elect George W. Bush assured the nation in a televised address Tuesday that "our long national nightmare of peace and prosperity is finally over."

"My fellow Americans," Bush said, "at long last, we have reached the end of the dark period in American history that will come to be known as the Clinton Era, eight long years characterized

see BUSH page 50

Rural Nebraskan Not Sure He Could Handle Frantic Pace Of Omaha

NORTH PLATTE, NE—Life-long North Platte resident Fred Linder, 46, revealed Monday that he doesn't think he could cope with the fast-paced hustle and bustle of Omaha, the Cornhusker State's largest city.

"Oh, sure, I bet it'd be exciting at first, going to see 9 p.m. showings of movies, shopping at those big department stores, and maybe even eating at one of those fancy restaurants that don't use iceberg lettuce in their salads," Linder said. "But I just don't think I could put up with all that hubbub for more than a day or two."

Added Linder: "And parking's a nightmare there."

Linder expressed doubts about Omaha's "hectic pace" while having dinner at the home of Pastor Bob Egan, the longtime spiritual leader of North Platte's Holy Christ Almighty Church.

"I'd just returned from a 'Prayer & Share' fellowship con-

Above: North Platte resident Fred Linder.

ference in Omaha, and I mentioned to Fred how much I enjoyed myself there," Egan said. "There's just so much to do: dining, shopping, seeing the sights—[wife] Margaret and I even saw a touring production of *Phantom Of The Opera*. But Fred just seemed uncomfortable with the whole idea of it."

The drawbacks to life in Omaha cited by Linder include crime, traffic, pollution, and the rudeness of Omahans.

"You read such awful stuff in

see OMAHA page 50

Corpse-Reanimation Technology Still 10 Years Off, Say MIT Mad Scientists

CAMBRIDGE, MA—Dead-tissue reanimation, projected in the 1980s to be standard medical practice by 2001, won't be possible for at least another decade, scientists at the Massachusetts Institute of Technology's Mad Science Research Center announced Monday.

Mad Science & Technology

"They laughed when we said we would rekindle the divine spark of life in flesh grown cold and lifeless," said MIT mad scientist Dr. Otto Von Verruchtheit, the nation's leading corpse-reanimation expert, speaking from the castle that houses the MSRC's state-of-the-art corpse-reanimation laboratory. "Oh, how they laughed! They said we were mad to attempt such an unholy ambition by the century's end. Fools! Fools, all of them! However, in this case, they were actually right."

Von Verruchtheit then raised his arms to the heavens, attempting to summon a lightning bolt and thunder crash to punctuate his remarks. After several unsuccessful attempts, he gave up.

Von Verruchtheit's colleagues in the mad-scientific community admitted that it may be decades before re-

see SCIENTISTS page 52

49

by unprecedented economic expansion, a sharp decrease in crime, and sustained peace overseas. The time has come to put all of that behind us."

Bush swore to do "everything in [his] power" to undo the damage wrought by Clinton's two terms in office, including selling off the national parks to developers, going into massive debt to develop expensive and impractical weapons technologies, and passing sweeping budget cuts that drive the mentally ill out of hospitals and onto the street.

During the 40-minute speech, Bush also promised to bring an end to the severe war drought that plagued the nation under Clinton, assuring citizens that the U.S. will engage in at least one Gulf War-level armed conflict in the next four years.

"You better believe we're going to mix it up with somebody at some point during my administration," said Bush, who plans a 250 percent boost in military spending. "Unlike my predecessor, I am fully committed to putting soldiers in battle situations. Otherwise, what is the point of even having a military?"

On the economic side, Bush vowed to bring back economic stagnation by implementing substantial tax cuts, which would lead to a recession, which would necessitate a tax hike, which would lead to a drop in consumer spending, which would lead to layoffs, which would deepen the recession even further.

Wall Street responded strongly to the Bush speech, with the Dow Jones industrial fluctuating wildly before closing at an 18-month low. The NASDAQ composite index, rattled by a gloomy outlook for tech stocks in 2001, also fell sharply, losing 4.4 percent of its total value between 3 p.m. and the closing bell.

Asked for comment about the cooling technology sector, Bush said: "That's hardly my area of expertise."

Above: Soldiers at Ft. Bragg march lockstep in preparation for America's return to aggression.

Turning to the subject of the environment, Bush said he will do whatever it takes to undo the tremendous damage not done by the Clinton Administration to the Arctic National Wildlife Refuge. He assured citizens that he will follow through on his campaign promise to open the 1.5 million acre refuge's coastal plain to oil drilling. As a sign of his commitment to bringing about a change in the environment, he pointed to his choice of Gale Norton for Secretary of the Interior. Norton, Bush noted, has "extensive experience" fighting environmental causes, working as a lobbyist for lead-paint manufacturers and as an attorney for loggers and miners, in addition to suing the EPA to overturn clean-air standards.

Bush had equally high praise for Attorney General nominee John Ashcroft, whom he praised as "a tireless champion in the battle to protect a woman's right to give birth."

"Soon, with John Ashcroft's help, we will move out of the Dark Ages and into a more enlightened time when a woman will be free to think long and hard before trying to fight her way past throngs of protesters blocking her entrance to an abortion clinic," Bush said. "We as a nation can look forward to lots and lots of babies."

Continued Bush: "John Ashcroft will be invaluable in healing the terrible wedge President Clinton drove between church and state."

The speech met with overwhelming approval from Republican leaders.

"Finally, the horrific misrule of the Democrats has been brought to a close," House Majority Leader Dennis Hastert (R-IL) told reporters. "Under Bush, we can all look forward to military aggression, deregulation of dangerous, greedy industries, and the defunding of vital domestic social-service programs upon which millions depend. Mercifully, we can now say goodbye to the awful nightmare that was Clinton's America."

"For years, I tirelessly preached the message that Clinton must be stopped," conservative talk-radio host Rush Limbaugh said. "And yet, in 1996, the American public failed to heed my urgent warnings, re-electing Clinton despite the fact that the nation was prosperous and at peace under his regime. But now, thank God, that's all done with. Once again, we will enjoy mounting debt, jingoism, nuclear paranoia, mass deficit, and a massive military build-up."

An overwhelming 49.9 percent of Americans responded enthusiastically to the Bush speech.

"After eight years of relatively sane fiscal policy under the Democrats, we have reached a point where, just a few weeks ago, President Clinton said that the national debt could be paid off by as early as 2012," Rahway, NJ, machinist and father of three Bud Crandall said. "That's not the kind of world I want my children to grow up in."

"You have no idea what it's like to be black and enfranchised," said Marlon Hastings, one of thousands of Miami-Dade County residents whose votes were not counted in the 2000 presidential election. "George W. Bush understands the pain of enfranchisement, and ever since Election Day, he has fought tirelessly to make sure it never happens to my people again."

Bush concluded his speech on a note of healing and redemption.

"We as a people must stand united, banding together to tear this nation in two," Bush said. "Much work lies ahead of us: The gap between the rich and the poor may be wide, be there's much more widening left to do. We must squander our nation's hard-won budget surplus on tax breaks for the wealthiest 15 percent. And, on the foreign front, we must find an enemy and defeat it."

"The insanity is over," Bush said. "After a long, dark night of peace and stability, the sun is finally rising again over America. We look forward to a bright new dawn not seen since the glory days of my dad." ∅

the papers about that place," Linder said. "Every month, it's another murder. Between the drugs and the crime and the street gangs, it's almost as bad as Wichita."

Those familiar with Linder say his anti-Omaha stance has deepened since his sister left North Platte in 1998 to take a job as human-resources director at an Omaha insurance agency.

"Don't get Fred started on Omaha," friend Ken Carlson said. "He's always resented Amy for going there. They're a lot less close now than they used to be, and Fred feels it's because she's gotten a bit of an attitude since moving to the big city, like she's superior or something."

"Let's just say the glamour of city life has changed Amy," Linder said. "She's definitely 'gone Omaha,' if you catch my drift."

Linder has visited the Nebraska metropolis three times in his life, most recently in 1996 for a farm-equipment show.

Above: The imposing Omaha skyline.

"I prepared plenty well before that trip, you better believe," Linder said. "I bought a money belt and travelers' checks to protect myself from all those Omaha pickpockets and con men. And I made sure I had a full tank before going, because I sure as heck wasn't about to pay Omaha prices for gas."

Linder said he has no plans to visit his sister in Omaha anytime soon.

"If Amy wants to come home only for Christmas, fine," Linder said. "If that means I only see her once a year, so be it. I just can't take the noise and commotion of Omaha. It gives me a migraine just thinking about it."

"That sort of running around at all hours of the day and night might appeal to some, but I believe there's more to life than the thrill-seeking, urban scene you find in a place like Omaha," Linder said. "The bright lights and fast cars may have seduced my sister, but they'll never get me." ∅

Clinton Not Expecting To Collect White House Security Deposit

WASHINGTON, DC—Surveying the White House's walls and bathroom fixtures in preparation for move-out, President Clinton said Monday that he expects to forfeit his security deposit. "It's just not worth it," Clinton said. "I'd rather lose the $575 than have to deal with fixing all the nail holes and chipped porticos and stuff." Noticing a small, brownish stain on the East Room's carpet, Clinton added: "It's not like the place is trashed, but eight years of summits and state dinners are really going to take their toll on a place."

New KFC Employee Takes 'Fry-Q' Test In Employee Manual

MITCHELL, SD—After a three-hour training session at the Berner Road KFC Monday, food-prep trainee Liz Falk took the "Fry-Q" test in the employee handbook. "It's to see how much you know about, like, breading and the different chicken parts and stuff," said Falk, 16, who has a Fry-Q of 127. "I think I messed up the section on potato wedges, but I did okay on the rest."

Impressed by Falk's high Fry-Q, KFC manager Dan Nies said he hopes to groom her for a shift-supervisor position.

English Teacher Obviously Hung Over

MARYLAND HEIGHTS, MO—In spite of attempts to conceal it from students, Eisenhower High School 11th-grade English teacher Matthew Geisinger was clearly hung over Monday. "Today, you're going to break up into groups of four to discuss that book you read over the weekend," Geisinger groggily told his first-period class. "The idea is to draw your own conclusions about the book without coming to me for any help." Geisinger then rested his head on his desk for the remainder of the period, occasionally taking a sip of coffee.

Ex-Girlfriend's Last Electric-Bill Check Remains Uncashed In Area Man's Wallet

BALTIMORE—Ten weeks after girlfriend Jessica Schroeder broke up with him and moved out, Richard Bluff, 24, continues to carry the check for her half of their final Baltimore Gas & Electric bill in his wallet. "Jess gave it to me the day she left, and I just couldn't bear to part with it," Bluff said Monday of the check for $75.92. "I know it shouldn't have any sentimental meaning, but, well..." Bluff has also not been able to bring himself to remove Schroeder's Lady Bic disposable razor from his shower.

Paul Hogan Keeps Pitching *Crocodile Dundee* Saturday-Morning Cartoon

LOS ANGELES—Continuing nine years of such efforts, Australian actor Paul Hogan pitched a *Crocodile Dundee* Saturday-morning cartoon to Fox Family Channel executives Tuesday. "In *Crocodile Dundee & His Outback Gang*, Dundee would travel the world in a hot-air balloon, having adventures with his outback pals Kenny Koala and J. Wellington Wallaby," Hogan told the executives. "This is an even stronger concept than the *Crocodile Dundee & The Magic Didgeridoo* idea I pitched you folks last year. Or was that UPN?" Hogan said that in addition to executive producing *Crocodile Dundee & His Outback Gang*, he would be willing to provide the voice for the title character. ∅

Man Who Thought He Was On Date Actually Just At Work-Related Get-Together

BOSTON—Thirty minutes into dinner with coworker Natalie Cooper, Matthew Rolen, a marketing manager at Novartis Pharmaceuticals, realized Tuesday that what he thought was a date was

Matthew Rolen enjoys a romantic business meeting with co-worker Natalie Cooper.

actually a work-related get-together.

"There Natalie and I were at Trattoria Il Panino, candles flickering and soft music playing. But somehow, the conversation kept turning back to the upcoming print campaign for [anti-fungal medication] Lamisil," the 32-year-old Rolen said. "Then it hit me: This is a business meeting."

Cooper, 26, and Rolen met last November when Cooper was transferred from Novartis' East Hanover, NJ, office, where she spent three years as marketing manager for the company's line of CIBA Vision contact lenses. Upon arriving in Boston, she was teamed with Rolen to head up the Lamisil campaign, and the two began spending a great deal of time together.

"Sure, everything we did was on the clock, but we were getting along really great—cracking each other up all the time and teasing each other about little things," Rolen said. "You know how it goes, sort of flirting but never saying anything too over the line. Then, one day, Natalie made a comment about how married she's been to our project, saying she really needed a night out on the town. I thought maybe that was her way of telling me she wanted to be more than friends."

While in Cooper's cubicle Monday going over ad specs, Rolen asked her to join him for dinner the next night. Noting how stressful it is to work against a deadline, Rolen suggested the two "get together and talk over some good food." Cooper agreed, and the pair met at Trattoria Il Panino at 7 p.m.

"As we were sitting there, I kept asking her all these questions about where she grew up and what kind of music she likes," Rolen said. "Then she'd turn around and ask me if I thought our media buys were too heavily concentrated in general-interest magazines. For some reason, I didn't catch on. I thought she was nervous and couldn't think of anything else to talk about."

Continued Rolen: "When I suggested we get some wine, Natalie said she wanted to 'keep a clear head' so we could really 'plow through this thing.' Looking back, I guess I should have seen that as a sign."

Rolen finally realized he was not on a date shortly after finishing the appetizers. "When the waiter cleared our gnocchi," he said, "Natalie took out a stack of papers and said, 'Well, should we get started?' I was like, 'On what?' She just laughed and said, 'Yeah, I wish I could forget about it, too.'"

The pair spent the next two hours working out details of the Lamisil campaign. While doing so, Rolen also dissected the evening's earlier exchanges in his head.

"I realized there were a bunch of times I must have looked like a real weirdo," Rolen said. "Like, she said to me, 'You look nice. Are you going somewhere later tonight?' and I said, 'Yeah, I've got another date.'"

As the evening wore on, Rolen became increasingly paranoid that Cooper would discover his original romantic intentions.

"Thinking I was covering my tracks, I said I had a thing for our supervisor, Michaela [Torres]," Rolen said. "I started babbling about how I like to date Hispanic women, because I find them very 'earthy' and 'spiritual.' I was out of control."

The final blow came toward the end of the meal. When Rolen insisted upon paying, Cooper relented but reminded him to save the receipt for reimbursement.

"By the time the check came, it was long clear that we were not on a date, but the save-your-receipt thing still hurt," Rolen said. "I wound up leaving the waiter an extra-big tip because I'd asked him to seat us at a private table next to the fireplace in their back room, which was closed off that evening. Actually, it

see DATE page 53

I'm Going To Be The Worst Father Ever

By Jim Jarrell

Well, Trish is now eight months pregnant. Before you know it, I'm going to be the father of a strapping baby boy. And you know what? I just know I'm going to be the worst father ever.

First of all, I'm not ready for this. Making another human being the center of my universe is not something I want to do. No doubt, I'll take my frustrations out on him. Not overtly. Just in lots of little passive-aggressive ways that undermine his sense of self-esteem and well-being. One day, in about 20 years, he'll trace it back to me while on his thera-pist's couch. But by then, it'll be way too late.

That won't be my only shortcoming. When it comes to discipline, I'll be weak and inconsistent. If he asks for candy right before bedtime, I'll say yes right after his mother says no. He'll quickly learn to come to me when he wants something he's not supposed to have. And, on the off chance I actually say no to something, I'll change my tune if he whines or throws a tantrum. That should help me lose his respect, not to mention undermine his mother's hard-earned authority.

Man, am I going to suck.

My kid's going to have all the things I never had as a child, whether he wants them or not. He'll take piano lessons, even if he'd rather play the trombone. He'll play Little League baseball, even if he'd rather play tennis. After a while, he'll become so resentful of my forcing him into things, he'll reject everything I try to give him, even the stuff he likes.

Sure, at first, I'll spend lots of time with him. But after the first few years of being a father, the novelty will wear off and I'll leave it to Trish to do the bulk of the parenting. While she's busy teaching him how to tie his shoelaces or build a snowman, I'll be hiding in the basement with my model boats. By the time he's in high school, it'll be too late to make up for all the lost time, so I'll overcompensate by smothering him with attention. That'll further drive a wedge between us.

As for the birds and the bees, for-get it. I don't even want to *think* about teaching him the facts of life. Hopefully, he'll learn what he needs to know from friends or *Hustler*, because I'm going to feel extremely uncomfortable talking to him about any of that stuff.

The teen years are a difficult time, and in addition to not having the slightest idea what he's into and what his interests are, I'll be fighting with him all the time. Unfortunately, once he's finally old enough that I can reason with him, I'll have resorted to yelling things like, "Because I'm your father and I said so!" I'll start snapping at him and harassing him about what he's up to and who he's hanging around with and what he's doing with his life. After all this, I'll still be sur-

see FATHER page 53

SCIENTISTS from page 49

animation technology becomes a reality.

"The truth is, there are certain forms of horrible knowledge that Man was not meant to possess," said University of Chicago mad scientist Dr. Hans-Klaus Menschesser. "A twisted mind lusting after the unclean power to play

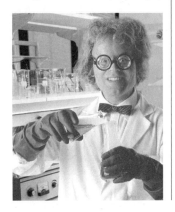

Left: Stanford University mad scientist Dr. Hugo Dammerung.

God is not enough to bring the dead back to life. Only through strict adher-ence to the scientific method can these hubristic and unnatural schemes be-come possible."

Still, others are more confident. "My plan to form a Modern Adam from the mere dust and clay of newly dead mat-ter is not yet lost," said Stanford Uni-versity's Dr. Hugo Dammerung, who predicted routine cadaver reanimation by 2000 in the October 1989 issue of *Mad Scientific American.* "True, I was unable to bring Helga, my beloved re-search assistant, back from the realm of death by the tenth anniversary of her fatal accident, but the problems are merely technical and will doubt-less be solved by more diligent re-search and grave-robbing. And, in-deed, why rush? Sweet Helga remains unwithered by the cruel ravages of

Time, still as fair and fresh as the day she fell from her horse on the misty moor."

Dammerung then tenderly embraced the moldering pile of des-iccated female remains on the stone dais of Stanford's Undergraduate Necrolab.

During the demented-tech boom of the '80s and early '90s, the mad sci-ences made great strides, including the development of high-voltage neck bolts and the discovery of a neon-green fluid that produces smoke when poured into beakers. But the past five years have witnessed a significant drop-off in federal funding for univer-sity-level mad-science programs.

"Just a few years ago, this field was booming," National Mad-Science Foundation director Dr. Gustav Blut-geist said. "In 1995, Cal Tech's mad-science Ph.D. program banished 39 brilliant-but-obsessed young men for practicing on non-living matter. By

last year, that number had dropped to just four."

The situation has been exacerbated by the elimination of hunchback-stud-ies programs at many technical col-leges. Since 1990, the number of schools offering a two-year hunch-backing degree has dropped from 492 to 39, leaving many mad scientists without much-needed grotesque lab assistants.

"I have been waiting with my large syringe of glowing blue fluid and a brain in a glass jar since 1994," said University of Colorado mad scientist Dr. Zunther Kornbluth, speaking from his hidden laboratory high in the Rockies. "I believe I have solved the problem of violent reactions to organ music which so marred my ex-periments with the rabbits. Now, all I need is one major research grant to fund my raised lightning-attractor table, and I will create life! Life, do you hear me? Life!" Ø

---

the ONION presents:

Firearm-Safety Tips

When operating a firearm, safety is paramount. Here are some tips to reduce the risk of mishaps:

- Instill in your children a healthy fear of guns by drunkenly waving one in their faces whenever you've had a few too many.
- If you shoot yourself in the foot, immediately contact a therapist to help you confront your fear of success.
- Dismantle your gun and melt it into a plowshare.
- Have spouse and children wear blaze orange and shout, "Family coming through!" when moving from room to room in your home.
- Unload gun each night by firing into ceiling, counting each bullet in screamed German.
- Store your gun at least four feet from your liquor cabinet.
- Never let your child play with a gun that is loaded.

- Stress to your children that guns are only for shooting bad people. Make sure they know the difference between good and bad people by having them name examples of each from their daily lives.
- Boil your bullets to prevent transmitting germs to people you shoot.
- Never use a firearm to settle a poker dispute, unless it's the absolute last option.
- Shoot a puppy at point-blank range to illustrate to your children the seriousness of guns.
- When preparing to pistol-whip someone, make sure the safety is on.
- Don't leave bullets on the floor where you can slip on them. That's the *real* killer.

OPINION

Eminem And The Grammys

Controversial rapper Eminem was recently nominated for four Grammys, sparking protest from groups such as GLAAD and NOW, who say his music promotes violence against gays and women. What do *you* think?

"Eminem should win. On *The Marshall Mathers LP*, he makes some very trenchant points about sawing off his mom's tits with a chainsaw."

Marc Andersen
Delivery Driver

"You didn't hear Jews complaining back in '89 when Professor Griff won Best Rap Song for 'Wicked Moneylending Vampire Kikes (Killum All).'"

Mel Dixon
Systems Analyst

"They could end this uproar by creating a separate category like Best Album That Never Should Have Been Recorded Because It Is An Affront To All That Is Decent."

Benjamin Reese
Carpenter

"This is a slap in the face to truly deserving nominees like Don Henley, up for Best Male Rock Vocal Performance for 'Workin' It.'"

Carl Weatherspoon
Investment Banker

"Eminem deserves to win after being so badly snubbed at last year's Tonys."

Linda Pulliam
Homemaker

"It's a trade-off. On the one hand, you risk alienating conservative Grammy voters, but on the other, the Grammys will actually be watched by people."

Liz Toffler
Student

The Inaugural Ball

What is being planned for Jan. 20's presidential inaugural-ball festivities?

- ★ 2,750 pounds of rich-white-guy food
- ★ Team of 75 Texan-to-English translators
- ★ Hank Williams Jr. to perform "Are You Ready For Some Inauguration?"
- ★ Four to five photogenic black Republicans
- ★ 3,000 balloons with "President Gore" crossed out and Bush written in
- ★ Special handler to assist Bush with pronunciation of word "inaugural"
- ★ Ballroom's color scheme to employ red, white, and possibly blue, as well
- ★ Five-man team of Laura Bush wranglers and feeders
- ★ 300 cases of Inaugural Edition Coors
- ★ The "real party" to go on in executive men's room

the ONION
America's Finest News Source

Herman Ulysses Zweibel *Founder*

T. Herman Zweibel *Publisher Emeritus*
J. Phineas Zweibel *Publisher*
Maxwell Prescott Zweibel *Editor-In-Chief*

FOUNDED 1871 • "TU STULTUS ES"

JUST FOR FUN

Your Horoscope

By Lloyd Schumner Sr.
Retired Machinist and
A.A.P.B.-Certified Astrologer

Aries: (March 21–April 19)
Awkwardness will prevail in your office this week as your coworkers try to pretend that the spontaneous Busby Berkeley number they walked in on never happened.

Taurus: (April 20–May 20)
You will learn the true meaning of the phrase, "Out of the frying pan and into the fire" during an incident involving an unusually large frying pan and a fire.

Gemini: (May 21–June 21)
In five to seven years, there will be increased demand for license-plate makers. Start job-training now by getting arrested for manslaughter.

Cancer: (June 22–July 22)
You're not going to be able to talk about this week without using the word "brutal" a lot.

Leo: (July 23–Aug. 22)
Relax: Everyone feels like a complete schmuck sometimes, though not for 28 straight years like you.

Virgo: (Aug. 23–Sept. 22)
A pop-cultural shift you are not equipped to understand will turn you into an object of high camp overnight.

Libra: (Sept. 23–Oct. 23)
Sharon may seem like a nice enough sort, but when she's named Secretary of Weights and Measures next week, you'll see her true colors.

Scorpio: (Oct. 24–Nov. 21)
Actually, there was nothing wrong with your design for tamper-resistant pants. You may, however, have overestimated demand for the product.

Sagittarius: (Nov. 22–Dec. 21)
You will become a modern Rip Van Winkle next week when you fall asleep under a tree and awake to a nightmarish world 11 hours into the future.

Capricorn: (Dec. 22–Jan. 19)
No one believes for a second that an evil hypnotist compelled you to eat all the doughnuts. Which is frustrating, because it's actually true.

Aquarius: (Jan. 20–Feb. 18)
The judge is moved by the accordion player's deep love and refuses to grant a restraining order. Just put up with the music until he gets over you.

Pisces: (Feb. 19–March 20)
No change for Pisces this week, except in the intensity and frequency of the fits.

DATE from page 51

proved really useful to have the extra space to spread out all our folders and printouts."

Compounding Rolen's embarrassment was the fact that he had spent much of Tuesday thinking about and preparing for the evening's

As the evening wore on, Rolen became increasingly paranoid that Cooper would discover his original romantic intentions.

non-date.

"I was so excited all day," Rolen said. "When I got home from work, I cleaned my apartment from top to bottom, just in case she wanted to drop by afterwards. I even got a haircut during my lunch hour. God, I'm pathetic."

Fortunately, the evening has not damaged the colleagues' working relationship, and Cooper remains blissfully unaware of the aborted wooing.

"That was a great idea to get together and finish up that project," Cooper told Rolen as they parted ways for the night. "I am so relieved to finally be done with that. Aren't you?" Ø

FATHER from page 52

prised when he moves out right after high school and hardly ever calls.

And I haven't even touched on how I'll fail to teach my son life lessons through positive examples. Or the high probability that he'll wind up a child of divorce. Or how my growing drinking problem will make the emotional chasm between us even harder to bridge, eventually causing him to take up the bottle himself. Or how all of this will make it almost impossible for him to have healthy relationships with his own kids.

Oh, well. Practice makes perfect, I guess. Trish wants the next one to be a girl. Ø

53

Ask A Former Touring Drummer For The Pointer Sisters

By Jeff Aufiero
Former Touring Drummer,
The Pointer Sisters

Dear Former Touring Drummer For The Pointer Sisters:

The other night, I came home from work to find my prize azalea bushes completely wrecked. I didn't witness it, but I'm sure I know who the culprits are: the children next door who are always running wild in our yard! How do I keep my bushes safe without permanently alienating my neighbors?

—Frustrated In
Freeport

Dear Frustrated,

By October of '84, "Neutron Dance" had hit number three, and things were getting seriously crazy. Every night, we'd hit the stage and be standing there in front of 1,500 wild, screaming fans. I remember this one show in Detroit, we were playing the Fox Theater, and it was so loud, I couldn't even hear Anita when she said, "Let's hit it, boys," which is the band's cue to launch into the "I'm So Excited"/"Jump (For My Love)"

encore set. And it didn't let up for the entire 90 minutes we'd be out there. Man, it was insane.

Dear Former Touring Drummer For The Pointer Sisters:

There's a big company dinner party coming up at the boss' house, and I can't decide whether to "dress to impress" or just go with the casual confidence of slacks and a sweater. The invitations say it's just an informal cookout, but this is my boss we're talking about! What do you suggest?

—In A Quandary In
Quincy

Dear Quincy,

For most of the "Break Out" Tour, we were on the road with Midnight Star, and, let me tell you, things got pretty wild. Backstage, after the shows, you'd have all kinds of groupies and freaks and God-knows-what-else hanging around. The girls

from Klymaxx used to swing by and party with us a lot, and so did Pat Sobriewski, a buddy of mine who used to play keys for Ray Parker Jr. and is now with Gloria Estefan. I really can't even get into most of what went on. With the double bill, we were drawing upwards of 2,000 people a night, so we were living pretty high, to be sure. I was pulling in some of the best scratch of my career, better than anything short of what I made with Billy Squier back in '80-'81. Those were good times, man, good times.

Dear Former Touring Drummer For The Pointer Sisters:

My mother's 75th birthday is coming up. I want to go all out and get her something really special, but I'm afraid I'll spend a fortune and end up getting her something she doesn't like. What would be an appropriate gift for an occasion like this?

—Unsure
In Utica

Dear Unsure,

All three Pointer Sisters were cool, but if I had to choose, I'd say Ruth was definitely my favorite. We'd tell jokes, play cards on the tour bus, and just generally have a real good time. I was with her in this hotel lobby in St. Petersburg when she came up with the basic chord structure for "Automatic," and after that, she'd always say I was her good-luck charm. But like I said, all three were real cool. Touring with them was one of the best times I've had in this crazy business. In '86, I left to tour with Richard Marx, and we had a lot of success, especially with the "Repeat Offender" Tour a few years later, but it just wasn't the same. I tell you, I really miss those gals.

Jeff Aufiero is a professional drummer whose weekly syndicated advice column, Ask A Former Touring Drummer For The Pointer Sisters, *appears in more than 250 papers nationwide.* ∅

My God, What Passes For Crunch-tastic These Days

Boy… I just wish there were a stronger word than "appalled."

While making my usual Wednesday grocery run, I was excited to see a new brand of snack chips next to the Sour Cream 'N' Cheddar Ruffles: Krunch Toobz, a lightly salted corn cylinder boldly labeled "crunch-tastic" in a red letters along the top of the bag.

By Mel Crowley

As any snack aficionado knows, crunch-tastic is the ultimate snack-chip adjective, outranking crunch-riffic, crunch-rageous, and even crunch-mongous. Needless to say, I was sufficiently intrigued to drop two full bags in my cart, for-saking my usual double-canister pack of Zesty Pizza Pringles.

Let me tell you, it took all the will power I had to keep from tearing open that bag on the way home! The promise of true crunch-tasticity is almost too much for any serious snacker to resist. But, determined to take my first taste of these

starchy wonders in a proper setting, I held out, tucking the bags into the bowels of my cupboard until after the opening credits of *Temptation Island*. Finally, at 9:03 p.m., I giddily opened Bag One and placed in my mouth a single Krunch Toob.

The moment my molars closed in on that first Toob, my faith in crunch-itude was shaken. My snacking soul was shattered like a Funyun beneath my blue-canvas Chuck Taylors. It only got worse with subsequent bites. No doubt, by the time this sees print, the dedicated snackhound will be well aware that Krunch Toobz nowhere near live up to their claims of being crunch-tastic.

On a good day, when absolutely fresh, these air-puffed-then-baked nuggets of processed corn could conceivably pass as unkommonly krispy. But to advertise Krunch Toobz as crunch-tastic is an insult to those who take such things seriously.

As a nation, we have seen an alarming deterioration in snacking standards. Am I the only one who remembers when crunch-tastic was a word not bandied about lightly, reserved only for those snack

chips possessing unsurpassed crunchworthiness?

I thought this trend of exaggerating the greatness of a snack treat had reached its nadir back when Nestlé dared tout its dubiously named Crunch Bar as "s-crunch-ous." Was no one in the corporation willing to stand up and shout, "Wait a minute! This is wrong! Crisped rice is crispy, not crunchy! We are trading a century of credibility for 30 pieces of silver!"? I shudder to think of the conspiracy of silence that taints the halls of the Nestlé Corporation.

Of course, this is merely indicative of a deeper malaise. Who among us remembers when Dairy Queen started using corn sweeteners in lieu of pure cane sugar, yet continued to label their treats "scrumpdilly-icious"? I thought their number was up that time, but, like sheep, the American public continued bellying up to the double-dip trough, as though they would rather believe that scrumpdilly-icious means using second-rate ingredients than vote with their dollars for a higher standard. And, to add insult to injury, Hank Ketcham continues to

whore Dennis The Menace to their unsavory cause.

Thank God for Frito-Lay. It did not market Cheetos as "dangerously cheesy" until after, and ONLY after, it had developed a Cheeto whose cheesiness exceeded acceptable safety standards. Such pride in one's craft, sadly, is all too rare in today's degraded snackscape.

This crunch-tastic fiasco: How far will it go before we as a people stand up and say, "Enough!"? Perhaps Doritos will have to be called "ecstatically radically crunch-o-matical" before Joe Average American is roused from his shameful slumber.

I, for one, will not sit around and wait for such a day to come. I wish to elevate the masses to a heightened awareness of the principles upon which America's snack industry was built. Only when we realize that crunch-tastic, choco-licious, and zestfully ranch-sational are words—words with meanings!—can we finally bring an end to snacking as usual and ascend to an exalted plane of Snack-vana. ∅

Winner Didn't Even Know It Was Pie-Eating Contest

see LOCAL page 3C

Ape Footage Causes Three-And-A-Half-Minute Interruption In Channel-Surfing

see TELEVISION page 4B

Britain Cleaned, Restored, Placed In British Museum

see WORLD page 10A

STATshot

A look at the numbers that shape your world.

Least-Used Exclamations During Sex

1. Mary Todd Lincoln! Mary Todd Lincoln!
2. Docking complete!
3. Lemme see here... righty-tighty, lefty-loosey.
4. Oh, yes! Change my long-distance service to Verizon!
5. Next stop, Santa Fe!
6. Once more into the breach!
7. Who's your legal guardian?!

THE ONION
VOLUME 37
ISSUE 02

$2.00 US
$3.00 CAN

0 74470 94595 6

---

the ONION®

VOLUME 37 ISSUE 02   AMERICA'S FINEST NEWS SOURCE™   25-31 JANUARY 2001

Area Man Likes To Think Of Own Past As Sordid

NORFOLK, VA—Ross Bingham, a married, 34-year-old professional videographer, likes to think of his own past as sordid, sources revealed Monday.

"I don't talk about it much, but I went through a pretty wild phase in my early 20s," Bingham told a group of coworkers at Outreach Communications, a corporate video-production company. "I'm lucky I straightened out, because if I'd kept heading down the path I was on, God only knows where I'd be now."

"Those first few years after college, there were times when I was going out drinking with my friends three or four nights a week," Bingham said. "The low point probably came when I woke up on the couch at my friend's apartment with my coat over me as a blanket. I could

see SORDID page 57

Right: Ross Bingham, who has put his dark days behind him.

'80s Retro Craze Sweeps Executive Branch

WASHINGTON, DC—Remember SDI, deregulation, and tax cuts? The new administration does. That's right, '80s retro fever is sweeping the executive branch, with President Bush and his nostalgia-crazed colleagues going wild for the people and policies of that "totally tubular" decade.

"The '80s were so awesome," said Bush, grabbing a handful of Jelly Bellys from a jar on his Oval Office desk. "They had, like, the best policies back then, like trickle-down economics and communist containment. And the Cabinet members were the coolest: Ed Meese, Caspar Weinberger, George Shultz. I'm so totally going to find a position for Donald Regan in my administration."

Bush has already begun indulging his love of all things '80s, nominating James Watt for

see RETRO page 57

Left: George W. Bush and members of his '80s-themed administration.

Developmentally Disabled Burger King Employee Only Competent Worker

MANCHESTER, NH—Despite his third-grade reading level and IQ of 71, developmentally disabled Burger King employee Andy Ehrman is the only competent member of the 22-person Frontage Road staff.

"I will help you with that!" the 28-year-old Ehrman told a drive-thru customer Monday, hustling to put the customer's order in a bag after cashier Daniel Genz dropped it on a tray and walked away. "There you go! Thank you! Have a nice day!"

As Ehrman waved goodbye to the customer, Genz leaned against the shake machine, making a cellphone call to his girlfriend.

"Don't forget to shut the

see BURGER KING page 56

Man Knows Unsettling Amount About Nationwide Age-Of-Consent Laws

HAGERSTOWN, MD—During a conversation at work last Friday, drill-press operator Pete Cromartie revealed a disturbing familiarity with various states' age-of-consent laws. "I mentioned to Pete that I'd be visiting family in Pennsylvania over the weekend, and he says, 'You oughta pick up some chicks there, 'cause they only gotta be 16,'" coworker Geoff Richardson said. "Then he says, 'South Carolina's the best: 15.' I mean, that's seriously creepy." Richardson said he later heard Cromartie talk about a bill pending in the Hawaii legislature that would lower the state's age of consent to 13.

White House Guidance Counselor Recommends Clinton Consider Career In Hotel Management

WASHINGTON, DC—At his mandatory post-presidency appointment with White House guidance counselor Larry Schecht, Bill Clinton was encouraged to consider a career in hotel management Monday. "Your Myers Briggs score suggests you would do well in a variety of job fields," Schecht told Clinton. "You could be anything from an architect to a food scientist, but your strong people skills indicate you would make an ideal hotel manager." To learn more about the field, Schecht recommended that Clinton set up informational interviews at some Washington-area hotels, as well as complete the exercises in the book *What Color Is Your Parachute?*

Bunch Of People Apparently Saw That Brendan Fraser Mummy Movie

SACRAMENTO, CA—A lot of people apparently saw that Brendan Fraser mummy movie, area resident Bill Whited said to himself Monday while watching a trailer for *The Mummy Returns*. "Wow, I guess a bunch of people out there saw that thing," Whited said of 1999's *The Mummy*. "I vaguely remember it being in theaters for a few weeks, but I guess it was big. What's next, *The Whole Nine Yards II*?" A sequel to 1999's *The Whole Nine Yards* is currently in pre-production at Paramount.

Explosion Used To Signify Big Savings

WORCESTER, MA—In an ad for Kearns Home & Garden Center in Monday's *Worcester Telegram & Gazette*, a violent explosion was used as a visual metaphor for low prices on thousands of items throughout the store. "Don't miss our once-a-year 'Explosion Of Savings' event," read the ad, which equated the destructive detonation of trinitrotoluene (TNT) with great savings on everything from Black & Decker wet-dry vacs to tulip bulbs. "Start the new year with a 'bang' of a bargain!"

Toilet-Paper Edge Given Classy Appearance With Triangular Fold

MISSOULA, MT—A roll of Charmin bathroom tissue in Room 316 of a Missoula Motel 6 was imbued with a regal air Monday when the maid service folded the edge of the first sheet into an eye-pleasing triangle. "I fell like a pampered duchess," motel guest Rachel Spencer said. "That's what I call 'living the high life.'" Spencer also gushed about the Motel 6 matchbook propped up in the center of a sparkling-clean ashtray. ∅

BURGER KING from page 55

drawer, Daniel, or someone can take all the money," said Ehrman, pushing the register closed and straightening the stack of trays under the counter. "Then we'd all get in trouble!"

In addition to his usual lunch-rush duties—making sure the dining area, condiment island, and restrooms are clean and stocked—Ehrman spent 11 a.m. to 1 p.m. Monday voluntarily sweeping and mopping the floor in the prep area, helping an elderly customer find her purse, and throwing salt on the icy walk outside the restaurant.

During the same two-hour stretch, 20-year-old Jenna Sanders, Ehrman's direct supervisor, incorrectly prepared three orders, spilled a jug of oil in the kitchen, and had a 25-minute conversation about the band Slipknot with coworker Debi Price.

"[Sanders] double-charged me for a BK Big Fish Value Meal," customer Terry Unger said. "Then she got my order completely wrong. I was about to storm out of there and never come back again when this retarded kid, all smiles, comes up and asks if I need help. Sixty seconds later, he hands me the correct order and change, and apologizes for the trouble. Finally, someone who understands how to treat a customer."

Unger added that in addition to having the only clean uniform in the store, Ehrman seemed to be the sole employee with basic interpersonal skills.

"Maybe they teach it in the specialed classes or something, but he's the only one who actually speaks in sentences as opposed to grunts," Unger said. "And when I asked for extra ketchup packets, he handed them to me and said, 'Here you go,' instead of rolling his eyes."

Ehrman is also willing to perform tasks beyond those in his job description, offering to help coworkers stock shelves or run the dishwasher when they fall behind. Most nights, he even volunteers to clean the grease traps.

"I don't mind," Ehrman said. "I'm helping!"

Willis Barnett, a delivery driver who makes twice-weekly dropoffs at the Frontage Road store, is among the many people impressed with Ehrman.

"I love it when I make a delivery and they've got that tard working in the back," Barnett said. "He always knows exactly where everything goes. Everyone else just says, 'Uh, I don't know—toss it on the floor or something.'"

Among his many other qualities, Ehrman boasts a near-encyclopedic knowledge of Burger King protocol and safety regulations.

"[Assistant manager] Kerri [Sheckley] said the dishwasher uses the green stuff, and [manager] Bob [Hundhausen] said it uses the purple stuff," Ehrman said. "But then I saw on the TV show [training video *Cleaning The Burger King Way*] that you use both, 'cause one is the stuff that kills germs and one is soap. So I use both."

Ehrman also makes an effort to bring potential safety hazards to coworkers' attention.

"Hey, Randy, we can't put cardboard boxes or anything paper under there," Ehrman told Randy Leyner, 26, upon seeing him put a stack of french-fry cartons under the fryer. "It could start a fire!" After being ignored by

Above: Employee Randy Leyner (left) sits while Ehrman clears a table.

Leyner, Ehrman dragged the cartons to the rear storage closet himself.

Unlike other members of the Frontage Road team, Ehrman never shows up late or asks to leave early. In fact, when Ehrman works the morning shift, he can usually be seen waiting in the front lobby by 5:30 a.m., 45 minutes before the morning manager arrives to unlock the door.

Despite working substantially harder than any of his coworkers, Ehrman bears no resentment toward them.

"I used to work at the hospital in the mailroom, but it was boring and people were mean to me," said Ehrman, plugging his nose and shaking his head to signify that the job "stank.""I like to work at Burger King better. There's always lots and lots to do. And

I get a free Whopper to take home!"

Miriam Donnelly, the social worker who placed Ehrman at Burger King, is extremely pleased with his success.

"Andy has trouble with basic addition and spelling his name, but he fits right in at Burger King," Donnelly said. "The work seems almost tailor-made for someone with special needs."

Donnelly added that everything at Burger King, from the touch-pad registers to the step-by-step diagrams for folding the apple-pie sleeves, is designed to help low-functioning individuals succeed.

"Andy may go a little slower than some of the other workers, but he does one thing at a time, focuses on it, and, in the end, gets it right," Donnelly said. "Actually, now that I think about it, he's not really any slower." ∅

barely even remember what had happened the night before. Then I realized I must've fallen asleep while we were drinking beer and watching *Fletch.* Kinda scary when you think about it."

Bingham characterized his living situation at the time as "pretty out of control," telling coworkers that they probably wouldn't even be able to comprehend how "crazy" it was, not having been there.

"One of my roommates was a total pothead," Bingham said. "He'd have guys dropping by to sell him drugs, right there in our living room. I smoked a little pot myself, but I didn't care for it all that much. Drinking, now that was *my* vice."

Continued Bingham: "I was working part-time at a video store, so I sometimes didn't go into work until noon or one in the afternoon. For a while there, it was 'get off work, go out and party, sleep late, and do it all again the next day.' I knew it was no way to live, but, you know, you get into a downward spiral and it's hard to crawl back out."

Bingham said his other roommate was good friends with the members of Dread Skatt, a popular local ska band, which meant that Bingham would accompany the friend to shows and social events, often staying out as late as 2 a.m.

"I was pretty much living to party," he said. "I didn't care about anything else."

Though alcohol was his primary vice, Bingham admitted that it was not his only one: He also had a strong weakness for the opposite sex. The now-reformed Bingham went through a "serious womanizing phase," dating numerous women with no intention of getting into a long-term relationship.

"There was this one girl," he said. "I met her at a bar and we went home together. The next day, I was going to call her, but I realized I couldn't even call information to get her number because I *didn't even know her last name.* It's probably a good thing we didn't go all the way, or it might have turned into a pretty bad situation."

Bingham also described a "near brush with death."

"I was out with the guys at a nightclub one night, and I'd had a few too many tequila shots," he said. "I started walking to my car when I realized I was way too 'altered' to drive home, so I called a cab. If I hadn't, that could have been it for me right there. To think how close I came to meeting my maker that night, it makes me shudder."

Luckily, at 23, Bingham had a spiritual awakening and realized it was time to turn his life around.

Above: An out-of-control Bingham (left) parties long past midnight during the dark days of the early '90s.

The wake-up call was the arrest of best friend and drinking partner Matthew Stackpole.

"Matt got really drunk one night and was goofing around on the walk home," Bingham said. "He decided to steal a 'No Parking' sign, and as he was pulling it out of the ground, a cop drove by. Matt got nailed for attempted theft of public property. Watching him stand in the harsh glare of the police lights, I realized it could have been me being handed that ticket."

Less than a month after his best friend's brush with the law, Bingham took his first steps on the road to recovery. He applied for and landed a job at Outreach Communications, where he prepares video presentations for corporations about to make initial stock offerings.

He hasn't looked back since.

"Sometimes, I miss hanging out with Matt and the old gang. But I know how easy it would be to slip back into my old ways if I did," Bingham said. "If I knew it wouldn't lead to trouble, I'd look Matt up again. It wouldn't be too hard to find him. I hear he's a systems administrator over at Novix Consulting." ∅

Secretary of the Interior.

"Remember in '83, when Watt didn't want The Beach Boys to play that Fourth Of July party because he said they were unwholesome?" Bush asked. "And then when he said the thing about his staff having a black, a woman, two Jews, and a cripple? That was hilarious."

Nearby, vice-president and fellow '80s-lover Dick Cheney reclined on a couch. "You know who else we should nominate?" Cheney asked. "Robert Bork for Supreme Court!"

"Bork? Who's that?" Bush responded. "Oh, wait—that's the arch-conservative judge with the funny little chin beard, right? God, I totally forgot about that guy! Yeah, we should definitely nominate him!"

Bush also tapped Donna Rice for White House press secretary but retracted the offer when he realized he was thinking of Fawn Hall.

"I always get those two confused," Bush told Cheney. "I know one was with Oliver North and the shredder, and the other was with Gary Hart and the Monkey Business, but I forget which was which. Then there's Jessica Hahn. She was the one with Jim Bakker, right? Or was it Jimmy Swaggart? Anyway, I want the Ollie North gal."

Bush praised Hall, calling her "a major-league babe." Cheney affirmed the appraisal, saying, "Yeah, big-time."

Though too young to remember much of the decade, Bush nevertheless said he had "tons of fun" in

Above: Bush shows off one of his many '80s-retro T-shirts.

the '80s.

"Once, when I was 36, my dad took me to the CIA to meet William Casey," Bush said. "It was one of the best days of my life: I got to watch a National Security Council meeting. Then, afterwards, Mr. Casey let me sit in his big leather chair. Even though I was really young at the time, I remember the whole thing like it was yesterday."

"Even the enemies were cooler in the '80s," Bush continued. "Back then, there was Russia, Libya, and Iran. Now, *those* were some bad guys. What do we have today? North Korea? How lame is that?"

"Know what else was awesome about the '80s? The respect for human life," said Bush, sporting a retro "Choose Life" T-shirt, made popular by George Michael during his Wham! days. "This is the same one [Michael] wore during the 'Wake Me Up Before You Go-Go' video."

Bush has vowed to pursue a number of '80s-retro initiatives while in office, including a revival of the Star Wars missile-defense system, the firing of 12,000 air-traffic controllers, and a boycott of the 2004 Summer Olympics. He is also organizing a Hands Across America event for later this year to commemorate the 15th anniversary of the 1986 original.

"As a uniter, not a divider, I recognize the importance of feel-good gestures like Hands Across America, USA For Africa, and that 'That's What Friends Are For' song," Bush said. "Back in the '80s, people used to come together and lend a hand to those in need. It's important to make the occasional token effort toward helping others."

Added Bush: "We also need more Americans like New Jersey's own Bruce Springsteen, in whose songs live the hopes and dreams of every one of us."

On Monday, in his first official act as president, Bush showed his love for the '80s by issuing pardons to convicted Wall Street figures Ivan Boesky and Michael Milken, as well as John DeLorean and Claus von Bulow. He also pledged $240 million in federal tax breaks to Union Carbide, whose Bhopal, India, chemical plant was the site of a 1984 chemical disaster that Bush "totally remember[s]."

Later in the day, Bush suffered his first retro international-relations gaffe, when, during an official greeting to the people of China, he said, "We begin bombing in five minutes." Bush apologized, explaining that he was only joking and did not realize the microphone was on.

Though committed to leading America into the future, Bush said he can't help but wish he could have been president back in the decade of Pac-Man, skinny ties, and illegal arms deals with Nicaragua.

"Man, that would've been so cool to be the leader of the free world back then," Bush said. "I was born 15 years too late." ∅

Vacationing Woman Thinks Cats Miss Her

VERO BEACH, FL—Annette Davrian, a 45-year-old Cedar Rapids, IA, bank teller, is spending her vacation time in a delusional haze this week, somehow managing to convince herself that her cats actually miss her.

"Buttons is so sensitive, I just know she's frightened without her Mommy by her side," Davrian told uninterested relatives Monday, just hours after arriving in Florida. "And Bonkers gets so cranky when he doesn't get his morning treats. I hope they'll be able to handle this emotionally. I've always gone to great lengths to assure them that they're loved, but they've never been left alone this long before. If they think I've abandoned them, I'd never be able to forgive myself."

Animal behaviorists agree that cats are incapable of feeling sadness over an owner's absence, asserting that their only reaction to such an event would be a brief adjustment period to claim household territory previously thought to be the owner's.

Davrian, who has lived alone since the death of her mother nine years ago, has considered cutting her vacation short because of the cats' nonexistent longing for her to return.

"Those poor, precious kitties," she told a man in an elevator. "I'm all they've got in this world. What will they do without me?"

According to coworker Phil Gross, Davrian began worrying about her cats' imaginary sadness over her Flori-da trip nearly three weeks before leaving. On Jan. 8, Davrian expressed concern to Gross that the cats might not sufficiently "bond" with a stranger entrusted with their care. Based on this worry alone, she delayed her trip for two weeks, paying a large rescheduling fee for her plane ticket.

"She asked me to look after the cats while she was gone," neighbor Janet Pullman said. "I said sure, figuring I'd just have to feed them. Turns out, she wanted me to go in there three times a day and stay at least 20 minutes each time so the cats would feel 'adequately socialized.' Then she hands me a list of things to do that's, like, 40 items long."

Pullman admitted that she has not followed the elaborate instructions, merely filling up the cats' food and water bowls when they are empty.

"I just dump some Purina in the bowl, and I'm gone," Pullman said. "And do the cats give a shit? No, they do not. Why? Because they're cats."

Hoping to ease the pain and loneliness of her asocial, predatory pets, Davrian has left numerous long messages on her answering machine, claiming that the cats will appreciate hearing her voice. She also wrapped one of her sweaters around a pillow before leaving so Buttons and Bonkers would 'have a bit of me to snuggle with,' unaware that the cats' motivation for 'snuggling' is to maintain body temperature, not to feel emotionally connected to their food provider.

Above: Annette Davrian with cats Buttons and Bonkers.

As a supplement to the answering-machine messages, Davrian left the clock radio playing in the bathroom "to keep the little ones company." Though the cats could not care less about the radio, the same cannot be said of neighbor Bob Franz, 49, whose bathroom shares a heating vent with Davrian's.

"I once heard [Davrian] say that [Bonkers] will get lonely without a human voice around to make him feel reassured," Franz said. "But the thing just sits in the window and watches birds all day, just the way it did before she left, and just the way it'll keep on doing after she gets back, every day until one of the two of them dies. Meantime, the damn radio yabbers on all day and night. That radio's probably more aware that the woman's gone than the cat is."

The Florida excursion is not the first time Davrian has ruined her leisure time fretting about the cats. Since 1996, she has failed to enjoy 219 activities or excursions, including two trips to Lake Winnepesaukee, a visit to a local botanical garden, 23 movies, and three dinners—each of which she spent worrying about being "out of phone contact in case something goes wrong."

Davrian could not be reached for additional comment, as she had just cut short a sailing trip in order to, as brother-in-law Don Koechley said, "make sure the damn cats are okay." ∅

---

the ONION presents

Super Bowl Party-Planning Tips

Jan. 28 is Super Sunday, a day for friends, food, and football. Here are some tips to help you score a "touchdown" with your Super Bowl party:

- Set aside a special area of the living-room floor to throw chicken bones.
- A complete and reverent silence should be maintained whenever Armen Keteyian speaks.
- Before guests arrive, be sure to hide any copies of *Harper's Weekly*, *The Atlantic Monthly*, and *The New Yorker* you may have lying around.
- Pre-soak all Doritos in Pabst Blue Ribbon.
- During commercial breaks, make non-stop sarcastic comments about the stupidity of Super Bowl ads. Rest assured, you'll be the first person in history to do so.
- If you do not know how to watch football on TV, ask an experienced friend to help you through the hard parts.
- The Super Bowl is the premier event of the entire sports year. Be sure to use the good chip bowl and your finest inflatable furniture.
- Provide "dip," into which chips can be dipped.

- If rooting for the Giants, openly question Ravens linebacker Ray Lewis' role in the stabbing deaths of two men outside an Atlanta nightclub following last year's Super Bowl.
- Do not wear a jersey featuring the name and number of an actual NFL player. Confused guests will wonder why a famous athlete is at the party, especially if that athlete is supposed to be playing in the Super Bowl.
- Urinate in each corner of room to mark your territory prior to the arrival of other males.
- At the end of the second quarter, switch over to the Lifetime Network for the Judith Light Halftime Spectacular.
- Select the cars you're going to overturn beforehand, because you're going to be really drunk afterwards.
- Leave nosehairs untrimmed for a minimum of three weeks before game.

Somehow, We'll Middle-Manage

By Rick Oberling
Departmental Supervisor

Times are tough, no question. There have been more layoffs in the past six months here at ProVantage Solutions than in the previous five years combined. Salaries have not increased to match inflation. Revenues have fallen off sharply. I do not need to tell you that the road ahead looks long and dark. But be brave, my friends: There is light at the end of the tunnel. Through it all, somehow, we will middle-manage.

I have tentatively scheduled a meeting for Monday the 29th for the purpose of compiling and preparing a report on potential strategies we might implement to ameliorate the situation. I can't say for certain if we will get the conference room for that day, as Doug is hoping to use it for an exploratory committee meeting on the possibility of upgrading the company from ISO 9000 to 9001, but I've put in my request. If we can't get it, my goal is to definitely meet by Wednesday the 31st, at the latest.

That meeting, actually, is the main reason I have called all of you here today. This is the informal meeting that precedes the formal one on the 31st. We could hypothetically have the formal meeting now, but Sharon is out of the office, and I'd really like to have her at the formal.

But to summarize my message in advance of the larger meeting, I want to say that we will face long, hard days in the coming months, days when we feel that the company will collapse at our feet. Days of tribulation and jammed copiers, days of seemingly insurmountable middle-management crises. Resolving the System 9 upgrade dispute between accounting and tech alone will take many long meetings, reports, and memoranda.

You will all have crosses to bear. Ruth, I know how badly you wanted to hire an assistant to handle the night deposit and miscellaneous filing. God in Heaven knows you deserve that much. But it will unfortunately have to wait. All the years you've been here, through every challenge and setback, you've always middle-managed, and I just know you'll do it now, too.

Kenny—brave, brave project coordinator Kenny—you have committed tremendous time and energy to streamlining interdepartmental communications, presenting the systemic improvements in report form, and getting that report stamped by all the department heads. Even on those days when you worked until you looked 'ike you'd drop, you would always walk that extra hallway to get Dave from Human Resources' okay. How I wish you could finally get your own cubicle and computer instead of just the desk in Larry's office. But for the time being, you'll middle-manage to get through the lean times just like the rest of us.

By tightening our belts, ProVantage Solutions will pull through these dark days. We will weather the storm with dignity and strength. Though we shall scribble memos with cost-cutting Bic Round Stics rather than the Uniball Visions we once enjoyed, we shall scribble them proudly. If we must, we will cut Post-It notes in half and write that much smaller. Even if we must use a single paperclip to hold 40 sheets together, we will scrimp and conserve every resource, right down to the last ebony particle of toner.

No one employee can bear the burden that is upon us alone. No temp worker could shoulder this great weight. You cannot outsource courage. But as a team, we will prevail. And in the process, we will learn a great deal about ourselves and how to resolve office crises in a swift and non-disruptive manner.

Exactly what will change, precisely what will deliver us from this long, dark night, I cannot say. But we must have faith, faith that we will middle-manage against all odds. Faith that we will keep this company running smoothly and maintain open avenues of communication between departments. Faith that the decisions made by the board of directors will be implemented in a timely and efficient manner. We have the mettle to put other departments to shame. We will not actually do this, because it would be bad for company morale, but make no mistake, we could.

And if any of you find the weight too heavy, if you feel yourself slipping, if you see no relief in sight, you know my e-mail address and should always feel free to articulate your concerns and remit them to me. Just make sure not to do so between 6 p.m. Wednesday and 6 a.m. Thursday, because the server will be down for maintenance.

We will do all of this, and we will be rewarded one day. There will be a tomorrow, and it will be bright, filled with company picnics and after-work get-togethers at J.P. McMuggery's. Company nights at Zany's Comedy Club shall come again. And there will one day be smiles around the water cooler. The laughter of children will fill these halls one glorious Take Your Daughter To Work Day. And there will be Christmas parties and Casual Fridays. And, when the storm clouds have gone and the sun has returned, there will be new, young employees who know not of these dark days.

But until such a time comes, let us turn our faces toward the soft, comforting glow of the Xerox machine and know in our hearts that if we can middle-manage just a little while longer, better days lie ahead. ⌀

I Bet I Wouldn't Be Laughing So Hard If It Was Me In That Fire

By Greg Gund

Listen, I know in my heart this isn't funny. If the tables were turned, I wouldn't be cracking up the way I am now. I definitely wouldn't be laughing so hard if it was me in that fire.

I mean, humor depends on one's perspective, right? To the guy who's running around shrieking, flailing his arms in a frantic effort to put out the flames enveloping him, a hearty chuckle is probably the last thing on his mind. But if that poor guy were a bystander like me, watching from a safe distance as a heating-fuel truck crashed into a church and turned someone who picked the wrong day to wear a nylon jacket into a human shish-ka-bob, he probably would've fallen down on the spot with helpless laughter, just like I did.

Life is short, so it's important to see the lighter side of things. But if it were me watching the spreading pool of flaming petroleum melt the soles of my shoes to the blacktop, I concede that I may not have seen the humor.

Would I laugh if it were my fillings liquefying in my mouth? Would I chortle as hard if it were my lungs filling with white-hot flames? I'd like to think so. But I realize it's tough to see the humor when your glasses are oozing like taffy across your boiling eyes.

It's moments like this, when I'm laughing so hard I feel like I might die shortly after this burning guy does, that I also try to take stock. Sure, there's something undeniably uproarious about a man engulfed in flames, but am I laughing for the right reasons? Am I cracking up because there's a little bit of me burning with him? Deep inside, is my own heart deep-frying in my chest? Can everyone around me smell the metaphorical roast-pork odor given off by the third-degree gasoline burns on my soul? If that's why I'm laughing, it's okay, isn't it? This is an important question.

And how far is too far to take a joke? Or, in this case, a fire? If the sight of this burning guy running out of the church is funny, where do you draw the line? Was it wrong for me to laugh at those two nuns welded together by the searing heat? Should I have suppressed my giggling at the three-foot-tall pack of human torches that used to be a Sunday-school class? If I do that, can I still grin at the guy punctured by thousands of smoldering shards of stained glass? I don't know.

I guess you could say I have a "sick" sense of humor. I see someone shrieking while the burning flesh bubbles off his bones, and I'm tickled. Is that so wrong? I mean, if you could have seen the terrified look on this guy's face, I think you'd have been in stitches, too.

Then again, maybe all those horrified witnesses just need to lighten up. Those firefighters, what with their fun-stopping hoses, are real wet blankets. Not one of those guys so much as cracked a smile the whole time they were pulling blackened, twisted victims out of the place. They may have been saving lives, but they were also ruining it for folks like me.

More than anyone, it's the EMTs who should know how to laugh at stuff like this. Haven't they heard the old comedy formula that comedy is tragedy plus time? Sure, less than 30 minutes have passed since First Methodist became a blazing inferno, but these are accelerated times. It only took the burn victims of the Great Chicago Fire a few weeks to gather around and share a hearty guffaw over the whole thing. And that was 1871. In this modern age, a person should be able to laugh about a church fire within four, five minutes, tops.

As I said, though, perspective is everything. I really hope that if I were the one on fire, I'd be able to see the humor in it. Judging from the way that guy who's on fire is screaming, he obviously doesn't. He's clearly in a great deal of mortal pain. But even so, he should feel good knowing he's brought a little levity into at least one person's life.

Perhaps I'm fooling myself, but if life ever handed me a straight line like being doused with a couple dozen gallons of flaming petroleum distillate, I'd like to think I'd do my level best to make the most of it. But for now, I'm glad to be sitting here safe on this comfortable park bench with my bottled water, just enjoying the show. ⌀

The California Blackouts

A state of emergency has been declared in California, where massive power shortages have necessitated cutting off electricity through much of the state. What do *you* think about the crisis?

Randy Toth
Painter

"It's all a sad lesson in the dangers of short-sightedness in civic planning. But the important question is: When should we commence looting?"

Michael Dupree
Systems Analyst

"Why don't they just hook the state up to the mega-watt star power of Hollywood's Charlize Theron? That blonde bombshell positively crackles with electricity."

Ken Brandt
Bond Trader

"Well, there's only one thing to be done. Nevada, Arizona: Give California all your power. Come on, it's not like you matter as much."

Adrienne Berner
Homemaker

"Gee, I hope San Francisco doesn't have to turn off its big fog machine."

Fred Nouri
Landscaper

"I'm sure the people of California will band together to get through this. Then they'll form a tofu cult."

Donna Rutt
Teacher

"Didn't California slide into the ocean yet? Can we find a way to speed that up?"

Your Horoscope

By Lloyd Schumner Sr.
Retired Machinist and
A.A.P.B.-Certified Astrologer

Aries: (March 21–April 19)
Though you've always believed that "everybody loves a good Polack joke," you will discover an entire nation of people who do not.

Taurus: (April 20–May 20)
You will be shocked to find your wife in bed with your best friend, even though he's been dead for eight years.

Gemini: (May 21–June 21)
You might think that a memorable handshake is the measure of a man, but it's easy to think that way when you have a hook for a hand.

Cancer: (June 22–July 22)
You know in your heart that nothing's really wrong with you. However, your heart is just a muscle. You "know" things with your brain.

Leo: (July 23–Aug. 22)
Your belief that laughter is the best medicine will be altered forever when you discover penicillin.

Virgo: (Aug. 23–Sept. 22)
Your fatuousness will be revealed to the world when a large sandwich is your downfall on CBS's *Contentment Island*.

Libra: (Sept. 23–Oct. 23)
You might have tons of emotional problems, but loving too much isn't one of them.

Scorpio: (Oct. 24–Nov. 21)
Your attempts to lighten the mood by organizing a little sing-along are not appreciated by anyone else in the smoke-filled cockpit.

Sagittarius: (Nov. 22–Dec. 21)
Despite your belief that you are basically a decent person, you will find yourself saying, "It's not you, it's me."

Capricorn: (Dec. 22–Jan. 19)
The Lutheran talking dog whose advice has helped you in the past will crack under pressure this week, taking you on a drunken, 10-day whoring binge.

Aquarius: (Jan. 20–Feb. 18)
Words can't describe the things that will happen to you this week. Fortunately, the mathematics of nuclear fusion can.

Pisces: (Feb. 19–March 20)
Pisces wanted to tell your future this week, but he had to get new tires and help Dave move, so there just wasn't time.

Police Baffled By Bottle-Shaped Paper Bag

Above: The mysterious paper bag that has confounded Sgt. Ted Vittorio (inset) and other police officers.

BRIDGEPORT, CT—Local police officials are "utterly baffled" by a bottle-shaped paper bag that local resident Jimmy Kilty held while sitting on an East Side strip-mall bench Monday.

"It's a real mystery," said Sgt. Ted Vittorio of the Bridgeport Police Department. "Judging from the way he kept putting the paper bag up to his mouth, you'd think he was drinking something out of it. But obviously he wasn't, since paper can't hold liquid. It would soak right through instantly."

Vittorio said he was patrolling the area when he noticed Kilty clutching the strange bag.

"It's part of my job to monitor for loitering and public intoxication, so when I spotted Kilty sitting on the bench, I slowed down to survey the scene," Vittorio said. "I thought maybe he was drinking, but, as it turned out, he was just repeatedly putting a paper bag up to his face. Such behavior may be strange, but it's certainly not illegal, so I moved on."

Kilty, 32, who remains on the bench as of press time, reportedly spent about three hours greeting passersby. At approximately 4:15 p.m., he was then joined by two male companions, who intermittently held the paper bag and took turns disappearing behind the thick hedges that border the parking lot.

With so few leads, police can only speculate as to what the bag contains.

"Whatever's in there, it's got to be pretty heavy, because otherwise why would the men need to take turns holding it?" police chief Edgar Rudolph said. "And we know it's not liquor, because everyone in town is well aware of Bridgeport City Ordinance Title 9, Chapter 4, Article 4, which clearly states that it is unlawful for any person within city limits to possess any alcoholic beverage in any public place, or to transport any alcoholic beverage upon any public street, sidewalk, pedestrian mall, alleyway, or thoroughfare where such alcoholic beverage is in a receptacle which has been opened, or the seal of which has been broken, or the contents of which

have been partially removed."

"Besides," Rudolph continued, "just for the sake of argument, let's say that those men were willing to risk arrest and a $110 fine for public drinking.

They certainly would have taken the extra 10 seconds to make it a little less obvious by simply pouring the alcohol into a soda can or paper cup or something. No one could be that stupid." ⌀

Clinton's Last Acts

What measures did Bill Clinton take in his final week as president?

- ☆ Inducted self into Pro Football Hall Of Fame
- ☆ Knighted Smokey The Bear
- ☆ Made a bunch of long-distance calls
- ☆ Signed yearbooks of graduating senior advisors
- ☆ Relocated White House to Gary, IN
- ☆ Set aside Sept. 15 as National "What A Fool Believes" Day, during which all Americans will take time to reflect on how cool that particular Doobie Brothers song is
- ☆ Finally made long-delayed guest appearance on *Buffy The Vampire Slayer*
- ☆ Cried out in anguish, "Eloi, eloi, lama sabachthani?"
- ☆ Had Minnesota renamed Clintonsota
- ☆ Left a big floater in toilet

Janice To Register Three; Janice To Register Three

see LOCAL page 7B

Germs Depicted With Menacing Little Faces

see PRODUCTWATCH page 6E

TV Muted While Neighbors Fight

see LOCAL page 10B

Quality Controlled

see BUSINESS page 4D

STATshot

A look at the numbers that shape your world.

New Candy Bar Sizes
- Glove-Compartment Size
- Chocomungus
- Horse-Choking Size
- Ungodly
- Depressed-Woman Size
- 2x4
- Mercator-Projection Size
- Dionysian

the ONION®

VOLUME 37 ISSUE 03   AMERICA'S FINEST NEWS SOURCE™   1-7 FEBRUARY 2001

Marilyn Manson Now Going Door-To-Door Trying To Shock People

Left: Manson knocks on a door in Grosse Pointe Farms, MI.

OVERLAND PARK, KS—Stung by flagging album sales and supplanted by Eminem as Middle America's worst nightmare, shock rocker Marilyn Manson has embarked on a door-to-door tour of suburbia in a desperate, last-ditch effort to shock and offend average Americans.

Accompanied by bandmates Twiggy Ramirez, Madonna Wayne Gacy, and Ginger Fish, Manson kicked off his 50-city "Boo" tour Jan. 26 in Overland Park, a conservative, middle-class suburb of Kansas City.

"When we first laid eyes on Over-land Park, with its neat little frame houses, immaculately landscaped lawns, and SUVs in the driveways, we couldn't wait to swoop down on it like the Black Death," said Manson, born Brian Warner in Canton, OH. "We were like, 'Welcome to our night-mare, you bloated, pustulent pigs.'"

Last Friday at 4 p.m., Mark Wesley, 46, a resident of Overland Park's exclusive Maple Bluff subdivision, heard the sound of "animal-like shrieking" coming from the vicinity of his front lawn. Upon opening his front door, he was greeted by the sight of a pale and shirtless Manson carving a pentagram into his chest

see MANSON page 63

Department Of Education: Metric System Thriving In Nation's Inner Cities

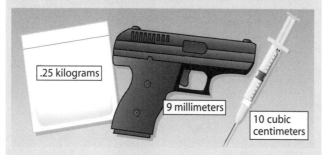

.25 kilograms

9 millimeters

10 cubic centimeters

WASHINGTON, DC—Despite other academic shortcomings, inner-city youths possess a firmer grasp of the metric system than their peers in suburban and rural areas, according to a Department Of Education study released Monday.

"While the typical teen has only a vague notion of what a kilogram is, teens in the Cabrini Green housing projects in Chicago and the Watts neighborhood of Los Angeles were thoroughly familiar with this unit of metric measurement," said Ira Danielson, the researcher who spearheaded the study. "They were able to identify a kilogram of weight by merely tossing it back and forth in their hands."

According to Danielson, young people in America's urban centers are so familiar with the kilogram that they have developed a system of abbreviations for the measure-ment, such as "kilo" or even "ki" (pronounced key).

"Most of the teens, even those reading at a fourth-grade level, were familiar with the gram as a base unit that can be either compounded or divided," Danielson said. "Finally, here's an area where at-risk urban youths can really shine."

In addition to their expertise with grams, urban youths proved knowl-edgeable about other metric units, including the millimeter, cubic cen-timeter, and liter.

"They were surprisingly familiar with metric measurements in the medical field, aware that liters of blood are used in an emergency room and that certain medications are injected in cc's or mls," Daniel-son said. "They also knew a great deal about ounces, but we preferred to focus on their metric expertise."

see METRIC SYSTEM page 62

Above: The fully prepared Lynn Paschal.

Area Man Proudly Accepts Exit-Row Responsibilities

CHICAGO—Air traveler Lynn Paschal feels physically and mentally ready to fulfill the duties of an exit-row passenger should tragedy strike United Airlines Flight 234 en route to Atlanta's Hartsfield International Airport, sources close to the 34-year-old confirmed Monday.

"The last thing anyone wants is an emergency landing," said Paschal, limbering up his forearms and checking his reach to the door handle. "But in case we do, I'll do everything in my power to make sure everyone gets out quickly and safely."

In the unlikely event of an emergency landing, Paschal may be called upon to open the escape door with the help of the O'Hare-based United flight crew.

"I certainly hope there will be at least one crew member left alive to help me, but there's no guarantee of

see EXIT page 66

Running Back's Buttocks Undulate Hypnotically In Sexuality-Challenging Slow-Motion Replay

ALBEMARLE, NC—The sexual identity of Super Bowl viewer Henry Bracken was challenged Sunday, when a slow-motion instant replay showed the sinewy buttocks of Baltimore Ravens running back Jamal Lewis undulating hypnotically through his high-sheen spandex pants. Bracken, 41, was watching the game at his Albemarle home when he became momentarily transfixed by the sight of Lewis' gluteal musculature rippling explosively as the player made a sharp cut to avoid a tackler. "I ain't gay," said Bracken upon snapping out of the trance, during which he tried not to notice the lines of Lewis' jock strap framing his powerful, magnificently sculpted ass. "I just ain't."

Annoying Coworker Precedes All Nouns With 'Quite The'

WICHITA, KS—Wichita Gas & Electric payroll secretary Patti Smolensk has thoroughly irritated coworkers with her habit of prefacing all nouns with "quite the," WG&E sources reported Monday. "She said, 'That's quite the mug you've got there' when I walked into the breakroom with a snowman-shaped mug," file clerk Cassie Taylor said. "And on Monday, she was talking about how she threw 'quite the shindig' over the weekend." Said sales representative Dianne White, whom Smolensk called "quite the sleepyhead" when she recently showed up half an hour late for work: "I'm gonna give her quite the punch in the face if she doesn't knock it off."

Diners Slightly Unnerved That Waitress Didn't Write Down Order

PORTLAND, OR—A Chili's waitress identified only as "Karen" made a six-person lunch party uncomfortable Monday when she didn't write down their orders. "We ordered a heck of a lot of stuff," diner Dennis Bernardo told his dining companions. "You think she'll actually remember the 'no olives' in Bob's Greek salad? And my request for marinara sauce instead of alfredo on my pasta? I'm sure she knows what she's doing, but I still kinda wish she'd written it down." Fellow diner Sandi Slocum said she was going to add a Coke to her order just as the waitress was leaving, but opted not to for fear of "complicating things."

Irish Wake A Blur

BOSTON—According to attendees, Saturday's wake for police officer Joseph "Joe" O'Malley was a total blur. "I think someone said something about remembering all the good times with Joe," said friend Patrick Monaghan, attempting to piece together details of the event Sunday. "Exactly which good times we remembered are lost to me now." Seamus McNamara agreed, saying, "I mainly recall making a lot of toasts and downing pint after pint of Guinness. Good ol' Joe."

Fucker Sure Taking Long Time To Download

MESA, AZ—That fucker sure is taking a long time to download, computer user Larry Eisen reported Monday. "What is taking this fucker so long?" asked Eisen, trying to download the fucker from amug.org, the web site for Arizona Macintosh Users Group. "I got a DSL line for this?" Spokespersons for AMUG, which offers the 145 MB, BinHex-encoded fucker for download off its FTP server, could not be reached as of press time. Ø

METRIC SYSTEM from page 61

Danielson said the discovery of the metric knowledge came as "a wonderful surprise."

"A few months ago, we were conducting a study to ascertain the basic skill level of high-school freshmen with poor attendance records—truant 14- to 15-year-olds who hadn't set foot in a classroom in months," Danielson said. "In the course of this study, an amazing pattern of metric expertise emerged among these kids. Upon discovering this pocket of knowledge, we knew we had to explore it further."

In a follow-up study titled "Metric Skills Among The Economically Disadvantaged," Danielson and his team of researchers discovered that not only did the youths score higher in metric knowledge than any other demographic, but many could also distinguish among the smallest variations in size and amount.

In one test, subjects were asked to follow a recipe for "metric-weight chocolate-chip cookies." Researchers found that the teens had a natural ability to estimate measurements of sugar, flour, and baking powder without using any measuring tools. When the use of a balance scale was required, the teens knew exactly how to operate it.

"Y'all need 500 grams of flour," said Erick Boykins, a 16-year-old study participant from Newark, NJ, scraping out a small pile of flour with a razor. "That's half a kilo right there. Now the recipe says we gotta cut it with 200 g's of sugar."

After combining all the ingredients, Boykins deftly divided the dough into 50 lumps of cookie dough almost identical in weight.

The cookie test was cut short by the disappearance of 25 scales, but results are still being called "conclusive."

Hoping to use the youths' metric zeal as "a springboard to further learning," the Department Of Education has launched "Da Math Skillz" program.

"As any good teacher knows, it's important to start with a foundation of knowledge and build on that," Danielson said. "Our plan is to begin with grams and millimeters, then move on to other metric units like newtons, amperes, and candelas."

The program, however, has run into some early snags.

"The youths seem to have some large blind spots in their knowledge," Danielson said. "For example, they know millimeters very well and can distinguish between something that's 9mm wide and something 7.62mm wide, but for some reason, not one of the teens had ever heard of a hectare. And though they know how much volume a cc represents, none knew it stood for cubic centimeter."

Nevertheless, metric-use advocates were pleased to hear about the new metric-education initiative.

"For some unfathomable reason, the U.S. is the only major industrialized nation in the world not using the metric system," said Dr. Michael Lenzi of UCLA's Center For Statistical Data. "At long last, it appears that the metric system is being embraced by a progressive segment of the population outside the scientific community."

Above: A Presidential Award For Metric Achievement hangs in an area of Detroit renowned for its metric use.

Such trends, Lenzi noted, often originate in major cities before spreading to the rest of the nation.

"While metric awareness is strongest in the cores of Chicago, Los Angeles, and New York, data indicates that it's spreading into smaller cities like Wichita, Portland, and Columbus, and even into the suburbs," Lenzi added. "That's an educational trend you've got to love." Ø

with a razor blade.

"Look at me, suburban dung," Manson told Wesley. "Does this shock you?"

When Wesley replied no, he said Manson became "petulant." Recalled Wesley: "He started stamping his feet and shaking his fists, saying, 'What do you mean, no? Aren't your uptight, puritanical sensibilities offended? Don't you want to censor me so you don't have to confront the ugly truth I represent?' So I say, 'Well, not particularly.' Then, after a long pause, he says, 'Well, screw you, jerk!' and walks off sulking."

That evening, Linda Schmidt was preparing to drive her daughter Alyssa to a Girl Scouts meeting when she found Manson standing on her porch draped in sheep entrails.

"I knew who he was, but I was kind of busy and didn't really have time to chat," Schmidt said. "He just kept standing there staring at me, expecting me to react in some way."

Added Schmidt: "I tried to be nice and humor him a little. I said, 'Yesiree, that sure is some shocking satanic imagery, no doubt about it. And that one eye with no color in the pupil, very disturbing. I'd sure like to suppress that.' I mean, what do you say to Marilyn Manson?"

A deflated Manson remained on Schmidt's porch as she and Alyssa drove off.

Subsequent attempts to provoke outrage were met with equal indifference.

"[Manson] was standing at my front door wearing those fake breasts he wore on the cover of *Mechanical Animals*," retiree Judith Hahn said. "He said, 'My name is Marilyn Manson, and I'm here to tear your little world apart.' I thought he was collecting for the Kiwanis food drive, so I gave him some cans

Above: A dejected Marilyn Manson ponders his next move.

of pumpkin-pie filling."

Undaunted, Manson and his entourage stepped up their assault on mainstream American sensibilities. On Tuesday, they arrived in the tony Detroit suburb of Grosse Pointe Farms, where stockbroker Glenn Binford answered his doorbell to find Manson hanging upside-down on a wooden cross as Ramirez performed fellatio on him.

"I just stood there thinking, now there's a boy who tries way too hard," Binford said. "I mean, come on: Homoerotic sacrilege went out in the late '90s."

Other provocative acts by Manson—including dismembering a chicken, bathing in pig's blood, and wearing a three-piece suit of human noses—failed to arouse anyone's ire, instead prompting comments such as "sophomoric," "trite," and "so Alice Cooper."

Manson's lone brush with controversy occurred in Edina, MN, a suburb of Minneapolis. An unidentified neighborhood-watch volunteer phoned police after seeing a nude, feces-smeared Manson being led around on a leash by a dwarf dominatrix. Officers arrived on the scene, but let Manson go with a warning for parading without a city permit.

"I could have given him a citation, but I figured, how much harm is he really causing?" Edina police officer Dan Herberger said. "I mean, he's just Marilyn Manson, for the love of Mike."

The "Boo" tour was dealt a further blow when Manson learned that Eminem's *The Marshall Mathers LP* had been banned from all Kmart stores. Manson's current album, *Holy Wood (In The Shadow Of The Valley Of Death)*, is still available.

"Why are all you people outraged by Eminem? He's not scary!" Manson said. "He doesn't sport ghoulishly pale skin or wear gender-bending make-up. He's just some regular guy. I'm the one people should be terrified by, not him! Me!"

"If you ban me," Manson continued, "I promise to rail against censorship and hypocrisy. Please? Pretty, pretty please?"

By Monday, the tour appeared to have lost all momentum. Sources close to Manson described him as "exhausted and discouraged," despite not having even completed the first leg of the three-month tour. By the time he arrived in Hoffman Estates, IL, Manson had resorted to leaving flaming bags of dog feces on doorsteps and shining a flashlight under his chin to make himself look "spooky." He was ultimately chased from a Hoffman Estates subdivision by a group of bicycle-riding teenagers who advised him to "get [his] chalk-white goblin ass" out of their neighborhood.

On Friday, Manson is slated to appear in Bethesda, MD, where many believe he will bring his tour to a premature end.

"Have you people forgotten already?" Manson asked *The Washington Post*. "You all thought I was responsible for Columbine two years ago. Well, I was! I was! I know I vehemently denied it at the time, but, really, I personally told those two kids to shoot up the school. I'm serious. I sent them an e-mail. And I told them to worship Satan, too. You hear that, kids? Marilyn Manson says you should shoot your friends in the head with a gun! And everyone should eat babies! And rape their dead grandparents! And poop on a church! There, now will someone please be offended?" ⌀

ARTS

Finest Opera Singer Of Her Generation Unknown By Her Generation

NEW YORK—Alessandra Coletti, the 22-year-old mezzo-soprano sensation, has stunned opera-loving octogenarians around the globe with her astonishing range, power, and upper-register control. Touted as the greatest female opera singer of her generation, the Milan-born, New York-bred Coletti is completely unknown among members of her generation.

"Alessandra who?" said Amy Sharper, 23, a self-described "total music freak" from Reston, VA. "I

think maybe that's the bassist for Nashville Pussy. I'm really not sure, though."

"A singer of this stature comes along once in a lifetime," said Thomas Sagal, 71, editor of *Opera Digest*, which boasts a circulation of nearly 38,000 elderly readers. "Her recent performance as the princess in Dorgomizhsky's *The*

see OPERA page 64

Right: Alessandra Coletti.

This Mug Exaggerates My Grandfathering Skills To An Embarrassing Degree

By Herman Fraser
World's Greatest Grandpa

My word. I still can't believe I was even nominated.

When I woke up Sunday morning, I never imagined that later that day, I'd be named World's Greatest Grandpa. I didn't even know there was such an award. But there it was, written on the mug I got from my grandson Josh. I just don't know what to say.

To be honest, I came very close to declining the award outright. How could I accept such a title when there are so many other deserving grandpas out there? What did I do to distinguish myself from them?

I mean, look at Ralph Fincher, just across town. He's got 16 grandkids in three states, and he never forgets a birthday. He knows each grandchild's favorite candy and always has a bedtime story at the ready. Just to be mentioned in the same breath as a grandpa like that is an honor. I've only got the one grandkid, and here I am being lauded as some sort of world champion in the field? I'm speechless.

And Charlie Quinn, over in Parkhurst! His daughter is raising her kids without a husband, so Grandpa Charlie picks them up from school every day with a big smile on his face. And, oh, how those grandkids squeal with delight when he plays the "got your nose" game with them! (A game I never play with my grandkid.) I hope Charlie at least got some special consolation award, seeing how he got snubbed for the big enchilada.

I mean, sure, I took Josh to the zoo once, but that's standard-issue grandfathering. Telling a wide-eyed 8-year-old that the South American capybara is the world's largest rodent hardly makes one a world-class grandpa, does it? I just read it off the sign on the cage.

Could I really have won the World's Greatest Grandpa award? Is this really happening? I feel like at any moment, someone's going to wake me from my afternoon nap and tell me it was all just a dream. I've searched every inch of that mug five times over looking for some qualifier, like, "World's Greatest Grandpa—Waupaca County Region," but no dice.

I can't help but wonder, who were the judges in charge of making this decision? And what criteria did they use? Were ballots mailed out? According to the inscription on the bottom, it was awarded by Continental Novelties, Inc. I guess that must be like the Motion Picture Academy for grandpas or something.

And since the award is "World's Greatest Grandpa," and not "America's Greatest Grandpa," am I safe to assume I was up against European and Asian grandpas, as well? Because I'm sure there are some pretty terrific grandpas in Burma.

There are so many people to thank. First and foremost, my supportive wife Connie. She's the one who bakes the chocolate-chip cookies when Josh is here and reads him stories. I certainly can't accept this honor without acknowledging her tireless efforts. Connie, this is yours as much as mine. Whenever the World's Greatest Grandma award is announced, my money's on you all the way.

My daughter Justine and her husband Paul should get some credit, too. If they didn't bring little Joshy around once a month, I never would've had the chance to hone my grandfathering skills. Justine and Paul, thanks for this opportunity of a lifetime.

And, quite frankly, Josh must share this award with me. Without him, I wouldn't even be a grandpa, much less the world's greatest. If I am number one, Josh, you are the one who makes it easy. Kudos, champ.

This really hasn't sunk in yet. It all seems strange and dreamlike. Like I'm out of my body looking down on some other, far greater grandpa. There's no way I could ever look at this mug and think, "Yes, that's me. That's the award I earned."

I'm certainly at a loss for where to display this thing. I could never drink out of it, that's for sure. This needs to go someplace befitting of an award this prestigious. I guess I could have some kind of cabinet or display case constructed for it.

My God, what if there's a formal ceremony later and they expect me to make a speech? I don't even have a nice suit. Are there some grounds on which I could just decline the award, like when Brando protested the plight of the Indians at the Oscars? But what would I protest? Maybe those new toilets that use less water. Those really frost my shorts.

Wait a second, what am I saying? This is not the sort of thing I should be trying to get out of. As the World's Greatest Grandpa, millions of grandpas around the globe will look to me as the embodiment of grandfathering. I have an obligation to uphold the responsibilities that come with such a title.

Besides, when Morrie and I get into one of our scraps about what's wrong with today's kids, and he gives me some guff, I can always whip the mug out and shut him up good. ∅

OPERA from page 63

Mermaid at the Leningrad Opera was electrifying. It must be thrilling for young people to know that one of their peers is such a prodigious talent."

During a recent performance of Mascagni's *Cavalleria Rusticana* at the Lyric Opera in Chicago, Coletti played to a capacity crowd of 4,600 old people. Of the 23 teenagers in attendance, 22 were ushers and one was dragged to the performance as punishment.

"My mom said if she ever caught me drinking again, she'd force me to go to an opera with her," said Courtney Weis, 15, who was not enthralled by Coletti's stirring vibrato and formidable coloratura agility. "Holy shit. Let's just say I'm never touching Jack Daniel's again."

Raised by symphony violinists Celeste and Antonio Coletti, young Alessandra grew up surrounded by opera and classical music.

"My earliest memories are listening to Enrico Caruso 78s

> **"Of the great female opera singers of today, few are comparable to Coletti," said near-death *Chicago Tribune* opera critic Arthur Sachs.**

on my parents' Victrola," Coletti said. "When I was 7, they took me to see Renata Babek in *La Gioconda*. What a thrill that was. I remember asking my mother why there were no other children in the audience. She told me they were all across town at Carnegie Hall watching Tchaikovsky's *Queen Of Spades*."

In 1997, after two years of study at the Rimsky-Korsakov conservatory in St. Petersburg, Coletti returned to the U.S. At the tender age of 18, she made her Metropolitan Opera debut as Inez in *L'Africaine*. Dazzling even the most jaded audience member with a bravura performance, Coletti received a five-minute standing ovation from people more than four times her age.

In attempting to describe Coletti's astonishing gifts, fans often invoke the legends of opera, from Emma Eames to Denyce Graves—names that would draw blank stares from anyone under 50.

"Of the great female opera singers of today, few are comparable to Coletti," said near-death *Chicago Tribune* opera critic Arthur Sachs. "If she continues to progress at her current rate, I might one day even put her in the class of a Maria Callas."

Widely considered the finest operatic voice of the 20th century, Callas is unknown among 18- to 24-year-olds, ranking behind rubber-faced '70s funnyman Charlie Callas in celebrity-Callas name recognition.

One of Coletti's few fans not born in the first half of the last century is Andrew Shermer, president of the Twentysomething Opera Appreciation Society (TOAS).

"I formed TOAS after seeing Alessandra Coletti's Violetta in *La Traviata*," said Shermer, 24. "I'd seen opera before and enjoyed it, but seeing her at the Met that night blew my mind. It inspired me to start up a web site, toas.com, to reach other people my age with interest in the opera."

Thus far, TOAS has attracted only five members. And while www.toas.com receives an average of 10,000 hits a week, an analysis of its traffic indicates that 99.999 percent of them are from people who misspelled "Taos," a popular New Mexico ski destination. ∅

Celebrity Couples Are Breaking Up!

Item! It's not just Oscar season, it's also break-up season! Among the Hollywood couples packing up their belongings and moving to Splitsville are **Kim Basinger** and **Alec Baldwin**.

**The Outside Scoop
By Jackie Harvey**

Rumors have it that both of them were unhappy with the other's ballooning weight, so they decided to split before the situation got worse. For a while, this couple had it all: looks, money, and **a commitment to numerous important causes**. But, like so many Hollywood clouds, this one had a dark lining.

As if that weren't bad enough, **Puff Daddy** and **Jennifer Lopez** are rumored to be on the outs. There's really no explanation for something like that. Puffy and J-Lo were America's perfect pair, he of the electric personality and she of the **triple-threat talent**. Just imagine the babies they could have had together. It could have been the start of an **entertainment dynasty**.

But wait, there's yet another glamour couple in trouble: **Helen Hunt** and **her husband**. Word is, if their relationship were a drink, it would be **on the rocks**! Say it ain't so, H.H.!

Item! The people have spoken and, as always, the people's voice is **The People's Choice Awards**! I don't know how many eyes were glued to the television that night, but you sure couldn't tear these two eyeballs away from it. All the stars came out to celebrate **the will of the people**. **Jim Carrey! Drew Carey!** And who could forget America's sweetheart, **Julia Roberts**? Right from the get-go, when co-host **Britney Spears** unexpectedly tore away her dowdy dress to reveal a super-sexy, belly-baring ensemble, I was riveted. I thought rapper **LL Cool J** was going to faint from surprise!

But the most touching moment came when **John Goodman** "came out" and accepted his award for Best New Comedy for the Fox gay-com **Normal, Ohio**. Even though the show had been canceled, he handled himself with the kind of **bravery and poise** that only a real star could pull off. I usually don't wear hats, but I will put one on just so I can tip it to you, Mr. Goodman.

Congratulations to the folks behind the **Terminator 2 DVD**, recently voted the number-four DVD of all-time in **Entertainment Weekly**.

Item! Speaking of Britney Spears, magician **Harry Blackstone** released his list of the **Year's Worst Dressed**, and she was on it. Now, I think Britney may make a few mistakes with her wardrobe, but I can think of a few gals who should come in well below her. Like **Marge**, the cashier over at the Amoco station near my house. Her awful blouse-and-sweatpants combos make Britney look like **Audrey Hepburn**! Mr. Blackstone was right on the money about that nasty **Courtney Love**, though. I don't even know why she's famous, but I just wish she'd go away already and leave fame to **the beautiful people**.

I just can't get the song from that **zoom-zoom-zoom commercial** out of my head. Help!

The X-Files has really taken a turn for the worse since they got **the liquid-mercury man** to fill in for **David Duchovny**. Word is that Duchovny and singer/wife **Teena Marie** are concentrating on raising their child. I just hope they remember that children aren't the only ones with needs... their fans have needs, too!

What's this **Tinker, Tiger, Soldier, Dragon** movie I hear so much about? Is it true there's no English in the entire thing? That's crazy.

Item! "Material Mom **Madonna** Married!" That's what we in the scoop-getting business call a **dream come true**. It's also a fine example of alliteration. Now, **Webster's Dictionary** defines alliteration as, "The repetition of the same letter at the beginning of two or more words immediately succeeding each other, or at short intervals." So, it didn't have to be all M's. The headline could have read, "Material Mom Madonna Gets Married!" and it still would have been alliteration. Wordplay is my favorite part of this job. But, yes, Madonna married **a British director** and it was very splendid.

Temptation Island... temptational! Tongues are a-waggin' across America over the tropical exploits of these four **sexy young couples** and the **sexy singles** designed to tempt them! Episode Three saw things heat up between hunky everyman **Billy** and **Perfect 10 model Vanessa** as they drank fruity margaritas and flirted. Meanwhile, Billy's girlfriend **Mandy** got back at him by having lots of fun on her date, drinking fruity margaritas and flirting! Which couple will be left standing in Episode 32? Only time will tell!

Item! Separated at birth? Rapper **ODB** (which stands for something a bit vulgar) and deeply talented actor **Morton Downey Jr.** were both captured by the long arm of the law within the same day. Did one tip the cops off to the other? Was there some sort of drug pact going on? Are the rumors about ODB's acting aspirations true? Is Downey marked for death? The rumors are swirling, and it will take a while, but trust yours truly to sift through the lies to bring you the truth.

So it turns out that **computers** weren't all the rage, after all! Go figure.

Item! She stole your heart in **Almost Famous**, but actress **Kate Hawn** is now married to a long-haired rock musician from **The Black Crows**. I guess she wasn't really acting when she portrayed a slavering groupie to a rock band of questionable talent. I don't get it: What's a red-hot Hollywood star like Hawn doing with a **homely guitar goon** like that? She should be with **Leonardo DiCaprio** or someone like that. That way, when she appeared at a **gala movie premiere**, photographers would get excited about shooting both of them, instead of just her.

PlayStation 2? I barely have time to keep up with my **Furby**!

As ever, it saddens me greatly to say goodbye to another edition of **The Outside Scoop**. But if you know me, you know that until my next column, I'll be a bloodhound sniffing out the scoop for you to drink in like a fine wine. By the way, that last sentence was a simile. See? Who says learning can't be fun? Until next time, I'll be sitting in **the aisle on the outside**!

Romantic-Comedy Behavior Gets Real-Life Man Arrested

Above: Police officers take Denny Marzano into custody following his latest romantic-comedy-like crime.

TORRANCE, CA—Denny Marzano, a 28-year-old Torrance man, was arrested Monday for engaging in the type of behavior found in romantic comedies.

Marzano was taken into custody after violating a restraining order filed against him by Kelly Hamilton, 25, an attractive, unmarried kindergarten teacher who is new to the L.A. area. According to Hamilton, Marzano has stalked her for the past two months, spying on her, tapping her phone, serenading her with The Carpenters' "Close To You" at her place of employment, and tricking her into boarding a Caribbean-bound jet.

Hamilton made the call to police at approximately 7:30 p.m., when she discovered that the bearded cable repairman she had let into her apartment was actually Marzano in disguise.

"Thank God he's in custody, and this nightmare is finally over," said Hamilton, a single mother struggling to raise an adorable, tow-headed boy all alone in the big city. "I repeatedly told him I wasn't interested, but he just kept resorting to crazier and crazier stunts to make me fall in love with him."

Marzano, who recently broke his leg falling off a ladder leaning against Hamilton's second-story bedroom window, said he was "extremely surprised" that his plan to woo the woman had failed.

"She was supposed to hate me at first but gradually be won over by my incredible persistence, telling me that no one has ever gone to such lengths to win her love," Marzano said. "But for some reason, her irritation never melted into affection."

In addition to the stalking charges, Marzano is accused of framing Stuart Polian, a handsome Pasadena attorney and chief competitor for Hamilton's hand, for arson. Marzano denied the charges.

"While it's true that I would love to have seen my main romantic rival out of the picture, I did not burn down that animal shelter and try to pin it on Mr. Polian," Marzano said. "I have always believed I could win Kelly's love without resorting to such illegalities."

Marzano had been arrested for engaging in romantic-comedy behavior on five previous occasions. The most recent arrest came in May 2000, when he pretended to be a confession-booth priest in the hopes of tricking a Fresno, CA, woman into unwittingly revealing her love for him.

Hillary In 2004?

The 2000 presidential election is barely in the books, but talk has already turned to the possibility of Hillary Clinton making a White House run in 2004. What do *you* think?

"A woman president? What if she menstruates all over some important legislation?"

Rich Durban
Machinist

"She's got a good shot, so long as no one blows her up, causing her faceplate to fall off and revealing the gears and diodes beneath."

Todd Tyler
Systems Analyst

"No, no—you don't understand: The 19th Amendment gives women the right to *vote* for a president, that's all."

Bob Van Eeghen
Lawyer

"Hillary would make a great president. But she'd probably ask her girlfriends for advice, and I just don't trust that Sharon."

Annette Petersen
Homemaker

"Would she have female Secret Service agents? Because that'd be pretty sexy."

Bob Houdel
Cashier

"We could do worse. You know, like we always have."

Lisa Rinaldi
Physical Therapist

JUST FOR FUN

Your Horoscope

By Lloyd Schumner Sr.
Retired Machinist and
A.A.P.B.-Certified Astrologer

Aries: (March 21–April 19)
Though you have always considered the difference psychological, you will be horrified to learn that men and women also have substantial physical distinctions.

Taurus: (April 20–May 20)
The only thing you'll be able to think during the entire 90-second multi-vehicle crash is how much your father would have loved it.

Gemini: (May 21–June 21)
You will look as good in a hundred years as you do today, thanks to recent advances in the field of taxidermy.

Cancer: (June 22–July 22)
Remember that trying to please everyone is impossible, except perhaps in the case of everyone just wanting you to stop singing show-tunes at your desk.

Leo: (July 23–Aug. 22)
As far as you can tell, the difference between the great and the near-great is their shoes.

Virgo: (Aug. 23–Sept. 22)
You will learn an important lesson about sharing over the course of 22 minutes, plus commercials.

Libra: (Sept. 23–Oct. 23)
While you have always considered yourself "lovable," this is true only in the narrowest, most clinical sense.

Scorpio: (Oct. 24–Nov. 21)
The technical term for what will happen to you next Tuesday is "trepanning," but that won't seem terribly interesting at the time.

Sagittarius: (Nov. 22–Dec. 21)
A good friend will see fit to share her darkest secrets with you shortly after placing a small but tasteful bouquet on your headstone.

Capricorn: (Dec. 22–Jan. 19)
You've got just one big collar to make in your two days before retirement, so be careful: Sewing clown clothing can be extremely dangerous.

Aquarius: (Jan. 20–Feb. 18)
Don't worry about posterity. Just because history is written by the winners doesn't mean you won't get a footnote somewhere.

Pisces: (Feb. 19–March 20)
Famous quotations are for people who have nothing of their own to say, so be sure to use a lot of them.

EXIT from page 61

that," Paschal said. "I have to prepare for the possibility that I'm the surviving passengers' only hope." Paschal noted that if need be, he could probably throw the door open himself, either by applying all his strength to the handle or by wrapping a seatbelt strap around it for leverage.

In addition to opening the exit-row door, Paschal's emergency duties would include helping his fellow passengers exit the plane and slide down the inflatable chute.

"That's the price you pay for having a little extra leg room here in the exit row," said Paschal, who stowed his carry-on bag in the overhead compartment so it wouldn't tangle the legs of escaping passengers. "Right now, it's leg room, but when the plane is engulfed in flames or sinking like a stone 30,000 feet above central Tennessee, it could be the path to life. And that's a path I want clear."

"Don't worry," said Paschal, turning to the woman seated next to him. "You're going to see your family again."

Paschal first learned of his exit-row responsibilities during the standard pre-flight safety video shown to passengers as Flight 234 prepared for takeoff. Paschal paid strict attention to the presentation, well aware that he could be unexpectedly called into service.

"When [chief flight attendant] Melinda [Garnock] directed my attention to the exit sign above my head, I was glad I made damn sure I had the procedure down," said Paschal, scanning the plane for any elderly passengers who might need special assistance. "Now, I'm basically a member of the crew. Until this plane lands, I'm no longer a civilian."

In addition to familiarizing himself with the large, clearly marked lever, Paschal made other preparations. After introducing himself to everyone in the immediate vicinity of seat 15E, he tucked the aircraft's crash card into the underside of his tray table for easy access. He also fixed his seat in its most upright position.

"Can't afford to relax on this flight," Paschal said. "No coffee, no soda. Got to stay ready. I might have to make my way around this bird in total darkness—or even underwater."

Paschal's zeal has not gone unnoticed by United personnel.

"I asked him about six times to stop removing his seat cushion," Garnock said. "He said he was practicing using it as a flotation device. He only stopped when I assured him we wouldn't be crossing any oceans from Chicago to Atlanta. He kept looking over at me and giving me the thumbs-up."

"He took me aside earlier and said he was pretty sure he could get everyone out himself, and that if it came to it, I should save myself," flight attendant Yvette Sanchez said. "It took me a while to realize he was talking about helping people out of the plane in an emergency."

Added Sanchez: "Apparently, the guy doesn't realize that in the unlikely event of a crash, we're all fucking dead." ∅

Rock's First Billionaire

With a net worth estimated at $1.07 billion, Paul McCartney recently became the world's first billionaire pop star. Among the former Beatle's holdings:

- $ Rights to the song "Michelle"; also, rights to the name Michelle
- $ Underground lab with Linda's head suspended in anti-aging fluids
- $ 51 percent stake in TravelingWilburycorp
- $ Ringo
- $ 10 percent cut of accidental March 1993 rental of *Give My Regards To Broad Street* at Des Moines, IA, Blockbuster
- $ Blue New World, Ltd. (a shadowy joint partnership created in 1969 by McCartney and the head Blue Meanie, purpose unknown)
- $ 600,000 boxes of Linda's inedible microwave vegetarian entrees
- $ "You Are The Walrus" Magical Mystery Family Funpark, English Midlands
- $ Humongous pile of unbelievably mind-blowing weed

the ONION
America's Finest News Source

Herman Ulysses Zweibel *Founder*

T. Herman Zweibel *Publisher Emeritus*
J. Phineas Zweibel *Publisher*
Maxwell Prescott Zweibel *Editor-In-Chief*

FOUNDED 1871 • "TU STULTUS ES"

the ONION®

VOLUME 37 ISSUE 04   AMERICA'S FINEST NEWS SOURCE™   8-14 FEBRUARY 2001

Dozens Of Glowing Exit Signs Mercilessly Taunt Multiplex Employee

see WORKPLACE page 10C

Elderly Woman Casually Mentions Wish To Die

see SENIORBEAT page 2E

Alex Winter Keeps Bugging Keanu Reeves About Third *Bill & Ted* Movie

see HOLLYWOOD page 7B

STATshot

A look at the numbers that shape your world.

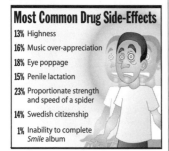

Most Common Drug Side-Effects

- 13% Highness
- 16% Music over-appreciation
- 18% Eye poppage
- 15% Penile lactation
- 23% Proportionate strength and speed of a spider
- 14% Swedish citizenship
- 1% Inability to complete *Smile* album

THE ONION
VOLUME 37
ISSUE 04

$2.00 US
$3.00 CAN

0 74470 94595 6

Above: Bill Clinton ponders his legacy in the den of his suburban New York home.

Clinton Vaguely Disappointed By Lack Of Assassination Attempts

CHAPPAQUA, NY—Reflecting on his presidency Monday, Bill Clinton expressed a "strange sense of disappointment" over the lack of dramatic attempts on his life.

"All the great ones had someone take a crack at them," Clinton said. "Lincoln, Teddy Roosevelt, FDR, Kennedy—even Reagan. An assassination attempt would have really elevated my status in the pantheon of presidents."

"Is this how I'm going to be remembered? As the president who wasn't worth a couple pot shots?" Clinton asked. "For God's sake, even Ford had Squeaky Fromme."

Clinton said an assassination attempt would have given the nation an opportunity to rally around its wounded leader.

"I would have inspired every American with my strength and bravery," Clinton said. "Giving the American people a heroic thumbs-up despite my side wound as they loaded me into the ambulance, attempting to walk before my doctors really wanted me to, passing legislation and signing executive orders from my hospital bed in Bethesda... I would have been terrific."

see CLINTON page 68

Receptionist At Chiropractor's Office Considering Pursuing Chiropractic Degree

BALTIMORE, MD—Paula Budig, 33, a receptionist at Liberty Heights Chiropractic Clinic since November, confirmed Tuesday that she is seriously considering returning to school to pursue a degree in chiropractic medicine.

"When I answered the want ad for this job, I didn't really even know what a chiropractor did," said Budig, straightening the magazines in the patient waiting room. "But after working at the clinic for a few months now, it seems like it would be a really great career."

Budig has already begun researching the possible career move. At lunch Monday, she talked to Dr. Wesley Lamp, one of the four chiropractors at the clinic, about what

see RECEPTIONIST page 69

Above: Chiropractic secretary Paula Budig.

Lava Lamps Revert From Passé Retro Kitsch Back To Novel Retro Camp

WASHINGTON, DC—Lava lamps, the once-popular, then passé, then popular again, then passé again novelty items that have cyclically taken various American subcultures by storm throughout their 35-year history, are back.

According to a report issued Monday by the U.S. Department of Retro, the status of the multi-colored, mildly psychedelic light fixtures changed again in 2000, reverting from a tired form of passé retro kitsch back into a novel form of retro camp. The switch marks the 17th time the government has changed the lava lamp's retro

classification since its initial resurgence in 1976 as an amusing, campy throwback to the then-outmoded '60s hippie drug culture.

"Lava lamps, which throughout the late '90s were seen as an irrelevant remnant of a relatively minor mid-'90s form of '60s retro, are once again retro in an exciting new way for millions of Americans unfamiliar with their previous kitsch-object incarnations," U.S. Retro Secretary Brian Setzer said. "That fallow period of the late '90s laid the groundwork for a revival within a subset of

see LAVA LAMPS page 71

New Country-Music Video Has Look Of 1991 Rock Video

NASHVILLE—The video for Lonestar's "How 'Bout That," which premiered Monday on TNN, bears an uncanny resemblance to a typical rock video circa 1991. "Dude, this looks like Bad English or something," Ryan Stearns, 24, told friend Jon Labine while watching the popular country band's video. "Check out the ripped jeans. And the long hair. And the mountaintop guitar-strumming." Said Labine: "No, wait—you know who this looks like? Damn Yankees. Or was it Extreme? Whichever did that 'High Enough' song, where they're rocking out in the junkyard." Labine also noted that Lonestar singer Richie McDonald kind of sounds like the guy from Mr. Big.

High-School Teacher Reluctantly Breaks Up Fight

IRVINE, CA—With great hesitation, Irvine West High School teacher Ted Broussard broke up a hallway fistfight Monday between students Rick Anders and Jeff Streed. "That would have been a great fight," Broussard said. "I would have loved to see those two go at it.

Too bad I was required to put a stop to it." Broussard noted that in spite of his smaller size, Anders "probably could've taken [Streed]."

Special 'Framers' Cut' Of Constitution To Feature Five Deleted Amendments

WASHINGTON, DC—The National Archives and Records Administration announced plans Monday to release a special "framers' cut" of the Constitution featuring five bonus amendments deleted from the original. According to NARA head John Carlin, the new document includes "more than 35 lines of never-before-seen provisions sure to thrill history buffs." Among the goodies: an early draft of the Fifth Amendment protecting citizens from being put in quintuple jeopardy and a rare, unnumbered amendment granting each member of Congress the right to "one concubine of his choosing per term served." The expanded version will also include "framers' commentary" by Alexander Hamilton and James Madison written in the margins, as well as a "Making Of The Constitution" document after the list of framers' signatures.

Woman Panics After Accidentally Getting Into Exact-Change Lane

DES PLAINES, IL—Motorist Gloria Eckstrom, 64, panicked Monday after accidentally entering an I-90 toll-booth lane explicitly marked "Exact Change Only." "Oh, my goodness," said Eckstrom, the flow of traffic carrying her toward a basket into which she would soon be expected to toss 40 cents. "I'm in the wrong lane." Eckstrom was able to merge into a nearby "Manual" lane at the last possible moment, averting disaster.

'Mr. Falafel' Owner Does Not Actually Like Being Addressed As Mr. Falafel

DETROIT—In a candid interview Monday, Elias Nawaz, owner of the Mr. Falafel restaurant on Telegraph Road, asserted that he does not like to be called Mr. Falafel. "Please call me Mr. Nawaz," he said. "Or, if you wish to be less formal, you can call me Elias. But my name is not Mr. Falafel." Nawaz added that anyone asking to speak to "Mrs. Falafel" would be ignored outright. ∅

CLINTON from page 67

Above: The scene following the jealousy-provoking March 1981 attempt on Ronald Reagan's life.

throng of people," Podesta said. "With TV cameras rolling, Bill rolls up his shirtsleeves and starts working his way through the crowd, shaking everybody's hands. After a few minutes, he leans over to me and says, 'Right now would be perfect.'"

Clinton Secretary of State Warren Christopher said he often tried to assure the president that he didn't need to be shot to be loved.

"I tried to tell him it's no big deal,

> **Secretary of State Warren Christopher said he often tried to assure Clinton that he didn't need to be shot to be loved.**

"The Reagan shooting, that made his presidency," Clinton said. "I still remember watching the coverage of it on TV back in Little Rock, thinking to myself, 'Man, that guy is playing this perfectly. Someday, I'm going to assure a shaken American people that it will take more than a bullet to stop me from leading this great nation.'"

Those close to Clinton are beginning to worry about his preoccupation.

"He'd never tell you this himself, but when it didn't happen in his last few months in office, he was inconsolable," former White House Chief of Staff John Podesta said. "He just kept staring out the windows, first at that little hill behind the Oval Office, then at the hedge in the Rose Garden, as if willing a lone gunman to appear. Saddest thing you ever saw."

Podesta said Clinton had high

hopes for a Nov. 14, 2000, visit to San Diego, a Republican-dominated city with a high number of ex-Marines. In addition to making three public speeches and waving to several large crowds in open areas, Clinton entered and exited numerous limousines and buildings during the trip. Not once, however, was he ever in any danger.

"At one point, we walked out of a hotel and were greeted by a

that plenty of the great presidents never got shot at," Christopher said. "Like Washington. Besides, no one remembers Charles Guiteau shooting James Garfield. Or McKinley getting plugged by that Polish guy in Buffalo. But he just looks at me with these sad eyes."

Continued Christopher: "Then I reminded the president of Francisco Duran, the Army vet who took shots at the White House in 1994. All he could say was, 'Whoopee, someone shot at the White House while I was nowhere in the vicinity. That's really gonna secure my place in history.'" ∅

Recently Born-Again Christian Finally Has Social Life

GASTONIA, NC—Eight months ago, Larry Dunne was alone. He didn't have a friend in the world. But all that changed with his baptism at the New Hearts Fundamentalist Church. Ever since becoming a born-again Christian, Dunne has a friend through Jesus.

"Let's see, there's Richard and Janet and Craig," said Dunne, a data technician at Quill Paper Distribution. "Oh, and Brent, too. He stands next to me in the choir. Now that I'm saved, I've got a whole bunch of friends."

Dunne said he has experienced a 180-degree turnaround since finding the Lord.

"Before I joined Christ's flock, everyone used to make fun of me and call me a weirdo," Dunne said. "But the people at New Hearts accepted me unconditionally—so long as I accepted Jesus Christ as my savior. Once I did that, all sorts of wonderful things followed, like having plans on Friday nights."

Dunne first became aware of the 37-member church during a Saturday-afternoon walk.

"I was wandering around the neighborhood by myself, much like Moses wandered the desert for 40 years, when I saw a sign for a church rummage sale," Dunne said. "I was only at the sale a few minutes and didn't find anything, so I was just going to buy a brownie and leave. The two women at the brownie stand started talking to me, asking me questions about my life and stuff. I was really taken aback by their interest in me. It was nice."

Eventually, the conversation turned to religion, a subject Dunne admitted he knew little about.

"They asked me if I was familiar with their denomination," Dunne said. "I said no but that I'd be open to learning about it. Then they invited me to their Monday Bible-study meeting. I thought, hey, we're really hitting it off here."

According to Dunne, his first Bible-study meeting went well, with parishioners enthusiastically welcoming him into the fold. By the end of the night, Dunne proved to be such a hit that he was invited to a church sing-along the next night.

"I've never met a group of people I get along so well with," he said. "Sometimes, we get together on the weekends to play basketball, but instead of playing 'horse' or 'pig,' we play 'Jesus' or 'God.' And then there are the bake

Above: Larry Dunne (second from left) enjoys a Saturday-night "Pizza 'n' Prayer" party with his new friends.

sales and other church fund-raisers. The gang never fails to invite me along to those, either."

According to Dunne, being born again has improved his love life, as well.

"I've been dating Linda for about a month now," Dunne said. "She joined the church a year ago, right after going through a messy divorce. She needed Christ's wisdom to get her through that tough time. Even though she's 16 years older than me, I really think we're soulmates."

"Everything's been so much better since I took Jesus into my heart," Dunne continued. "For the first time in my life, I'm surrounded by people who actually want me to hang out with them. In Christ, I am liked." ❡

RECEPTIONIST from page 67

it's like to be a chiropractor. Upon returning to the office, she logged onto the web site for Baltimore Chiropractic College, Lamp's alma mater.

"They have a program at Baltimore Chiro where I could finish in three and a half years," Budig said. "The first year and a half can be done in night classes, so I wouldn't even have to stop working until after my third semester. Best of all, the campus is only 25 minutes from my apartment complex."

According to Budig, working at Liberty Heights Chiropractic Clinic gives her a considerable head start over any future classmates.

"Just being in this office, I've soaked up a ton of knowledge about the field," Budig said. "I mean, all day long, I'm writing down messages from patients regarding the condition of their backs and then relaying them to the doctors. You can't help but learn when you're doing stuff like that."

Though Budig did not continue her education after high school, she said she has "always known that option was there."

"When I graduated, I was offered and accepted a managerial position at the Safeway where I'd been working," Budig said. "I really wanted to buy a new Fiero at the time, so I figured school could wait."

After three years as assistant manager at Safeway and then four years at the Falls Road Roy Rogers, Budig decided to move out of the retail field.

"For a while, I was pretty serious about going into law," Budig said.

"I felt it was time to get out and explore some other options," Budig said. "I was working in the floral department at Safeway, and for a time I considered becoming a florist, but that never quite came together."

Within three months of leaving Roy Rogers, Budig landed a job as a receptionist at the law firm of Higgins, Damisch & Davis.

"For a while, I was pretty serious about going into law," Budig said. "I even got some brochures from one of the local law schools. But then I got a job as a secretary at an advertising firm and found that field much better suited to my skills."

After numerous career detours and false starts, Budig believes she

Above: The institute of higher learning Budig hopes to attend.

has found her true calling.

"I think I'm really well-suited to being a chiropractor," she said. "For example, I give amazing back rubs, so I know I'd be good at working the various spinal bones. I just have, like, a natural aptitude with the human body."

Budig admitted that the lucrative nature of the profession is also a plus.

"Right now, I make $22K per year," she said. "A chiropractor's starting salary is easily $35K. Plus, they get paid vacations and great benefits and all that. I get paid for holidays, but that's it. And I have a 30 percent co-pay for my insurance."

Budig said she would likely be able to do her six-month internship at Liberty Heights Chiropractic Clinic, and that upon graduation, she would have an inside track to a job at the clinic.

"The doctors are always complaining about how they're understaffed," Budig said. "They seriously need more chiropractors working here. Believe me, I should know: I do patient scheduling." ❡

I Can't Seem To Find The Moline Gay District

By Lance Cuellar

As a gay man, whenever I'm in a new city, the first thing I do is seek out the gay district. Whether it's New York's Greenwich Village, The Castro in San Francisco, or Chicago's Boystown, a gay district has the stores, cafés, and clubs that fit my lifestyle. But I've been here in Moline for two whole days on business and, God help me, I can't find the Moline gay district anywhere.

I just don't get it. I've driven all over town with no luck at all. Where are the gay bars? The vintage-clothing shops? The lesbian book stores? I swear, it's like Moline is trying to keep the gay part of town a big secret. You have to be a regular queer Columbo to find a single upscale erotic-art gallery in Moline, much less an entire gay district.

My first stop was downtown, which I quickly redubbed Lametown. No vegan restaurants, no scented-candle shops—not so much as a single inverted pink triangle in a window. Only fast-food chains, auto-supply stores, and a Kmart. Can't get much straighter than that.

Convinced that I missed something, I scoured the entire downtown area again, this time with my gay-dar turned up a good three notches. Once again, nada. For a second, I thought I saw a rainbow flag, but it was just a sign in the window of a paint store.

It was time for drastic measures. I marched into Ray's Feed & Farm and asked if there were any thrift shops, massage parlors, or holistic pet-

---

I just don't get it. Where are the gay bars? The vintage-clothing shops? The lesbian book stores?

---

food stores nearby. Those farmers looked at me like I was balancing a Buick on my dick. After a few moments of awkward silence, one guy in a John Deere cap cleared his throat and directed me to Bridgewood Antiques. I thanked them for their help and got out of the store quickly. I hope I don't ever have any need for feed or farming supplies, because I don't think I'd want to go back in there any time soon.

After going through all that trouble, Bridgewood Antiques turned out to be a major bust. All they had were old magazines and Craftsman tools. No Shaker rocking chairs, no Japanese screens, no chintz drapes. What's worse, the customers were all just a bunch of gray-haired old grandmas. Where were the immaculately dressed gay professionals trying to find that perfect, one-of-a-kind floor rug for their sunroom? Where were the flamboyant hipsters buying campy early-'60s kitchen tables? They must be somewhere in Moline, but *where*?

I finally realized where I needed to look: the local college campus. That's always a reliable gay hotbed. I marched right up to the entrance of the Black Hawk College student union and asked a man where I might find any "Friends Of Dorothy." All I got was a blank stare. The next 250 people I approached just offered more of the same.

I'm not giving up yet. I know there's a gay district somewhere in Moline. There *has* to be. I mean, it's a city of more than 40,000 people, for heaven's sake. Ten percent of that works out to 4,000 people. That's a heck of a lot of gay people to keep hidden and districtless.

This morning, while leaving my hotel, I got a tip from the front-desk clerk. He said there's a drag show on the outskirts of town tonight. Hallelujah! If I can get out there, I should be able to find my kind of folks. I just have to remember the directions to the raceway where it's being held, and I'll be home free. Keep your fingers crossed. ∅

---

the ONION ParentCorner presents

Helping Your Kids Succeed In School

Now more than ever, parents need to be active and involved in their children's education. Here are some ways you can give your kids the support they need to thrive in the classroom.

- If at all possible, set a good example for your kids by learning to read and write.

- Make your child the envy of the school by buying him or her Trapper Keeper®-brand portfolios.

- If you currently live in a community with high-quality schools, consider moving your family to an impoverished rural or inner-city area to improve your child's class standing.

- Many television shows are actually valuable educational resources disguised as entertainment. For example, *Gilligan's Island* is a great way to learn about Gilligan's island.

- Develop a working model for a reformed educational system that addresses the needs of every child at a reasonable taxpayer cost. Then become powerful and implement that system.

- Get to know your child's schoolteacher. Ask why he or she can't drum some sense into the little shit.

- Fostering a strong sense of self-worth is crucial to academic success. Send your child to school bedecked in precious jewels and carried aloft in a gilded chair by four loinclothed slaves.

- Underfeed your child so he or she will become skinny and awkward. The child will then pursue academia instead of sports and social channels.

- While education is important, make sure your child doesn't get all uppity with his or her book-learning.

- There's no teacher like life: Lie about your child's age and enlist him or her in the army.

- Children perform better in classrooms of smaller size. Lure your child's classmates away from school by dressing up as a clown and promising them candy and balloons from a great, big circus wagon on the other side of town.

- In the future, knowledge will come in pill form. Wait.

Mass Of Unfreshened Air Moving In From Arctic Circle

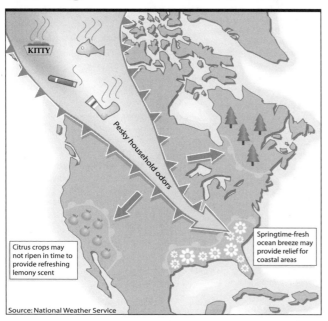

KITTY

Pesky household odors

Citrus crops may not ripen in time to provide refreshing lemony scent

Springtime-fresh ocean breeze may provide relief for coastal areas

Source: National Weather Service

WASHINGTON, DC—The National Weather Service issued a severe musty-odor advisory Monday for a majority of the U.S., as a massive front of stale, unfreshened air sweeps down from the Arctic region.

"While no state of emergency has yet been declared, we are cautioning all citizens to be on alert for problem odors which, even as we speak, are moving through the Dakotas and gaining strength as they head east," National Weather Service director James Auslander said. "These embarrassing, lingering smells show no sign of dissi-

pating any time soon, and it is vital that Americans prepare themselves."

The wave of unfreshened air is believed to be connected to a recent "poker night" get-together in the Arctic region, complete with big, smelly cigars and a fried-fish dinner. According to Auslander, shoes were removed during the gathering, contributing foot odor to an already unpleasant front.

Working closely with Renuzit officials, the National Weather Service is taking steps to freshen the approaching air mass.

see WEATHER page 72

I'm A Dinner-Party Animal

Whoo-hoo! It's Friday night, people! Time to shake off the week, crack open a carafe of Zinfandel, get my hands in the canapés, and let loose. It's dinner-party time!

By Stephan Tewksbury

After a long, hard week at the office, I am ready to let off some serious steam at Ethan's dinner party tonight. A buddy of mine invited me to a cheese-tasting on the West Side, but I was like, "Sorry, Oliver—tonight's my night to rage." From the mouth-watering hors d'oeuvres to the palate-cleansing sorbet, it's going to be one full-throttle banquet. Shit, yeah!

Ethan's blowouts are where I first earned my rep as the ultimate dinner-party animal. I'm the guy who arrives with a bottle of Chardonnay *and* Pinot noir. I'm the guy who gets the Debussy pumpin' on the stereo when things slow down. There's no greater compliment than a high five from yours truly for a beautiful centerpiece or for having enough escargot forks for all. Those are the things that make a dinner party a dinner *par-tay*. Otherwise, you might as well be having people over for an after-dinner grappa.

Man, I cannot wait for tonight. I am going to be dinner-partying 'til the break of 11:30 p.m. When I see lit candles, folded cloth napkins, and matching place settings, it makes me want to throw my hands in the air and shout, "Come on, all y'all dinner-party people in the house! You ready to make some pleasant conversation? Let me hear you say *yeah!*"

I've lived this dinner-party lifestyle so long, my friends say my heart pumps bouillabaisse. Some people think my stomach's going to fail, or I'll become lactose intolerant and be forced to give up this 24-7 dinner-party lifestyle. That's never gonna happen. I come from a long line of over-the-top gourmands. My dad was—and still is—a dinner-party animal, even though he recently developed a seafood allergy that's taken a bit of the gusto out of him. But back in the day, man, he could really put away those ladyfingers. I'm the same way.

I remember this one time, my friend Hamilton came down to visit from Newport. We went to this dinner party my friend Chance was throwing. Now, Chance throws a mean dinner party, the kind that sends most potluck wimps crying to Mama. But I don't think even anyone there was prepared for the dining-room roof Hamilton and I would raise that night. It was insane. Hamilton out-ate, out-toasted, and out-chatted everyone in the room. He's a dinner-party legend. Even the so-called "Dinner-Party Kings" were humbled by his knowledge of flatware placement. When everyone else was slumped in the couches with their belts loosened, Hamilton and I were still scarfing Russian tea cakes.

Yeah, I'll probably slow down someday. But until then, I'm gonna rock out at every dinner party I can. So, if you wanna kick your own dinner party into high gear, just send me an invite and strap yourself in. Because I don't stop until the last slice of lemon-meringue pie is gone.

Just don't call me if you're throwing a cocktail party. They're for pussies. ∅

LAVA LAMPS from page 67

retro consumer for whom the novelty factor of floating bulbs of wax suspended in water and lit from below had not yet worn off."

Setzer—who made his name in the '80s playing retro '50s rockabilly with The Stray Cats and subsequently enjoyed a comeback in the '90s, both for playing '40s big-band music with the Brian Setzer Orchestra during the retro swing revival and as the subject of retro appreciation himself during a concurrent '80s retro wave—praised the pop-cultural tenacity of the lava lamp.

"One of the few pop-culture fads to weather a significant number of lame-then-cool-again changes in the fickle American retro landscape, the lava lamp has proven itself the rare retro phenomenon that will not die," Setzer said. "Whether this is good or bad, or what it even says about our society, is largely unknowable."

As noted in the Retro Department report, the popularity of lava lamps at any one moment is difficult to gauge due to their varying status

> **In 1998, computer dweebs considered lava lamps "CyberKewl," while swing-dancing hipsters dismissed them as "lame-a-roony-toony."**

within different subcultures. As a result, the lamps often simultaneously occupy many different points along the retro-cycle curve, causing confusion among retro cognoscenti. For example, in 1998, computer dweebs considered the lamps "CyberKewl," while swing-dancing hipsters dismissed them as "lame-a-roony-toony."

Further complicating matters are

the complex meta-retro aesthetics of pop-culture-obsessed Generation Xers for whom the lamps represent a form of "retro-retro." For such individuals—who enjoyed the lamps in the late '80s as a retro throwback but then grew out of this "pure" retro phase and rejected them, only to eventually develop nostalgic affection for their original retro feelings—it is hard to assess how they truly feel about the lamps.

"Remember back in '88, '89, when everybody had lava lamps in their dorm rooms because they were so hilariously evocative of the late '60s, early '70s?" said Todd Wakefield, 31, a recent lava-lamp re-reconvert. "That was awesome."

"Lava lamps? Please. I remember back in '88, '89, when everybody had one in their dorm room because they were trying to be all late '60s, early '70s," said Jen Cushman, 31. "Talk about over. Having a lava lamp now is *so* late-'80s late '60s/early '70s."

Still others say they view the matter altogether differently.

"It all depends whether you're talking about straight, unironic, revivalist retro or one of the numerous strains of pre-X and Gen-X irony," said Seth Burks, 29, author of the award-winning Athens, GA-based 'zine *Burning Asshole*. "I've identified 22 distinct varieties of irony-informed retro and non-retro aesthetics, including camp, kitsch, trash, schmaltz, post-schmaltz, and post-post-schmaltz. It's time we addressed the woeful inadequacies of the government's current retro-classification system."

The report marks the latest in a string of controversies for the embattled Department of Retro, which is still feeling the effects of 1998's bitter infighting over the still-unresolved issue of "classic" rock. The department was further rocked in May 1999, when Setzer replaced then-Retro Secretary Donny Most, who stepped down after refusing to endorse *That '70s Show.* ∅

The Return Of Mad Cow

Mad-cow disease is once again sweeping Europe, prompting renewed fears on this side of the Atlantic, including a New York-area recall of Mamba, a candy that contains beef gelatin. What do *you* think?

"So long as Mallo Cups remain untainted, I care little about this."

Matt Maldonado
Bartender

"Mad Cow? Isn't that the guy on the Z-106 Morning Nuthouse? I always knew there was something wrong with him."

Victoria Ewart
Legal Secretary

"Does this candy knock children unconscious for an hour or so? Oh. Never mind, then."

Benjamin Ruff
Machinist

"Now I can finally unload all this mad-cow-related merchandise."

Oscar Kinnard
Systems Analyst

"People are overlooking an important aspect of this crisis: Have you actually seen a cow staggering around drooling? It's hilarious."

Warren Hough
Civil Engineer

"Germany is being forced to slaughter 400,000 cattle. Luckily, they're pretty good at that sort of thing."

Susan Royce
Hairstylist

Celine's Baby

After years of publicly wishing for a child, Celine Dion finally gave birth to a son on Jan. 25. How is the world reacting to the blessed event?

15% Shedding tears, so many joyous tears

22% Awarding Dion medal of honor from La Société Des Chanteuses Québécois Anorexiques Avec Les Svengalis Anciens

11% Grabbing pitchforks, amassing at base of Castle Angélil to demand destruction of monstrous spawn

8% Recoiling in abject horror

10% Hand-knitting booties specially tailored to fit baby's terrifying mutant flippers

14% Sending letters of congratulations to Dion, condolence cards to child

20% Accidentally stepping between mother and offspring, provoking attack from Dion's powerful clawed forelegs

⌀ the ONION
America's Finest News Source

Herman Ulysses Zweibel *Founder*

T. Herman Zweibel *Publisher Emeritus*
J. Phineas Zweibel *Publisher*
Maxwell Prescott Zweibel *Editor-In-Chief*

FOUNDED 1871 • "TU STULTUS ES"

Your Horoscope

By Lloyd Schumner Sr.
Retired Machinist and
A.A.P.B.-Certified Astrologer

Aries: (March 21–April 19)
Though you'd like to think of it as a triumph of the human spirit, it's really just the opening of a Krispy Kreme doughnut shop three blocks from your office.

Taurus: (April 20–May 20)
Soon your 15 minutes of fame will be up, and people will only know you as "that freaky-looking guy who survived the barbed-wire-plant explosion."

Gemini: (May 21–June 21)
This week will be noteworthy for your whirlwind tour of the American criminal justice system.

Cancer: (June 22–July 22)
The stars would love to tell you your fortune for next week, but it lacks the tinge of verisimilitude that would make it believable.

Leo: (July 23–Aug. 22)
You will go down in snowboard history for accidentally inventing the "540 Goofy-Foot Christa McAuliffe" while nailing siding on your mountain cabin.

Virgo: (Aug. 23–Sept. 22)
Nothing can stop you this week as you accelerate to a considerable fraction of the speed of light.

Libra: (Sept. 23–Oct. 23)
Please stop telling your coworkers you've been "nailing" your new secretary. The polite term is "nailing love to."

Scorpio: (Oct. 24–Nov. 21)
You can claim anything you want in your song, but, truth be told, by the time you get to Phoenix she'll have forgotten all about your hick ass.

Sagittarius: (Nov. 22–Dec. 21)
Remember: That which does not kill you makes you stronger—even if it paralyzes you from the neck down and necessitates the removal of your renal system.

Capricorn: (Dec. 22–Jan. 19)
You're eventually going to get tired of people comparing next Thursday to the Flying Wallenda Tragedy of 1963.

Aquarius: (Jan. 20–Feb. 18)
After next week, you will no longer wonder where the phrase "I'll be dipped in shit" came from.

Pisces: (Feb. 19–March 20)
Perhaps the color and positions of the stains on your boyfriend's mattress can offer a clue as to how he earned the money he's stuffed inside it.

WEATHER from page 71

"While we cannot turn back the clock and prevent this malodorous incident from taking place," Auslander said, "we can take action as soon as possible to save Americans from exposure to the resultant common household odors."

Emergency air-freshening measures being implemented include the planting of more than 50,000 pine-scented trees along the U.S.-Canada border, the distribution of 35 million cans of Glade Mountain Spring spray to those citizens most at risk, and Operation Airwick, a full-frontal airborne assault on the wave of stale air.

But even with all these efforts, some experts say it will likely be too little, too late. "Even if 50 million pounds of potpourri were spread across American soil, it would merely be a flowery cover-up," said James Valentine of the D.C.-based Americans For Freshness. "Ventilating and re-scenting the ecosystem will take months and bring federal votive-candle and incense resources down to near-critical levels. This nation needs fresh, pleasant air now."

"In reality," Dr. Martin Hargreaves of Cornell University said, "we would need a Stick-Up the size of Vermont to adequately address this crisis."

Across the U.S., the damaging effects of the unfreshened air are already being felt. "Yesterday, when I woke up, I wasn't greeted by the usual light, flowery breeze blowing in through my window," said Georgia Wells of St. Petersburg, FL. "Instead of a fresh rose-petal scent, I could distinctly detect a staleness in the air. It was horrible."

"As an American, if there's one thing I can't stand, it's a lack of freshness," Marcia Palmer of Sunnyvale, CA, said. "That's why this current crisis is so terrible. Cigar smoke, fish odor, smelly old sweatsocks—it's all too much to bear."

Palmer then wrinkled her nose and added, "Oh, I see the Arctic Circle still has that cat."

Responding to the public outcry, President Clinton has pledged to work with the National Weather Service toward the goal of having the nation completely aired out by the end of next week. Clinton also acknowledged that his interest in solving the problem is to some degree personal.

"Next Friday, I will be hosting an important state dinner, at which there will be numerous foreign dignitaries," Clinton said. "If these high-level diplomats arrived with the United States smelling like old sneakers and tell-tale pet odors, I could never show my face at a world summit again." ⌀

Cottonelle Introduces New 'Piping-Hot' Toilet Tissue

see PRODUCTS page 12D

Violinist Sick Of Doing Mozart Covers

see ARTS page 4B

4-Year-Old Dressed Nicer Than Local Man

see FASHION page 1E

Dildo Washed

see LOCAL page 7C

STATshot

A look at the numbers that shape your world.

Top Regional-Interest Fiction
1. Hot Winnemucca Nights
2. Bury My Heart In Kentuckiana
3. Murder On Washtenaw Avenue, Right Where It Veers Left By The Water Tower
4. Frankenstein & Dracula Meet Da Yoopers
5. Are You There God? It's Us, Southcentral Missouri
6. Magnum, WI
7. The Bridges Of Western Madison County, Not The Obviously Inferior Ones In The Eastern Part

THE ONION
VOLUME 37
ISSUE 05

$2.00 US
$3.00 CAN

0 74470 94595 6

09

the ONION

VOLUME 37 ISSUE 05   AMERICA'S FINEST NEWS SOURCE ™   15-21 FEBRUARY 2001

Report: Mankind's Knowledge Of TV Trivia Doubling Every Three Years

NEW BRUNSWICK, NJ—According to a report released Monday by Rutgers University's Center For Media Studies, mankind's collective knowledge of TV trivia is increasing at an astounding rate, doubling every three years.

"Our species' familiarity with the details of specific *I Love Lucy* episodes is 16 times what it was during the show's ratings peak in 1955," said Dr. Timothy Klennert, director of the Center For Media Studies. "For example, 80 percent of Americans are able to name the bogus health tonic that got Lucy drunk during the episode 'Lucy Does A TV Commercial,' compared to 5 percent the day after the program's original airing."

Klennert attributed the trend to the rise of such rerun-driven cable

networks as Nick At Nite and TV Land, as well as the increased availability of classic TV episodes on home video. Also cited was the proliferation of Internet sites offering TV-trivia quizzes and books crammed with statistics and factoids about the history of the medium.

"In today's media-rich environment, a person pretty much has to

live in a cave not to be exposed to TV trivia," Klennert said. "There are infants who haven't even watched television who can name all six Brady kids. It's practically genetically encoded."

Klennert praised the dedication of U.S. television viewers, who have "tenaciously studied and absorbed TV trivia in the face of so many other forms of information competing for their attention."

"In 1987, only 16 percent of Americans could sing the entire *Family Ties* theme song, including the 'Sha-la-la-la' ending, compared to the 67 percent who can sing the *Friends* theme today. If we continue at our current pace, it is not inconceivable that by 2010, there will be a TV theme song that achieves 100

see TRIVIA page 77

Congress Holds Weekend Trust-Building Retreat

LURAY, VA—Seeking to foster a spirit of unity and teamwork between Democrats and Republicans under the new Bush Administration, members of Congress attended a trust-building retreat in Virginia's Shenandoah National Park this past weekend.

"For years, Congress has been sharply divided along party lines, with Democrats and Republicans fighting against one another to further partisan goals," President Bush said. "But this weekend, the congressmen came to realize that the only way to accomplish anything—whether it's reforming

see CONGRESS page 74

Left: Speaker of the House Dennis Hastert (R-IL) leads Sen. Russ Feingold (D-WI) and Rep. Dick Gephardt (D-MO) on a blindfolded walk through the woods.

Irrepressible Bad Boy Slays Seven

WEST HOLLYWOOD, CA—Watch out, ladies: Irrepressible bad boy Jordan Jeffries, that hard-partying Hollywood hunk who's on everybody's A-list, is at it again.

Paroled Jan. 19 after spending six months in Los Angeles County Jail for cocaine and gun posses-

sion, the club-hopping cut-up and legendary lothario was once again in hot water Saturday after gunning down seven bystanders at the red-hot L.A. nightspot Skybar, dispatching his victims "mercilessly and at point-blank range," according to police reports.

see BAD BOY page 75

Above: Jordan Jeffries flashes his killer smile.

Pantomimed Lasso Motion Fails To Pull Woman Across Dance Floor

SCOTTSDALE, AZ—Russ Bakke, 37, unsuccessfully attempted to pull an unnamed female across a nightclub dance floor Saturday with a pantomimed lasso motion. "After making eye contact with the young lady and giving her a seductive smile, I attempted to rope her in with my invisible lasso of love," Bakke said. "But for some reason, when I threw the lasso toward her and mimicked a pulling motion, she was not drawn my way." Subsequent attempts to capture the woman with a pantomimed fishing rod and butterfly net also met with failure.

Jerry Lewis Undergoes Emergency Gefloigel Surgery

LOS ANGELES—Less than an hour after doctors discovered that the gland had become all screwy with the infections, legendary comedian Jerry Lewis underwent emergency surgery to remove his gefloigel Monday. "We had to go in through Mr. Lewis' schlaphlecky system, bypassing the oy-hayvel," said Dr. Jacob Weisz, Nice Mister Chief of Surgery at Cedars-Sinai Medical Center. "But in the end, we were able to get him all being better and healthy, you know." Doctors have prescribed Lewis several weeks of bedrest, with the sleeping and the flowers and the nice music and hrrrrrn.

Star Wars Gamer Magazine Boldly Claims To Be The Leading Magazine For *Star Wars* Gamers

NICASIO, CA—The debut issue of *Star Wars Gamer*, which hit newsstands Monday, audaciously boasts that the magazine is "the world's leading publication for *Star Wars* gaming fans." "Whether you're looking to take your character on an adventure on Yavin IV, soup up your B-wing fighter, or paint an army of Stormtrooper miniatures, *Star Wars Gamer* is the only *Star Wars* gaming source you'll ever need," the issue brashly proclaims. Said Chad Burnley, an Athens, GA, *Star Wars* gamer: "They are certainly going out on a limb to make this claim. If a second *Star Wars* gaming magazine were ever to be published, they'd have to work really hard to maintain their number-one status."

'Army Of One' Campaign Attracting Troubled Loners To Military

WASHINGTON, DC—The Army's new "Army Of One" campaign is attracting millions of troubled loners, recruitment officials said Monday. "Historically, Army enlistees are creepy, antisocial drifters," said Sgt. Glenn Decinces of the Army's Recruitment Office. "After years of trying to attract stable, achievement-oriented young patriots with the slogan 'Be All You Can Be,' we finally gave up and decided to consciously go after the freakos we've always drawn."

Movie Deemed Acceptable For Mom And Dad

LOCK HAVEN, PA—Looking for a video to watch with his parents during a weekend visit, 28-year-old Steve Berg rented *Small Time Crooks* Sunday. "This seems good—no sex or violence," said Berg, studying the back of the box. "I could get *Analyze This*, but there's an outside chance it has some bad language." While home last Thanksgiving, Berg squirmed through *Double Jeopardy* with his mother, unaware that it contained brief nudity. ∅

CONGRESS from page 73

Social Security or getting three people over a 20-foot wall with just a yard of rope and an old milk jug—is through cooperation."

Upon arriving at the orienteering cabin, Speaker of the House Dennis Hastert said he heard a great deal of complaining from fellow legislators about being taken away from important lawmaking work.

"[Sen.] Sam [Brownback (R-KS)] was bellyaching about having a ton of bills to read. [Rep.] Earl [Hilliard (D-AL)] was saying the retreat was 'gay' and 'for babies,'" Hastert said. "However, a quick bicameral game of Build-A-Song soon broke the ice and had everyone clapping."

Build-A-Song, in which each participant contributes a line about him or herself to a growing song, was well-received by virtually all of the 535 lawmakers, with only Sen. Strom Thurmond (R-SC) showing difficulty keeping meter.

Subsequent exercises offered the legislators physical activity and fun, but also challenged them to reevaluate the way they look at themselves and their peers.

"I was really scared to lean back and fall into Orrin Hatch's arms," Sen. Carl Levin (D-MI) said of Saturday afternoon's "Open Arms" workshop. "After all, this was a man who blocked countless pieces of legislation I'd tried to pass over the years. But when I finally worked up the nerve to do it and he caught me, I realized I'd just been saved from physical harm by someone I thought was my enemy. Right then, my eyes were opened, and I thought, hey, I'm around good

Above: Sen. John McCain (R-AZ) falls into the arms of Sen. Ted Kennedy (D-MA), learning about the importance of bipartisan trust.

people in Congress."

Another exercise, in which the legislators sat Republican-Democrat in a circle and had to say one nice thing about the person to their left, proved embarrassing at first, but ultimately strengthened the bonds between the participants.

"I was really touched when Rep. Bill Jenkins (R-TN) told me he admired the way I stood up for my constituents' interests by fighting so hard for H.R. 2403, which would bring $197 million in infrastructure upgrades to my home district," Rep. Paul Kanjorski (D-PA) said. "During House debate, he called the bill 'pork-barrel politics at its worst.' But when we were sitting in that circle, he apologized and admitted that he only said mean stuff about the bill because he was trying to impress a senior Republican who was head of a subcommittee he wanted to get on. That meant a lot to me."

Added Kanjorski: "Ever since the retreat, Bill and I have been inseparable. We're even going to co-sponsor a bill."

The final challenge of the weekend, in which members of Congress were forced to "buddy up" across party lines and build a log bridge across a 75-foot-wide creek, proved the most trust-building experience of them all.

"When they told us we were supposed to build a bridge across that huge creek, we thought, no way, that's impossible," Rep. Dick Gephardt (D-MO) said. "But with a little imagination and a whole lot of teamwork, we actually did it. Now we feel like we can forge a better, more cooperative U.S. government—as long as we remember to trust each other."

"When we finally finished, [Sen.] Jesse [Helms (R-NC)] started jumping up and down on the bridge yelling, 'Yes! We did it!' and then he slipped and fell in the water," Sen. Tom Daschle (D-SD) recalled with a smile. "It was a little scary, because at first he didn't come up to the surface. But when he finally did, he just started laughing. Then I started laughing and, before long, everybody was laughing. And when I reached into the creek to pull Jesse out, he pulled me *into* the water instead! You better believe everybody was cracking up after that happened. And, boy, did we ever splash each other."

On Monday morning, members of the newly strengthened 107th Congress were sent home with their experiences, their memories, and T-shirts featuring caricatures of all the participants.

"As President Bush kept saying on the bus ride back to D.C., whether Democrat or Republican, deep down, we are all the same," Daschle said. "And to have fun working together is the only way to make America great." ∅

Customer's Attempt To Complain To Manager Thwarted By Employee

ELGIN, IL—A customer's repeated attempts to complain to the store manager about Mama Z's Pizza employee Matt Wheaton were successfully thwarted by Wheaton, restaurant sources confirmed Monday.

"At about 10 p.m., this guy calls up bitching about how he got sausage on the pizza we delivered, going all apeshit because he's, like, a vegetarian or something," the 20-year-old Wheaton told reporters while mopping behind the counter. "So I was like, 'Tough break, man'—you know, trying to sympathize with him. But that just totally pissed him off for some reason."

Wheaton said he attempted to determine whether the customer, Gary Marchese of 344 Gloria Street, could "deal" with the pizza as is or if he wanted to go through the trouble of having another one delivered.

"He got all mad about that, as if I was insulting him by saying he should just pick the sausage balls off," Wheaton said. "He told me

that even if he picked them off, the meat juice was still all over the pizza. Finally, I was like, 'Okay. What the fuck. I'll send the driver out with another one right away, sir.'"

An hour and a half later, Wheaton answered the phone to

> ## "That guy didn't just want his money back," Wheaton said. "He wanted to rat on my ass."

find Marchese, 54, inquiring as to the whereabouts of his replacement pizza. He informed Marchese that "someone" must have forgotten to put in the order.

"So [Marchese] says, 'Well, Matt, you are the person I spoke

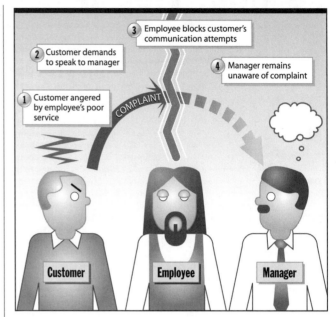

with, aren't you?'" Wheaton said. "Right then and there, I knew this guy was gonna be trouble, remembering my name like that. Sure

enough, he cuts loose with, 'Could I please speak to the manager? Perhaps he can help me get my

see CUSTOMER page 78

BAD BOY from page 73

Witnesses said the sexy and oh-so-single Jeffries—best known for his role as daredevil test pilot Johnny Spade in the blockbuster *G-Force* movies—committed the murders "for no apparent reason," mowing down his terrified prey "with cold-blooded precision, deaf to their desperate pleas for mercy." Ouch!

Jeffries, 29, who has been romantically linked to everyone from Charlize Theron to James King to Amanda Peet, has slayed plenty of women with his drop-dead-gorgeous looks. But with five males among his seven victims, this notorious ladykiller seems to be a mankiller, too.

"He has all the markings of a sociopathic psychotic, showing no remorse for this brutal mass slaying," said LAPD profiler Dr. Leila Briedel-White, who conducted a psychological examination of the homicidal heartthrob following his arrest.

"What he did is beyond the capacity of a normal human being."

"That certainly sounds like the Jordan Jeffries millions of viewers loved to hate as the duplicitous ladies' man Gregg Grant on *To Have And To Hold*," said *Soap Opera Digest* editor Ellen Bright. "But unlike the character he played on *THATH*, Jordan isn't just breaking hearts—he's firing .38-caliber slugs into them, as well."

The arrest marks the latest in a string of brushes with the law for Jeffries, dubbed "The Multiple-Convicted Felon Who Cannot Be Tamed" by *Us* magazine in its May 2000 cover profile. Past charges range from misdemeanor reckless endangerment and disturbing the peace to such A-list crimes as felonious assault, vehicular manslaughter, and transporting a minor across state lines for immoral purposes.

In 1997, the free-spirited Jeffries was nearly extradited to France for his involvement in a Paris hotel fire that left four dead, but his lawyers managed to get him off with a $50,000 fine. This time, LAPD authorities say, if he's convicted of the shootings, the hot-blooded actor and part-time bassist for the band Rocketdog will face stiffer penalties, including seven consecutive life sentences and/or up to 40 hours of community service.

Lew Adelman, Jeffries' longtime manager, remains optimistic. "Jordan is a sensitive, deeply fragile creative talent, and he's had his share of hard times," Adelman told *Daily Variety*. "Yes, he's a troubled soul, but we're confident that if we can sufficiently prove psychological instability, an insanity verdict can be reached in

time for him to complete shooting on *G-Force IV: Maximum Thrust*. If the trial goes well, his six-week guest spot on ABC's *Whizzer & McDeal* should be unaffected."

Lawyers for the talented but troubled actor expressed confidence that they can have the multiple homicide charges reduced to a lesser offense, provided the recidivist Romeo—recently spotted at the ultra-hip Hollywood S&M dungeon and sex club Der Vault with his bodyguard and two unnamed models in tow—agrees to drug and alcohol rehabilitation and psychological counseling.

Will Jeffries curb his notoriously wild ways? Don't count on it. As he was led away by police after a 45-minute armed standoff, the ever-quotable Casanova told reporters: "I killed them all! And I'll do it again! Do you hear me? I'll keep on rampaging like an unstoppable murder machine until I breathe my last breath on this accursed Earth!"

Even if found not guilty, Jeffries has more legal hurdles to clear: He still has two other trials pending, one stemming from a much-publicized fistfight with a transvestite prostitute in a Burbank alleyway in May 1999, and the other for allegedly assaulting a photographer after a night of drug-fueled partying with rapper Ol' Dirty Bastard and teen socialite Nicky Hilton at music mogul David Geffen's Aspen bungalow. He also faces a $23 million civil suit stemming from a March 2000 incident in which he allegedly kidnapped, tortured, and sodomized three Santa Monica teens. ∅

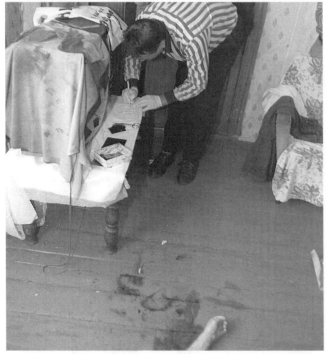

Above: The scene of a 1997 double homicide many believe was committed by the notorious bad boy.

Fashion Victim

A few days ago, if you'd asked me what "nepotism" meant, I would have guessed it was some sort of eye disorder. But boy, oh, boy, Jeanketeers, since then I've learned what the word really means! (The hard way!)

A Room Of Jean's Own
By Jean Teasdale

When I began working at Fashion Bug, I thought I'd finally found my dream job: decent pay, flexible hours, and the chance to have truly important responsibilities. I was even given my own keys to the cash-register drawer and a special register code so I could correct any cashiering errors I made! I never had that privilege at any of my other retail jobs. I always had to wait for the supervisor to come and delete the error, getting an icy glare in the process!

Best of all, I was almost up to 40 hours a week. And you know what being full-time means: Yup, employee discount!

Then, out of nowhere, came trouble with a capital T. Or, in this case, a capital E! Her name was Ellen. (Actually, that's not her real name. My editor recommended I change it to avoid getting sued for libel. So her real name begins with a different letter.)

A few weeks before Christmas, Ellen was hired as an entry-level sales associate, just like I'd been three months earlier. The more the merrier, I figured. With the Christmas rush on, we sure needed the extra help.

Anyway, Ellen was the best friend of the store manager, Roz. She was divorced with two kids and really needed a job because the state was cutting off all her assistance if she didn't go back to work. (A policy I wholeheartedly supported—until I saw what Ellen's presence at Fashion Bug meant for me!)

On Ellen's very first day, a Monday, Roz had me train her on the cash register. You know, being a cashier may look easy, but it's not. You have to pay attention to giving out the correct change, remember to itemize each sale correctly as a check, cash, or credit card, and change the register tape before it runs out. And if you don't balance at the end of the day, you have to go through the tape and try to find your mistake.

So here I was, trying to train Ellen. Notice how I said "trying," because Ellen hardly paid any attention at all!

"I had a lot of these type jobs before my marriage," she told me, "so I know what I'm doing." When I told her that if she made an error, I'd

delete it with my special code so she could do the sale over again, she stifled a laugh. I asked her what was so funny. She said she couldn't help it, but that I was just acting so serious about everything. Well, that irked me a little. I like to think of myself as a fun-loving person, but I was trying to train her, so I couldn't be all happy-go-lucky, now, could I? (Maybe she should've gone to work with those cutups over at Hot Sam's a few doors down. I can't even order a pretzel there without hearing people tittering in the back kitchen!)

So, after lunch, Ellen got on the second register. And, sure enough, at the end of the day when we rang out the totals and counted everything, Ellen had recorded two credit-card sales as check sales and was $5 short. That meant Ellen had to go down on the employee-error ledger. Because she was new, she was entitled to three major cashiering mistakes a month instead of the customary two. But if she committed any more than that, she could have her probationary period lengthened by a month.

The following Monday, I was scheduled for the afternoon shift. I walked in and saw Ellen at the register. I couldn't believe my eyes: Not only was her "trainee" badge replaced with an "Ellen" one, around her wrist on a stretchy cord was a key: her own register-drawer key! I rushed into the back office and confronted Roz.

"Ellen's only been here a week," I said. "How come she got a key so soon?"

"This seasonal rush has me swamped, and I'm too busy to check on the cashier area all the time," Roz replied. "Ellen is doing well enough

that if she needs extra cash, she can sign it out from the vault herself. Oh, and I gave her correction privileges, too. She knows what she's doing, Jean. She used to be my boss when we both worked at Merry-Go-Round."

I was speechless. I had to wait until the end of my probationary period to get my keys and correction privileges! Ellen loses $5 for the company, and within days she's given what it took me three whole months to earn? What's the point of even having a probationary period if the rules can be flouted like that?

I tried to look on the bright side. After all, if Ellen kept to the register, she couldn't fold clothes in that sloppy way of hers. One time, I practically had to redo an entire table of women's shaker-knit sweaters because she let the sleeves stick out. Sheesh! (Boy, that Merry-Go-Round of hers must have been a real mess!)

For about a month, I hardly ever saw Ellen, because she worked mornings while I worked afternoons and evenings. Then, last Friday, when I arrived at work, I saw her chatting with Roz. At first, I thought Ellen was there to pick up her paycheck, but I noticed she was dressed a little nicer than usual, with a blazer and pearls. Then I spotted her nametag. It was managerial red, not sales-associate black.

You guessed it: Ellen got hired for the long-vacant assistant-manager position! Now, she was my boss! Worst of all, Ellen would get the coveted employee discount, while I worked just two fewer hours per week than her and had to pay full price!

I'm not exaggerating when I say that my world was shattered. I was so close to getting that assistant-manag-

er position, I could taste it! Granted, Roz never officially promised it to me, but it just seemed natural that I would get it after giving so much of myself to Fashion Bug. Didn't Roz remember when I volunteered to stay three hours after closing to assist with inventory? Or that time I helped her unpack and organize that larger-than-expected shipment of misses' rayon career blouses? Or when I showed up at the Christmas party with my notorious Ecstasy In Chocolate Surprise, which everybody said was the best dessert they'd ever tasted, hands down?

Suddenly, Fashion Bug didn't seem like a fun place with cute, kicky, affordable clothes and plentiful opportunities for advancement. It was almost like it became this depressing place that offered cheap clothing of inferior quality in an underpatronized strip mall in an economically depressed part of town.

That evening, as I told hubby Rick what I just told you, his eyes started to glaze over like he was hearing the most boring story in the world. When I finished, he just looked at me and said, "So? I've been passed over for tons of promotions over the years, but I don't get all worked up about it. Like I always say, life's a bitch and then you die." Then he returned to his all-important living-room-floor slot-car race. Gee, thanks for the loving support there, Rick!

I think folks like me who get passed over for promotions they clearly deserve should form a union. Can you imagine how powerful we'd be if we all banded together and demanded that our voices be heard? Maybe there's already a union like that. If there is, could someone please let me know how I can join? Solidarity, Jeanketeers! ✐

the ONION presents a Valentine's Day Kids Page!

Gasp! It's Valentine's Day, and you still haven't found the perfect valentine for your special little friend. Not to fret! Here are some dear little valentines, all ready for delivery. Use a safety scissors to cut them out, then affix them to cardboard with school glue or sticky tape. Remember to have Mom help you. Have fun!

My Collection Of Cassingles Is Second To None

Kassingle Korner
By Larry Harroway

In the realm of the true musical aesthete, there are some who rise above the madding crowd. At the risk of seeming immodest, I must confess that I am a member of this elite upper strata. I have put my love of music before all else in my life, and I feel supremely confident in asserting that my collection of cassingles is second to none.

I will stake no less than my reputation on this claim. No cassingle I have sought has ever eluded me. Ever.

Sigue Sigue Sputnik's impossible-to-find cassingles from its critically reviled 1988 sophomore effort *Dress For Excess*? Some deny that any were released, but I've got them both.

The complete run of every Howard Jones cassingle ever produced, including the ultra-rare "Life In One Day" promo cassingle—mint in shrink-wrap, no less—issued two months prior to the official release of the megaselling *Dream Into Action*? I am proud to say I own two such runs in their entirety.

I treasure my comprehensive libraries of such Cassingle Era giants as Hall & Oates, Mr. Mister, and Laura Branigan in equal measure to my extensive archive of such one-cassingle wonders as T'Pau, Nu Shooz, and Boys Don't Cry. In all the world, is there a collection of cassingles equal to my own? No. No such collection exists, except in dreams.

In the history of civilization, has there ever been a medium of musical expression to rival that pearl of elegant simplicity, the mass-market cassingle? I care for CDs and MP3s no more than I do 8-tracks and 45s. Keep your so-called "perfect" digital-sound reproduction of the post-cassingle age: Nothing can top the unpolished grit of omnipresent tape hiss for sheer, visceral impact on the listener. Until you've heard Ready For The World's "Oh Sheila" on cassingle, you haven't truly heard it.

I hold the same disdain for full-length cassettes that I do for other non-cassingle formats. Why would anyone want to taint the emotional purity of a lyric like Steve Perry's immortal, "Oh, Sherrie / our love / holds on / holds on," by burying it within the sad tangle of lesser works that is *Street Talk*? To soil "Oh Sherrie" with such musical miscarriages as "Captured By The Moment" and "Running Alone" is tantamount to blasphemy. Nay, heresy.

The cassingle separates the wheat from the chaff, zeroing in on the one song that truly deserves our undivided attention. And there is no awkward rewinding process, as identical programs are presented on both sides, so that the chosen song may be heard over and over again without stopping, until the very soul itself is illuminated in its glory.

I am in possession of the complete Thompson Twins cassingle *oeuvre*. I own all four hit cassingles spawned by Huey Lewis & The News' *Sports* album. I have Thomas Dolby's entire cassingle canon meticulously catalogued and annotated. And I don't mean only those from the *Golden Age Of Wireless* sessions. I mean everything, including his promotional cassingle from the *Howard The Duck* soundtrack.

Klymaxx? Shalamar? Atlantic Starr? The Deele? The solo careers of such former frontmen as Michael McDonald, Peter Cetera, and Colin Hay? I have always treasured them—they will always be a part of my collection.

Now, I realize that my cassingles collection—lo, the cassingle format itself—is not without its detractors, particularly my brother Doug. He says they take up too much space for just one song. As if any price to enjoy the greatest musical format known to man could ever be too great! He resents the flimsy paper sleeves that protect the precious music within. But as I gently run my fingertips along the warm, softly textured cardboard spine housing Animotion's "Obsession" cassingle—so much more inviting than a cold, hard CD jewel case—I am acutely aware that Doug could not be more wrong if he had asserted that the Earth is flat.

And, of course, some grouse that cassingles deteriorate rapidly after only a handful of listens. They say they melt when you leave them on a dashboard in summer. They say they are easily chewed by an angry boom box. Fools! Do they not see that the poignant inevitability of such decay only serves to make each listen all the more bittersweet?

I will never be able to erase the memory of that heartbreaking day when the clerk at Sam Goody told me that the commercial manufacture of cassingles had been discontinued forever. But I know my collection will live on. For as I comb thrift stores and church bazaars for cassingles, as I tirelessly search the Internet for them, as I rifle through boxes in my cousin Jeffrey's attic, I know that the breathtaking experience of hearing Dennis DeYoung belting out "Desert Moon" on spooled magnetic tape shall be preserved for future generations.

My cassingles collection is the finest in the land. Believe that. Ø

TRIVIA from page 73

Above: Some of the once-obscure TV shows that a majority of today's Americans can easily identify.

percent saturation."

Some complain that the TV-trivia explosion has come at a cost, contributing to a general decline in interest in subjects such as math, science, and history. For others, however, the trade-off has proven enormously profitable.

"I have no idea what a proton is," said *Who Wants To Be A Millionaire* contestant John Carpenter, who won $1 million for correctly identifying the U.S. president who appeared on *Laugh-In*, becoming the subject of a TV-trivia factoid in his own right. "Fortunately, the million-dollar question had nothing to do with such basic scientific knowledge."

According to Mark Bennett, author of *TV Sets: Fantasy Blueprints Of Classic TV Homes*, not only are more Americans trivia-savvy than ever before, but the quality of the trivia itself is increasing.

"It's no longer all that impressive to know that two different actors played Darrin on *Bewitched*," Bennett said. "To impress these days, you'd have to know that there were two Mrs. Kravitzes. Or two Louise Tates. Or that Jerry Seinfeld was on the second season of *Benson*."

Pondering the future of TV trivia, Bennett said: "One day, I envision a world in which every American knows that *Happy Days* was a spin-off from a 1972 *Love, American Style* episode. A world in which the phrase 'No whammies!' is instantly associated by all with the '80s game show *Press Your Luck*. A world in which the importance of TV trivia is as universally undisputed as the greatness of the first three seasons of *St. Elsewhere*." Ø

Clinton And The Fugitive Financier

Congress is investigating Bill Clinton's pardon of Marc Rich, a major Democratic Party contributor who since 1983 has been living in Switzerland to avoid trial for racketeering, tax evasion, and trading with Iran. What do *you* think?

Hugh Carter
Math Teacher

"A powerful politician doing favors for a corrupt business crony? America has lost its innocence."

Patrick Poulon
Systems Analyst

"Would you do any less for a loved one or major campaign contributor?"

Jessica Smith
Graduate Student

"Marc Rich's plight is a lot like that of Native American activist Leonard Peltier, except Rich has eleventy gazillion dollars and isn't in jail."

Harriet Swann
Guidance Counselor

"I'm sure living a luxurious lifestyle in Switzerland for the past 18 years showed Rich the error of his ways."

Marc Cowart
Electrician

"Come on, let him go. The poor guy's done his time. He was president for eight years, for God's sake."

Henry Thalacker
Custodian

"I wish Clinton could have pardoned my ass out of jail for robbing that camera store. Oh, and also for my oil deals with Iran."

The Cruise-Kidman Divorce

After 10 years of marriage, Hollywood power couple Tom Cruise and Nicole Kidman announced their divorce on Feb. 5. What were the reasons for the split on each side?

Cruise's Complaints:

Kidman grew nearly one foot since beginning of marriage

Forced to carry bulk of family's financial burden, earning $140 million a year to Kidman's $19 million

Mental image of wife making love to a sailor drove him into seamy underworld of sexual obsession and desire

Misses early days when it was just he, Kidman, and collected writings of L. Ron Hubbard

Kidman, despite protests, continued to age

Kidman's Complaints:

Abusive "I'm prettier/No, I'm prettier!" arguments would go on for days

Cruise always insisted on renting his movies at video store

Can't stand dealing with actors

Unlike Cruise, wanted to raise children as statuesque redheads

Alienation of affectation

the ONION
America's Finest News Source

Herman Ulysses Zweibel *Founder*

T. Herman Zweibel *Publisher Emeritus*
J. Phineas Zweibel *Publisher*
Maxwell Prescott Zweibel *Editor-In-Chief*

FOUNDED 1871 • "TU STULTUS ES"

Your Horoscope

By Lloyd Schumner Sr.
Retired Machinist and
A.A.P.B.-Certified Astrologer

Aries: (March 21–April 19)

Your admirable decision to lead a life of honesty and moral rectitude will bring your career in advertising to a sudden and drastic end.

Taurus: (April 20–May 20)

You will be pursued by millions of hungry nutrition-conscious Americans when it is revealed that you are part of a complete breakfast.

Gemini: (May 21–June 21)

After six weeks, you still haven't figured out how Jonah got so much done from inside one of these things.

Cancer: (June 22–July 22)

Your habit of standing on your desk and flailing about with a fire ax will continue to be distracting and divisive at your office.

Leo: (July 23–Aug. 22)

Your striking resemblance to TV's Craig T. Nelson will somehow fail to get you laid for yet another week.

Virgo: (Aug. 23–Sept. 22)

You've always said that premature baldness never killed anybody, but the tragic events of next week will force you to eat those words.

Libra: (Sept. 23–Oct. 23)

After 12 years of living alone in the bush, you're beginning to think the damned snipe is never going to show.

Scorpio: (Oct. 24–Nov. 21)

You will go down in linguistic and polar history next week when it is discovered that the Eskimos have more than 600 words for what a big jerk you are.

Sagittarius: (Nov. 22–Dec. 21)

Next week's trials and tribulations will force you to stand tall and be a man, even though you were born short and female.

Capricorn: (Dec. 22–Jan. 19)

Though you'll certainly be proud to have your own action figure, you would have rather had one that didn't feature realistic spastic-colon action.

Aquarius: (Jan. 20–Feb. 18)

The nation is stunned by Amelia Earhart's miraculous return, especially when she knees you in the groin and shouts, "Thanks for nothing."

Pisces: (Feb. 19–March 20)

Remember, the impressive thing is not how well the bear dances. It's how incredibly sexily the bear dances.

CUSTOMER from page 75

money back.'"

Wheaton said he wasn't fooled by the customer's request. "That guy didn't just want his money back," he said. "He wanted to rat on my ass."

Though manager Vance Endries was in the back of the store facing dollar bills, Wheaton told the irate customer that he had stepped out for a few minutes "to go to the bank or something."

"Normally, I wouldn't care if somebody bitches me out to the boss," Wheaton said, "but after skipping work twice last week, I was an ass hair from getting canned."

Vowing to call back later, Marchese asked for Wheaton's last name. Wheaton told him it was Jones. As an added protective measure, for the remainder of his shift, Wheaton answered the phone with an accent somewhere between French and Jamaican. Though Marchese did not call again, he showed up in person the following day.

"This guy comes in and is stand-ing by the door sort of checking everyone out," Wheaton said. "Then I hear him ask Katie [Sullivan] if the manager is in. I knew it had to be that guy from the night before. This time, Vance really was gone, but I ran to the back and got Sid."

Though only a dishwasher, Sid Bricken, a 42-year-old recovering alcoholic and the oldest member of the general staff, was someone Wheaton believed could pass for a manager. Bricken listened to the customer complain about Wheaton for nearly 10 minutes while nodding sympathetically.

"I told the guy I'd put Matt on probation, and I also gave him a bunch of gift certificates and a two-liter bottle of whatever soda he wanted," Bricken said. "He wanted to keep complaining, but I told him I had to go do some manager stuff in the back."

"[Marchese] thought he could outsmart me," said Wheaton, opening an industrial-sized can of sliced black olives. "Well, think again, dude. Think again." Ø

the ONION®

VOLUME 37 ISSUE 06   AMERICA'S FINEST NEWS SOURCE™   22-28 FEBRUARY 2001

Brad Pitt Bored With Sight Of Jennifer Aniston's Naked Body

see PEOPLE page 10D

Area Man Fills Important 'Demand' Role In Economy

see COMMERCE page 2E

Cub Scout Wishes They'd Taught Him How To Chew Through Ball Gag

see LOCAL page 4C

STATshot

A look at the numbers that shape your world.

Top Spin-Off Series

1. Sipowicz's Place
2. Acquaintances
3. She's The Daughter Of The Sheriff And Now Is The Sheriff Herself
4. Mannix Babies
5. Yan Can Clean Up Afterwards
6. Family Law Nights
7. Star Trek: A New Journ—You Know What? Fuck This

THE ONION
VOLUME 37
ISSUE 06
$2.00 US
$3.00 CAN

Nigeria Elects Black President

AFRICAN FOCUS

Above: Bilikisu Adewale waves to supporters after becoming the next black man ever to lead Nigeria.

ABUJA, NIGERIA—In a historic triumph for Nigeria's African-African community, Bilikisu Adewale, a 49-year-old black man, was elected president Monday.

"Today is a great day for the people of Nigeria," Adewale told a cheering crowd in his 30-minute acceptance speech. "But even more so, today represents a tremendous victory for this nation's black citizens, who came to the polls in full force to put one of their own in power."

"I am overwhelmed," Adewale added. "This is truly precedented."

Addressing the largely black crowd, Adewale, who served as Nigeria's Foreign Minister from 1993 to 1998, pledged to defend the interests of the nation's sizable black community. Among his chief campaign promises was to increase funding for schools in Nigeria's inner cities, outer cities, and middle cities—areas with a high concentration of blacks.

"I grew up in an extremely poor, all-black section of Lagos and attended schools that were overcrowded and horribly equipped," Adewale said. "For many blacks of my generation, the experience was the same. I want every member of the current generation of black youths to read from new textbooks and learn in state-of-the-art facilities. We must leave no child behind."

As a further measure, Adewale said he planned to declare March

see NIGERIA page 82

Grueling Household Tasks Of 19th Century Enjoyed By Suburban Woman

SAUSALITO, CA—Ellen Brinkworth, a 37-year-old homemaker from the upscale San Francisco suburb of Sausalito, enjoys spending her free time engaged in the back-breaking labors of a 19th-century pioneer woman.

"My friend Linda came over Saturday and we spent the whole day making soap," Brinkworth said. "We made some absolutely gorgeous shell-shaped pink hand soaps and some wonderful oatmeal facial-scrub bars. And it was so easy: All you do is dissolve lye in water, weigh out the hard and liquid oils, melt it on the stove to 110 degrees, stir until smooth, add fragrances, pour it into the molds you've pre-lined, wait for it to

see WOMAN page 81

Above: Brinkworth and one of her handmade candles.

Guy At Bar A Little Too Into Stevie Ray Vaughan

EUCLID, OH—According to Main Street Tavern employees and patrons, the guy at the end of the bar is a little too into deceased blues guitarist Stevie Ray Vaughan.

Bar-goer John Menke said that the guy, an unidentified beret- and denim-vest-wearing man in his early 30s, should be avoided "unless you want to talk about Stevie Ray Vaughan for at least an hour."

"I go up to get another pitcher of beer, and this guy at the bar just stares at me, biting his lip and nodding his head to the Stevie Ray Vaughan song on the jukebox," Menke said. "I try to look away, but then I accidentally make eye contact for a split second. That's when he says to me, 'Man, there'll never be another SRV.' Before you know it, I'm trapped listening to

see VAUGHAN page 84

Above: The guy (right) discusses Stevie Ray Vaughan with an uninterested stranger.

Bush Still Getting Clinton's Mail

WASHINGTON, DC—More than a month after moving into the White House, President Bush continues to receive former occupant Bill Clinton's mail, Bush reported Monday. "Is it so hard to fill out a change-of-address form at the post office?" asked Bush, waving a copy of *Rolling Stone* addressed to Clinton. "I suppose he expects me to mail all this to him." Bush added that if one more Sierra Club newsletter arrives for Clinton, it is going straight into the trash.

Ostensibly Heterosexual Man Constantly Threatening To Put Objects Up Coworkers' Asses

IRVING, TX—Though married and ostensibly heterosexual, Westech Data Systems office manager Douglas Briar is constantly threatening to anally penetrate male coworkers with office supplies. "Keep it up," Briar warned coworker Trent Lonegan Monday, "and I'll ram this toner cartridge up your ass." Briar has made similar threats involving staplers, three-hole punches, coffee pots, and rolls of fax paper.

New Energy Secretary Guesses He Ought To Read Up On Energy

WASHINGTON, DC—Spencer Abraham, the newly installed U.S. Energy Secretary, admitted Monday that he probably ought to read up on energy. "I know energy is really important, and that there was a big crisis back in the '70s, but other than that, I'm in the dark," Abraham said. "I was hoping to be appointed Secretary of Transportation, which I know a lot more about, but that one was already taken." The former Michigan senator said he plans to go to the library Thursday to look up "Energy" in *The World Book Encyclopedia*.

Australian Forced To Flee Homeland To Sell His Microwave Omelet Cooker

BURBANK, CA—Mick Hastie, Australian political refugee and inventor of the Perfect Omelet microwave omelet cooker, recently fled his native land for the U.S., where he is free to sell his amazing new device without fear. "I am a man without a country, forced out by a corrupt regime that thinks omelets can only be prepared the old-fashioned way, in a greasy skillet," Hastie told a studio audience from the set of his infomercial Monday. "I fled in a leaky tramp steamer, risking death but knowing I'd at least be free of the tyranny of the stove-top omelet." Hastie added that you cannot imprison an idea, and that clean-up is a snap.

Pre-Teen Moves From Giggling-At-Everything Phase To Never-Smiling Phase

WATERVILLE, ME—Cori Schmidt, 12, went through a substantial life change Tuesday, moving from the giggling-at-everything stage of adolescence to the never-smiling stage. "My goodness, just the other day, I accidentally left a pair of old pantyhose on the couch, and she was jumping all over the living room giggling hysterically," Hannah Schmidt, 41, said of her maturing daughter. "But now, everything I say to her is met with a gloomy scowl." Asked if she was aware of her passage into sullenhood, the younger Schmidt said "I don't know" without making eye contact. ∅

Human Tragedy Tops Nielsens

LOS ANGELES—The Fox network's Feb. 15 broadcast of a shark attack on a shipwrecked boatload of Haitian refugees garnered a Nielsen-topping 27.6 rating and 48 share, dominating its 8 p.m. time slot and positioning itself for a 13-week series option, television-industry insiders reported Monday.

The win caps a yearlong trend of human tragedy as the top prime-time ratings grabber for the four major networks.

"We are pleased the shark-attack footage has struck such a chord with viewers," Fox Entertainment chairman Sandy Grushow said. "Of course, we knew people would tune in to watch real-life Haitians struggling desperately among flotsam and wreckage in the open sea, only to be eaten alive by ravenous, blood-crazed schools of sharks in a feeding frenzy, but we never expected these kinds of numbers."

"I'd just like to thank all the fans for helping us realize our dream of being number one," Grushow added.

The shark attack is the latest in a string of human tragedies to top the Nielsens. Among previous winners: CBS's November 2000 special on the cannibalization of a stranded Norwegian research team in Antarctica, ABC's *PrimeTime Thursday* report on villagers being dissolved by molten lava during recent volcano eruptions in Indonesia, and *Dateline NBC*'s five-part special *Crushed By An Enraged Bull Elephant*.

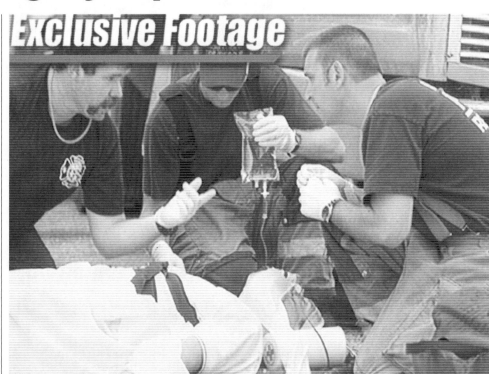

Above: A scene from a Fox special about parents who are killed in car accidents on their daughters' birthdays.

The success of such fare has cemented human tragedy's status as the primary programming directive for the coming season.

"When networks announce their Fall 2001 schedules in May, the watchwords are going to be 'pain and suffer-ing,'" *Los Angeles Times* television columnist Howard Rosenberg said. "CBS has already gotten a jump on the trend by greenlighting *Widowed By War*, and NBC is reportedly in negotiations for an as-yet-untitled series about earthquakes that orphan small chil-dren, leaving them to wander alone through rubble, howling in confusion and despair as they scrounge for food like animals."

Human tragedy, a mainstay of the dramatic arts for thousands of years,

see NIELSENS page 81

You And Me And Baby Minus Me Makes Two

By Len Datillo
Expectant Father

Honey, a miracle has happened—you've got a bun in the oven. How wonderful! Before long, this family is going to be bigger by none. After all, you and me and baby minus me makes two.

It's hard to believe that soon there are going to be two people in our little brood. Nothing brings two people closer together quite like one of them being a mother and the other a child. No, there's nothing in the world more special than that.

You and I are going to have so many good times together until you start to show! And after that, you and the baby will have so many good times together, too. Of course, I'll be having great times on my own. I know that might be hard to believe right now, but don't worry—it's true. I'll be having an absolute blast.

> You and I are going to have so many good times together until you start to show! And after that, you and the baby will have so many good times together, too.

Just think of the happy, loving family we'll make: You and the baby, plus me 700 miles away. That's the kind of family I've always wanted, and you've made it possible. It's truly a dream come true.

A woman plus her child minus a man there to provide support; now, that's what I call the perfect couple. And let's face it: The whole idea of couplehood is kind of ruined by a third person, isn't it? But I wouldn't want you to be the one who has to give up all that beautiful couple stuff. So I'll do the responsible thing and bow out. I'll be a man about it. Do you think you'd even want me around? I know I wouldn't. It just wouldn't be right.

A pair of little feet running around the house. That's exactly what you need! And I need my own pair of feet to run out of the house as quickly as possible. I can't believe how wonderful this is going to be for at least one of the three of us.

Oh, wow, this is such a magical time! You're really, really going to have a baby! And I'm not! Not in the physical sense, of course, and not in the "couples' ubiquitous we" sense, either. I'm just plain not going to be there at all, and I can't tell you how great that makes me feel.

Watching our child's birth, seeing it grow, hearing its first word and seeing its first step—I'm going to burst with joy over not seeing a single one of these things. I can hardly wait for the blessed event of me moving far away, someplace where all this baby business is just a memory, and a short-lived one at that.

You and the baby have made me the happiest man in the world. Not long ago, I didn't know what I was going to do with my life. But now, you and the baby have given me the strength and courage to high-tail it out of town as fast as humanly possible. Thank you, from the bottom of my heart, for making my life complete again. I love this so much. ∅

NIELSENS from page 80

has in recent decades been overtaken in the televisual arts by wacky pratfalls and bawdy sexual innuendo. But tragedy is making a big comeback, industry insiders say. Funny and sexy are out; horrific and senseless are in.

"Since the time of Aeschylus, human tragedy has captivated the human mind," said media and pop-culture analyst Kurt Andersen, founder of Inside.com. "Yet the current popularity of televised atrocity—beheadings, disembowelings, and immolation by chemical fires at the sites of industrial accidents—is something new. Never before have we seen such flaunting of the misfortunes of innocents by the major television networks. Because of content restrictions which hampered TV throughout most of its history, raw unedited footage of, say, a Afghan peasant mother and her five screaming children being hacked to pieces by Taliban militiamen was considered 'inappropriate' for viewer consumption."

However, Andersen said, with the advent of the Internet and the effect it has had on traditional television broadcasting, all that has begun to change.

"Now that these constraining standards of propriety have at long last loosened, we are in the middle of a 'Golden Age of Human Tragedy,'" Andersen said. "And it has made for some great TV."

Industry observers expect human tragedy to continue drawing big audiences—and big revenues—in the coming years. CBS just wrapped shooting on the series *Venereal Archipelago*, which will feature 16 young, single islanders slowly succumbing to worsening stages of syphilis. NBC's *Tragic Event Sunday* will document massacres by Third World despots and train accidents involving chemical spills. And ABC News' much-hyped six-part series on Angolan child amputees disfigured by abandoned land mines is expected to wrap up during November sweeps. Other hot topics coming to the small screen in 2001 include starvation, killer-bee attack, and gang rape. ∅

TV Ratings: The Nielsen Leaders
Week of Feb. 5, 2001–Feb. 11, 2001

Program	Network	Rating	Share
1. *The Final Minutes Of Flight 283*	Fox	27.1	40
2. *Watching Grandma Fade*	CBS	23.6	33
3. *Amanda: Gone Too Soon*	ABC	19.0	31
4. *ER*	NBC	17.4	26
5. *My Son's Eyes Are Mrs. Griffith's Now*	NBC	14.6	23
6. *Law & Order*	ABC	14.3	21
7. *Everybody Loves Raymond*	CBS	13.9	21
8. *The Make-A-Wish Foundation Presents: Blow Out The Candle*	Fox	13.8	20
9. *They're Going To The Prom In Heaven—The Fitchburg High Disaster Remembered*	NBC	13.7	22
10. *Becker*	CB...		

WOMAN from page 79

harden, cut it into blocks, and presto!"

In all, Brinkworth devoted nearly 10 hours to soap-making, a task which, until the late 20th century, was not considered an enjoyable leisure-time activity. She also spent all day Friday shopping for the necessary ingredients and supplies, which included eucalyptus oil, fresh rosemary leaves, lavender essential oil, colored wax, lye, coconut oil, palm oil, glycerin, rubbing alcohol, various fruits and dried flowers, and a soap mold.

Soap-making is not the only arduous 19th-century chore Brinkworth enjoys in her spare time. She also dips her own candles, re-upholsters foot stools, and makes her own clay pots.

"It's so neat to make something with your own hands," Brinkworth said. "There's nothing more pleasurable than spending a lazy Sunday afternoon churning butter."

According to Brinkworth, her love of grueling chores was inspired by author and television personality Martha Stewart. Brinkworth religiously watches *Martha Stewart Living*, a throwback to a time when women spent upwards of 14 hours a day maintaining the home. On last week's episode, Stewart showed viewers how to hand-dye cloth with the natural coloring found in flowers, plant roots, and bits of bark—a grinding, laborious task still performed in developing nations where commercial dyes are not available.

"I absolutely adore Martha," Brinkworth said. "I've gotten so many terrific ideas from her, like how to pick your own wild berries and make preserves out of them and how to refinish antique garden hand tools. I even saw an episode which showed Martha in her own hen house. Raising your own chickens—wouldn't that be so fun?"

According to Danielle Huson of the Bay Area Historical Society, for thousands of years, raising chickens was not considered "fun."

"Women used to do things like dye cloth, spin wool, and make candles as cost-saving measures, or because they lived too far from a major town to purchase these items," Huson said. "They certainly didn't do it for pleasure. In the 1800s, the average frontierswoman toiled all day long, and on the rare occasion that she had a moment of free time, she usually spent

> For thousands of years, raising chickens was not considered "fun."

it letting her bloody calluses heal."

Brinkworth's favorite activity is quiltmaking, an eye-straining, finger-numbing task which originated as a way to make use of small scraps of leftover cloth.

Said Huson: "In centuries past, many women didn't have a lot of fabric for blankets, so they were forced to make quilts out of whatever bits and pieces were lying around. Of course, to mimic these elaborate patterns, modern quilters buy yards of brand-new cloth from fabric stores and cut them up to resemble precious scraps."

"It's so fun to make quilts and do different crafts," said Brinkworth, removing a hand-sewn quilt from the washing machine and tossing it into the dryer. "I swear, sometimes I think I was born in the wrong century." ∅

81

"Black History Month." Throughout the month, he said, the nation will celebrate "the remarkable and oft-overlooked contributions of Nigerians of color."

"Do you realize that in this nation of 123 million people, there is not a single black-history museum or black cultural center?" Adewale asked. "Did you know that at the University of Nigeria, there are no black fraternities and no black student union? This must change. And it will, starting today."

But in spite of his optimism, Adewale cautioned that many daunting challenges lie ahead.

"Yes, this election is a great step forward for black Nigerians," Adewale said. "But there is much work to be done: A shocking 50 percent of our nation's blacks earn an income below the national average. The ever-present specter of black-on-black violence continues to loom over our communities. Our prison population is virtually 100 percent black. And each year in Nigeria, the dread disease of AIDS kills more blacks than all other ethnicities combined."

The Adewale win, which many are calling the greatest political victory for black Nigerians since the previous election, did not come easily. Throughout the seven-month campaign, Adewale tirelessly canvassed the nation, targeting predominantly black areas in an effort to capture the highly coveted African-African vote. During speeches, Adewale frequently emphasized issues of special concern to black Nigerians, including the economy, education, health care, and foreign policy.

As Adewale began to rise in the polls, his opponent, longtime Nigerian parliamentary leader Nshange Oduma, also attempted to court black voters, visiting numerous Hausa and Yoruba neighborhoods. But in the end, analysts said, such efforts proved too little, too late.

"The black vote is often the key to Nigerian elections," said Bikot Ughegbe, a reporter for *The Guardian*, the country's largest newspaper. "If you can win their support, you have an excellent chance of winning the presidency. Oduma simply waited too long to focus on black voters, and that cost him dearly."

The election now over, attention is turning to Adewale's cabinet nominations, which he is expected to begin announcing as early as Friday. Already, rumors are swirling that

Above: Black voters turn out in force to support Adewale.

Adewale will tap Bitek Kashoba, a high-ranking black general, for Minister of Defense. In addition, the new president is believed to be strongly considering Nolo Okoye, also black, for Minister of Transportation.

Throughout the presidential campaign, Adewale promised that, if elected, he would appoint a significant number of majorities to his cabinet, creating "a government that looks like Nigeria." Ø

---

the ONION presents

Stargazing Tips

The night sky holds countless wonders. Here are some tips to help you make the most of your next stargazing experience:

- Be in the know about which stars are hot and which are not. Rigel: hot. Betelguese: not. Polaris: hot. Pleiades: not.

- If the evening you choose to take your kids stargazing turns out to be overcast, maintain their interest by announcing that it is an extremely rare "eclipse of everything."

- Though astronomy is a relatively safe hobby, keep in mind that stars are very, very hot and will burn for millions of years if left unattended.

- Remember the "ABCs" of learning about constellations: **A**lways **B**e learning about **C**onstellations.

- When contemplating the ineffable grandeur of the universe, nothing sets the mood quite like the airy, transcendent synthesizer sounds of Vangelis.

- Do not gaze directly at white-hot star Kate Hudson. Instead, poke a pinhole in a sheet of paper and look at Hudson's outline on another sheet of paper.

- Some may scoff at the hobby of astronomy, but sitting in an empty field in the middle of winter is a great way to see tiny little dots.

- Name your baby after a constellation. No one has ever thought of that before.

- Locate the Virgo cluster. Is it still there? Good... you're like the cop of the universe!

- Remember: Galileo was an astronomer, and they threw his ass in the clink. Exercise caution.

- There's one star that's incredibly easy to find. You have to wait until the daytime, though.

- When stargazing in South Florida, be sure to steer clear of territory controlled by Jack Horkheimer.

- Next time you go stargazing, bring a girl along. Set up in a field far from the city lights and take turns looking through the telescope. Then, when the right moment comes, kiss her. Kiss her! Don't let the opportunity pass you by—it may never come again! Kiss her! *Kiss her!*

Ask An Upscale Gift Catalog

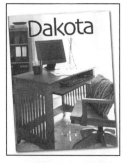

By Dakota, Spring 2001

Dear Upscale Gift Catalog,

My boyfriend and I have been dating for a year, and I think he could be The One. But there's one thing about him that drives me nuts: Whenever we eat out, he always insists on ordering for me. He says he's just being chivalrous, but I feel like it's his way of showing he's the one "wearing the pants" in the relationship. Am I overreacting, or is he showing signs of chauvinism that may rear its ugly head later?

—**Capable In Cape May**

Dear Capable,

It's 3 o'clock in the morning on a moonless night. Your wife is sound asleep. You suddenly have a million-dollar idea. The light is not an option. Your wife, the light sleeper, would surely be awakened. The pen and paper you keep on your nightstand seem a thousand miles away. Then you remember the Lexmore Lumiwriter. With a twist of the wrist, this remarkable pen emits a readable glow from its mushroom-like base, enabling one to write discreetly in complete darkness. Even in daylight, this sleek, ultra-modern tool is built for maximum function and beauty. Hand-crafted from a stunning mix of aluminum and mahogany and engraved with designs inspired by Aztec craftsmen, each pen is equipped with the patented Lexmore Ink-Flo distribution system and a lifetime guarantee. So you can go to sleep knowing that your idea is safely on the page and that your wife will wake up the next morning none the wiser.

Dear Upscale Gift Catalog,

My birthday is coming up, and every year, my mother-in-law insists on giving me some horrible outfit I would never, ever wear. Then, the next time my husband and I go out with her, she expects me to wear the thing. Is there an easy way to let her know I don't want to receive clothes from her anymore? Her heart is in the right place, but her fashion sense is all wrong.

—**Fashion Victim In Farmington**

Dear Fashion Victim,

A solitary backpacker in Milan. A sudden downpour. You seek shelter from the rain in a charming little café. You order a cup of the local blend and sit on the aged leather furniture. You look for something to read while you wait out the storm. Then you notice the bookcase. Sturdy. Handsome. Classic. The honey-stained oak lovingly lacquered by hand and covered in embossed leather. The Italian craftsmen who passed down this design for generations reveled in the beauty of the simple, strong lines that catch the eye but don't stand out. From the Italian countryside to the den, this bookcase exudes the wisdom of a man well-read and well-traveled. Also available in natural or chocolate.

Dear Upscale Gift Catalog,

When I'm at work, I'm constantly being bugged by coworkers to fix every little mechanical problem that arises. I was hired to be a data technician, but I spend most of my time fixing paper jams and replacing toner cartridges. I hate to tell my fellow employees to buzz off, but I need to do the work I'm being paid to do. Help!

—**Used In Utica**

Dear Used,

A Moroccan bazaar. The aroma of exotic spices fills your nose. The clangor of a thousand voices rattles your ears. You brush past vendors as they try in vain to get your attention. You duck into a back alley to catch your breath. Away from the chaos of the street, you spy an entrance to a lonely shop. You walk in. Immediately, you are drawn to the bundle in the corner. Unfurling it, you realize it's a Kashan-style Persian rug. You run your hands across its surface, knowing each thread was painstakingly woven by master craftsmen. The simple, muted earthtones belie a complex design unique to the region. Each rug is hand-knotted from 100 percent wool using only vegetable dyes. Equally at home on marble or hardwood floors, this rug takes center stage in any room. This one-of-a-kind rug won't last. It cannot possibly.

Persian Rug #PR50035.....................$5,740

Dakota, Spring 2001 is a nationally syndicated advice columnist whose weekly column, Ask An Upscale Gift Catalog, appears in more than 250 newspapers nationwide. ∅

Man Who Fought For Americans' Rights Demands Americans Stop Exercising Their Rights

WASHINGTON, DC—Speaking before the U.S. Senate Tuesday, Herbert Macallum, a retired Wichita, KS, insurance salesman and Navy veteran who fought during WWII to protect the inalienable rights of all Americans, demanded that U.S. citizens stop exercising those rights.

"As someone who risked his life for this country, I am infuriated when I see protesters exercising their First Amendment rights by burning the U.S. flag," Macallum told legislators during a Senate debate over a proposed anti-flag-burning amendment. "I didn't fight the Japanese at Midway to save democracy for a bunch of long-haired jerks who want to freely express their views."

"I love the Constitution, and I nearly lost my life defending it," Macallum added. "That's why it angers me so much to see malcontents exploiting it for their own purposes."

Macallum is president of the Kansas Veterans' Council for

Above: WWII veteran Herbert Macallum, seen here marching in a Wichita, KS, Memorial Day parade.

Liberty & Restraint, one of a number of veterans' organizations calling upon Congress to pass anti-rights-use legislation. Under the provisions of the proposed legislation, any U.S. citizen convicted of exercising his or her constitutional rights in a manner deemed controversial would face a fine and/or imprisonment.

Said KVCLR member Walter Mickleson, 81: "Wherever you look today, you see people using the First Amendment to openly criticize or protest the U.S. government. I don't think that's what the framers of the Constitution had in mind. And I, for one, didn't storm the beach at Normandy so I could see America dragged through the mud."

"Men gave their lives for the U.S. Constitution," WWII veteran Robert Schumer said. "I'm sure they would weep if they were alive to see it being followed so shamelessly. If you ask me, protesters who object to our government should not be allowed to vote."

KVCLR spokespersons cite such "societal ills" as flag-burning, pornography, public assembly for the purpose of protest, and the pursuit of "certain forms of happiness" as their motivation for founding the organization.

"The disorder that plagues American society today is rooted in our gross indulgence in civil liberties," said KVCLR treasurer and former Army pilot Donald Morrow, 79. "Servicemen fought and died for this great nation, and servicemen know that discipline, obedience, and blind faith in one's superiors and country are the key to domestic harmony. Civil disobedience is disrespectful to our government and has no place in a democratic society."

"I firebombed Dresden in 1943, and I lost a son in Vietnam," Morrow added. "What have protesters ever done for this country?"

Clarence Johnson, a retired Marine lieutenant who served in the Korean War, agreed.

"When I entered the United States armed forces, I gave up my constitutional rights in order to be a soldier," Johnson said. "It was one of the proudest days of my life. I had never exercised my rights much before then, anyway. Let me tell you, if you'd fought and seen friends die to protect the God-given rights of all Americans, you'd want to keep them from exercising them, too." ∅

The Tax-Cut Proposal

In his first major initiative as president, George W. Bush is lobbying hard for a controversial $1.6 trillion tax cut. What do *you* think?

Sunil Bardeekian
Forklift Operator

"Finally, the burden of raising a family on a meager factory-job salary will be lifted slightly. What? It won't? Damn."

Jill Yablonsky
Homemaker

"I'm not sure what to make of all this. Can I get back to you after tonight's *O'Reilly Factor*?"

Bill Bohnert
Custodian

"Income tax? Geez, I thought that highway toll I paid when we went to Taste Of Chicago last year took care of everything."

Hillary Green
Art Historian

"Is this one of those things that sounds great but only benefits the rich? Or is it one of those genuinely great, fairytale things that never really happens?"

Frank Muncie
Systems Analyst

"A 10-year, $1.6 trillion cut to revive a softening economy and rein in spending impulses in Congress? Four words: *Party at my place!*"

Tom Wilhoyte
CEO

"This would be a tremendous boon to me and my fellow corporate titans if any of us actually paid taxes."

Your Horoscope

By Lloyd Schumner Sr.
Retired Machinist and
A.A.P.B.-Certified Astrologer

Aries: (March 21–April 19)
Your conviction that there is meaning and purpose to life is shattered when you are reminded of the existence of Phyllis Diller.

Taurus: (April 20–May 20)
Though you know the difference between a pseudopod and a blastula, you can't figure out why you would suddenly sprout so many of them.

Gemini: (May 21–June 21)
Until next Thursday, you would have sworn on a stack of Bibles that unicycles couldn't explode.

Cancer: (June 22–July 22)
You will enjoy increased attention when you are chosen as the site of the 2008 Summer Olympics.

Leo: (July 23–Aug. 22)
You will finally achieve lasting peace of mind this week, moments after a wayward icepick removes your frontal lobe.

Virgo: (Aug. 23–Sept. 22)
Your whole view of the universe will change drastically when you learn you have been greatly overestimating the strength of the weak nuclear force.

Libra: (Sept. 23–Oct. 23)
No one can say you don't have good all-American values. After all, you're the House Of All-American Values off Route 40 in Davenport, IA.

Scorpio: (Oct. 24–Nov. 21)
Your conspiracy theory about a shadowy cabal of high-ranking Hardee's executives who run the Hardee's restaurant chain from behind the scenes turns out to be frighteningly close to reality.

Sagittarius: (Nov. 22–Dec. 21)
The worst thing about the bloody events of next week will be that Penn and Teller feel no need to apologize for any of it.

Capricorn: (Dec. 22–Jan. 19)
Though you're not sure why people are always telling you to go screw yourself, there's no real reason not to.

Aquarius: (Jan. 20–Feb. 18)
The derisive laughter of others is silenced when your deed to the Brooklyn Bridge turns out to be legal and ironclad.

Pisces: (Feb. 19–March 20)
Try to keep things in proper perspective this week, even after you lose your left eye to marauding longbowmen.

VAUGHAN from page 79

him go off about Vaughan's blistering guitar solo [on 'Cold Shot']."

After expounding on Vaughan's "fiery, impassioned guitar work" on "Cold Shot" for several minutes, the guy explained to Menke the song's origins.

"The guy says to me, 'Stevie used to sing this to the women he felt had wronged him, but he realized *he* was the one who was cold to women because of his addictions,'" Menke said. "I definitely got the feeling that this wasn't the first time this guy had ever told a complete stranger that story."

The guy was about to explain to Menke that the title of the album *In Step* was a reference to the 12-step program Vaughan had completed, but Menke excused himself to go to the men's room. After waiting in the bathroom the approximate length of time it would take to urinate, Menke ordered a pitcher of beer at the other end of the bar and returned to his table.

Main Street Tavern patron Bill Raychek, who later in the evening encountered the guy at the bar's pool table, said he "went on and on" about how Vaughan had finally begun to turn his life around and conquer his demons when he was tragically killed in the summer of 1990.

"I don't recall asking the guy to tell me about the night of Stevie Ray Vaughan's death in great detail, but he did," Raychek said. "As you no doubt know, Vaughan had just finished a show with Clapton, Buddy Guy, Robert Cray, and his brother Jimmie at Alpine Valley Music Theater in East Troy, WI, and was going to drive back to Chicago. At the last minute, though, he decided to board a helicopter instead. Shortly after take-off, in a thick fog, the chopper crashed into a nearby hillside, killing all five on board, including numerous members of Clapton's management team."

Continued Raychek: "When the guy told me that, I responded by saying, 'Wow,' in as uninterested a manner possible. But he just plowed on ahead, telling me how ironic it was that the last song Stevie ever played was a transcendent 20-minute version of 'Sweet Home Chicago,' almost as if he knew he'd be called home to the Lord that night."

Bartender Frank Aufiero said the guy's habit of steering any conversation toward the subject of Stevie Ray Vaughan was "extremely irritating."

"For some reason, I was talking to someone about Annette Funicello," Aufiero said. "Out of nowhere, the guy chimes in about how the soundtrack for the Funicello movie *Back To The Beach* has Vaughan collaborating with Dick Dale on a version of 'Pipeline.' It's almost like he's playing Six Degrees Of Stevie Ray Vaughan."

Aufiero acknowledged that he himself likes Vaughan, but said he finds the guy at the bar's enthusiasm "a bit much."

"Stevie's great, but there are other things to talk about in this world," Aufiero said. "I mean, when I go out someplace, I don't sit around saying things like, 'Without Stevie Ray Vaughan, there is no Jonny Lang or Kenny Wayne Shepherd.' If I didn't know better, I'd think this guy was hired by Vaughan's PR firm, but his territory is only this bar." ∅

The McVeigh Execution

The execution of Oklahoma City bomber Timothy McVeigh, recently set for May 16, is expected to be broadcast via closed-circuit TV to hundreds of the victims' loved ones. What else is being planned for the big event?

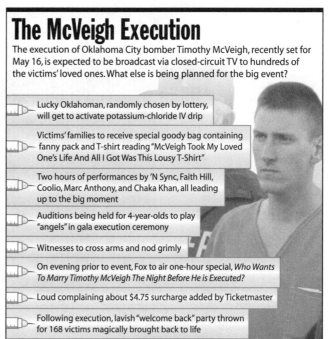

- Lucky Oklahoman, randomly chosen by lottery, will get to activate potassium-chloride IV drip

- Victims' families to receive special goody bag containing fanny pack and T-shirt reading "McVeigh Took My Loved One's Life And All I Got Was This Lousy T-Shirt"

- Two hours of performances by 'N Sync, Faith Hill, Coolio, Marc Anthony, and Chaka Khan, all leading up to the big moment

- Auditions being held for 4-year-olds to play "angels" in gala execution ceremony

- Witnesses to cross arms and nod grimly

- On evening prior to event, Fox to air one-hour special, *Who Wants To Marry Timothy McVeigh The Night Before He is Executed?*

- Loud complaining about $4.75 surcharge added by Ticketmaster

- Following execution, lavish "welcome back" party thrown for 168 victims magically brought back to life

the ONION ®

VOLUME 37 ISSUE 07   AMERICA'S FINEST NEWS SOURCE™   1-7 MARCH 2001

Bush Seeking Non-Masturbating Surgeon General

see PEOPLE page 10D

Area Man Participates In 21st-Century Cashless Economy

see COMMERCE page 2E

Lighthearted Romp Filmed

see MOVIES page 4B

Wrong Midriff Bared

see LOCAL page 7C

A look at the numbers that shape your world.

Where Are We Hiding Our Money?

1. In fake can of Heinz Pork 'N' Cash
2. Between cheek and gum
3. Under mattress at Don's Discount Bed Warehouse
4. Mir space station
5. Anal column of unsuspecting loved one
6. Sunshine Community Credit Union

THE ONION
VOLUME 37
ISSUE 07

$2.00 US
$3.00 CAN

0 74470 94595 6

Video-Game Violence Blamed In Giant-Robot Shooting Spree

OLD MURAKUMO DOME, MARS—A concerned parents' group is blaming a tragic shooting in the Martian Colonies on "excessive and reprehensible video-game violence."

Parents Against Robot-On-Robot Violence (PARORV) is calling for a ban on the giant-robot-themed PlayStation 2 game "Armored Core 2," which the group claims inspired a 17-year-old giant robot's Feb. 22 slaying of 13 giant robots and himself.

According to Martian authorities, the young assailant was obsessed with the violent game.

"From what we've seen, this appears to be a case of a giant robot who, through excessive exposure to giant-robot-battle video-game scenarios, lost the ability to distinguish fantasy from reality," PARORV spokeswoman Marianna Cutchek said.

The giant robot, a heavily armored high-end Zio Matrix AC, became addicted to the video game over the past year. Described by neighbors as "quiet" and "sullen," he played

Right: A 1999 yearbook photo of the young robot who committed the shooting. Left: The video game that allegedly inspired him.

"Armored Core 2" for upwards of nine Martian hours a day, avoiding contact with other giant robots his own age and becoming progressively more withdrawn.

Despite the presence of warning signs, no one

see ROBOT page 89

Supportive Gay Friend To Counsel American People On Ways Of Romance

WASHINGTON, DC—Reeling from countless relationships gone awry, blind dates from hell, and one-night stands that were about one night too long, the American people received help Monday in the form of tart-tongued but shrewdly perceptive gay friend Garrett Blaine.

At a White House Rose Garden ceremony, President Bush named Blaine, 30, U.S. Romance Counselor-General. Charged with dispensing no-nonsense relationship advice to more than 250 million Americans, as well as providing citizens with a shoulder to cry on, Blaine will summon every ounce of his

see FRIEND page 86

Left: Sassy, supportive gay man Garrett Blaine vows to be there for the American people.

Beauty Of National Forest Enjoyed By Logger

SAWTOOTH NATIONAL FOREST, ID—The rugged natural beauty of Idaho's Sawtooth National Forest was thoroughly enjoyed by logger Steve Orton Monday.

"This sure is beautiful country," said Orton, admiring the lush foliage surrounding him in most directions. "Just smell that fresh air."

An employee of the Northwestern Logging Company, Orton was dispatched as part of a team of 350 loggers to Sawtooth last Thursday after the company outbid dozens of competitors for a lucrative government contract.

"I could never work all cooped up in an office," said Orton, placing his coffee mug on a stump grinder, a three-ton machine used to pulverize tree stumps into sawdust.

see LOGGER page 87

Right: Logger Steve Orton takes in the breathtaking majesty of Sawtooth National Forest.

Bankrupt Dot-Com Proud To Have Briefly Changed The Way People Buy Cheese Graters

SAN FRANCISCO—Egraters.com, an Internet retailer that filed for Chapter 11 last week, announced on its homepage Monday that it is proud to have briefly made people rethink the way they buy cheese graters. "Unfortunately, we were not able to see our revolution all the way through," read the message from CEO Jeff Bell, 29. "But for a brief, shining moment, we showed the world that there *is* a better way to buy graters." Bell said he hopes to one day relaunch Egraters.com and "smash the tyranny of traditional brick-and-mortar cheese-grater-tailing."

6-Year-Old Cries When Told MTM Productions Kitten Dead By Now

RYE, NY—Following a *WKRP In Cincinnati* rerun Monday, 6-year-old Megan Connor was devastated to learn that the mewling orange kitten in the MTM Productions logo has almost certainly been dead for years. "All I said was that that kitten was around back when I was a kid, so it probably died 15 or 20 years ago," said father Bruce Connor, 39. "Now she won't come out of her room." Megan's parents plan to forbid Megan from watching *Family Ties* reruns for fear of having to explain the whereabouts of Ubu.

U.S. Changes Motto To 'America... We're Gonna Make Ya Smile'

WASHINGTON, DC—After a focus group determined "In God We Trust" to be "boring," the U.S. introduced a new motto Monday: "America... We're Gonna Make Ya Smile." "We feel the new motto projects a more playful image for the nation," State Department spokesman Marlon Harris said. "This new slogan tells the world that America Is Fun Country." Harris added that "E Pluribus Unum" will be replaced on all currency with "U.S. Fever—Catch It!"

Architect Asks Self How Le Corbusier Would Have Designed This Strip Mall

TOPEKA, KS—Architect Curtis Winter, designer of the planned Fox Plaza strip mall in downtown Topeka, found himself wondering Monday how influential 20th-century Swiss architect Le Corbusier would have approached the retail center. "I could imagine Le Corbusier using more sculptural roof-lines on the Play It Again Sports," Winter said. "And I could see the FuncoLand making a stronger impression from afar and evoking a modernized classicism if it were raised up on stilts." Winter previously made headlines for a Laundromat that echoed the abstract geometric designs of I.M.Pei.

Menu Describes Diner's Pancakes As 'World Famous'

FT. COLLINS, CO—A laminated paper menu for Smitty's Diner on Hwy. 32 describes the eatery's pancakes as "world famous," patron Annette Larouche discovered Monday. "Well, I guess I've been hiding under a rock," Larouche said. "I can't believe I made it this far in life without hearing of Smitty's World Famous Pancakes. Apparently, this is something people throughout Europe and Asia know all about." The menu also praised the eatery for "The Best Apple Pie Ever To Touch The Lips Of A Mortal." ∅

FRIEND from page 85 ▪

energetic, outgoing personality and gift for outrageous one-liners.

"All Americans—not just stylish urbanites—should have access to a sassy, supportive gay sidekick with whom they can share their romantic trials and tribulations," Bush said. "It is as basic a right as a good education or complete medical coverage."

Blaine, who when not attending to wounded veterans of the dating wars works at the Racy Stamen Floral Boutique & Oxygen Bar in Los Angeles, attempted to explain his knack for helping heterosexuals with their love woes.

"A lot of people ask me, how does a gay man know so much about solving straight people's romantic problems?" Blaine said. "Honey, if I knew the answer to that, I'd be God. And I know I'm not God, because I'm not black or female! Well, not black and only about a quarter female."

Continued Blaine: "I can always tell when something's wrong with the U.S. populace when they come into my shop. Their posture's drooping, or they avert their eyes, or they tell me they love my new turquoise polka-dotted shoes. Oh, boy! That's when I know something's wrong. So I roll up my sleeves, brew up a big pot of java, haul the cheesecake out of the fridge, and say, 'Okay, American people, this is Garrett you're talking to here. What's eating you? And don't say 'a Brazilian cabana boy,' because I won't believe you.'"

In the years prior to his appointment, Blaine tirelessly supported nearly 8,000 Americans as they braved the roller-coaster ride that is modern romance.

"If it weren't for Garrett, I'd probably be with yet another guy who's

Above: Blaine offers support and encouragement to La Crosse, WI, brewery worker Bob Sharpe, whose wife recently cheated on him.

more committed to his health-club membership than to me," said Alyssa Ennis, an insurance-claims adjuster from Saginaw, MI. "Instead, he told me to take a chance on that nerdy-but-nice tech-support guy at work, because, as Garrett put it, 'He may wear a *Star Trek* necktie, but he's better than those Klingons you've been dating!'"

Continued Ennis: "Neil and I have been together for more than a year, and we just got engaged! Thanks, Garrett!"

Another American who has benefited from Blaine's help is Santa Fe, NM, bookstore employee Andrea Adkins. In 1996, Adkins was 100 pounds overweight and involved with a man who constantly derided her appearance.

"I was very unhappy with this guy," Adkins said, "but I felt that, looking the way I did, beggars can't be choosers."

Outraged by Adkins' predicament, Blaine closed his shop and moved in with her. "I took one look at Andrea," Blaine said, "and I immediately thought, now, there's a gal who needs a flamboyant, frank-talking sidekick."

Over the course of the next year, Blaine coached, coaxed, and cajoled Adkins down to a svelte 110 pounds. He also encouraged her to pursue the open position of children's-section manager at her bookstore and helped her gain enough self-respect to dump her no-good boyfriend once and for all.

"Garrett saved my life," Adkins said. "There has been a 180-degree turnaround in the way I look at things. Instead of being the beggar, now I'm making them beg. As Garrett says, 'You go, girl!'"

Blaine's clientele is not entirely female. Brad Cochrane of Shreveport, LA, contacted Garrett in November after a second attempt to reconcile with his girlfriend failed.

"When I picked up Garrett at the airport, the first thing he did was put his hands on his hips, cluck his tongue, and say, 'Brad, old buddy, do we ever have our work cut out for us,'" Cochrane said. "I had no idea what he was talking about. But then he gave me the news."

Blaine, Cochrane recalled, bluntly informed him that his number-one roadblock to reconciling with his girlfriend was his slovenly wardrobe.

"We went straight to the mall, where I tried on clothes as ZZ Top's 'Sharp Dressed Man' blasted over the P.A.," Cochrane said. "Garrett chose enough Armani suits and Hugo Boss casual wear to outfit an army. I told him I didn't have enough money for all that stuff, but Garrett just said, 'Baby, you just need to hop on board a certain train called the American Express.'"

After receiving a crash course in etiquette from Blaine, Cochrane unveiled his new look to his girlfriend at a fancy French restaurant. Sure enough, she agreed to give him another chance.

"I'd still be sitting home alone in my pizza-sauce-stained sweatpants if not for Garrett," Cochrane said. "He's a real straight shooter."

Informed of Cochrane's use of the adjective "straight" in describing him, Blaine emitted a mock shriek.

Though Blaine is renowned for his skills as a pal and confidante, little is known about his own love life.

see FRIEND page 88

New Parents Desperately Seeking Other New Parents For Socializing

BETHESDA, MD—New parents David and Diane Huber, both 28, remain locked in a desperate search for other parents with whom they can talk exclusively about children, child-rearing, and their beautiful eight-month-old son Tyler, sources said Monday.

Despite a few tentative signs of progress—including the discovery of a new-parent Internet bulletin board, a brief conversation with a new father in their pediatrician's waiting room, and a possible get-together with Marc and Allison Wofford, new parents they met through their pastor's aunt—the Hubers' quest has been slow going.

"I really liked Rob and Kim, didn't you?" Diane asked David, referring to a couple the Hubers cornered near the swingsets at a Bethesda-area park upon spotting them with a stroller. Absent-mindedly musing as she folded tiny pieces of cloth, Diane added, "We really should get together with them sometime. It seems like we have a lot in common." Diane knows nothing about the couple that is not baby-related.

"We should all go out to dinner," David replied. "Although, maybe it would be easier just to have them over to the house for dinner, because I'm still not all that comfortable with the whole babysitter thing."

> "I really liked Rob and Kim, didn't you?" Diane asked David. "We really should get together with them sometime."

David and Diane then concluded that it would be great if the other couple, whose last name they failed to obtain, brought over their baby, too.

Friends and neighbors see no end in sight for the Hubers' quest, which has produced few viable candidates for new-parent socializing due to the lack of

see PARENTS page 88

Right: David and Diane Huber with son Tyler at age three months.

LOGGER from page 85

"I only feel at home when I'm surrounded by nature in all her magnificent splendor."

One of the largest national forests in the U.S., the 2.1 million-acre Sawtooth boasts an astonishing variety of terrain, from wildflower-covered meadows to towering mountain peaks. With many areas only accessible by helicopter, Sawtooth is considered one of the most pristine old-growth forests in America.

"I've been a logger all my life," Orton said. "I've worked in a lot of areas, but this was definitely one of the most awe-inspiring. It was so beautiful and untouched, it was almost like we were the first people to set foot here. I know that's not true because people used to camp out here, but they cleaned up after themselves so well, you'd never know it."

Orton, a self-proclaimed "nature lover and all-around outdoorsman," reported that the first tree they felled was especially impressive.

"For some reason, we decided to start with this enormous western hemlock," said Orton, motioning to what is now a 15-foot-wide stump. "During a break, Wally [Dassle] decided to count the rings and there were 160 of them, which means that

Above: A section of forest that Orton said "was absolutely awe-inspiring."

tree had been here since 1841. Just think about all the history that's happened since that tree was a sapling."

In addition to admiring the trees, Orton said he has "a real soft spot" for the local wildlife.

"You wouldn't believe how many elk we saw over there," said Orton, pointing to what is now a pock-marked, heavily eroded field. "Every

morning, before we started work, one or two would come out of the trees into the clearing to say hello."

"Most days, we see animals while we're setting up camp, but after we begin we don't see them anymore," Orton said while filling the gas tank on a professional-grade chainsaw. "I keep forgetting to take a camera with me to snap some shots."

For nearly a week, Orton has been working on clearing 1,200 acres of the Sawtooth National Forest, with the lumber to be turned into 2x4s or presswood.

"This is an incredible area," said Orton, patting the bark of a Sitka Spruce. "Sometimes, when we're on break and everything's quiet, the rustling of the remaining foliage almost seems to be talking to me."

Orton said that even though he and the other loggers are working, they have set aside time for fun.

"When we first got out here, we'd fish during our lunch break," Orton said. "Russ [Keely] caught a 30-pound Steelhead, and we all got pretty excited. We haven't been able to fish the last few days, what with the logs and all, but it sure was fun while the river was still clear."

With the logging project scheduled for completion March 4, Orton is determined to enjoy his remaining time in the forest.

"Russ and I talked about seeing who can scale that huge one over there the fastest," said Orton, pointing to a 100-foot-tall spruce. "We'll have to do it soon, though, because we're taking it out right after lunch tomorrow." ∅

I Have Expensive Taste In Trucks

By Karl Wineke

Call me stuck-up. Call me a snob. That's fine with me. Because what you call snobbery, I call refusing to settle for anything less than the best. Yes, for me, nothing but the finest trucks will do.

It's true. I have no patience for anything but the absolute crème de la crème in trucking hardware. And if you don't have a top-quality truck, well, I have no patience for you, either. You can take your chintzy Ford Rangers and your gauche Chevrolet S-10s and just sweep them under the rug for all I care. Don't bother me with them. They might be decent trucks if you're a migrant worker or on welfare, but they certainly aren't the kind of vehicles I would ever be caught dead in. A true truck connoisseur like myself requires the sort of pick-up that makes men nod in appreciation and women go weak in the knees.

Show me a late-model F-150 Lightning Flareside with the optional Pearlcote Metallic two-tone paint and performance suspension package. Or a Silverado Z-71 Indy 500 edition Dualie. Those are the sorts of trucks that will make a refined truck aesthete like myself take notice. Even your stock Dodge Ram 1500 is nothing to sneeze at. (Although you really need a lift kit and a bedliner, if not a topper, before you can really call it a capital-T truck.) But even without such accoutrements, it's still a vehicle that says you have some measure of self-respect.

Sometimes, I wonder if people have any standards anymore. All over my hometown, I see people driving some of the tackiest trucks you've ever seen. Now, I'm not made of money, although I have a decent-paying job down at the plumbing supply. But if you're not going to spend what money you have on a classy truck, what *are* you going to spend it on?

Yes, it can be hard to have such discriminating tastes. But high standards are important to me. Only the finest trucks have ever graced the Karl Wineke garage. (Except, I suppose, for that regrettable bit of Subaru Brat-slumming I did in trade school. But, Jesus, I was just out of the Navy and looking for any trashy bit of cargo-hauling capacity I could find, and I never regretted it for a moment.) Of course, nothing worth having ever comes cheaply. I worked hundreds of extra hours for the 30-horse winch, the fully appointed crew cab, and the comprehensive towing package, and I am proud to have done so.

You have to sacrifice to get the kind of rolling stock that's worth driving. When I wanted the XLT luxury package on the Ford, that meant Janice and I had to keep the old bedroom a while longer. Checking the chrome-trim option box on the order form meant we had to put off having kids for a few years. And, though it's gone unspoken, Janice and I both realize that installing the full fog- and driving-light package means we're not taking that second honeymoon to Florida any time soon.

But when you're a true aficionado, it's worth any price to have a good truck, a proper truck, a truck that's just right. I have no idea how the other guys at the plumbing supply can look at themselves in the mirror knowing that their trucks lack accessory electrical outlets and that big Triton V-10. But when I look in the mirror, I see the face of a man who appreciates the finer things in life, and has the truck to prove it. And if you ask me, that's all that really matters. ✍

PARENTS from page 87

other new parents in their extended social circle.

"David used to go bowling every Sunday night with the league at Bumper's Bar and Grill," said onetime friend Carl Henkins. "We always got along real well because we both like boats. Plus, I'm a big Philadelphia Eagles fan, and David went to college in Philly. But now, the few times he comes down to bowl, it's always, 'When Tyler was born, he weighed almost as much as this bowling ball,' or 'Speaking of shoe rental, you should see the booties we bought Tyler last week' or some other such nonsense."

"I mean, come on, I've got a 5-year-old girl myself," Henkins said. "But that doesn't mean I can't keep my bowling life and my family life separate."

The primary cause of the Hubers' inability to relate to their former friends, David said, lies in their friends' unwillingness to talk exclusively about parenting.

"Ever since the baby arrived, my old buddies have been acting really weird around me," said David, warming a bottle of formula. "Like, just the other day, I met Jason [Niering] for a game of racquetball, which I hardly ever have time for anymore. When I got there, I started telling him how Tyler had been lying on his back that morning, grabbing his ankles and swinging his legs up over his head, and how it was noteworthy because neither Diane nor I had ever seen him do that particular move before."

After pausing for approximately four minutes to remove a messy diaper, clean Tyler's soiled backside, find a Wet-Nap, apply powder, put on a fresh diaper, and return to warming the now-cold bottle, David continued: "So, anyway, I'm not more than four or

> ## "Ever since the baby arrived, my old buddies have been acting really weird around me," David said.

five minutes into the story when all of a sudden, Jason says, 'What does this have to do with anything? Will you serve, already?' Totally out of the blue. I mean, what provoked that outburst?"

Henkins and Niering are not the only friends from whom David has "grown apart."

"Me and Tony [Lake] used to hang out all the time because we were both into cars," he said. "Now, it's just not the same. Every time we get together, it seems like all he ever talks about is cars."

Diane has noticed an increased distance from her old friends, as well. Over the past several months, she has frequently remarked that none of them seem to share her interests anymore. The lack of conversation with others her own age, Diane said, has made her feel lonely at times.

"What with all the work I have to do taking care of Tyler, I'd sure like to spend some time with other adults every now and again," Diane recently told her mother, in between anecdotes about Tyler, during a long-distance phone call. "I'm a well-rounded person, and I have lots of interests: like where the best public schools in the area are, when is the right time to introduce pets into the home, what is the best way to set up a college fund, the whole issue of immunizations—you name it."

As pathetic and self-deluding as it may seem, the Hubers' plight, experts say, is actually quite common.

"It is not unusual for the parents of a new baby to feel terrible isolation, as the demands of parenting force them to spend less and less time with friends," said noted family therapist Dr. Eli Wasserbaum. "Yet it is possible to cope with these changes. All the Hubers need is to find someone—pretty much anyone with a pulse, really—they can spend a little time with away from the baby, yet with whom they can talk about nothing but the baby for hours on end, without making the other person feel like tearing his or her hair out and screaming. That's all." ✍

FRIEND from page 86

"Garrett has been out of the closet for years, but I can't remember him ever having a steady boyfriend or even a date," Adkins said. "In fact, I've never even seen him kiss a man. Isn't that strange? It's almost like he's asexual."

"At first, I was kind of uneasy about Garrett's homosexuality," Cochrane said. "But after I found out he probably never actually does it with a man, he became safe and non-threatening."

Blaine will have his work cut out for

> ## Though Blaine is renowned for his skills as a pal and confidante, little is known about his own love life.

him Thursday, his first official day in his new position: Karyn Robles of Grand Junction, CO, has not yet told her boyfriend that she hates his new mustache. Joe Barents of Huntington, NY, is still waiting in vain for a phone call from a lingerie model with whom he had a blind date two weeks ago. And Meredith Crouch of Durham, NC, was recently asked to dinner by her boss, with whom there has long been a simmering mutual attraction, but she feels it might jeopardize her career. Should she or shouldn't she?

"Hold the fort, buckaroos," Blaine said. "It's Garrett to the rescue!" ✍

A Homey In Need

By Herbert Kornfeld
Accounts-Receivable
Supervisor

All y'all disciples of tha H-Dog know that The Man always be tryin' to playa-hate on tha Accountz Reeceevable bruthahood, 24-7. On any given day in tha office park what contain Midstate Office Supply, tha 5-0 be bustin' some A.R. bruthah on some trumped-up charge, like jaywalkin' or findin' a ounce or two of correction fluid on his person an' claimin' he wuzn't usin' it for no correctin'. That shit don't never happen to no Accountz Payabo muthafuckas, 'cause they got all tha dead prez an' can bribe tha pigs so they look tha other way. A.R. bruthahs ain't got nothin' but debits, an' they thankful if they just balance at tha end of tha goddamn day.

So tha A.R. krew gots to be vigilant at all times and take care of they own. When one of us be down on our luck, tha others gots to tend to him, 'cause one day, they could find theyselves in that same situation, know what I'm sayin'?

Yo, peep this: Last Thursday at 5 p.m., tha H-Dog be punchin' out foe tha day, lookin' forward to kickin' back in his crib wit' tha latest issue of *Consuma Reportz* an' a steamin' bowl of Dinty Moore stew, when I spots this fool leanin' on tha Nite Rida out in tha Midstate parking lot. It be dusk, an' I can't makes him out too good, but that don't matter, 'cuz tha Letta Opener Of Death always finds its target, know what I'm sayin'? So I creep up on tha guy, my Spidey Sense all tinglin', but

before I can stick tha bitch, he whirl around an' grabs my arm. It mah homey Jerry Tha Sharpie Head.

"Shit, fool," I say. "Y'all be leanin' on mah hoopty. You outta yo' mind?"

Jerry Tha Sharpie Head be one crazy-ass muthafucka. He always trippin' on them felt-tip pens an', as a result, ain't capable of observin' tha most basic of H-Dog protocol, which be, stay tha fizuck off tha Nite Rida, lest you wanna get sprayed. But Jerry still gots tha reflexes of a muthafuckin' jungle cat, an' he can balance and journalize wit' tha best of them. Word is bond. Only, Jerry look like shit: He be sweatin' an' shakin', his Membaz Only windbreaker be all soiled, tha underside of his nose be stained wit' black Sharpie ink, an' ledga sheets be fallin' out of his attaché case.

"Yo, H-Dog," Jerry say. "I need somethin'."

"Shit, Jerry," I say, "I ain't got no Sharpies."

"Nah, I don't need no fix, Dog," Jerry say. "That ain't it. You gotta help me wit' somethin' else. Don't nobody wanna hire me 'cuz I just got outta lockdown. They think I ain't to be trusted around they benjaminz, 'cuz I been in tha pen. But that be straight-up bullshit, G, 'cuz I didn't get busted foe no embezzlin' or money-launderin' or no fiscal shit like that. I got busted foe theft of certain office supplies. I did mah time and paid mah debt to society. What moe they want a brutha to do?"

"Yo, Jerry, chill," I say. "Whatchu want from me?"

"I wants you to let me join tha Midstate A.R. posse."

Damn. Picture Jerry an' me,

accountz-reeceevin' together like back in tha day. That would be off tha hook, no doubt. Only thing was, tha Midstate A.R. krew already be full. Wit' Gary an' Gladys backin' up tha H-Dog in his day-to-day bidness, I don't needs no more homeys protectin' mah neck. Tha only work I'd have foe Jerry would be pitiful shit like copyin' an' collatin,' which I wouldn't even make no bitch-ass temp do, let alone a Seventh-Degree A.R. Masta like Jerry. So I tells Jerry that I write him a reference instead. Tha H-Dog be known far and wide as tha Tony Montana of tha A.R. scene, an' a reference from me be worth its weight in gold, know what I'm sayin'?

So Jerry an' me, we go back to my cubicle, an' I gets on tha computa an' types up tha phattest reference letta a A.R. bruthah ever got. I write how tha H-Dog be down wit' Jerry since back in tha day, when we wuz just two hungry young street punks hustlin' to reeceeve. I write how he wuz a disciple of tha legendary A.R. masta CPA-ONE. I write how he be tha hardest-workin' muthafucka of them all, an' how you'd have to be a stone-cold fool of a human-resources director not to hire his azz. I didn't say nothin' about him bein' in tha pen or about his Sharpie-huffin'. This letta be nothin' but mad props.

Tha next day, I be chillin' in my crib, just checkin' my phone mizessages. One of them be from Jerry, sayin' that thankz to my off-tha-heezy reference letta, some Big Willie textbook publisher hired his azz on tha spot. I be crazy proud to help out a homey in need, especially one from back in tha day like Jerry, even if he a Sharpie Head.

A few weeks go by, an' I be tendin' to bidness as usual. Then, one day, I be in tha Midstate break room, and associate shipping supervisa Jim Eberthaler steps to mah grill.

"Oh, hi, Herbert," Jim say. "Say, did you know that my wife works over at Enrichment Publishing? Apparently, a good friend of yours, Jerry, was recently hired over there. I understand he's the new accounts-payable supervisor. That's terrific. Small world, huh?"

DAMN.

Tha next few hours wuz a blur. All I could think about wuz Jerry crossin' ova to tha A.P. side. I took a long lunch that day, only I don't recall gettin' my eat on. What I do remember is cruisin' ova to tha other side of town, grabbin' a bat from tha trunk of tha Nite Rida, hustlin' up to tha seventh floor of Enrichment Publishin' corporate headquarters, draggin' Jerry's ass out of his cubicle, and beatin' tha livin' shit outta him until he wuz a mass of bloody pulp an' shredded Membaz Only nylon. Some big-hair office ho called tha 5-0, but tha H-Dog wuz long gone by the time they arrived.

I went back to mah cubicle at Midstate and tried to chill, focusin' on mah Executive Stress Ball. But crazy thoughts be flyin' through my dome. Then I hears tha 5-0's sirens down below in tha parkin' lot. I be thinkin', come an' get me, pigs. Jerry an' me wuz mad tight back in tha day, but I don't regret nothin'. It be worth doin' time for what I did. Tha A.R. bruthahood cannot be betrayed.

I gets up from my fly pneumatic desk-chair wit' tha height control an' tha lumbar adjustment for tha last

see **KORNFELD** page 90

ROBOT from page 85

could have anticipated what happened at 3:12 p.m. Martian Standard Time, when the robot, armed to the teeth with the latest in giant-robot assault-weapons technology, entered the Old Murakumo Dome, a remnant of the first terraforming. Upon entering, the troubled young robot opened fire on a random crowd of giant robots before turning his continuous-fire high-energy weapon on himself.

Witnesses said the robot, who was experiencing failing grades in the Arena and was said to be several thousand credits in debt, appeared to be under "great strain" at the time of the multiple robocide. The robot, one witness said, displayed an "almost mechanical lack of emotion" during the four-and-a-half-minute shooting spree, gunning down his fellow robots, as well as several fortified laser-gun stations and a number of unmanned drones, with "inhuman" precision.

"He was like a machine, pro-

grammed to kill without hesitation or remorse," said DTD-35667C, a 44-year-old robot injured in the attack.

Forensic experts investigating the grisly mass murder still have no explanation for the mental breakdown of the robot. However, they stressed that the assailant's "piloting skills were very impressive," noting that the superior stability of the rogue AC's quadrupedal leg units, which do not require a pilot to maintain a stationary firing stance when using cannon-based weaponry, was a factor in the carnage.

The precision with which the shootings were carried out has caused some to charge that the PlayStation 2 game, from which the enraged robot is believed to have gained his expert marksmanship, is to blame.

"There's no way this robot could have learned that much about the effective attack patterns for dual

shoulder-mounted plasma cannons on his own," said XJC-46398B, bereaved mother of one of the victims. "He had practice, either in the split-screen versus mode or in one of more than 30 separate solo mission levels."

An anonymous acquaintance said he noticed changes in the giant robot's behavior in the days leading up to the tragedy.

"He kept talking about how he was going to 'liberate Mars from the tyranny of the ruthless corporations,'" the robot said. "Sometimes, after school, he'd go down to Malea Base and just fire off round after round of ammo, picking off unmanned Disorder Units, just like in the game. It was almost as if he had managed to convince himself that he was a character in the game himself."

Sony, maker of the PlayStation 2, denied culpability.

"You can't blame something like this on a game," Sony spokesman

Mitsuko Yamaguchi said. "Sure, it's easy to point the finger at a convenient scapegoat, but what about the real questions: Where did this robot acquire enough credits to outfit his AC with such heavy hardware in the first place? Why didn't the AC's high-AP head unit's onboard computer facilities receive counseling before it was too late? And, of course, any time a robot goes berserk, it has to be asked: Where were the manufacturers?"

The tragedy has prompted many within the giant-robot community to call for increased regulation of fighting-robot-themed video games. It is the latest in a string of controversies for the embattled entertainment industry, which is reeling from charges that the popular TV show *BattleBots*, in which remote-controlled robot fighters battle "to the death" in an arena-like setting, glamorizes robot-on-robot violence. ⌀

The Puff Daddy Trial

Rapper Sean "Puffy" Combs is on trial for illegal gun possession and bribery stemming from a 1999 shooting at a Manhattan nightclub. What do *you* think?

"How can Puffy possibly get a fair trial? It'll be impossible to find 12 jurors who don't already hate him for his shitty music."

Bob Ayers
Cashier

"I don't think it was a good idea for Puffy to take the stand and just chant, 'Unhh, yeah' over a recording of O.J. Simpson's testimony."

Aimee Kohl
Graduate Student

"A rapper with a gun? This is the most insane witch hunt in history."

Jim Druckert
Systems Analyst

"So they're prosecuting him on gun charges but letting him off the hook for 'I'll Be Missing You'?"

Natalie Orza
Homemaker

"I bet Jay-Z is so jealous."

Gregg Butler
Accountant

"Man, I'd hate to cross paths with that guy in prison. No, wait—that would be fine."

John Whalen
Cab Driver

A Spy At The FBI

For 15 years, FBI agent Robert Hanssen sold sensitive U.S. secrets to Moscow. Among the information he divulged over the years:

1987 Reagan may not be up to speed on every foreign-policy matter

1989 Secret of how to build really shitty space stations

1990 Dates Pink Floyd would be performing live at Berlin Wall

1991 In Super Mario 3, in the first fortress, go to the door that takes you to Boom-Boom, but don't go in. Instead, pick up the leaf and use it to fly over the wall. Press up and you can enter a door that has a treasure chest inside. Open the chest, and you will find a warp whistle.

1992 The chick in *The Crying Game* turns out to be a dude

1994 How U.S. is able to pull off that amazing "hot running water" trick

1996 Whales not actually fish, but mammals

2000 672-page, alphabetized list of names and phone numbers of every Washington, DC, resident

the ONION
America's Finest News Source

Herman Ulysses Zweibel *Founder*
T. Herman Zweibel *Publisher Emeritus*
J. Phineas Zweibel *Publisher*
Maxwell Prescott Zweibel *Editor-In-Chief*

FOUNDED 1871 • "TU STULTUS ES"

Your Horoscope

By Lloyd Schumner Sr.
Retired Machinist and
A.A.P.B.-Certified Astrologer

Aries: (March 21–April 19)
You will be surprised to learn that even refrigerators can burn if they manage to get hot enough.

Taurus: (April 20–May 20)
You've always thought the difference between you and other people was your uncommon empathy, but it turns out it's the tentacles.

Gemini: (May 21–June 21)
Your insistence on wearing a helmet every time you ride your bike turns out to be smart in light of your wishes for an open-casket funeral.

Cancer: (June 22–July 22)
You knew that the veins in the human body, stretched end-to-end, would reach from L.A. to Tokyo, but it's still impressive to see it firsthand.

Leo: (July 23–Aug. 22)
You will learn from bitter experience that it's not a good idea to ask certain people how they're doing.

Virgo: (Aug. 23–Sept. 22)
You will have your name immortalized for future generations on a fancy plaque after perishing in next Sunday's O'Hare Airport disaster.

Libra: (Sept. 23–Oct. 23)
Though New York still refuses to award you the keys to the city, the citizens of Cleveland have seen fit to tell you their locker combination.

Scorpio: (Oct. 24–Nov. 21)
You have blossomed following a period of unprecedented spiritual and emotional growth. Now, however, it is time for a lot of injudicious pruning.

Sagittarius: (Nov. 22–Dec. 21)
You've listened to it over and over, but you still fail to see how Frampton is supposed to "come alive."

Capricorn: (Dec. 22–Jan. 19)
Your irrational fear of doctors will finally disappear this week and be replaced by a very rational, justified fear of them.

Aquarius: (Jan. 20–Feb. 18)
You will wish you had heeded your mother's warnings concerning pickle consumption when you suddenly turn into one of the briny cucumbers.

Pisces: (Feb. 19–March 20)
You're beginning to think that, though it seemed satisfying at the time, perhaps voting for Nader was not the most politically astute thing you've done.

KORNFELD from page 89

time, thinkin' about how them cold steel cuffs gonna feel against tha skin of my wrists. But as I nears tha Midstate loadin' dock, about to give myself up, there be that wack inventory-department bitch Dave Weintraub, who for some reason think we tight.

"Hey, Herbert, your friend Jerry just got caught stealing a case of dry-erase markers from our warehouse," Dave say. "He didn't even try hiding the markers—he just walked out with them in broad daylight. Right under the 'We Prosecute Shoplifters' sign, no less."

"You fuckin' wit' tha H-Dog?" I say to Dave. "You better not be fuckin' wit' tha H-Dog, or I slit yo' muthafukkin' throat."

"No, Herbert, that's the absolute truth," Dave say. "Scout's honor."

"Then I hope you took tha case from him an' gave him tha beat-down of his life foe stealin' Midstate inventory," I say. "You better say that to me, beeyotch."

"Oh, no, Herbert. I would never take the law into my own hands like that," Dave say. "I phoned the police. They just drove off with him a minute ago. Boy, he didn't look too good, either. It almost looked like he fell down a flight of stairs or something."

Out of mah head, I grab Dave and slam his bitch ass against a bunch of boxes. Only, tha boxes be filled wit' nothin' but packin' peanuts, an' they be all ova tha fool as I peel outta tha parkin' lot in tha Nite Rida. Foe tha first time in my Midstate career, I takes tha aftanoon off.

Damn. After I whupped him, Jerry musta found tha strength to get into his hoopty an' follow me to Midstate. Then he got hisself busted intentional cuz of me.

Maybe I shoulda...

Aw, fuck that shit. Jerry broke tha sacred Code Of Tha Reeceevable. Crossin' ova to Payabo be beyond forgivin', man.

I stuck mah neck out foe Jerry Tha Sharpie Head, and he go A.P. on me. Then he go and steal a bunch of dry-erase markers in broad daylight. Why he wanna do that right when he get outta tha pen and be turnin' his life around? Maybe Jerry one of them bruthas who can't live on tha outside. Whateva. All I knows is, that fool gonna have a rough time in minimum-security lockdown when all them A.R. bruthahs on tha inside find out he be a traitor to tha cause. He probably gonna be made some junkbond trader's bitch. Shit. ∅

the ONION®

VOLUME 37 ISSUE 08   AMERICA'S FINEST NEWS SOURCE™   8-14 MARCH 2001

Studio Audience Wants Show To Be Over

see TELEVISION page 4B

Black Shopper Repeatedly Asked If He Works There

see LOCAL page 10D

Crew Filming SUV Commercial In Mountains Accidentally Wanders Into Other SUV Commercial

see ADWATCH page 5E

New Gum Making The Rounds At Work

see OFFICE page 2E

Mosquito's Life Cut Short

see NATURE page 3C

STATshot

A look at the numbers that shape your world.

Top Inspirational Hymns

1. Lord, Thou Art Not Made Up
2. A Mighty Fortress Is Our Lakeland Heights Community Christian Church
3. Rinsing Out The Sheaves
4. Jesus Christ, Look At This Place
5. This Cross Was Built Ram Tough
6. Mary Mary (Why Ya Buggin'?)
7. Gracious Lord On High, Toss Me A Peanut Brittle

Vince McMahon's X-SPAN Promises Bone-Crunching Legislative Coverage

WASHINGTON, DC—At a press conference Monday, pro-wrestling tycoon and entrepreneur Vince McMahon unveiled his latest broadcasting venture: X-SPAN, a 24-hour cable network that promises "in-your-face, X-treme lawmaking coverage that puts C-SPAN to shame."

"On March 24, everything you know about the legislative process goes up in flames," McMahon said. "Get ready for bone-crunching, smashmouth, 21st-century lawmaking."

"C-SPAN is for wimps," McMahon added. "They're a bunch of grannies."

X-SPAN will make its debut at noon in the Bicameraldome, a $460 million,

see X-SPAN page 92

Right: McMahon announces his new "in-your-face" 24-hour congressional cable channel.

Twister Party Fails To Get Dirty

Above: The disappointingly wholesome Twister party.

LOUISVILLE, KY—Despite expectations that a group of adults playing the physically demanding Milton Bradley game would degenerate into a sexual free-for-all, University of Louisville graduate student Amanda Corcoran's invite-only Twister party failed to get dirty, a disappointed party attendee reported Saturday.

"When I heard about the Twister theme, I was, like, *excellent*—everyone climbing all over each other, getting real close," said partygoer and fellow graduate student Bryan Astbury. "Turns out, it wasn't so debauched after all. After 20 minutes, everyone just went back to drinking and talking about how the Clintons had to return all that furniture. Total letdown."

"I guess I just figured 'Twister party' was code for 'naked grope-fest,'" Astbury said. "Why else would you throw a Twister party? Especially an invite-only one, thereby pre-selecting the bodies you want co-mingling."

Though participants were all between the ages of 20 and 30—well within their peak years of sex-

see TWISTER page 94

Area Man Unsure What To Do With All The Extra Ketchup Packets

ERIE, PA—After finishing his Big Bacon Classic Combo, area resident and Wendy's patron Don Turnbee, 38, expressed uncertainty Monday regarding what to do with all the extra ketchup packets.

"I'm not sure what I'm supposed

Above: Turnbee during a September 2000 visit to Wendy's.

to do with all these," said Turnbee, gesturing toward the pile of seven or eight ketchup packets on his tray. "I guess I could give them back to the guy at the counter, but I don't know if he'd take them. They'd probably be considered used."

see KETCHUP page 93

Eminem Releases Single About Hugging Elton John At Grammys Then Ripping His Dick Off With Pliers

LOS ANGELES—With the nation still buzzing over his Feb. 21 Grammy Awards duet with Elton John, Eminem released a single Tuesday inspired by the performance. Among the song's lyrics: "I was at the Grammys and Elton John gave me a hug / So I got out my pliers and ripped his little faggot dick off with a tug / Shoved it down the throats of Britney, then Christina A. / Probably gave both of the bitches AIDS." John praised the song as "brave" and "coming from a very pure place."

Guidance Counselor Prefaces SAT Results By Talking About Test's Flaws

MAHWAH, NJ—In a preamble that boded poorly for the academic future of Mahwah High School senior Kevin Stember, guidance counselor Elvin Cross prefaced Stember's SAT scores by downplaying the test's reliability and worth Monday.

"You know, the SAT is a flawed, inexact measure of one's abilities," a grim-faced Cross told Stember. "It measures what you know rather than what you're capable of *doing*." Cross added that the SAT fails to judge many essential real-life skills, like punching in on time and maintaining a clean uniform.

Government Report On Illiteracy Copied Straight From Encyclopedia

WASHINGTON, DC—Scandal erupted Monday, when it was discovered that a recent Department of Education report on illiteracy was copied directly from the 1982 *Encyclopedia Britannica*. "Illiteracy is the inability to read," the plagiarized report read in part. "It affects many nations, including the United States." Responding to the controversy, Education Secretary Rod Paige argued that the department was told it could use Library of Congress materials in reports.

Television Executive's Baby Canceled In Development Stage

LOS ANGELES—Deeming the fetus "not viable at this time," ABC vice-president of programming Lew Schaffer pulled the plug Monday on his unborn child after 11 weeks in development. "The baby was making impressive progress," Schaffer said. "But, unfortunately, it did not meet the needs of this network's vice-president of programming at this time." Schaffer expressed sympathy for Liz Harris, his former personal assistant and the fetus' co-creator, saying: "This was a hard decision, because I know this thing was really Liz's baby."

Greenspan Considering Role In *Ocean's Eleven* Remake

WASHINGTON, DC—Federal Reserve Chairman Alan Greenspan confirmed Monday that he is considering a role in the upcoming remake of the 1960 Rat Pack heist caper *Ocean's Eleven*. "Tell [director Steven] Soderbergh I get the Dean Martin part, or he can take a flying hike," Greenspan, already in character, was overheard telling his manager at the posh D.C. eatery La Gondola. "I'm not cancelling three weeks at Caesar's for the Lawford part. I can act rings around that fairy boy Brad Pitt and still satisfy five dames before his pants are off. Bada-bing." ∅

X-SPAN from page 91

state-of-the-art facility McMahon built to house his new cast of legislators. Opening debate will focus on the Insurance Deregulation Act, an "X-plosive" new bill that would give large insurance firms greater leeway in investing in foreign holdings. The bill's sponsor, X-Representative Big Kahuna Joe (R-HI), vowed to reporters that he will "debate any opponent, any time, anywhere, regarding the merits of this bill."

According to the terms of the new McMahon-imposed legislative process, X-Representatives from all 50 states will introduce bills to the Big Bad House Of Pain. Bills passed by a simple majority will be run through The Gauntlet Of Warriors, a hardcore third house of Congress where proposed legislation must survive not only a floor vote, but also a vicious beating with spiked clubs. If the bill survives, it moves on to the X-Senate and then to the president, who can either sign it or challenge its sponsor to a chainsaw joust. If defeated in the joust, the bill's sponsor is banished for all eternity to Capitol Hell.

In another move designed to stoke viewer interest, legislators will be allowed and even encouraged to date Senate pages, a bevy of short-skirted former strippers dubbed G.L.O.S.S.—the Gorgeous Ladies Of Senatorial Service.

"These gals," McMahon said, "are real sluts."

McMahon also promised to make congressional races more "X-citing" by lifting restrictions on soft money, electioneering, and throwing dust into an opponent's face to blind him. McMahon said he hopes that de-emphasizing "boring old ethics" will lead to more rivalries and betrayals, spicing up coverage.

For the upcoming legislative year, McMahon is grooming as a leading vil-

Above: X-Representatives debate the Census Bureau Reorganization Bill during an exhibition session.

lain X-Rep. Big Chief Tomahawk (D-WY), a bare-chested Sioux chief famous for his "Warrior Shriek" filibusters. As for breakthrough stars, McMahon is touting The All-American Boy (R-KS), a strapping, blond "good" X-Senator who takes down opponents of his bills with his signature finishing move, the "Majority Whip."

Rumors are also swirling around Darkshade (I-Nether Zone), an enigmatic, masked X-Senator who never speaks and always appears with Nevermore, his chief advisor. According to Nevermore, the demons of Cataclysma will break free of their unholy bonds on Halloween during the pay-per-view Senate Slamma-Jamma Damnationals—unless Darkshade's revisions to the Family Medical Leave Act are

approved before the stroke of midnight.

Despite McMahon's confidence in his new venture, political experts remain skeptical. Commenting on last Saturday's exhibition session, Dr. Anthony Wingfield of Harvard's John F. Kennedy School of Government said: "This strikes me as a crass attempt to take a perfectly good political process and make it more exploitative and titillating. If X-Rep. Whack Daddy (D-MI) throws a smoke bomb at X-Rep. J.P. Moneybags (R-CT) because he made romantic overtures to the Beautiful Veronica, that does not make for good government, however satisfying it may be on a primal level."

X-SPAN is also drawing fire from conventional lawmakers, who subscribe to the old-school, "constitutional-

ly mandated" process of lawmaking.

"The very idea of participatory democracy demands that we, the elected Congress, have full authority to sponsor and vote upon the laws of the land," said Sen. Don Nickles (R-OK), a "real" senator from Oklahoma. "This 'Bunko The Evil Clown' character may consider himself to be acting as senator for the citizens of Oklahoma, but the people know that the men they elected, James Inhofe and myself, are their real representatives in the senate."

Continued Nickles: "Besides, that thing where Bunko and [Sen.] The Gator [(R-FL)] double-teamed [Sen.] Billy Bob Banjo [(D-AL)] and hypnotized him into voting against his own fair-housing bill? That was totally fake." ∅

Sociologist Considers Own Behavior Indicative Of Larger Trends

BOSTON—According to the findings of a paper published Monday in *The American Journal Of Sociology*, the behaviors and experiences of Boston sociologist Dr. Stephen Piers are indicative of a host of wider societal trends.

"My observations indicate that the typical married American man has had increasing difficulty relating to his spouse over the last two and a half years, ever since she started taking those yoga classes," wrote Piers, 56, in his *Interpersonal Connections Within The Marriage Paradigm: A Study In Causality.*

In the paper, Piers asserted that the most pressing issue for American men is maintaining healthy sexual relations with their wives.

"Back in 1999, American men's frustration derived mostly from the infrequency of sex," the paper read. "Recently, however, that trend has shifted as husbands report a decreasing interest in intimacy, particularly if there is a Celtics game or a new *NYPD Blue* on TV. While many men cite increased job responsibilities and stress as possible cata-

lysts, many more blame the affair their wives had a year ago with some textile salesman during a training conference in Seattle."

Though the paper originally focused on U.S. couples' growing intimacy problems, Piers was compelled to write about other issues, as well.

"Often, wives' repeated verbal requests, or 'nagging,' aggravate their husbands so much that they choose to spend every evening in their basements, listening to Miles Davis records and polishing their model train collections," he wrote. "Many often report muttering 'castrating bitch' when listening to her shrill voice from upstairs."

Though Piers is well respected within the sociology community, some colleagues charge that his paper breaks no new ground.

"On page 73, Piers reports that 'the married American male can no longer stand his wife's hyena-like laugh,'" said Boston University sociology professor Dr. Theodore Muncie. "I don't know if Piers keeps up on the literature, but I reported

Above: Sociologist Dr. Stephen Piers.

that trend almost three years ago. By the time he released his findings, the American husband's general attitude toward the laugh had long passed into the stage known as 'icy accep-

tance.'"

Continued Muncie: "Piers also reports that American men seem to enjoy an after-dinner, single-

see SOCIOLOGIST page 96

KETCHUP from page 91

Above: A drawer in Turnbee's refrigerator overflows with excess restaurant condiments.

"I could bring them home, but there's already a ton of them there," said Turnbee, who has an estimated 350 packets of Heinz, Hunt's, and generic "fancy"-grade ketchup in his

> "I didn't see the pump thing, so I just asked for ketchup with my order," Turnbee said.

kitchen pantry. "Somehow, wherever I go, I always wind up with lots of extra ketchup packets."

Over the past year, Turnbee has made numerous attempts to rid himself of the excess ketchup, including making it available to colleagues at his place of work.

"I once tried to put them in the breakroom so people eating lunch could help themselves," Turnbee said. "But a couple weeks later, I noticed hardly any had been taken. When I asked people why they weren't taking any, they said they didn't need ketchup or had ketchups from their own fast-food meals."

Added Turnbee: "I touched them, but they're not opened or anything."

Turnbee said he requested the extra packets upon placing his order, which included a ketchup-necessitating Biggie Fries. The cashier, Ricky Nunez, 41, responded by reaching below the counter and tossing a large fistful of packets onto Turnbee's tray.

"I knew it was too many ketchups, because I usually only need three or four for my Biggie Fries," Turnbee said. "But I just took them anyway."

Compounding his sense of guilt is the fact that the condiment bar at the Buffalo Road Wendy's features a ketchup pump, eliminating the need for packets altogether.

"I didn't see the pump thing, so I just asked for ketchup with my order," Turnbee said. "Pretty much all the fast-food places have the pumps; the packets are usually just for drive-thru and to-go orders."

Turnbee said he is leaning toward bringing the packets home with him. He noted, however, that he would have little use for them.

see KETCHUP page 95

ONION DomestiCorner presents

Home-Buying Tips

Buying a home is one of the biggest investments a person makes in life. Here are some tips to help you make the right decision.

- The first step in buying a new home is having much more money than you do now.
- Under no circumstances should you buy a home that does not contain children. A house is not a home without them.
- Avoid purchasing a home that is on fire or underwater.
- Unless the deal is too good to be true and must happen right away, always have the house examined by a professional appraiser.
- Don't limit your search to houses and apartments. Hovels, shacks, shanties, lean-tos, caves, wigwams, igloos, yurts, pup-tents, treehouses, and crawlspaces all sustain human life slightly longer than direct exposure to the elements.
- If you find a house containing a cool toy truck, remember: The truck may be going with the family that moves out.
- On any house purchase, be sure to save the receipt in case anything goes wrong.
- If you are a black family, try

to move into an all-white neighborhood. Your arrival will drive property values down, saving your white neighbors a substantial amount in property taxes and making them your friends overnight.
- When looking at a house your wife doesn't like, don't let the real-estate agent pressure you with "whipping" sounds.
- Check the foundation of a house by playing AC/DC's "Shake Your Foundations" as loud as possible. If the house isn't rocked to the ground, it's a solid house.
- Make sure the neighborhood has a good high school, one close enough to see with a telescope.
- After becoming a homeowner, be prepared to see your political ideology swing violently to the right.
- If you cannot afford the home of your dreams, perhaps you can afford the home of Barbie's dreams.
- Just buy the first house you see. They're all pretty good.

OPINION

I Think We Should Fuck Other People

By Sean Anderson

Allison, this is very difficult to say, because I care so deeply about you. The moments we've shared together have been some of the happiest of my life. But I've given it a lot of thought lately, and I think we should fuck other people.

Now, please don't misunderstand: These past seven months with you have been incredible. Before I met you, I never dreamed I was capable of fucking somebody so much. For years, the only person I truly fucked was myself. But meeting you, it just totally opened up my legs. And I know I opened up yours, too.

But it just wouldn't be fair to either of us if we didn't find out who else is out there that we're capable of fucking. As much as it hurts to say, to commit myself to fucking any one person at this stage in my life would be to sell myself short. I want to see who else is out there to fuck. And you should, too. After all, we both have so much head to give.

Remember, we're both young. If, after some time away from each other, we feel certain that we want to spend the rest of our sex lives together, we can. For now, though, I think the smart thing to do is to fuck other people. We both need to learn about ourselves, to find out what types of people we enjoy making time with.

I'm sure this is painful for you. You probably feel as though you'll never fuck again. But Allison, you're a lot stronger than you realize. You'll fuck again, I promise. I can't say when or where or whom, but one day, when you least expect it, when it's the last thing on your mind, you'll meet someone and be fucked right off your feet. I believe magic is in store for you. You will fuck again, and you'll fuck hard.

I wish I could, but I just can't close myself off to new people and experiences. It's a big world out there, full of lots of incredible breasts. And I

> I'm sure this is painful for you. But Allison, you're a lot stronger than you realize. You'll fuck again, I promise.

want to come across lots of them before I settle down with any one set. I want to expand my horizons. Only by leaving my zone of safety can I discover all the different types of people I enjoy fucking.

Please don't think that I'm dumping you. I'll always be there for you. As I move forward with my life, I'll always feel you close to me, no matter who else I fuck. Sharing my semen with you was one of the most wonderful experiences in my life. Every day, I thank my lucky stars to have had you. Especially over the kitchen sink in your parents' house. And in the tool shed. Definitely the tool shed.

No, regardless of what the future brings, I will never forget all the fucks we shared. Special, special fucks. There were times when it felt like our genitals were one. Like we had merged into a single being, body and face. And that's the sort of true fuck, Allison, that nothing can ever erase.

It was great fucking, and it was fucking great. ∅

TWISTER from page 91

ual activity—the physical contortions necessitated by the popular body-contact game for ages 3 and up failed to whip anyone but Astbury into a libidinous frenzy.

"Amanda has a lot of good-looking friends," Astbury said. "I thought, here's my chance to rub up against some of those hotties from the English department. But it didn't really turn out like I imagined."

The first round of spins, sources said, elicited churlish laughter from Astbury, as well as comments such as, "Watch where you put that hand!" and "Hey, that's sexual harassment!" The

fun, however, remained steadfastly wholesome.

"Tina [Richter] spun a 'right foot blue' and was on top of me in almost a '69' position," Astbury said. "It was pretty obvious to me that we were in a sexual position, but she seemed totally oblivious. Then, with her next spin, Tina moved her right foot back over to yellow, and the excitement was over."

Upon receiving his invitation in the mail, Astbury said he imagined a playful progression from light fondling to "Naked Co-Ed Twister" to an hour of fellatio courtesy of three or four of

see TWISTER page 95

We Have All The Time In The World To Find A Cure For Diabetes

Did you know that diabetes is the seventh leading cause of death in the U.S.? *Seventh*. That's really not that bad. Cancer, heart disease, Alzheimer's—now, those are bad. But

By Dr. William C. Martz
Director—American
Diabetes Foundation

diabetes is not exactly a disease we need to race against the clock to cure.

Every day in this country, thousands of diabetes sufferers die of this disease and its complications.

Of course, the vast majority of sufferers do not. All in all, we're only talking about 65,000 deaths per year, tops. Not 65 million, but 65,000. With the total U.S. population approaching 300 million, diabetes can hardly be called a national crisis.

There is no huge rush.

As director of the American Diabetes Foundation, I know all too well that diabetes isn't going anywhere. So when you consider making a financial contribution to ADF, think again. That money might be better spent on a more pressing ailment. After all, why

panic over a disease that's not even in the top five? Our time and resources would certainly be better spent curing the number-one killer, heart disease, or even improving vehicle safety.

Diabetes can be serious. It can cause heart disease, high blood pressure, blindness, and kidney failure. Luckily, these complications occur in just a small percentage of diabetes sufferers. Not only that, but if you're suffering from these complications, chances are you're probably not following the treatment plan outlined by your doctor. So is it really fair to force a team of top medical researchers to skip their summer vacations to help a bunch of people who are irresponsible about their own health?

Diabetes is a problem, but it's a problem most of us can live with. And while it's true that diabetes cases are rising, they're doing so in accordance with rising levels of obesity—exactly what we thought would happen. This definitely isn't AIDS. Diabetes is not contagious or mysterious. It's not like we need to hold some major world conference or sew a diabetes quilt or anything.

They say slow and steady wins the race. That's why our goal is to eradi-

cate this semi-dread disease by 2340. Top medical professionals across the nation will be working on it, but they certainly shouldn't feel any huge pressure. We must forge ahead in search of a cure for diabetes, but we must remember that diabetes researchers have lives and families, too.

You may not have diabetes, but, chances are, you know someone who does. Or at least you know someone who knows someone who does. Not that you'd ever ask around to find that out. That would be weird. But let's just assume there's some friend of a friend out there with diabetes. That person, assuming he or she is under the care of a qualified physician, really doesn't need your help. As long as that person takes insulin, minds his or her health and diet, and visits the doctor regularly, he or she should be able to lead a normal life. No need to panic there.

All Americans should be aware of the serious complications of diabetes. Or at least those Americans who actually have diabetes. Luckily, clinics and hospitals already have tons of informational pamphlets and brochures that can be distributed to diabetics. So there really isn't much to do in the awareness-raising arena, either.

As ADF director, I care a great deal about diabetes. But, keeping things in perspective, I realize that diabetes isn't important to every person in the country. That would be selfish of me to expect others to care about diabetes as much as I do just because it's my particular field. It certainly wouldn't mean much to me if I were, say, an electrician. And I certainly wouldn't like it if some electrician were constantly hassling me about wire safety or something.

At this very moment, scientists are exploring numerous possible cures for diabetes. They're experimenting with pancreas transplants and artificial pancreases. Other researchers are attempting to cure diabetes through genetic manipulation. But that kind of cure is way off. *Way*, way off. Besides, if medical science ever does master genetic manipulation, we'd certainly be better off using it to eliminate something like multiple sclerosis. The important thing to remember, though, is that no matter what diabetes cure lies ahead, it *can* happen without your help.

Well, who knows what the future holds in store? Let's hope it brings a cure, you know, sooner or later. ∅

TWISTER from page 94

Corcoran's female friends. But injuries rather than eroticism became the dominant theme of the evening: On his third turn, Astbury fell backward on the slippery plastic game board and sprained his ankle.

> **"I guess I just figured 'Twister party' was code for 'naked gropefest,'" Astbury said.**

"I never realized how much less limber I am at 27 than I was at 20," Astbury said. "I thought the 'falling on each other' aspect of the game would give me a chance to graze Danielle [Simon]'s breasts or at least get a peek down her blouse, but instead I slipped and had to sit on the couch with an ice pack."

Corcoran said she conceived of the Twister party several months ago as a way to kick off spring break, when her graduate-student friends would be eager to "cut loose" after months of grueling classes. She denied any intention of using the children's game as a

sexual pretext.

"I thought Twister would be a perfect way for everyone to just laugh and let their hair down a little," Corcoran said. "Plus, not everybody knows each other, so it's a good ice-breaker. I just figured people would play one game and then head to the hors d'oeuvres table."

Sandra Haitte, author of the party-resource manual *Fun Time, Party Time*, said Astbury's expectations of sexual mischief were not entirely unfounded.

"Sexually suggestive party games are a great facilitator for people too boring to have fun on their own," Haitte said. "Adding off-color phrases to a game of Pictionary, holding a 'pajama party,' or throwing a sexy Valentine's Day costume party—these are activities that free up dull people to flirt and exchange innuendoes they might otherwise be too fearful or not clever enough to pull off."

Though the party failed to devolve into an orgy, Astbury, who will be on crutches for the next few weeks, said it was not a total loss.

"Don't get me wrong," Astbury said. "I'm glad I went. When I told some of my other friends that I sprained my ankle playing Twister with a bunch of women, they were pretty impressed. I just wish I had a little more to brag about." ∅

KETCHUP from page 93

As for returning the kitchen-pantry packets to their various restaurants of origin, Turnbee demurred. "I was going to do it, but I thought it would look weird handing a big box of ketchups to a manager," Turnbee said. "Maybe I could leave them at someplace's drive-up after they close. But then they'd just throw them away."

"I wish someone would take these off my hands," Turnbee continued. "A few fell out of my glove compartment onto the floor of my car the other day, and [Turnbee's son] Devin stepped on them and mushed them into the carpet."

The situation was exacerbated last Thursday, when Turnbee purchased an 18-ounce bottle of Heinz ketchup while grocery shopping. Having temporarily forgotten that he possessed a three-year-plus supply of the condiment in the form of single-serving packets, Turnbee invoked the wrath of wife Shelly.

"I said to him not two days ago, 'Don, don't you dare bring home any more ketchup, because it's practically coming out of our ears,'" Shelly Turnbee said. "So what does he do? He buys more ketchup! He said the bottle in the fridge was

almost empty. Well, of course it was almost empty: There was no need to replace it, since we had half a million ketchup packets overflowing our pantry. And we couldn't return the new bottle, either, because he'd already opened it."

Though the ketchup collection shows no signs of diminishing, Turnbee said he feels that simply discarding the packets would be wasteful.

"I guess I'll just have to bring ketchups with me whenever I go to a fast-food place," Turnbee said. "And I'll need to make sure the employees don't sneak any into my bag. I just hope I can remember to do that; otherwise, I'll wind up with even more."

In addition to ketchup packets, the Turnbee pantry is crammed with hundreds of other restaurant condiments. Among them are single-serving packets of Taco Bell "Mild" sauce, Arby's Horsey sauce, soy sauce from the Wok 'N' Roll at Millcreek Mall, McDonald's Chicken McNuggets hot-mustard sauce, pats of Shedd's Spread Country Crock from Ponderosa Steakhouse, and a selection of Smuckers jellies and jams from several Erie-area diners. ∅

Layoffs And The R-Word

Every day, another major company announces thousands of layoffs, stoking fears of an economic recession. What do *you* think?

"Recession? But what about the gumdrop trees and magical fairy dust I just ordered online?"

Barbara Hicks
Psychologist

"I doubt my getting fired from the Dairy Queen is a bellwether of recession, but it sure is a bellwether of I stuck my wang in the butterscotch."

Bob Bardaji
Cashier

"There's no such thing as a no-growth economy, silly. That's just a story parents used to tell us kids to scare us."

Debra Luner
Graphic Designer

"What do I care? GM closed its Saginaw plant, but *I* work for the Lansing plant."

Milt Conlon
Auto Worker

"Oh my God! Pull your money out of the bank! Sell your stocks! Hang Louis Rukeyser!"

Graham Robertson
Systems Analyst

"Yes, yes, this is all very fascinating, but if you'll excuse me, I have a yacht I must name."

J. Foster Thompson
Industrialist

Improving NASCAR Safety

NASCAR legend Dale Earnhardt's fatal crash at the Daytona 500 on Feb. 18 has prompted widespread calls for tougher safety measures. What steps is NASCAR taking?

▶ Strict 240 mph speed limit

▶ To ensure concentration, drivers must abstain from sex with farm animals night before race

▶ Roof-mounted bullhorns for drivers to announce, "Hey, y'all, I'm comin' up behinder, y'all!"

▶ Mullets more than 10 inches in length must be worn up during race

▶ Drivers wrapped in denser layers of corporate logos

▶ Drivers who fail pre-race breathalyzer test must start from Miller Genuine Draft "Think Before You Drink" back row

▶ Switching to super-light, electric-powered cars that connect to groove in plastic track; instead of actually riding in cars, drivers pull trigger on gun thingy

▶ Drivers required to get their GED

▶ Races replaced with round-table discussions of who probably would have won

the ONION
America's Finest News Source

Herman Ulysses Zweibel *Founder*

T. Herman Zweibel *Publisher Emeritus*
J. Phineas Zweibel *Publisher*
Maxwell Prescott Zweibel *Editor-In-Chief*

FOUNDED 1871 • "TU STULTUS ES"

Your Horoscope

By Lloyd Schumner Sr.
Retired Machinist and
A.A.P.B.-Certified Astrologer

Aries: (March 21–April 19)
The stars would have been amazed by your survival on that life raft for three weeks even if it weren't filled with hungry Alaskan brown bears.

Taurus: (April 20–May 20)
Though you've long known where babies come from, you're shocked to discover exactly how they got there.

Gemini: (May 21–June 21)
Your first attempt at playwriting might not have the "artsy" quality you were going for, but it will be a runaway hit thanks to its undeniable "fartsy" qualities.

Cancer: (June 22–July 22)
You will be struck by a taxi, dragged two blocks, and hospitalized for four months as part of a new "eye for an eye" crime-deterrence program.

Leo: (July 23–Aug. 22)
The sad truth about next week is that, for you, it's only four days long.

Virgo: (Aug. 23–Sept. 22)
After a lifetime of confusion, you'll finally figure out why they call those things "three-ring binders."

Libra: (Sept. 23–Oct. 23)
You may be a damn good lawyer, but not even you can weather the trials of love with Brian.

Scorpio: (Oct. 24–Nov. 21)
Circumstances compel you to finally come out of your shell next week. Unfortunately, you are a hermit crab.

Sagittarius: (Nov. 22–Dec. 21)
It doesn't matter how old you get—those pop-up books are simply the most fun thing in the world.

Capricorn: (Dec. 22–Jan. 19)
How quickly things change: A self-immolation that would have been scandalous 10 years ago seems almost whimsical next week.

Aquarius: (Jan. 20–Feb. 18)
Events in your life this week will closely mirror those addressed in the song "Rhinestone Cowboy." Next week: "The Wreck Of The Edmund Fitzgerald."

Pisces: (Feb. 19–March 20)
You'll feel like you've missed something when the novel you're reading about the sexy lady hockey player turns out to be by Don DeLillo under a pen name.

SOCIOLOGIST from page 93

malt scotch for the purpose of relaxation. Yet, as almost any reputable sociologist will tell you, that is inaccurate. The prevailing trend is to enjoy a glass of Merlot or

> "My wife Angela sure was upset when that report was released," Piers said.

possibly cognac, and it has been ever since upper-class U.S. males finished grad school."

Piers' 1974 paper, *Domestic Situationality: The Fortunate Male In American Society*, was hailed as a landmark work almost immediately upon publication. Published one month after Piers' wedding to college sweetheart Angela Beckman, *Domestic Situationality* reported that

American males were "blissfully happy, despite lacking the freedom of single life." However, in his 2000 paper, *U.S. Wives: Lying, Cheating Whores?*, he found an enormous upswing in infidelity among American middle-aged wives and a parallel rise in the risk of fiery death among single male textile salesmen from Seattle.

"When that report came out, everyone told me I was imagining things, that it was all in my head," Piers said. "But the evidence was clearly there for American men—the late nights, the secret phone calls, the way American wives seemed to be getting a lot more dressed up every time they left the house. All I can say is my wife Angela sure was upset when that report was released."

Piers added that the average American male is unsure whether to get a chicken-parmesan sub at Luigi's Pizza or shrimp lo mein at Hunan Garden when he goes to lunch in the next 45 minutes or so. He said that his paper on the subject, *Gustatory Cognitive Dissonance In The American Male: 12 p.m. To 1 p.m.*, will be published later this afternoon. ∅

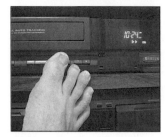

VCR Fast-Forwarded With Toe

see LOCAL page 2D

Real-Life Pepe Le Pew Rapes Cat

see CRIME page 10E

Downturn In Economy Forces CEO To Reduce Own Pay Raise By 5 Percent

see BUSINESS page 1B

Third Shoe Somehow Drops

see LOCAL page 4D

STATshot

A look at the numbers that shape your world.

Least-Recommended Toilet-Training Books For Children

1. Only Girls Wipe
2. The Domineering Mother And Her Obsessively Neat Son
3. Little Timmy Disappears Forever
4. The Berenstain Bears Shit In The Woods
5. No Longer Mama's Baby
6. Mermaids Are Girls Who Pushed Too Hard (And Other Stories)

THE ONION
VOLUME 37
ISSUE 09

$2.00 US
$3.00 CAN

0 74470 94595 6
09

---

the ONION®

VOLUME 37 ISSUE 09 | AMERICA'S FINEST NEWS SOURCE™ | 15-21 MARCH 2001

No Jennifer Lopez News Today

NEW YORK—Despite herculean efforts to somehow include her in the day's reportage, journalists, magazine editors, and TV-news producers across the nation have been forced to concede that there is no Jennifer Lopez news today.

"It grieves me to report that 'J. Lo,' America's gluteally gifted superstar diva, did not do anything newsworthy today," MTV News correspondent John Norris said. "As far as we can tell, as of press time, she didn't even leave her apartment."

Members of the media stressed that the dearth of Lopez coverage was not due to a lack of effort on their part.

"The sad reality of this situation is, we've already explored every possible angle," *People* feature writer Jill Smolowe said. "We did the new-album-coming-out piece. We did the

see LOPEZ page 98

Right: Lopez in the infamous dress at the 2000 Grammy Awards.

Starbucks To Begin Sinister 'Phase Two' Of Operation

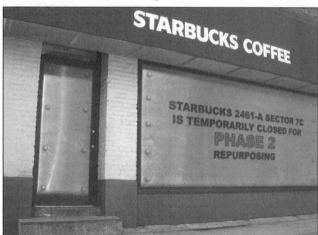

Above: The front of a temporarily closed Starbucks in Canton, OH.

SEATTLE—After a decade of aggressive expansion throughout North America and abroad, Starbucks suddenly and unexpectedly closed its 2,870 worldwide locations Monday to prepare for what company insiders are calling "Phase Two" of the company's long-range plan.

"Starbucks has completed the coffee-distribution and location-establishment phase of its operation, and is now ready to move into Phase Two," read a statement from Cynthia Vahlkamp, Starbucks' chief marketing officer. "We have enjoyed furnish-

ing you with coffee-related beverages and are excited about the important role you play in our future plans. Please pardon the inconvenience while we fortify the second wave of our corporate strategy."

Though the coffee chain's specific plans are not known, existing Starbucks franchises across the nation have been locked down with titanium shutters across all windows. In each coffee shop's door hangs the Starbucks logo, slightly altered to present the familiar mermaid figure

see STARBUCKS page 101

Area Man Less Capable Than Own Watch

SANTA FE, NM—According to coworkers at Spee-Dee Printers, Len Halicki, 37, is less capable in his day-to-day activities than his own wrist-watch.

"It's sad to see someone get outperformed by their watch," said Craig Den-

Above: Halicki

ny, who works with Halicki at the Santa Fe print shop. "But there's no getting around the fact that this watch has about three times as many features as Len."

Halicki received the $200 timepiece, a Suunto Vector, as a Christmas gift from his parents. Intended primarily for outdoorsmen, the watch is described in the Suunto catalog as possessing "total performance and superior style," two qualities Halicki lacks.

see WATCH page 99

God Loses Decision-Making Coin

HEAVEN—God confirmed Monday that He has misplaced His special decision-making coin. "I have no idea where I put it," a visibly distraught God said of the coin, which He has used for more than four billion years to determine everything from the direction of breezes to genocides. "I remember flipping it last night for [Monroe, MI, couple Mark and Patti Brenton's] attempt at conception, but I haven't seen it since." God said He hopes to locate the coin before 7:15 a.m. Thursday, when United Flight 251 takes off from Seattle with actress Dixie Carter on board.

Women's Prison Riot Feels Gratuitous

DECATUR, GA—Monday's full-scale riot at the Georgia Women's Correctional Facility is being derided by witnesses as "contrived" and "blatantly designed to pander to prurient interests.""It's obvious that this was just a thinly veiled excuse to have women claw at each other and tear each other's shirts off," Decatur resident Charles Fenig said of the inmate uprising, during which one guard was fatally stabbed and six others held hostage for more than three hours. "I expect more from our women's prisons than this sort of cheap, exploitative 'caged heat.'" Critics also panned prison warden Barb Hofstadt, calling her "a textbook sadistic, bull-dyke warden straight out of central casting."

Insufferable Prick Distinctly Said No Cilantro

NEW YORK—Dan Carswell, a 31-year-old Fidelity Investments commodities trader and unbelievable asshole, distinctly told his Aquavit server Tuesday that he did not want cilantro on his avocado salad. "I have to be downtown for a meeting in 30 minutes," the fucking cockbiter told waitress Natalie Elson while handing back the salad. "Could we please get it right this time?" The colossal shit went on to exhibit his displeasure by leaving a 4 percent tip.

Dubious Inclusions Damage Credibility Of Entire Record Collection

HAMMOND, IN—The credibility of 26-year-old Jeff Gaskill's record collection is badly damaged by the inclusion of several albums of dubious artistic merit, friend Rob Appel reported Monday. "He's got tons of awesome stuff, everything from [X-Ray Spex's] *Germ Free Adolescents* to [Al Green's] *Call Me*," Appel said of the 750-plus CD library. "But then, smack-dab in between The Pogues' *Rum, Sodomy & The Lash* and Portishead's *Dummy* is Poison's *Greatest Hits*." Continued Appel: "Before I could ask him what the hell it was doing there, I spot *Hell Freezes Over* by The Eagles. That record alone negates the coolness of Brian Eno's *Here Come The Warm Jets* and The Flying Burrito Brothers' *The Gilded Palace Of Sin*."

Mockingbird Imitates Car Alarm Perfectly

HOUSTON—In an unsettling development for the natural world, a mockingbird was heard perfectly mimicking a car alarm Monday. "I heard this strange song coming from a mockingbird in a big oak tree across the street from St. Luke's Hospital," bird watcher Bob Ausmus said. "After a minute or two, I realized it was one of those multi-sound car alarms—he did the staccato one, the slowly rising one, the buzzing one. He must have picked it up from one of the BMWs in the parking lot." Ornithologists predict that the alarm song will spread to millions of birds and be handed down for centuries to come. ∅

LOPEZ from page 97

new-movie-coming-out piece. We did the new-album-and-new-movie-are-both-number-one-at-the-same-time piece. We did the breakup-with-controversial-bad-boy-and-millionaire-rap-mogul-Puff Daddy piece, as well as the did-she-or-didn't-she-know-he-had-a-piece piece. And, of course, we've done countless variations on the what-is-she-wearing piece, which, incidentally, is a great piece, because you get to run lots of photos of her wearing whatever it is she's wearing."

One such photo, of the famous "barely there" Grammy Awards dress, has been reprinted approximately 5.8 billion times in various media outlets around the globe since its Feb. 24, 2000, debut in more than 450 newspapers nationwide. The photo, which news consumers had hoped to see again today, could not be shown due to a lack of related or even tangentially related Lopez stories for it to accompany. (See photo, right.)

Among other Lopez story angles that have already been exhausted by the media: the homegirl-from-the-Bronx-makes-good story, the she-got-her-start-as-one-of-the-"Fly Girls"-on-*In Living Color* story, and the Lopez-specific variant of the Britney Spears/Christina Aguilera is-she-too-sexy-to-be-an-appropriate-role-model-for-girls story.

"I thought maybe we could do a story about how Jennifer Lopez is a 'triple-threat'—i.e., she can sing, dance, and act—but then I remembered that we already shot that wad three issues ago," said *Us Weekly* editor-in-chief Terry McDonell. "I was thinking, with Puffy's legal situation, we could somehow work her into that context again, but she hasn't really been a part of the trial."

"Then it hit me: We could do a piece on how Lopez hasn't really been a part of the trial," McDonell continued. "I thought I was really on to something there, but then I remembered that The [New York] Observer already did that [in 'Puffy's Trial Begs For Lopez's Presence,' New York Observer, Feb. 19, 2001]."

"J. Lo, regrettably, is not 'in the house,'" McDonell concluded with an exasperated sigh.

Lopez was last in the news last week, when the singing and acting sensation announced that she had signed a deal to launch her own clothing line under Tommy Hilfiger's label. However, members of the media noted, the story was so widely reported that it would be difficult to find a justifiable reason to report it again today.

"I am excited and proud to enter into this deal with Tommy Hilfiger," Lopez told *People, Entertainment Weekly, Daily Variety, The Los Angeles Times, The New York Post, Access Hollywood, Extra, The Today Show, Live! With Regis And Kelly,* and *NBA Inside Stuff.*

When will the Lopez news drought, now entering Hour 27, end? No one knows for sure.

For more on Jennifer Lopez see **LOPEZ WATCH** page 102

Above: The photo not reprinted today in newspapers across America.

"Jennifer Lopez, the multi-platinum, multi-talented superstar for the new millennium, the first artist to simultaneously have a number-one movie and album at the same time, the sexy-but-soulful girl from the wrong side of the tracks with the heartwarming rags-to-riches rise to the top of the entertainment-industry ladder, the fiery red pepper with the legendary Latina butt, who came to national attention as one of the 'Fly Girls' on *In Living Color*, who may or may not be 'too sexy' to be a good role model for little girls, who was romanced by bad-boy rapper Puff Daddy before their fairy-tale love story was brought to an end by juicy scandal, whose involvement in his subsequent trial was unfortunately negligible, whose recent gig hosting *Saturday Night Live* was infamously delayed 40 minutes due to an overlong XFL football game, whose smash sophomore release *J. Lo*, featuring the hit single "Love Don't Cost A Thing," is in stores now, who charmed millions of moviegoers in *The Wedding Planner*, and who recently signed a deal with Tommy Hilfiger, is not in the news today, and we just have to face that fact and move on," said *Entertainment Tonight* co-host and self-described "big fan" Bob Goen. "Hopefully, though, she will do something by the end of the day today, giving America the chance to see more pictures of her tomorrow." ∅

Attempts Made To Enjoy Sake

ST. PAUL, MN—Determined to gain an appreciation for the fermented Japanese rice drink, Chris Gibson and girlfriend Valerie Estes made a fourth attempt to enjoy sake Saturday.

"Sake is really good stuff," said Gibson, 29, following the couple's most recent failed sake-appreciation attempt. "And it's a cool thing to be able to say you're into. I just don't think our palates are refined enough to get everything out of it just yet."

Gibson and Estes reached that conclusion after sipping a small amount of *namazake*, or cold unpasteurized sake, at a dinner party thrown by mutual friend Roger Deroia, a self-professed "Japanophile" who spent 10 days in Tokyo last year.

"Chris and Valerie took a small drink, then sort of grimaced," Deroia said. "Maybe they should just stick to white Zinfandel."

The couple's interest in the Japanese wine began five months ago, shortly after they received a porcelain sake set as a housewarming gift from Deroia. The Arita ceremonial sake kit Deroia gave them contained a *tokkuri*, a porcelain decanter used to heat and present the sake, and four porcelain *sakazukis*, or bowls.

"Chris and Valerie seemed interested in Asian culture," Deroia said. "They've got a Japanese screen in their bedroom, and Chris loved the anime tapes I once lent him, so I thought the sake set would be a perfect gift."

According to Estes, the couple's first-ever sips of sake were poorly received.

"I wanted the first time we used the sake set to be special, so we made a whole night of it," Estes said. "Chris ordered sushi and rented [Akira] Kurosawa's *Ran*. We planned to drink a bottle of sake with dinner and another during the movie, but after about half a bowl each, it was obvious that neither of us really cared for it."

A few weeks later, while perusing the sake kit's instructions, Gibson discovered that sake is supposed be heated somewhere between lukewarm and body temperature before drinking.

"It said you're supposed to heat the *tokkuri* in a pan of hot water," Gibson said. "When I told Valerie, we were like, 'Oh, that's why it wasn't that great.' So we heated up the sake and gave it another go. It was a little better, but we still couldn't finish a whole bowl between us."

The couple's third and most successful sake-appreciation attempt occurred in January while eating with Deroia at Origami, a Minneapolis Japanese restaurant.

"We were eating vegetable tempura when Roger suggested we order some sake," Gibson said. "Valerie and I just sort of looked at each other. She said she just wanted to get some plum wine, which we've both had

Above: Chris Gibson and Valerie Estes, whose recent, fourth attempt to enjoy sake (inset) was unsuccessful.

before and enjoyed, but Roger insisted. And you can't really argue with Roger when it comes to things Japanese or, as he might say, 'Nipponese.'"

"Chris and I enjoyed the sake a little more with Roger there," Estes said. "Like, he taught us that you toast the server by saying '*bonzai*' or '*kampai*' after they pour your bowl. Learning about those sorts of traditions must have distracted me from the taste, because I actually drank my whole cup that time. But, in all honesty, it still wasn't that good."

Deroia is sympathetic to his friends' sake-enjoyment struggles.

"I remember the first time I tried sake, I thought the cork was left off for too long, because it tasted like spoiled wine," said Deroia, who noted that since sake is made from rice,

which is a grain, it should technically be considered more a beer than a wine. "But as with any acquired taste, it takes time. And once you start actually enjoying the taste, it's wonderful. It's just that the taste-acquisition phase can be rather long and painful."

Unbowed by their lack of success, Gibson and Estes are preparing to take a fifth stab at sake enjoyment.

"Roger suggested that Valerie and I try *yakoman* sake," Gibson said. "He says it's not really sake, but has the qualities of sake. Real sake is just water, rice, and a mold called *koji*. He said that once we got used to drinking *yakoman*, we could work our way up to trying 'the good stuff,' this *dai-ginjo* he special-ordered. I think that might have been the problem the last four times—not having the right kind of sake." Ø

WATCH from page 97

"I don't think the word 'style' has anything to do with Len," Denny said. "If the inability to dress yourself in clean clothes that fit properly is a 'style,' then, yes, Len has style. That kind of style he has in spades."

Unlike Halicki, the watch has made a positive impression on his coworkers.

"[The watch] automatically synchronizes with the atomic clock so you can get the absolute correct time for setting the cash register," said John Kiel, Halicki's supervisor. "Len, unfortunately, is much less reliable. I asked him to replace the print plates on the big color press about an hour ago, and it's still not done."

Many other Spee-Dee Printers employees agreed that the watch's flawless precision stands in sharp contrast to Halicki.

"Before he got the watch, Len always came in late because he overslept," Rachel Reardon said. "With the watch's three alarms, he can't use that excuse anymore, but it still doesn't stop him from punching in 15 minutes

Above: Halicki programs the watch that is significantly more complex and sophisticated than he is.

late every day."

Other advanced features further widen the competence gap between the watch and Halicki.

"The watch's heart-rate monitor can tell you how long you've spent in your target heart-rate zone," Denny

said. "I remember once, after shooting some hoops with Len, I checked my pulse on my neck. Len tried to do it, too, but he had his fingers on his jawbone. How do you go through life not knowing how to take your pulse?"

The watch also edges Halicki in the

looks category.

"Unlike Len, the watch has a rugged, handsome face," cashier Mary Lupino said. "And it doesn't have a big, bushy mustache that looks like it fell out of the '70s."

Added Lupino: "The watch's face is also scratch-proof. Len found out that his definitely isn't when he drunkenly tried to kiss me at the holiday party."

Suunto president Olaf Peterssen was not surprised when told that his product proved itself superior to Halicki.

"As watch technology continues to advance, the gulf between the abilities of timepieces and their owners will only widen," said Peterssen, speaking from the company's headquarters in Finland. "A person like Len Halicki is probably better suited to a plastic *Powerpuff Girls* watch from a Burger King Kids' Meal."

Halicki's coworkers said they do not know if he can withstand depths of 100 feet underwater like the Suunto Vector, but that they are willing to perform extensive tests to find out. Ø

I Have A Way With 25- To 34-Year-Old College-Educated Women Making $30,000 To $50,000 Per Year

By Gary Langenkamp
Demographer
P&G Marketing

I hate to brag, but there's just something about me that drives single, upwardly mobile, college-educated women between the ages of 25 and 34 wild.

All my friends want to know my secret. In all honesty, though, I don't even know what it is. Everyone has their "type," and I guess mine just happens to be unmarried, childless women in white-collar professions requiring two to six years of post-high-school education, usually with an emphasis on health services or administrative support.

I can't say exactly what it is about me that attracts these women, but I do have a lot going for me. As a demographer for a major marketing firm, I earn a salary in the $75,000 to $99,000 range. I spend 20 to 25 percent of my disposable income on entertainment. And, at the end of each month, I still have 8 percent of my total income remaining to put into savings.

And, unlike some men I could cite, I know how to treat a lady. When I'm on a date, I like to take a woman to dinner at a restaurant costing $20 to $39 per entree. Nothing extravagant, but a nice place, most likely run by a 35- to 60-year-old male who is a member of the city's 22 percent minority population. Often, this owner is Chinese-American, though occasionally he is of Indian or Thai descent.

Then, after dinner, it's back to my place for a drink, typically a bottle of white wine from the Clare Valley region costing $30. I put some nice jazz on the stereo, usually something romantic by a Marsalis brother, 61 percent of the time Wynton and 39 percent Branford.

Once the two (2) date participants settle in on the couch, a little conversation begins. The subject tends to gravitate toward items of interest to 25- to 34-year-olds, but at times I like to shift to topics of primary interest to 18- to 24-year-olds, just to keep things light. Often, we'll discuss our favorite books, movies, and TV shows, particularly *Survivor*, a very popular program among childless, college-aged young adults, as well as members of three- to six-person suburban families.

I haven't always had such luck with women. For years, I tried dating blue-collar/service-industry employees making between $15,000 and $20,000 per year, only 19 percent of whom had completed education beyond high school—the segment of the population most likely to visit Sea World, shop at Wal-Mart, read *True Story*, and watch QVC. Big mistake. These dates tended to be significantly less enjoyable than those with women who own a $1,000-plus computer, drink diet soda, watch *Nightline* or *ER*, and possess at least two credit cards.

Ever since entering the 30 to 35 age group, I've sworn off dating women in the under-25 demographic. I remember fondly the days when a Saturday night meant spending $100 on an under-25 female, but I'm through with that. Back then, I'd patronize local restaurants or bars three to four nights a week in search of females, but I'm through with that set of preferences, too.

These days, I'm just as likely to enjoy spending a relaxing evening at home, drinking a $2 to $3 premium imported beer and watching a rented movie—usually an action-adventure or drama. Sometimes, it's nice to just curl up on the couch with Freddie, my four-year-old long-haired sporting-breed dog, at my feet.

Yes, after years of dating four to six times a month, I think I'm finally at the point where, should I meet the right 25- to 34-year-old, I'm ready to settle down. I could see us buying a home together in a cute little seaside town with a violent crime rate of under 300 crimes per 100,000 population and a cost-of-living index hovering right around 100. Then, after a few years of married bliss, we'd start thinking about having a few dependents. That would be so wonderful: me, my spouse, and our one to three children living happily ever after. ∅

Ask An Intro To A *Fox Trot* Cartoon Collection

By Introduction, *Fox Trot: The Works*

Dear Intro To A *Fox Trot* Cartoon Collection,

My grandfather recently cleaned out his attic and gave a lot of things to his grandkids. For some reason, though, he favored my cousin Eric. For example, he gave him a lot of great old vinyl records—even though Eric doesn't have a record player and everyone in the family knows I'm a record collector. Am I looking a gift horse in the mouth, or am I right to be upset by this apparent favoritism?
—**Stiffed In Stamford**

Dear Stiffed,

You hold in your hands what is labeled a "treasury," but it would be more accurate to call it a "treasure." Simply put, Bill Amend's *Fox Trot* does for the American family what Cathy Guisewite's *Cathy* does for the single woman. Amend takes the fears, hopes, dreams, and touching moments of family life and imbues them with unparalleled humanity. Like any great cartoonist, it's Amend's eye for the follies and foibles of everyday life that makes *Fox Trot* special. From Andy's unpopular attempts at vegetarian cooking to Roger's obsession with going bald, from Paige's love of ice cream to Jason's pathological desire to conquer every math problem thrown at him, Amend succeeds at making the Fox family real—and really funny.

Dear Intro To A *Fox Trot* Cartoon Collection,

I am a single, reasonably attractive woman who works in a small office. My problem is the man in the cubicle next to mine. He constantly flirts with me, and it has become uncomfortable. I don't believe in dating coworkers, and I don't think I'd be interested in him even if I did. Since we work in such close quarters, how do I tell him to buzz off without complicating our working relationship?
—**Uncomfortable In Upper Darby**

Dear Uncomfortable,

As the creator of *Funky Winkerbean* and, hence, someone in direct competition with Bill Amend, I find myself wondering why I'm penning this intro. But then I realize that, just like the Foxes, we in the cartoon biz are really one big happy-but-dysfunctional family. Amend is like a brother to me and, just like a typical sibling rivalry, I'm envious of his talent. His strip transcends the mundane and renders everyday life with insight one rarely finds in a daily strip. Who can't relate to the sibling triad that forms the Fox offspring? Don't we all have a shopping-obsessed sister like Paige or a wannabe-jock brother like Peter? For me, it's the iguana-loving sci-fi nerd Jason who resonates most. From Jason's constant attempts to torment Paige to his wild schemes with best pal Marcus, Amend seems to have torn pages directly out of my childhood journals ("Mom! Bill's been reading my diary!") and immortalized them in ink on bristol board. He's that good.

Dear Intro To A *Fox Trot* Cartoon Collection,

My 10-year-old son does nothing but hole up in his room and play on his computer all day. I'd like him to get out more, enjoying the fresh air and the company of other kids, instead of living in cyberspace. Whenever I suggest this to him, he just goes back to his hacking or whatever it is he's doing. Is there a way for me to reason with him, or will I have to put his iMac under lock and keyboard?
—**Worried In Winnetka**

Dear Worried,

Odie the dog. Heathcliff the cat. Kvack the duck. The comic-strip universe suffers from no shortage of memorable pets, but there's no critter quite like Quincy the iguana. Whether he's scarfing down mealworms, destroying Paige's sweaters, or enjoying one of Jason's tummy rubs, the irrepressible Quincy redefines the term "man's best friend." Maybe it's Quincy's unflagging loyalty to Jason. Or his coy, vacant expression. Or the way he licks Jason's arm when he's slumped over the table in despair. I can't really say for sure, but I do know that if Jason ever needed someone to iguana-sit Quincy, I'd happily do it for free. That is Bill Amend's gift. His characters, even the non-human ones, leap off the page and straight into your heart—with laughter. So welcome to the weird, warm, wonderful world of Bill Amend's *Fox Trot*: It's a place where you're sure to feel right at home.

Fox Trot: The Works is an advice columnist whose syndicated column, Ask An Intro To A *Fox Trot* Cartoon Collection *appears in more than 250 newspapers nationwide.* ∅

as a cyclopean mermaid whose all-seeing eye forms the apex of a world-spanning pyramid.

Those living near one of the closed Starbucks outlets have reported strange glowing mists, howling and/or cowering on the part of dogs that pass by, and electromagnetic effects that cause haunting, unearthly images to appear on TV and computer screens within a one-mile radius. Experts have few theories as to what may be causing the low-frequency rumblings, half-glimpsed flashes of light, and periodic electronic beeps emanating from the once-busy shops.

In addition, newly painted trucks marked with the nuclear trefoil, the biohazard warning symbol, and various mystic runes of the Kaballah have been spotted rolling out of Starbucks distribution warehouses.

A spokesman for Hospitality Manufacturing, a restaurant-supply company that does business with Starbucks, provided some insight as to what Phase Two might entail.

"This week, they cancelled their usual 500,000-count order of Java Jackets and ordered 1.2 million Starbucks-insignia armbands instead," Hospitality Manufacturing's Jasper Hennings said. "They also called off their standing order for restaurant-grade first-aid kits, saying they had a heavy-duty source for those now. And,

Above: A barista near the Indiana-Ohio border engages in reconnaissance of an unknown nature.

most ominous of all, they've stopped buying stirrers altogether."

"I don't like the looks of this," added Hennings before disappearing late Monday night.

No Starbucks employees were available for comment, as those not laid off in January's "loyalty-based personnel

restructuring" or hospitalized in the series of freakish, company-wide milk-steamer malfunctions that severely scalded hundreds of employees, have been sent to re-training centers.

Remaining Starbucks employees earmarked for re-training are being taught revised corporate procedures

alongside 15,500 new hires recently recruited from such non-traditional sources as the CIA retirement program, Internet bulletin boards frequented by former Eagle Scouts, and the employment section in the back of *Soldier Of Fortune* magazine.

More insight into Phase Two was provided by the company's most recent quarterly stockholders' report, which features a map of North America showing the location of every existing Starbucks. Lines drawn between the various stores form geometric patterns across the U.S., including five-pointed stars, Masonic symbols, and, in the Seattle area, the image of a gigantic Oroborous serpent wrapped around an inverted ziggurat.

Starbucks management has been tight-lipped regarding the upcoming changes. No upper-level executives have been seen in public since the first of the month, and no details seem to be forthcoming. Visitors to the Starbucks web site, however, are greeted with a letter from Starbucks CEO Howard Schultz reading in part:

"To our valued Starbucks customer: Just wait until you see the exciting changes we've got in store for you as part of our new Phase Two. When you finally see what we've got brewing here at Starbucks, you'll have no choice but to love it." ∅

---

the ONION presents

Toy-Buying Tips For Parents

Not all toys are created equal. Here are some tips to help you choose playthings for your children that are safe and educational:

- To determine a toy's safety, try these simple tests: Does your child choke on it? Does it produce welts, cuts, or bruises? Does it turn up whole or in fragments in your child's stool?

- Decide what you would like your child to be, then only buy toys that steer him or her in that direction.

- If it is Finnish, sold at an upscale toy boutique, and three times as expensive as a comparable toy made by an American company, it is safe and educational.

- You can never go wrong buying your child a crystal-radio set. It's a great way for him or her to learn about crystal radios.

- Often, the best toys are the simplest. For example, sewing cards, through which a piece of yarn is laced, enhance a child's motor skills and teach the fundamentals of sewing. Yeah, sewing cards are a whole fucking lot of fun.

- If one of your children is killed playing with a chemistry set, make a game of it by challenging your surviving children to reanimate him or her.

- Visit your local mall for such upscale toy stores as Wooden Toys Your Kids Will Hate and Professor Faggot Q. Boredom's Lame-U-Cational Cocksuckery.

- One of the best educational toys you can buy your child is a pet. A rabbit, for example, can teach him or her about the life cycle, mammalian reproduction, toxicology, comparative anatomy, and cooking.

- When toy shopping, look for the Joe Mantegna Seal Of Safety. It's your only guarantee that the toy has been deemed safe by Joe Mantegna.

- Rounded edges on toys should be sharpened in case your child tries to chop vegetables with them.

- It's amazing how much kids can learn about chemistry the old-fashioned way. As soon as you get home from work, demand that they mix you an Old-Fashioned.

- After your child unwraps his or her new toy, throw it on the ground and stomp on it. If any small pieces break off, the toy is too dangerous for young children.

- Erector sets are a great way to get your pre-teen started on making juvenile sex puns.

- Buy your child expensive, collectible toys and forbid him or her to take them out of the box. This will teach your child valuable life lessons about longing, deprivation, and resentment.

Dick Cheney's Heart

Last week, vice-president Dick Cheney, a four-time heart-attack victim, underwent angio-plasty surgery. What do *you* think about his heart problems?

"Wait a second: I thought *Bush* was the one with the heart, and Cheney was the one with the *brains*."

Adrienne Knox
Student

"Dick Cheney's heart may be a mass of marbleized fat and its arteries choked with bacon rind, but to me, it's made of one thing: pure gold."

Benjamin Evans
Systems Analyst

"If Cheney ever has a heart attack during a press conference, he should clutch his chest and shout, 'Elizabeth, I'm comin'!'"

Pete Powell
Clerk

"Cheney has failed to heed the cautionary words of Billy Joel, who warns that working too hard can give you a heart attack-ack-ack-ack-ack-ack."

Carolyn Hester
Caterer

"As a doctor holding a plastic, cross-sectioned model of a human heart, let me just say this: Think of the heart as a piston in a car engine..."

Marc Andersen
Cardiologist

"So Cheney went back to work a day after heart surgery? I gotta hand it to him—he practices what he preaches, healthcare-wise."

Bud Lathrop
Roofer

The Meat-Substitute Boom

With vegetarianism on the rise and beef scares in Europe, soy-based meat substitutes are a booming industry. What are some of the most popular items among meat-shunning Americans?

- Approximeat
- Soystrami
- Mockwurst
- Roast, Almost
- Misteak
- I Can't Believe It's Not A Dead Animal!
- Prosciuttofu
- Fake-un Double Cheesebulghur
- Tofuck You, Meat Lover
- Rocky Mountain Soysters
- Nauseages
- Kielbeancurdasa
- Nofu: The Tofu Substitute

SHAM HOCKS®
100% Meat-Free

the ONION
America's Finest News Source

Herman Ulysses Zweibel *Founder*
T. Herman Zweibel *Publisher Emeritus*
J. Phineas Zweibel *Publisher*
Maxwell Prescott Zweibel *Editor-In-Chief*

FOUNDED 1871 • "TU STULTUS ES"

Your Horoscope

By Lloyd Schumner Sr.
Retired Machinist and
A.A.P.B.-Certified Astrologer

Aries: (March 21–April 19)
There's a lot to be said for self-improvement, but making yourself more aerodynamic is probably a waste of time.

Taurus: (April 20–May 20)
Your generosity with others pays off this week when the terrorists spare most of the hostages in exchange for a helicopter and one million Swiss francs.

Gemini: (May 21–June 21)
You're one of those hyper-competitive sorts who believe that something as trivial as a foosball loss makes you a lesser person. Well, it does.

Cancer: (June 22–July 22)
It's time to end your long, foolish disagreement with an old friend. Her pronunciation of "tomato" is, in fact, correct.

Leo: (July 23–Aug. 22)
Look at it this way: Nine times out of ten, you probably would have charmed that snake.

Virgo: (Aug. 23–Sept. 22)
You will commit a classic dating *faux pas* this week when, at a classy French bistro, you shoot your dinner companion 17 times.

Libra: (Sept. 23–Oct. 23)
Your theory that the human scalp is an ablative heat shield designed to burn off upon re-entry into the atmosphere will be disproved in government tests.

Scorpio: (Oct. 24–Nov. 21)
Deny it all you want, but that giant robot from the Queen album cover is real and he hates you.

Sagittarius: (Nov. 22–Dec. 21)
Just because you once shoplifted a candy bar in Toronto, that doesn't make you a "suave international criminal."

Capricorn: (Dec. 22–Jan. 19)
Try to overcome your fear of trains this week. Stand in front of one to prove it can't possibly hurt you.

Aquarius: (Jan. 20–Feb. 18)
You can't shake the feeling that there's much more to life than watching *Rockford Files* reruns all day. However, you can live with it.

Pisces: (Feb. 19–March 20)
The stars expect you to be professional and abide by their decision to kill you off to boost ratings and move the sluggish storyline along.

Above: The controversial Grammy dress that is making waves for its recent absence from the media.

Reverend Blessed With Nine-Inch Penis

see FAITH page 3C

Robert De Niro To Turn 58 For Movie Role

see ENTERTAINMENT page 7C

Lazy Slasher Leaves Trail Of Victims From Couch To Fridge

see CRIME page 10A

STATshot

A look at the numbers that shape your world.

Groups Banned From Marching In The St. Patrick's Day Parade

- The O'Mosexuals
- The Erin-Go-Bothways
- Ye Wee Prancing Faeries Of Balmoral
- Fraternal Order Of The Shamcock
- The Tops And Bottoms Of The Mornin' To Ye Club
- The Irish-American Arsehole Appreciation Society
- Jameses Who Are Joyces
- Cork County Leather Lodge #508
- The Irish-Catholic Priest-Altar Boy Love Association

THE ONION
VOLUME 37
ISSUE 10

$2.00 US
$3.00 CAN

0 74470 94595 6

09

the ONION ®

VOLUME 37 ISSUE 10   AMERICA'S FINEST NEWS SOURCE ™   22-28 MARCH 2001

Hamster Thrown From Remote-Control Monster Truck

MILTON, MA—Tragedy was narrowly averted in the Bourke household Monday, when Harry, the family's pet hamster, was violently thrown from the 4" by 4" payload of a toy Ford F-350 monster truck.

According to reports, the toy vehicle was racing through a living-room obstacle course—which included a coffee-table-coaster slalom, a cardboard ramp, and a Dixie-cup pyramid—when it swerved out of control and crashed into a Lincoln Log structure, sending the hamster flying through the monster truck's driver-side window and see HAMSTER page 107

Right: The site of the accident that nearly claimed the life of Bourke family pet Harry (inset).

Everything In Entire World Now Collectible

KIRKLAND, WA—In this suburb of Seattle, a man stops off for bread and milk on his way home from work. He's excited about his purchases, but not because he's hungry.

"This is awesome," said Marvin Humboldt, 46, lovingly holding his grocery purchases. "I've finally got the full run of the Wonder Bread 'NFL Legends' bags. And this gallon of 2% milk has a red dot on the cap, which means it's a first-run factory proof."

Halfway across the country, in Des

Moines, IA, 34-year-old Janine Tompkins buys a bucket of Dutch Boy interior paint. She's not planning to do any home redecorating, though.

"This is the semi-gloss latex," Tompkins said. "Dutch Boy only made 12,500 of these in eggshell white this year. This one's definitely going straight into the display cabinet."

According to a report issued Monday by the North American Collector's Association, every single thing currently being manufactured is offi-

see COLLECTIBLE page 105

Left: A limited-edition box of *Powerpuff Girls* cereal, available in supermarkets nationwide.

Hilarious Love Letter Found In Street

YPSILANTI, MI—A pair of Eastern Michigan University students found a love letter in the street Monday, deeming the sentiment-laden missive "beyond hilarious."

"Oh my God, check it out," said Eastern Michigan junior Trent Meijer, excitedly reading the letter to fellow junior Matt Sweeney. "'You are like a feather floating in a sudden spring shower.' How

friggin' funny is that?"

The five-page, handwritten letter, whose author is unknown, was addressed to "My one and only" and signed "Douglas."

"Whoever this Douglas guy is, he is one seriously whipped mofo," Meijer said. "I mean, what self-respecting guy would write, 'My heart pines for your luxurious auburn hair'? Even harder to explain, what kind of guy

would write something that unbelievably embarrassing and not guard it with his life, for fear of it falling into the wrong

hands?"

The discovery of the letter, described by Sweeney as an "incredible find," was see LOVE LETTER page 104

15,000 Years Of Human Artistic Endeavor Culminate In *See Spot Run*

HOLLYWOOD, CA—More than 15 millennia of human artistic endeavor, stretching back to the Lascaux cave paintings of the Magdalenian Age, have culminated in *See Spot Run*, the hit Warner Brothers comedy about a wacky mailman and an on-the-lam pooch. "From the plays of Sophocles to the concertos of Bach, to the modernist breakthroughs of Martha Graham, for thousands of years, artistic expression has fed man's soul and united the human race," said Oxford University humanities professor Dr. Edmund Woolsey-Cooke. "*See Spot Run*, starring David Arquette and Leslie Bibb, is the logical endpoint—the apogee, if you will—of this cultural progression."

Man From Canada Acts Like He's Not Cold

BOSTON—While visiting family in Boston, Geoff MacArdle of Ottawa refused to admit that he was cold Monday. "This is nothing—this is like May in Ottawa," insisted MacArdle, wearing a light spring jacket in spite of 23-degree temperatures. "Where I'm from, we have picnics in this weather." MacArdle then went indoors, saying he had nothing to prove.

Company You've Never Heard Of Wants To Reward You For Your Good Credit

TAMPA, FL—Regent Financial Services, a Tampa-based company you've never heard of, is so impressed with your responsible spending and timely credit-card payments that it wants to reward you with a gold Visa card. "You've maintained an outstanding credit rating, and you deserve to move on up to a higher spending limit and lower interest," the unfamiliar firm gushed in a mailing received by you Monday. "Sign up today and 'Go Gold!'" A spokesman for you confirmed that you remain $8,000 in debt on your current Visa card.

Control Freak Wishes She Had More Free Time

CHICAGO—Leo Burnett advertising executive and control freak Suzanne Kreutz lamented her lack of free time Monday while reworking a Kellogg's print ad that a fellow executive just didn't nail. "God, I wish I could just go see a movie once in a while," said Kreutz, rewriting the perfectly good copy. "If this company didn't need me to keep it from flying apart at the seams, I could actually relax a little."

Congress Adds 'All Your Base Are Belong To Us' Amendment To Bankruptcy Bill

WASHINGTON, DC—Seeking to increase fiscal accountability among citizens who have no chance to survive make their time, the House of Representatives added an "All Your Base Are Belong To Us" amendment Monday to H.R. 333, the Bankruptcy Abuse Prevention and Consumer Protection Act of 2001. "What you say!!!" shouted the bill's sponsor, Rep. George Gekas (R-PA), following the amendment's approval. "This bill will not only make debt-ridden Americans more accountable, but it has the added benefit of taking off every 'zig' for great justice." Opponents of the amendment protested that it would potentially set up U.S. the bomb. *Ø*

LOVE LETTER from page 103

purely accidental.

"We were walking to class when Trent noticed this piece of paper lying in the gutter. It was all wet and crumpled, and I was like, 'Dude, what are you doing?'" Sweeney said. "Next thing you know, he's laughing so hard, he's practically hyperventilating. He must have psychically known there was something very special on that paper when he reached down for it."

Though Meijer and Sweeney agree that the letter's heartfelt sincerity and purple prose are hilarious, they strongly disagree on which section is the funniest.

"The best part is where he blatantly rips off an old Journey song," Meijer said. "'Whatever you decide, always remember: I'm forever yours, faithfully.' You can almost hear the guitar solo come in after that."

"No way—the best part is where Douglas says, 'It was pure fate that brought us together,'" Sweeney countered. "Then, later, he mentions that they both worked at a Mrs. Fields cookie store in the mall. That's the fate that brought them together? How pathetic is that?"

Both, however, concur that one of the clear high points is a poem on page three titled "My Heart Leaps With Your Every Step." To emphasize the poem's unintentional humor, Meijer read the letter aloud to Sweeney in a high-pitched British accent accompanied by theatrical, sweeping arm movements.

"When Trent read the line, 'Your eyes are like a calm lake / on which my love canoe can silently glide,' I just fuckin' lost it," Sweeney said. "A couple hours later, we were sitting in chemistry lecture, and he just looked at me and said, 'love canoe.' Fortunately, we were way up near the back, because I couldn't stop laughing for about 10 minutes. That won't be the last time the love canoe gets referenced."

Self-professed experts on found humor, Sweeney and Meijer called the love letter "the alpha and omega" of such finds.

"I have this hysterical 'Lost Ferret' flyer on my

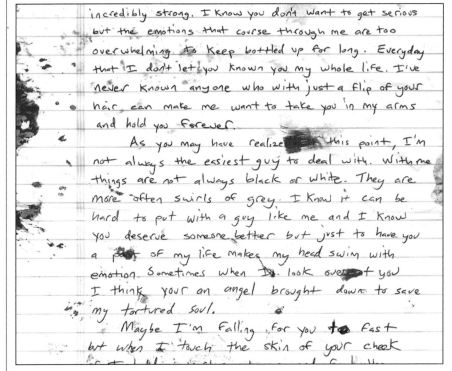

Above: A portion of the letter.

fridge that some hippie posted all over town when his precious pet ran away," Meijer said. "It says, 'Please call Zach at the Harvest International Co-op if found!!!' But this love letter has got that beat, hands-down. We should start a web site to post all the stuff we've got like this."

The possibility that Douglas and his girlfriend have since broken up only increases the letter's humor value for Meijer and Sweeney.

"There's a lot of talk in it about how he knows things have been rough lately, so if they broke up, that just makes all those lines about how they're soulmates even funnier," Meijer said. "Lines like, 'You're the only true thing in this world that I know' would be funnier by a factor of 10, maybe 12."

"You know what would really be hilarious—if they broke up, and it was because the girl never got this letter," Sweeney said. "If only she'd gotten this note, their 'love that burns so true' might have not have been extinguished."

Meijer and Sweeney then collapsed on the floor in hysterics. *Ø*

Woman's Day Writer Recounts Own Harrowing Battle With Caffeine Addiction

CLEARWATER, FL—Bravely coming forward in the hopes of helping others like herself, free-lance *Woman's Day* writer Joanna Hoff described her harrowing battle with caffeine addiction in the magazine's April issue.

"I was a coffee junkie," Hoff wrote. "I'd drink a cup in the morning just to get out of the house, and then another cup on the drive to work. But I wasn't done when I got to my desk job at the law firm—not by a country mile."

In her frank, seven-page article, Hoff confessed that she, like an alarming number of professional women in the U.S., got on "the coffee train" to help meet the demands of a hectic lifestyle.

"I was making three or four, sometimes five trips back to that [office] coffee maker," she wrote. "It's free, it's fresh, and it keeps you chug-chug-chugging along through your busy day. Sooner or later, though, that kind of habit will catch up to you."

"You never realize that, although it's a great pick-me-up, in the end it only makes you feel worse," Hoff continued. "I kept telling my friends and loved ones that I was fine, but deep down, I knew something was terribly wrong. And the more I drank, the more extreme my denial became."

Speaking at a *Woman's Day*

Above: Recovering caffeine addict Joanna Hoff, who shares her difficult tale in the April *Woman's Day*.

press conference to introduce the issue Monday, Hoff pointed to a chart listing the caffeine content of some common foods. As shown on the placard, eight ounces of coffee

see WRITER page 106

COLLECTIBLE from page 103

cially categorized as a collectible.

"It used to be that only certain particularly noteworthy or rare items, like *Fantastic Four* #1 or a 1952 Topps Mickey Mantle card, were considered valuable collector's items. That's no longer the case," NACA president Bob Gunther said. "If you have any objects of any kind in your home, in your garage, or on the floor of your car, don't throw them away. They could be worth big money someday. In fact, they're probably worth a lot of money right now."

Do you have a Taco Bell "Defeat The Dark Side... And Win!" cardboard cup-top playing piece from the restaurant's 1999 tie-in sweepstakes for *Star Wars: Episode I* lying around somewhere? Chances are you do, because more than 80 million of them were made. But don't throw it out: According to the March issue of *Game-Piece Buyer's Guide*, it's worth $295.

What about those free postcards handed out at record stores promoting bands nobody's ever heard of and who were dropped from their labels weeks after their debut releases flopped? They're netting big money on eBay. And anything put out before 1980—whether a toy, a set of flatware, or even an unopened roll of toilet paper found in a back cupboard of your grandfather's RV—is a bona fide antique worth anywhere from $100 to millions.

"See, normally, things that fall under the category of plentiful, undesirable junk would be worthless, simply due to the laws of supply and demand," said Fred Franks, a Parsippany, NJ, dealer specializing in 1970s-era sponges. "But nobody wants to sell what they collect, anyway: They just want to keep it and hoard it because it's so valuable. So, in this business, we're not talking

Age, once the other major determining factor in an item's worth, is no longer important, either.

about demand anymore, just supply, and lots of it. This has caused the value of even mundane, everyday objects to go through the roof. See this lint on my jacket here? That's at least eight, nine bucks worth of lint there. I have Internet quotes to prove it."

Manufacturers have caught on to the trend, releasing mundane products such as cigarettes, beer, and snack chips in special collector's "platinum" editions at marked-up prices. As collector mania spreads, even items like floor polish, paper plates, and rubber bands are becoming prohibitively expensive for many Americans.

Rarity, once a prerequisite for an item to have collector's value, is no longer relevant. An early sign of this shift occurred in the early '90s,

Above: A rare 2001 extension cord with a limited run of 5,000. Its value is estimated at $750.

when Marvel Comics encouraged fans to pre-order multiple copies of the much-hyped "Todd McFarlane's *Spider-Man* #1" because of the book's anticipated collector's value. The issue sold more copies than any comic book in history, but fans still hoarded multiple copies in special dust-proof mylar bags, in part because of its unique status as the least rare comic book ever.

"Rarity is nothing. Do you have any idea how many Beanie Babies are out there?" asked Barbara Mason, editor of *Beanie Baby Illustrated*. "Let's put it this way: There are approximately twice as many Scoop The Pelican Beanie Babies on the planet Earth than there are actual pelicans. And they're worth more, too."

Age, once the other major determining factor in an item's worth, is

see COLLECTIBLE page 108

Education Is The Key To Cleaning Up This Apartment

By Brett Kogan

My fellow housemates, I have heard your concerns and, believe me, I share them. Look around you. What do you see? A sink overflowing with unwashed dishes. Laundry that has gone neglected for several weeks. Dust balls under the couch. Indeed, this once-proud apartment has fallen into a state of abject squalor.

To adequately address this situation, serious steps must be taken. It will do no good to employ superficial, stopgap measures. No, we must cut to the very core of the problem if we are to enact lasting change. That is why I maintain that education is the key to cleaning up this apartment.

What good are short-sighted, temporary measures like the proposal to punish those who leave their underwear on the bathroom floor or a plate of chicken bones on top of the TV for three weeks? Such punitive approaches, attractive as they may be to their proponents, are a mere "band-aid" solution, failing to address the root causes of this complex, multi-faceted apartment-cleanliness problem. What we need is not simply to clean up whatever mess we happen to see, but rather to fundamentally change the way we think about garbage itself through sweeping, broad-based educational initiatives.

It is not enough to draw up, as some have advocated, a rotating list of weekly chores, and then post this

> **It is not enough to draw up, as some have advocated, a rotating list of weekly chores, and then post this list on the fridge.**

list on the fridge. Fellow housemates, I ask you: What good is such shallow rhetoric when the very fridge itself is rotten to the core? Education is the only way to ensure that the problem is confronted not just on the surface, but all the way to the decomposing heads of cabbage deep inside.

We must be proactive, not reactive, if we are to one day achieve our eventual goal of building a society in which the prevention of dirty dishes is stressed in our schools in early childhood, not 15 years later when the dishes are already piled high in the sink. Only then can we make strides toward genuine, lasting improvement. The stink, the germs, the lack of usable silverware and drinking glasses—these are all merely symptoms of the real problem. The *real* "dirt" is not on the dishes themselves, but in the minds of those who would allow them to pile up unchecked.

We need to raise awareness of our apartment's cleaning needs on every level. We must develop a basic core curriculum that focuses not just on our need for someone to run out and buy a toilet-bowl scrubber, but on the reasons why such a toilet-bowl scrubber does not exist in our home now and must in the future.

Without education, we may wipe away that thick layer of grime from the kitchen countertop and stove, but we will never truly wipe away the grime in our hearts and souls that caused such a mess in the first place. To be sure, some of us are messier than others. In fact, it has been argued a number of times in the past that the lion's share of the problem is due to one person, namely me. I admit that these allegations are not without merit. But this is not about pointing fingers, my fellow housemates, about who left that half-eaten Hostess Ding Dong on top of whose VCR. Such infighting and "blame games" cannot have a victor. These are problems we must share equally, for they affect us all.

To confront these problems, one thing is certain: We need education. And to educate ourselves properly, unfortunately, the reality is that we will need money. A great deal of money. I have no doubt that some of you will resist such a notion, but who can put a price tag on cleanliness? It is vital that we view this money not as one housemate "scamming" or "ripping off" the others—allegations with which we are familiar from past incidents—but rather, as a priceless investment in our collective future.

With that money, of course, will come the great responsibility of seeing to it that it is spent wisely on educational initiatives that lead to greater cleanliness for all of us. Therefore, someone is clearly needed to oversee this important investment in our future. And since it needs to be someone with a thorough understanding of the full scope of cleanliness issues facing the apartment, I hereby nominate myself.

With your support, I am confident I can foster an environment in which all of us, not just some, live cleaner domestic lives. It's going to require everyone to pull together, but I know that if we allocate enough energy and resources to this cause, it can happen. It may take a long time. It may not even happen in our lifetimes. But remember, lasting change never happens overnight. So please pledge generously for my proposed housemate-based cleanliness-education initiative. Nothing less than the eventual cleaning of this apartment is at stake. ∅

WRITER from page 105

contains between 30 and 300 mg of caffeine, depending on its preparation, while black tea contains 45 to 75 mg of caffeine.

Caffeine, Hoff noted, is also added to certain soft drinks. Among the most dangerous is Mountain Dew, a standard 12-ounce can of which contains 55 mg of "the evil stuff."

"I wish I could say my addiction was limited to coffee," Hoff said. "But when I wasn't pounding the java, it was Mountain Dew. At my low point, I was drinking four cans a day. And even though I hated myself for it, I didn't want to stop."

Though caffeine is a natural stimulant, it can have many adverse side effects, including anxiety, insomnia, irritability, and headaches. Hoff said she experienced them all.

"There were nights when I'd lie in bed tossing and turning for hours," Hoff said. "Even when I'd come home from work exhausted and just want to go straight to bed, the caffeine made it almost impossible. I never knew that my inability to fall asleep could be caused by caffeine I'd ingested up to 12 hours earlier. Looking back, it's frightening how little I knew about this beast that was controlling my life."

Perhaps the most alarming aspect of caffeine addiction, Hoff said, is the fact that many people—even doctors—assume the substance is harmless because it is not regulated by the FDA.

"The truth is that it is a drug like any other," Hoff said. "It can alter moods and change behavior. That's a drug."

In her article, Hoff candidly confessed that her caffeine binges also caused severe mood swings.

"One day, my 8-year-old son was making noise playing in the next room," she wrote. "It was the weekend, and I had a pounding, five-alarm headache—unbeknownst to me at the time, it was due to my not having had my regular dose of caffeine that day. Before I even knew what was happening, I'd snapped at my child... *my own child.*"

The very next day, Hoff phoned Arlene Lewis, an old high-school friend who was now a nurse. After hearing Hoff describe her headaches, insomnia, and irritability, Lewis diagnosed her as a caffeine addict. Then she recommended that Hoff read *Caffeine Freed* by Dr. Charlotte Kelsey.

Reading *Caffeine Freed*, Hoff learned that caffeine may exacerbate such conditions as migraine headaches, coronary heart disease, fibrocystic breast disease, prostrate trouble, or cardiac arrhythmia. It also is a diuretic and can be the

> **Said Hoff: "Looking back, it's frightening how little I knew about this beast that was controlling my life."**

cause of urinary-tract infections.

Most important, the book taught Hoff that to kick the habit, a caffeine addict needs to begin to limit intake to between 100 and 1000 mg a day, depending on weight, eating habits, and personal bodily responses to caffeine.

Armed with her newfound knowledge of her addiction, Hoff was finally able to take her first steps down the long road to recovery. Over the course of the next several months, she slowly reduced her intake, keeping a "caffeine journal" in which she jotted down the caffeine content of the foods she consumed throughout the day.

"I had no idea just how much caffeine I was taking in until I started to keep track," Hoff said. "A piece of chocolate here, a can of Pepsi there—it was scary. Thank God I'm no longer that person."

Hoff said she is grateful that, as a *Woman's Day* writer, she has a platform to share her story with other caffeine addicts.

"Yes, this was difficult to talk about," Hoff said. "But if there's just one woman out there who reads this article about what I went through and, as a result, gets the help she needs, it's all worth it."

Hoff has been a regular contributor to *Woman's Day* since 1991. In that time, she has written candid, first-hand accounts of her harrowing battles with such conditions as Carpal Tunnel Syndrome, seasonal afflictive disorder, and PMS. ∅

Don't Talk To Me About Problems

Hola, amigos. What's the deal behind your steering wheel? I know it's been a long time since I rapped at ya, but I've had some shit to contend with. I was supposed to write

**The Cruise
By Jim Anchower**

this column last Wednesday, but I did a few too many o n e - h i t t e r s and wound up spending the whole afternoon trying to figure out what was making this horrible smell under my sink. I pulled out all the rusty tools and bottles of Windex from under it and wound up finding a dead mouse. I was like, "Shit! Mouse!" Then, I was like, "Shit! Dead thing!"

But that wasn't the end of it. After seeing the mouse, I started thinking all these deep thoughts about how, in a way, we're all like mice, and how that could have been me under the sink. It freaked me out for a few days. I had to call in sick to work and everything. Not that calling in sick was a huge deal. I'm getting sick of that damn job, anyway.

But you know what? I'm not gonna bitch about that anymore. During those days I stayed home, I came to the realization that I bitch too much about stuff. From now on, I decided, I was gonna be a man of action.

If something comes along that I don't like, I deal with it. Pow! Just like that. For example, let's say I scope out a parking space in front of

> **During those days I stayed home, I came to the realization that I bitch too much about stuff. From now on, I decided, I was gonna be a man of action.**

the White Hen and some guy whips in from out of nowhere and takes it. What do I do? As a man of action, I simply find another parking space and key the guy's car. See? I don't cry like a baby about the problem, I take concrete steps to deal with it.

I got a long list of problems to deal with. Like, what the hell is the deal with all the crappy rock these days? It's all watered-down wimped-out bullshit. I tell ya, some people I come across are all like, "I love Third Eye Blind," or whatever. These feebs wouldn't know a hot Randy Rhoads guitar lick if he was to come back

from the dead, knock on the door, and deliver it in person. I only got one solution when somebody says they like that Eve's Vertical Match-box shit, and that is to kick 'em out of my car so they can walk home and think about the error of their ways. But they'd have to be riding with me for that to happen, and there's no way I'd even let a puss like that in my car in the first place.

Another problem I got is high gas prices. My cousin Matt fought in Iran so we could have low gas prices, and I gotta pay $1.40 a gallon? Milk costs, well, something like that, and that stuff doesn't even grow in the ground like oil. If you want my opinion, high gas prices are for suckers. But, again, I'm not just sitting around bellyaching about it, I'm taking action by siphoning gas out of my neighbor's car. I ain't paying for gas until it goes back down to around a buck. That's action for you!

People drive like morons, too. But while, in the past, I would just gripe about it to Ron and Wes, now I just lay on my horn whenever someone does something stupid. And, if it's warm out, I yell something, too. At Spencer Gifts, they got this awesome sign you can put in your car window that says things like, "Nice Job, Asshole!" and other stuff like that when you come across some idiot driver. Next time I'm at the mall, I'm picking one up for sure.

Another problem that's been bothering me for a long time is that when I go to a store to pick up a pack of rolling papers, the clerk always looks at me like I'm just gonna use it to smoke weed. I mean, yeah, that is what I'm going to use it for, but I sure don't need some creepy clerk staring at me like I got an extra head. Next time that happens, the new Jim is going to grab a handful of Zig-Zag packs from the counter and throw them on the floor and say, "Now you've really got something to stare at, old man!"

I also have sloppy friends that don't have any respect for me or my space. Ron in particular is always eating my food and leaving crumbs all over my couch and car seat. I'm not the cleanest person, but Ron eats about half what he gets in his mouth, and the other half winds up in places I gotta sit. Then he complains about how he never gets a chance to pick the music when we're cruising. Man, that guy is the biggest whiner in the world.

Okay, I just want to make something clear. All this stuff I'm saying, it's not bitching. I'm just passing along my story. And as far as me calling Ron a dumb-ass, hey, that's just the plain truth. It's no different than if I'd said the sky is blue or that Jimmy Page is the world's greatest musician. It's an unarguable fact. No one can take that away. ✍

HAMSTER from page 103

knocking over three nearby Fisher-Price Little People.

The scene quickly devolved into pandemonium, with the launched hamster tumbling humorously in mid-air several times before landing at the foot of the sofa and fleeing in shock. A frantic, living-room-wide search for Harry ensued and, after extensive search efforts behind the sofa, under the recliner, and behind the bookcase, the hamster was found between the vertical blinds and the sliding glass door, shaken but alive.

As of press time, Harry was resting in his cage, his condition described as "skittish but stable."

"This is a tremendous shock," said Bourke next-door neighbor Paula Gates upon learning of the mishap. "Harry is well-liked by all the neighborhood children, and for his life to be jeopardized in this manner is terribly upsetting."

Parental investigators have determined that the toy's two operators, whose names are being withheld due to their ages, successfully navigated the monster truck through the obstacle course numerous times before adding the hamster in an attempt to increase the

activity's entertainment value. If found guilty, the boys, 7 and 9, could be sentenced to an evening in their rooms and fines of up to two weeks' allowance.

> **As of press time, Harry was resting in his cage, his condition described as "skittish but stable."**

The accident's cause has been the subject of much debate. While many blame the toy's manufacturer, Playcorp Unlimited, for making a substandard product, others say the monster truck's operators are at fault. Angry at the boys, an unnamed Bourke parent is pressing for a strict

ban on the use of family pets in play activities, with a penalty of three days without PlayStation for those found guilty.

Playcorp spokesperson Paul Ionesco expressed "deep dismay" over the crash.

"This is a flagrant and obvious misuse of our product," Ionesco said. "No Playcorp product is intended for the transportation of live cargo, no matter how cute and humorous the spectacle of a little hamster driving along in his little truck may be."

Monday's crash marks the fourth time that Harry, 1, has found himself involved in dangerous play. In October 2000, Harry was placed on the back of family dog Raggles, who ran through several rooms within the house before being stopped by mother Lorraine Bourke. On Feb. 20, he was strapped to an army-man parachute and dropped from a second-story window. Three days later, the hamster was placed inside his glow-in-the-dark run-about ball and pushed down a flight of stairs. Both acts occurred with no parents in the vicinity, and no perpetrators were ever brought to trial. ✍

GAGGLE from page 2

of blood. Passersby were amazed by the unusually large amounts of blood. Passersby were amazed by the unusually large amounts of blood. Passersby were amazed by the unusually large amounts of

> **You'll never guess what I've got strapped to myself.**

blood. Passersby were amazed by the unusually large amounts of blood. Passersby were amazed by the unusually large amounts of blood. Passersby were amazed by the unusually large amounts of blood. Passersby were amazed by the unusually large amounts of blood. Passersby were amazed by the unusually large amounts of blood. Passersby were amazed by the unusually large amounts of blood. Passersby were amazed by the unusually large amounts of blood.

see GAGGLE page 118

How Real Is Reality TV?

Survivor and other reality-based TV shows have come under fire of late, with former participants charging that aspects of the programs are rigged. What do *you* think?

Richard Polk
Systems Analyst

"How far the journalistic integrity of reality TV has fallen since the first season of *The Real World*."

Audra Andrews
Student

"Reality TV is nothing but LIE$. By the way, when you print that, make sure the 'S' is a dollar sign, so my provocative statement is rendered all the more cutting."

Gail Pennington
TV Critic

"Love it or hate it, one thing's for certain: Reality TV makes us the ultimate voyeurs. Hi, I'm Gail Pennington, TV critic for the *St. Louis Post-Dispatch*."

Robert Lau
Physicist

"This is the classic Heisenbergian situation in which the behavior of the observed is altered by the act of observation. Nonetheless, Kimmi is my favorite."

Manu Apalakian
Dishwasher

"I'm glad they tinker with these shows. Real life is fuckin' boring."

Ed Munson
Machinist

"So these shows were set up to ensure that the most attractive people would come out on top? And how is that different from reality?"

Preventing Military Mishaps

The U.S. military has committed numerous deadly blunders of late, including the accidental sinking of a Japanese fishing trawler and the bombing of U.S. servicemen during a naval exercise in Kuwait. What measures are being taken in response?

☆ Cancelling Navy's "Steer A Sub For 20 Bucks" fundraiser

☆ Rethinking decision to teach high-school dropouts to work with computers

☆ Rigging subs to emit loud, piercing klaxon when backing up

☆ Adopting new "Don't ask, don't tell" policy in all cases of accidental vessel-sinking

☆ Encouraging safety with "11 Days Since Last Accidental Bombing Of Our Own Troops" sign

☆ Removing Japanese fishing trawlers from official U.S. enemies list

☆ Banning over-aggressive, type-A men from military bases

☆ Launching $30 million "Think Before You Sink!" awareness campaign

☆ Passing strict regulation prohibiting soldiers from dying as result of military error, to be enforced with deadly force

☆ Taking right to fly helicopter gunships away from Beetle Bailey

☆ Adding another $1 trillion to military budget

⌀ the ONION

America's Finest News Source

Herman Ulysses Zweibel *Founder*

T. Herman Zweibel *Publisher Emeritus*
J. Phineas Zweibel *Publisher*
Maxwell Prescott Zweibel *Editor-In-Chief*

FOUNDED 1871 • "TU STULTUS ES"

Your Horoscope

By Lloyd Schumner Sr.
Retired Machinist and
A.A.P.B.-Certified Astrologer

Aries: (March 21–April 19)
You will find yourself torn between two lovers, one who is giving and kind and refuses to let you go, and another who chains you to the bumper of his truck.

Taurus: (April 20–May 20)
While it's true that deciding to begin is half the battle, the rest turns out to be a bloody contest of attrition in the treacherous Khyber Pass.

Gemini: (May 21–June 21)
The stars thank you for your interest, but you do not fit their needs at this time. Good luck in future endeavors.

Cancer: (June 22–July 22)
Your hatred of the strange and unfamiliar leads you to open hundreds of identical fast-food restaurants.

Leo: (July 23–Aug. 22)
Sooner or later, you're going to have to stop and think about whose money it is, what the girl's name might be, what's in the bags of white powder, and why that helicopter sound keeps getting louder.

Virgo: (Aug. 23–Sept. 22)
You will be disproportionately rewarded for your ability to manipulate a standard-issue baseball.

Libra: (Sept. 23–Oct. 23)
Events that will eventually win you fame as the Human Tiddlywink are starting to come together in a Pittsburgh manhole-cover factory.

Scorpio: (Oct. 24–Nov. 21)
You will never completely overcome your murderous rage at the people who turned an anti-corporate Devo song into an ad jingle for Target.

Sagittarius: (Nov. 22–Dec. 21)
Look on the bright side: After the next four years, they probably won't elect another Republican in your lifetime.

Capricorn: (Dec. 22–Jan. 19)
Attempts to bring you to justice will ultimately prove fruitless, forcing justice to come to you with its own fruit.

Aquarius: (Jan. 20–Feb. 18)
Though the moon seems large in the night sky, you can cover it up with a nickel. However, this will cause an eclipse, so don't do it casually.

Pisces: (Feb. 19–March 20)
You will be worshipped as a god when you demonstrate your lighter to the natives, all of whom smoke but forgot to bring matches.

COLLECTIBLE from page 105

no longer important, either. Items used to only get valuable over long periods of time. Not so anymore, says TransUniverse Collectibles, makers of the official *Star Trek: Voyager* Officers' Club individually wrapped toothpick assortment, which retails for $79.95 and is sold directly to collectors.

"Old? Are you kidding? Everything we sell here at TransUniverse goes straight to collectors with no middlemen the day we make it, because these Trekkie types insist on buying [the items] the first day they're out," TransUniverse co-founder Wayne Spoerl said. "We don't need to wait for it to become a collector's item over time—we just print the words 'Collector's Item' right on the package. They're valuable because we only make a limited run of, say, 500,000. Okay, more, but still."

With everything on the planet officially collectible, collectors have more items to choose from than ever. Objects such as plastic twist ties from speaker-wire packaging, the tin-foil lining of chewing-gum wrappers, and the little rubbery residue left in magazines when attachments are removed have all jumped sharply in value—and investors see no signs of a slowdown.

"I just sold some guy 3,000 gallons of factory runoff from a waste-processing plant in central Illinois," said collectibles dealer Gary Hammond of Louisville, KY. "The government tried unsuccessfully to get the stuff zoned for burial in three states, but now it's in this guy's basement in a glass case. Why? Because it was banned in three states, so now it's collectible. That's the beauty of this business: Even stuff that absolutely nobody wants, somebody wants." ⌀

the ONION®

VOLUME 37 ISSUE 11   AMERICA'S FINEST NEWS SOURCE™   29 MARCH-4 APRIL 2001

Phalanx Of Lawyers Stares Hungrily From Back Cover Of Phone Book

see LOCAL page 9C

Prairie Dog Town Rezoned For Commercial Use

see BUSINESS page 3E

Student Secretly Giving The Finger In Yearbook Photo

see EDUCATION page 12B

THE ONION
VOLUME 37
ISSUE 11

$2.00 US
$3.00 CAN

0 74470 94595 6   09

57 Lawmakers Feared Dead In Senate Mine Disaster

WASHINGTON, DC— Hopes of finding more survivors of Monday's Senate Mine disaster are fading, as a second full day of rescue efforts proved futile Wednesday.

In all, 57 legislators remain buried deep within the Senate Mine, the southern shaft of which collapsed without warning at 7:57 a.m. Monday.

Left: The body of a senator is carried from the disaster area.

Rescue workers say the likelihood of finding survivors is slim.

"The area where the senators were digging is one of the narrowest in the entire mine," said Tom Asheton of the Red Cross. "We know for sure that the passageways on both sides of the corridor were sealed off in the initial blast, so the senators probably ran out of oxy-

see SENATE page 112

THE ROAD TO THE VATICAN

Cardinals Blasted For Negative Campaign Tactics In Papal Race

VATICAN CITY—As the health of Pope John Paul II erodes and the next papal election draws near, many Catholic Church officials have expressed dismay over the prevalence of negative campaigning among those vying for Catholicism's top post.

"This papal campaign is one of the nastiest in recent memory, characterized by slander, smear tactics, and ad hominem

attacks," said *Catholicism Today* editor Bruno DeGaetano. "Everyone knows His Holiness will soon be called to join The Heavenly Father, and there are a lot of cardinals out there who've been waiting since 1978 to run for pope, so the stakes are incredibly high."

The papal election, expected to occur in late 2001 or early 2002, has already sparked a flurry

Above: Archbishop Eugenio Vitti of Genoa greets supporters during a campaign stop in Milan.

of negative campaign ads on TV.

"Cardinal Norberto Rivera Carrera has been

archbishop of Mexico City since 1995," says the voiceover of one ad cur-

see CAMPAIGN page 110

Girlfriend Changes Man Into Someone She's Not Interested In

CHARLOTTE, NC—After two and a half years of subtle prodding and manipulation, Jill Nickles has finally molded boyfriend Brendan Eiler into the sort of man in whom she's not interested.

"When I first met Brendan, he was a guitarist for [local rock band] The Heavy Petters, and I couldn't take my eyes off him," said Nickles, 28. "I used to go to Tramp's every Thursday night just to watch him play. He wasn't even the most handsome guy in the world, but he just had this mystique, this air of danger about him. He was really exciting. It's too bad he's not like that anymore."

After several months of watching him from the crowd, Nickles finally introduced herself to Eiler after a show in September 1998. They soon began dating.

"Brendan was everything I wanted in a man," Nickles said. "He was unpredictable, smart, and passionate. I knew he wasn't perfect, but he was really fun to be around—which is more than I can say for him now."

Just weeks into the relationship, Nickles began to notice changes.

"It started pretty early," Nickles said. "Instead of being the wild man he'd been, more and more he'd just

see GIRLFRIEND page 111

Above: Jill Nickles and Brendan Eiler.

109

Fifth-Grader Writes 'Mrs. Alan Greenspan' All Over Her Notebook

INDEPENDENCE, MO—Brianna Kilgore, 11, a fifth-grader at Westlake Elementary School, was observed scribbling "Mrs. Alan Greenspan" an estimated 200 times in her notebook during class Monday. "She was totally writing 'Mrs. Alan Greenspan' and 'Brianna Greenspan' all over her spelling notebook—big and small, in cursive and block letters, everything," said Ashley Taylor, who sits directly behind Kilgore in Mrs. Schukal's class. "Then she took out a pink marker and wrote 'B.K. + A.G.—4EVA' inside a heart." When confronted by Taylor, Kilgore denied being in love with the Fed chair and told her classmate to mind her own beeswax.

Man Won't Stop Coming Up With New Sniglets

STOCKTON, CA—Nearly 20 years after the briefly popular lexicographic fad made its debut on HBO's *Not Necessarily The News*, local resident Paul Appleby continues to create new Sniglets. "I was drinking coffee with Paul in the breakroom, and he informs me that the non-dairy-creamer residue at the bottom of the cup ought to be called the 'cremorass,'" coworker Gail Farner said Monday. "Then, a few minutes later, he says, 'You know that little pop-up safety button on the cap of juice drinks? That's a snubbler.'" Added Farner: "He's working on these things like there's still someplace you can send them. Is that Rich Hall guy even still alive?"

Giant Blood Clot Dislodges From Your Femoral Vein

YOUR CIRCULATORY SYSTEM—According to lower-extremity sources, a blood clot two to three times larger than necessary to cause a pulmonary embolus has broken loose from your femoral vein and is migrating up your leg at this very moment. "In light of the size of this clot," your doctor said, "calling 911 would only waste city resources." Your doctor recommended that you lie down near the front door so the coroner's office can more easily remove your body from your home.

Repressed Molestation Memory Not What It Was Built Up To Be

WEEHAWKEN, NJ—After 22 months of thera-py, Kathy Stebbins' long-repressed childhood memory of sexual abuse at the hands of her uncle finally surfaced Tuesday in a thoroughly anti-climactic breakthrough. "That was it? That was the big molestation we've been trying to draw from her subconscious for almost two years?" disappointed therapist Dr. Anderson Gruber said. "She can't open herself up emotionally to men because some hug from Uncle Gordon went on too long? Give me a break."

Pillsbury Doughboy Killed By Skittish, Broom-Wielding Housewife

BOWIE, MD—Kenneth Fresh, 34, son of original Pillsbury doughboy Marv "Poppin'" Fresh, was killed Monday when a startled housewife beat him to death with a broom. "I was sweeping the kitchen floor and lamenting our family's usual humdrum breakfast biscuits when I heard a strange, high-pitched voice directly behind me," said a shaken Debbie Combs, 44. "All he could say was 'Try my new flaky Cres—' before my instincts took over and I pounded him with all my might." Rescue workers frantically poked Fresh for nearly 20 minutes in an effort to revive the doughboy, but were unsuccessful. ∅

CAMPAIGN from page 109

rently airing in North America. "But in that time, he twice opposed the canonization of Our Lady of Guadalupe, one of Mexico's most beloved religious figures. If Our Lady isn't fit to be a saint, Cardinal Carrera, who is?" The image of Cardinal Carrera is then shown superimposed over a shadowy image of a horned, fork-tailed man holding a pitchfork.

The ad was paid for by the Committee To Elect Pope Egan, an organization that supports New York Archbishop Edward Egan.

"This is absurd," Carrera said. "I never opposed the canonization of Our Lady of Guadalupe. I merely noted that several others were at least as deserving. I'd also like to note that it's more than a little ironic that Cardinal Egan, a known consort of moneylenders and fraternizer with sodomites, should take the moral high ground against a man with a proven track record of piety like myself."

Egan, who recently hired longtime Bill Clinton advisor Dick Morris as a consultant, denied involvement with the ads or the Committee To Elect Pope Egan.

"In the past six months, various advocacy groups, nominally in the pay of my opponents, have questioned my stance on drugs and birth control," said Cardinal Antonio Innocenti, Archbishop of Eclano, speaking to various assembled cardinals in St. Peter's Basilica. "I resent that we must stoop to such secular levels in our quest for the papacy, and I promise that if it pleases God that I am chosen, I shall issue a papal edict banning such behavior."

Cardinal Innocenti's campaign promise isn't the only one stirring controversy in the Vatican. Archbishop Emeritus Giovanni Canestri of Genoa was recently slammed for promising to reduce confessional penances for all Catholics by at least 10 Hail Marys, 10 Novenas, and 5 Our Fathers by 2004. And, in a controversial interview in the March issue of the German magazine *Stern*, Archbishop Joachim Meisner of Cologne stated that, if elected pope, he would loosen the definition of a "viable fetus," allowing abortions for Catholics well into the second trimester. In the weeks since the interview's publication, Archbishop Meisner's approval rating among Catholics has doubled, prompting outrage from lesser-known cardinals.

"The backstabbing among these holy men has grown fierce," United Catholic League president Frank Donovan said. "Take Ash Wednesday just a few weeks ago. Cardinal Claudio Hummes was presiding over a live televised mass in São Paulo when, right in the middle of the recounting of the Third Station of the Cross, an unidentified man in the crowd repeatedly yelled for Hummes to 'tell them about the shame of Sister Maria.' Then the man started screaming that sodomy is a mortal sin and that he 'had pictures.' It created quite a stir, particularly when Hummes lost his temper and denied knowing any Sister Maria. After the man was apprehended and questioned, he said that a man in a red hat had promised him liquor if he yelled those things within earshot of reporters."

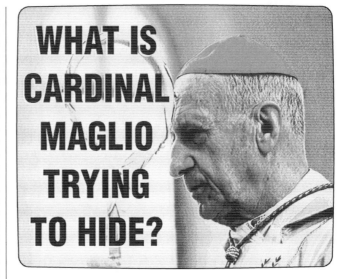

Above: A campaign ad attacking cardinal Vittorio Maglio. The ad was paid for by the group Catholics For Ennio Antonelli For Pope.

Other recent examples of dirty tactics include a doctored photo of Cardinal Honore appearing to drop a premature infant at a Tours clinic, the infamous "Do we really want a Pope Darmaatmadja?" TV spots, and the anti-Archbishop of Canterbury newspaper ads funded by "the Friends of Cardinal Thomas Joseph Winning of Glasgow," a nonexistent organization subsequently revealed to be a front for Desmond Connell, the Archbishop of Dublin.

Despite all the negative campaigning, Pope John Paul II expressed confidence that cooler heads will prevail when the process of choosing his successor begins.

"Back in 1978, when Pope Paul VI fell ill, I went out of my way to expose Cardinal Albino Luciani's drinking problem and predilection for impure thoughts to the Vatican Council," His Holiness told reporters. "But in spite of such attacks, I lost the election. Later that year, the new pope died and I was in the running once again, this time determined to run a clean race. I did, and I won. I have faith that, as I did, today's papal candidates will eventually see the wisdom of eschewing slander and sticking to the issues that matter to everyday Catholics." ∅

Why Can't We Have A Nice Igloo Like The Meekitjuks Next Door?

By Komangapik Mukpa

This so-called "igloo" of ours, dear, is a complete embarrassment. Some days, I don't even want to be seen crawling out of the entrance. Now, the Meekitjuks next door, they've got a beautiful place—perfectly cut blocks of ice, a nice, wide entrance, and a two-sled snow rampart built into the back. Why can't we live in a decent igloo like them?

Just take a look at this poor excuse for an igloo: there are ice shavings all over the floor, the ceiling is filthy with smoke, and the wall that faces the rising sun is so uneven, it looks like it's ready to cave in at any second. I wouldn't be surprised if we came home one day to find the whole dome collapsed! Yes, we're the laughingstock of the whole neighborhood.

Yesterday, I had some of the gals from the neighborhood over for a bit of blood soup. I didn't even have a decent hammered-copper bowl to serve it in. On top of that, do you think they didn't notice the worn-out condition of our qipiik? It's more hole than caribou hide! And this old polar-bear-skin rug—it's an ancient hand-me-down from my grandmother, and we're still using it.

All the other women in the village enjoy the latest modern conveniences: blades made of metal, coffee cans to cure the blubber dip. Meanwhile, I don't have so much as an *ulu* knife to butcher the darn seals.

Not that I've had much to butcher lately. Yesterday, I was peeking out the front entrance and saw Pauloosie Meekitjuk come home after a day of hunting. He was dragging two seals home on his sled! When was the last time *you* brought two seals home? Last week, it was a few skinny little otters. You're always giving the same lame excuse, telling me it's a "hard winter." Well, we must have some real strange weather patterns around these parts, because it doesn't seem to be a hard winter 20 feet away over at Chez Meekitjuk.

You come home every night, complaining about how exhausted you are from standing over the ice all day with a harpoon, waiting for a seal to surface. And that's not even counting all the nights you come crawling in the front hole at 2 a.m., armed with some phony-baloney story about how you've been out all night following caribou tracks across the frozen tundra. Please. I'm not stupid. I know you're down at the kashgee listening to the shaman stories with the guys. And you know what? I'm really starting to get tired of it.

This coming Sunday, we're invited to the seal-sharing feast over at the Meekitjuks. You'll be happy to know that there will be a whole feast of sliced flipper and blubber and caribou-stomach contents. And I'm sure you'll enjoy it every bit as much as the Meekitjuks' last feast. But we're not going to be invited too many more times if you don't bring home a seal soon to return the favor. Then where will we be? We'll be shunned and have to move our igloo to the bad part of the village, out where the anthropologists live.

I know what you're thinking: "But Komangapik! We just got a new kayak this year! Doesn't that count for something?" Some kayak! The Meekitjuks have a 14-foot kayak, and ours is barely 10 feet long. And what about the caribou-skin interior you keep saying you'll put in it as soon as you get the time? You promised to do it 20 moons ago!

The only thing you care about is that stupid sled of yours. Did we really need another dog? I think Qallunaaq and Kitikmeot were more than adequate, but you insisted we needed Nujuattaittut and Nujuattaittuttuta, too.

My mother warned me about you. She said, "Komangapik, that man has the spirit of the mighty humpback whale in his soul, but nothing but dust in the pockets of his parka." What did I know? I was only 14. Now that I'm older, I understand all too well what she was saying.

Don't I deserve a decent igloo? Do you think I just sit around all day chewing dried salmon while you're away hunting? Yesterday, I spent all day repairing last year's sealskin boots with sinew thread and bone needles, just so I'd have something decent to wear to storytelling sessions around the group fire. If only I could have something besides the same old fox-fur coats.

You spare no expense when it comes to your precious harpoons and knives. You just had to have that toggle harpoon made out of ivory when the antler one would have done fine. But as soon as I want a few small things for around the igloo, we suddenly don't have the skins to trade for them.

Did you see the wooden mask Amik Meekitjuk has on her wall? I asked her where she got it. She said she bought it during an umiak trip to Baffin Island and that it cost only a pot of seal oil. *Only!* We barely have enough seal oil to keep our igloo lit through the winter, and they're trading away a whole pot of oil! The fact that she got it during a trip to Baffin Island only makes it worse. Every year, you promise that the whole family will migrate there for the summer to fish and capture birds. Then, when it's time to go, you take off with the other men and say there's not enough room in the umiak for me and the kids.

Do you think I enjoy sitting home, staring at the same one wall day after day? Of course not! Then, when I offer to accompany you on the hunt, you say I talk too much and prevent the seals from coming to the surface! Well, maybe if I had more otter to skin, I'd have less time to talk. Hmmph. ∅

GIRLFRIEND from page 109

stay home like a lump, even on nights I told him it was okay if he went out."

Four months to the day after their first date, Nickles moved into Eiler's one-bedroom apartment. The move only accelerated the changes in him.

"Jill and I weren't living together long before she started getting irritated by how small the apartment was," Eiler said. "She was always complaining about how she didn't have space anymore. Then, she got this idea to get a bigger place, but I couldn't afford it, because I was just barely scraping by with what I earned bartending at Mickey's. I really liked bartending, and it allowed me flexible hours for band practice and gigs. But, like Jill said, I was 25 now and shouldn't be living hand-to-mouth."

At Nickles' urging, Eiler quit his job at Mickey's and landed a position at SFR Solutions, a Charlotte-area web-design firm. The job paid nearly $4,000 a year more than bartending,

enabling the couple to move into a larger apartment.

With a full-time job and a live-in girlfriend, Eiler's relationship with his bandmates soon began to deteriorate.

"They kept wanting to play more and more gigs, and I felt like if we wanted to land a record deal, what I needed to do was stay home and write some strong new material," Eiler said. "Even Jill had stopped going to see us because she said she was getting sick of hearing the same songs—and she was our number-one fan. Finally, they said I had to make more time for shows or they'd get a new guitarist. I was like, 'Screw you guys,' and left. Jill pointed out that the band wasn't really going anywhere anyway, and that I was better off in no band at all than one made up of a bunch of unambitious losers."

Upon quitting the band, Eiler's lifestyle changes accelerated. In September 2000, he cut his long mane of hair in an effort to land a

promotion to associate design director at SFR Solutions. Nickles also convinced him to become a vegetarian and sell his customized leather jacket to put a down payment on a new Toyota Camry.

"When we first started dating, Jill loved how I looked in that jacket," Eiler said. "But then, a few months later, she said I was getting too old to wear something like that. Plus, it didn't really gibe with my new vegetarian beliefs. So, with Jill's full support, I decided it was time to put my old ways to rest."

Now a self-described homebody, Eiler said he finds his domestic lifestyle "really satisfying."

"If you told me two years ago that I'd be thinking of marriage, a house with a picket fence, and kids, I would have said you were nuts," Eiler said. "All I used to care about was hanging with my friends and having a good time. I guess it's true that the love of a good woman can really change you for the better."

In spite of Nickles' success in sculpting Eiler into "husband material," she found her attraction for him beginning to wane.

"The reason I fell so hard for Brendan was that he was totally different from the guys I used to date," Nickles said. "He had beautiful long hair, and he was really smart and cynical. Now he reminds me of my boring ex-boyfriend Kevin, who's an accountant in Raleigh."

Even though Nickles' nights of going out to see The Heavy Petters are long over, she still enjoys going out on occasion.

"A couple of weeks ago, I was at the bar Brendan and I used to go to all the time," Nickles said. "I ran into Rob, the bassist for Brendan's old band and, I have to tell you, he looked really good. We hung out and talked for hours and just had a great time. Drinking and laughing with him really reminded me of the way it used to be with Brendan. I think I'm developing a little crush on Rob." ∅

As Real-Estate Agent, Area Man's Appearance Crucial

Above: Gregg Rafalski, who understands the importance of a good first impression.

GRANGER, IN—Looking good is an essential component of Gregg Rafalski's success as a real-estate agent, the 35-year-old RE/MAX employee asserted Monday.

"As a real-estate agent, my appearance is crucial," Rafalski said. "On any given day, I'm interacting with a large number of people: clients, property owners, business associates. It's of the utmost importance that I convey professionalism to my customers and colleagues at all times."

To this end, Rafalski said he always wears a freshly pressed shirt, a "smart-looking" tie, well-polished shoes, and a minimal amount of carefully chosen jewelry, usually a watch and one ring. He also makes sure that his fingernails are clean and neatly trimmed.

"Buying a home is one of the most important decisions a person can make—many are sinking their entire life savings into it," Rafalski said. "That's why I need to project an air of confidence to my clients. Rumpled khaki pants and an untucked polo shirt are simply not going to cut it when you're looking to say, 'I am fully in control of this situation.'"

Though he graduated from high school with only a C average, Rafalski "aced" his subsequent 54-hour real-estate pre-licensing course at Michiana College in nearby South Bend. After completing the course, Rafalski passed the Indiana Real Estate Commission examination and gained his licensure in 1984. He has spent the past 17 years in commercial and residential real-estate, including the past six at RE/MAX.

Rafalski said he learned the importance of looking good early in his career.

"I attended quite a few [Indiana Commercial Board of Realtors] conferences during those first few years on the job, and I was lucky enough to meet some tremendous salespeople to serve as my role models," Rafalski said. "Because of the way they looked and carried themselves, these guys could walk into a room and, within two seconds, all eyes would be squarely on them. They could sell a drink of water to a fish."

It was at these early conferences that Rafalski learned "the true meaning of sales."

"Many people mistakenly think the success of a salesman is determined by your knowledge of the product," Rafalski said. "Sure, you need to know how old this house is or what the property taxes are on that one, but that's what briefcases are for. It's not the house, it's *you* that you're really selling to a customer."

Added Rafalski: "Speaking of briefcases, this one is imported Italian leather."

To look his best, Rafalski keeps abreast of current fashions. Two Fridays a month, he leaves work early and drives down to Glenbrook Square Mall in Fort Wayne, nearly 70 miles away.

"The Marshall Field's at University Park doesn't always carry the Hugo Boss shirts I like," Rafalski said. "So, every so often, I like to take a little trip down to Fort Wayne. I know that sounds crazy, but, believe me, when a potential home buyer is on the fence, the right shirt can turn an 'I'll pass' into an 'I'll take it.'"

Unlike his less successful colleagues, Rafalski doesn't waste his office hours keeping track of property values or brushing up on zoning changes. Instead, he browses online for hard-to-find items from his favorite brand names, including Kenneth Cole, Calvin Klein, and Ralph Lauren.

"If you dress cheap, you are cheap—it's that simple," Rafalski said. "Same thing goes for houses: Cheap houses, cheap commissions. That's just not my mindset."

In addition to his wardrobe, Rafalski's choice of transportation plays an important role in the impression he makes. He drives a red 2000 Chrysler Sebring convertible, which sends a strong message when he arrives for a house showing.

"What would a potential home buyer think if I pulled up in a dinky little Honda?" Rafalski asked. "Would that instill confidence in my abilities as an agent? I don't think so."

Rafalski also puts care into the appearance of his office at RE/MAX, which he keeps meticulously clean and decorated with silver curios and framed art prints.

"When someone walks into my office and sees the Waterford vase and Nicoletti leather chair, they know I know what I'm doing," Rafalski said. "Why would you entrust your search for a home to an agent who doesn't even care what his own office looks like?"

Rafalski's attention to detail has

see APPEARANCE page 114

SENATE from page 109

gen sometime yesterday afternoon. We'll give it another go first thing tomorrow, but at this point, it doesn't look good. Lord help those brave lawmakers."

Asheton then called upon all Americans to pray for the senators.

At 7 a.m. Monday, as they do every week, the nation's 100 senators donned their lantern helmets, took up shovels, and descended the main shaft by rope elevator to excavate the rich seam of coal recently discovered in the mine's Great Southern Drift. *Congressional Mine Record* transcripts of intercom communications indicate that operations were proceeding smoothly, with drill operators encountering no more than the normal resistance from rocky occlusions, when a sudden rumbling was heard.

"From way down the shaft, I could hear [Sen.] Judd [Gregg (R-NH)] shouting, 'The pilings! The pilings!'" said senate majority foreman Trent Lott (R-MS), whose leg was badly contused by falling mine tailings and who had to be restrained by aides from reentering the mine to save his colleagues. "Then there was this incredible roar, and all the lamps blew out. I remember thinking, 'Please, God, no: There's still so much important legislation to pass—and coal to dig.'"

At 8:08 a.m., the mine whistle on the Capitol dome sounded the emergency warning. Within minutes, sen-

Right: Senate majority foreman Trent Lott (R-MS) talks to reporters shortly after the mine collapse.

Oh, I'm No Good With Soap

By Roger Ayala

Barely a day goes by when someone doesn't scrunch their nose at me and say, "Hey, Roger, don't you believe in using soap?" To which I reply, "Oh, I believe in it. I'm just no good at it."

You'd think people would understand. All the time, I hear folks say things like, "I'm not a math person" or, "I'm terrible with names" or, "I can't golf to save my life," only to be chided goodheartedly. Yet when I say, "I'm really bad with soap," you should see the odd looks I get.

I mean, people who have difficulty with math don't get calculators left on their desks. But you offhandedly mention to your coworkers that you just don't "get soap" and what happens? Little "gifts" of soap, shampoo, and bath beads start showing up in your cubicle. What the heck am I supposed to do with them? It's like giving a ratchet set to a guy who's just told you he's lousy with cars. I either give these so-called presents to the homeless or toss them in the trash where they belong.

It's hard enough dealing with the hairy eyeball at the office, but getting grief from my family—well, that just stings. Every time I call Mom, she asks me if I'm taking showers, which I am. Then she asks if I use soap, and I'm like, "Come on, Mom, you know how it is with me and soap." I don't see her giving my brother Gene grief for being a terrible bowler, so why do I always have to get harassed about my little soap weakness?

Is it really the end of the world that I'm a lousy soaper? I mean, can't we focus on my positives? I don't chew with my mouth open. I speak clearly. I get my work done in a timely, efficient manner. I just have this mental block when it comes to soap. It's not like I urinate in the sink or talk about abortions while everybody's eating. Gee whiz.

I used to think this whole soap thing might have something to do with me being left-handed. You know how left-handed people are more creative because they're dominated by their right brain? Well, I asked my doctor if the part of the brain that controls your ability to use soap is the right or left side, and he said he didn't know. I thought doctors had to know stuff like that before they started operating on people.

Rather than get down on myself, I try to look at my lack of soaping skills as something that makes me unique. Sometimes, as a joke, someone will call me Pig Pen, like the guy from the *Peanuts* comic. I'm pretty sure they're trying to hurt my feelings, but I just remind myself that Pig Pen was pretty cool, pretty laid-back and sure of himself. He was always doing his own thing, just like me. Plus, most of the other characters in the strip seem to accept that he's just a dusty kid. (Except Lucy, but she's just a crank nobody really likes anyway.)

When I was a little kid, a lot of my friends were bad with soap. But then, sometime around age 13, they all started getting really good at it. Except me. My parents figured I'd start using soap when I hit puberty. But I'm 27 now, and my soaping abilities have not developed at all. I've decided to not worry about it, though. After all, if I don't have it by this point, I'm never going to have it.

Maybe one day, a meteor will crash to Earth, and I'll touch it and it will magically turn me into a tenth-level master soaper. But until that day comes, I guess I'll have to make do with tap water and the forcible hose-downs I get from time to time. ∅

---

the ONION presents
Bicycle-Safety Tips

Warm weather is just around the corner, and soon it will be time to dust off those bicycles. Here are some tips for safe riding:

- Always use hand signals when turning at intersections. There's nothing motorists pay more attention to than hand signals from bicyclists.
- Leaving your bike out in the ice and cold all winter may cause serious damage. But it makes a nice subject for the cover illustration of a short-fiction quarterly.
- Always wear a helmet. If this makes you uncomfortable, think of the helmet as a crown and yourself as King Dorko.
- Placing your feet firmly on the pedals of the bike will help reduce the "Wheee" sound emitted from your mouth while going downhill.
- Insist on a bicycle made of solid matter. Liquid and vapor bikes are a passing fancy; argon frames are particularly shoddy.
- Taking your bike in for a professional tune-up is a great way to waste $25.
- Be sure to wear your seatbelt, even if just biking down to the corner store.
- Fat-bottomed girls may be riding today, so look out for those beauties, oh, yeah.
- Visibility is crucial when biking. Ride with a lit highway flare in each hand.
- Every three to four weeks, lightly oil the chain. Then dip it in flour and fry it for a real taste treat.
- As soon as you buy a bike, talk to your friends about how great Shimano crank sets and STX hubs are.
- Does your city have adequate bike paths? If not, consider bitching about it to your local government for the next 40 years.
- If rich, spoiled Francis Buxton steals your bike, go on a hilarious and heartwarming journey through the American Southwest to get it back.
- Bike safety can never be stressed enough. If you doubt this, try stressing it as much as you possibly can. It won't be enough—guaranteed.

---

ators' loved ones began assembling at the mine's entrance to watch rescuers going about their grim work. One after another, the grimy, blue-suited bodies of senators were dragged from the mine.

"These are brave men," said Lott, his face still blackened with soot. "Despite our ongoing bipartisan struggles, with the Democrats arguing for shorter hours downshaft and Republicans supporting less restrictive mining regulations, there has been nothing but brotherhood today."

The cause of the mine's collapse remains unknown. No smoke or heat has been detected emanating from the shaft, ruling out the possibility that a hammer-drill struck sparks and ignited the abundant coal dust that fills the senatorial chambers.

Senators who had been working

> **Unsafe as congressional mining may be, few other options are available to unskilled elected officials.**

in the mine's central shaft say oxygen levels were normal. They also noted that congressional pages positioned in the mine to monitor air quality were chatting happily just seconds before the disaster. Survivors' accounts seem to point to a straightforward collapse, which, experts note, is an ever-present danger when legislators excavate in the wet rock near the Potomac.

"Of all the industrial ventures run by the federal government, the coal-mining operations of the legislative branch have always had the worst safety record," said Cliff Stephney, president of the United Senatorial Mine Workers of America. "Just last year, we almost lost the entire Senate Armed Services Committee when the hay bales they feed the cart-horses 'down the hole' somehow caught fire."

Stephney noted that Supreme Court & Southern Railroad brakemen, statistically the second most dangerous job in American government, had a 17 percent better chance of seeing retirement without injury.

Unsafe as congressional mining may be, few other options are available to unskilled elected officials.

"Every year, we say we're going to pass laws that make our jobs safer," said senator and rock hog Mitch "Mule" McConnell (R-KY), who has the distinction of surviving both Monday's collapse and the infamous Library of Congress Foundry Explosion of 1999. "But when a man gets down to voting, he remembers how much he owes to the Capitol store, and that's usually

see SENATE page 114

Hispanic U.S.A.

In a historic demographic shift, Census officials reported last week that Hispanics have passed African-Americans as the nation's largest minority. What do *you* think?

Richard Polk
Systems Analyst

"I don't care what you say, Hispanics are not a bigger minority than blacks. Have you seen those guys? They're barely five feet tall."

Robert Lau
Physicist

"I had no idea there were so many Hispanics in this country. They must all be in the back."

Manu Apalakian
Dishwasher

"I guess those good-luck candles with the bloody dude on them are actually good for something."

Ed Munson
Machinist

"Luckily, I am prepared for this, thanks to bilingual educational programming on PBS. *Abierto!... cerrado! Abierto!... cerrado!*"

Gail Pennington
TV Critic

"Boy, if it's not the blacks, it's the Hispanics. That's it. That's the summation of my feelings on the matter."

Audra Andrews
Student

"There are still tons more whites than any of these minorities, right? Whew."

20 Years Of MTV

MTV is celebrating its 20th anniversary this year. Among the music channel's highlights:

1982 Contest winner Janet Arbus of Evansville, IN, given Dexys Midnight Runners

1983 MTV airs "Billie Jean," first video by black artist; designation later rescinded

1985 That one time they played that Power Station video

1987 Downtown Julie Brown sort of semi-delights nation with "wubba wubba wubba" catchphrase

1988 MTV superstar Sting defects to VH1

1990 *Remote Control* host Ken Ober kills Neil Young, setting up trick question for game show's popular "Dead Or Canadian?" segment

1992 "Weird Al" Yankovic sentenced to 40 years in federal prison for illegally hacking MTV signal with "AL-TV" pirate satellite

1995 Regular programming stopped for 24 hours to help teens cope with death of Shannon Hoon

1997 "Smack My Bitch Up" controversy rages for nearly 40 minutes

2001 The Buggles reunite for last-ever video on MTV, "Adolescent-Targeted Prime-Time Programming Killed The Video Star"

the ONION
America's Finest News Source

Herman Ulysses Zweibel *Founder*

T. Herman Zweibel *Publisher Emeritus*
J. Phineas Zweibel *Publisher*
Maxwell Prescott Zweibel *Editor-In-Chief*

FOUNDED 1871 • "TU STULTUS ES"

Your Horoscope

By Lloyd Schumner Sr.
Retired Machinist and
A.A.P.B.-Certified Astrologer

Aries: (March 21–April 19)
Stop worrying so much about what your friends think. You should only care about the opinions of decent people.

Taurus: (April 20–May 20)
You pride yourself on learning something new every day, but next Wednesday will provide you with a greater education in primate anatomy and high-energy physics than you really wanted.

Gemini: (May 21–June 21)
The monsters that rampage through your slumber party will be different from the ones that terrorized Party Beach just a few days ago.

Cancer: (June 22–July 22)
You might be feeling down about your choice of careers this week, but look on the bright side: You're still the best deal in town.

Leo: (July 23–Aug. 22)
The story of your life turns out to be a ripoff of Donald Westlake's 1975 crime-caper novel *Two Much!*

Virgo: (Aug. 23–Sept. 22)
Just keep telling the officers "*No hablo Ingles.*" Unless they're Mexican. In that case, run.

Libra: (Sept. 23–Oct. 23)
When the girl you picked up at the bar said she could "peel a banana with it," she was actually talking about the Peelerator, a handy, labor-saving device she sells out of her bedroom.

Scorpio: (Oct. 24–Nov. 21)
There's just something about you that screams gay. But that's okay, as it's your voice, and you're doing it on purpose.

Sagittarius: (Nov. 22–Dec. 21)
A word of advice: Though drywall cement is a substance, it is not the kind that can be abused.

Capricorn: (Dec. 22–Jan. 19)
You've always thought that kicking the tires on used cars was smart, but next week you'll encounter a dealer who fills them with nitroglycerine.

Aquarius: (Jan. 20–Feb. 18)
You just don't have time for any so-called "rocking" song that doesn't have cowbell-banging in the chorus.

Pisces: (Feb. 19–March 20)
Two-time Academy Award winner Jack Lemmon will call you at home next Thursday to inform you that he has no intention of ever portraying you.

APPEARANCE from page 112

not gone unnoticed among clients.

"Gregg always looks so nice," said Adrienne Bauer, whom Rafalski is helping find a larger location for her Wicks 'N' Wax store. "I wish my husband would wear some of the newer tie styles, but he won't. He always says, 'I'm a pediatrician, not Regis Philbin.'"

Rafalski's coworkers are equally impressed.

"The clients really seem to like Gregg," said Granger RE/MAX senior real-estate broker Jonathan Quirk. "He's not necessarily our best agent when it comes to knowing his way around the neighborhood, but he still gets a heck of a lot of referrals and repeat customers. I think it might be his hair or something. He's got real nice hair." Ø

SENATE from page 113

the end of that. I mean, times being what they are, a senator can't really afford to just cash out and risk starving his family."

"Boss Thurmond always says there are tons of immigrants right off the boat who aren't afraid to serve a six-year term in elected office hauling out the coal," said Sen. Russell "Rusty" Feingold (D-WI). "I hate it like poison, but as soon as we get the slag out of that drift, I know I'm back to the shaft again."

In a nationally televised address Tuesday, President Bush paid tribute to the lost senators.

"We pray for the souls of each of these brave men, and we humbly thank them for toiling to provide our nation with badly needed laws and coal," Bush said. "We are with their families in their time of grief and promise a full congressional investigation just as soon as the mine—and Congress itself—can be reconstructed." Ø

Jenna Elfman Mentally Prepares Answer To Inevitable Question About Her Outfit

see PEOPLE page 3E

Yak Chews Thoughtfully

see LOCAL page 2C

Sean Combs Changes Name To P. Puff Diddly-Dang Doofus

see MUSIC page 6D

STATshot

A look at the numbers that shape your world.

Least-Common Tax Deductions

1. Monetary losses resulting from purchases of Skittles..........1
2. Bait..........2
3. "Bidness expense"..........3
4. Lighter fluid for client..........4
5. Potty training..........5
6. Medical expenses incurred while avenging dis to L'il Kim..........6
7. Leotard depreciation..........7

THE ONION
VOLUME 37
ISSUE 12
$2.00 US
$3.00 CAN

0 74470 94595 6

the ONION®

VOLUME 37 ISSUE 12   AMERICA'S FINEST NEWS SOURCE™   5-11 APRIL 2001

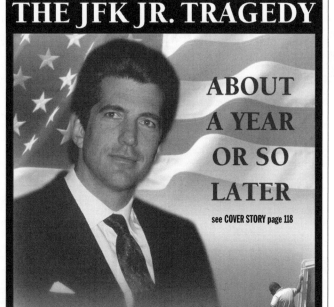

THE JFK JR. TRAGEDY

ABOUT A YEAR OR SO LATER

see COVER STORY page 118

Above: The GMC Whim.

General Motors Reports Record Sales Of New Disposable Car

DETROIT—In a report released Monday, General Motors announced 56 percent growth for the first quarter of 2001, a profit increase company officials attributed to February's wildly successful launch of the GMC Whim, the first-ever non-refillable, disposable automobile.

Making their debut at a cost of $1,100 each, the vehicles are flying out of showrooms as quickly as dealers can stock them. Featuring factory-

see CAR page 116

Action Figures Set Cubicle Apart

FAIRFIELD, OH—Ron Pelinka, a designer at Cincinnati's K&G Media Concepts, sets his cubicle apart from those of coworkers with an impressive collection of action figures.

"Here's The Creech," said Pelinka, 33, picking up one of the 57-and-counting toy figures that adorn his workspace. "This guy is from *Spawn*, series 12. Pretty creepy, huh? Roar! Seriously, though, this one is one of my favorites."

Pelinka said the creative nature of his work—designing instruction booklets for clock radios and other household electronics—demands a casual, free-thinking environment.

"I'd go crazy working in a sterile cubicle all day," Pelinka said. "Just take a look around this place. Desk, computer, chair. Wall, wall, door, wall. Management might as well drop us in a sensory-deprivation tank and say, 'Get to work.' Now, my cubicle, on the other hand—nobody's going to mistake it for any other around here, that's for sure."

see ACTION FIGURES page 118

Above: Just a few of the action figures that make Ron Pelinka's workspace distinctive.

Citizens To Vote On Young Or Old Reagan For $15 Bill

WASHINGTON, DC—On the heels of the Ronald Reagan Airport and U.S.S. Ronald Reagan aircraft carrier, citizens can now vote for one of two portraits of the former president to adorn the U.S. Mint's upcoming $15 bill. "Choose either the young, *General Electric Theater*-era Reagan or the older, second-term-president Reagan," U.S. Mint Deputy Director John Mitchell said Monday. Citizens may cast ballots at any FDIC-member bank. All voters will receive a commemorative LeRoy Neiman poster of Reagan delivering his 1981 inaugural address.

Oscar Countdown 2002 Begins

HOLLYWOOD, CA—With just 50 weeks to go before the big event, buzz surrounding the 2002 Academy Awards is beginning to build. "Will Tom Hanks turn in a performance that completes his Oscar hat trick? Will *Pearl Harbor* be the night's big winner, assuming it's a film of artistic merit?" Rebecca Ascher-Walsh wrote in *Entertainment Weekly*'s "Oscar '02 Preview!" double issue, which hit newsstands Tuesday. "These are some of the questions sure to be answered in just 341 days." Ascher-Walsh said *Entertainment Weekly* will run exclusive photos of the Versace gown to be worn by the radiant newcomer who will nab a Best Actress nomination for her surprise, star-making turn "the very moment" she becomes known.

Everything A Goddamn Ordeal In Area Family

HUNTINGTON, WV—Absolutely everything, from ordering a pizza to going out to the movies, has to be a huge goddamn ordeal for the Flemings, father Bryce Fleming reported Tuesday. "Just once, could we maybe sit down and watch some goddamn TV together without the whole thing devolving into an all-night screaming match?" Fleming asked wife Tanya Fleming. "Could we?" Fleming went on to ask if that could happen once in the history of their goddamn household.

Tenants Feel Guilty Asking Elderly Maintenance Man To Fix Anything

BOSTON—Tenants in the apartment building at 437 Market St. reported Monday that they experience a gnawing feeling of guilt every time they ask Hank Hudson, the 82-year-old maintenance man, to repair anything. "The other day, my sink was clogged and, at first, I was going to ask Hank to fix it," Apt. 4B tenant Julie Winters said Monday. "Then I remembered the time he repaired the furnace and coughed for weeks afterwards. In the end, I just bought a snake and did it myself."

Abandoned Mall Retains Eerie Vestiges Of Fun Shopping Atmosphere

ROSEVILLE, MN—The silent hull of Northlands Mall disquieted Erik Sandvig Monday, when the local man gazed through the locked glass doors of what was, in happier times, "Roseville's One-Stop Shopping Fun Zone." "Man, it's really creepy," Sandvig said of the once-thriving mall's mausoleum-like stillness. "There's the Sam Goody where you could get all the hottest new releases. And right next door is the Foot Locker that had all your favorite gear from Nike and Adidas." His nostalgic longing satisfied, Sandvig walked on, leaving the ghosts of former fun-seeking shoppers to roam the aisles undisturbed. *∅*

CAR from page 115

Above: The Whim's dashboard, which features a gas gauge that lets drivers know when to discard the car.

installed gasoline, an AM/FM radio with two preset stations, and a nine-volt battery to power the ignition, the Whim is attracting motorists looking for convenient, hassle-free transportation.

"I'm a busy mother of four," said Winston-Salem, NC, homemaker Hannah Plunkett, who buys a new Whim Grande minivan every seven to ten days. "I don't have time to change the oil, rotate the tires, fill up the tank, or deal with any of the other maintenance headaches you have with old-fashioned reusable cars. But with my Whim, the parts never have time to age."

"The Whim is the wave of the future," said enthusiast Glen Shriver, who recently drove from his home in Eden Prairie, MN, to Daytona Beach, FL, for the First Annual Whim Owners' Convention, consuming four of the vehicles in the process. "I've already collected all eight colors."

"Finally, I can feel comfortable teaching my kids to drive the family car," said Harold Sperber of Chillicothe, OH. "And when my oldest misbehaves, I can threaten to throw his car away."

Introduced to the nation in an ad aired during Super Bowl XXXV, the Whim's "Hi.... And Bye" spot features a rapid-fire succession of slogans touting advantages of the new car, including "Enjoy That New-Car Smell All The Time," "No Rust, No Repairs, No Fooling," and "Never Pay For A Car Wash Again. In Fact, We Urge You Not To Wash The Whim, As Hot Water Can Melt The Glue Holding The Frame Together."

When out of gas, the car can either be abandoned at the side of the road or returned to the dealer for a $10 deposit. For $100 extra, buyers can purchase the Whim Distinct, a premium model that boasts roomier seating, super-unleaded gasoline, and a tape deck with a pre-inserted, non-ejectable tape of the owner's choice. The Whim Distinct will also offer drivers the added option of going in reverse.

"We here at GM are delighted with the success of the Whim," CEO G. Richard Wagoner said. "America's love affair with the car, combined with its love of disposable products, has spelled tremendous success for us. As long as American industry keeps producing aluminum and polystyrene, we'll keep making Whims as fast as we can."

The vehicle has also given a boost to GM employment figures. Though faulted in recent years for rampant layoffs, GM has hired thousands of new assembly-line workers to meet demand for the Whim, which can take upwards of 450 man-minutes to assemble. Wagoner also noted that the Whim costs substantially less to manufacture than conventional automobiles due to the fact that it requires no fan belt, oil-distribution system, or other parts integral to the long-term functioning of a vehicle.

Responding to the Whim's success, rival automakers are preparing to counter with their own lines of disposable cars, including the Ford Temporaire and the Chrysler Dumper. The 2002 Mitsubishi Ditch will be unveiled later this year, with a projected sticker price of $799. *∅*

Neurotic Woman Turns To Neurotic Friends For Support

ANNAPOLIS, MD—In times of crisis, local neurotic Beth Haller is thankful to have a support network to turn to: her group of equally neurotic friends.

"My friends are so important to me," said the 36-year-old Haller, tearing up as she spoke. "They're always there for me, and I do my best to be there for them."

Haller and her three closest friends, Shannon Olbrich, Jennifer Beech, and Leslie Chevik, are in near-constant contact, sharing stories of hardship over the phone, at local coffee shops, and during intense weekly get-togethers over multiple bottles of wine—a Sunday-night ritual they refer to as their "recharging sessions."

"Do you think my wearing my hair like this is some sort of subconscious cry for attention?" Haller asked the trio of fellow neurotics at a recent recharging session. "I know I said I wanted to be happier with my self-image, but then I realized, how can I be truly comfortable with the inner me when the outer me doesn't match my image of the me I see when I form a mental picture of the person I think I truly am?"

"Oh, totally," Olbrich said. "That's

see WOMAN page 119

Right: Beth Haller (right) discusses her relationship issues with her closest neurotic friends.

Russell Crowe Has Something To 'Crowe' About... An Oscar Win!

The Outside Scoop By Jackie Harvey

Item! In case you're on **Mars** or something, here's a news flash: **The Oscars** happened! I always get cable this time of year so I can watch that catty **Joan Rivers** and her **lovely but retarded daughter** dish on the fashions. Well, after last year's debacle, I was determined not to miss the Oscars, so I recorded them, and I even took notes so I could recall some of the highlights. Here they are!

Russell Crowe has something to "crowe" about... an Oscar for **Best Male Actor**! The hunky star of **American Gladiator**, who was seated in the front "crowe" with **an unnamed blonde**, slayed the competition with his sword of talent and charisma. **Another Crowe**, whose first name I forget, also won an Oscar for writing or directing or something like that, so he had something to "crowe" about, as well.

That's the only bad thing about the Oscars: Why do they have to interrupt all the glamour of **Hollywood's hottest actors and actresses** with these **nerdy behind-the-scenes people**? Who wants to look at them?

And **Julia Roberts**? Oh, my! She looked stunning in a dress that looked like it floated down from heaven! But jeers to **Beeork** and **Jennifer Lopez** for their dresses. Beeork looked like a clown in her duck dress, and J. Lo didn't even notice that her gown was see-thru. How embarrassing! The winner of **Best Supporting Actress** from the movie about **the artist who just splashes paint like any monkey could** also looked good in her red ensemble.

And the **Britney Spears Pepsi commercial**? Ooh la la! It's okay to

> Another Crowe, whose first name I forget, also won an Oscar for writing or directing or something like that, so he had something to "crowe" about, as well.

say that now that she's 18. A year ago, that sort of talk would have been inappropriate and perverted, but now, hubba-hubba! Britney has "it"... and then some! I don't know about you, but I can't wait until Britney starts her acting career.

For my money, **Steve Martin** was an all-right host, but he was no **Whoopi Goldberg**. I mean, **Father Of The Bride 2** is one of my all-time faves, but I think Steve Martin has a bit too much restraint and dignity these days to host the Oscars. No offense, Steve, but where was that **"Wild And Wacky Guy"** we fell in love with in the '70s? Where was the "Excuuuuse me!" and the meat-cleaver-through-the-head thing? I say we bring back my personal choice: **Billy Crystal**! Now, *there's* a man who doesn't know the meaning of the word "restraint."

And, once again, the Oscars snubbed the comely **Sharon Stone**. Sheesh! What does a gal have to do to win an Oscar these days?

see HARVEY page 119

'I Can Still Sort Of Remember Where I Was When I Heard'

It's hard to believe, but it has been maybe a year or so since America lost its prince, John F. Kennedy Jr.

An entire nation mourned on that fateful day—probably last spring, but maybe even the summer before—when the plane he was piloting to some relative's wedding on one of those islands off the coast of Massachusetts like Nantucket or Martha's Vineyard plunged into the body of water it was flying over.

Within hours of the crash, journalists and TV news crews from around the world had descended upon the scene. The networks suspended their regular programming as millions of us watched the monumental story unfold at home, glued to our televisions for the latest word on the status of JFK Jr. and his wife, whose name escapes us at the moment. It may have started with a "C." Or maybe a "K." Kathryn? No, that's not it.

As with the death of his father, every one of us can remember exactly where we were when we heard the news.

"I think I was driving with my girlfriend to her parents' place, and we heard about it on the radio," said Andy Zeigler of Tarrytown, NY. "Actually, I think I'm thinking of Princess Di. I definitely remember it was a huge deal at the time, though."

"When I got home from work, my roommate told me that JFK Jr. had died in a plane crash," said Richard Pollian of Duncanville, TX. "I distinctly remember thinking to myself, 'Huh.'"

A year or so after the tragedy, in spite of exhaustive efforts by federal investigators and the media, many questions remain: Wasn't there somebody else on board besides JFK Jr. and what's-her-name? What was the cause of the crash, again? And did those avia-

Above: John F. Kennedy Jr. at the *George* launch maybe two or three years before his death.

tion experts who were all over the news that whole week after the crash say it could have been averted or not? Some of these questions have been answered. Still others have been answered, too, but those answers cannot quite be recalled at the moment.

The questions do not end with the crash. The loss of John-John has left us with a host of what-ifs to ponder. One can only wonder what might have been, had he lived: Would his *George* magazine, which folded several months ago, have survived slightly longer than it did without its leader? Some believe it was poised to hang on another year

or two. Would he have been photographed rollerblading shirtless in Central Park? Likely, though he hinted at a shift toward shirtless frisbee-throwing. Would he have gone on to make more allusions to the possibility of maybe one day running for public office? He showed signs. Tragically, we will never know for certain.

Come to think of it, maybe it was Cape Cod they were headed to.

Yes, John F. Kennedy Jr., the one remaining crown jewel in America's royal family, was cruelly taken from us 10 to 18 months ago. It probably was summertime, most likely the summer before last, since

the summer of 2000 was too recent. But summertime definitely sounds right. For who among us can't faintly recall those indelible televised images of onlookers milling about the shoreline in shorts and tank tops as Coast Guard officials or somebody like that went about their rescue efforts? The millions of us who clung to our television sets in those unforgettable hours following the crash sort of can.

But regardless of when the crash occurred, or where, or who was on board, one thing is certain: John Fitzgerald Kennedy Jr. may be gone, but he is not completely forgotten. ✐

ACTION FIGURES from page 115

Most of Pelinka's coworkers personalize their cubicles in some way, adorning them with items ranging from pictures of loved ones to humorous cartoon calendars. Few, however, have gone to the lengths that Pelinka has.

"Whenever someone new starts here, they inevitably come up and ask me about my collection of *Dragonball Z* series five mini-figures," Pelinka said. "I guess they really

make my cubicle stand out, don't they?"

Pelinka's action figures lean against his phone, sit atop his computer's CPU tower and monitor, and litter his desk. A shelf to the right of Pelinka's computer is reserved for action figures that are valuable or otherwise irreplaceable.

"This is an Ultraman in its original packaging that I ordered through the mail," Pelinka said. "And this is a very

collectible Aquaman figure from 1976. And Boba Fett. No one gets to touch the Boba Fett. That's why he's in that bag."

Pelinka's action figures reveal his wide range of interests, from comic books to science-fiction films. Included in his collection are Tomb Raider's Lara Croft, Lieutenant Worf from *Star Trek: The Next Generation*, Trixie from *Speed Racer*, Morpheus and Cypher from *The Matrix*, and two

different poses of Austin Powers from *The Spy Who Shagged Me*.

The collection even contains a figure of John Lennon from *Yellow Submarine*.

"I'm not into The Beatles all that much," Pelinka said, "but I saw this and I thought, 'Hey, an action figure of a musician. That's pretty cool.'"

Pointing to *Battlefield Earth*'s Terl slow-dancing with Princess Leia atop

see ACTION FIGURES page 119

Bereaved? Come Bathe In The Healing Light Of My Cock

By Lowell P. Thurber

Are you bereaved from the loss of a loved one? Are you all alone in this world, with nowhere to turn? Are you one of the billions of wounded souls who have suffered a deep and unnameable anguish? Well, there is someone out there who understands. Or, to be more precise, *something* that understands. Something far bigger than you can possibly imagine.

You need to know that no matter how low you are feeling, you have a friend right now. A friend named My Cock.

My Cock will be there for you always, and My Cock does not judge. It just loves. Can you imagine being loved more than you ever thought possible? And more fre-

quently? That is a joy you can know today, simply by inviting My Cock into your heart and various other parts of yourself.

Does it feel like the whole world has turned against you? My Cock would never turn against you. My Cock is loving and gentle. It will ease your pain and bathe you in Its healing glory, because My Cock understands, and It wants to love you as much as you want to be loved.

I know you are going through some hard times right now. But as hard as these times are, you must understand that there is something out there that is even harder. Let My Cock show you that you can know joy once again. You can know a deep and long-lasting joy. A deep, deep, deep and long-lasting joy. All night long, I would imagine.

You've probably heard of My Cock, but maybe you haven't given serious thought to what It could do for you. You doubtless figured, "I'm

young. I have plenty of time to start a relationship with Lowell's Great Big Cock." But we only go around once, and you can never know when your time will be up. Life can end in the blink of an eye. Do you really want that to happen without knowing the everlasting joy that is My Cock? Thousands slip into a Cockless eternity every hour. Please do not be one of them.

But as important as it is to start and nurture a personal relationship with My Cock, you need to know that you have an enemy, as well. An enemy who pretends to have your best interests in mind but is really just out to use and destroy you. That enemy is called Jerry Smidlap's Cock. And it will lead you down a path to destruction.

My Cock does not discriminate. My Cock does not care whether you are rich, poor, young, old, black, white, red, yellow, or plaid. There is room for everyone—with the possible exception of fatties—

in the Kingdom of My Cock. And there is nothing you can do that would make My Cock turn Its back on you. And not merely because It has no back. For even if It had a back, My Cock would never turn it on you because of something you did, no matter how bad the deed was.

My Cock has had Its detractors. There were people who hated My Cock. They persecuted It, they mocked It, they beat It, and they pounded nails through It. But My Cock is still here. Behold, My Cock has risen! It has risen time and time again, gazing down upon the entire world from on high. So those of you who have fallen from grace, who have lost your way, let My Cock point the way to your destiny.

In closing, suffer the little children to come unto My Cock, and I invite you, as well. Won't you accept My Cock today, or maybe Friday night? ∅

HARVEY from page 117

As for creepy musical performances at this year's Oscars, I'd have to give the nod to **Vincent Price** for his live-via-satellite performance from Australia. (Although, if you ask me, it looked more like he was live-via-satellite from **beyond the grave**!)

Item! If you're like me, you spell comedy with a big letter M, as in The Divine Miss M—**Bette Midler**. But in this case, the 'M' is silent because the villains at ABC have silenced Bette, pulling **Midler!** right out from under her. Who could believe the chutzpah (or nerve, as we goyim might say) of those bigwigs?

But just when I'm down on television, I see that **Dennis O'Leary** has a new show where he plays a **gruff, fast-talking, straight-shooting cop**. Now I

can see him on a weekly basis. I hope he'll stick it to **those uptight PC people** about smoking (not that I am a smoker or advocate smoking, but it sure is funny to hear him cut loose) or share some insights about being a father.

Say, does anyone ever wonder why every time you slip into a hot bath, **some telemarketer** calls trying to sell you something? And why is it usually something good?

Item! Survivor is now in Australia, and you know what? I don't care! The only one I like is **Kimmi** because she stands for something, even if it is as nutty as vegetarianism. Other than that, it's just an island full of Richards. Yuck. Here's a prediction about the last episode: I won't be watching.

Item! Madonna has a new video! Is it just me, or is everyone getting a little freaked out about **Mad Cow Disease** these days? Heck, I'm not even sure what it is, but I sure do know that I don't want to get it myself! Just the idea of mad cows makes me feel a little queasy.

Item! Puff Daddy is Puff Innocent! It turns out that he never had the gun that numerous people (or "liars," as I like to call them) claim they saw him carrying. Nor did he throw a gun out the moving car window. Nor did he try to bribe his bodyguard to claim the gun was his. It just goes to show you: No one who dresses that nice could ever be guilty of assault or attempted murder. Way to go, Sean John!

Forget your keys? Here's a special **Jackie Harvey Home Tip**: Make sure your neighbor has an extra set so you can get back in. If they're not home, make sure you have another set hidden under a rock by your back door. Of course, a good key rack can really cure a lot of your key woes.

In the spirit of the Oscars, I'd like to thank you all for dropping by Jackie's Place for The Outside Scoop. Make sure you stop by again next time. I think you'll be pleasantly surprised about some information regarding sparks between **a certain pop sensation** and **a supermodel**! That's all I can say for now, but I think you have a pretty good idea what I'm talking about. Until then, I'll see you… on the Outside! ∅

ACTION FIGURES from page 118

his Zip drive, Pelinka said he sometimes likes to pose the figures in humorous positions. He is also fond of creating accessories for them, such as when he recently teased coworker Angela Rachert by fashioning a tiny sign for Austin Powers that read, "Angie is shaggadelic [sic] baby!"

Though some might assume that such antics result in decreased productivity, Pelinka said the exact opposite is true.

"Working in an environment where I'm free to express myself really helps me get into my zone," Pelinka said. "I look at these figures, and it reminds me of all the cool adventures these characters have had. That really fires me up to design brochures. Otherwise, half the time, I'm about ready to drop off to sleep."

Not everyone is so enthusiastic about Pelinka's cubicle collection, however.

"I keep telling Ron to tone it down with the action figures," design supervisor Lisa Mendes said. "But no matter how many times I've told him, he just keeps adding new ones, so now it's kind of a joke around the office. Still, I just hope no one from corporate ever swings by unannounced, or he might get written up or put on probation."

"That's the price you pay for being a rebel," said Pelinka, leaning back in his chair with his hands clasped behind his head.

Pelinka said he has no intention of scaling back the collection any time soon.

"I gotta be me," he said. "I gotta be me." ∅

WOMAN from page 117

why I got the interior of my car reupholstered. Something just wasn't right until I did. But now I wish I would have gotten black. Do you think the tan

> **"Beth is such a special person,"** the Prozac-taking Chevik said.

looks stupid? At first, I really liked it, but now I think maybe it just looks cheap. You don't think so, do you?"

Haller said that her close friends "have literally saved [her] life" on countless occasions.

"I know this isn't how it's supposed to be, and I feel guilty about it, but my friends are more like a family to me than my actual family," Haller said through subsequent tears. "That's okay, right? I mean, I love my family, but Jen, Shannon, and Leslie are the ones I spend real Q.T. with."

Though members of Haller's family care about her well-being, most maintain little contact with her.

"I just couldn't stand it anymore," said Haller's sister, Deborah Barkum, who lives in nearby Edgewater. "I'd get frantic phone calls in the middle of the night about some meaningless comment her boss made. She'd drop by for dinner, and I'd spend six hours listening to her go on about how she has to find a new apartment because the

see WOMAN page 120

Global Warming Heats Up

Last week, President Bush rejected the 1997 Kyoto Protocol, which requires industrialized nations to curb greenhouse-gas emissions. What do *you* think?

"I'm sorry, but it's vital to the health of the U.S. economy that we destroy the entire Earth."

Chris Stratton
Delivery Driver

"As a Nader supporter, I'm thrilled to see the Green Party's master plan working so perfectly."

Debbie Honig
Student

"I'm with Bush: What have future generations ever done for me?"

James Burkholtz
Mechanical Engineer

"I'm against global warming. I'm also against altering my lifestyle in any way whatsoever to reduce it."

Patricia Volk
Homemaker

"SUV owners can help reduce toxic emissions by parking in enclosed garages, stopping up their exhaust pipes, getting back into their cars, and tightly sealing all windows and doors."

Frank Toomer
Systems Analyst

"As a resident of Greenland, I only have one thing to say: goodbye."

Larry Blunstone
Shopkeeper

Disney's Cost-Cutting Measures

Disney recently laid off 4,000 workers in an effort to reduce costs. What other steps is the company taking to improve its bottom line?

- Pluto only getting dry dog food
- Robots in Hall Of Presidents reprogrammed to roam through the park mugging visitors between shows
- Suing self for copyright violation
- Holographic ghosts in Haunted Mansion replaced with janitor wearing vampire teeth
- CEO Michael Eisner's annual salary reduced from $60 skajillion to $54 skajillion
- Theme parks instituting a two-sweatshirt minimum
- Re-edited *Peter Pan*, in which Peter urges children to mail in money to save Tinkerbell's life
- Wide-eyed childlike wonderment of Magic Kingdom reduced by 15 percent
- Exploring possible new revenue stream by permitting manufacture of select merchandise items based on certain Disney films
- Stealing the sorcerer's magic hat, creating more and more money until it spins out of control in a destructive whirlpool, providing a valuable lesson about greed

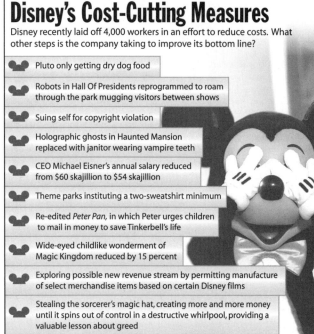

the ONION
America's Finest News Source

Herman Ulysses Zweibel *Founder*

T. Herman Zweibel *Publisher Emeritus*
J. Phineas Zweibel *Publisher*
Maxwell Prescott Zweibel *Editor-In-Chief*

FOUNDED 1871 • "TU STULTUS ES"

Your Horoscope

By Lloyd Schumner Sr.
Retired Machinist and
A.A.P.B.-Certified Astrologer

Aries: (March 21–April 19)
There comes a moment in every person's life when one must honestly evaluate one's worth as a human being. You should put this moment off indefinitely.

Taurus: (April 20–May 20)
Your replacement by more than 10,000 miles of super-efficient fiber-optic cable is scheduled to begin next week.

Gemini: (May 21–June 21)
No one will catch your witty, conversational George Romero reference next week, embarrassing you and the entire courtroom.

Cancer: (June 22–July 22)
You will inspire a disappointing, half-hearted Lifetime Channel original movie after waking from an eight-hour coma.

Leo: (July 23–Aug. 22)
You will go down in medical history as the first North American to succumb to foot-and-mouth-and-kidney-and-eye-socket-and-lung disease.

Virgo: (Aug. 23–Sept. 22)
Armed government agents will again prohibit you from attending Milan's oh-so-very Spring Fashion Week.

Libra: (Sept. 23–Oct. 23)
All the time and effort you've put into preparing for your future should come in handy over the next nine days.

Scorpio: (Oct. 24–Nov. 21)
After years of using, selling, and enjoying the stuff, you still can't figure out why they call it "dope."

Sagittarius: (Nov. 22–Dec. 21)
Though you've never even heard of the "Cool-O-Meter," you'll score a measly three on it next Wednesday.

Capricorn: (Dec. 22–Jan. 19)
You'll set the custom of open-casket funerals back years when you demand that a rather non-traditional part of your casket be left open.

Aquarius: (Jan. 20–Feb. 18)
Your flagging interest in the arts will be rekindled by the realization that there is a Bat-*girl*.

Pisces: (Feb. 19–March 20)
Though it's demonstrably true that "[you] do not have problems; everyone in the rest of the world does," knowing this will do nothing to help you get along with the other members of human society.

WOMAN from page 119

landlord refuses to do anything about the dogs down the hall. I finally made a rule: I'll talk to her on weekends, but that's it."

For years, Barkum was frustrated by her sister's emotional neediness, but most of Haller's neurotic behavior is now addressed by her cadre of neurotic friends, from whom she receives constant affirmation and reinforcement. As a bonus for Haller, her friends' own neuroses make it easier for her to view her perpetual state of anxiety as normal.

"Beth is such a special person, so complex and multi-layered," the Prozac-taking Chevik said. "I'm happy to be there for her when she needs a shoulder to cry on."

"It is truly amazing how she's held on after the split," Beech said of Haller's 1991 divorce, still a major source of pain, heartache, and confusion for her 10 years later.

Beech herself knows the pain of love lost. Six years ago, she dated a man for two months and then suddenly never heard from him again. According to Haller, the experience has made it impossible for her friend to trust any man.

"Poor Jen," Haller said. "She was badly wounded by someone who said he'd call and then never did, and, as a result, she's built up this wall to protect her from ever leaving herself vulnerable like that again."

Added Haller: "It seems like some of us have our load to bear in life, and no matter what we do, it never gets any lighter."

Haller was cryptically alluding to any one of her own crises, including her strained relationship with her mother, caused by an offhand comment her mother made in 1979 about never having expected to have a third child; her indecision about whether to return to school to receive a Masters degree in English; her "demeaning and demoralizing" research-assistant job, one of the few positions in publishing that a divorced woman her age can get; her home computer's hard-drive crash, which wiped out nearly five pages of notes for the novella she intends to write someday; and her new relationship with a man who is obviously a commitment-phobe, making her wonder what the point is of even proceeding to a third date. ∅

the ONION®

VOLUME 37 ISSUE 13   AMERICA'S FINEST NEWS SOURCE™   12-18 APRIL 2001

New Grill To Revive Foreman-Ali Rivalry

see PRODUCTWATCH page 11B

That Same Guy With The Glasses At Every Rock Show

see LOCAL page 1C

Psychiatrist Cures Patient

see HEALTH page 4E

STATshot

A look at the numbers that shape your world.

Most Popular Easter-Sermon Topics

1. "The Miraculous Gift Of Marshmallow Peeps"
2. "Redeemed By The Blood Of The Walking Undead"
3. "Good Versus Emo Philips"
4. "A Preaching To The Choir"
5. "The Jew Who Couldn't Be Killed"
6. "See You At Christmas!"

Accountants Pack Times Square For Fiscal New Year

NEW YORK—Amidst a blizzard of white, yellow, and pink forms in triplicate, a jubilant crowd of more than 800,000 accountants jammed Times Square Saturday night to ring in the fiscal new year.

"Fiscal Year 2001–02!" shouted one unidentified CPA, a tie wrapped around his forehead and a paper-bag-covered bottle of caffeine-free Diet Coke in his hand. "The expense-accrual forms are completed and the statutory salary recovery requests are in. Now it's time to par-tay!"

The man then climbed atop a garbage can and wildly waved a copy of a PricewaterhouseCoopers end-of-year report before falling back into the crowd.

"Oh, yeah!" yelled 49-year-old Deloitte & Touche accountant David Gelfand, tearing off his shirt to reveal the phrase "In The Black" painted on his chest. "Anyone looking for final approval for payment vouchers subject to post-payment audit can forget it. The Office of Accounting is offi-

see ACCOUNTANTS page 124

Above: Admiral McManus.

Navy Admiral Considers Death Of Son Within Acceptable Loss Range

SAN DIEGO—At a Monday press conference from the steps of his home, Navy Admiral William McManus categorized the death of his son in a weekend car crash as "a casualty within the acceptable loss range for this family."

"The unforeseeable death of my son is tragic," said McManus, clad in full Navy dress. "No one ever wants to see a young life lost. However, even as the family weeps, we must keep in mind that the damage to our unit is minimal. We have the personnel and emotional reserves necessary to move forward."

At approximately 7:25 p.m. PST Saturday, while driving to a movie in a heavy downpour, Matthew McManus, 17, spun out of control and collided with a tree, killing the teenager and girlfriend Alicia Reginio, 16.

The elder McManus said that, had one of his other three children been in the car with Matthew instead of his

see ADMIRAL page 125

Teacher Of The Year Awards 'A Fashion Nightmare'

RALEIGH, NC—The 2001 North Carolina High School Teachers Association Awards ceremony, held Saturday at the Raleigh Civic Auditorium, was proclaimed "a fashion nightmare" by style pundits covering the event.

"I haven't seen this much plaid since I was in Edinburgh," said comedian and E! commentator Joan Rivers, standing outside the auditorium. "Forget the fashion police—this event needs a fashion SWAT team."

see AWARDS page 122

Right: Teacher Of The Year honoree and "fashion disaster" Angela Schroeder.

Nation Awaits Word On Today's Slam Dunks

BRISTOL, CT—As of press time, an anxious nation continues to wait for word on today's NBA slam dunks. "The moment we have any information on any dunks, we will pass it along to the American people," said Dan Patrick, speaking from ESPN's Bristol headquarters. "We do know that the Mavs and Hornets tip off at 3 p.m. EST, so hopefully sometime shortly after that, we'll know more." Patrick urged citizens to stay close to their televisions for the latest developments.

Report: Clinton Accepted Rebate While In Office Depot

WASHINGTON, DC—According to a report in Monday's *Washington Post*, on Jan. 14, Bill Clinton accepted a $60 rebate on an O'Sullivan office workcenter while in Office Depot. "In his final days as president, Mr. Clinton knowingly took money as an enticement to purchase a $300 desk, leveraging his status as a valued customer of Office Depot for personal gain," the report stated. "The sales associate who orchestrated the deal, Marc Ryback, has a history of dealings with the president dating back to a November 1995 photocopier-for-cash exchange." Said a spokesman for the former president: "Mr. Clinton regrets any wrongdoing that may have occurred."

Fifth Level Of Video Game Reached During Phone Call To Mom

LONGMONT, CO—While speaking on the phone with his mother Monday, Sega Dreamcast enthusiast Jon Grebe, 22, defeated Sarge to reach the fifth level of Quake III Arena. "Mom was telling me about Aunt Gail's thyroid condition when I finally got the Quad Damage powerup I needed to kill Sarge and get to the end of level four," Grebe said. "I yelled out, 'Yes! Awesome!' Fortunately, Mom was right in the middle of telling me the good news about my aunt's goiter getting smaller, so I was sort of able to cover it up."

Role Of Tree Ineptly Played By Second-Grader

POPLAR BLUFF, MO—Critics savaged Monday's underwhelming stage debut of second-grader Kimberly Bauer, who "fumbled and stumbled her way" through the role of the Happy Little Pine Tree in Mrs. Shore's class production of *Our Forest Friends*. "What is supposed to be an eloquently simple role was bludgeoned into the ground by Ms. Bauer's ham-fisted delivery and clunky sense of timing," said *Poplar Bluff Gazette* theater critic Meredith Woodson. "One might have leaned her cardboard-cutout tree costume against the wall for a superior display of thespianism."

Bruce Vilanch Sodomized By Homosexual

HOLLYWOOD, CA—In an act "so heinous, it defies the imagination," famed awards-show joke writer and *Hollywood Squares* regular Bruce Vilanch was sodomized by an unnamed homosexual Monday. Authorities are still at a loss as to what could have motivated the homosexual—whom Vilanch met at a dinner party before accompanying him home—to commit the act. "How could anyone do such a thing?" asked Vilanch's distraught *Hollywood Squares* co-star Whoopi Goldberg. "What sort of inhuman monster could bring himself to do this?" Vilanch, who described himself as "perfectly fabulous" following the incident, told reporters: "I felt like Monica Lewinsky... at a cigar store!" ∅

AWARDS from page 121

The three-hour event honored 21 teachers from around the state and featured a performance by the Gastonia High School Swing Choir, as well as a presentation by North Carolina Mothers Against Drunk Driving. Spirits ran high throughout the evening as award recipients collected their plaques and enjoyed an evening of camaraderie with their fellow educators.

"This is our one night of the year to pat ourselves on the back," said Roaring Gap High School history teacher Sherry Spinks, who wore a red polka-dotted dress and brown Hush Puppies to the event. "It's always a fun time for everyone."

Reporters and photographers were stationed outside the auditorium to snap pictures as the nominees arrived in Ford Tauruses and Ford Windstar minivans.

"Frumpy and unflattering were definitely the watchwords for the night," *People* style editor Steven Cojocaru said. "Outfits ranged from drab, shapeless pantsuits to headache-inducing floral-print frocks. Most shocking, though, was the dearth of name designers: Other than one Liz Claiborne dress from her abysmal '92 career-wear collection, everyone went with complete unknowns."

Added Cojocaru: "These teachers could use a few lessons themselves—in accessorizing."

Rivers, flanked by her daughter Melissa, was even less charitable. Throughout the evening, she dished out critiques of everyone from Eng-

see AWARDS page 123

Above: Rivers reacts to the outfit worn by Lenoir, NC, special-education teacher Sharon Grunwalt.

Hero Citizen Can Name All 50 States

FAYETTEVILLE, AR—Local resident Carl Sutton was recognized by Fayetteville officials Monday for his "unique and patriotic" ability to name all 50 United States.

"I am proud to call Carl Sutton one of Fayetteville's own," said Mayor Gordon Semple, who awarded Sutton a special citation at the city's American Legion Hall. "Very few people possess the skill to name all 50 states of the Union without consulting reference materials. Yet, relying only on his intellect and his powers of retention, Carl has achieved the near-impossible. He is a true American hero."

Sutton's state-recitation aptitude has drawn national attention, resulting in guest spots on TV talk shows, lecture dates in elementary and secondary schools, and goodwill visits to hospitals, nursing homes, and military bases. However, the 46-year-old delivery driver for Tyson Foods remains modest and somewhat bewildered by the acclaim.

"I only graduated from high school and never attended college, so when people say I'm a hero or a genius, I have a hard time believing them," Sutton told reporters. "I did not have the advantages others have, so I'm just grateful to God for endowing me with this gift. I do not take it for granted, because I know how much it means to so many people."

Sutton then concluded his remarks with his customary, keenly anticipated recitation of the 50 states in alphabetical order.

"Alabama, Alaska, Arizona, Arkansas, California, Colorado, Connecticut, Delaware," Sutton said. "Florida, Georgia, Hawaii, Idaho, Illinois, Indiana, Iowa, Kansas, Kentucky, Louisiana, Maine."

Added Sutton: "Maryland, Massachusetts, Michigan, Minnesota, Mississippi... uh... Missouri, Montana, Nebraska, Nevada, New Hampshire, New Jersey, New York—no, wait—New Mexico, then New York... North Carolina, North Dakota, Ohio."

Following a 10-second lapse accompanied by a pained expression, Sutton said, "Oklahoma, Oregon, Pennsylvania... er... Rhode Island, South Carolina, South Dakota, Tennessee, Texas, Utah, Vermont, Virginia, Washington... um... West Virginia, Wisconsin, Wyoming."

Reporters in attendance then broke into enthusiastic cheers and gave Sutton a standing ovation as he left the room.

Those who have heard Sutton's celebrated recitation inevitably express wonderment.

"I have a hard time just remembering which states border my own," said Joseph Russo, an insurance-claims adjuster from Harwich, MA. "Heck, I can't remember how to spell my own state. But this Sutton guy, he's amazing."

"I want to be just like Mr. Sutton when I grow up," said 8-year-old Wendy Sperling of Casper, WY. "Right now, I know California, Florida, and New York. Oh, and

Above: The heroic Sutton at home.

Wyoming!"

But for all the adulation, Sutton refuses to rest on his laurels. Not content to dazzle others with his perfect state recall, he has taught himself the names of the territories currently under U.S. jurisdiction.

"Guam, Puerto Rico, U.S. Virgin Islands, American Samoa, and the Commonwealth of the Northern Mariana Islands," Sutton told Katie Couric during a recent appearance on *Today*.

With Sutton's rise to fame has come a growing number of rivals eager to challenge his throne. Danielle Claussen, a bartender from Amherst, NY, claims to have memorized not only all 50 states, but also their capitals. A 12-year-old Taiwanese-born, San Francisco-raised prodigy named Yan-Zhou Li is rumored to know all the major American rivers and their

tributaries, as well as the number of congressional representatives per state.

In spite of the competition, Sutton received more good news Monday, when he learned that he has won a MacArthur Foundation "Genius Grant." He said he plans to use the $500,000 prize to study and memorize all the state mottos, nicknames, and birds.

"It seems overly ambitious, but with this financial assistance, I think I can pull it off," Sutton said. "I already know Montana's state bird is the Western Meadowlark, and that Arizona's motto is *Ditat Deus*, which is Latin for 'God enriches.' And that Connecticut is known both as 'The Constitution State' and 'The Nutmeg State.' Now I can afford to take an extended leave of absence from my job to devote the proper time and attention to this project." ∅

AWARDS from page 122

lish Teacher Of The Year Frederick Bowles, whose tweed sportcoat was "about as colorful as Barbara Bush and almost as wrinkled," to 50-Year Service Award recipient Florence Webb, whose gray poly-cotton dress "made her look like a battleship—one on the verge of sinking."

According to Rivers, some of the biggest sartorial sins of the evening were committed by NCHSTA president Bernadette Karcher, 68.

"In that white ruffled collar, Mrs. Karcher was a dead ringer for George Washington," Rivers said. "I cannot tell a lie: That's the *worst* outfit I've ever seen. Ack!"

Added Rivers: "Apparently, not all teachers have class."

Karcher was not the only target of Rivers' scathing fashion eye. Lenoir High School teacher Sharon Grunwalt, who took home a plaque for her development of a summer-science

program for learning-disabled students, was given the thumbs-down upon arriving at the ceremony in an

> ### Said Cojocaru: "These teachers could use a few lessons themselves— in accessorizing."

oversized beige sweater.

"Perhaps Mrs. Grunwalt thought the extra-large sweater would camouflage her size-20 backside," Rivers said. "Sorry to tell you, honey, but there's not enough fabric in China to hide that caboose."

"And next time," Melissa chimed in, "try shopping for your jewelry somewhere other than the row of gumball machines at the supermarket."

According to fellow fashion commentator Mr. Blackwell, Social Studies Teacher Of The Year Janice Ranieri was the biggest fashion victim of the evening.

"Ms. Ranieri should have dug a little deeper in her closet, past the hideous maroon stirrup pants and oh-so-'80s shaker sweater," Blackwell said. "And, although some women can pull off the no-makeup look, Ms. Ranieri simply does not have the classic good looks required. Ms. Ranieri, I sentence you to six weeks of fashion detention."

In her acceptance speech, Ranieri dedicated her award to "all the wonderful students and faculty members of Greensboro South High School," where, in addition to teaching, she

serves on the scholarship committee, the student-teacher mentorship program, and the standardized-testing goal-setting committee. She made no reference to her critically panned ensemble, which Rivers said "made me wish I was Stevie Wonder for a night."

Ranieri, like most of the evening's winners, was unavailable for comment following the ceremony, reporting that she needed to head directly home "to finish grading papers."

Reflecting on the event, Cojocaru recommended that a five-block radius surrounding the Raleigh Civic Auditorium be closed off and declared a Federal Fashion Disaster Area.

"Talk about your horror shows," Cojocaru said. "I finally understand why the Teacher Of The Year Awards generally aren't televised and receive no attention from the media at all." ∅

I've Got A New Soup That Will Knock Campbell's On Its Ass

By Trudy Schiff

When you think soup, who do you think of? Campbell's. Everyone does. They're considered the masters. That's why they have soup in every goddamn grocery store in this country.

Unfortunately, being so good at what they do and all, they've gotten a little bit comfortable over the years. That's where Trudy Schiff comes in, because I've got a soup that is going to knock Campbell's on its fucking ass. *Boom*.

You know their slogan, "Soup Is Good Food"? Well, my soup is goddamn great food. I haven't been cooking for 30 years for nothing. I raised three kids on that soup. I know what I'm doing when it comes to pots of broth.

When I make soup, I don't screw around. You open a can of Campbell's soup, what do you see? The same old shit. It's good, but it's not all that interesting, is it? In their chicken noodle soup, you get chicken, noodles, a few chunks of carrots and celery, and that's it. Yawn.

When I make chicken noodle soup, I *make* chicken noodle soup. You can see the vegetables. You can put them in your mouth and chew them. And I sure as hell don't stick to Mom's recipe. Carrots? Whoop-dee-fucking-doo. Have a little goddamn creativity, will you?

I put in whatever I feel like eating that day. Potatoes, nice big chunks with the skins still on. Northern beans. Yes, I said beans. Why is everyone so afraid to add beans to anything other than a bean soup? They're an excellent source of protein, they thicken the soup naturally, and they taste great, for shit's sake. Christ.

Whoa there, cowboy. Don't think that this new soup I'm telling you about is just some minor variation on chicken soup. No way. My soup is a totally new, utterly unheard-of soup. And, like I said, it's going to send Campbell's flying through the back door and right out into the street on its complacent rump. See ya, Campbell's. Nice knowing you, but you are history.

Now, clam chowder, it's a good soup, right? Sure. And, granted, Campbell's makes a decent version. The problem is, we've all had it a million times before. But still, they keep cranking out the same tired stuff, day after day, year after year. Me, on the other hand, I've taken the very concept of clam chowder and turned it on its fucking head. That's what I did when I made—drum roll, please—Trudy's Crab & Corn Chowder. *Boo-yahhh!*

I didn't set out to make the best soup in the world. It didn't come to me in a dream or anything, either. I developed this soup in the kitchen over the course of countless hours of trial and error in the kitchen. But, believe me, it was worth it. Because this soup is like a goddamn chowderquake. It's got crabmeat and corn and a whole bunch of other fresh and tasty veg-

see SOUP page 126

ACCOUNTANTS from page 121

cially closed for the year! Whoooooo!"

Many present for the annual Times Square mayhem wore hats and carried noisemakers, and floating through the air were thousands of balloons emblazoned with the logo of the Big Five accounting firm Ernst & Young, the event's official sponsor.

Accountants began to gather as early as noon in anticipation of the official countdown to midnight, April 15. At first, the mood was calm and genial, with accountants discussing tax code and sharing their Fiscal New Year's resolutions with one another. But as day turned to night, the scene changed, with celebrants yelling, climbing onto parked cars, and throwing items from their briefcases, including pocket calculators, spill-proof coffee mugs, and Parker pen sets. By 9 p.m., the size of the roiling throng had forced police to close off Broadway from 34th Street to 57th Street and reroute all vehicular traffic.

Shortly after 10 p.m., a portion of the crowd began to chant, "Excel! Excel!" in unison, prompting another group to defend its preferred spreadsheet software with shouts of, "Lotus 123! Lotus 123!" As the two sides' intensity increased, the impassioned yelling turned to shoving, and police had to escort several accountants out of the crowd.

Throughout the evening, the Times Square Jumbotron showed clips of accounting highlights from FY 2000–01, as well as reflections on the past fiscal year by celebrities such as Gerard Truman, author of *The Truman Formula For Estimating Loss Leader Profitability Returns*.

"There's no question that 2000–01

was one incredible fiscal year," said Truman, his words echoing through Times Square. "Microsoft released Windows 2000, everyone changed their methods to accommodate the Euro, and Office Max released its biggest catalog ever. But now, after a long, hard year of accounting, it's time to turn off our NQS batch queues and just enjoy ourselves."

One minute before midnight, the traditional countdown began as the three-ton, Tiffany-made Fiscal Ball slowly descended from the sky at One Times Square.

"That Fiscal Ball is the most beautiful thing I've ever seen," said Peter Timmins, 38, a KPMG budget analyst from Philadelphia. "Back when I was getting my Master's in accounting at Georgetown, we'd all sit glued to the live annual broadcast of *John Kenneth Galbraith's Fiscal New Year's Rockin' Eve*. And now I'm actually experiencing it in person."

Lou Dobbs, former star of CNN's *Moneyline*, officially closed the ceremonies, addressing the crowd from atop a giant adding machine shooting reams of number-filled streamers into the crowd below.

"Let us now, for but a moment," Dobbs said, "look back fondly on FY 2000–01—the mergers and acquisitions that made it special, the new information systems that came into our lives, the new tax strategies we may have discovered in places we weren't even looking."

Dobbs paused shortly, waiting for the crowd to quiet, before bursting into song.

"Should auld accountants be forgot..." sang Dobbs, lifting his voice as

Above: The Fiscal Ball drops, ushering in the new year.

the swaying crowd of accountants linked arms and joined him in song.

"This is so amazing," said Amanda Lakewood, a tax-code accountant who traveled all the way from Merced, CA, to be part of the Times Square festivities. "When we're all here together, it doesn't matter if you

work in budget analysis, auditing, or management accounting. It doesn't matter if you work for the government, a privately held corporation, or a public accounting firm. When we're together here like this, we're all just accountants, every one of us. Happy Fiscal New Year!" ∅

Ask The Voice-Over From *The Dukes Of Hazzard*

By The Voice-Over From *The Dukes Of Hazzard*

Dear Voice-Over From *The Dukes Of Hazzard*,

I recently moved to Florida from Minnesota for my career, and I'm very unhappy. My job is fine, and the weather here is beautiful, but the people are really different from what I'm used to. To make a long story short, I'm having trouble finding a Florida man with good old-fashioned Midwestern values. Should I move back, or should I tough it out and learn to adjust?

—**Confused In Coral Gables**

Dear Confused,

Well, it sure is lookin' like a beautiful day in Hazzard, the little town where any old thing can happen… and usually does. Today, though, Hazzard's as quiet as a cat in socks. The sun is out, the sky is blue, and the Hazzard Ladies Auxiliary is lookin' prettier than ever. Daisy's busy as any beehive makin' her famous huckleberry pie, Ol' Cooter done gone and fell asleep while workin' under Uncle Jesse's truck again, Sheriff Roscoe is giving out phony parking tickets, and the Duke boys, Bo and Luke, are makin' this month's farm mortgage payment at the Bank of Hazzard. But, uh-oh… what's this here? Fetch a look over yonder. It's that low-down mean ol' Boss Hogg putting somethin' in the General Lee, something that looks a powerful lot like bank bags. If I was them poor Duke boys, I'd get a-ready for some slick shuckin'.

Dear Voice-Over From *The Dukes Of Hazzard*,

I love him, but my boyfriend is the worst dresser! He only has about three shirts he actually wears, and they're all worn out and faded. Now, he's in line for a possible promotion at work, and I think it's time to whip his wardrobe into shape. I don't expect him to become a fashion plate, but I do think having a neat and professional appearance counts in the eyes of an employer… and a girlfriend. Don't you agree?

—**Exasperated In El Paso**

Dear Exasperated,

Now, mind you, blowin' up the Boar's Nest outhouse was the dirtiest thing them Duke boys ever pulled besides a plow, but doggone if it weren't necessary. Sure, it made a bar full of good ol' boys madder than a weasel in a gum-bush, and pretty near scorched the skivvies right off of poor ol' Deputy Wilbur Fudge, but there's more than plain meanness to this here deal. In fact, in all the ruckus, I reckon no one noticed Daisy switchin' the counterfeit money bags on poor ol' Enos—and it's an unusual day in Hazzard County when a body don't notice the finest legs in Georgia. I guess dynamite in the two-holer does get folks' attention right quick. Ain't them boys slick?

Dear Voice-Over From *The Dukes Of Hazzard*,

I'm what you'd call a "neatnik." I like to have absolutely everything in its place. Problem is, the woman I love (I'll call her "Nicole") is the kind of person who can't be bothered to shelve books, rack CDs, or keep files organized. And now she wants us to move in together! How can I get her to change before she drives me nuts?

—**Organized In Orchard Park**

Dear Organized,

Look out, Bo! That low-down snake-belly-mean Sheriff Roscoe done set him up one of his genuine impenetrable roadblocks across Possum Gulch! And if them federal boys catch you with Boss Hogg's funny money in the General Lee, you can forget about havin' any of Daisy's huckleberry pie for a while. And what's this? Seems some ol' body left his farm wagon up against the gulch all tilted-like. Now, can any y'all guess what ol' Bo is thinkin' right about now? Stay set, folks, and we'll see if Luke manages to break himself into jail… and if Bo here ever comes down.

Dear Voice-Over From *The Dukes Of Hazzard*,

I've been married for 30 years, and I still love my wife very much. But, recently, I found out that she had a brief affair in the '70s. It's water under the bridge, and I don't want to ruin a good marriage, but adultery is adultery! What should I do?

—**Betrayed In Bethlehem**

Dear Betrayed,

Well, seems like everything done turned out all right, leastways for now. Them federal boys believed Boss Hogg's story about the money bein' lost in the Boar's Nest outhouse fire—or maybe they just don't want to be around, come sundown. Ms. Lulu Hogg got down out the tree before her britches could burst. Uncle Jesse gets to keep his farm until next month. And Enos found them counterfeit money-makin' plates inside Daisy's prize huckleberry pie… by breakin' off a couple of his favorite eatin' teeth. Oh, well, just another day in Hazzard County.

The Voice-Over From The Dukes Of Hazzard *is a syndicated columnist whose weekly advice column,* Ask The Voice-Over From The Dukes Of Hazzard, *appears in more than 250 newspapers nationwide.* ∅

ADMIRAL from page 121 ■

son's girlfriend, the damage to the family would have increased by "at least a factor of two."

"Luckily, only one of the Dodge Daytona's crew members, the pilot, was a member of the McManus family," McManus said. "Had there been multiple family members on board, the loss would have been more difficult to sustain. But as such, only one of six, or 17 percent of total McManus family members, were lost."

According to McManus, the death of either himself or his wife Rose would have been far more devastating.

"Last night, Rose said she wished she'd been the one who died in that crash," McManus said. "But, from a purely tactical standpoint, this is absurd. Under such a scenario, the family would lose not only a valuable income source, but also parental leadership for the remaining children. Also, Rose is still within reasonable child-bearing years, making it possible for us to rebuild our ranks with another child. Matthew, as an unmarried teen, would not have been able to do that within the bounds of God's laws for a number of years."

Even though casualties were "minimal and contained," McManus acknowledged that the accident has weakened family morale. The admiral has attempted to boost his surviving children's spirits by increasing their weekly allowances, doubling dessert rations, and extending weekend curfew. Efforts to provide his wife with back-up and support, however, have met with less success.

"I keep telling Rose that not getting past Matthew's death is a disgrace to his memory and to what he did for us and this great country of ours," McManus said. "But she just keeps saying I shouldn't have let him take the car out in that driving rainstorm. No matter how many times I tell her that visibility was 200 feet and the terrain on South Bay Freeway navigable, she remains steadfastly unconvinced."

McManus said both he and his wife knew the risks when they entered into Project: Offspring, and that she should have expected, at the very least, minimal casualties.

"I'm a pragmatic father," McManus said. "I realize that in this life, you are never going to have a 100 percent target-strike rate. So I decided long ago that if at least two of my four children graduated from Annapolis, I would be

> ## "I'm a pragmatic father," McManus said. "I realize that in this life, you are never going to have a 100 percent target-strike rate."

happy. I'm just glad that our family still has the numbers to make this happen."

Fellow officer and friend Lt. Roger Trimble expressed regret over the death of McManus' son.

"I know that Matthew's passing upset Admiral McManus a great deal," Trimble said. "I don't think I've ever seen him take a leave of absence, but after his son's death, he took off two full days."

"In terms of the strength of the unit, Matthew's death was the least damaging," Trimble continued. "To be blunt, Matthew was strictly 4-F. The other two boys are more responsible with brighter futures. And I know Rose really hopes that Michelle will get married and bear grandchildren in the next few years. Matthew was always getting into trouble. Even though he was a valued member of the family, he certainly wasn't going to win any medals."

McManus said he loved his son in spite of his weaknesses.

"I would love my son even if he decided to join the Marines," McManus said. "But when I look at the situation, I think back to what Admiral William R. Booker said when his daughter fell off a cliff during a hiking trip. 'You can't make an omelet without breaking a few eggs,' he said. These words still ring true today." ∅

The U.S.-China Standoff

Last week, China detained 24 Navy officers after their spy plane collided with a Chinese jet. What do *you* think about the escalating tensions between the two nations?

"Tell me about it. One of my spy planes went down over China once, and I had a bitch of a time getting it back."

Ben Carlson
Welder

"Can't we just send China a fruit basket or something?"

Yvonne Goltz
Librarian

"And Bush was so close to world peace before this, too."

Will Franklin
Systems Analyst

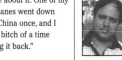

"If a Chinese spy plane crash-landed in California after knocking down one of our jets, I'm sure we'd give it right back."

Bob Rolen
Cashier

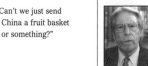

"Damn Truman! We should cross the Yalu River and invade the Chinese mainland! We must halt the spread of Communism at all costs!"

Richard Grolier
Consultant

"This is a great chance for Bush to show the world that he appears to be tough."

Gina Jeffries
Violinist

Rosie The Magazine

The debut issue of *Rosie*, talk-show host Rosie O'Donnell's new magazine, hit newsstands April 2. What are some of its features?

- 10 Days To A Shriller You
- Great Koosh Recipes
- Nathan Lane Or Elmo: Which Should You Talk About Next?
- The Cruise-Christ Connection
- Rave Reviews Of All The Latest Movies
- Chocolate, Church, Or Cats?: Rating The Middle-Aged Woman's Sex Substitutes
- Making Your Deep Political Convictions Known
- Craving Attention? Belt Out A Show Tune
- Hairdos For Today's Sexually Neutral Woman
- Diet All You Want...Without Actual Weight Loss!
- Dealing With Your Incompetent Staff Of Underlings
- Keeping Up With Oprah And Martha
- Dramatic True-Life Tales From Rosie Readers: "The Day I Almost Forgot To Pick Up My Kids From Soccer Practice"
- Rosie's "Being Loud And Overbearing With Other Celebrities" Corner

the ONION
America's Finest News Source

Herman Ulysses Zweibel *Founder*

T. Herman Zweibel *Publisher Emeritus*
J. Phineas Zweibel *Publisher*
Maxwell Prescott Zweibel *Editor-In-Chief*

FOUNDED 1871 • "TU STULTUS ES"

Your Horoscope

By Lloyd Schumner Sr.
Retired Machinist and
A.A.P.B.-Certified Astrologer

Aries: (March 21–April 19)
When you said no one could tell you how to live your life, you forgot about the warden and all those guards.

Taurus: (April 20–May 20)
You will receive an urgent transmission from the Martian government informing you that Mars does not, in fact, need women, so please stop sending them.

Gemini: (May 21–June 21)
The people who brought you *Beethoven* and *Beethoven's 2nd* have had time to think about it and are now willing to take them back.

Cancer: (June 22–July 22)
Your insistence that mere psychology is behind the recent stock-market swings will go largely unheeded by the other panhandlers.

Leo: (July 23–Aug. 22)
Does anybody want a perfectly good coffeemaker? The stars are giving up coffee and just want to get rid of the thing. It's a nice one, barely used.

Virgo: (Aug. 23–Sept. 22)
You'll learn from experience that appointing a 10-member steering committee isn't the best way to drive a truck.

Libra: (Sept. 23–Oct. 23)
Be assured that the gods of Love and Mercy have heard your pleas for help. They have taped them and enjoy playing them for huge laughs at their god parties.

Scorpio: (Oct. 24–Nov. 21)
Scorpio would like to point out that it's a lot easier to predict exciting futures for people who leave the house sometimes.

Sagittarius: (Nov. 22–Dec. 21)
You will be struck with an incredible flash of near-divine insight next Tuesday, suddenly making you aware of the reason the chicken crossed the road.

Capricorn: (Dec. 22–Jan. 19)
Your biting, acerbic sense of humor will be magically transformed into a lightly irreverent, playful one by Hollywood executives.

Aquarius: (Jan. 20–Feb. 18)
You just can't shake the feeling that, while he might not have shot anybody, Puffy must be guilty of something.

Pisces: (Feb. 19–March 20)
Money woes will continue to plague you for the foreseeable future. But, gee, you should be used to it by now, right?

SOUP from page 124

etables. My secret blend of spices, too, some of which Campbell's probably ain't ever even heard of. I shit you not.

Classic appeal, with a brand-new twist—that's what Trudy's Crab & Corn Chowder has. But I'm not dumb enough to tell you what that twist is, because I'm going to sell this soup to Campbell's and make a fuckload of money. *Ka-ching!* Back the truck up to my front door and drop it off, baby.

You know what? On second thought, maybe I won't sell it to Campbell's. Sure, I could retire on the kind of dough they'd pay, but it's just not worth it. I'd much rather watch those bitches slowly squirm as they watch their soup cans collecting dust on supermarket shelves across the nation while everybody stampedes to get their mitts on a can of Trudy's Crab & Corn Chowder. No amount of money could give me that much pleasure.

Hear those footsteps, Campbell's? Yeah? You can? That's me coming after you. ∅

LOVITZ from page 112

large amounts of blood. Passersby were amazed by the unusually large amounts of blood. Passersby were amazed by the unusually large amounts of blood. Passersby were amazed by the unusually large amounts of blood. Passersby were amazed by the unusually large amounts of blood. Passersby

If this doesn't spark a flurry of anti-animal-cruelty legislation, nothing will.

---

were amazed by the unusually large amounts of blood. Passersby were amazed by the unusually large amounts of blood. Passersby were amazed by the unusually large amounts of blood. Passersby were amazed by the unusually large amounts of blood. Passersby were amazed by the unusually large amounts of blood. Passersby were amazed by the unusually large amounts of blood. Passersby were

see LOVITZ page 134

the ONION®

VOLUME 37 ISSUE 14   AMERICA'S FINEST NEWS SOURCE™   19-25 APRIL 2001

Milosevic Confesses To Crimes Against Subhumanity

see WORLD page 3A

6,000-Year-Old Culture Now A 'Developing Nation'

see WORLD page 5A

Lite Brite Peg Extracted From Ear

see LOCAL page 7C

A look at the numbers that shape your world.

Worst-Selling Specialty Magazines

1. Dry-Erase Marker Huffer
2. Mauled By Bears Magazine
3. TRS-80 World
4. Monkeybone Insider
5. Grease Trap Aficionado
6. Eye Schmutz Collector's Weekly
7. Two-Weeks-To-Live Illustrated

Pebble Sorting Today

THE ONION
VOLUME 37
ISSUE 14

$2.00 US
$3.00 CAN

0 74470 94595 6

09

Bush Regales Dinner Guests With Impromptu Oratory On Virgil's Minor Works

Above: An effervescent Bush delights friends with tales of the poet Virgil.

WASHINGTON, DC—President Bush delighted an intimate gathering of White House dinner guests Monday, regaling the coterie of dignitaries, artists, and friends with a spirited, off-the-cuff discussion of the Roman poet Virgil's lesser-known works.

"Ah, W. was in top form tonight," Spanish foreign minister Josep Pique Camps said. "We were all held captive by his erudition and charm. First, a brief history of the opium trade, then a bit of Brahms on the piano, then a rousing discussion of Virgil. That boy is a wonder, isn't he?"

According to guests, the subject of Virgil arose serendipitously, when a servant opened a window in the Red Room, to which the group had retired for after-dinner drinks. Noticing the breeze, Bush raised his glass and delivered a toast to the changing of the seasons. He then apologized to "lovely Winter," explaining that he "meant no slight against her."

"The first blush of Spring always reminds me of Virgil's words," Bush said. "In early spring-tide, when the icy drip / Melts from the mountains hoar, and Zephyr's breath / Unbinds

see BUSH page 129

Asshole Proud Of Asshole Son

SUNDERLAND, MA—Gordon Ostrove, a 51-year-old Sunderland-area asshole, said Monday that he is very proud of his son Keith, 18, who is growing up to be a fine young asshole in his own right.

"Keith is a real chip off the old block," said the elder asshole, beaming with pride. "Just like his old man, he appreciates all the finer things in life—beer, Beemers, and broads. And, like me, he doesn't take shit from anybody: The other day, some kid at school made some smart-assed remark to him, and Keith mopped the floor with him."

Before Keith was born, Ostrove said he'd never thought he would have such a special relationship with his child.

"To be honest, [wife] Jackie was the one who wanted kids," Ostrove

Above: Asshole father-son duo Gordon and Keith Ostrove.

see ASSHOLE page 131

Report:
Stuffed-Animal Biodiversity Rising

WASHINGTON, DC—According to a World Wildlife Fund study released Monday, stuffed-animal biodiversity is rapidly rising, with the number of species available in plush form up nearly 800 percent since 1990.

"While the number of living species continues to plummet, the exact opposite is true of their toy counterparts," WWF director Ruth

Above: A rich spectrum of stuffed animal life is found under a leafy canopy in New York's FAO Schwarz.

Aberg said. "This is particularly true in America, where polyester-fiber-filled replicas of even the most endangered species can be found in glorious abundance."

According to the WWF report, 885 animal species are in danger of extinction worldwide, and another 165 are classified as threatened. Of these 1,050 at-risk species, however, an estimated 970 can be found in mass quantities in children's toy boxes and on collectors' shelves.

Stuffed-animal biodiversity, Aberg said, has not always been so robust. Ten years ago, the number of species produced by toy manufacturers was "abysmally low," mainly restricted to North American wildlife and a few select jungle animals. The past decade, however, has seen a proliferation of all manner of synthetic fauna.

see BIODIVERSITY page 130

Bill Up And Dies In Tennessee Legislature

NASHVILLE, TN—Democratic supporters of H.R. 3470, the Shelby County Millage Act, were right sorry Monday when the bill up and died in the Tennessee General Assembly. "We done supported that bill like a mama possum supports her young 'uns," said Rep. Clem McCombs (D-Pikeville), the bill's sponsor. "But the committee process was just too ornery." Rep. Lefty Perkins (R-Pigeon Forge), chairman of the House Committee On Looking After Your Own Business, celebrated the death of the bill by firing his shotgun into the air.

Sitcom Resorts To *Wizard Of Oz*-Themed Fantasy Episode

BURBANK, CA—Desperate for plotlines as its fifth season winds down, NBC's *Just Shoot Me* resorted to the time-honored *Wizard Of Oz*-themed fantasy episode Thursday. "David [Spade] gets hit over the head, and when he wakes up, he's in Oz," head writer Alex Cohen said. "Laura [San Giacomo] is The Tin Man, George [Segal] is the Cowardly Lion, Wendie [Malick] is the Scarecrow, and David—here's the best part—is Dorothy." Cohen said plans are already in the works for a late-December *It's A Wonderful Life* fantasy episode.

Bus Passenger Suspects Man In Next Seat Might Be Having Conversation With Him

SPOKANE, WA—An hour after pulling out of Spokane Monday, Greyhound passenger Ed Comello began suspecting that the man in the next seat was having a conversation with him. "I was gazing silently out the window," Comello said, "and I could hear the guy next to me going on about having to get to Tacoma tonight and how 'if your mama's sick, you got to go visit her.' I assumed he was talking to the person across the aisle, but when I looked across, the seat was empty." Comello added that he was afraid to acknowledge the possible conversation for fear of prolonging it.

St. Jude Swears Off Ever Answering Another Personals Ad

HEAVEN—Exasperated after a string of bad dates, Catholic martyr St. Jude vowed Monday never to respond to another personals ad. "Man, talk about hopeless causes," the holy figure said. "Do I have a sign on my head saying, 'Losers of the world, contact St. Jude?' I mean, these were some big-time desperate cases." Jude added that, from now on, he will respond only to direct prayer delivered in a Roman Catholic Church.

Ironic-Kitsch-Appreciation Subculture Excited About New Britney Spears Novel

AUSTIN, TX—Across the nation, Gen-X ironic-kitsch aficionados are racing to bookstores to pick up the new Britney Spears novel *A Mother's Gift*. "Holy shit, check it out: It's about a teenage girl who becomes a pop superstar thanks to the love and support of her mother," Mike Romanoff, 29, told friend Darius Grace, 30, while perusing the book at an Austin-area Barnes & Noble. "This is an instant classic on par with *Fabio After Dark*." Added Tim Edwards, operator of the popular "Mr. Sarcastic" web site: "I cannot wait to read this 'timeless, universal story as written by the girl who actually lived it.' Awesome." ∅

---

the ONION AcademiCorner presents

Choosing A College

The college years are a pivotal time in a person's life, not to mention a major financial investment. Here are some tips to help you choose the right school:

- You can never go wrong choosing a college you saw advertised on public transportation.

- There are many fine single-sex colleges where the emphasis is squarely on academics. Attend one of these only if you are a homosexual.

- Examine the school's official crest. If it has a big pot leaf in the center, you are on the right track.

- Find a college that will nurture your talents. For example, if you have an aptitude for dressing up in drag, penning witty quatrains, and awarding celebrities prizes as a way to draw attention to yourself, you may want to consider Harvard.

- If you fail to get accepted at a good school, you have brought shame upon not only yourself, but also your entire family. Committing ritual *seppuku* is the only way to save face.

- Schools that boast about their outstanding academic reputation are probably insecure about their inadequacies in other areas.

- The Armed Forces Scholarship Program is a great way to earn a considerable amount of money toward college, but it has a small "joining the goddamn army" downside.

- When consulting *Playboy*'s annual party-school rankings, be sure to look closely at the students-per-hot-tub ratio.

- Be wary of colleges where the chair of the history department keeps using the phrase "olden times."

- If you are having a hard time deciding between Princeton and Yale, cry me a fucking river, Fauntleroy.

- Avoid colleges where the previous year's commencement speaker was Burt Ward.

- College? Aw, man, what are you thinking about college for? You're the best metal guitarist in Winneshiek County.

Song About Heroin Used To Advertise Bank

Above: A scene from the new Metrobank ad, which features a song by longtime heroin addict Iggy Pop (inset).

BOSTON—The soul-wrenching experience of recovery from heroin addiction was used to evoke the financial security of a major banking institution Monday, when Boston-based Metrobank launched a high-profile ad campaign featuring "Lust For Life" by seminal '70s proto-punk Iggy Pop.

"We needed something that conveyed Metrobank's global financial presence, high-powered transaction capabilities, and respected position throughout the business community," said Jared Morris, president of Ogilvy & Mather, the spot's creator. "So, we thought, what better way than to call to mind punk forefather Iggy Pop's long, terrifying struggle with a near-fatal heroin habit?"

The 30-second spot, which premiered Monday during *Everybody Loves Raymond*, features images of gleaming skyscrapers, money changing hands, and businessmen on cell phones striding confidently down marble hallways. Notably absent from the ad is any footage of a shirtless, bleeding Iggy Pop in skintight leopard-print pants, repeatedly bashing himself in the face with a microphone onstage at the legendary New York punk venue CBGB.

Ian Hammond, who masterminded Global Tetrahedron Financial's acquisition of Metrobank earlier this year, rolled out the new campaign with a reception at the company's headquarters.

"We at Metrobank are proud to welcome Mr. Pop to the Global Tetra-hedron family," said Hammond, reading from a prepared statement. "We feel confident that this new commercial, much like Mr. Pop's exploits as the rolling-through-broken-glass frontman for The Stooges, will greatly appeal to our valued customers' 'lust for life.'"

Added Hammond: "Putting your trust in a financial institution other than Metrobank, well, that's like hypnotizing chickens."

The spot is part of a growing trend among advertisers to utilize songs associated with hardcore needle drugs. Among the notable heroin-themed songs featured in recent commercials: Jane's Addiction's "Jane Says," with its chorus of "I'm gonna kick tomorrow," for Motorola two-way pagers; The Velvet Underground's copping-heroin-in-Harlem anthem "I'm Waiting For The Man," for the 2002 Jeep Grand Cherokee; and Neil Young's "The Needle And The Damage Done," for the men's hair-replacement medication Rogaine.

"When The Rolling Stones sing, 'The sunshine bores the daylights out of me' on *Exile On Main Street*'s 'Rocks Off,' they're singing about the deadening effects of narcotics addiction and their powerlessness to escape it," said Dennis Frazier, creative director of Foote, Cone & Belding. "Such sentiments resonate profoundly with the American consumer. That's why 'Rocks Off' is perfect for Procter & Gamble's new line of children's shampoos."

Whether Metrobank's $11 million ad gamble will pay off in the long run remains to be seen, but so far, focus-group feedback has been overwhelmingly positive. The campaign has

The Motorola campaign has helped cement the mainstreaming of heroin-themed advertising.

already helped cement the mainstreaming of heroin-themed advertising, with more ambitious campaigns currently in the works.

"As junkie author William S. Bur-roughs conveyed in his hallucinatory prose, the staggering physical and emotional emptiness of drug addiction represents the escapist impulse turned savagely back upon itself, leading inexorably to nihilism, anhedonia, and the eventual nullification of the addict's essential humanity," said Ellen Weston, a media consultant for C&C Marketing in L.A. "This is why we're seeing passages from *Naked Lunch* featured in the new print campaign for Reebok."

Continued Weston: "Perhaps Lou Reed put it best when he said, 'Heroin will be the death of me / It's my wife, and it's my life.' For Reed, life and love become the same as death, and this 'living death,' if you will, really resonates with the American buying public in a deep and powerful way. It's not surprising, then, that there's such a huge bidding war between Coke and Pepsi for rights to Johnny Thunders' 'Chinese Rocks.'" Ø

BUSH from page 127

the crumbling clod, even then 'tis time / Press deep your plough behind the groaning ox / And teach the furrow-burnished share to shine."

"Book One of *The Georgics*, of course," Bush added.

Bush arranged the small, informal dinner in honor of Camps' unexpected arrival in America.

"It had been too long since I'd heard one of W.'s anecdotes, so I simply got on a plane," Camps said. "I showed up at his doorstep with a watercolor by Ignat Bednarik, whom I know he adores, just to make sure he'd let me in."

Bush confessed that he has "long held a fascination with the classical world," noting that his love of Roman history influenced his decision to enter politics.

"Virgil was born in the year 70 B.C.—let's see, that would be during the consulship of Gnaeus Pompeius The Great and Marcus Licinius Crassus, if I'm not mistaken," Bush said. "It is said that while Virgil's mother was with child, she dreamt she gave birth to a laurel branch, which, upon touching the ground, sprang up into a full-grown tree, its branches laden with ripe fruits and flowers. The next morning, she gave birth to Virgil. The legend goes that Virgil was born without crying, so mild was his countenance."

According to White House regulars, it is not uncommon for Bush to engage guests in discussions of whatever subject strikes his fancy, from the symphony playing in the background to the history of a style of jewelry a guest happens to be wearing.

"I love to hear George hold court on this or that," said Bush family friend and world-renowned physicist Norberta Münter. "I tell him he is such a spoiled brat, the way he demands our attention, but I must confess I can't take my eyes off him when he does."

As the group sipped apple martinis and, in Bush's words, "recovered" from the Chilean sea bass, the president continued.

"Most primarily associate Publius Vergilius Maro with *The Aeneid*," Bush told guests. "Yet so much pleasure is to be found in his lesser-known works—*The Eclogues*, completed in 37 B.C., and *The Georgics*, in 30 B.C., both of which praise the idyllic rural life."

"You have to remember I'm a bit of a farm boy myself," chuckled Bush, referring to his 1,600-acre ranch in Crawford, TX.

"*The Bucolics* are my personal favorite," Bush said. "They were basically a thank-you to Asinius Pollio for preventing the seizure of Virgil's land by the Triumvirate when they ordered the lands on the far banks of the river Po distributed to veterans of the victory at Philippi. They are so sublime, so inspirational. But why should I speak, when Virgil can do so himself? And far more eloquently, I might add."

Bush then recited a selection from *The Bucolics* in the original Latin, pausing occasionally to translate into French out of respect for his friend Amélie du Maurier, a young Parisian concert violinist in attendance. Earlier in the evening, a blushing du Maurier admitted to Bush that she did not know Latin. Bush eased the young woman's embarrassment with a joke.

"I wouldn't be surprised if your father forbade you from learning Latin, out of sheer distaste for *res publica*," said Bush, alluding to du Maurier's ancestors' place in the ousted French aristocracy.

Despite urging from dinner guests to continue his *Bucolics* recitation, Bush declined.

"I have already taken up far too much of your valuable time with my classical natterings," Bush said. "I dearly wish I could give you back this hour during which you so graciously indulged my dilettantism, but, as Plautus said, 'Factum est illud, fieri infectum non potest.' Done is done, it cannot be made undone." Ø

You Will Suffer Humiliation When The Sports Team From My Area Defeats The Sports Team From Your Area

By Bill Brodhagen

As you can see from the calendar, the game is coming up this weekend. I'm sure you are as excited for it as I am, as our cities are rivals and have been for quite some time. Your confidence in your team is high, but rest assured, you will suffer humiliation when the sports team from my area defeats the sports team from your area.

On numerous occasions, you have expressed the conviction that your area's sports team will be victorious. I must admit that every time I hear you make this proclamation, I react with both laughter and disbelief. "Ha!" I say to myself with laughter. "What?!" I say to myself in disbelief. How could you believe that your sports team could beat my sports team? It is clear that yours is inferior in every way.

When the sporting contest begins, the players on your team will be treated as though they are inconsequential. It will be remarkably easy for my team to accumulate more points than yours. There are many reasons for this, starting with the inferior physical attributes of the players representing your area. Strength, speed, and agility are just three of the qualities that the players on the team from your area lack. The players representing my area, on the other hand, have these traits in abundance.

I would not be a bit surprised if the individuals on the team from your area were sexually attracted to members of their own gender. That is how ineffective they are on the field of battle.

Underscoring your team's inferiority is its choice of colors. It is ludicrous to believe that your team's colors inspire either respect or fear. Instead, they appear to have been chosen by someone who is colorblind or, perhaps, bereft of sight altogether. The colors for my team, on the other hand, are aesthetically pleasing when placed in proximity to one another. They are a superior color combination in every way.

While we are on the subject of aesthetics, let us compare the respective facilities in which our teams play. While my team's edifice is blessed with architectural splendor and the most modern of ameni-

We will win and you will lose.

ties, yours is a thoroughly unpleasant place in which to watch a sporting contest. I know of what I speak, for I once attended a game between our respective teams in your facility. Let's just say the experience left me wishing that my car was inoperable that day due to mechanical problems, rendering it impossible for me to get to your area to attend the game.

If you need another reason why the sporting franchise representing my area is superior, look no further than the supporters for the two sides. Not only are the supporters of the team from my region more spirited, but they are also more intelligent and of finer breeding than you and the rest of your ilk. In addition, the female supporters of the team from my area possess more attractive countenances and figures than yours. Some of the women from my side that I have observed could make a living by posing for pictures for major men's magazines. The women who cheer for your team, I'm afraid, are far too unattractive to do so.

One of the more pathetic aspects of the team from your area is the fact that only people in your immediate area possess an affinity for it. By means of contrast, the team from my area inspires loyalty and affection in individuals who live in many other geographic locations.

To illustrate this point, let me tell a brief story: Recently, I was on vacation in an area of the country far away from my own, and I saw many individuals wearing items of clothing that bore the insignia of my team. I approached one such
see TEAM page 132

BIODIVERSITY from page 127

"There are an estimated 41,000 species of vertebrates on Earth, yet until recently, only a small handful were available for purchase—tigers, bears, lions, penguins, giraffes, and perhaps an owl or a duck," Aberg said. "Even then, only the most common species within a particular genus was represented. In the case of bears, for example, you'd have the brown bear, but rarely the polar bear and never the sun bear or sloth bear."

Today, by contrast, consumers regularly encounter river otters, hedgehogs, hammerhead sharks, warthogs, capybaras, opossums, tarantulas, and rare caimans found only in remote regions of the Amazon.

"Look at sea turtles, a species rapidly disappearing due to pollution and poaching," Aberg said. "Several years ago, EcoToys Inc. introduced Sam The Super Sea Turtle, a green turtle, or *Chelonia mydas*, complete with a tag describing its natural habitat and status as an endangered species. It was so well-received that the company then introduced Louie The Loggerhead, a large-headed, brownish-red turtle better known as *Caretta caretta*. That, in turn, was followed with *Lepidochelys kempi*, a small, gray Atlantic ridley named Bo Ridley. Store shelves that were once devoid of sea turtles are now teeming with all manner of them."

Our Plush Planet

Over the past 10 years, many exotic species of stuffed animals have experienced a population explosion. Among them:

1. Siberian ground fox
2. Cook Islands kiwi
3. Blue-backed musk turtle
4. Long-breasted mountain vulture
5. Three-toed trotting armadillo
6. Spiny pocket gopher
7. Sand leopard
8. Hungarian bearded pig

The rise in stuffed-animal biodiversity, experts say, has been made possible by humans' growing interest in environmental issues: Science-themed toy stores have popped up in malls across the nation. Entire shelves of such retail giants as Toys 'R' Us are devoted to animals from around the world. Beanie Baby manufacturer Ty can barely keep up with consumer demand for plush biodiversity.

Wild Republic, a major manufacturer of stuffed animals, produces more than 100 species of animals, including Halima The Snow Leopard, Brunei The Probiscus Monkey, and Adoncia The Poison Dart Frog. Several of the company's more pop-

ular species are also available as backpacks.

"As rainforests continue to disappear at a rate of one and a half acres every second, I thought there was no hope for the leopard frog," Sierra Club associate director Dianne Wilmot said. "But Wild Republic just announced that there will be 5,000 more *Rana pipiens* in existence by Christmas. A walk through the aisles of any toy store reveals what a diverse world we used to live in."

While Wilmot is encouraged by the stuffed-animal boom, some see cause for alarm.

"The number of species is rising way too quickly," said South Bend, IN, wildlife enthusiast Wendy Elias. "I wanted to get all the animals in the Jack Hanna collection: They're so cute, and I knew I could give them a good home. But they keep introducing new ones faster than I can make shelf space. My husband will absolutely kill me if I bring another one home."

Manufacturers, however, do not regard overpopulation as a threat.

"We have a plan, should the animals on store shelves become too numerous," said Adrian Rohn, a spokesman for Wild Republic. "We will simply employ a systematic reduction of prices to encourage bargain hunters to thin the herd." Ø

Odds 'N' Ends

A Room Of Jean's Own
By Jean Teasdale

Your old pal Jean has never claimed to be an expert on journalism, but there's one thing I do know: When you write a newspaper column, you have to pour your heart out. You loyal Jeanketeers out there know all about my battle with my weight, my troubles with hubby Rick, and my series of lousy, low-paying jobs. I admit that some of that stuff is a little embarrassing. It's not the kind of thing you usually tell total strangers. But being so open and honest in my column helps me get things off my chest, and I always feel a whole lot better for it. (For a little while, at least!)

Well, lately, my face has been even redder than usual. You see, I've been reading my local paper, *The Herald-Clarion*, a lot because Roz, my manager at Fashion Bug, buys a copy for the breakroom every morning. Besides "Dear Abby," the obituaries, and good ol' Cathy (natch!), I've been checking out the weekly column by *Herald-Clarion* features editor and star columnist Nancy Feeney. Now, I'm not saying I'm a washout in the writing biz, but after studying Nancy's column, "Nancy's Fan-cies" (how cute!), I realize I've still got a lot to learn about writing a professional column.

Like me, Nancy writes about her personal life in her column. But, like a true professional, she never gets too personal. (Unlike some columnists I could name, she never would have told her readers that she got arrested for shoplifting circus peanuts at the Pamida. Or that her kitty Arthur choked to death on a Pinchers The Lobster Teenie Beanie Baby.) No, before Nancy gets too deep into any gory details, she always changes the subject to something going on in the community. Or she talks about some local person's triumphant battle with a disease. Or she mentions that a local WWI veteran recently celebrated his 105th birthday. (The names of the people she writes about are always in bold-face, so it's really easy to read! Isn't that clever?) Then she ends her column with an inspirational quote or a funny but tasteful joke she'd overheard. Get it? Very professional.

Remember those old TV commercials where the woman slaps her forehead and says, "Wow! I coulda had a V-8!"? Well, after reading a few of Nancy's columns, I said to myself, "Wow! I coulda written about stuff besides my life!" So, from now on, instead of rambling on about my own daily doings, I think I'll devote my col-umn to little miscellaneous observations about the world around me. I'm calling it "Odds 'N' Ends."

So here it is, Jeanketeers. My first "Odds 'N' Ends" column...

I read recently that **Fred Lass-well**, the cartoonist behind *Snuffy Smith*, died. Now, get this—he had drawn *Snuffy* since 1942. Wow, that's nearly 60 years! I only hope that **Cathy Guisewite** can last that long! Actually, she probably can—*Cathy* doesn't look all that hard to draw.

Speaking of death, **Dale Earn-hardt**'s fatal accident at the Day-tona 500 was a huge shock to racing fans. The shock could be felt in the Teasdale household, too, since Dale was hubby Rick's favorite NASCAR driver. After Dale died, Rick swore he'd never watch another Winston Cup race again. "There will never be another Intimidator," he said. That seemed kind of extreme to me—I mean, there are always a whole bunch of racers on the track, and surely they must have talent, too. So I brought up that one cute hunk who wins a lot, **Jeff Gordon**. "What about him? Couldn't he be your new favorite driver?" I asked Rick. You'd think I'd asked him to jump off the Golden Gate Bridge! He went on this tirade about how totally clueless I was, saying I had absolutely no understanding of NASCAR or anything else that didn't involve kitties or a bunch of TV-talk-show ladies "on the rag" drinking tea and crying their eyes out about preemies on respirators.

Yikes! What brought that on? (Cue the *Twilight Zone* theme!) Don't get me wrong: I'm sorry Dale Earnhardt died. But, after all, he did race cars at speeds approaching 200 mph. There are loads of far safer sports he could have chosen. Like soccer, for example.

Nancy Feeney talks about ordinary yet inspiring local citizens, which I think is great. It just goes to show that you don't have to be famous to be a superstar! Unfortunately, I don't know a lot of people in the community. I tend to not leave the house much, except to work and shop, so I'm not really as well-connected as Nancy. But she did say something in her column the other day that practically bowled me over, because it reminded me of a very similar event in my own life. Observing the generation gap between Baby Boomers and their parents, Nancy mentioned that her mother had criticized her for wearing too informal an outfit to a church gathering.

Talk about uncanny! Several years ago, my own mother and I attended my cousin Heidi's wedding, and Mom didn't like the fact that I was wearing an electric-blue rayon pantsuit. Throughout

see TEASDALE page 132

ASSHOLE from page 127

said. "But on the day Keith was born, I walked into the delivery room to have a look at the little turd. When I leaned over, he grabbed my finger. Everything changed at that moment. I thought to myself, 'You're gonna be a tough bastard, just like your pop.' And you know what? He is."

Among the many qualities Ostrove has passed on to his son is his sense of humor.

"When Keith was 8, we stopped at the Kwik Trip for some Pepsi," Ostrove said. "The clerk short-changed us, and right in front of him, Keith says, 'Hey Dad, that towelhead gave you the wrong change.' I was just about to lay into the stupid Pakistani, but instead I just hugged Keith and laughed. Where did he get that stuff at that age? He's got the Ostrove genes, that's for sure."

The younger Ostrove has also inherited his father's gift for communicating with the opposite sex.

"One time, Keith asked me why Mommy was crying," said Ostrove. "I told him that mommies sometimes get upset when you remind them of their proper role in a marriage. Now that Keith has a girlfriend of his own, I see the impact of my words: Whenever [girlfriend] Traci gets out of line,

> **Said Ostrove: "The clerk shortchanged us, and right in front of him, Keith says, 'Hey, Dad, that towelhead gave you the wrong change.' He's got the Ostrove genes, that's for sure."**

Keith straightens her right out with the old Ostrove stare. And if that doesn't work, he just threatens to dump her. The kid is in charge of that relationship, that's for sure."

Ostrove, who said he has always been "extremely close" with his asshole son, is there for Keith in times of trouble.

"Last week, Keith and his friends were keying that Pfister kid's car when a cop caught them," Ostrove said. "He brought Keith to the house and told me what he'd done. I said, 'I'm very sorry about this, officer. You can be sure I will deal with this matter,' and shut the door. Keith actually seemed scared that I was going to punish him, but I just patted him on the back and said, 'Good job, son.' That was the same goddamn cop who'd given me a $100 speeding ticket a few days before."

In spite of the exceptional closeness of the father-son duo, some Sunderland residents do not appreciate the love and support Ostrove gives his offspring.

"A few summers ago, that Ostrove brat was shooting fireworks into my yard," said neighbor Julia Shaw. "So I grabbed him and dragged him home by his ear." Shaw said she was surprised when the elder Ostrove demanded to know why she was touching his son. Even after Shaw recounted the fireworks incident, Ostrove threatened her with a lawsuit.

"He told me that if I ever touched Keith again, there'd be 'dire fucking consequences,'" Shaw said. "I couldn't believe it. People like that should be castrated at age 12 so they don't pass that gene on to others."

According to noted therapist Dr. Eli Wasserbaum, Ostrove should be applauded for his commitment to parenting.

"In a world of deadbeat dads, Ostrove's devotion to his son is remarkable," Wasserbaum said. "Most men like him would have left their family by now for some young bimbo. Yet there he is every day, spending lots of quality time with his son, shaping his young mind with his ignorant opinions on sports, women, and politics. Say what you will about Mr. Ostrove, but this is one asshole who cares." ∅

Executing The Mentally Disabled

The U.S. Supreme Court is currently hearing a case challenging the constitutionality of the death penalty for retarded individuals. What do *you* think?

"The notion of executing retarded people is deeply offensive. It should be called the execution of the *developmentally disabled*."

Anita Welch
Homemaker

"I'd rather see these killers executed than force the American taxpayer to spend thousands on lemon cookies and safety scissors for the next 50 years."

Robert Ready
Banker

"You'd think judges would be lenient, since they probably were pretty easy to catch."

Irfan Clarence
Cashier

"How can we execute criminals for actions they don't even fully comprehend? They just wanted to pet the pretty lady's soft hair."

Don Duquette
Truck Driver

"Do we really need to waste money and resources killing the retarded when sending them into a hedge maze would be just as effective?"

Art Gordon
Systems Analyst

"Even more shocking is the fact that hundreds of these executions were carried out by a Texas governor with a 57 IQ."

Mindy Andersen
Reference Librarian

The Hoof And Mouth Panic

Hoof and mouth disease is a major problem in Europe. What precautions are being taken to prevent the spread of the disease here?

- Surgically removing hooves, mouths from all livestock
- Interrogating cattle passing through U.S. customs regarding their intended business in the country
- Getting cows to eat healthy, quit smoking
- Requiring animals grazing in fields to wash hooves thoroughly before returning to barn
- Banning importation of Cap'n Killarney's Olde Hoof 'N' Mouth Brisket
- Urging nation's farmers to halt practice of tongue-kissing cows for good luck
- Placing strict limitations on immigration from Hüffenmauthia
- Boiling all British beef until gray and flavorless, the way the British do

the ONION
America's Finest News Source

Herman Ulysses Zweibel *Founder*

T. Herman Zweibel *Publisher Emeritus*
J. Phineas Zweibel *Publisher*
Maxwell Prescott Zweibel *Editor-In-Chief*

FOUNDED 1871 • "TU STULTUS ES"

132

Your Horoscope

By Lloyd Schumner Sr.
Retired Machinist and
A.A.P.B.-Certified Astrologer

Aries: (March 21–April 19)
The stars indicate that you will meet an attractive Aries the next time you look in the mirror. Sometimes, those stars are just a little too precious.

Taurus: (April 20–May 20)
There are certain species of bear which mind their own business and don't attack or eat humans. You will not meet any such bears this week.

Gemini: (May 21–June 21)
You will fall prey to a strange sexual condition which leaves you unable to achieve orgasm unless certain nerves are repeatedly stimulated.

Cancer: (June 22–July 22)
Venus ascending in your sign may sound sexy, but it's really just a function of its orbit. So don't get all excited.

Leo: (July 23–Aug. 22)
Though your sign has always been known as The Lion, your tireless work has changed it to The Mattress King.

Virgo: (Aug. 23–Sept. 22)
Let's do Virgo! Virgo, Virgo, bo birgo, banana fanna, fo firgo, fee fi mo mirgo— Vir-go!

Libra: (Sept. 23–Oct. 23)
You will be unable to stop yourself from falling unconscious for seven hours at a time this week.

Scorpio: (Oct. 24–Nov. 21)
It's time to put some spice back into your relationship. The stars suggest you might consider having sex once in a while.

Sagittarius: (Nov. 22–Dec. 21)
After years of trying, you are finally able to quit drinking next Monday, only to die several days later of advanced dehydration.

Capricorn: (Dec. 22–Jan. 19)
You will achieve a modicum of fame as a supermodel for the unspeakably ugly plus-sized woman.

Aquarius: (Jan. 20–Feb. 18)
Your life will be thrown into disarray when you find yourself loving an epic science-fiction film that you know in your heart was really bad.

Pisces: (Feb. 19–March 20)
The biggest mistake of your life was asking the exact wrong people to write your letter of recommendation.

TEAM from page 130

individual and asked him if he originated from my area. He said no, explaining that he simply liked the team from my area and had for many years. Interestingly enough, during this trip, I saw no clothing or other paraphernalia bearing the insignia of your team.

Do you still doubt that the team from your area is inferior to the one from mine? Just look at our teams' respective histories. In the past, we have defeated you on any number of occasions. Granted, there were times when your team beat my team, but those were lucky flukes.

The day of the game will soon be at hand. And no matter how hard you pray to a higher power or how many foam accoutrements you wear in support of the team from your area, your team will be defeated. We will win and you will lose. This is your fate.

Prepare for humiliation. It shall be upon you at the designated hour. Ø

TEASDALE from page 131

the ceremony and reception, she kept sniping to me about how "immodest" and "informal" it was. Then, during the car ride home, we got into a screaming match that rivaled something you'd see on the WWF show! She called me slovenly, and I accused her of being a loveless, abusive, hypocritical witch. That got her so mad that she kicked me out of her car near the outskirts of town, forcing me to trudge one mile across this marshy field in patent-leather pumps to the nearest bus stop, bawling all the way.

Oops. I suppose I'm getting carried away again, talking about personal stuff. Well, I promise that in my next "Odds 'N' Ends" column, I'll shape up and be more professional. But I'll need your help. If you know of any disease-sufferers in my area who are probably going to live, or any 105-year-old WWI veterans, or anyone else of that ilk, please write me care of this newspaper. Ø

the ONION®

VOLUME 37 ISSUE 15   **AMERICA'S FINEST NEWS SOURCE**™   **26 APRIL-2 MAY 2001**

Mason-Dixon Line Renamed IHOP-Waffle House Line

see NATION page 5A

First Chapter In History Of Sino-American War Of 2011 Already Written

see WORLD page 9A

Spelling-Bee Runner-Up Bursts Into Tears Whenever Anyone Says 'Proprietor'

see LOCAL page 10C

STATshot

A look at the numbers that shape your world.

What Are We Talking About Other Than *Survivor*?

1. That show that comes on after *Survivor*
2. That show that comes on before *Survivor*
3. The *Survivor-Boot Camp* lawsuit
4. *Survivor's* time slot
5. What's up with *Survivor 3*?
6. That Pepsi ad they showed during *Survivor*
7. That Destiny's Child song "Survivor"
8. Why anyone would want to watch *Survivor*

Gay-Pride Parade Sets Mainstream Acceptance Of Gays Back 50 Years

WEST HOLLYWOOD, CA—The mainstream acceptance of gays and lesbians, a hard-won civil-rights victory gained through decades of struggle against prejudice and discrimination, was set back at least 50 years Saturday in the wake of the annual Los Angeles Gay Pride Parade.

"I'd always thought gays were regular people, just like you and me, and that the stereotype of homosexuals as hedonistic, sex-crazed deviants was just a destructive myth," said mother of four Hannah Jarrett, 41, mortified at the sight of 17 tanned and oiled boys cavorting in jock straps to a throbbing techno beat on a float shaped like an enormous phallus. "Boy, oh, boy, was I wrong."

The parade, organized by the Los Angeles Gay And Lesbian And Bisexual And Transvestite And Transgender Alliance (LAGALABATATA), was

Left: Participants in Saturday's Los Angeles Gay Pride Parade, which helped change straight people's tolerant attitudes toward gays.

see PARADE page 134

Area Father Must Have Read Some Drug-Slang Brochure Or Something

DECATUR, GA—Rodney Dunbar, a 46-year-old civil engineer and father of two, "must have read some drug-slang pamphlet or something," his children reported Monday.

"Dad and I were watching the NBA playoffs Saturday," 14-year-old son Dylan said. "Someone missed a pass, and he goes, 'Sometimes, I get the feeling that some of these basketball players are smoking the rock.' Then, a few days later, he sits down on my bed and asks me if I'd ever been 'pressured into attending a raver party, where kids dance and take party drugs like truck driver, co-pilot, Georgia home boy, and doctor.' It's like he picked up a health textbook or something. Or maybe he found some weird talking-to-your-kids-about-drugs web site."

A discussion between Dylan and his sister Megan, 16, revealed that she had been asked similar questions.

"He asked me if any of the kids at school 'do crystal.' I just stared at him, dumbfounded," Megan said. "Then he

Above: Rodney Dunbar holds a rap session with his son.

says, 'It's also called crank. It's very dangerous.' Okay, dad."

Dr. Allen Mayhan, a local family therapist, explained Dunbar's clumsy

see FATHER page 136

Best-Laid Plans Of Mice And Men Faulted In 747 Crash

WASHINGTON, DC—Representatives of the National Transportation Safety Board, their "bosoms heavy with melancholia," announced the findings of their investigation of American Airlines Flight 251 Monday, citing "fate's cruel hand" as the cause of the Apr. 10 crash that claimed 411 lives.

"The best-laid plans of mice and men go oft astray," NTSB spokesman Frank Whelan said, "and leave us naught but grief and pain for promised joy. Such was the case when the 747 unexpectedly burst into flames and plummeted to the ground at 7:14 a.m., shortly after take-off from Chicago's O'Hare Airport."

According to NTSB investigators, the London-bound Boeing 747 relayed a distress call at 7:07 a.m., just 12 minutes after leaving O'Hare. Three minutes of desperate radio communication between the pilots and air-traffic controllers

see 747 page 135

Above: The smoldering wreckage of Flight 251, which crossed the Stygian ferry.

Bananas Again Sweep Primates' Choice Awards

LOS ANGELES—In a gala, chimp-studded affair at the Shrine Auditorium, bananas swept the Primates' Choice Awards for the 42nd year in a row Monday, winning such categories as Best Food, Best Fruit, and Best Dessert. "This year, as in so many years past, bananas delighted and nourished the primate world," said Dole CEO David Murdock, who accepted the award for Best Potassium Source on behalf of bananas. "It is only fitting that we pay tribute in kind." The fruit's sweep proved popular with the 3,200 simians in attendance, who shrieked and jumped up and down in their seats each time it was announced as the winner while a photo of bananas was projected onto a giant screen.

Depressed NRA Member Half-Hoping Son Will Accidentally Shoot Him

ROUND ROCK, TX—Despondent from the loss of his job and his recent divorce, National Rifle Association lifetime member Patrick Schramm is half-hop-ing for an accidental shooting death at the hands of his 10-year-old son. "I don't know what the point is anymore," Schramm said Monday. "Sometimes, I find myself wishing that Jeffrey would mistake me for a robber late at night and put me out of my misery." Schramm then absent-mindedly released the safety on his Browning 10 gauge and left it on the kitchen counter a foot from the cookie jar.

Grimacing Congressman Quickly Drafts Legislation For Charley-Horse Research

WASHINGTON, DC—Grimacing in considerable pain Monday, Rep. William Delahunt (D-MA) quickly drafted and introduced the 2001 Charley Horse Research Appropriations Act, which would allocate $100 million for "immediate research" to find a charley-horse cure. "Charley horses are a serious—oh, Jesus—medical condition that afflicts thousands of Americans every day," Delahunt told House colleagues. "And so let us—Christ, this kills—pass this bill as soon as possible." When informed that the earliest the bill could be passed and signed into law is next Monday, Delahunt moaned and pounded the podium.

Restaurant, Staff Patronized

BOSTON—Attorney Derrick Carlisle patronized the Riverside Café and five members of its staff Monday. "Excuse me, but I've always been under the impression that Manhattan Clam Chowder is red, not white," Carlisle told server Diane Ptacek. "And, when you get a second, please tell the bartender that a proper Old Fashioned is made with a dash of bitters, not a whole ounce. Thanks so much."

Antarctic Observational Comic Running Out Of Ideas

BYRD, ANTARCTICA—Brad Swithers, three-time winner of the Molson Ice/Edge Gel South Pole Laff-Off, said Monday that he is running out of ideas for observational humor about life in Antarctica. "I've already made tons of 'What's the deal with those ice chunks that form between the huskies' toes?' jokes," Swithers said. "And, of course, I've done the whole penguins-and-smelt thing to death." Swithers added that he's currently working on a bit about the differences between Amundsen Bay and Voyeykov Ice Shelf women. ∅

PARADE from page 133

intended to "promote acceptance, tolerance, and equality for the city's gay community." Just the opposite, however, was accomplished, as the event confirmed the worst fears of thousands of non-gay spectators, cementing in their minds a debauched and distorted image of gay life straight out of the most virulent right-wing hate literature.

Among the parade sights and sounds that did inestimable harm to the gay-rights cause: a group of obese women in leather biker outfits passing out clitoris-shaped lollipops to horrified onlookers; a man in military uniform leading a submissive masochist, clad in diapers and a baby bonnet, around on a dog leash; several Hispanic dancers in rainbow wigs and miniskirts performing "humping" motions on a mannequin dressed as the Pope; and a dozen gyrating drag queens in see-through dresses holding penis-shaped beer bottles that appeared to spurt ejaculation-like foam when shaken and poured onto passersby.

Timothy Orosco, 51, a local Walgreens manager whose store is on the parade route, changed his attitude toward gays as a result of the event.

"They kept chanting things like, 'We're here, we're queer, get used to it!' and 'Hey, hey, we're gay, we're not going to go away!'" Orosco said. "All I can say is, I *was* used to it, but now, although I'd never felt this way before, I wish they *would* go away."

Allison Weber, 43, an El Segundo marketing consultant, also had her perceptions and assumptions about gays challenged by the parade.

"My understanding was that gay people are just like everybody else—decent, hard-working people who care about their communities and have loving, committed relationships," Weber said. "After this terrifying spectacle, I

Above: Members of the Laguna Beach Leatherdaddy Association make their final pre-march preparations.

don't want them teaching my kids or living in my neighborhood."

The parade's influence extended beyond L.A.'s borders, altering the attitudes of straight people across America. Footage of the event was featured on telecasts of *The 700 Club* as "proof of the sin-steeped world of homosexuality." A photo spread in Monday's *USA Today* chronicled many of the event's vulgar displays—understood by gays to be tongue-in-cheek "high camp"—which horrified previously tolerant people from coast to coast.

Dr. Henry Thorne, a New York University history professor who has written several books about the gay-rights movement, explained the misunderstanding.

"After centuries of oppression as an 'invisible' segment of society, gays, emboldened by the 1969 Stonewall uprising, took to the streets in the early '70s with an 'in-your-face' attitude. Confronting the worst prejudices of a world that didn't accept them, they fought back against these prejudices with exaggeration and parody, reclaiming their enemies' worst stereotypes about them and turning them into symbols of gay pride," Thorne said. "Thirty years later, gays have won far greater acceptance in the world at large, but they keep doing this stuff anyway."

"Mostly, I think, because it's really fun," Thorne added.

The Los Angeles Gay Pride Parade, Thorne noted, is part of a decades-old gay-rights tradition. But, for mainstream heterosexuals unfamiliar with irony and the reclamation of stereotypes for the purpose of exploding them, the parade resembled an invasion of grotesque outer-space mutants, bent on the destruction of the human race.

"I have a cousin who's a gay, and he seemed like a decent enough guy to me," said Iowa City, IA, resident Russ Linder, in Los Angeles for a weekend sales seminar. "Now, thanks to this parade, I realize what a freak he's been all along. Gays are all sick, immoral perverts."

Parade organizers vowed to make changes in the wake of the negative reaction among heterosexuals.

"I knew it. I said we needed 100 dancers on the 'Show Us Your Ass' float, but everybody insisted that 50 would be enough," said Lady Labia, spokesperson for LAGALABATATA. "Next year, we're really going to give those breeders something to look at." ∅

Area Woman Judges Everything By Whether It's Cute

EAU CLAIRE, WI—Sharon Sczerba evaluates everything on the basis of cuteness, sources close to the 36-year-old Eau Claire woman reported Monday.

According to friends, Sczerba uses the word "cute" more than 150 times a day, applying it to everything from such traditionally cute items as infants and stuffed animals to such non-traditional items as board games, soft-drink bottles, and art.

"I remember one time, she said she liked Van Gogh," said neighbor and longtime friend Emily Cone. "I thought it was great that she was getting into art other than Anne Geddes photos, but then I found out she just thought his 'Sunflowers' painting was 'really cute.'"

When informed that Van Gogh had cut off his ear in a fit of madness, Sczerba reversed her opinion of the Dutch master's work, calling the painting "not so cute anymore."

When judging music and movies, cuteness is again the overriding factor, weighing more heavily than style, substance, or meaning.

"I know I'm a little old for them, but how could you not love 'N Sync—they are just darling," Sczerba said. "Speaking of darling, have you seen *Bridget Jones's Diary* yet? It's such a cute movie. Renée Zellweger is absolutely adorable in it."

Sczerba recently purchased an iMac for her home finances, despite the fact that a PC would have better suited her needs.

"Isn't this computer the cutest thing? It's tangerine," Sczerba said. "When I saw it, I just had to have it. Why would you get a boring old gray box when you can get a precious little see-thru one like this instead?"

Cuteness was also the major determining factor in Sczerba's recent car purchase.

"When I saw the VW Bug, I thought it was the most adorable car in the world," Sczerba said. "Everyone told me I shouldn't get it because I'd need more trunk room to carry things to work and back, but

Above: Sharon Sczerba.

when they showed me one in the cutest shade of yellow, I couldn't help myself."

Added Sczerba: "Know what Volkswagen should do? They should make a red VW Bug with black dots so it would look like a ladybug. That would be the cutest thing ever."

A donor to numerous charities,

see **CUTE** page 136

747 from page 133

ensued before contact was lost and passengers and crew "shuffled off this mortal coil."

Speaking at the press conference, American Airlines CEO Donald Carty expressed sympathy for the victims' families. He stressed, however, that American Airlines accepts no responsibility for "this swipe of God's mighty hand."

"I am deeply sorry this tragedy occurred," Carty said. "But let us ask ourselves, what is so tragic about awaking to life immortal?"

Carty praised the members of the doomed 747's cockpit crew, who "struggled mightily to right the listing ship but were ultimately destined to go to a far better place."

"Exult, O shores, and ring, O bells!" Carty said. "But I, with mournful tread, walk the deck my Captain lies, fallen cold and dead."

Based on air-traffic-control records and eyewitness accounts, the crash may have been caused by an explosion in the plane's left engine. Neither the NTSB nor American Airlines, however, plans to investigate.

"The call of death is a call of love," Whelan said. "Death can be sweet if we answer it in the affirmative, if we accept it as one of the great eternal forms of life and transformation."

Victims' loved ones traveled from across the country to attend the press conference, hoping to learn more about the crash or simply share their pain with others.

"Why? Why?" asked Teresa Salton, 34, clutching a hand-knitted sweater

her deceased sister had given her last Christmas. "Angela doesn't deserve this. It just makes no sense. It can't be."

Whelan urged Salton and other grief-stricken loved ones not to cry, telling them that they should envy the victims, who "now sing in the choir invisible."

"Out, out, brief candle!" Whelan said. "Life's but a walking shadow; a poor player, that struts and frets his hour upon the stage, and then is heard no more: It is a tale told by an idiot, full of sound and fury, signifying nothing."

A *Chicago Tribune* reporter asked Carty to respond to rumors that the plane's inspection record reveals a history of left-engine problems, and that service documents may have been falsified to allow scheduled flights to continue. Carty shook his head and gazed upward.

"How ridiculous to think we humans can control our own life and death as if setting a clock," Carty said. "One's days are numbered, one's hour is come, one's race is run, one's doom is sealed."

Of the plane's 411 passengers, 53 were children. Carty spoke briefly to the families of these particular victims.

"In *To An Athlete Dying Young*, A.E. Housman explained best why we should not shed tears upon the graves of these little ones," Carty said. "'Smart lad, to slip betimes away / From fields where glory does not stay / And early though the laurel grows / It withers quicker than the rose.'"

Despite the words of comfort, families of victims expressed anger and

Above: American Airlines CEO Donald Carty asks reporters, "Who am I to question Flight 251's destiny?"

confusion over the NTSB's decision to forgo an investigation.

"How can they just do nothing?" asked Elgin, IL, resident Pamela Robinson, whose husband Anthony was on Flight 251. "Something needs to be done. We need to know why this happened."

The NTSB, however, remains steadfast in its refusal. Whelan said he has

no interest in searching the crash site for the plane's black box.

"There is special providence in the fall of the sparrow," Whelan said. "If it be now, 'tis not to come; if it be not to come, it will be now; if it be not now, yet it will come. The readiness is all. Since no man of aught he leaves knows, what isn't to leave betimes? Let be." ∅

These Nerf Guns Really Liven Up The Office

By Robert Ulm
Tech Support Manager
Redfire Software

When you're a manager at a software company, boosting employee morale is a full-time job. The best way to keep everyone focused and productive, I believe, is to strike a careful balance between hard work and whimsy. That's why, last Thursday, I ran over to KB Toys on my lunch break and bought a dozen Nerf guns. And, boy, let me tell you, those Nerf guns really liven up the office!

Upon returning from KB, I called my team into the conference room for an "emergency meeting." You should have seen the look on their faces when they walked in and found a large particle-board sign with a big red bullseye and the words, "Take Aim... At Productivity!" For the next eight or nine minutes, the only thing on anyone's mind was having fun. I handed out the Nerf guns and everyone took a shot at the bullseye. For added enjoyment, I encouraged everybody to cheer the shooter on.

I had faith that my people would use the Nerf guns to keep the office from getting too uptight and stifling. And you know what? I was right! Before long, they were shooting up each other's cubicles and

After letting off a sufficient amount of steam, they returned to their cubicles, batteries recharged.

having a grand old time. Then, after letting off a sufficient amount of steam, they returned to their cubicles, batteries recharged. Those Nerf guns sure did the trick.

You might think boosting morale is an easy task—a kind word here, a pat on the back there. But if that were the case, anyone could be a manager. No, a good manager is constantly finding new ways to keep his or her folks happy. And sometimes, that means thinking outside the proverbial box.

The Nerf guns were hardly the first initiative I'd enacted to improve morale and stimulate creativity. But it was the most successful. Take the foosball table I brought in last September. I thought it might bring a little competitive spirit to the office, but Greg and Andrew were such ace players, they completely hogged the table. Not a great way to encourage teamwork.

Then there was my idea for a bi-weekly mid-afternoon ice-cream break. Everybody likes ice cream, I figured, and it might provide a nice, relaxed forum for people to exchange ideas on their current projects without calling a formal meeting. But because we were so busy eating ice cream—and I could still kick myself for this—a bunch of customer calls went unanswered. Well, the head office got wind of that, and you can bet I got a first-class butt-kicking. To make matters worse, it turned out that a lot of my workers were lactose-intolerant. How was I to know?

One of the great things about the guns is that my team can have their Nerf battles and get a little crazy without getting too carried away. After a few Nerf-gun volleys, the tension is broken and the monotony of staring at humming computer screens for hours on end is broken.

Then my troops can go back to work refreshed. And it sure beats a cup of stale afternoon coffee and a dried-out bagel!

Granted, the guns cost $19 each, for a grand total of $228. That may seem like a lot of money, but you really can't put a price on employee morale. In the end, those guns will more than pay for themselves in new energy and ideas, believe you me.

I'm sure the higher-ups will be pleased with my efforts. One of the memos from the head office specifically instructed us to tailor morale-boosting to our individual teams. If Nerf isn't my tech-support team all over, then, by golly, I don't know my team. I just know that when the district manager comes by and notices the high spirits in the office, I'll be in line for a promotion. Maybe I'll even get a corner office, or at least something farther away from that noisy paper shredder.

As big a success as the guns have been, though, I can't sit back and rest on my laurels. Morale doesn't stay up on its own. Sure, nominal raises and attractive new business cards help some, but it's the little things a manager does that keep an office fresh and vibrant. But the big question is: Are the Super Soakers I ordered going a little too far? ∅

FATHER from page 133

efforts to incorporate contemporary slang into his drug talks.

"By using current slang terms, Dunbar is trying to tell his children, 'I'm "hip" or "down," and you can talk to me about anything,'" Mayhan said.

"He asked me if any of the kids at school 'do crystal.' I just stared at him, dumbfounded," Megan said.

"He is unaware that his stilted speaking style, belabored references, and frequent incorrect usage of terms leave his children more confused than reassured."

Mayhan mentioned an April 3 incident in which Dunbar alluded to "Special K," the newly popular club drug Ketamine, during breakfast.

"As Dylan was eating a bowl of cereal, his father told him, 'Product 19 is fine, kiddo, but stay off the Special K,'" Mayhan said. "Dylan wouldn't have even known he was talking about a drug if he hadn't punctuated the reference with a raised eyebrow."

Said Dylan: "I had no idea what 'Special K' was. I had to ask White Jimmy, this guy in my history class who deals. Turns out, it's a dog anesthetic that people take. Then White Jimmy showed me his stash. Man, that guy has a lot of wild stuff."

According to Dr. Mary Putnam-Ellis, author of *Speedballs, Spliffs, And Spores: How NOT To Talk To Your Teen About Drugs*, parents have attempted to use drug slang for generations, despite the fact that there are no known cases of the tactic being effective.

"Recent studies indicate that knowledge of slang does not improve communication between parents and children," Putnam-Ellis said. "Instead, statistics show that hearing parents use the street names of drugs leaves teenagers feeling vaguely creeped out."

In the past, parents would use drug slang from their own generation, assuring their children that they "don't have to smoke doobies to be cool." More parents, however, are turning to current slang, picked up from articles about drugs in *Time* and *Newsweek*, investigative pieces on *60 Minutes*, and movies such as *Traffic*, as well as from drug-slang brochures.

"Parents feel that, by exhibiting knowledge of street names, their children will see them as an informed, experienced peer who is worth listening to, rather than an out-of-touch authority figure," Putnam-Ellis said. "This tactic *never* works."

Despite its ineffectiveness, Dunbar said he has no plans to stop using contemporary drug slang any time soon.

"I read an article in the paper about that new drug Ecstasy and its long-term effects on the brain," Dunbar said. "I wanted to talk to the kids about it, but then I forgot what the article said they call it. Is it 'E' or 'X'? Or is it both? And I can't remember if you use 'E' as a noun or verb—do you 'do E' or do you 'get E'd up'? I'll have to make sure to get that straight." ∅

CUTE from page 135

Sczerba evaluates organizations' worthiness on the basis of adorability.

"I joined PETA, because every time I see a baby seal, I just want to hug it and never let it go," Sczerba said. "But then, in the latest PETA newsletter, they were going on and on about how they're trying to save this rare species of crab, and I was like, 'Why? That thing is disgusting!' Before long, it became clear that half the things they wanted to save were either scary-looking or slimy, so I stopped giving to them."

According to psychologist Dr. Harold Backlund, Sczerba's cuteness fixation may prove destructive in the long run.

"Sharon's need to immerse herself wholly in that which is precious is indicative of an inability to deal with conflict and pain," Backlund said. "One day, she is going to face an ugliness in her life that she cannot turn away from, and when that happens, it will send her entire world into a massive, irreversible tailspin."

Sczerba is unfazed by the possibility.

"Whenever I'm feeling down in the dumps, I just take one look at the picture I have of a baby dressed up as a pumpkin, and everything's all right," Sczerba said. "There's no problem a picture of a baby in a pumpkin suit can't fix. Talk about *cute*!" ∅

All Women Don't Know What They're Missing

By Justin Stroebel

It's a situation we've all been in before: You see a pretty woman in a bar, mall, grocery store, restaurant, library, Laundromat, bowling alley, car dealership, post office, student union, tattoo parlor, or hospital. Smiling suavely, you move in and strike up a conversation using whatever means you have at hand. But every time, you somehow wind up striking out. It's happened to me, and I'm as eligible a bachelor as they come. These ladies would be lucky to land a guy like yours truly, but still they say no. I'm telling you, all women don't know what they're missing.

Sometimes, I look in the mirror and say, "Wow, Justin, women should be falling all over you." But whenever I approach a girl and tell her that I'm the type of guy she should be having sex with, she begs to differ. What's the deal with every single woman in the entire world?

It's not like I don't have a good job. I work for a prominent lawn-furniture distributor and make well over $41,000 a year. One would think women would appreciate a man with financial stability. And, since I usually bring it up within the first three sentences, it's not like they don't know. You'd expect the ladies on this planet to realize I'm perfect for them, but it seems like every woman in any given place at any given time completely misses that fact.

Who knows what crazy things go on in the head of everyone who isn't a man?

Take, for example, the 200 or so women I've asked out in the last year. Every single one of them had some sort of problem that made them not want to date me. I guess they all must have been frigid.

Not only am I well-off, but I'm also well-muscled. I spend at least three days a week at the gym, so you'd think the ladies would be all over me like shit on a shoe. You would be wrong. Often, I'll see a beautiful woman on a park bench, and I'll take off my suede jacket and start flexing, saying things like, "Oh, yeah!" and "You want a piece of this, sweetheart?" Nine times out of ten, they'll grab their belongings and get the hell out of there as fast as they can. I wish I could say that the other one time in ten, the woman was interested in me, but almost always, they call for the police or deploy pepper spray. To be honest, I prefer the pepper spray.

You know, women say they want a man with a sense of humor, but from what I've seen, they don't. I'm always telling jokes. I know a bunch of hysterical jokes about the differences between blondes and beer, but whenever I tell one, women leave or throw a drink in my face. Geez, talk about all women being on the rag all the time. Well, at least I know it isn't me. All I can say is, your loss, ladies of the world.

Obviously, I'm just not meeting the right type of women. The only sort of woman I ever seem to meet is either short, tall, thin, smart, serious, overweight, ditzy, career-driven, aggressive, fun, shy, family-oriented, or of medium height. It's hardly worth the effort talking to that kind of girl.

Well, what can I do? I just happen to have been born on a planet where half the population can't recognize a good thing when they see it. Bum luck, I guess.

Don't worry about me, though. Justin Stroebel's always got an ace in the hole. If the 3,121,833,445 females on this planet don't see what they're missing, fuck 'em. ∅

Ask The Cheat Guide To BloodLair

By The Cheat Guide To BloodLair

Dear Cheat Guide To BloodLair,

My recent job change has brought me more money—and more headaches! I used to see my friends several times a week, but lately I'm too strapped for time. This has many of my friends accusing me of being "too good" for the old gang. How do I make them believe that's simply not true?

—Stressed Out In Stamford

Dear Stamford:

After the opening sequence, in which you meet the other members of the Lycanthro-Vampire Suppression Task Force and board the chopper, you'll be automatically taken to the Equip screen and given a chance to choose items. If you choose to play as Gerhard, your choice is limited to the Combat Axe or three Flasques of Holy Water. Choose the Axe, which works adequately on both Fiends and Angry Villagers and can be upgraded to the Hellbard once you reach the Darkwell. Gerhard can always use his extra Soulpoints to buy Holy Water later in the game—and the Flasques you find in the BloodLair itself hold either Holy Water or the supernaturally powerful X-Ichor. If, on the other hand, you decide to brave the Darkling Mountains with Aurelia, the brutal and buxomly Brit, you are automatically equipped with her grandfather's Moon Amulet—a useless encumbrance at first, but by expending Soulpoints, you'll eventually be able to control the Changelÿng attribute granted by Aurelia's weregenes. Equip Aurelia with the game's most useful early weapon, the Double-Blessed Shotgun, and a box of Cruciflares. Leave the Magnum for now. (When you reach the Tavern of the Damned, you'll find one hidden under the defiled roulette wheel.) Now, board the chopper for Fanngustan.

Dear Cheat Guide To BloodLair,

My son is being bullied by an older boy at school. But that's not all: It just so happens that this unruly child's parents are old friends of the family. My husband Jeff and I have spoken to the parents several times, but the teasing continues. Jeff says it's a little extreme to break off our friendship with the couple for the actions of their son, but I'm not so sure. What do you think?

—Peeved In Peekskill

Dear Peeved:

In Stage Four, as you regain consciousness atop Mount Darkling, you'll immediately see that the Priest's daughter has been abducted—by the same BlasphoDaemon that attacked the other members of your LVSTF team and crashed your helicopter. Immediately kill the Villager who's trying to impale you on the sharpened cross, then talk to his frightened pals to get an apology and some game info. They'll also tell you the way to East Magwych, which will be added to your MAP screen. After the ShadowFiend scares them off, vanquish it (by using your combo attack of L2+D-up+X, O, X, you gain extra Soulpoints) and then search the bodies of your team members for extra Holy Water. Proceed to the Moonwell, which is just past the Bridge in Magwych.

Dear Cheat Guide To BloodLair,

My 67-year-old mother recently got a computer. At first, the whole family was thrilled, but now we're beginning to worry. It seems like she's dropped all of her old hobbies, like painting and mall-walking, to spend all of her time staring at a screen. Should I urge her to get offline?

—Concerned In Columbus

Dear Columbus,

Congratulations! You've finally made it to the BloodLair. Look carefully during the movie, and you'll recognize the chopper pilot, the villagers from Stage 11, and Gruppenführer Von Steudel. The Priest's daughter is chained to the Black Obelisk at the BloodKing's feet. The object is simple: Defeat the king, avert the Apocalypse, and save the girl to preserve the legacy of the Morgansterns. As you go about this, be sure to keep in mind the following:

• Combo, combo, combo! Use Fist of Holiness if playing Gerhard, or the Fang of Contention if you drank enough X-Ichor to transform yourself into Dark Gerhard. Aurelia should use her Queen's Gambit Slash to reduce the king's Soulpoints and block his Essence Drain attack.

• Don't transmorph into wereform! It may be your most powerful offensive tactic, but the BloodKing will use the priest's daughter to trigger your BloodLust and affect the ending of the game.

• Don't try to save Holy Water, Starbolts, or Cruciflares! Once you've reached this final stage,

see BLOODLAIR page 138

The Cincinnati Riots

Riots erupted in Cincinnati last week following the shooting death of an unarmed black man by police officers. What do *you* think about the latest such incident?

"It's no surprise that these types of situations occur. Our police are overworked and underpaid and mostly really stupid."

Dianne Chester
Piano Teacher

"If black people are going to act like animals every time they're treated like animals, racists like me will never respect them."

Ira Richmond
Business Owner

"Riots are tragic releases following years of pent-up rage and despair. Unless they occur after a sports championship. Those rule."

Bob Edmondson
Plumber

"This is the worst thing to happen in Cincinnati since that radio station dropped all those flightless Thanksgiving turkeys from a helicopter."

Amil Gopalakian
Cashier

"I know there's racism, but the police are under a lot of pressure. So the next time a cop is braining me, I'm going to relax, count to 10, and try my best to see his point of view."

Jerome Barker
Systems Analyst

"I'm sure that if Cincinnati's blacks and whites just sat down and talked honestly about their feelings, it would combust into violence 10 times worse than those riots."

Anita Holcomb
Speech Therapist

The Organ-Donor Crisis

The U.S. is critically low on organ donations. What is the nation's medical community doing to address the shortage?

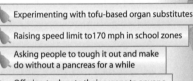

- Experimenting with tofu-based organ substitutes
- Raising speed limit to 170 mph in school zones
- Asking people to tough it out and make do without a pancreas for a while
- Offering to donate their organs to anyone in critical need, if you catch their drift
- Removing David Crosby's new liver and giving to more deserving person
- Wondering if nation's homeless problem, organ-shortage problem can't be solved simultaneously
- Splitting up available organs so at least everyone in need gets a little piece
- Allowing recipient's body to reject maximum of two hearts; after that, no more favors for Mr. Picky
- Introducing special edition of *Dawn Of The Dead* ending with zombies turning to camera and saying, "We've had some fun tonight, but ripping organs out of people's bodies is no laughing matter," followed by web address for shareyourlife.org

Ⓞ the ONION

America's Finest News Source

Herman Ulysses Zweibel *Founder*

T. Herman Zweibel *Publisher Emeritus*
J. Phineas Zweibel *Publisher*
Maxwell Prescott Zweibel *Editor-In-Chief*

FOUNDED 1871 • "TU STULTUS ES"

Your Horoscope

By Lloyd Schumner Sr.
Retired Machinist and
A.A.P.B.-Certified Astrologer

Aries: (March 21–April 19)
You will learn that you are 1/64th Chippewa. Honor your heritage by finding a use for every part of the burrito.

Taurus: (April 20–May 20)
Strangely, no one will congratulate you when you finally win your life-long battle with oxygen addiction.

Gemini: (May 21–June 21)
A vision of Christ will appear before you, page through His Heavenly Book Of Geminis, read your chapter to Himself, and disappear laughing.

Cancer: (June 22–July 22)
You will make *People*'s list of the 25 Most Fatiguing People Of 2001.

Leo: (July 23–Aug. 22)
This will be a lucky week, indeed, since no one enjoys a good concussion more than you.

Virgo: (Aug. 23–Sept. 22)
When you boasted last week that "nothing can stop me now," you apparently forgot about syphilis.

Libra: (Sept. 23–Oct. 23)
The Publishers Clearinghouse Prize Patrol will cruelly prank you this week by presenting you with an enormous novelty check for 63 cents.

Scorpio: (Oct. 24–Nov. 21)
Your near-illiteracy and slavish devotion to '70s retro kitsch lead you to shock and disturb your friends when you unveil your new Pet Cock.

Sagittarius: (Nov. 22–Dec. 21)
Investigators from several federal agencies will conclude that the failure of an 89-cent O-ring caused you to explode over Florida.

Capricorn: (Dec. 22–Jan. 19)
Your innocent inquiry regarding the origin of the term "panhandler" incites three bums to beat you to death with cast-iron skillets.

Aquarius: (Jan. 20–Feb. 18)
Your attempt to double-cross the mob ends badly when you discover that most crooks are not as bumbling as Disney had led you to believe.

Pisces: (Feb. 19–March 20)
Your fascination with the Vietnam War, combined with your love of romance novels and vampire myths, cause you to produce the worst work of fiction ever.

BLOODLAIR from page 137

you have no reason to hold anything back.

Once the BloodKing is banished again to Asmodaeus' dungeon, sit back and enjoy one of the game's eight cinematic endings. Then save to play again as the other character. Or, if you're going through BloodLair for the third time with a rating of 85 or better, you can select ArkAngel as a playable character, complete with bonus game ending!

Confidential To Stalked In Stoughton:

To get Aurelia's sexy Union Jack armor, go to the EQUIP screen while in the Temple of Withered Hope. While holding Select, press L2, R2, O, and X. You should hear Aurelia say, "Pip pip cheerio, Vic!" Now select Whitemail in her Armor slot and... wow!

The Cheat Guide To BloodLair is a syndicated advice columnist whose weekly column, Ask The Cheat Guide To BloodLair, *appears in more than 250 newspapers nationwide.* Ⓞ

GLUGGED from page 133

large amounts of blood. Passersby were amazed by the unusually large

Have I mentioned that I'm a vegan?

amounts of blood. Passersby were amazed by the unusually large

amounts of blood. Passersby were amazed by the unusually large amounts of blood. Passersby were amazed by the unusually large amounts of blood. Passersby were amazed by the unusually large amounts of blood. Passersby were amazed by the unusually large amounts of blood. Passersby were amazed by the unusually large amounts of blood. Passersby were amazed by the unusually large see GLUGGED page 165

Attorney, Client Privileged

see LOCAL page 4C

That One McDonald's Plate From The '70s: Holy Shit, There It Is

see NOSTALGIA BEAT page 2B

Dwarf Falls Equivalent Of 10 Stories

see LOCAL page 6C

STATshot

A look at the numbers that shape your world.

What Did We Think We'd Be Doing With Our Lives By Now?

1. Dancing professionally
2. World famous truck driver
3. Overseeing vast empire of some sort
4. Making at *least* assistant manager
5. Presenting own line of designer handbags
6. Owning a car with gull-wing doors
7. Not this telemarketing shit, that's for sure

THE ONION
VOLUME 37
ISSUE 16

$2.00 US
$3.00 CAN

0 74470 94595 6

---

the ONION®

VOLUME 37 ISSUE 16   AMERICA'S FINEST NEWS SOURCE™   3-9 MAY 2001

Lowest Common Denominator Continues To Plummet

American Focus

WASHINGTON, DC—The lowest common denominator (LCD), the leading cultural indicator for American mass-market tastes, continued its precipitous drop last week, fueling worries about the future of the U.S. marketplace for ideas and stoking fears of a long-term cultural recession.

The ill health of the LCD, in steady decline since the advent of television, has been cause for concern among the intelligentsia for decades. But double-digit drops in the LCD since October 2000 have alarmed even the most pandering members of the entertainment industry.

"Quite simply, the collective intelligence level is dropping so rapidly that it's becoming increasingly difficult for producers to insult the intelligence of the American public," said News Corp president and COO Peter Chernin. "Without a way to set a floor for the lowest common denominator, even the stupidest material we can develop is not stupid enough for audiences to enjoy."

As examples of the accelerating descent of the LCD, experts cite Chyna's best-selling wrestling biog-

see DENOMINATOR page 141

God Diagnosed With Bipolar Disorder

Above: The Lord, found to be manic-depressive by Rev. Dr. Jurgens (left).

NEW HAVEN, CT—In a diagnosis that helps explain the confusing and contradictory aspects of the cosmos that have baffled philosophers, theologians, and other students of the human condition for millennia, God, creator of the universe and longtime deity to billions of followers, was found Monday to suffer from bipolar disorder.

Rev. Dr. J. Henry Jurgens, a practicing psychiatrist and doctor of divinity at Yale University Divinity School, announced the historic diagnosis at a press conference.

"I always knew there had to be some explanation," Jurgens said. "And, after several years of

see GOD page 140

Local Man Exhausted After Long Day Of Video Games

SAGINAW, MI—Jon Broskowski, a 32-year-old Saginaw liquor-store clerk, described himself as "completely wiped" Monday after a long, hard day of video games.

"I'm totaled," said Broskowski, tossing his PlayStation 2 controller onto the floor following one last "cool-down" game of Madden 2001. "That shit really takes it out of you."

Broskowski, who has logged two decades of back-breaking toil on systems ranging from Intellivision to Sega Genesis, woke up at the crack of noon and went straight to work.

Left: A visibly drained Broskowski gathers the strength for one more game.

"I had the whole day off from the liquor store, and I thought, today's the day I roll up my sleeves and earn all the extra characters in SSX Snowboarding," Broskowski said. "Man, it was a grind."

"They make you snowboard over the same course and do the same tricks, like, a thousand times to get a new character," said Broskowski, who, through discipline and a strong work ethic, was able to earn the snowboards Sumo Stick, Chaos

see VIDEO GAMES page 143

First-Grade Teacher Apprehends Urinator

NEWARK, DE—The mysterious Coat Room Urinator, who for weeks terrorized Mrs. Collinsworth's first-grade class at Lakeview Elementary School, was brought to justice Monday, when student Danny Culver was caught in the act of voiding his bladder by the lost-and-found box. "The elusive urine fiend has been apprehended and will be dealt with accordingly," Collinsworth said. "We as a class no longer have to live in constant fear of discovering a warm puddle by the Simba cutouts along the back wall." Culver is being held without bail in his room at 294 Maplewood Drive after being released to the custody of his parents.

Asian Man Has Thing For Asian Women

TOKYO—Shoji Furukawa, a 33-year-old Tokyo man, confessed Monday to a fetish for Asian women. "For some reason, as long as I can remember, I've always been into Asian chicks," Furukawa said. "I don't know what it is about them, but they just totally do it for me." Furukawa said the preference may be a familial trait, noting, "My dad was really into Asian girls, too."

Trucking Industry Honors Methamphetamines

KANSAS CITY—At its national convention Monday, the National Trucking Association bestowed its highest honor on methamphetamines. "Methamphetamines, you are the substance that keeps our nation's truckers 'speed'-ing along to their appointed destinations," NTA president Larry Herrick said. "Without you, American trucking would not be the world leader it is today." Herrick then downed a fistful of pills and climbed into a rig, saying he had to be in Fresno, CA, by sun-up.

Maxim Skimmed

DALLAS—A copy of *Maxim* magazine was skimmed Monday by subscriber Steve Reiger, who briefly flipped through the May issue before tossing it onto the floor near his bed. "I glanced at the thing about *Buffy* bad girl Eliza Dushku and read a little of the interview with the guy from Korn," Reiger said. "They also had something about motorcycles I caught a little of and this thing called '100 Things To Do Before You Die.' I think there was also something about that new *Mummy* movie, but it may have been an ad." Reiger looks forward to skimming the May issues of *FHM* and *Men's Health* when they arrive.

Slight Inconvenience Avoided

ST. LOUIS—Area resident Jim Shaffer avoided slight inconvenience Monday, thanks to Jhirmack's new "upside-down" shampoo bottle. "If I'd been using a traditional shampoo bottle, I'd have had to turn the thing over and shake it when it started to run low," Shaffer said. "But, with the Jhirmack bottle, the shampoo collects at the bottom, making shaking unnecessary." Shaffer plans to use the time saved by the shampoo to "catch up on [his] reading."

Former American Gladiator Still Insists Friends Call Him 'Turbo'

LIMA, IN—More than five years after his last appearance on the syndicated program *American Gladiators*, Dale "Turbo" Brandt continues to insist that friends refer to him by his on-air name. "Please," Brandt told acquaintance Lynn Crane at a dinner party Monday. "Call me Turbo." In recent years, Brandt has bought a "TURBO" vanity plate for his 1990 Honda Del Sol, placed a "Turbo" nameplate on his mailbox, and attempted to make restaurant reservations under the name "Turbo." ⌀

GOD from page 139

patient research and long sessions with God Almighty through the intercessionary medium of prayer, I was able to pinpoint the specific nature of His problem."

Bipolar, or manic-depressive, disorder is a condition that afflicts millions. Characterized by cycles of elation followed by bouts of profound depression and despair, the disorder can wreak havoc on both the sufferer and his or her loved ones, particularly if it goes undetected and untreated for an extended period. Though the condition is estimated to affect, in one form or another, 5 percent of the world's population, Monday marks the first time it has been diagnosed in a major deity.

Evidence of God's manic-depression can be found throughout the universe, from the white-hot explosiveness of quasars to the cold, lifeless vacuum of space. However, theologians note, humanity's exposure to God's affliction comes primarily through His confusing propensity to alternately reward and punish His creations with little rhyme or reason.

"Last week, I lost my dear husband Walter to the flood," said housewife and devout churchgoer Elaine Froman of Davenport, IA. "I asked myself, 'Why? Why would God do something like this, especially when He had just helped Walter overcome a long battle with colon cancer, and we were so happy

Above: Taken on the same day, these photos offer evidence of God's mood disorder.

that we finally had a chance to start our lives anew?'"

New York attorney Ruth Kanner also gained firsthand knowledge of God's wild mood swings.

"Last Saturday, on a gorgeous spring afternoon, I was jogging in Central Park with my daughter. We were marveling at the beauty and majesty of nature, and I remember thinking what a wonderful world we live in. Then, out of nowhere, I heard the gunfire," said Kanner, speaking from her hospital bed at

Columbia Presbyterian Medical Center. "All they took was a measly $17, and for that, the doctors say my daughter will never walk again. If only Our Holy Father didn't have those mental problems, my precious Katie might not be confined to a wheelchair for the rest of her life."

Jurgens stressed that God's earthly subjects need to understand that, because of His bipolar condition, He is not in control of His actions and does not realize how

they affect others.

"What He needs from us is understanding and patience," Jurgens said. "To paraphrase the words of the Lord God Himself, 'Humans, forgive Him, for He knows not what He does.'"

While such drugs as Paxil, Prozac, and Zoloft have proven effective in the treatment of bipolar disorder among humans, there is no modern earthly medicine that can be prescribed for a deity see GOD page 142

Area Man's Free Time Monopolized By Friend With No Other Friends

PHILADELPHIA—A disproportionate amount of area resident Chris Blakely's free time is monopolized by Spencer Reuss, whose only friend is Blakely.

"I like Spencer and everything, but our friendship is way skewed," Blakely said Monday. "I have about 20 friends, so, statistically speaking, I should only be hanging with Spencer, like, 5 percent of the time. But I see him way more than that—more than I see anybody else—because I have to carry the entirety of his friendship load."

The problem began in November 2000, when Reuss, who attended high school with Blakely in New Castle, PA, moved to Philadelphia for a job with a graphic-design firm. Upon arriving in Philadelphia, Reuss knew no one except his old high-school acquaintance.

"In the beginning, I knew he was pretty lonely, so I tried hard to make him feel welcome, telling him he should feel free to stop by any time," Blakely said. "Big mistake: Four months later, he's still feeling free to stop by any time."

see FRIEND page 143

Above: Blakely (left) exits a movie with the single-friended Reuss close behind.

DENOMINATOR from page 139

raphy, the elephant-sperm-filled Tom Green film *Freddy Got Fingered*, and MTV's *Dude, This Sucks*, in which performers defecate explosively onto audience members. In spite of efforts to raise national interest rates in more sophisticated fare like *The Sopranos*, *Memento*, and Michael Chabon's Pulitzer Prize-winning *The Amazing Adventures Of Kavalier & Clay*, the demand for increasingly inane cultural output has rendered efforts futile.

"We face a real crisis in mainstream society's media preferences," said James W. Northrup, special appointee to the recently established LCD Emergency Federal Task Force. "Things that were once base enough for the notoriously undemanding American public are now considered too highbrow for mass consumption. The bar is on the floor, but everyone still wants it lowered."

As the LCD drops, competition for the stupidity dollar grows ever more fierce. *Entertainment Tonight*, once the nation's standard-bearer for hollow, insipid celebrity journalism, has been rendered respectable by the likes of *National Enquirer TV* and E!'s *Mysteries And Scandals*. *Survivor*, derided by critics upon its debut last year, now stands as the Old Gray Lady of reality television,

Above: A popular, LCD-lowering video that features teenagers pounding each other with folding chairs.

towering over such crass knock-offs as *Boot Camp* and *Chains Of Love*. Even Hollywood, America's primary provider of sub-literate pabulum for nearly a century, must compete with hyper-violent video games, Internet sites featuring foul-mouthed animated genitalia, and mail-order

Girls Gone Wild: Sexy Sorority Sweethearts videos for the lucrative stupid-person market.

"It's a real nightmare," said Jerry Bruckheimer, producer of such critically reviled smashes as *The Rock*, *Con Air*, and *Armageddon*. "These

> ## The test group also took issue with *Happy Days'* "boring," non-fatal motorcycle crashes and confusing lack of gunplay and/or graphic nudity.

days, it's getting harder and harder to underestimate the intelligence of the American public."

In a Syracuse University study conducted last month, reruns of *Happy Days*, a show derided by 1970s critics as "targeted to third-graders," were deemed "beyond comprehension" by 75 percent of present-day third-graders. The surveyed students expressed frustration with the show's characters, some of which exhibited more than one trait.

"Fonzie rides a motorcycle, but he also likes girls," one subject said. "I don't get it."

The test group also took issue with *Happy Days'* "boring," non-fatal motorcycle crashes and confusing lack of gunplay and/or graphic nudity.

Dr. George Lowell, director of Syracuse's Center For The Study Of Television & Popular Culture and one of the study's organizers, expressed concern about the test subjects' inability to follow even the simplest stories.

"The biggest problem is not that TV shows' plots are too complicated, but that shows have any plots at all. The presence of a plot, however hackneyed, is not palatable to viewers accustomed to programs like *Total Request Live* or *Jackass*, which contain no story structure whatsoever," Lowell said. "What's worse, in two or three years, even *TRL* will be too hard for most people to grasp, because the e-mail requests scrolling across the screen require them to read."

The media are attempting to respond to the crisis. The eight-minute attention-span limit on network TV programming, a longtime staple of the medium, has been

see DENOMINATOR page 142

I'm Such A Shitty Senator

By Sen. Max Baucus (D-MT)

I've been "serving" the great state of Montana in the U.S. Senate since 1978. You'll notice I put "serving" in quotes, because, let's face it, I suck. My wife has been pleading with me not to say this publicly, insisting that it's not true, that I'm a capable and dedicated public servant, blah, blah, blah. Bless her dear heart, but she's just being nice. Because, folks, I am telling you, I am hands-down the shittiest senator in the history of the Senate. *The* worst.

The other day, I was in my office, thumbing through some old pieces of legislation I'd either authored or co-sponsored. The whole time, I was thinking, "Christ, what a hack I am." Take my 1993 masterwork, S.915, the Semiconductor Investment Act. Section 2a of the bill states, "IN GENERAL— Section 168(e)(3)(A) of the Internal Revenue Code of 1986 (relating to three-year property) is amended by striking 'and' at the end of clause (i), by striking the period at the end of clause (ii), and by inserting at the end of the following: '(iii) any semiconductor manufacturing equipment.'"

What the hell is that shit? As I recall, it had something to do with semiconductor manufacturing equipment. But you'd never know, what with the way I buried its meaning under a tidal wave of I-know-all-the-fancy-schmancy-bill-

writing lingo. I was trying to look like Mr. Big Shot, but little did I know what a conceited ass I came off as. When the bill was pitched, Sen. Bob Packwood (R-OR) was nice enough to say some introductory words of support on the floor. But now I think he was just embarrassed for me and wanted to help a fellow senator save face, however little I deserved it. I forget what happened to that bill. Hopefully, it died without ever coming to a vote.

There's a huge stack of old bills in my office, each containing tons of that sort of hackwork. I'm tempted to burn down the entire Hart Office Building and cleanse the planet of every physical trace of my senatorial presence. But, no, that wouldn't do any good, because every facet, every aspect of my incredible suckiness is piledriven into the memories of those I so ineptly represent.

God. *God.* I am so, so, so sorry, folks.

Here's another stupid-ass thing I did. Every Wednesday, when the Senate is in session, I invite Montanans who happen to be in Washington to stop by my office to enjoy an informal breakfast with my staff and myself. It's a way for me to keep abreast of the needs of my constituents. A neat idea, right? Well, it would be, if I weren't actually there, *fucking things up.*

Anyway, one morning, this very nice woman named Shirley Besser, who is from my hometown of Helena, stopped by while vacationing in D.C. She wanted to know why I supported permanent normal trade relations with China, given its

oppressive government and history of human-rights violations. I thought this was a good question, and I started to say, "Well, Sheila..." But, before I could say

> **When the bill was pitched, Sen. Bob Packwood (R-OR) was nice enough to say some introductory words of support on the floor. But now I think he was just embarrassed for me and wanted to help a fellow senator save face.**

another word, she interrupted to point out that her name was Shirley. *Stupid, son-of-a-bitch, no-listening-skills senator.* She had just told me her name a second ago, and here I was, already forgetting it! I apologized profusely, but she just smiled politely and said it was okay. It wasn't.

Whether ladling too much stew onto the tray of a homeless person at a Missoula soup kitchen or making repeated mixed metaphors during a speech praising the efforts of those who fought Western wildfires last summer, I can't imagine why the people of Montana continue to put up with my crap.

I should just quit. Actually, I

should have quit a long time ago. But I never did, because the people kept insisting I run for another term. I've been re-elected three times, and every time I am, I get the notion that maybe, if I made a real conscious effort, I could stop being such a lousy legislator.

I sometimes make an effort, but every time I do, before I know it, I've made another inexcusable flub like mentioning, during an appearance on *Montana Politics Today,* that the Gallatin Land Consolidation Act Of 1998 was introduced during the 104th Congress instead of the 105th. Christ on a crutch!

No, don't try to talk me out of it. I'm definitely quitting this time. I'm not sure what I'm going to do with myself once I leave the Senate, though. I can't go back to Montana, that's for sure. Facing all those constituents I failed so badly day after day, year after year? I don't think so. Maybe I'll go to Maine instead. No one knows me there. Set up a small law practice, hang my shingle, buy a quaint little saltbox on the outskirts of Bangor. Of course, I'm sure I'd somehow manage to fuck up everything there, too. What the hell was I thinking? God, I'm such a bonehead. I should go live in a cave somewhere, someplace far away from all humanity where I can't poison everything I touch.

So, people from the great state of Montana, forget you ever even heard the name Max Baucus. Max Baucus... more like Trash... Ruckus.

I can't even pun well. ∅

GOD from page 140

as vast and complex as God. Jurgens is in the process of forming a support group, "Living With A Bipolar Creator-Deity," for all of humanity to "get together and discuss their feelings about living in a universe run by an Omnipresent Loved One not fully in control of His emotions."

Jurgens said he believes God's essential condition is seasonal, as evidenced by the bursts of energy and elation associated with springtime and summer, followed by the decay and bleak despair of fall and winter. Sometimes, however, the condition cycles even faster.

"The average person with bipolar disorder may go through 10 or 12 cycles of mania and subsequent depression in a lifetime. In severe cases, a sufferer may experience

four or more per year, which is known as 'rapid cycling,'" Jurgens said. "We believe God suffers from the even rarer 'ultra-rapid cycling,' which would account for the many documented cases in which He alternates between benevolence and rage toward humanity within a matter of seconds. For example, last week, He brought desperately needed, life-giving rain to southern Mali while simultaneously leveling Turkey with a devastating earthquake."

Further evidence of God's manic-depression can be found in the Bible, in which the erotomania of the Song of Songs sharply contrasts with the sadness and existential despair of the Book of Ecclesiastes. The Book of Job, Jurgens noted, marks the best example of His condition. The book begins with the bleak lamentations of Job and ends

with a full-blown manic episode by God, complete with such classic bipolar symptoms as the illusion of omnipotence and delusions of grandeur.

"One of the major 'heresies' of Christian history is the Gnostic belief that the Creator, or 'demiurge,' of this troubled world is a blind, idiot god who is insane," Jurgens said. "This idea surfaces in many religious traditions around the globe. As it turns out, they were only half right: God has His problems like anyone else, but He is essentially trying His best. He just has a condition that makes His emotions fly out of control at times."

"So it's up to us to make the best of God's emotional problems," Jurgens continued. "Thus, mankind is born to trouble, as surely as sparks fly upward." ∅

DENOMINATOR from page 141

lowered to four minutes. Radio personality Howard Stern has been warned by producers to "dumb down" his daily radio show. And Pamela Anderson Lee's syndicated action program *V.I.P.* will be retooled to a dialogue-free all-kung-fu/bikini format starting this fall.

In spite of the challenges, many remain optimistic. "America has stood tall as the world leader in spoon-feeding mindless swill to the uneducated, sub-literate masses, and we will continue to do so," Viacom president Mel Karmazin said. "Nobody is better at pandering to people's basest tendencies than this great nation's entertainment industry, and if our material isn't stupid enough for them, then, by God, we'll use good old American know-how to make the product even worse." ∅

FRIEND from page 141

Because Blakely's apartment is just a few blocks from Reuss' place of employment, Reuss often drops in unannounced.

"He can see my car parked out on the street, so there's no way I can just pretend I'm not home," Blakely said. "I've tried telling him I need some time alone, but that always leads to 10 phone calls where he asks me if I'm okay. One time, he even sent me a card."

Blakely has tried to introduce Reuss to his other friends, with less than favorable results.

"I figured, maybe if he hit it off with some of my other friends, I could pass him off to them," Blakely said. "Well, one night, after hanging out at a bar with six or seven of them, Spencer informed me that he doesn't like my friends because they're 'too mainstream' for his tastes. Yet, he'll still want to tag along any time I make plans with them. And he always finds a way to corner me into a conversation about the things he wants to talk about, like his kite-building or his obsession with WWI. So, even when I'm with others, I'm still only with him."

Compounding the difficulties of the social babysitting are Reuss' depressive tendencies.

"Spencer really gets lonely and down on himself," Blakely said. "It makes just ditching him that much harder."

On any given night, whether spending time at a bar, concert, or movie, Blakely is 650 percent more likely to be socializing with Reuss than with any of his other friends. Blakely is 95 percent assured of spending time with Reuss during holidays.

"Take this past New Year's Eve," Blakely said. "As much as I wanted to, I just couldn't leave the guy sitting in his apartment alone, so I was like, 'Hey, why don't you come along with me to my buddy Jonathan's party?' But then Spencer surprises me with these expensive tickets for a KC & The Sunshine Band New Year's show. So, instead of going to Jonathan's party, I end up spending New Year's with Spencer, KC, and the goddamn Sunshine Band."

Though it is still three weeks away, Blakely is already dreading Reuss' upcoming birthday.

"I'm going to have to spend about $100 on drinks just to bribe my friends to show up at the bar," Blakely said. "If I have to sit there alone, with Spencer across from me wearing one of those stupid 'It's My Birthday!' pins, I'm going to slit my wrists." ⌀

VIDEO GAMES from page 139

Crippler, and Bloo Goo after four hours of labor. "I must've traveled 50 miles before I got complete brain fade."

After a brief lunch of toast, jelly, and a Coke, Broskowski turned to Tomb Raider 2, a game he admitted he had put off finishing for more than a year.

"It was time to hunker down and get it done," Broskowski said. "I'm kind of sick of the whole Lara Croft thing, but I decided I'd procrastinated long enough. I was determined to get to the end of this game, even if it killed me."

Though he "guess[es]" he enjoyed himself, Broskowski said the three-hour session of Tomb Raider 2 was by no means easy.

"I must've dragged about 2,000 blocks around and climbed over the damn things," he said. "And I kept getting killed, so in the end I wound up doing it 11 times on the Tibetan Catacombs level alone. And those blocks they made me drag were as big as me."

"As big as Lara, I mean," Broskowski added.

At approximately 7:30 p.m., he finally completed Tomb Raider 2. After watching the game's 90-second closing video, a reward he called "hardly worth all the effort," Broskowski tidied up his memory-card files and resumed the robot quest he began last Thursday on the rented game Zone Of The Enders.

"I wanted to finally kill Tempest without wrecking all those buildings," said Broskowski, his fingers numb from prolonged exposure to DualShock controller vibrations. "I had, like, $9 in late fees on the game, but I wasn't taking it back until I got an A rating on all the missions, rescued all the colonists, and got to the versus mode. It takes about eight hours, but it's the best part of the game. It sucks that I had to fight about 200 other Orbital Frame Robots to get there, though. I'll be paying for that tomorrow, that's for sure."

Sometime shortly after midnight, Broskowski decided he was "in a major robot rut" and opted to "cleanse his tired palate" with a sports game.

"If I went right to bed [after Zone Of The Enders], I knew I'd be seeing robots in my sleep, so I decided on a quick game of Madden 2001," said Broskowski, who played half a season as the Baltimore Ravens before noticing the VCR clock reading 4 a.m.

"Christ, am I blown out," said Broskowski, twisting and stretching to ease the strain on vertebrae which had not moved appreciably for an entire day. "My eyes feel like they're on fire, and I never did unlock the last two hidden arenas in Zone Of The Enders. It never ends."

"I suppose I should return that game to Blockbuster tomorrow, if I have the energy," he continued. "Sure is a long walk, though." ⌀

Your Horoscope

By Lloyd Schumner Sr.
Retired Machinist and
A.A.P.B.-Certified Astrologer

Aries: (March 21–April 19)

You tend to fly into a rage over the smallest problems. Fortunately, you'll encounter only huge disasters this week.

Taurus: (April 20–May 20)

Sun Tzu said that victory without conflict is the ultimate success for any general. That said, be prepared to lose a bloody battle with your weight.

Gemini: (May 21–June 21)

What you're feeling now hurts, there's no denying that. But try to remember that, when he died, Joey Ramone was writing songs about his stock portfolio.

Cancer: (June 22–July 22)

You tend to hate and fear that which you do not understand. But since you're such a big genius, your hatred and fear of soap must come from some other source, Mr. Stinky.

Leo: (July 23–Aug. 22)

This week, you will find that, contrary to popular belief, the unexamined life is quite worth living.

Virgo: (Aug. 23–Sept. 22)

Sometimes, you have to do things you just don't want to do. Try to figure out a way not to do these things.

Libra: (Sept. 23–Oct. 23)

The problem with people like you isn't that you love too much. It's what you love that gets you brought up on charges.

Scorpio: (Oct. 24–Nov. 21)

You're more than just a collection of annoying, loosely bundled neuroses. There are some entertaining, tightly wound psychoses in there, too.

Sagittarius: (Nov. 22–Dec. 21)

To answer your repeated queries: Yes, the stars *can* see your house from up here.

Capricorn: (Dec. 22–Jan. 19)

Attempts will be made to compare thee to a summer's day, but after the part about the temperature being 98.6°, the metaphor breaks down.

Aquarius: (Jan. 20–Feb. 18)

You will be reincarnated as a being whose status is commensurate with your behavior in your last life. Enjoy governing Texas, you nurse-murdering bastard.

Pisces: (Feb. 19–March 20)

Remember: Just because you read it in a book doesn't mean it's true. There's no such thing as a "John Updike."

RIDDLE CARD

1. How many peas in a pint?
2. Why is a battleship like a star?
3. What well-known animal drives a car?
4. Why is a crash of thunder like a jeweler?
5. Why is a hat on the head like a bucket full of water?

Answers: 1. One. 2. Both contain T, A, R, S. 3. The head hog. 4. Because both make the ear ring. 5. Because they are both filled to the brim.

DON'T SCRUB OUT ON THIS ONE! In this back-to-school wardrobe problem, you must replace the letters on the board with the digits 0 through 9 so that you have a correct addition problem. The same letters get the same digits.

(429 + 237 + RaR, D47, N42, S=8, A=2, WaR 'JewsuA euO)

THE "G" PYRAMID! As you move down the word pyramid shown, each word contains the same letters as the word above it, plus a new letter. We give you all the G's. Here are some hints from the top down:

1. Slang for $1,000 (given).
2. Inspector general.
3. To fit with sails.
4. A facial expression.
5. What a king does.
6. To get back again.
7. A family member.
8. Provoking, displeasing.

Junior Whirl by Charles Barry Townsend

FIND THE BIG WORDS! It's not OK to be KO'd by this puzzle! Using the definitions and the anagrams below, find the eight, eight-letter words that fit into the framework pictured on the left. For each definition, the letters in the two anagram words must be unscrambled and used to form the word asked for.

DEFINITIONS:	ANAGRAM:
1. A sudden eruption.	tour + beak
2. Type of shared meal.	puts + lock
3. Incited to anger.	pork + dove
4. More frightening.	rook + pies
5. An easy win.	veal + work
6. Type of tests.	bolt + skin
7. Supporting framework.	elks + note
8. North American Indian tribe	cook + pika

Answers: 1. Outbreak. 2. Potluck. 3. Provoked. 4. Spookier. 5. Walkover. 6. Inkblots. 7. Skeleton. 8. Kickapoo.

W's First Hundred Days

Last week, George W. Bush reached the 100-day mark of his presidency. What do *you* think of the job he's done so far?

"So much has happened these past 100 days. Let's see, there was the Clinton-pardon thing, the Clinton-furniture thing, the Clinton-in-Harlem thing..."

Alan Choudhury
Electrician

"Oh, Christ. I'm supposed to have an opinion on Bush's first 100 days? Geez, I dunno, what all did he do?"

Pete Terrell
Cab Driver

"Well, he did lower drinking-water standards, revive hostilities with China, and endanger the budget surplus, so I guess that's all good."

Mary Ellen Bolz
Guidance Counselor

"Has it been 100 days already? Wow, it seems like only yesterday that Bush cut off funding for overseas abortion providers."

Danielle Ormond
Art Dealer

"Since Gore really won the election, I've only been following what he's been doing these past 100 days. It hasn't been much."

Rodger LaPierre
Systems Analyst

"Sixty-three percent of the American people approve of the job Bush is doing. Then again, 98 percent of the American people are fucking morons."

Rick Dandridge
Chemical Engineer

Bracing For The Writers' Strike

May 1 was the deadline for the Writers Guild Of America strike. What have TV and movie executives been doing to prepare?

- Shopping around for cheap translators for *Dos Mujeres, Un Camino*
- Encouraging TV viewers to call in and suggest what next line of dialogue should be
- Airing live, all-improv season of *Law & Order*
- Quickly knocking out *Joe Dirt 2, 3,* and *4* over next few days
- Checking to see if Jane Austen has anything new out
- Inserting spaceships and explosions into old *Hill Street Blues* episodes, airing them as *Hill Street Blues: The Next Generation*
- Unused sitcom scripts to be related orally by jovial Jamaican storyteller
- Desperately searching for scabs who can write on level of *Moesha* scribes
- Hiring one million non-WGA monkeys, buying them typewriters, rejecting resultant works of Shakespeare as "too brainy"

America's Finest News Source

Herman Ulysses Zweibel *Founder*

T. Herman Zweibel *Publisher Emeritus*
J. Phineas Zweibel *Publisher*
Maxwell Prescott Zweibel *Editor-In-Chief*

FOUNDED 1871 • "TU STULTUS ES"

I Have Returned, Baby

Girl, you knew I could not stay away for long.

Although I have not been in contact with you in a great many months, let me assure you that you were in my

By Smoove B
Love Man

thoughts every second of every day. As I ate, as I slept, as I showered, and as I folded my laundry, rest assured that your fineness was the predominant matter on my mind. Even during Christmas.

Believe me when I say that I would have given anything under the sun to be able to stay by your side instead of leaving without even a note or a phone message. Let us just say that I was involved in some deep personal problems and a family crisis that required a great deal of my time.

But, now that I have returned, I would like to take this opportunity to promise to stay by your side forever. You are my everything and, as a result, I do not want to leave you ever again. I do not ever want to look in any direction in which you are not standing. From the moment I wake up to the moment I go to bed, I want you to be in my line of sight.

And, now that you have been un-Smooved for so many months, I expect with reasonable certainty that you will greatly wish to freak with me this Friday night.

With your approval, I will ride to your apartment in the most beautiful white stretch limousine in the entire city. Upon my arrival, rather than expect you to just be there waiting in the vestibule, I will take the elevator or stairs to your apartment and personally fetch you. This magnificent white limousine will then whisk us away to the finest restaurant available. During the limo ride, we will enjoy an assortment of complimentary Pepsi products from the limo's refrigerator.

You can also play the radio if you wish.

As soon as we arrive at the restaurant, immaculately dressed waiters will appear and place glasses of water upon our table. They will ask whether we want a drink to start. Even though there will already be water on the table, I will order more liquids for you. This additional liquid will be the finest wine in all of France. Mere seconds will pass before we have this exemplary wine before us.

These waiters will also place rolls on the table, with pats of fresh creamery butter. This butter will be served at slightly below room temperature so as to spread easily.

Whatever you desire that is printed upon that restaurant's menu, you may order with no thought as to the expense. That will be for Smoove to worry about.

As we dine on our respective meals, I will tell you how beautiful you look while looking directly into your sweet eyes. I will tell you how lovely your particular dress looks upon your finely tuned body.

I will pay for the meal with my Gold Visa, and we will then go to my place and retire to *le boudoir*, which is French for "my bedroom." There, as the music of Peabo Bryson plays, I will hit you doggy-style all night long.

The next morning, I will serve you breakfast in bed, featuring eggs, two kinds of meat, toast, and your choice of hash browns or grits. You will also receive a tumbler of orange juice.

Aw, girl. I cannot believe how long it has been since I have gazed upon you, the most lovely rose in all of creation. In my mind, I am envisioning you right now. I am envisioning you laughing warmly at my every witticism, returning my loving gazes, and whispering in my ear. The various items you are whispering involve the freak-nasty things we will do together following our meal.

I am also envisioning you hitting the uppermost dimension of ecstacy as I propel you through the universe of my love aboard the spaceship of my strong back, with myself as the captain of this cosmic journey through the sexual stratosphere to our passion meteor.

If this scenario is to your liking, you have my number. If you have lost it, simply dial 555-1212 for directory assistance.

Damn. ∅

PRONGS from page 21

large amounts of blood. Passersby were amazed by the unusually large amounts of blood. Passersby were amazed by the unusually large amounts of blood. Passersby were amazed by the unusually large amounts of blood. Passersby were amazed by the unusually large amounts of blood. Passersby were

How was I supposed to know you didn't want a trepanning?

amazed by the unusually large amounts of blood. Passersby were amazed by the unusually large amounts of blood. Passersby were amazed by the unusually large amounts of blood. Passersby were amazed by the unusually large amounts of blood. Passersby were amazed by the unusually large amounts of blood. Passersby were amazed by the unusually

see PRONGS page 149

After Careful Consideration, Bush Recommends Oil Drilling

Televised Sporting Event Completely Obscured By On-Screen Graphics

see WORLD page 5A

Best Friends Make Eye Contact While Singing Along To 'Summer Lovin''

see HEALTH page 4E

A look at the numbers that shape your world.

Rejected Euphemisms For The Disabled

1. The unnerving
2. The conveniently parked
3. Go-tards
4. The differently pleasant to be around
5. Stumbly-wumblys
6. Prey
7. The just-a-tad off
8. Cincinnati Bengals
9. Pinnacles of human perfection
10. Ingredient "D"

THE ONION
VOLUME 37
ISSUE 17

$2.00 US
$3.00 CAN

0 74470 94595 6

09

---

the ONION®

VOLUME 37 ISSUE 17   AMERICA'S FINEST NEWS SOURCE™   10-16 MAY 2001

Nation's Porn Stars Demand To Be Fucked Harder

WASHINGTON, DC—Seeking to reverse a "decades-long trend toward shamefully inadequate underfucking in our nation's adult-entertainment industry," a coalition of U.S. porn stars gathered in the nation's capital Monday to voice their demand to be fucked

Above: Jenna Jameson, co-chair of Porn Stars For Being Fucked Harder.

harder.

"Uggh! Come on, give me that cock, jungle stud. Fuck me! Fuck me harder!" said Jenna Jameson, co-chair of Porn Stars For Being Fucked Harder and star of Wicked Pictures' *Up And Cummers #10, #11,* and *#17.* "Deeper! Deeper! Oh, *fuck.*"

The D.C. summit arrives on the heels of years of complaints from dis-
see PORN STARS page 148

Above: Artificial flowers and a $7.99 teddy bear adorn the site of the tragedy.

Site Of Fatal Auto Accident Tritely Commemorated

MOUND CITY, KS—A ribbon of blacktop called Hwy. 52 runs through the heart of this tiny eastern Kansas town. Not much distinguishes this road from countless others, except for the violent, head-on collision that, on the evening of April 24, claimed the lives of five people from the town of Mound City.

It is on the shoulder of this otherwise ordinary road that a makeshift shrine to the victims has been erected. With plastic flowers, stuffed animals, and hand-painted signs, the grieving citizens of Mound City resolved to
see ACCIDENT page 147

The grieving townspeople resolved to consecrate the death site in the most hackneyed way possible.

Work Avoided Through Extensive List-Making

FORT WAYNE, IN—Julie Smalley, a 43-year-old Fort Wayne-area office manager, avoided completing any work whatsoever Monday, when she spent a majority of the day composing to-do lists.

"I've got a stack of mail up to here, I need to get the new schedule out by Wednesday, and department supervisors are breaking down my door for my signature," said Smalley, sitting at her desk at One World, a mail-order retailer of maps and other travel-related goods. "That's why I knew I had to lock myself in my office today, put my nose to the grindstone, and draw up a detailed list of all the things I need to do."

Upon arriving at the office at 8 a.m., Smalley got right to avoiding work, drawing up an extensive list of everything that needed to be accomplished. Among the pressing tasks she itemized: scheduling a meeting with One World promotions director Terry Connell, processing a stack of employee-reimbursement requests, and locating previous to-do lists and transferring any still-uncompleted items to the new list.

Above: Listmaker Julie Smalley.

"I was supposed to get together with [coworker] John [Tribley] to finalize some prices for the new catalog, but I cancelled because I have so much to do," Smalley said. "That
see LISTS page 146

145

North Dakota Drinks Itself To Sleep Again

BISMARCK, ND—Exhausted from another hard day in the wheat fields, the state of North Dakota drank itself to sleep Monday with the bottle of Old Thompson it keeps hidden in Fargo. "Oh, they've been doing this a lot lately," South Dakota Gov. William Janklow said. "Every night, they fall asleep on their respective couches with the local TV stations on all night." Janklow expressed concern about waking the state, as North Dakota is known for its violent outbursts when hung over.

Man Nods Knowingly At Mechanic

GREENSBORO, NC—Attempting to conceal his ignorance of car repair, area resident Dave Snell, 39, nodded knowingly Monday as mechanic Bill Kreuter explained the precise nature of Snell's automotive problem. "He was telling me that the car had, like, a faulty alternator plug," Snell said. "So, you know, that's something that definitely needs to be fixed." Snell said his risky bluff almost backfired when Kreuter asked him how he gaps his plugs, to which Snell responded, "About the usual amount."

Health-Food-Store Worker Dies Of Vitamin Lung

SAUSALITO, CA—Duane Cristopher, longtime manager of the Brooks Street Health Food Co-op, died Sunday following a three-month battle with vitamin lung. "Decades of inhaling a trace dust of vitamin supplements caused particles to accumulate over time in his lungs, ultimately cutting off his oxygen supply," said Dr. Arthur Washington, Christopher's physician. "We also suspect bee pollen may have been a factor." At Christopher's funeral Tuesday, family and friends commented admiringly on how natural the 57-year-old's body looked.

Child Lies For Parents' Own Good

CONCORD, NH—Area 9-year-old Andrew Mota lied to his parents Monday, telling them that he was at the park after school and sparing them the unpleasant truth that he was setting off fireworks at the quarry with friends. "[Parents] Patrick and Adrienne are very fragile emotionally," Mota said. "Telling them something like that would only cause them undue stress." He added that he may tell them one day when he is older.

Guy On Racetrack P.A. Sounds A Little Depressed Today

SARATOGA SPRINGS, NY—Gordon Asheton, public-address announcer at Saratoga Racetrack, seemed a bit distant Monday, track regular Brad Herman reported. "Usually, [Asheton]'s totally enthusiastic, firing up the crowd," Herman said. "But today, after he said, 'And they're off,' there was kind of a pause and a heavy sigh before he gave the running order. When he announced Daddy's Little Prizefighter as the winner, he barely seemed to care. I hope everything's okay at home."

New Dog Sick Of Being Compared To Old One

PRESTON, MO—Patches, the Layden family's new dog, expressed frustration Monday over the constant comparisons to his predecessor, who died in February. "No matter what I do, I can't escape the long shadow cast by Sneakers," the five-month-old Patches said. "I go for a walk, I hear about the way Sneakers went for walks. I chew on the rug, I hear about the way Sneakers chewed on rugs. They need to realize that I can't be Sneakers." ∅

LISTS from page 145

went straight to the top of my list: 'Reschedule meeting with John T. re: catalog prices.'"

Smalley's list was meticulously arranged, its more detailed tasks subdivided into numerous line items. Instead of simply writing a reminder to speak to the company's three department supervisors about hiring new employees, Smalley listed separately, "Talk to Sarah W. re: hiring," "Talk to Roger M. re: hiring," and "Talk to Howard B. re: hiring."

"I have my own little notation system to help me make sense of everything," Smalley continued. "I add an exclamation point next to especially important items, a question mark next to things I'm only considering doing, and a star next to things I should do as soon as possible. Next to some of the starred items, I also write ASAP. Or, if it's a phone call I need to make, I sometimes draw a little phone. But, if there are too many phone calls, I make a separate 'Phone calls to make' list."

Several of the list's items were cross-referenced to other lists. One such list detailed 32 tasks for planning the company's summer picnic, including number 16, "Look up different caterers in phone book," number 17, "Decide which caterer to use," and number 18, "Call caterer (see list 5B)."

After completing her extensive list, Smalley went to the employee lounge, where she discussed the chaotic state of the office with coworkers.

"They gave me great suggestions for things that needed to be done," Smalley said. "I went back to my office and compiled them into a list called 'Long-Term Company Goals.' I plan to turn that into an animated PowerPoint slide presentation we can

show at our next organizational meeting, time permitting."

Smalley then did more near-work, sending e-mails to various coworkers promising she would send longer, more detailed responses to their previous e-mails when she had time. She also addressed envelopes for several letters she needs to write.

"Figuring out everything that needs to be done in the office made me realize we really have to step up the level of productivity here at One World," Smalley said. "I was so concerned about that, I spent the rest of the afternoon online, checking out the different incentives that successful companies use to motivate employees."

Besides her main list, Smalley has a Day Runner filled with everything from grocery lists to lists of possible birthday presents for her husband to lists of hair colors she is considering the next time she goes to the beautician. She also has a bulletin board covered with notes reminding her to call her parents, buy a teal purse for her niece's wedding, and send thank-you cards for Easter cards she'd received, as well as such personal-improvement notes as "Get more sun" and "Drink eight glasses of water a day."

Smalley insisted that not all of her work-avoidance tactics were of her own invention.

"I've gone to several management-skills seminars over the years," Smalley said. "They taught me the need to set goals, make projections, and use graphs and charts to strategize. In fact, in June, I'm taking a week off to go to another seminar in Indianapolis."

"Which reminds me," Smalley added, "I should really get a packing list started." ∅

Code: ! = important   * = ASAP   ? = Maybe   # = Can do later

AT·A·GLANCE QuickNotes TO DO TODAY Date 5/8/01

Priority	Activity	Complete
!	Write out bills · Buy stamps · Mail bills	
*	Clean kitchen · Do dishes · Clean out refrigerator · Sweep floor in kitchen · Mop floor in kitchen · Clean oven (dirty?)	
*	Call June about dinner and movie	
?	Read movie reviews online - Chocolat? Bridget Jones Diary?	
#	Decide on movie	
#	Dinner with June	
#	Movie with June	
!	Water plants	
*	Separate vitamins into vitamin holder	
!	Take vitamins (everyday!)	
?	Find blue pants	
#	Try blue pants on	
*	Recharge cell phone	
!	Set clock in living room	
#	New light bulb in hallway	
!	Lotion on feet tonight	
*	Bring new mug to work	
?	Take other mug home	
!	Clean off table by door	
*	Sort mail · Throw out old magazines	
#	Put photos by other photos	
*	Put candy/others in purse	

QuickNotes
?	Light bulb key chain - try to fix?
?	Sunglasses - leave there?
*	Set watch calendar to correct day or ask Joel at work to do it
!	Think about if I should renew lease for next year
*	Look in car for missing yellow sweater - Back seat? Trunk? Under seat?

♻ Recycled Paper with 30% Post-Consumer Waste

E403-16

New Technological Breakthrough To Fix Problems Of Previous Breakthrough

COLLEGE STATION, TX—Agricultural scientists around the world are hailing what is being called "the biggest breakthrough in biotechnology since the breakthrough it fixes."

On Monday, Texas A&M chemists unveiled Zovirex-10, a revolutionary new fungicide capable of halting the spread of a fungus unexpectedly spawned by a July 2000 breakthrough, an advanced soy hybrid that grows 10 times better in soil over-saturated with chemical herbicides.

The fungus, which, if left unchecked, would likely have destroyed 98 percent of Earth's soy crop and wrought untold environmental havoc, made the latest scientific advance possible.

"It's an extraordinary development," said Dr. Nathan Oberst, project coordinator and the man responsible for both breakthroughs. "At the time, we thought the soy hybrid was a fantastic thing. When the resultant fungus started wiping out other soybean plants at an alarming rate, we thought we might have blundered, but now it's clear that this potential global disaster was just the precondition we needed for a major leap forward."

Oberst dismissed charges that the development of new biotechnological advances to counteract unexpected side effects of prior biotechnological advances constitutes a dangerous Moebius loop.

"It may seem dangerous to tinker with nature without knowing the long-term effects," he said. "But without the threat of environmental disas-

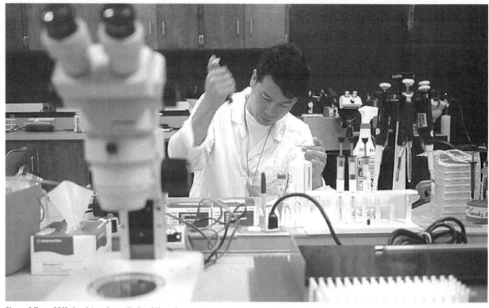

Above: A Texas A&M chemist works on the breakthrough.

ter caused by the short-sighted unbalancing of natural forces, how are we to bring about positive change in the world around us?"

Oberst downplayed claims that if Zovirex-10 were to seep into the groundwater, it would kill off 70 percent of fish and aquatic plant life, poison 35 percent of the human population, and raise the temperature of the sea by seven degrees.

"If this is true, it shouldn't be thought of as a disaster," he said. "Modern science has a long, proven

track record of correcting the mistakes it inadvertently unleashes on the world. I'm confident that if the worst ever came to pass, science would find some way to fix it. That's what science does."

According to Oberst, flawed and dangerous technological advances have helped broaden understanding in all fields of science.

"Just think about the hydrogen bomb," Oberst said. "Not only was it a tremendous breakthrough in physics, but it broadened our knowledge of

everything from radiation containment to bomb-shelter construction to hair loss. Science has been coming up with breakthrough after breakthrough to fix the problems that the H-bomb has created. Without the H-bomb, we would know significantly less about the potential problems associated with the H-bomb."

"People shouldn't see man-made global disasters as a bad thing," Oberst added. "They should see them as scientific breakthroughs waiting to happen." ∅

ACCIDENT from page 145

consecrate the death site in the most trite and hackneyed way possible.

"This is a truly tragic event," said Mound City resident Trudy Pierstorff. "It's painful enough to lose one person you know, but five, well, it boggles the mind. I'm going out to the site today to pay my respects and leave a few mylar balloons."

According to the Linn County Sheriff's Department, Jason Gullickson, 18, was heading north to nearby Pleasanton at a speed approaching 90 mph when he lost control of his 1992 Plymouth Sundance and collided with a Ford Taurus in the opposite lane driven by 42-year-old James Drabeck. Drabeck, his wife Alma, 40, and daughter Kelly, 13, died instantly. Gullickson and a passenger, Kimberly Femia, 17, died later of massive head injuries. A second passenger, 17-year-old Michael Allen, survived the crash but remains in critical condition at Methodist Medical Center in Pleasanton.

To cope with this incalculable loss of life, within hours of the accident, the citizens of Mound City responded with a spontaneous outpouring of crappy mementos. Despite the presence of such disturbing reminders of

the crash as tire marks, headlight shards, and blood-stained pavement, Mound City residents have come here day after day, adding more tacky shit to the steadily growing pile.

"It's staggering to think we won't be seeing Jason and Kimberly anymore," said Mound City High School English teacher John Pentland, who laid two synthetic red roses with plastic baby's breath atop the ever-growing heap of embarrassing kitsch.

"I've been having nightmares every night since the accident," said Lynette Searcy, 38, sister of James Drabeck. "But somehow, I know that Jim, Alma, and Kelly are with God in Heaven now." Searcy then honored her deceased family members with a crocheted clown doll in a tiny Kansas City Chiefs T-shirt.

Passersby on Hwy. 52 also stopped to pay their respects. Off-duty sheriff's deputy Scott Tierney was moved by the tribute.

"I'm a family man like [James Drabeck], and it's sobering to think that everything can disappear like that in the wink of an eye," Tierney said. "He must have been quite a guy to warrant that purple horse piñata."

It is not just tasteless bric-a-brac that makes up the shrine: Ill-conceived signs and corny poems

> Said Pierstorff: "It's painful enough to lose one person you know, but five, well, it boggles the mind. I'm going out to the site today to pay my respects and leave a few mylar balloons."

abound, as well. Friends of Gullickson felt the best way to tell the world how much they missed him was with the words "See You At The Crossroads" written in glow-in-the-dark

green paint on a slab of cardboard. Bordering the sign was a collage of items representing Jason's favorite things, including a Mound City Mustangs logo, several Icehouse Beer labels, and a crudely cut out image of Jesus Christ.

"You and Jason were so great togeather [sic]," reads a poem to Femia from classmate Danielle Schoyer. "I liked having DECA and Choir with you / You were looking so forward to the senior class trip to Washington / I will throw a coin in the Potamac [sic] for you."

Though the remainder of the poem was illegible, its ink washed out by an overnight drizzle, it no doubt continued in this mawkish vein.

Allen, the lone survivor of the crash, has not been spared the tawdry tributes. Stuffed pandas, bouquets of carnations, and "Stone Cold" Steve Austin balloons adorn his hospital room, as well as a construction-paper placard bearing the proclamation "U R A Hero!!!" spelled in macaroni and glitter.

"I'm sure once Michael regains consciousness, he'll be glad so many

see ACCIDENT page 150

Beer Commercials Aren't What They Used To Be

By Ed McIntosh

In these modern times, the concept of workmanship, of taking pride in one's craft, has gone the way of Nagel paintings, the Thompson Twins, and Vision Street Wear. And nowhere is this more evident than in the sorry state of our beer commercials.

What? You say the beer commercials of today are just as good as those of the past? Nonsense! Peel back the scales from your eyes and gaze unblinking into the gaping maw of inarguable truth.

Let us go back to the 1980s, the Golden Age of beer advertising, to see how far we have fallen.

Take the gloriously whimsical Miller Lite campaigns. In one classic spot, comedian Rodney Dangerfield is called upon to win a celebrity bowling tournament. His team implores him, "We only need one pin, Rodney!" thereby setting up a moment of high drama. Can lovable loser Dangerfield pull off the seemingly simple task under intense pressure from his middle-aged cronies? Our hero proceeds to roll the ball dead-center down the middle of the

lane and, though it appears he is headed for a triumphant strike, in a surprising turn of events, the ball bounces harmlessly off the head pin, toppling not a one and losing the game. This defies our expectations, for we know that a bowling ball is a good deal heavier than a bowling pin. The resultant response of the viewer is one of delighted laughter and merriment.

Now, compare this bit of levity to the recent Budweiser campaign featuring the talking frogs and lizards. It is common knowledge that lizards and frogs can't talk, so this freakish defiance of nature's laws provokes a confused reaction. Where did these lizards learn the English language? Where did they pick up the regional dialect? And since when do amphibians of any sort consume beer? How could the producers of these ads expect the public to buy into the ludicrous premise of beer-swilling iguanas with powers of speech?

Have the higher minds at Budweiser forgotten their own Spuds MacKenzie, the beer-drinking "party animal" of the fraternity Tappa Kegga Bud? Spuds never uttered a single syllable and went on to become an internationally recognized icon of the go-go '80s. Who, meanwhile, cares a whit about the Bud frogs?

Nary a soul.

And what about human personalities? In the '80s we had Dangerfield, Bob "I Must Be In The Front Row" Uecker, Bubba Smith, Ed "Too Tall" Jones, Joe "Python" Piscopo, and pool-player extraordinaire Steve Mizerak. And what have we today? Those faceless shills who prattle "Wazzup" as they remain lethargically splayed on the davenport. Can our beer-commercial standards sink any lower?

And what sort of catchphrase is "Wazzup"? It is not even a proper English word! In my day, the slogans were at least complete sentences, like the poignant, "It just doesn't get any better than this." But even phrases that weren't full sentences were infectiously catchy. Sports enthusiasts of today still chant the "Tastes Great, Less Filling" slogan of the '70s and '80s. Meanwhile, "Wazzup" has already been supplanted in Budweiser ads by the shamelessly derivative "What are you doing?" Appalling!

Most importantly, to paraphrase Pete Seeger, where have all the hot chicks gone? In the glory days of the beer commercial, we had the Swedish bikini team and the Amazonian babes playing volleyball using the Rocky Mountains as a net. All the recent Corona ads offer is a faceless woman lounging in a beach

chair propped up by cell phone.

As a male viewer, I want to be reassured that drinking a certain beer brand will make me desirable to supermodels and other unattainable women. Once upon a time, the simple act of cracking open an MGD or an Old Milwaukee held the promise of scantily clad young ladies mobbing a man to bathe in his alcohol-tainted essence, with strains of Eric Clapton's reworked "After Midnight" playing in the background. Sadly, an entire generation of boys is now growing up unaware that there exist harsh deserts that, at the twist of a bottle cap, turn into snow-covered party paradises, complete with bikini-clad sex kittens and caravans of 18-wheelers fully stocked with ice-cold Bud.

Hear my plea, beer-commercial directors. We can fix this problem. Next time, instead of making another Coors ad with a faux web-browser look, try putting that creativity to constructive use. Give us Pete Sampras or Norm Macdonald spouting a few zingers. Or, better yet, a fraternity pool party with two guys shotgunning a couple of beers, only to be attacked by the U.S. Women's Naked Soccer team. Only then will our beer commercials once again achieve greatness. ∅

PORN STARS from page 145

gruntled female sex-industry workers, many of whom had repeatedly argued that, as cock-crazed nymphomaniacs who can never get enough, they weren't receiving the deep-dicking they needed.

"Give it to me! Oh, God, give it to me harder," said PSFBFH spokeswoman Christy Canyon, bent over the press-conference podium. "I fucking need it so bad."

Canyon's sentiments echoed those of many PSFBFH members, who are such nasty sluts that moderately hard fucking is not enough to satisfy their

constant craving for hot fuck action.

As living embodiments of unrealistic male fantasies, porn stars, experts say, possess extraordinarily high libidos that cannot be satisfied by anything less than full-throttle, no-holes-barred banging. For these women, being such fantasy objects comes at a price: the near-impossibility of attaining the level of full-on pussy pounding they desire, even when lustily worked over by one or more trained professionals.

"The sexual frustration of many porn stars," said noted porn expert Bob

Guccione Sr., "is further complicated by the fact that their desires often go beyond traditional vaginally penetrative sex to include a heartfelt need to be repeatedly pounded in the ass, as well."

Tiffany Mynx, PSFBFH co-chair and America's Anal Princess, agreed. "Oooh, baby," read Mynx's testimony before Congress during recent hearings on substandard fucking within the U.S. porn industry. "I want you to slide that big, hungry dick of yours all the way up my tight asshole right now."

According to congressional sources, meeting the porn stars' demands will

not be easy.

"Quite simply, no man alive could give it to these wet, horny bitches in the manner they require," said Senate Majority Leader Trent Lott (R-MS). "They represent a fictional, media-created standard of sexual appetite that nobody, male or female, can possibly satiate."

Despite such skepticism on Capitol Hill, the porn stars remain fully committed to their cause.

"Fuck me!" said porn star Asia Carrera during a recent demonstration in downtown Washington. "Goddamn it, I said fuck me harder!" ∅

---

the ONION Kids Page presents

A Glimpse Into Yesteryear With
Old Victorian Greeting Cards!

Today, it's common to exchange greeting cards to commemorate a birthday or holiday. But did you know that the concept of mass-produced greeting cards first arose in the mid- to late 19th century, known as the Victorian Age? Made possible through improvements in postal efficiency and the development of a quick, inexpensive method of art reproduction known as chromolithography, greeting cards reflected the sentimental values and artistic tastes of the period. Enjoy!

English birthday card, 1878

May Day card, c. 1875-79

148

Ask The Minutes From A Heated Kiwanis Club Meeting

By The Shawano Kiwanis Club Minutes, 5/5/01

Dear Minutes From A Heated Kiwanis Club Meeting,

I recently married a wonderful woman and, in the process, became stepfather to her three young children. These kids were raised to be strict vegetarians, but I still eat meat. I respect their parents' beliefs, but I think I should be able to enjoy a hamburger once in a while without being made to feel guilty about it. What should I do?

—**Meat Lover In Merrick**

Dear Meat Lover:

I. Call to order.
  The meeting of the Shawano Kiwanis called to order at 6:46 p.m. on 5/5/01 by Vice Chair Louis Rollings.
II. 6:49 p.m. - Roll call.
  Members absent: Commissioner Fred Lee, Commissioner Thom Alicea, Treasurer Bill Jarvis, John Pope.
III. 6:51 p.m. - Pledge Of Allegiance led by Chairman Ronald Burroughs.
IV. Meeting
  6:59 p.m. - Commissioner Edward Selsby moves to approve the minutes of 4/14/01. Vice Chair Rollings seconds.
  7:04 p.m. - Minutes approved.
  7:10 p.m. - Jarvis arrives.
  7:13 p.m. - Roger Lambert motions for the dismissal of Jarvis as Treasurer on grounds of chronic absenteeism.
  • Motion seconded by Commissioner Selsby.

• Motion passes 15 to 3.
7:14 p.m. - Jarvis requests recent divorce to be noted in minutes as reason for absences.
• Request denied.
7:15 p.m. - Motion to forgo other meeting itinerary in lieu of inquiry of Jarvis made by Lambert.
• Motion seconded by Edward Holian.
• Motion passes 15 to 3.

Dear Minutes From A Heated Kiwanis Club Meeting,

I bought tickets for a friend and me to see *The Producers*, but she got sick at the last minute and had to cancel. I couldn't find anyone else to go with, and I charged them on my credit card, so I got stuck with a big bill. I told this to my friend, but she didn't offer to reimburse me. Since I bought the ticket for her, shouldn't she pay for it whether she goes or not? I'd like to know the proper etiquette before I say anything.

—**Stiffed In Staten Island**

Dear Stiffed:

7:16 p.m. - Inquiry into status of Treasurer Jarvis. Jarvis motions to have inquiry tabled until next meeting.
• Motion not seconded.
7:17 p.m. - Motion made by Lambert to have Jarvis' absentee record read by Kiwanis Secretary.
• Motion seconded by Allen

Holian.
• Motion passes 15 to 3.
7:18 p.m. - Evidence against Treasurer Jarvis read by Lambert.
1. Missed three out of four meetings in months of February and March.
2. Has had 'bad attitude' at meetings.
3. Refused to step down when asked by various Kiwanis members.
4. Volunteers forced to buy supplies for Pivet Park clean-up project due to Jarvis' absence. Many still not reimbursed.
7:20 p.m. - Reading of evidence interrupted by Jarvis' request to respond to charges personally.
• Request denied.
• Heated argument between Jarvis and Chairman Burroughs.

Dear Minutes From A Heated Kiwanis Club Meeting,

Every morning, I carpool to work with some of my coworkers. We generally get along, but whenever one particular man drives, he insists on tuning the radio to a local morning DJ that I find offensive. I've told him several times that I'd rather not listen to it, but he just laughs it off. I know it's his car, but I think we should try to listen to things that all of us can enjoy.

—**Offended In Oberlin**

Dear Offended:

7:31 p.m. - Reading of evidence continues. Lambert alleges Jarvis may have come to at least two Kiwanis meetings under the influence of alcohol.
7:32 p.m. - Reading of evidence interrupted by request to have "Fuck you, Roger" uttered by Jarvis added to minutes.
• Request denied.
7:33 p.m. - Lambert asks that "Fuck you, Roger" be kept in the minutes as further evidence against Jarvis.
• Request granted.
7:34 p.m. - Motion by Jarvis to Lambert to "take this outside."
• Lambert requests to note in the minutes that Jarvis is "an asshole."
• Jarvis requests to note in the minutes that Lambert's wife committed suicide three years ago.
7:36 p.m. - Motion by Chairman Burroughs to force Lambert to stop punching Jarvis.
• Motion defeated 16-2.

The Shawano Kiwanis Club Minutes, 5/5/01, is a syndicated advice columnist whose weekly column, Ask the Minutes From A Heated Kiwanis Club Meeting, appears in more than 250 newspapers nationwide.

Card commemorating the slaying of a boy's first passenger pigeon, 1885

Christmas card with early image of Santa Claus, 1872

Card for mother, c. 1882-1883

Kerrey's Secret Shame

Last week, former senator Bob Kerrey admitted that a raid he led in the Vietnam War resulted in the deaths of at least 13 unarmed women and children. What do *you* think?

"Geez, you'd think he could make a run at the presidency without resorting to this kind of grandstanding."

Myron Kannell
Systems Analyst

"Come on. If that had really happened, he'd have an ear necklace like McCain."

Pete Terrell
Cab Driver

"What I want to know is, when he realized what had happened, did he throw back his head and yell, 'Nooooo!' in pain and rage?"

Paulette Arnold
Homemaker

"We all have skeletons in our closets. Of course, in Kerrey's case, it's a whole pile of Vietnamese child skeletons, but still."

Peter Odomes
Banker

"There are many good reasons to kill: money, revenge, that satisfying 'thwump' sound... but not to advance one's political career."

Ike Brophy
File Clerk

"I suppose next you're going to tell me that Senator Calley was involved in this sort of thing, too."

Denise Pillers
Florist

TiVo Fever

TiVo, which enables TV viewers to customize programming to their tastes, is proving to be wildly popular. What are some of the system's features?

- Emits loud beep whenever Comedy Central airs *Revenge Of The Nerds IV: Nerds In Love*
- Automatically relays to advertisers detailed information about what you're watching, when you're fighting with your spouse, and what you look like in your underpants
- Watches shows for you, saving hours of valuable time
- Plants idea in your head to use bone as weapon against rival ape tribe
- Pop-up box lists better things you could be doing with your time
- Compresses commercials into three-second subliminal blocks for maximum ad exposure
- Flashes helpful "pay-per-view porn time" reminder whenever you go more than three days without masturbating
- Lets you watch *Yes, Dear* when *you* want, not when some Nazi network bigwig tells you to

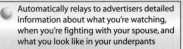
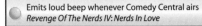
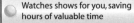
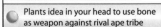
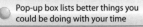
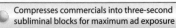
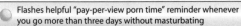
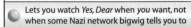

the ONION
America's Finest News Source

Herman Ulysses Zweibel *Founder*

T. Herman Zweibel *Publisher Emeritus*
J. Phineas Zweibel *Publisher*
Maxwell Prescott Zweibel *Editor-In-Chief*

FOUNDED 1871 • "TU STULTUS ES"

Your Horoscope

By Lloyd Schumner Sr.
Retired Machinist and
A.A.P.B.-Certified Astrologer

Aries: (March 21–April 19)
Please help clean up your world! After all, your mother doesn't live here, at least not after next Thursday.

Taurus: (April 20–May 20)
It might not be a comfort, but if we lived in a parallel universe where bulldozers are sentient beings, a certain one would be apologizing profusely right now.

Gemini: (May 21–June 21)
The stars aren't exactly Cole Porter, but "If I Can't Have You, I'd Like A Small Order Of Fries" doesn't seem to have "hit" written all over it.

Cancer: (June 22–July 22)
You will meet dozens of people as cold and unfeeling as yourself after taking out an ad in the impersonals section of your newspaper.

Leo: (July 23–Aug. 22)
Try not to beat yourself up over your failings. After all, there are plenty of people willing to do the job for you.

Virgo: (Aug. 23–Sept. 22)
There's no easy way to say this, but a falling plate-glass window will shear you in half next Friday. Actually, that was pretty easy, come to think.

Libra: (Sept. 23–Oct. 23)
After all these years, the arresting officers still get a little flustered when you try to tip them.

Scorpio: (Oct. 24–Nov. 21)
Though you may never actually find your soulmate in this lifetime, any decent supermarket will provide you with a lifetime supply of Coffee-Mate.

Sagittarius: (Nov. 22–Dec. 21)
Sometimes, you think that becoming a corporate lawyer stained your soul and destroyed your faith in humanity. However, there is the money.

Capricorn: (Dec. 22–Jan. 19)
Your ex-wife says you're six feet of stunted emotional growth in a bad tie. Better get a new tie.

Aquarius: (Jan. 20–Feb. 18)
Remember those less fortunate than yourself next week. You can find them in burn wards and leper colonies.

Pisces: (Feb. 19–March 20)
You will be the 37th overall pick in this week's NFL Slow-Old-Guy Supplemental Draft.

ACCIDENT from page 147

people are pulling for him," said Andrea Allen, Michael's mother. "A few days ago, he was awake long enough to see the sign and ask, 'How was I a hero, Mom? I was in a car accident.' Then he slipped out of consciousness again. I'm sure the painkillers are clouding his reasoning."

As the people of Mound City try to rebuild their lives, psychologist and grief counselor Dr. Elizabeth Calloway said their makeshift shrine is a positive sign that they will weather this crisis.

"Mourning is part of the healing process, and people express their grief in many ways," Calloway said. "Leaving unorthodox tokens of their love for the deceased is sometimes the only way people can articulate their sorrow."

Continued Calloway: "I just wish these mourners would give their tributes a little more thought, because some of it is pretty cheesy. I mean, I don't question the depth of their grief, but there's got to be a better way to show it than with a beanbag frog." Ø

FROG from page 92

large amounts of blood. Passersby were amazed by the unusually large amounts of blood. Passersby were amazed by the unusually large amounts of blood. Passersby were amazed by the unusually large amounts of blood. Passersby were amazed by the unusually large amounts of blood. Passersby

I think I really pissed off that carny.

were amazed by the unusually large amounts of blood. Passersby were amazed by the unusually large amounts of blood. Passersby were amazed by the unusually large amounts of blood. Passersby were amazed by the unusually large amounts of blood. Passersby were amazed by the unusually large amounts of blood. Passersby were amazed by the unusually large amounts of blood. Passersby were amazed by the unusually large amounts of blood. Passersby were amazed by the unusually large

see FROG page 168

New Ford SUV Holds Eight Passengers And Their SUVs

see AUTOMOTIVE page 3C

John Ashcroft: 'Obey'

see WASHINGTON page 3A

Christian Led Down Path To Iniquity By Yahoo! Search For Bush-Trimming Tips

see CYBERBEAT page 14B

Roof Accessed

see LOCAL page 7D

STATshot

A look at the numbers that shape your world.

Least Requested Personalized License Plates

MINNESOTA **IMDYIN**
OHIO **INXS4EVA**
TEXAS **GUNNUT**
NEVADA **RIMMER**
FLORIDA **DPSHT-1**
DELAWARE **CRDSHRKS**
IOWA **FREEMUMIA**
NEBRASKA **MID40S**
ARIZONA **HELPME**

THE ONION
VOLUME 37
ISSUE 19

$2.00 US
$3.00 CAN

0 74470 94595 6

---

the ONION®

VOLUME 37 ISSUE 19   AMERICA'S FINEST NEWS SOURCE™   10-16 MAY 2001

Russia Acquires Amway Distributorship

Above: Russian citizens set up a makeshift Amway table on the streets of St. Petersburg.

MOSCOW—The struggling nation of Russia took a major step toward getting out of debt and achieving financial independence Monday, when it became an official Amway distributor.

"I can't express how wonderful it feels to finally be in control of our destiny," Russian president Vladimir Putin said. "To be able to start up our own company in our spare time with only a small up-front investment is an incredible opportunity."

Russia's involvement with Amway began when longtime Putin friend Elaine Pendergast, a 44-year-old Skokie, IL, homemaker, told him about the program during a recent visit to Moscow.

"Elaine started by asking me and some of the top parliamentary lead-

ers to write down Russia's goals and dreams," Putin said. "Many of them were things we'd all talked about before, like increasing the GNP, paying off our overseas loans, and rebuilding our crumbling industrial base. After we did that, Elaine showed us 'The Plan.' It said that by working only eight to ten hours in our spare time, we could not only be making money from regular sales of products people need in daily life, but within a few years, we could also have a network of distributors making money *for us.* With Amway, there

see RUSSIA page 153

CLASS OF 2001

High-School Senior Marvels At What A Long, Strange Trip It's Been

FREDERICK, MD—Brian "Bri" Moeller, 17, poised to graduate from Frederick West High School next month, reflected on what a long, strange trip it's been Monday while signing his fellow seniors' yearbooks.

"Looking back, I can't believe how naïve I was when I first arrived here as a freshman, so many untold epochs ago, with no real understanding of what the world was like," said Moeller, pausing to take a long, contemplative sip from his Capri Sun juice pack. "Man, my eyes have been opened since then, let me tell you."

Attempting to capture the essence of his journey from fresh-

man-year innocence to senior-year wisdom and worldliness, Moeller signed his friends' yearbooks with the phrase, "What a long strange trip it's been," a line from the song "Truckin'" by The Grateful Dead—a band he was not even aware of four years ago, but whose greatest-hits album he now owns.

"As a younger man, I'd heard those words but never truly understood them," Moeller said. "Now, after all I've seen and done, they resonate deeply within me."

Drawing a "Steal Your Face" logo on the signature page of classmate Aaron Aberg's yearbook, Moeller added: "Those innocent years of the Z-108 'Friday Top Five At Five'

Above: Brian Moeller stands outside Frederick West High School, where "so much crazy stuff went down, I can't even begin to explain."

countdown—back in, what, '97? '98?—they're so far behind me now."

Gathered with friends on a bench near the spot where the bus driver used to pick them up after school, back in the days before they had driver's licenses, Moeller and his friends reflected on how far they'd come.

"The cafeteria—can you believe we actually used to eat lunch there?" said Michelle Benson, 17. "God, I feel so bad for all the little

see TRIP page 152

Pro Athlete Lauded For Being Decent Human Being

MILWAUKEE—Ray Allen, Milwaukee Bucks guard and budding NBA superstar, is drawing raves on and off the court, hailed by admirers as "not an asshole" and "a reasonably decent human being."

The recipient of the NBA's inaugural Magic Johnson Ideal Player Award, Allen was praised by Bucks coach George Karl as "a true standout individual, the kind of person who treats others with a basic level of respect."

"Ray Allen is a great player, but he's an even greater person," said Karl, who is accustomed to reporters asking him about Allen's normalcy. "I

remember this one time during his rookie season, he was walking back to his car from practice, and a woman nearby slipped on a patch of ice and fell. He could have kept walking, but instead he asked the woman if she was okay. Right then and there, I knew this kid was something special."

Allen, 25, who came to the NBA from the University of Connecticut in 1996, is among the NBA's best at shooting three-pointers, defending the perimeter, and going home quietly after games. A hardworking athlete, Allen has raised eyebrows

see ATHLETE page 154

Supreme Court Agrees To Disagree On Abortion Issue

WASHINGTON, DC—After decades of divisive debate, the U.S. Supreme Court finally agreed to disagree Monday on the hot-button issue of abortion. "It is the opinion of this court that we could go on and on arguing about this forever," said Justice Antonin Scalia, who wrote the opinion in the 9-0 decision. "But in the end, that serves nobody. So, finally, we threw up our hands and said, 'Let's just agree to disagree.'" The court's ruling contains language that specifically prohibits justices from bringing up the matter again.

Man Hoping To Accidentally See Roommate's Girlfriend Naked

ATLANTA—Steve Smidlap, 23, roommate of Andy Cordova, admitted Monday that he is hoping to "accidentally" catch a glimpse of Cordova's girlfriend naked. "Every now and then, I'll just sit in the living room with the TV off and hope they think I'm in my room or out of the apartment altogether," said Smidlap, keeping an eye on the hallway between the bathroom and Cordova's room. "I think I have a decent shot of at least seeing Valerie's ass if I stay diligently to the task."

Vast Array Of Lip-Balm Options Paralyzes Shopper

PLANT CITY, FL—Looking for relief for her dry, chapped lips, Walgreens shopper Danielle Liddle was paralyzed with indecision Monday upon confronting the store's vast, intimidating array of lip balms. "I just wanted some simple lip balm, and there was this entire wall," Liddle said. "Blistex, Carmex, Chap Stick, Bonne Bell Lip Smackers, Vaseline Lip Therapy, Burt's Beeswax—I didn't even know how to begin the selection process." After nearly 30 minutes of browsing, Liddle narrowed her choices down to Blistex mint, Walgreens cherry medicated, and Chap Stick Ultra SPF 30.

Area Woman Can't Understand Concept of Suggested Donation

NEW YORK—During a Tuesday visit to the American Museum of Natural History, Omaha resident Mary Stefano, 49, struggled to understand the concept of suggested donation. "So, if the sign says $10 is the suggested donation, that means I have to pay $10, right?" Stefano asked the admission-counter cashier. "Because, if you could pay less, why wouldn't everyone pay less?" After the cashier explained that $10 is what most adults pay, but that museum visitors have the option of paying more or less depending on their ability, Stefano replied, "But if I don't pay $10, I won't get to see the whole museum, right?" After another 10 minutes of queries, Stefano was escorted out of the museum by security.

Family Not Appreciably Enriched By Trip To Mount Rushmore

KEYSTONE, SD—Despite predictions to the contrary, the Lurmans' visit to Mount Rushmore failed to enrich the Portage, MI, family or bring its members closer together. "I guess I thought we'd all bond a little," father Tom Lurman said. "But, aside from lending [daughter] Katie $5 to get something at the snack bar, we didn't really even interact all that much." Lurman said he was prepared to share details of the construction of the monument with his children, but they never asked. ∅

TRIP from page 151

freshmen and sophomores too young to drive to Stella's [Pizza]."

"Remember how everybody thought Janelle was going to be B.F.F. [Best Friends Forever] with Andrea, but she ended up being B.F.F. with Stephanie instead?" Renee Marks chimed in. "We were so young back then... so foolish and young."

His face growing pensive, Moeller mused on some of the many experiences he and his friends shared during their years at West, including that time they endured two whole hours with no electricity when the school's power went out; the time the school janitor lost his temper and yelled, exposing them to the harsh realities of working-class existence; and the time they confronted, head-on, the disturbing truths of modern urban life during a class trip to Chicago to see a touring production of *Rent*.

"I'll never forget my long talks with Gina, the foreign-exchange student, junior year," said Brett Kogan, Moeller's best friend. "I learned so much from her. Up until then, I'd never realized there were no Hardee's in Italy."

"Of course, we're older and wiser now," said Moeller, wistfully touching the Dave Matthews Band patch he placed on his bookbag last year. "After that crazy weekend at Matt's dad's cabin last fall, I doubt anything could faze me."

Though the years offered more than their share of good times, Moeller noted that it was not always wine and roses. There was the time he left his term paper in the breakfast nook and had to call his mother to have her drop it off at school, mere hours before it was due. There were those long student-council meetings that were "a living hell." And there was the hard-earned lesson gained from the time he went to Jeff Rossum's party instead of studying for the following day's algebra midterm and wound up flunking the test.

"At the time, that really seemed like the end of the world," Moeller told Julie Duchamp, with whom he bonded during Mr. Kannenberg's second-period algebra class, becoming "so unbelievably close" in the process. "But now, after coming through the other side, I know that whatever doesn't kill me only makes me stronger."

Moeller said he cannot believe how much happened during his long and storied time at West.

"After graduating from eighth grade, I was thinking, 'Okay, I'm in high school now,'" Moeller said. "I thought I knew everything there was to know. But I was wrong, so wrong. Over the last eight semesters, I've seen it all: Kristin and Justin's soul-shattering breakup, the tragic futility of drunk driving portrayed at that one school assembly with the gruesome slide show, the true bonds that form among brothers in arms as they face unthinkable odds at State Debate."

"Four years ago, I was but a boy. But now, I am a man," Moeller said. "It's a sad and beautiful world." He then went home to eat Fruit Roll-Ups in the den while watching MTV. ∅

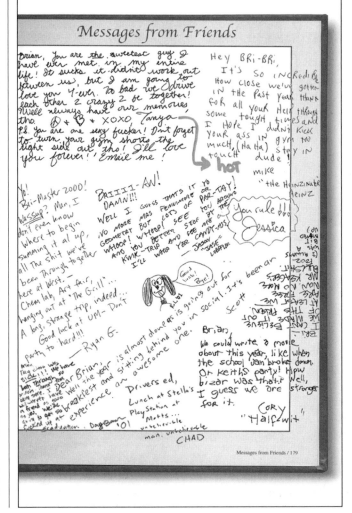

Messages from Friends / 179

Mom Brought To Tears By Thing Picked Up At Airport

COLUMBIA, MO—Joan Hadler, a Columbia-area mother of three, wept tears of joy Monday over a cheap, last-minute present her visiting son Troy bought at an airport gift shop en route home.

"I had a layover in St. Louis and had about an hour to kill. There was a gift shop called 'That's Something Else' in the C Concourse, so I figured, 'Hey, I should pick up something for Mom,'" said Troy Hadler, 25, who now lives in Alexandria, VA. "I picked her up this little teapot, and when I gave it to her, she was so touched, there were tears running down her face. I was glad she liked it, but she liked it so much, I kind of felt sorry for her."

Upon being handed the gift, wrapped only in a plastic bag, Joan protested that her son's visit home was "all the present [she] needed." After opening the bag and seeing the teapot, however, her eyes welled up with tears, and she hugged Troy repeatedly.

"Mom cradled it in her arms like it was a Faberge egg," Troy said. "It made her so incredibly happy. I guess I made the right decision when I chose it over the pewter replica of the St. Louis Arch."

Though Troy said he loves his mother "very much," he admitted that he rarely buys her gifts. On Monday, however, he went the extra mile and spent approximately 60 seconds picking out the $29 flow-ered enameled teapot.

"I'm sure it was stupid to get something like that at an airport," Hadler said. "It's obviously just some overpriced, crappy version of an actually nice teapot, but I wasn't about to run all over St. Louis comparison-shopping for teapots."

Compounding Troy's guilt, his overjoyed mother told him that the teapot would have "a place of honor" among the decorative tea cups she displays in her home's dining-room cabinet.

"Maybe I subconsciously knew she collected teacups and that's why I got it, but that's unlikely," Troy said. "Pretty much, I was just looking around and saw the teapot and thought, 'Hey, I think Mom drinks tea.'"

Despite Troy's insistence that the gift was "no biggie," his mother continued to treat it as a special event well into the next day.

Said next-door neighbor Francine Geis: "I was watering my azalea bushes Tuesday when Joan saw me over the fence. She waved me over and said, 'You've got to come inside and see what Troy brought me all the way from Washington, DC!'"

The neighbor stood by as Joan "oohed and aahed" over the teapot, talking at length about what a thoughtful son she has.

"I wanted to yell, 'Stop! No, I'm not!'" said Troy, who was present for the sad display of unjustified maternal pride. "The only effort I expended in buying the gift was the two-

Above: Joan Hadler proudly displays the inexpensive teapot her son purchased as an afterthought.

second struggle I had trying to pull the credit card out of my wallet."

"I know Mom wasn't trying to make me feel guilty by overreacting," Troy continued. "She genuinely did love it. Just like she loved the Washington, DC sweatshirt I got her last year and the Blue Mountain e-card I sent her on her birthday in 1999."

To assuage his guilt, Troy has made a pact with himself to buy his mother "a nice necklace or some-thing" from a non-airport gift shop the next time he visits.

"I've got to get her a gift that's actually decent next time," Troy said. "The look of joy on her face from that crappy teapot, man, I felt like the worst son in the whole world."

"Mom said she'd think of me whenever she used the teapot," Troy added. "In turn, I guess I'll think of her whenever I'm in an airport gift shop." Ø

RUSSIA from page 151

are 10 different ways to make money."

Even though Putin was enthusiastic about this potentially lucrative business venture, he said he would not have signed on if the products his people were selling were not things they themselves would use.

"Russia has plentiful oil and natural gas reserves and one-sixth of the world's iron ore deposits," Putin said. "We don't need to sell inferior products to make a quick buck. Everything Amway sells is strictly top-of-the-line. And even though many might balk at the higher-than-average prices, many Amway products are highly concentrated, making the cost per use actually less."

Added Putin, "Did you know that Amway deals with 90 percent of the Fortune 500 companies?"

Shortly after ordering 147,700,000 "opportunity kits" from the Amway home office in Ada, MI, Russia began embracing the Amway lifestyle, removing all other brands from its store shelves and stocking only Amway products, such as Active-8, a juice drink, and SA-8, a laundry detergent.

"It just doesn't make sense to have our own business and still buy prod-ucts from other companies," Russian Prime Minister Mikhail Kasyanov said. "If Russia owned a car company, would we go out and buy a Ford if we needed a car? I don't think so. Plus, with our 30 percent distributor discount, we'd be crazy to buy from anyone else."

To generate enthusiasm among the populace, Russian television stations are airing Amway videotapes featuring motivational speeches made by top-selling, or "Diamond," distributors.

"After seeing those tapes, I'm all fired up to get to Silver Distributor status. It won't be long before we're on the cover of Amagram," said Kasyanov, referring to the monthly newsletter for Amway distributors.

As further motivation, Russia has erected billboards bearing such phrases as "Show The Plan" and "Go Diamond" in town squares across the nation. In addition, the Russian national anthem has been changed to "Tough Times Don't Last, Tough People Do."

To stay on top of the latest Amway developments, a coalition of top Russian leaders will travel to Pender-gast's home for monthly meetings.

"At first, it seemed like traveling to Skokie every month would be an enormous hassle," Putin said. "But Elaine pointed out that Russia can't

Added Putin, "Did you know that Amway deals with 90 percent of the Fortune 500 companies?"

let that kind of 'stinking thinking' keep us from our goals. We have to look to the future and take whatever steps are necessary to make our dreams reality."

Despite Russia's excitement, some of its neighbors are skeptical. For nearby Tajikistan, the lure of easy money for minimal effort is one it has heard before.

"The proud nation of Tajikistan is sad to say it was once an Amway dis-tributor," Tajikistan president Emomali Rahmonov said. "After the collapse of the Soviet Union, all the other republics seemed to be doing so much better than us. Amway waved a golden carrot in front of us, and we reached out for it. But after two years, we found ourselves in debt to Amway. Our sponsor, Roger, just kept on telling us that we had to try harder. But the harder we tried, the deeper in debt we got. And being an Amway distributor certainly didn't help our relations with our neighbors: It's hard to form alliances when countries are afraid you're going to try to sell them Estée Lauder knockoffs."

"I wish Russia had talked to us before committing to Amway," Rahmonov continued. "At this point, though, they're too brainwashed to reason with. If you try to warn them, they'll just say you're bringing in negative thoughts and that they have to be like a rhino and bust through all of that. I can't believe we were once that way, too. I'm just glad Iran didn't call for a jihad on Tajikistan, what with the way we were constantly bugging them to buy toothpaste from us." Ø

153

I Guess You Could Say Lying On Couches Has Been A Lifelong Love Of Mine

By Tony Kaner

There are some things in life we all enjoy: the beauty of an ocean sunset, a tall glass of lemonade on a hot summer's afternoon, the warm glow of a roaring fire with a mug of steaming cocoa at Christmastime. But, while all of those things are nice, they don't hold a candle to the joys of a big, comfy four-piece sectional. Or a soft-cover three-seater with extra-wide arm pads. Sure, everybody likes lying on couches, but in my case, I guess you could say it's been a lifelong love of mine.

I was thinking about this just the other day. As I lay on my couch, staring up at the ceiling cracks, the afternoon sun making beautiful sunbeams in the smoky haze rising from the overflowing ashtray on my coffee table, I realized that lying on couches has always been a profound part of who I am. Though I'd long sensed this, it hit me full-force at that moment, just before I nodded off for a nap.

Even as a small child, that love was there. How vividly I recall my parents' old couch. To a small boy, it was as special as a couch could be. It was lime green and covered with an embossed pattern of stitched leaves and Fleurs de Lis in darker green, with a stiff fringe running along the bottom. When I was four, I could actually fit under that couch—yes, all the way underneath! I spent many a blissful hour lying under it, my face pressed into the deep-pile shag carpet below, lost in some solitary game of hide-and-seek.

Ah, but those hours spent squeezed under the couch were nothing compared to the ones I spent on top. I loved burying my face in the space between the cushions. The scratchy synthetic poly-blend upholstery bothered me not the slightest bit. The couch was my playroom, my playmate, my confidant. When I needed a quick place to store a stolen cookie, the cushions' soft, pillowy insides were my trusted hiding spot. How I can still remember lying on my back with my head hanging over the side, imagining I lived in an upside-down world. Then, after several minutes of reverie, I would drift off to sleep. And how wonderful it felt to wake up to discover the cushion, along with the whole right side of my face, soaked in boyhood drool.

When I was 9, my family moved to Arizona, and the old green couch was replaced. I was sad to see it go, but my sorrow was short-lived. Soon, the furniture men delivered an L-shaped, white-corduroy couch that took up nearly two full walls of our new home's basement rec room. What joy! Because it was white, Mom made us take off our shoes before lying on it, but this was a small price to pay for such luxury.

What an exhilarating multitude of cushions! What forts we made of

> **Wherever I lived, the couch was the place where it all went down. The couch, always the couch.**

them! What adventures my siblings and I had climbing its length and breadth! But, still, no adventure was quite as thrilling as the simple act of reclining on it, feeling its womblike softness envelop me while I read my *Thor* comic books or watched *Battle Of The Planets*.

Many times was I chided for monopolizing the couch. When necessary, I moved my feet to make room for others, but I did so reluctantly: Sitting on a couch, however comfy, is nothing like lying fully stretched. Do not the Chinese have a proverb, "Better to sit than to stand, better to lie than to sit"? Truly, a couch's truest purpose lies in the lying.

As time went on, many couches touched my life. In ninth grade, it was on my friend Brian's couch that I played Atari 2600 games into the wee hours. In high school, long after the L-shaped couch had been consigned to oblivion, a brown plaid couch was where I read *Catcher In The Rye*, watched history unfold with the first-ever MTV Video Awards, and stayed up until 2 a.m. furtively masturbating to brief nudity and strong sexual content on HBO. And, not long after, it was on my girlfriend Angela's couch where I first became a man.

As my teenage years wore on, more couches came into my life. My freshman year at Ohio State, countless Saturday nights were spent drunkenly consuming pizza after pizza on couches stained with generations of beer and God knows what else. And, though the old couch in my dormitory's commons area was stinky, battered, and broken beyond repair, I loved it still.

After college, there was such a succession of apartments, I dizzy to think of them all. But wherever I lived, the couch was the place where it all went down. The couch, always the couch. I watched the entire Gulf War on CNN from my couch. At my old job at the community radio station, the couch that had been in the back room since 1965 doubled many late nights as my bed. Each of these couches, every one, holds a special place in my heart.

Some say the couch is the one true symbol of my generation. In fact, one of the greatest moments of my life happened on a couch. I was 26 and living with four buddies in a run-down student-ghetto apartment. It was 2:30 a.m. and I was watching TV, as I did every night. Suddenly, the late-night stillness was broken by a loud bang as my roommates burst drunkenly through the door. It was bar time and, without a word, they hoisted me up to a standing position and hauled the couch away. Before I had a chance to protest, they brought in a second couch that they'd found on the street on the way home. Pausing only momentarily to sweep aside the accumulated debris from the floor where our old couch had been, they dropped their newest find in the same spot, plopped me down on it, and headed to the kitchen to raid the fridge, leaving me exactly as they'd found me. What rapture!

I'm older now, but my love of couch-lying goes on. I have a

see **COUCHES** page 156

ATHLETE from page 151

around the league by never going AWOL or skipping practice.

"I knew when he came into this league that he had the potential to be a standout player," said *Sports Illustrated* basketball writer Marty Burns. "He had a reputation as a guy who would not only hit the clutch shot down the stretch, but also make eye contact with the towel boy. He has the potential to be a decent human being in this league for another 10 or 15 years if he stays healthy."

"I'll never forget what he said to me before the first interview I did with him," Burns said. "He said, 'Hello, Mr. Burns.' Then he extended his hand for me to, you know, shake. That's just the type of guy he is."

Allen's remarkable normal-human-being behavior carries over into his personal life. Though unmarried, he spends a respectable amount of time with his 8-year-old daughter and is rumored to be on good terms with the girl's mother. He is also said to be close with his own mother.

Such decency has not gone unnoticed: Never accused of sexual assault, Allen has earned high praise for his lack of hostility toward women.

"When he was in college, Ray voluntarily went to several UConn women's basketball games and has been quoted as saying that he'd play for a female coach," Bucks public-relations director Cheri Hanson said. "Ray Allen isn't merely in the top 1 percent of NBA players; he's in the 51st percentile of human beings."

In addition to being a media darling, Allen's civility makes him a fan favorite. Though many pro athletes are abusive toward their supporters, Allen has, on numerous occasions, praised a home crowd as "good" or "great." Last week, after a tough home playoff loss to the Charlotte Hornets, he smiled and signed three or four autographs in the Bradley Center parking lot.

"That's unbelievable," said Karl, whom Allen has never threatened physically. "To come off a tough loss like that in the Eastern Conference semifinals and still be willing to interact with people, you just don't see that sort of thing very often."

"Acting reasonably nice, exhibiting basic common decency, having a general awareness of other people's feelings… that's what sets Ray Allen apart from your run-of-the-mill NBA player," said ESPN's Dan Patrick, who called his November 2000 interview with Allen "possibly the most civil" of his career. "Here I am, an interviewer asking him questions, and instead of taking a swing at me or showering me with verbal abuse, he politely responds to my queries. He didn't have to, but he did."

Continued Patrick: "It's nice to know that in this day and age, there are still athletes out there who say 'thank you' when you give them a new car for making the all-star team." ∅

154

My Weed Connection Is Dried Up

The Cruise
By Jim Anchower

Hola, amigos. Whaddaya say? I know it's been a long time since I rapped at ya, but I've been tied up lately. Actually, I meant "pissed off," not "tied up." It's hard for me to think straight these days. It seems like every little thing is stacking up against me, like the universe has got something against your old pal Jim Anchower.

Like, I just left this job yesterday at this big insurance company where I had to run around the building delivering mail and water bottles to all the different offices. They made me wear a tie, and if the money hadn't been so sweet, I never would have done it. But you know I ain't the type that can live in that buttoned-down world for long, even at $10.35 an hour. They wanted to hold me down. After two days, I was like, "Fuck that noise," and I was gone.

Here's a little insight into the deep mind of Jim Anchower. The way I figure it, there may be a lot of trouble in your life, but in the end, life just keeps on keepin' on. So you've got to learn to roll with it.

Like, when your car breaks down in the middle of nowhere, and it's 3:30 in the morning, and you walk a mile to get to a phone you can use, but you can't get any of your friends on the phone 'cause it's so late, and the one friend you do get on the phone is so out of it he don't even remember you calling, let alone agreeing to pick you up, so you wind up sleeping in your car with the stick shift jabbing you in the nutsack until somebody finally comes by and gives you a lift into town. When that happens, you've got to remember that today won't happen again, and that you've got another day ahead of you that can go right.

You should pause right here to let that soak in, hombre.

Sometimes, though, there are things you simply cannot turn the other cheek to, even if it's your ass cheek and you're hanging it out a car window at a bunch of dorks. Right now, I've got something like that in my life, something that's really getting to me on a profound level: My weed connection is all dried up.

I used to buy it from this guy Randy Rasmussen. I probably shouldn't have told you his name, but I will because he pussed out so bad. He used to get some awesome stuff, and he always seemed to have it on hand, even when other people couldn't find it to save their lives. Plus, he'd always be willing to split a joint from his own stash when I stopped by so we could hang out and shoot the shit.

The problem started when Randy started settling down with a girlfriend and a real job. Pretty soon, he wasn't up for smoking and hanging out. It was all business. Next thing you know, he's got a kid coming, and he says he wants to set a good example, so he doesn't want to be selling weed. What the hell? Like a baby can tell you're selling weed and that it's illegal? I tried to tell him, but he just wasn't listening. Personally, I think the guy's whipped, but he's all like, "No, man, I just want to do right by my kid." Whatever, tool.

So, my connection gone, I decided to grow my own stash. I have to say, amigos, I was pretty hard up by the time I stumbled onto this plan. Since I'd smoked most of my stems and seeds, I went over to Ron's place because he has legendary amounts of shake lying around. He said he's saving up for the big weed drought that's supposed to be coming. He's been saying that for almost four years now, so he's got, like, a whole Ziploc bag full of it. After giving Ron a six-pack and my solemn word to share some of the weed when it sprouts, he forks over, like, a dozen seeds, telling me that if I planted four of them in the same pot, the contact high alone would knock me on my ass.

That was almost two weeks ago. I planted them in all these little containers around the house, making sure they got plenty of light and water. I even bought a hydroponics guide at the head shop, but I haven't had time to check it out too much. I mean, how hard can it be? Out in nature, plants grow all the time without any help. All I could do is walk by them and go, "Looks good."

Problem is, I've got no weed until it grows and gets sticky. And, believe you me, that's a real problem because, without weed, I've been getting pissed off at the littlest things. This one time, I dropped a sandwich and almost lost my shit. I was gonna throw the sandwich across the room, but I was pretty hungry, so I picked up a beer bottle and threw that instead. Hey, I didn't say it was a good idea, I said I was pissed.

So, until the homegrown's ready, I'm looking all over the place for a new connection. I found a high-school kid who sells, but I ain't doing that—I've got to have some respect left when I look in the mirror. Besides, the shit he sold me turned out to be real weak stuff. It took about four pulls from my three-footer before I even caught a buzz. Made me cough like a dog, too. So, if you've got a connection I could get some off of, hook me up. I ain't an addict or nothing, but some decent weed right about now would make life go down a whole lot smoother. ∅

---

the **ONION** presents

Moving-Day Tips

Moving can be a major hassle, but with proper planning, it doesn't have to be. Here are some tips to make your next move as smooth as possible:

- To avoid breakage, glass items should be melted down, then re-blown after moving into your new home.

- Six weeks before moving day, fill one small box with books, seal it tightly, and write "books" on top in permanent marker. Then do nothing more until the day before your move.

- If using friends to help move, show your gratitude by buying them a pizza. Don't mention that a professional mover would have cost about 300 times more than a pizza.

- It is heartless and cruel to leave a pet at the humane society because of a move. Smother it in the bathtub and bag it up for trash day.

- Throw smoke grenades into every room of your new home to flush out any possible Viet Cong.

- Get a jump on things by cancelling electricity and water service several weeks before moving.

- Move to Portland. It's a really cool city. They've got all these awesome parks downtown.

- Waiting until the truck is pulling away to say goodbye to neighbors will make moving day a very moving day, indeed.

- Instead of writing "Fragile" on boxes containing breakables, place a copy of Yes' *Fragile* on top.

- Let professional movers take care of large, heavy items such as furniture and my cock.

- Boxes are an unnecessary expense. Place all possessions in the truck and fill it to the top with packing peanuts.

- Don't get too excited when you see a U-Haul truck that says "Moves Only $19.99" on the side. These signs are only intended as a joke.

- After relocating to your new home, remember that you are legally obligated to go door-to-door informing your new neighbors that you are a convicted sex offender.

- Rushing the previous tenants out of the apartment you're moving into is a great way to score free toiletries.

- For the love of God, don't ever move.

The Medical-Marijuana Ban

Last week, the Supreme Court ruled 8-0 that federal law does not allow a "medical necessity" exception to the ban on marijuana use. What do *you* think?

"Good. Medical marijuana is a gateway drug, and many who use it go on to use stronger stuff—even engaging in full-blown chemotherapy."
Diane Denkinger
Realtor

"You know, those Cheech & Chong movies come off as very warm and human if you see them as simple dramas about two dying friends."
Patti D'Andrea
Tour Guide

"The terminally ill need to learn that you can have fun without all the drugs."
Burt Allenby
Systems Analyst

"Luckily, people with health problems still have the healing powers of alcohol at their disposal."
David Dawson
Mechanic

"What? I can't believe I voted for David Souter in the *High Times* Hemp 100."
Radu Manogian
File Clerk

"If they really wanted to stop people from smoking pot, they *should* legalize medical marijuana. Under this country's health-care system, nobody would be able to get it."
Marlon Edwards
Civil Engineer

China's Olympic Bid

Beijing is in competition with Toronto and Paris to host the 2008 Summer Games. What are the Chinese doing to win over the International Olympic Committee?

- Giving IOC members complimentary "Beijing 2008" testicle-electrocution kits
- Building state-of-the-art hospital in Beijing to remain open for duration of Olympics
- Renaming decathlon Happy Family Combination Event #10
- In gesture of goodwill, Olympic flame to be lit by political prisoners, who are conveniently already on fire
- Pointing out to IOC that some of the fastest, most dedicated running in the world has occurred in China
- Temporarily lifting nationwide ban on printed materials to print souvenir programs
- Subtly hinting to IOC members that there might be pandas in it for them if they play their cards right
- Will release doves in opening ceremony to showcase aerial-gunnery skills of Chinese Red Army
- Guaranteeing that all athletes will be tested for steroids, MSG
- Informing IOC officials, "We *will* host the 2008 Olympics" in flat monotone, followed by several minutes of hard, unblinking stares

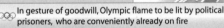
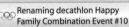
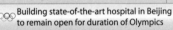
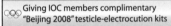

the ONION
America's Finest News Source
Herman Ulysses Zweibel *Founder*
T. Herman Zweibel *Publisher Emeritus*
J. Phineas Zweibel *Publisher*
Maxwell Prescott Zweibel *Editor-In-Chief*
FOUNDED 1871 • "TU STULTUS ES"

Your Horoscope

By Lloyd Schumner Sr.
Retired Machinist and
A.A.P.B.-Certified Astrologer

Aries: (March 21–April 19)
You won't be aware that there's a Citizens' Coalition To Stop The Igniting Of Cats until they knock on your door next Wednesday.

Taurus: (April 20–May 20)
You have no grounds for a lawsuit: The label on the vegetarian buffalo wings said "meatless," not "contains no chicken parts."

Gemini: (May 21–June 21)
For the last time, Brad isn't right for you. Stop breaking into his house and waiting naked in his closet.

Cancer: (June 22–July 22)
You'll no longer wonder if you have what it takes after finding out that it takes a weak will, a pot belly, and a full complement of cable channels.

Leo: (July 23–Aug. 22)
The grim spectre of Death will appear before you next week and hint that, though you're not supposed to die for years, it never hurts to be nice to the man who makes the schedule.

Virgo: (Aug. 23–Sept. 22)
We're pretty sure that the fortune cookie was wrong about your lucky numbers.

Libra: (Sept. 23–Oct. 23)
The pride you feel when your superiors choose you as the best man for the job will fade when you discover how much raw sewage the job involves.

Scorpio: (Oct. 24–Nov. 21)
Preparation is the key to success. For instance, you can save yourself a lot of pain and stress next Friday by studying how pins go back into grenades today.

Sagittarius: (Nov. 22–Dec. 21)
The stars were going to tell you to stop playing your little head games. Then again, that's how soccer, the world's most popular sport, was invented.

Capricorn: (Dec. 22–Jan. 19)
There's a chance you're being melodramatic about next week's events. Three giant Nazi Martian women do not necessarily constitute a threat to the planet.

Aquarius: (Jan. 20–Feb. 18)
Take some time out to appreciate all the not-exactly-horrible things in your life.

Pisces: (Feb. 19–March 20)
You thought Texas had already unleashed all the evil it could upon the world, but you forgot about the Dell layoffs and the killer bees.

COUCHES from page 154

PlayStation 2/DVD player and a great surround-sound speaker system. I have not one but two couches, one for guests and one exclusively for me. It's not the greatest couch in the world, a foot too short and possessing so many busted springs that I had to stick a piece of plywood under the cushions. But it's good enough for me.

I don't think I'll ever stop lying on couches. Last month, when I visited my friend Jimmy in Minneapolis, I amazed him and his roommates by spending 36 straight hours on their couch, enjoying conversations with various people as they moved in and out of the room. They said I was a true "hall-of-famer." I hope I can live up to that honor. Years from now, when death arrives, as it does for all men, I hope I go comfortably and willingly into that great darkness, dying as I have lived, entering death's silent embrace with arms—and feet—outstretched. ∅

KLUGMANESQUE from page 144

large amounts of blood. Passersby were amazed by the unusually large

Man, that funeral sucked.

amounts of blood. Passersby were amazed by the unusually large amounts of blood. Passersby

were amazed by the unusually large amounts of blood. Passersby were amazed by the unusually large amounts of blood. Passersby were amazed by the unusually large amounts of blood. Passersby were amazed by the unusually large amounts of blood. Passersby were amazed by the unusually large amounts of blood. Passersby were amazed by the unusually large amounts of blood. Passersby were amazed by the unusually large amounts of blood. Passersby were amazed by the unusually large

see KLUGMANESQUE page 172

Promotional Jacket Worn Everywhere

see LOCAL page 6C

Destiny's Child Referred To As 'Feminist Icons' With Straight Face

see PEOPLE page 10D

Modern-Day Jesus Says He'll Come Back To Fix Everything But Never Does

see LOCAL page 7C

STATshot

A look at the numbers that shape your world.

Why Aren't We Able To Feel Anything In Our Toes?

1. That seventh scotch and soda
2. Are Christopher Reeve
3. No toes
4. Kangaroo on toes refuses to leave
5. Overdid it on ToeNumm™, the topical analgesic for pedal extremities

THE ONION
VOLUME 37
ISSUE 20
$2.00 US
$3.00 CAN
0 74470 94595 6
09

---

the ONION®

VOLUME 37 ISSUE 20   AMERICA'S FINEST NEWS SOURCE™   31 MAY-6 JUNE 2001

Bush Actually President, Nation Suddenly Realizes

WASHINGTON, DC—More than four months after his Jan. 20 inauguration, the realization that George W. Bush is actually president of the United States finally hit the American people this week.

The fact of the Bush presidency, which sunk in with most Americans sometime between 11 a.m. Sunday and 4 p.m. Tuesday, has stunned citizens of all races, ages, income levels, and party affiliations.

"Whoa," said Bill Wylecszki, 38, an Odessa, TX, grocery-store owner. "George W. Bush, former owner of the Texas Rangers and failed oilman, is president. This is too weird."

"I guess with the media circus and all the other craziness surrounding the election-recount fiasco, I just kind of looked at it like

see BUSH page 159

Right: George W. Bush looks around his new office.

Dot-Commers To Receive Unemployment Benefits In Form Of Stock Options

WASHINGTON, DC—Offering unemployment aid with "a huge potential upside" to the approximately 100,000 Americans who lost their jobs in the New Economy collapse, the government's new eBenefits stock-option plan is proving wildly popular among dot-commers.

"Instead of settling for a little cash to help them through rough times, victims of the Internet crash have the option of receiving valuable stock in a number of fast-growing U.S. companies," Secretary of Labor Elaine L. Chao said Monday. "In place of a traditional unemployment check for a few hundred dollars a week, laid-off dot-commers can receive stock options valued at five, ten, even *twenty thousand dollars*."

see DOT-COM page 158

Right: Laid-off dot-commers wait in line for their eBenefits at a San Mateo, CA, unemployment office.

Best Friends Each Secretly Think Of The Other As Sidekick

Left: Mutual sidekicks Morrell and Rotham.

OXFORD, OH—Though neither has openly acknowledged it, Marc Morrell and Justin Rotham, longtime best friends and sophomores at Miami University of Ohio, each regard the other as a sidekick.

"Me and Marc, we're like Batman and Robin," said Rotham, 19, who met Morrell when both were freshmen at Canton (OH) McKinley High School. "Wherever I lead, I can count on him to follow."

Morrell expressed similar affection for his sidekick.

"Justin and I make a great team," Morrell said. "No matter what crazy plan I come up with, I always know that he's gonna be right there to back me up. If this were *Ferris Bueller's Day Off*, I'd be Ferris and he'd be Cameron Frye."

Added Morrell: "Chuck D and Flavor Flav, Johnny Carson and Ed McMahon, me

see FRIENDS page 160

Hidden Valley Ranch Bombed By Balsamic Extremists

HIDDEN VALLEY, CA—A radical Balsamic fundamentalist group detonated an estimated 800 pounds of TNT at the Hidden Valley Ranch compound Monday, killing 11 and injuring dozens more. "Let no salad again be foully tainted by the corrupt regime of Hidden Valley," said Martin Pulaski, leader of the Nation Of Balsam, in a statement claiming responsibility for the deadly attack. "We shall not rest until every salad's flavor is enhanced by a light and tangy vinaigrette, not buried in a shameful avalanche of buttermilk."

Longtime Sexual Fantasy Awkwardly Fulfilled

LEXINGTON, KY—The longtime sexual fantasy of Andrew Marcone was awkwardly fulfilled Saturday, when the local record-store clerk participated in a clumsy, embarrassing *ménage à trois* with girlfriend Karen Wagner and her roommate Shelley Peelen. "Well, I finally did it, for what it's worth," said Marcone, 27, following the long-dreamed-of sexual encounter, six minutes into which he ejaculated. "So much for wondering what it would be like, I guess." After achieving orgasm,

Marcone spent the next half hour "trying not to get in the way" of his companions.

America A Fascist Police State, Stoned Underage Drunk Driver Charges

SMYRNA, GA—Outraged by the brutal suppression of civil liberties that has defined the nation's history, stoned 15-year-old Corey Shifflett denounced America as a "total fascist police state" following his drunk-driving arrest Saturday. "This whole country is, like, totally Hitlered-out," Shifflett told friend Glen Withers, who posted his $500 bail. "These cops, they're just looking for any excuse to pull us over and hassle us, just to feel like fuckin' Superman." Shifflett then knocked over an orange highway cone and vowed to move to Amsterdam.

Mediocre Painter's True Talent Lies In Acting Like A Painter

LOS ANGELES—According to art critics, mediocre painter James Augustiniak has proven

masterful at cultivating the self-centered, womanizing demeanor of an art-world *enfant terrible*. "Augustiniak's latest exhibition, featuring dozens of paintings of melting eyeballs and hearts, was a staggering achievement in clichéd, pseudo-pretentious banality," said *Los Angeles Times* art critic Christopher Knight. "But I went anyway, just to see him throw a fit over the lighting in the gallery. He's very good at that sort of thing."

Average Age Of Wacky TV Neighbors Dropping

ATLANTA—According to a Center For Media Studies report released Monday, the average age of wacky TV-sitcom neighbors has steadily declined over the past half-century. "In the '50s, during the days of Ed Norton and Fred and Ethel Mertz, the median age was a mature 53," the report read. "By the late '70s and early '80s, with the likes of Larry on *Three's Company*, Monroe on *Too Close For Comfort*, and Lenny and Squiggy on *Laverne & Shirley*, the average had dropped to 36. Today, the wacky-neighbor landscape is dominated by twentysomethings, typified by Jack on *Will & Grace* and all the friends on *Friends*." At the present rate, the report added, wacky TV neighbors will primarily be toddlers by 2015. ∅

DOT-COM from page 157

In lieu of traditional unemployment benefits, out-of-work dot-commers have the option of receiving stock in their former company, if still existent, or a mutual fund drawing from a diverse pool of Internet companies. Among the companies offered are getupandgo.com, "the world's largest online razor-scooter-accessory retailer," and naturalpet.com, "an oasis of information and communication for informed and enlightened pet owners."

Chao said 80 percent of unemployed tech-industry workers are choosing the stock option, jumping at the chance to "double, triple, or even quadruple the value of their unemployment checks."

"This is an extremely exciting, innovative form of unemployment," said Justin Reed, 27, one of 1,000 workers recently laid off at eToys. "It's going to totally revolutionize the way people think about government checks."

Susan Reyes, director of development for the now-defunct online sporting-goods retailer eZoomaboom!, agreed.

"This is a radical re-imagining of unemployment and, frankly, I'd be a fool not to get in on the ground floor of it," said Reyes, leaning on the mailbox outside her San Jose, CA, home while waiting for her monthly unemployment portfolio to arrive. "The future of unemployment benefits is bright—really bright."

While eBenefits recipients are not permitted to cash in or trade their stock for at least a year, Reyes spends much of her ample free time calculating her projected earnings at local coffee shops.

"Before I signed up for eBenefits, I was living check-to-check, stretching out my pitiful unemployment funds while looking for a new job," Reyes

> ## "This is a radical re-imagining of unemployment and, frankly, I'd be a fool not to get in on the ground floor of it," Reyes said.

said. "Now, my situation has completely changed. I've got nearly unlimited future earning potential."

The unemployment package has proven so popular that a cottage industry of eBenefits-related web sites has sprung up in its wake.

"Governmentcheck.com is the first company to offer a full range of online services in tracking, trading, and projecting the growth potential of state unemployment checks," recently re-employed webmaster Sunil Parekh said at the site's launch party, held Saturday night at the Masonic Auditorium in San Francisco. "This is going to be big."

While a few laid-off dot-commers have sworn off the Internet sector altogether, most say their experience has not deterred them from trying again.

"Excuse me, but haven't you ever

Above: Marcus Todd, founder of now-defunct clothing retailer Thingamajig.com, checks his eBenefits on his Palm.

heard of the concept 'buy low, sell high'?" laid-off DrKoop.com employee Shawn Bennett asked. "Well, the market is at its lowest point in years."

Bennett went on to note that today's tech companies are "leaner" than ever.

"Companies like perfumewarehouse.com and crosswords.com have literally cut their budgets and payrolls by 90 percent in the last year," Bennett said. "They're primed for profit after reining in overspending and eliminating tons of dead weight by firing people like myself."

According to Chao, eBenefits was "a natural" under current economic conditions.

"While tech companies had no cash to pay into the unemployment

system, they did have ample stock," Chao said. "That put the government in a unique position to offer this stock to the workers themselves. Bingo. A New Economy way of looking at the old problem of massive layoffs."

Fans of eBenefits also point out that owning thousands of dollars in stock has given laid-off tech workers the collateral needed to procure additional loans to cover their day-to-day expenses.

"At DotComCasualties.com, we specialize in providing pre-approved, no-questions-asked loans to recently unemployed programmers, network administrators, and outsourced content providers," company president and CEO Rodney Woods said. "Best of all, you can apply online." ∅

Wal-Mart Opens Store In Winesburg, Ohio

WINESBURG, OH—In a move retail-industry insiders are calling "thematically fitting," Wal-Mart opened its newest store Monday in Winesburg, a town of 25,000 in northern Ohio.

"We chose Winesburg due to its convenient location, relative lack of competing retail superstores, and the darkly powerful inner lives of its residents," said Thomas Coughlin, president and CEO of Wal-Mart Stores Division, which oversees more than 2,500 locations nationwide.

Since the turn of the century, the citizens of Winesburg have developed a national reputation for spiritual and emotional frustration and dashed ambitions. Wal-Mart's decision to open a store in Winesburg underscored those feelings.

"Target scouted the Winesburg area last year but decided against locating there," *Wall Street Journal* retail analyst Julia Faber said. "Their control-group data showed that the town's residents were filled with a rarely articulated yet palpable anguish that meshed poorly with the exuberant image of the Target Corporation. The bankrupt Montgomery Ward, which closed its Winesburg location late last year, seemed more in tune with Winesburg residents' somber, conflicted psychological state. Wal-Mart, with its proven track record of leaving economic devastation in its wake, should be a good fit."

Winesburg residents responded positively to Wal-Mart's October 2000 announcement that it would open a store there the following spring: More than 3,000 people

Above: The Winesburg Wal-Mart.

applied for some 150 new jobs. Among the first to be hired was 19-year-old George Willard IV. A restless yet circumspect boy with a keen curiosity about the world, Willard manages the housewares department.

"If you can bring us a lower price from another store, Wal-Mart will match it," Willard told a customer. "We won't be undersold. Yet

see WAL-MART page 160

BUSH from page 157

it was some sort of funny TV show," said Amanda Milner, 37, a Red Wing, MN, bank teller. "I never really thought about it as something that was actually happening. And once Bush finally got sworn in, I don't know, I suppose I must've just subconsciously assumed that there would be another recount or another election in a few months or something."

Americans hit with the sudden realization have reported feelings of nervousness, confusion, and disorientation. The effects are said to be fairly uniform across the nation, with a particularly high concentration in Florida.

"A few nights ago, I was watching *The Tonight Show*, and [Jay] Leno was making some typical joke about Bush—you know, the kind we've all heard a thousand times before—and I was thinking, 'Boy, wouldn't it be bizarre if he actually got elected?'" said Ocala, FL, homemaker and mother of four Janis Niering.

"Then it hit me: 'Wait a minute—I think he *was*.'"

Even months after Inauguration Day, the presidential situation never really dawned on most Americans. This, political experts say, was largely due to the fact that former president Bill Clinton continued to dominate the news through much of February, March, and April, while the media paid little attention to Bush.

"The stolen White House furniture, the missing Ws from the White House computers, the Clinton office in Harlem, the whole Marc Rich pardon thing… it just seemed like Clinton was still president," said Mary Ellen Buis of Salina, KS. "I know that doesn't make sense, but that's what it was like."

"Evidently, I should have taken it all a lot more seriously," Buis continued. "I mean, he's apparently going to be our leader for the next four years, minimum. But who knew?"

Even Republican Party leaders have expressed surprise over Bush's occupancy of the White House.

"Early in the presidential race, we all expected Bush to get stomped by

Pausing to rub his eyes and shake his head, Hatch added, "Wow."

Al Gore," U.S. Sen. Orrin Hatch (R-UT) said. "But once the race got tight, we were so excited that we might actually win, it was sort of unreal. But I'm not sure we ever really gave much thought to the idea that it might actually happen. It was more like some strange dream or something."

Pausing to rub his eyes and shake his head, Hatch added, "Wow."

For the first 24 hours after the mass realization, Bush remained silent on his status as president. This, political analysts say, was because the full scope of the truth had only begun to dawn on him, as well. After conferring with top advisors in a six-hour closed-door session, Bush finally addressed the nation Tuesday evening.

"My fellow Americans," Bush said. "God, it sounds so weird to actually be saying that. Anyway, I know we've all had a bit of a shock lately. To be honest with you, I'm a bit blown away by it all myself. But it appears that, for whatever reason, I am now the leader of the free world. And that's something we're all, myself included, going to have to get used to."

Added Bush: "Any comments or advice anyone might have would be welcome at this time." ∅

159

There's More To Life Than Just Traveling The World And Marveling At Its Varied Peoples And Cultures

By Dr. Peter Masterson

I guess we inherit a certain worldview from our parents. My father was a reporter for *National Geographic*, and my mother was the photographer on his assignments. We spent 11 months out of the year seeing the world and taking in its various wonders. Since that's the way I was raised, I just figured that's what families do; that's how life is lived.

My folks retired when I was 19. Not long after, I joined the Peace Corps, in which I helped a remote Honduran village develop an irrigation system. Along the way, I got to know the locals, learned their traditional folk songs and tales, and saw how their strength comes from their closeness and interdependence. Why did I do this? Frankly, because I knew no other way. I was just copying what I'd seen my parents doing.

Today, I'm one of the world's leading anthropologists, an accomplished archaeologist, and an award-winning novelist. And, at 41, I'm only now becoming aware of the globetrotting rut I've been in my entire life. Looking back on everything I've seen and done, I can't help but ask, "Is that all there is?"

If this is such a great life, traveling the world and drinking deep of its bountiful cultural and historical well, then why am I the only guy doing it? It's time for me to wake up to the real joys life has to offer.

Every weekend, in malls across America, guys hit on girls and dine on food-court Chalupas and Mountain Dew, then go off to buy the new Tool CD. Why am I not among them? Because while they're spending genuine quality time in fluorescent-lit shopping corridors, stupid me is off becoming a blood brother of the Blackfoot Indians or observing a Haitian voodoo ceremony. Well, I'm sick of it! I want better. I want to watch the DVD of *Miss Congeniality* in my bathrobe!

I want to blow my money on scratch-off lottery tickets! I want to make my ass go numb sitting on the floor playing Donkey Kong 64 all day! I don't think that's so much to ask.

Everywhere I turn, I see ads for a corn chip called "Fritos." I think, "My God, this must be a truly remarkable corn chip, to be so widely and confidently touted." My thoughts often turn to Fritos while eating the obscure regional cuisine on which I invariably subsist. Like when that Chilean peasant village held a banquet to thank me for showing them how to dam the river and create a fishing reservoir. They made this local delicacy called "Pastel del Choclo" with corn, meat, and spices. But if it were as good as Fritos, wouldn't Pastel del Choclo be on billboards in every city? Why am I getting shorted? Will I die not having tasted Fritos?

Recently, I was with the Wapemba tribe in Zanzibar, and I heard their chieftain recite the mythology of creation that these people had known for thousands of years. And I was struck by its similarities to other creation myths, including the Judeo-Christian model. Then I thought to myself, *so what the fuck am I doing here in Zanzibar?* Why did I slog all the way to Africa to hear a story that I could have heard at the Baptist church two blocks from my house? You get what I'm saying? If all people are the same on the inside, why did I spend a year learning Swahili when I could just talk to the girl at the Tast-E-Freez? It's all the same shit, folks. Save your plane fare.

I'm not saying you should never go places and meet people. I'm just saying don't get too carried away with it. Sure, visit Paris and chat up a local in a coffee shop. But stay home, too. Get drunk and sleep until noon. Before studying the coastline of Sicily, learn the shape of your own mattress.

Sometimes, I just want to draw the blinds, tell the Explorer's Club to fuck off, and order two large pizzas and the Spice Channel. Now, *that's* living. ∅

WAL-MART from page 159

something tells me there has to be something out there beyond Winesburg. Something besides all this decay and loneliness and broken dreams."

Doc Reefy, 72, works at the new Wal-Mart as a greeter and stockperson. A physician for nearly 50 years, Reefy grew bored with the quiet routine of retirement and now uses his large, gnarled hands—which resemble clusters of unpainted wooden balls fastened together by steel rods—for rolling back prices.

"Doc Reefy is a quiet sort," Willard said. "We aren't the kind of folks who involve themselves in each other's business, but legend has it that he was once married to a tall, dark girl who'd had many suitors. They had an understanding. They were married less than a year before she took sick and died."

Willard's mother, Elizabeth Willard, works as a cashier. A silent, frail woman whose ashen complexion gives no indication of the vivaciousness and idealism of her youth, she only exhibits fire when her son's happiness is threatened.

"George's father come to the breakroom on the second day of business," Elizabeth said. "I heard him tell George he wasn't aggressively promoting himself within the company enough, that Ezra Hardy's son Victor would practically snatch the associate-manager position from him before George could have a chance at it. He accused him of wool-gathering, of errant thoughts. 'What ails you?' he asked him."

Continued Elizabeth: "I could not bear to see George's youthful dreams wither and die as mine had so long ago. I have always hated my ambitious, swaggering husband, who thinks himself one of the chief men of town despite his many failures, but it was always an impersonal hatred, because he was only a small part of a far larger problem. But now he was this thing personified. So incensed was I that I grabbed a cheap Swiss Army knife from the impulse-purchase rack flanking my register, and with great determination strode to the breakroom, intending to stab my husband. When I killed him, something would snap inside myself and I would die, too. It would have been a great release for all of us."

Before Elizabeth could commit the act, however, a voice over the store's P.A. system called her to the front registers, where a long line of customers had formed. Her anger subsiding as fast as it had risen, Willard returned to the front of the store with only a little broken sob in her throat betraying her emotion.

Other Wal-Mart employees have

see WAL-MART page 161

FRIENDS from page 157

and Justin... standing beside every great man is a great sidekick."

Like many best friends, Morrell and Rotham have similar tastes, sharing an affection for *The Simpsons*, Kurt Vonnegut, and the BBC series *Black Adder*.

"I love Rowan Atkinson as Black Adder," Rotham said. "I can't even watch *Mr. Bean*. It's okay, but it's not like Atkinson's in his prime anymore."

"I'm not surprised he'd say that," Morrell said later. "He'd never even heard of *Black Adder* before I got him into it. Now, he's the world's greatest expert on it. Like I said, wherever Marc leads, Justin follows."

While Morrell claims superior knowledge of *Black Adder*, Rotham says he's the authority when it comes to music.

"I'm the one who got him to stop listening to all that Top 40 crap and turned him on to electronica and trance stuff like John Digweed," Rotham said. "Now, he compares everything to Digweed, and I have to set him straight when it's more like Paul Oakenfold. He's still learning."

The duo's mutual sidekicksmanship often manifests itself during road trips.

"Whenever we drive down to Cincinnati to see bands, I take the wheel," Morrell said. "Me being the leader, not to mention the one with the car, I'm always the one who drives."

Rotham, however, sees it differently.

"As the man with the plan, I choose to take the role of navigator on road trips," he said. "Marc couldn't find his ass with a homing device, so that means I've got to man the maps. And, let's face it, even though Sulu pilots the Enterprise, he still takes orders from Kirk. I am captain, and Marc is my first lieutenant."

"Without me, Marc would be totally lost," Rotham said.

Though Morrell and Rotham generally enjoy having a sidekick, both acknowledged that it occasionally has its downside.

"Justin's a great guy and all, but sometimes it's tough to make my moves when he's always hanging on my sleeve," Morrell said. "Like, last weekend, we were at this house party, and I was trying to chat up this cute girl Amy from my psych class, and he wouldn't leave my side for a second."

Rotham expressed similar frustration over his friend's reliance on him in social situations. "If not for me, he'd nev-

see FRIENDS page 162

Just Being Neighborly

You know, you'd think a genuine people-person like me would have friends coming out the wazoo. But other than Patti and Fulgencio, and my two sweet kitties Priscilla and Garfield, I don't have a whole heck of a lot of buddies. I've never understood it: I'm always eager to initiate a conversation (even with a complete stranger), I'm always smiling, and I'm ever-ready to lend a helping hand or shoulder to cry on. I'm serious! If any of you Jeanketeers out there ever need a favor, just let me know. Heck, if you're real nice, I'll even help out with the housework! (Only, I don't do windows—ha ha ha!)

A Room Of Jean's Own
By Jean Teasdale

I wish I could befriend some of my neighbors, but the apartment complex where I live has a month-to-month lease arrangement, so there's constant turnover. In fact, the only permanent residents seem to be me and hubby Rick, and this elderly lady who sits on her little balcony porch and stares down at me as I walk to and from the driveway. So, sometimes, your old pal Jean got a little lonely at her digs on good old Blossom Meadows Drive.

That is, until recently, when the Jean Teasdale Official Fan Club opened downstairs!

A couple weeks ago, while misting my fern, I glanced out the window and noticed two young men and a young woman taking boxes out of a moving van and walking toward the downstairs entrance of my unit. I didn't think much of it until I noticed what was sticking out of one of the boxes: a cardboard "Love Is" placard! I was soooo knocked out to see a "Love Is" placard! Am I the only one who remembers "Love Is"? It was this darling comic strip of observations about love featuring two adorable little naked kids! Anyway, after spotting that placard, I just had to drop in on my new neighbors!

When I walked downstairs to meet them, I couldn't believe the stuff these kids were carrying! Leif Garrett and Shaun Cassidy posters! Scads of old Barbie dolls! And they must have had at least half a dozen paintings of children, puppies, and kitties with huge eyes! The girl was even wearing a Holly Hobbie T-shirt! I can't tell you how thrilled I was to finally meet some people who shared my interests!

"I love your stuff!" I cried.

One of the young men stared at me for a couple seconds. "Really?" he said. "Well, we love your stirrup pants."

I was floored. It's not often I get compliments on my clothes!

I offered to help the trio move the rest of their stuff in. They were kind of reluctant at first, but I wouldn't take no for an answer!

"I can't get over the fact that you guys have a 'Love Is' poster," I said. "I gotta include that in my column."

"Column?" the girl asked. "What column do you write?"

I told them who I was and, judging from their reaction, you'd think I said I was Madonna! They let their boxes drop to the floor and stared at me all slack-jawed and wide-eyed.

"*You're* Jean Teasdale?" one of the young men asked. "You mean, Jean Teasdale? 'A Room Of Jean's Own' Jean Teasdale?"

"Hey, don't wear out my name… it's my only one!" I replied.

The three froze, saying nothing. Suddenly, the girl clapped her hand to her mouth and squealed. The two boys' eyes shone. For a minute there, I thought they were going to burst into tears! One of them finally gathered the wits to step up and shake my hand.

"Mrs. Teasdale, this is truly an honor," he said. "We are Jeanketeers of the highest order."

Greg, Sean, Marni, and I have been buddies ever since.

The three are all students at nearby Concordia College and were looking to get out of the dorms, so fate (and cheap rent!) brought them to my apartment complex. That evening, they came over for pizza and ice cream. They took great interest in seeing all the things I've mentioned in my column over the years, like my kitties, my Precious Moments collection, and my curio cabinet full of dolls, including my coveted Miss Beasley. But their biggest thrill came when hubby Rick came home from work. "How are things at the tire center, hubby Rick?" they exclaimed in unison when he walked in the door. I hadn't seen Rick that befuddled since he woke up next to me after our first night together!

I've spent time at their place, too. I must admit, though, that even though we share similar tastes, some things they do are kind of strange. For example, Marni, who's an art student, took this really adorable clown painting she'd found at a garage sale and painted a blood-covered ax over the flower the clown was holding. Then, she painted the bloody corpses of two children at his feet. Even though I like Marni, I don't think this was really necessary. Besides, I think

---

> **It's great to meet people who see the humor in life. I mean, whenever I'm around Greg, Sean, and Marni, it seems like they're trying their darnedest to stifle a laugh.**

---

she did herself a real disservice in the long run, because clown paintings are really collectible, and an original in good condition could be worth a lot of money.

There's another strange thing that's been happening lately. Ever since I met Greg, Sean, and Marni, people their age have been passing by the Fashion Bug where I work and peering into the front window. Whenever I see them, I always smile and wave. But instead of waving back or going into the store, they nervously giggle and dart away. Except for this one guy. He strolled by the store and yelled in a loud voice, "Hey, Jean! Let's go shopping someday! I'm just mad about Patrick Swayze and chocolate, too!" I hustled to the entrance to see who he was, but by the time I got there he'd disappeared. That confused me. If we had so much in common, why didn't he come in to talk to me? But I suppose I shouldn't look a gift horse in the mouth. I'd always wondered if anyone out there cared about my column, and now I was getting my answer. And, from all appearances, that answer was a resounding YES!

Besides, it's great to meet people who see the humor in life. I mean, whenever I'm around Greg, Sean, and Marni, it seems like they're trying their darnedest to stifle a laugh. I'm always encouraging them to laugh as much as they want! Let it out! Don't be so bashful! There are too many Gloomy Gusses in this world anyhow!

Tonight, my new friends and I are going to watch my VHS copy of *Ice Castles*. When they told me they'd never seen it, I just about flipped. I mean, they call themselves Jeanketeers, and they've never seen *Ice Castles*? But I forgave them pretty quickly. After all, it's not every day you forge such a strong bond with people! ∅

WAL-MART from page 160

even more enigmatic pasts. Wing Biddlebaum has quick hands, making him an ace cashier and stockperson, yet it was those same hands that may have led to a violent and tragic misunderstanding many years ago between himself and the father of a boy Biddlebaum instructed as a schoolteacher. Misses-department supervisor Alice Hindman still waits in vain for a long-gone suitor. Only recently has she realized that some people are destined to live and die alone in Winesburg.

Perhaps most disturbing of all is the new Wal-Mart's manager, the foul-tempered, malodorous Wash Williams III, who nevertheless commands a perverse respect.

"This Sam's Choice Cranberry Apple Juice was spoiled before it was shipped here. It was a foul thing come out of a factory more foul," Williams told a complaining customer before refunding her money.

Mitch Ennis, Wal-Mart's director of north-central Ohio operations, is confident that the Winesburg Wal-Mart will fast become one of the top-performing retail stores in his region.

"Wal-Mart wants small communities like Winesburg to thrive, and what better way than to give jobs and livelihoods to its deserving townsfolk?" Ennis said. "Some naysayers claim that Winesburg is but a procession of grotesques—grotesques who so ardently embrace certain truths that these same truths sour into falsehoods. But we at Wal-Mart cherish the American Dream, and nowhere does it manifest itself so deeply as in small-town America."

If the Winesburg store proves successful, Wal-Mart next plans to open stores in Spoon River, IL, and Gopher Prairie, MN. ∅

The Jeffords Defection

Last week, U.S. Sen. James Jeffords of Vermont left the GOP to become an independent, handing control of the Senate to the Democrats. What do *you* think?

"Wow, this could shift the balance of power in the Senate. It has? I was right."

Bud Manwaring
Truck Driver

"It's rare when a senator does what he thinks is right. It's even rarer when the rest of the Senate notices."

Angela Aldrete
Piano Teacher

"Now that the Democrats are in control, know what that means? Ping-pong table in the rotunda! Ping-pong table in the rotunda!"

Hal Uribe
Cashier

"We can't have people changing parties all willy-nilly. This nation was founded on principles of non-willy-nillyness."

Paul Dravecky
Systems Analyst

"Why would anybody want to leave the Republican Party? It just doesn't make sense."

Donna Thompson
Homemaker

"A senator defected? Oh, no—now the Russians will learn all the secrets to how we make our government run so smoothly and efficiently."

Larry Mitchell
Banker

Pearl Harbor's Historical Inaccuracies

Pearl Harbor, the Jerry Bruckheimer blockbuster that opened May 25, is not 100 percent historically accurate. What are some of its flaws?

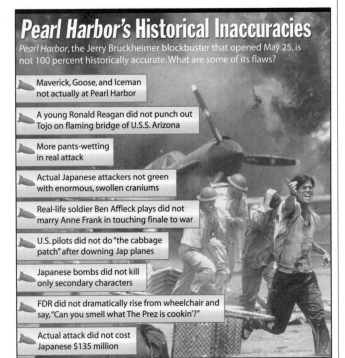

- Maverick, Goose, and Iceman not actually at Pearl Harbor
- A young Ronald Reagan did not punch out Tojo on flaming bridge of U.S.S. Arizona
- More pants-wetting in real attack
- Actual Japanese attackers not green with enormous, swollen craniums
- Real-life soldier Ben Affleck plays did not marry Anne Frank in touching finale to war
- U.S. pilots did not do "the cabbage patch" after downing Jap planes
- Japanese bombs did not kill only secondary characters
- FDR did not dramatically rise from wheelchair and say, "Can you smell what The Prez is cookin'?"
- Actual attack did not cost Japanese $135 million

the ONION
America's Finest News Source

Herman Ulysses Zweibel *Founder*

T. Herman Zweibel *Publisher Emeritus*
J. Phineas Zweibel *Publisher*
Maxwell Prescott Zweibel *Editor-In-Chief*

FOUNDED 1871 • "TU STULTUS ES"

Your Horoscope

By Lloyd Schumner Sr.
Retired Machinist and
A.A.P.B.-Certified Astrologer

Aries: (March 21–April 19)
You're known to all as a person who doesn't bother hiding her feeling. That's not a typo. You've only got one.

Taurus: (April 20–May 20)
Don't go around wondering what people say about you. If you knew, you'd only learn a lot of unpleasant things about yourself.

Gemini: (May 21–June 21)
Remember, really cool people don't need drugs to have a good time. They need to *take* drugs to have a good time.

Cancer: (June 22–July 22)
The funny thing about next Monday won't seem very funny to you, but rest assured that it'll be hilarious to the bartender, the coroner, and all the monkeys.

Leo: (July 23–Aug. 22)
A prospective employer, during the course of a job interview, will ask you what you believe to be your worst quality, a question which leads inexorably to his suicide some days later.

Virgo: (Aug. 23–Sept. 22)
All things considered, it's a good thing you aren't in the prostitution business for the money.

Libra: (Sept. 23–Oct. 23)
Your superhero career is born when a knock on the head from a radioactive evergreen tree gives you the proportionate strength and speed of a Douglas fir.

Scorpio: (Oct. 24–Nov. 21)
The next few days will be a good time for the Zodiac to take some time for itself and get things done. Scorpio has a life outside of you, you know.

Sagittarius: (Nov. 22–Dec. 21)
Surprisingly enough, the end of your life will include 20 minutes of credits, copyright information, and a rather sad zither-based closing theme.

Capricorn: (Dec. 22–Jan. 19)
You will have a sudden flash of insight in the bathtub and run down the street enlightened, exultant, and naked, only to find out it's been done.

Aquarius: (Jan. 20–Feb. 18)
The old saying, "It'll never heal if you pick at it," will save your life this week.

Pisces: (Feb. 19–March 20)
Don't worry: There will be very little pain, and it will be over almost instantly. However, "it" in this instance refers to lunch.

FRIENDS from page 160

er even talk to girls," Rotham said. "He counts on me to steer the ladies his way. Usually, I'm happy to, but every now and then it'd be nice if he could make things happen on his own."

Neither Morrell nor Rotham are dating, but both expressed confidence that they have some "hot leads." Those who know the pair, however, have their doubts.

"Those guys are sort of cool in their own way, but mostly they're dorks," said Renee Callahan, a friend of the two. "I mean, they go everywhere together, have all these retard-ed inside jokes, and even dress almost identically. And they definitely share a lack of success with the ladies. I don't know why they don't just admit they're in love with each other."

Morrell and Rotham concede that the affection is mutual, though not equal.

"I love Justin like a brother," Morrell said, "but he definitely needs me a lot more than I need him."

"Without me, Marc would be totally lost," Rotham said. "It's like if this were *Ferris Bueller's Day Off,* I'd be Ferris and he'd be Cameron."

SOCKS from page 2

were amazed by the unusually large amounts of blood. Passersby were amazed by the unusually large amounts of blood. Passersby were amazed by the unusually large amounts of blood. Passersby were amazed by the unusually large amounts of blood. Passersby were amazed by the unusually large amounts of blood. Passersby were amazed by the unusually large amounts of blood. Passersby were amazed by the unusually large amounts of blood. Passersby were amazed by the unusually large amounts of blood. Passersby

were amazed by the unusually large amounts of blood. Passersby were amazed by the unusually large amounts of blood. Passersby were amazed by the unusually large amounts of blood. Passersby were amazed by the unusually large amounts of blood. Passersby were amazed by the unusually large amounts of blood. Passersby were amazed by the unusually large amounts of blood. Passersby were amazed by the unusually large

see SOCKS page 213

NEWS

the ONION®

VOLUME 37 ISSUE 21 | AMERICA'S FINEST NEWS SOURCE™ | 7-13 JUNE 2001

Ben Stiller Peels Banana With Own Feet

see PEOPLE page 7B

Foul Play Suspected In Destruction Of World's Second-Largest Ball Of Twine

see LOCAL page 10D

Cliffs Notes Skimmed

see EDUCATION page 9E

STATshot

A look at the numbers that shape your world.

Least-Used Kitsch References

1. *Madame's Place*
2. Aqualad
3. *Hardcastle & McCormick*
4. Odyssey 2 video-game system
5. The Asian maid from *The Courtship Of Eddie's Father*
6. Rubik's Snake
7. *O.C. & Stiggs*
8. Fruit Brute cereal
9. Balki from *Perfect Strangers'* catchphrase, "Get out of the city!"

Mr. Bubble

THE ONION
VOLUME 37
ISSUE 21
$2.00 US
$3.00 CAN

0 74470 94595 6

Mom-And-Pop Loan Sharks Being Driven Out By Big Credit-Card Companies

PHILADELPHIA— Frankie "The Gorilla" Pistone leans wistfully on his bat. Then, without warning, he picks it up, swinging it furiously toward his deadbeat client's leg. Just before the Louisville Slugger makes contact with the man's kneecap, he pulls back, as only a real pro can, leaving the $250-in-the-hole man gasping in fear and relief. "Just get it to me by tomorrow, because next time, I ain't gonna let up," Pistone says.

As the thankful man scurries off, Pistone pulls the cigarette out of his mouth and drops it to the ground. "I'm going to miss this," he says.

Frank Pistone is part of the dying breed known as the American

Above: Loan shark Frankie Pistone, whose way of life is endangered by the likes of American Express.

Loan Shark. Not so long ago, the loan shark flourished, offering short-term, high-interest loans to desperate people with nowhere else to turn.

Today, however, Pistone and countless others like him are being squeezed out by the major credit-card companies, which
see LOAN SHARKS page 164

Haggar Physicists Develop 'Quantum Slacks'

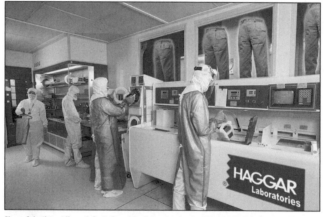

Above: Scientists at Haggar's Pants Propulsion Laboratory bombard khakis with high-speed pleat particles.

DALLAS—At a press conference Monday, Haggar physicists announced the successful development of "Quantum Slacks," attractive, wrinkle-free pants that paradoxically behave like both formal and casual wear.

"With this breakthrough, pants enter a whole new dimension," said Dr. Daniel Chang, head of the Haggar team. "Conventional notions about the properties and possibilities of slacks have been completely turned on their head."

Though long dreamed of by theoretical physicists and science-fiction authors, the quantum slacks represent the first wearable pair of non-Newtonian pants, bringing America one step closer to a complete casual wardrobe that transcends classical physics.

"For decades, we conducted level-one physics experiments in which we collided individual subatomic particles in a highly controlled laboratory setting," Chang said. "But an array of technical hurdles kept us from taking the next logical step: colliding pants."

Preliminary tests conducted last month at the Haggar Pants Propulsion Laboratory in Dallas indicate that the quantum slacks, generated by smashing together two larger sizes of slacks at near-light speeds, defy scientific explanation.

Said Chang: "We placed the pants in a casual lawn-party setting and discovered them to be functional and comfortable. But, against all logic, in subsequent tests the pants per-
see SLACKS page 165

Author Wishes She Hadn't Blown Personal Tragedy On First Book

SANTA FE, NM—Author Jessica Kingley expressed regret Monday that she had "pretty much used up all the hardship" from her early life in her recent first novel *Bitter Root*, leaving her nothing to write about for her follow-up book.

"In writing *Bitter Root*, I drew heavily on my experiences growing up poor and neglected by my alcoholic parents in an economically depressed small town in southern Oklahoma," the 36-year-old Kingley said. "Apparently, I drew a little too heavily, because I don't have any personal trials and tribulations left for the next one."

Bitter Root, the fictional story of

Above: Kingley in her Santa Fe home.

a young woman named Jessie Strong growing up in the desolation of an economically depressed small town in southern Oklahoma, was
see AUTHOR page 164

163

Bush Picks Up 20 Copies Of *Washington Post* He's In

WASHINGTON, DC—President Bush made a special trip to his local newsstand Monday to purchase 20 copies of that day's *Washington Post*, the cover of which featured a story on him. "I'm definitely going to want a copy for my wall and one to send Mom, just for starters," Bush said of the article, which concerned his efforts to renew normal trade relations with China. "Did you see the article? They quote me five or six times. And there's a big color picture." The president last expressed this level of excitement in April, when he saw footage of himself on CNN Headline News throwing out the first pitch at a Baltimore Orioles game.

Church Member Not The Same Since Unsuccessful Choir Tryout

PORTLAND, ME—According to parishioners at St. Luke's Episcopal Church, Mary Raines, 58, has "not been the same" since her unsuccessful audition for the church choir last month. "Ever since Mary failed to make the cut, she sits in the back row for Sunday services and barely sings along," fellow parishioner Bill Genzler said. "Last weekend, she left the church bazaar an hour before it ended. That's just not like her."

Area Man Wants Something Made Of Titanium

PENDLETON, OR—Anthony Schilling is hoping to acquire something made of titanium, the 43-year-old claims adjuster reported Monday. "I can't afford a new titanium bike, but maybe I could get a pen or a watch," Schilling said of his lust for the low-density, corrosion-resistant element. "Or maybe I could get a pair of super-strong titanium binoculars. Whatever I wind up getting, though, it'll be really lightweight and last forever."

Heroic Cancer Sufferer Inspires Others To Get Cancer

SAN DIEGO—Diagnosed three months ago with terminal lymphoma, David Bradley, 46, has stood as such a stirring example of courage in the face of disease that he is inspiring others in his community to get cancer. "Seeing David and the way he's bravely battled this thing, I couldn't help but follow his lead," said neighbor Timothy Willis, injecting himself with a concentrated dose of the carcinogen trichloroethylene in an effort to contract the disease. "David understands that every day is a precious gift. Pretty soon, I'm going to realize that, too." Said Mandy Pitnick, 14, chain-smoking three unfiltered Camels: "I want to be a symbol of hope just like David."

Woman Wonders Whatever Happened To Those Rainforests She Gave $5 To Save That One Time

NORTHGATE, CO—Audra Smoller, 39, who donated $5 to the Save The Rainforests organization in 1997, was struck with curiosity Monday about the fate of her arboreal beneficiaries. "I wonder how those forests wound up making out with my five bucks," Smoller said. "I guess they were saved, because I never read anything in the paper about them getting cut down." Smoller added that, should another ecological crisis arise, concerned parties should not hesitate to approach her for assistance. ∅

LOAN SHARKS from page 163

can offer money to the down-and-out at lower rates of interest and without the threat of bodily harm.

"It's a damn shame," said Joseph Stasi, 61, a South Philadelphia loan shark whose business is down 90 percent from its mid-'70s heyday. "These days, there's just no place for the small businessman. My kind, we just can't compete with the Visas and MasterCards of the world."

"The old customers don't come 'round here no more," said Felix Costa, 59, speaking from the Elizabeth, NJ, pool hall that has served as his place of business since 1972. "Time was, a guy who needed a quick $400 for a new refrigerator or some car repairs would come straight to me. Now, he just puts it on his Discover card."

Though their client lists are dwindling, the loan sharks still have their champions.

> Asked Johnny Toothpick: "How can we compete with rates as low as 18 to 26 percent a year?"

"Call me old-fashioned, but I prefer the loan sharks to the credit-card companies," said Gene Hobson of Detroit. "When I borrow money from Three Knuckles Benny, I know there's going to be a personal touch, whether it's a dead animal on my doorstep or one of my kids coming home with a missing toe. The credit cards just don't give you that sort of individualized attention. And, if you're late with them, it's a form letter and maybe—*maybe*—an irate call from the accounts-receivable department."

"With our overhead, we need to charge a 50 percent weekly interest rate just to break even," said a Chicago loan shark identified only as "Johnny Toothpick." "We've got rent, pay-offs, and switchblade maintenance, not to mention travel expenses. How can we compete with rates as low as 18 to 26 percent a year?"

Continued Toothpick: "These [credit-card companies] are monsters. They care nothing about the damage they're doing to the American landscape by driving us out. Loan sharking was about more than giving people money and roughing them up when they didn't come through. It was about ruffling a kid's hair on the street, helping out a local fella who needed a break, and occasionally letting somebody off easy with just a couple of punches to the gut instead of a glass-filled sock to the face. It's a unique part of our shared national experience that, once extinct, will never come back."

With nearly 200,000 new credit-card solicitations going out every week, the loan sharks have little hope of regaining the ground they've lost.

"We were going by word of mouth, and we did pretty good around the neighborhood," Pistone said. "But these credit cards? With direct mail and the Internet, they reach a customer base we can only dream about. In this business climate, how can a small, independent goon possibly compete?" ∅

AUTHOR from page 163

heralded by *The Chicago Sun-Times* as "a searing, painfully honest portrait of a young girl's hardscrabble adolescence on the plains."

The success of *Bitter Root*, which climbed to #16 on the *New York Times* bestseller list, netted Kingley a second-book deal with Viking Press worth a reported $450,000. Kingley said the prospect of writing a follow-up seems daunting.

"I've already used the time my dad, in a drunken rage, burned down the house," Kingley said. "I used the time my grandmother died and everyone in my family missed the funeral. I used the stuff about the summer the river dried up. I even used that corrupt police officer my cousin dated, even though I only met him once. I

> Said Kingley: "I just don't have any more memories with that kind of dramatic heft."

just don't have any more memories with that kind of dramatic heft."

During her painful years growing up in Oklahoma, "where oppressive heat bears down on chained dogs longing to run—*run!*—and never look back," Kingley experienced a number of other hardships firsthand. At 16, she ran away from home the night her father threatened her with a gun. At 18, she fell into a string of unhealthy relationships that led to a near-fatal bout with bulimia. At 19, she underwent the physically and emotionally wrenching experience of having an abortion.

Unfortunately, the protagonist of *Bitter Root* underwent every last one of these tragedies, as well.

"Jessie is a troubled spirit," Kingley said. "She's the type of person who's too strong-willed to listen to others. She's a woman who has to make her own way in this world. So, what happens after she survives her traumatic childhood and, at 20, finally leaves Oklahoma behind to create a new life for herself in New Mexico? A bunch of stuff way too boring to write about."

Kingley has already taken several unsuccessful stabs at a second novel. First, she tried writing about a young woman facing adversity growing up on the Louisiana Bayou. Discovering she knew little about Bayou culture, Kingley changed the setting of the book to an economically depressed town in Appalachia, but ultimately found she had a hard time identifying with the characters she created.

"After those false starts, I thought maybe I needed to branch out and try something totally different," Kingley

see AUTHOR page 167

Actually, On-The-Job Safety *Is* A Laughing Matter

By Garry Krumenacher

As a factory metalworker, I enjoy almost limitless opportunities to be maimed or killed. The Red River plant where I work has its own foundry, smelting plant, steel-forming works, welding line, pipe-bending assembly room, and dozens of other accumulations of heavy industrial equipment capable of removing fingers and heads. It's a good thing, then, that management makes the effort to post signs reminding us that "On-The-Job Safety Is No Laughing Matter!" Thanks for the heads-up, guys.

What the folks at corporate HQ don't seem to realize is that, for those of us who have to work with all this incredibly dangerous machinery every day, the idea of on-the-job safety *is* a laughing matter.

Let's set aside, for the moment, the obviously hilarious sight of watching a 12,000 RPM band-saw blade launch some idiot's fingers across the factory floor. Or the lifetime of Jesus impressions awaiting the poor slob who takes his eyes off

the drill press for even a second. Miss your mark, and it's instant stigmata. But the funny thing about on-the-job safety is how the higher-ups act like its importance never crosses the minds of the actual on-the-job people.

Have you seen the signs? They're pretty funny, really. "WARNING! MOLTEN STEEL!" "DANGER! HIGH-SPEED BLADES!" "ATTENTION! HIGH-TEMPERATURE, HIGH-VOLTAGE WELDING TIP IN USE!" As if we weren't aware. Excuse me, but I'd been working here three seconds when I noticed the searing wall of heat coming off the vat of liquid steel, the insane shriek of the diamond-toothed bar-stock saw, and the eyelid-piercing white glare of the arc welder.

On the other hand, I'd been working here maybe a month before I noticed the safety signs. Couldn't afford to, really: Look away from the arc-welder tip for two seconds to read the warning on the manipulator arm, and you're a textbook case of workplace casualty. Usually an advanced medical textbook case, too.

Listen, I know what a pinch point between two gearwheels is. I know what acid does to a human hand. And I know what happens if I get caught in a 440-amp electrical

arc. The last thing I need is a sign reminding me about it every time I turn around. I've seen guys get

> ## Excuse me, but I'd been working here three seconds when I noticed the searing wall of heat coming off the vat of liquid steel.

their hands caught in the spot-welding jig, and it wasn't pretty. When Jorge lost his arm in the snipper, it wasn't for lack of a huge, day-glo sign reminding him to "Take Care!!!" There's a kind of callous, premeditated malice to those signs that's just plain laughable. If you're laughing in a high-pitched, sanity-eroding kind of way, that is.

The slogans are hilarious: "No Job Is Too Small For Safety At All!" I got a good chuckle out of that one,

especially when they put it on the sheet-steel roller mill, a machine that squeezed Bob Atherton's left arm like a zit until his fingers popped off. "Skip That Beer… We Need You Here!" is another good one. First of all, no one who wants to keep their bones on the inside will be operating the high-speed metal lathe drunk. Second, if someone does slip and put a two-inch dovetail joint in his forehead, anyone who witnesses it is going to need something a hell of a lot stronger than beer to erase the image.

And let's not even get into the filmstrips and lectures. Sheer comedy. Anyone who's been here at Red River for a while has seen a lot of stuff they'll never put in the films, like the difficulty of cleaning off the blood stalactites you get on the ceiling over the carborundum saw when something goes a little squirrelly. And the lectures are always given by "safety experts" with fancy college degrees—not to mention intact sets of fingers and toes. I suspect they're the same guys who, at the end of the year, have all kinds of laugh-out-loud reasons why trip guards and face shields can't be installed on the forge press.

Yeah, on-the-job safety is a laughing matter, all right. It's a big fucking joke. *∅*

SLACKS from page 163

formed equally well at a formal business luncheon. This represents a baffling, 'Schrödinger's Pants' duality. The results even fly in the face of Einstein, who preferred wool trousers."

Subsequent experiments yielded even more puzzling results.

"We have attempted to measure the exact dimensions of these counterintuitive slacks, if only to know what rack to store them on," Haggar physicist Dr. Mattias Kohl said. "But we've learned, to our dismay, that if we measure length, we lose sight of waist size and vice versa. These slacks defy all traditional means of measurement."

Added Kohl: "Additional study and data-gathering is proceeding at a slow pace, as the pants have a strange tendency to vanish and reappear elsewhere. Understanding and harnessing this trait is essential before we can find a way to distribute the slacks to stores."

More exciting, Kohl said, is the potential for gaining insight into the very origin of trousers itself—a breakthrough he described as "within walking distance."

see SLACKS page 166

Right: Some of the attractive quantum slacks featured in Haggar's Spring 2001 catalog.

Every Brand Of Alcohol Reminds Man Of A Different Story

HALLANDALE, FL—Randy Streeter, a 32-year-old sales associate at Guitar Center, has a different anecdote for every brand of alcohol.

"Oh, man, Malibu. That takes me back," said Streeter, browsing the shelves of a liquor store while picking up a bottle of wine for a dinner party. "At Mardi Gras one year, me and my buddy Mo got totally smashed on that stuff at Pat O'Brien's. I woke up on the floor of the hotel room the next day with a fucking 'No Parking' sign on my chest. I must've ripped it down when I was drunk, but, I swear, I had zero recollection of doing it. And Mo had this girl's number written all over his arm, like, 100 times. Stay away from that stuff, man."

Streeter, who said his "hardcore drinking days are mostly behind [him]," remains a fount of wisdom on the inebriating powers, relative merits, and after-effects of such brands as Jameson's Irish whiskey, J&B scotch, and Jose Cuervo Gold tequila.

"Drinking tequila is like playing with fire: It warms you up nice, but if you're not careful, you get burned," Streeter said. "One night back in college, this guy Andy Nardo got so polluted on tequila shots that he thought he was Mr. Fantastic. He kept going on about how he could stretch his arms out like rubber. We had to pile on him to stop him from knocking shit down. Nardo was so sick the next day, he thought he was gonna die. Leave the Cuervo alone if you know what's good for you."

Continuing to browse the liquor store's shelves, Streeter noticed a bottle of Jägermeister, which inevitably reminded him of another tale.

"Oh, man, Jäger," said Streeter, shaking his head. "Graduation week at the University of South Florida is the beer blast of all time, and the guys and I were mixing Jägermeister with vodka for the crazy, mellow drunk it gives you. They say there's opium in it—or there used to be, at least—and deer's blood. But whatever's in it, for some reason, made me act like a lion tamer. All night, I'd walk up to girls with a chair and, like, do this circus act. Of course, I don't remember any of it. I had to be told about it later while nursing the king hell hangover of all time at the

Above: Randy Streeter.

graduation ceremony. Just say no to that shit, my friend."

Not all of Streeter's stories function as cautionary tales. Noticing a bottle of Bombay Sapphire behind the store counter, he recalled a wonderful, long-ago experience with the premium gin.

"Back in '91, I was working at this True Value over in Hialeah. On my very last day there, just before quitting time, the guys surprised me with this really expensive bottle of Bombay Sapphire," Streeter said. "We all went in the back of the store and finished off the whole thing. Man, it was like drinking diamonds. We nearly kicked this one guy's ass for trying to mix it with orange juice. It was too good for that. I'd almost say I liked it better than the Oban scotch my girlfriend gave me for my 21st birthday, but I don't know. Bombay is a breed apart, that's for sure."

Streeter went on to note that Bombay Sapphire and other "topshelf stuff" would never cause a hangover unless the drinker were abusing it.

"Hangovers, now, that's a whole other topic," Streeter said. "There's a bunch of stuff you shouldn't do,

like mix booze and beer. Then there are all the different cures, like spicy Mexican food and stuff. Actually, that reminds me of the time my buddy and I accidentally dis-

covered the magic cold-calzone-and-Dr. Pepper cure after spending all night drinking at this topless bar down in Cabo. Oh, man, that's a great story." ❧

SLACKS from page 165

"Scientific law holds that any given piece of clothing becomes less fashionable over time," Kohl said. "However, at the quantum level, we have found that certain styles of Haggar slacks actually grow *more* fashionable, suggesting the existence of 'slachyons,' theoretical pants that travel backward in time."

According to Chang, just as Einstein showed matter, energy, and pants to be essentially the same, the Haggar team may soon prove that space, time, and fashion are bound together as unified elements of the cosmos.

"If we can stabilize a pair of these slacks long enough for in-depth study, perhaps by confining them in a radiation belt powerful enough to stop them from slipping into other dimensions, we have a good shot at proving our theory," Chang said.

The only danger, he noted, is the prospect of creating anti-pants. This would derail the experiment by

annihilating any pants the original pair comes into contact with, leaving only nude space.

"Further," Chang cautioned, "if these slacks do, in fact, travel through time, we risk altering the history of slacks and endangering the present state of comfortable, affordable daily-wear. This could potentially collapse the probability weave and create a 'casual loop' from which we might never escape."

But, dangers notwithstanding, the Haggar physicists remain optimistic.

"Mankind's knowledge of pants technology has been advanced immeasurably," Kohl said. "We cannot overstate the revolutionary nature of this breakthrough. We are on the verge of unzipping the secrets of creation and peering into the pants of God Himself. We are about to discover the very fabric of the universe, and it appears to be a smart cotton-twill weave." ❧

Guard Yo' Grill Against Them Computa Bitchez

By Herbert Kornfeld
Accounts Receivable

Yo, whassup, Gs? H-Dog in tha house. Do all y'all recall, back in tha day, tha beef between tha Accountz Reeceevable posse an' tha west-wing Tech Support krew? Them computa bitchez wuz fuckin' wit' mah flow, switchin' mah software on me an' tellin' me I can't put no desktop image on mah computa screen. Well, I called bullshit on that. I won't go into all tha detailz again, but suffice it to say I had them computa bitchez runnin' scared an' didn't have no mo' trouble wit' them. That is, until yestidday.

Turns out, there be a whole new posse o' computa suckas to contend wit'. Only, they ain't on tha Midstate Office Supply payroll. They do freestyle consultin' wit bidnesses, tellin' them how to run they computas better. And they be rollin' in tha scrilla, flashin' tha mad bling-bling, 'cause they problem-solvin' skeelz an networkin' solutionz be in crazy demand. What's worse, they got it in foe Daddy H an' all tha other officin' peoples what crunch numbas.

It all started afta work. I was in tha Nite Rida, cruisin' ova to Agnes' crib to pick up mah li'l shortie, Baby Prince H Tha Stone Col' Dopest Bizook-kizeepin' Muthafukkin' Badass Supastar Kornfeld II. Only, his no-good, dirty-ass ho of a mama call him by tha wack name she gave him, "Tanner." Huh. That boy ain't gonna do no tannin'. He gonna be a white-colla office highrolla like his daddy. Matta of fact, I wuz plannin' on takin' him to mah crib to show him mah computa wit' all tha def Microsoft Office 2000 software an' shit. Uh-huh. I even got Minesweeper on mah hard drive. I got it goin' ON.

But that wasn't tha only reason I went ova to Agnes' crib. I got wind from one a them fine bitchez in Marketing that Agnes be backin' that azz up foe some free-style computa consultin' sucka. Course, I ova her long ago, but I still don't like hearin' 'bout some fool gettin' his freak on wit' mah ex-bitch. So I head ova to Agnes' crib, figurin' he probably ova there an' that I can scares him off with a li'l flexin', know what I'm sayin'?

As I'm gettin' out of tha Nite Rida, I peeps some movement behind tha chain-link fence in front of Agnes' yard. I whips around wit' a quickness and see this pitiful li'l man starin' back at me like he a deer caught in tha headlights. Then he take off behind tha house, runnin' scared. Tha computa bitch! I leap tha fence like a muthafukkin' ninja an' trail his ass to

tha backyard patio, where mah shortie be kickin' back in his bassizinet an' Agnes be tendin' to tha gas grill an' stirrin' a big pitcha of Hi-C. So I says to tha computa bitch, "Time to throw down, muthafucka, 'cause y'all be bumpin' uglies wit' mah boo." Shit, he so scared, he looked like he wuz gonna piss his Cool-Max travel shorts. I wuz jus' messin' wit' tha fool, seein' what he wuz made of. But Agnes starts buggin' out, sayin', "Herbert, what are you doing here? I cannot believe you would come here uninvited and act like this around the baby! Leave right this instant, or I'm calling the police."

So I be like, "Yo, chill, bitch. S'cool. Show yo' shortie's babydaddy some respect."

Agnes want me gone, but mah bidness wit' Mr. Computa Bitch ain't finished. I aks tha fool his name, and he say it be Neil Sundquist. Then he try to impress tha H-Dog wit' some o' his computa jive, but I ain't havin' it. Save it foe tha suckas that be innerested in that boo-ya. Don't get me wrong: Lotus software be tha BOMB, an' a big shoutout to all tha homiez at Dell, 'cause all y'all help tha H-Dog do his thang in STYLE. But a real man don't make his livin' wit' his ass parked in front of a computa all day, know what I'm sayin'? It one thing to use a computa to assist you in yo' day-to-day bidness, but when tha computa be yo' whole hustle, that shit be WACK. Ever see what them computa bitchez do to numbas? It ain't natural. Numbas ain't supposed to be code, they supposed to quantify shit. I could go into it mo', but all that deep shit's probably way ova yo' head.

Anyway, I turns to Agnes an' say, "Get me a Hi-C, bitch." But instead of gettin' me a Hi-C, she start in on me again.

"Do you know what, Herbert?" she say. "Neil says that within the next five years, bookkeeping operations are going to be completely computerized in all but the smallest businesses, and Accounts Receivable and other such accounting departments will be rendered obsolete. Herbert, you haven't got a future."

"Izzat true, muthafucka?" I aks Neil.

"Well, I wouldn't have put it in quite the way Agnes did, Herbert," Neil say, all sweatin' an' stammerin'. "I mean, people still program the computers, and having people around with a solid foundation in accounting can only be a plus. What if there were a problem? An unforeseen glitch? Something not balancing? Someone with the keen troubleshooting skills borne of years of experience in accounting work could come in very handy in such situations."

"Ain't no errors now, muthafucka,"

I say. "I see to that. What tha point of havin' a fuckin' computa do all your accountin' if it gonna fuck up anyhow?"

Before Neil can say anythin', fuckin' Agnes butt in: "The answer is simple, Herbert: speed. A computer can crunch far more numbers than the fastest human in just a fraction of the time. Get with the program."

Now, normally, y'all, if a bitch mouthed off to me, I'd give her a smackdown. But there wuz sumthin' in what Agnes say that got me thinkin'. Ten yearz ago, when I wuz accountin' on tha streetz wit' mah homie an' mentor CPA-ONE (R.I.P., bro—mourn you 'til I join you), we wuz kickin' back wit' some Bartles & Jaymes wine coolas in tha parkin' lot of Northcentral Family Insurance. Tha quittin' time whistle blows, an' all tha flunkies come out, hop into they hooptys, an' blow outta there wit' a quickness. Tha last sucka to leave be this old-ass geeza. He had this hangdog look on his face, like he about to keel ova. He look even older than Myron Schabe an', man, thass OLD.

I start laughin' at tha geeza. "Check out that ol' dude," I say to CPA-ONE. "He belong in diapas."

"That ain't funny," CPA-ONE say to me. "Dog, I brought you to this 'hood so you could peep this guy. Back in tha day, he be tha king pimp of all tha accountantz. But now, they lettin' him go 'cause he can't get used to computas. He insists on kickin' it old school, an' he can't keep up wit tha young, computa-literate hustlas. So they canned his ass. Today his last day. He lost his retirement pension, his health benefitz—ev'rythang. He too old to get hired anyplace else. Shit, he be lucky if he land a gig mannin' tha condiment station at Taco John's."

CPA-ONE wanted to learn me a lesson, which wuz that you gotta stay on top of that computa shit if you wanna be a true playa on tha accountin' scene. So what Agnes say made me wonda if I wuz goin' tha

way of that Northcentral Family Insurance geeza. I always figured that by tha time computas an' robotz be doin' ever'body's work, I'd already be retired and livin' large in Branson, MO, chillin' wit' mah homies Roy Clark an' Jim Muthafukkin' Stafford.

But if what this computa-consultin' sucka say be true, tha H-Dog in trouble. Shit. An A.R. bruthah like me, I always looked at them Accountz Payabo foolz as tha enemy. I ain't never considered that maybe tha real enemy be computas.

But then it hit me: If mah hustle be threatened 'cause computas be makin' it obsolete, why can't tha same shit go down on muthafuckin' Neil Sundquist? One a these dayz, some young punk gonna step to him an' say, "Fuck all y'all, I gots tha mad skeelz, I know shit y'all ain't never even heard of, so step tha fuck OFF."

Yeah, H-Dog gonna be a-ight. Besides, it ain't tha H-Dog's style to doubt his skeelz.

Peep this: Accountz Receevable be my reality, y'all, and I'll put mah old-school accountin' skeelz up against a computa's any day. A computa may crunch numbas fasta, but it gonna have to go tha distance wit' me, 'cause tha H-Dog don't surrenda, know what I'm sayin'? It be like John Henry an' tha Inky Poo all ova again. Except I ain't gonna die like John Henry, Gs. I can journalize an' troubleshoot foreva, 'cause it my CALLIN'.

Numbas. Numbas. Numbas. They my true love anyway. Fuck everybody and everything else. Fuck them two-timin' freak-o'-the-weeks. Fuck them computa-consultin' bitchez who wanna wreck mah rep. Fuck computas. 'Cause when y'all get down to it, it only about one thing: tha ACCOUNTIN'. And, by tha way, don't think I about to go soft on them Accountz Payabo bitchez. Daddy H still has mad beef with all y'all. Fuck wit' me, and you WILL get sprayed Danny Lee-style. H-Dog OUT. ∅

AUTHOR from page 164

said. "I started a sci-fi novel about a young woman and the hardships she faces growing up in a uranium-mining colony on a sparsely populated planet in the Andromeda Galaxy. It didn't really pan out."

Kingley also attempted, without luck, to find inspiration in her more recent struggles.

"I thought I could get at least a short story out of the time my car broke down last year," Kingley said. "The opening paragraphs about the smoking, stalled car sitting on the shoulder of the highway were pretty good, but it kind of lost momentum when I got to the part about

being approved for a loan and picking out a Saturn with my friend from grad school."

The experience of trying to finish "Curls Of Smoke On A Highway" made Kingley realize her recent life may not be suitable for novelization.

"Pretty much everything after 1990 is a wash," Kingley said. "That's when I landed my writing residency at the University of New Mexico. After that came my book deal. Then I got married, and my husband and I bought a house. So, right now, my only hope is giving birth to an autistic child. I'll keep my fingers crossed." ∅

Human Rights And The U.S.

Recently ousted from the U.N. Human Rights Commission, the U.S. is no longer the world's human-rights leader, according to Amnesty International. What do *you* think?

"Doesn't Amnesty International realize we have covert black-op specialists who shoot people for saying that kind of stuff?"

Allen Andrews
Systems Analyst

"I'd like to applaud the forward-thinking nations of Angola, Sudan, and Syria for helping vote the U.S. off the U.N. commission. Truly, your countries are examples to us all."

Duane McHenry
Doctor

"Fine, I'll let the guy out of my basement. Will that fix this up?"

Stan Tocchet
Landscaper

"I guess our nation's leaders have given up trying to impress sexy, politically active college chicks."

Ron Bass
Cashier

"I support whatever Amnesty International has to say. I have to: They sent me those free return-address labels."

Paulette Wilson
Librarian

"America makes the best movies, the best TV shows, and the best snack foods. We can't do *everything*."

Dana Milbank
Real-Estate Agent

Yoga Nation

Yoga is more popular than ever in the U.S. Why are so many Americans taking up the practice?

- Want to tap into ancient wisdom of Californians
- Heard yoga helps improve breathing; cannot currently breathe
- Have been trapped in full lotus position since 1989 bicycle accident, decided to make the most of it
- Hoping to one day fit into small plastic box
- Enables many Americans, for first time, to sit very still without watching TV
- That dishy Indian prime minister Atal Behari Vajpayee is into it
- Features slightly better music than step aerobics
- Went vegetarian last year, but life still doesn't suck enough

the ONION
America's Finest News Source

Herman Ulysses Zweibel *Founder*

T. Herman Zweibel *Publisher Emeritus*
J. Phineas Zweibel *Publisher*
Maxwell Prescott Zweibel *Editor-In-Chief*

FOUNDED 1871 • "TU STULTUS ES"

Your Horoscope

By Lloyd Schumner Sr.
Retired Machinist and
A.A.P.B.-Certified Astrologer

Aries: (March 21–April 19)
You will realize that just because an idea comes to you in a dream doesn't make it any good after spending millions establishing a projectile-flooring business.

Taurus: (April 20–May 20)
You've stuck to your diet and deserve a reward. Let yourself come between an enraged mother polar bear and her cubs just this once.

Gemini: (May 21–June 21)
After discovering the lost manuscript to George Orwell's *1975*, you are silenced by the government for knowing subversively kitschy secrets.

Cancer: (June 22–July 22)
Some things only become funny when you look back on them years later. Next Wednesday, however, will seem funny almost instantly.

Leo: (July 23–Aug. 22)
Your impromptu conga line across the Mideast will somehow fail to bring peace to the region.

Virgo: (Aug. 23–Sept. 22)
Not to make you feel any worse, but even Virgo knows that drawing to fill an inside straight is a bad idea. Idiot.

Libra: (Sept. 23–Oct. 23)
You will be praised by needy upper-middle-class families everywhere when you found the first charity dedicated to helping the vacation-home-less.

Scorpio: (Oct. 24–Nov. 21)
You will be metaphorically drawn and quartered after misusing the word "literally" four times in one conversation.

Sagittarius: (Nov. 22–Dec. 21)
Your word will never be bond again when you violate your age-old vow never to be caught dead in beige pumps.

Capricorn: (Dec. 22–Jan. 19)
You will witness many instances of comedy as a delightful, if unexpected, secondary benefit of next week's floor-buttering experiment.

Aquarius: (Jan. 20–Feb. 18)
Remember: You didn't become a screen-door-factory worker for the money or the fame. Remind yourself of this constantly.

Pisces: (Feb. 19–March 20)
You will spend an entire day in New York City without meeting a soul. You will, however, meet dozens of actual people.

PLOVIS from page 47

were amazed by the unusually large amounts of blood. Passersby were amazed by the unusually large amounts of blood. Passersby were amazed by the unusually large amounts of blood. Passersby were amazed by the unusually large amounts of blood. Passersby were amazed by the unusually large amounts of blood. Passersby were amazed by the unusually large amounts of blood. Passersby were amazed by the unusually large amounts of blood. Passersby were amazed by the unusually large amounts of blood. Passersby were amazed by the unusually large amounts of blood. Passersby were amazed by the unusually large amounts of blood. Passersby were amazed by the unusually large amounts of blood. Passersby were amazed by the unusually large amounts of blood. Passersby were amazed by the unusually large amounts of blood. Passersby were amazed by the unusually large amounts of blood. Passersby were amazed by the unusually large amounts of blood. Passersby were amazed

by the unusually large amounts of blood. Passersby were amazed by the unusually large amounts of blood. Passersby were amazed by the unusually large amounts of blood. Passersby were amazed by the unusually large amounts

My plasma should be worth more than that.

of blood. Passersby were amazed by the unusually large amounts of blood. Passersby were amazed by the unusually large amounts of blood. Passersby were amazed by the unusually large amounts of blood. Passersby were amazed by the unusually large amounts of blood. Passersby were amazed by the unusually large amounts of blood. Passersby were amazed by the unusually large amounts of blood. Passersby were amazed by
see PLOVIS page 176

Federal Prison System Retires McVeigh's Number

see NATION page 5A

Hammered Office Depot Manager Thrown Out Of Chili's

see LOCAL page 7C

Married Paramedics Bickering Over Best Way To Restart Heart

see LOCAL page 4C

STATshot

A look at the numbers that shape your world.

How Big Are Our Bongs?

1. Like, *this* big
2. Huuuuge
3. 1,000 millibongs
4. So big I'm just an atom in it
5. Same size as Mrs. Butterworth
6. Four Jerrywidths
7. Oh, wow

the ONION®

VOLUME 37 ISSUE 22   AMERICA'S FINEST NEWS SOURCE™   14-20 JUNE 2001

Non-Controversial Christ Painting Under Fire From Art Community

Above: Members of the art world gather outside the Whitney Museum to protest "Jesus Rising #4" (below).

NEW YORK—Miguel Nunez, a Brooklyn-based artist, has sparked protest and outrage within the art community with his "Jesus Rising #4," a non-controversial, non-feces-smeared painting that in no way defiles or blasphemes Jesus Christ.

"Jesus Rising #4," included in Nunez's new *Divinity* exhibition at the Whitney Museum, has received harsh criticism from artists and

academics since its June 6 debut. The painting has been picketed nearly around the clock by angry protesters, who say they are stunned by its lack of obscene imagery metaphorically conveying a provocative, highly charged theopolitical message.

"Why isn't this [painting] splattered with donkey semen?" asked sculptor India Jackson, one of the

see ART page 170

Above: Metzler behind the Slipped Discs counter.

Nation In Love With Girl From Record Store

ATHENS, GA—Captivated by her adorability and off-the-charts hipness, the U.S. populace sheepishly admitted a deep infatuation with 22-year-old Danielle Metzler, that amazing girl with the multi-colored hair who works at Slipped Discs in Athens.

"God, she is so fucking unbelievably cute," Sam Kiefer of Euclid, OH, said Monday. "The last time she was wearing these super-tight silver pants and this rhinestone-studded New York Dolls half-shirt, and I was just like, 'Wow.'"

Metzler was first spotted at Slipped Discs, an independently owned store stocked with a wide selection of indie rock, hip-hop, electronica, and otherwise hard-to-find music, in September 1999. Ever since, the nation has had a major crush on the girl.

see GIRL page 171

Gay Man Really Respects Dolly Parton For All She's Been Through

KANSAS CITY, MO—Rich Fontenot, a Kansas City-area homosexual and longtime Dolly Parton fan, announced Monday that he "totally respects" Parton for all she's been through.

"Dolly's been to hell and back, and she's come out smiling," said Fontenot, holding up a glossy 8x10 photo purchased at Silver Screen Memories, a Kansas City movie-memorabilia store. "That woman is a true survivor."

The country-music legend,

Fontenot said, grew up with 10 siblings in a tiny shack in Sevierville, TN, her family barely having enough to eat.

"Now Dolly has, like, a zillion dollars, and everyone in the world knows who she is," Fontenot said. "She owns that whole Dollywood thing up in Pigeon Forge. But she started with absolutely nothing. Nobody gave her a thing when she

see PARTON page 172

Right: The Parton-loving Fontenot.

169

Everything Better Now In Oklahoma City

OKLAHOMA CITY, OK—Timothy McVeigh's death by lethal injection Monday has made everything perfect in Oklahoma City, his 168 victims' loved ones describing themselves as feeling "100 percent better." "I just know my baby girl is up there in heaven, smiling down on this execution, happy as can be," said a beaming George Browne, whose 7-year-old daughter Brianna died in the 1995 federal-building blast. "Her death is avenged, and everything's great." Said Oklahoma City schoolteacher Sherrie Olsacher, 37, who was blinded in the bombing: "You can't imagine how healing this is. My eyesight's even returned." Moments after McVeigh was pronounced dead, 168 white doves were seen soaring over the city, racing toward a suddenly cloudless horizon that beckoned the dawn of a glorious new day.

Woman Puts Cool Whip Containers To Every Conceivable Use

TERRE HAUTE, IN—According to neighbors, Terre Haute homemaker Barb Lake puts empty Cool Whip non-dairy whipped-topping tubs to a staggering array of uses. "She stores leftovers in them, pots plants in them, keeps sewing supplies in them," next-door neighbor Paula Brearly said Monday. "Last year, she made Halloween masks with them. Oh, and she turned them into musical instruments for her daughter's Brownie troop." Brearly added that she has "no clue" how Lake manages to go through so much Cool Whip in the first place.

Partygoer Vows To Fix Keg

CHARLOTTESVILLE, VA—Insisting that calling the liquor store for assistance is "totally unnecessary," University of Virginia sophomore and house-party attendee Josh Pelham heroically vowed to fix a broken keg himself Monday. "Everybody, just have the MGDs in the fridge for now—I'll figure this out quick," said Pelham, standing over the far-from-tapped keg. "My brother did this once with, like, a wrench. Is there a wrench around?" Over the course of the next hour, Pelham went on to request a coat hanger, a kitchen knife, and a crowbar.

Astronomers Admit They Made Neptune Up

LONDON—An elaborate, 155-year-old hoax was revealed Monday, when the Royal Astronomical Society confessed that the planet Neptune does not exist. "It appears to have begun in 1846, when Johann Galle needed a big discovery to give his career a jump-start, so he fabricated this new planet," said Royal Astronomical Society president N.O. Weiss. "Ever since, every astronomer who's wanted some attention has come up with some new report on 'Neptune' and made up some rubbish to support it. I swear, we meant to come clean eventually, but the whole thing just kind of snowballed."

Vatican Declares Hours Between 3 A.M., 5:30 A.M. 'Ungodly'

VATICAN CITY—In the first papal edict against a time of day since 1560, Pope John Paul II declared the two-and-a-half-hour interval between 3 and 5:30 a.m. "wholly ungodly." "If a man dares to come home during these demonic hours, he shall be declared anathema," said His Holiness. "Likewise, anyone calling during these hours shall face excommunication." The Pope added that in some cases, devout Catholics may receive special dispensation from a priest in a different time zone. ∅

ART from page 169

protesters. "And I defy anyone to find a trace of urine, human or otherwise, on this entire canvas. The piece does not appear to be an enraged howl against Christian patriarchal hegemony at all.

> "The piece does not appear to be an enraged howl against Christian patriarchal hegemony at all."

Frankly, I'm shocked."

"It's the duty of all artists to expose Judeo-Christian brutality through images of Christ engaged in acts of masturbation, rape, and torture," said Diana Bloom-Mutter, curator of New York's Rhone Gallery. "When I look at a painting of Christ, it's supposed to make me say to the person standing next to me, 'Yes, this is obscene, but do you know what's *really* obscene? Two thousand years of white, male oppression in the name of God.'"

Other detractors point out the "outrageous, inexcusable absence" of subversive commentary on the pervasiveness of materialism in our consumer culture.

"[Nunez] could have had a field

Above: Jean Arbus' celebrated 1997 mixed-media piece "Crucifuckwad," a work the art community says stands in sharp contrast to Nunez's "repulsive non-filth."

day with this subject," said Martin Meyer, a 1960s art-world sensation who made his name with such Pop Art works as "Mother (Rheingold Beer Ad)" and "General Le Duc Tho Wouldn't Trust Anything Less Than Oxydol For His Wash." "Divinity and materialism are practically one and the same in today's world. Instead of Jesus on his throne, why not place him atop a pile of DVD

see ART page 173

Surgeon General: Americans Have Gigantic Fat Asses

WASHINGTON, DC—According to a report released Monday by the Surgeon General's office, 67 percent of U.S. citizens have gigantic fat asses, with that number projected to climb significantly in the next decade.

The report is the latest in a string of dire findings from Sur-

Wellness Watch

geon General David Satcher concerning the high percentage of Americans who suffer from fatness of ass.

"The state of the American derriere has reached crisis proportions," Satcher said. "Without immediate steps to rectify this problem, we can only foresee even more hideously huge backsides as we continue to blimp out into the 21st century."

The strongly worded report, in which Americans are alternately described as "porkers," "wide loads," and "friggin' whales," attributes the fat asses primarily to poor eating habits, with diets heavy in sugar, starches, and saturated fats.

Above: One of the 185 million fat asses that dot the American landscape.

It also cites Americans' lack of exercise and sedentary lifestyles as factors in the trend toward "huge bucket-butts."

In addition, the report found that roughly 185 million Americans are "flab-ass flabbos who couldn't say no to a candy bar if their fat, stupid lives depended on it." It went on to warn that those with "gargantuan, sun-blocking rear ends" stand at greater risk of conditions ranging from heart disease to hideousness.

The Surgeon General said the solution to the national health crisis lies in obese citizens "somehow dredging up the shred of dignity needed to drag their rotund, repellent posteriors to a gym, for Christ's sake." He also encouraged

see FAT ASSES page 172

GIRL from page 169

"[Metzler] works at the coolest record store in Athens, and she's totally up on all the latest stuff," said Ryan Griggs, 48, a television repairman from Salem, OR. "You have no idea how many people go in there every day and buy some obscure Go-Betweens B-sides collection or the latest Stephin Merritt side project just to try to impress her."

Griggs recently purchased Toby Dammit's vinyl-only *Gopher Edits* EP—a highly successful move which prompted Metzler to ask about the record.

"I couldn't believe it," Griggs said. "For 45 glorious seconds, it was just me and her talking about bands like Tipsy and Jazzanova."

Residents of the Florida panhandle admitted that their own attempts to impress Metzler were less successful.

"I heard her talking to someone about these great new Boredoms remixes, so I bought the one by U.N.K.L.E.," Pensacola's Andy Nichols said. "I don't even own a single original Boredoms album, but I now have an import remix I paid $30 for."

Continued Nichols: "When she

> **Upon discovering they were not the only ones with a long-standing crush on Metzler, residents of the Midwest came forward with their own tales of longing for the girl.**

was ringing up the U.N.K.L.E. thing, I said, 'These are supposed to be really good.' So she says, 'Yeah, but if you're not going to get them all, the DJ Krush is really the one to go with.' I was like, oh, great. But then she gave me this really big smile, and it was all worth it."

Upon discovering they were not the only ones with a long-standing

crush on Metzler, residents of the Midwest came forward with their own tales of longing for the girl, sharing everything from the time she wore that really tight Le Tigre T-shirt to the time she danced to Cheap Trick's "Southern Girls" as it played on the store's stereo.

"Once, she was reaching up to grab a CD for a customer, and I noticed maybe half an inch of leopard-print underwear peeking out of the back of her hip-huggers," said Carl Mills, a Beloit, WI, truck driver. "That was a year ago, and I still remember it."

Josh Starkes of Boise, ID, is among the few Americans who know the girl's name.

"I was hanging around the store one afternoon, and I heard one of her coworkers say, 'Hey, Dani, could you grab me a few of the new Dirty Three/Low from the back?'" Starkes recalled. "Turns out, her name is Danielle, but she goes by 'Dani,' and sometimes even 'Dan.' On the employee-suggestion rack, it says, 'Dan's Pick Of The Week.' I mean, how cool is that?"

According to millions of Americans, unlike many of the other

clerks at Slipped Discs, Metzler never asks if you need help finding anything. Even if you make it obvious that you are struggling to find a particular record, she will remain by the front counter, talking and laughing with a select crowd of visitors.

"I was in there, and I recognized this one guy talking to her as the lead singer from [Athens band] Corky Thatcher," said Dave Douglas of Riverside, CA. "I can never figure out if all these people hanging out are her actual friends or just people she's deemed cool enough to talk to her. And, if the latter is the case, how do I become one of those people? Oh, who am I kidding? I don't stand a chance."

Despite such insecurities, the people of Southern California say the mixture of desire and insecurity associated with a trip to Slipped Discs is "exhilarating."

"I wanted to get the first Modern Lovers album, but I didn't want her to know I didn't already own it," said Jody Osbourne of San Diego. "To cover up, I told her some big, long story about how my friend is such a jerk because he borrowed it a long

see GIRL page 173

You Hurt Me Just Now When You Hit Me With That Shovel

By Louis Granger

We've known each other for a long time now, and I think you know I'd never try to stop you from expressing what you feel. But I also have to express what *I'm* feeling, and what I'm feeling is hurt. Badly. I just want you to know that you really hurt me when you hit me in the face with that shovel.

I've tried hard not to let my pain show, but it's not easy. Maybe you can tell by the sad, confused expression I wear these days. Or the rivers of blood streaming down my face. But since you don't seem to realize what you've done, I guess I have to come right out and tell you that your actions have caused harm.

I realize empathy isn't your strong suit. Let me assure you, though, that getting walloped in the side of the face with a steel shovel hurts. Is that what you intended to do—hurt me? Believe me, I've tried my best to give you

What you've given me is a wound that may never heal.

the benefit of the doubt. Maybe you were just trying to get my attention. Maybe you were showing off how good you are at swinging shovels. Or maybe you were signaling an airplane with it and lost control, sending it careening into the side of my skull. I hope so. But my gut instinct says your intent was to cause me pain, and I think you should know you did.

It's going to take a long time to get over this. This isn't something that just goes away. It'd be nice if the healing process were fast, but it'll probably be at least six months. This isn't the first time I've been hurt by someone I cared for, so I know what I'm talking about. What you've given me is a wound that may never heal. Even if it does, the scars will remain.

You owe it to me to at least talk about why you did what you did. Something like this will just fester if we try to pretend it never happened. If we ignore it, the six-inch gash in my cheek will get infected, bubbling over with gangrenous pus. But if, on the other hand, we work hard to make things better, with some time, understanding, and good old-fashioned reconstructive surgery, things might one day go back to the way they were. Especially around my left eye socket.

It's really just a matter of trust.

And right now, I honestly don't trust you with a shovel anymore.

Okay, so maybe you didn't mean to hurt me as severely as you did. In moments of anger, people often don't realize the power of their actions. They don't understand that braining someone with a blunt object can really do harm. They just want to lash out, figuring you're more resilient than you really are. But now you can see that human beings, at their core, are fragile creatures. They *can* break. They *can* have their cheekbones shattered.

Look, we're all wounded creatures in our own way. No one goes through life without enduring his share of hurt and pain. But we owe it to each other to try to minimize that trauma, be it heart or head. So, next time you feel the urge to lash out at me, be it with a cruel remark or a nine-pound spade, remember that I bleed, just like you. ∅

PARTON from page 169

was first coming up."

"You've got to have some pretty tough skin to make it in this world," Fontenot added. "Well, Dolly said, 'I'm not gonna let anybody knock me down,' and she didn't. Talk about courage."

In addition to her wildly successful singing career, Parton has made a name for herself in acting, an achievement Fontenot attributes to her "take-no-crap" attitude.

"Instead of being all worried about fitting into some Hollywood-prescribed mold of what a star is supposed to be, she just said, 'I'm me, and if you don't like it, you can stick it where the sun don't shine!' And you know what? It worked! In *9 To 5* and *Steel Magnolias*, she was simply fabulous."

A major part of Parton's appeal, Fontenot said, is her willingness to take risks with her image.

"Every time you see Dolly, she's totally working it with the spangles and the sequins and the full-on hair up to here," said Fontenot, motioning nearly a foot above his head. "It's as if she's saying, 'I don't care what you think—I'm doing this for *me*.' It just makes you want to shout, 'You go, girl!' You have to respect someone who's not afraid to be herself like that."

Though he generally prefers dance music, Fontenot admitted that he has a "major soft spot for the

country divas."

"Besides Dolly, there's Wynonna and Reba and, of course, Patsy," Fontenot said. "That woman was the queen, absolutely the queen. But Dolly can belt them out just like Patsy could. And whom do we owe

Though he generally prefers dance music, Fontenot admitted that he has a "major soft spot for the country divas."

for writing Whitney Houston's 'I Will Always Love You'? That's right, Dolly Parton. I love Whitney's version, but nobody can do that one like Dolly. She owns that song."

Most of Fontenot's friends agreed with his assessment of Parton.

"Me, Todd, and Marco were hanging out at Rods one night, and a see **PARTON** page 173

FAT ASSES from page 171

those with American Fat-Ass Syndrome, or AFAS, to "lay off the sour-cream-and-chive Ruffles."

The report has provoked outrage among the public at large.

"Okay, so we could all stand to lose a few pounds, but I don't see the need for such insulting language," said Nancy Goode, 48, a morbidly obese St. Cloud, MN, housewife with diabetes, knee problems, and an ass so ludicrously huge it looks like some sort of mutant, land-bound dugong. "Besides, lots of people in this country are very slim and attractive. I see them on TV every day."

Experts say Goode's response is symptomatic of the severe denial inherent in most Americans' self-images.

"Because of what they see on television and in advertising, many Americans are convinced that the nation is largely populated with hot, hard-bodied models who consume nothing but Pepsi and Cheetos," said Secretary of Health and Human Services Tommy Thompson. "This notion, however, couldn't be further from the truth. All you need to do is look around to see that we are, in the main, grotesque, repulsive fat fucks who have long ago given up maintaining a mote of basic pride."

Though the alarmist tone of the report may come as a shock to Americans accustomed to the enor-

mous asses of themselves and their neighbors, the rest of the world has long been aware of Americans' ovoid lower halves. This is apparent in the translations of various languages' popular slang terms for Americans, such as "two-sacks-of-

"The time has come for Americans to face the truth about our collective fat ass," Satcher said.

suet-in-skirts," from Swedish; "bloated round-eye balloon-buttocks," from Mandarin Chinese; and "hideous, hellbound hippo-humans," from Swahili.

"The time has come for Americans to face the truth about our collective fat ass," Satcher said. "For too long, we have sat on our massive rump, mindlessly consuming 90 percent of the world's resources and growing steadily bigger by the decade. It's time to get off that fat ass and face the harsh reality of our enormous, distended, disgusting hind ends." ∅

I Have Been Too Generous With My Gum

By Roger Barney

I love gum. Anyone who spends time around me knows this to be true. No matter where I am, whether in my home or office or car, I always have at least three or four packs around me. From Big Red to Chiclets, from Trident to Plen-T-Paks of Juicy Fruit, I'm never far from a fresh stick of delicious chewing gum. Yes, I love gum and always have plen-T of it on hand.

But, as rich as I am in gum, I'm equally rich in friends and acquaintances who are aware of my gum supply and don't hesitate to ask for a piece if the need arises. This is usually not a problem: I am a generous man by nature and feel gum should be shared freely among those in need. However, there are times when the line between generosity and exploitation is crossed, and steps must be taken to drive the line-crossers back.

I must hold fast to my gum.

I admit, I'm partially at fault. I've established myself as someone who is extremely charitable with his gum, always holding it aloft and asking if anyone is in need of a piece. Always asking those around me if they, too, would like a chewy strip seemingly forged in heaven itself. In the face of such temptation, it is only natural for

> ## Many around me seem to think that I am the planet's sole gum distributor.

one to be seduced by its minty or fruity allure.

Who among you can resist a piece of gum? Apparently, very few, for when I raise the blue, gleaming beacon that is a package of Wrigley's winterfresh Extra, virtually all heed its call. Like jackals descending upon a fresh kill, a crowd forms around me, arms outstretched and mouths open, eager to wrap their tongues around Extra's sweet, refreshing blend of sorbitol, gum base, glycerol, mannitol, acesulfame k, softeners, aspartame, BHT, Maltitol, and natural and artificial flavors. I admit, it's a difficult recipe to resist, and I, for one, wouldn't ask anyone to. I merely ask for a little courtesy and respect.

Many around me seem to think that I am the planet's sole gum distributor. No, I am merely a fan, a gum enthusiast who savors the sweet allure of a freshly unwrapped stick. While I am more than happy to share my bounty, I do not wish to be depended upon 100 percent of the time. Why is it that no one has the temerity to pick up their own gum at the local shop? Is a man really a man who does not equip himself with his needs at the beginning of the day? Why, then, do those who often crave gum not procure themselves some, instead of relying solely upon the generosity of those with the forethought to do so?

A clarification is in order: Most do not take my gum for granted. Most of my family, friends, and coworkers are decent folk who do not abuse my charitable nature, taking my gum sparingly and with a good measure of appreciation. It is that small handful of others, however, upon whom I train my wrath, those who feel that a daily stick of my gum is their birthright, earned merely by being in my presence. They're the ones who promise to return the favor with sticks and entire packs of gum, to be given to me at some unspecified future date. I must say, for the record, that not a single piece of Everest or Dubble Bubble has been repaid by these charlatans, their lies laid bare by the passage of time.

The burden placed upon me by my own magnanimity is one I can bear. I am repaid merely by the smiles, the happy chewing and sweetened breath of those around me. But the frenzy of demand for my gum has gotten out of control. My only thought to correct this is to decrease the supply so that I run out. However, logic and simple economics suggest this might not be the best course of action, as it would only serve to further drive up demand. Plus, I delight in the knowledge that one can rely upon me for a piece of icy cool gum when needed. Yes, for now, I shall suffer the indignities of the few for the good of the many. As a true gum lover, this is my stick to bear. ∅

ART from page 170

players? Instead of gold, frankincense, and myrrh, why not three wise men bearing Cuisinarts, Nokia cell phones, and PlayStations?"

Still others criticized Nunez's failure to make himself part of the work.

"In my 1997 piece 'Shitrock Salad (Eat 'Em Upp) #79,' I placed myself in a sealed plexiglass coffin for eight days with only a slender tube providing me air, while maggots writhed about my ranch-dressing-covered body," performance artist Eugene Weaver said. "While I admit 'Jesus Rising' shows some skill in composition and color, I think Nunez could have made a far more powerful statement by scourging his naked flesh with broken glass, rolling in a bed of salt, and crucifying himself on an old metal mattress frame."

Among the few members of the art community to come to the embattled painting's defense is *New York Times* art critic Michael Kimmelman, who called it "a friskily post-postmodern tour-de-force."

"At first glance, 'Jesus Rising #4' seems to be a competent if unremarkable devotional work," Kimmelman said. "But look deeper, and you find that Nunez's main objective is to challenge our preconceptions to the very core. The beatific visage of Jesus seems to echo the most shopworn Sunday School homilies, but the clichés of religious art are so vigorously rendered that the viewer comes to realize that this is not a work of slavish iconography at all, but a shrewd comment on our spiritual limitations."

Continued Kimmelman: "Yet Nunez does not spare the Existentialists and the Modernists, either. They once somberly proclaimed that 'God is dead,' but Nunez rejects this, too. His conclusion? 'God is nice.'"

In spite of the uproar over "Jesus Rising #4," Whitney Museum director Maxwell Anderson said he is committed to keeping the work on display. He is, however, willing to "open a dialogue" with the protesters.

"Perhaps we can reach some sort of compromise," Anderson said. "I don't want to go so far as to soak the painting in the menstrual blood of a 13-year-old girl, as some have demanded, but I'm open to other suggestions. We might be able to scare up a pint or two of rhino vomit to splash on the canvas. And I know candied yams can be mashed into a nice, viscous paste and spread pretty easily. Personally, I like the painting as it is, but if a little shock is all it takes to calm everybody down, I'm all for it." ∅

GIRL from page 171

time ago and never gave it back. When I was done with this four-minute spiel, she just said, 'I hate Jonathan Richman.' I wanted to curl up in a ball and die."

While it's unknown whether Metzler has a boyfriend, the American people have always assumed she does.

"Whenever I see her out at a show, she's always surrounded by this pack of slim-hipped, good-looking hipster guys," said Jesse Avery of Roseville, MI. "She's never hanging on any one in particular, but one of them has got to be her boyfriend."

The nation has no plans to try to advance its relationship with Metzler beyond that of customer and clerk, saying it prefers to worship her from afar.

"She's way out of my league, and even if I could get her to like me—which I couldn't—it would only cause problems," said Earl Shaw, 36, a Gulfport, MS, actuary. "When a girl has so many guys fawning over her, she's bound to want her way with everything."

Continued Shaw: "That is, unless she was sick of all the rock 'n' roll assholes she dates and was ready for someone who doesn't fit into that mold. Maybe she is. Maybe she's looking for someone a little smarter than those guys—someone like me."

Shaw added that maybe he could even learn to play bass guitar.

Informed of the nation's crush, Metzler shrugged her shoulders. "That's cool," she said, "but lately I've been more into British guys." She then returned to sorting CDs. ∅

PARTON from page 172

Dolly Parton Christmas special came on TV," said close Fontenot friend Andrew Lord. "We all sat there completely mesmerized. I swear, that woman's got as much stage presence as Cher. Maybe more."

Despite Parton's glamorous image, Fontenot noted that she is remarkably down-to-earth. This, he said, is central to her appeal.

"For all her fame and fortune, Dolly's never lost touch with her roots," Fontenot said. "At heart, she's still that same old country girl from Sevierville. I even heard that her husband is just a regular guy, a construction worker. You know, rough hands and big muscles and the whole bit. Who wouldn't want to be Dolly?" ∅

The $3 Billion Judgment

Last week, a Los Angeles jury ordered Philip Morris to pay $3 billion in punitive damages to a longtime smoker who has lung cancer. What do *you* think?

"Three *billion* dollars? I'm switching to non-filters right away."

Vijay Thakker
Cashier

"When this guy started smoking 40 years ago, people had no idea it was bad for you. People had to guess based on the hacking cough, shortness of breath, and bloody phlegm."

Donna Lafarge
Interior Decorator

"Shouldn't Bic have to pay for making the lighters that made the cigarettes deadly in the first place?"

Marcus Alberts
Systems Analyst

"Three billion for endangering the guy's life? Christ, Philip Morris could've had him killed for a measly ten grand."

Paulette Wilson
Librarian

"Finally, America's educational system is getting the funding it so desperately needs. What? The $3 billion is going to a smoker? Oh."

Lisa Koenig
Cellist

"This is a victory for everyone without a shred of common sense."

Donald Astbury
Investment Banker

Energy-Drink Mania

Sales of high-caffeine "energy drinks" like Red Bull are soaring. Why are the beverages so popular?

- Slightly less expensive than crystal meth
- Just like Mountain Dew, but healthy because of some Chinese thing called gualooga or something
- Give users strength of 10 lumberjacks who have also consumed energy drinks
- Easier to open than a battery
- Tired of getting energy in pill or powder form
- Vaguely recall reading something about taurine in June issue of *Men's Health*
- Want to get in on trend before negative side effects discovered
- Temporarily endows drinker with sense of drive and purpose
- Tiny little cans make drinkers feel like giants among men
- Combines secrets of Eastern medicine and Western marketing

the ONION

America's Finest News Source

Herman Ulysses Zweibel *Founder*

T. Herman Zweibel *Publisher Emeritus*
J. Phineas Zweibel *Publisher*
Maxwell Prescott Zweibel *Editor-In-Chief*

FOUNDED 1871 • "TU STULTUS ES"

Your Horoscope

By Lloyd Schumner Sr.
Retired Machinist and
A.A.P.B.-Certified Astrologer

Aries: (March 21–April 19)
Your decision to put on a show to save the old malt shop will result in your arrest for public nudity, indecent behavior, and violation of six health codes.

Taurus: (April 20–May 20)
The stars indicate that this is a good time to start new projects. At the same time, your neighbor's dog indicates it's a good time to kill young couples.

Gemini: (May 21–June 21)
A cake, some candles, and a few token gifts will soon mark your passage into an exciting new demographic.

Cancer: (June 22–July 22)
Though you're getting pretty good at interpreting your dreams, you're still piss-poor at interpreting things that happen when you're awake.

Leo: (July 23–Aug. 22)
The story of your life has been quiet so far, but don't worry: They've decided to cut out a bunch of boring exposition and get right to the final bloody chase scene.

Virgo: (Aug. 23–Sept. 22)
Your decision to go back to nature conveniently ignores the fact that you're not from nature, but Los Angeles.

Libra: (Sept. 23–Oct. 23)
Being a parent is a new challenge every day. The specific challenge next Monday is explaining why you had to nail the puppies to the ceiling-fan blades.

Scorpio: (Oct. 24–Nov. 21)
After sleeping with someone who is not your spouse, you will suffer horrible guilt, which would be understandable if you were married.

Sagittarius: (Nov. 22–Dec. 21)
You're known as a really decent character. This is because you are a D&D character named Gryth The Decent.

Capricorn: (Dec. 22–Jan. 19)
James Joyce's *Ulysses* put forth the idea that every one of us is a hero just for getting through an average day in our lives. Congratulations, hero.

Aquarius: (Jan. 20–Feb. 18)
It's said that life is like a bowl of cherries. But for most people, the metaphor breaks down faster than it does for you.

Pisces: (Feb. 19–March 20)
It turns out that intellectual awareness of the consequences of putting your hand in a meat grinder is very different from the actual experience.

TONGUE from page 29

were amazed by the unusually large amounts of blood. Passersby were amazed by the unusually large amounts of blood. Passersby were amazed by the unusually large amounts of blood. Passersby were amazed by the unusually large amounts of blood. Passersby were amazed by the unusually large amounts of blood. Passersby were amazed by the unusually large amounts of blood. Passersby were amazed by the unusually large amounts of blood. Passersby were amazed by the unusually large amounts of blood. Passersby were amazed by the unusually large amounts of blood. Passersby were amazed by the unusually large amounts of blood. Passersby were amazed by the unusually large amounts of blood. Passersby were amazed by the unusually large amounts of blood. Passersby were amazed by the unusually large amounts of blood. Passersby were amazed by the unusually large amounts of blood. Passersby were amazed by the unusually large amounts of blood. Passersby were amazed by the unusually large amounts of blood. Passersby were amazed by the unusually large amounts of blood. Passersby were amazed by the unusually large amounts

of blood. Passersby were amazed by the unusually large amounts of blood. Passersby were amazed by the unusually large amounts of blood. Passersby were amazed by the unusually large amounts of blood. Passersby were amazed by the unusually large amounts

I like to think that, overall, I'm a pretty intolerant person.

of blood. Passersby were amazed by the unusually large amounts of blood. Passersby were amazed by the unusually large amounts of blood. Passersby were amazed by the unusually large amounts of blood. Passersby were amazed by the unusually large amounts of blood. Passersby were amazed by the unusually large amounts of blood. Passersby were amazed by the unusually large amounts

see TONGUE page 189

Jenna Bush's Federally Protected Wetlands Now Open For Public Drilling

see NATION page 3A

SORRY YOU ARE NOT A WINNER

Opening Soda Bottle Inadvertently Makes Man Loser

see LOCAL page 4D

Keebler Elves Multiracial All Of A Sudden

see PRODUCTWATCH page 10B

THE ONION
VOLUME 37
ISSUE 23
$2.00 US
$3.00 CAN

74470 94595 6

the ONION®

VOLUME 37 ISSUE 23   AMERICA'S FINEST NEWS SOURCE™   21-27 JUNE 2001

Nobel Fever Grips Research Community As Prize Swells To $190 Million

STOCKHOLM—The Nobel Prize in Physiology or Medicine, unclaimed in 2000, has climbed to a staggering $190 million, setting off a frenzy of research and publication among scientists.

"This is very exciting," said Sweden's King Carl XVI Gustaf, who will announce the winner of the Nobel Prize at a gala July 20 ceremony in Stockholm. "One lucky scientist will never have to do another research project for the rest of his life."

Scientists around the globe are submitting their studies to the Nobel committee in the hopes of striking it rich.

"I think I've got a real shot at the grand prize with my genomewide scan of 200 families with hereditary prostate cancer that can be used to identify regions of putative prostate-cancer-susceptibility loci," said Dr. Henry Chu, a Duke University geneticist. "Man, if that comes through, I'm hanging the 'Gone Fishin'' sign on my laboratory door and never looking back."

Medical and scientific journals have been deluged with submissions from researchers clamoring to be published before the Nobel drawing.

see NOBEL page 179

Above: King Carl XVI Gustaf keeps an eye on the Nobel jackpot.

WORLD FOCUS

Northern Irish, Serbs, Hutus Granted Homeland In West Bank

The New Homeland

SYRIA

Mediterranean Sea

JORDAN

Tel Aviv

ETHNIKLASHISTAN

Jerusalem

Gaza Strip

ISRAEL

Basques
Chechens
Greek Cypriots
Hutus
Kashmiris
Kurds
Moros
Northern Irish
Papuans
Serbs
Sikhs
Somalis
Tajiks
Tamils

UNITED NATIONS—In a bold gambit hoped to resolve dozens of conflicts around the world, the U.N. announced Monday the establishment of Ethniklashistan, a multinational haven in the West Bank that will serve as a new homeland for Irish Protestants, Hutus, Serbs, and other troubled groups.

"For far too long, these groups have been locked in prolonged strife with their former neighbors, unable to achieve a lasting peace," U.N. Secretary-General Kofi Annan said. "Now that these various peoples have a new homeland where they can find refuge, all the years of fighting and bloodshed can finally be put behind them."

Former Serbian leader Slobodan Milosevic, now presiding over a Serb settlement near the Jordanian border, was optimistic about the future. "All Muslim scum must die," he said. "Death to all enemies of Serbian purity!"

The various groups, transported to Ethniklashistan by a massive U.N. airlift, will share their new homeland with the roughly two million Palestinians and Israeli settlers who cur-

see HOMELAND page 176

Guests Forced To Pretend Wedding A Good Thing

MINOT, ND—Suppressing their feelings about the doomed couple, guests at Saturday's wedding of Jerome Sykes, 23, and Madeline Pirone, 26, pretended the marriage was a good thing.

"Madeline looked so beautiful today," said mother of the groom Betsy Sykes, who once threatened to disown her son if he married "that manipulative bitch." "She looked positively radiant. They're going to give me such beautiful grandchildren one day."

Willfully ignoring the eight months of screaming, pleading, and threats that marked the couple's courtship, both families were outwardly positive about what they secretly called a "horrible disaster waiting to happen."

"Jerome and Madeline said they were in love and wanted to spend the rest of their lives together," said Dorothy Pirone, the bride's mother, who reacted to the October 2000 announcement of the engagement by throwing a porcelain cookie jar at Sykes' head. "It's so wonderful to see a young couple so in love."

In spite of near-constant fighting

see WEDDING page 177

Above: Sykes and Pirone after their secretly disapproved-of wedding.

Bush Trying To Decide How To Spend His Tax Refund

WASHINGTON, DC—Four days after signing a $1.35 trillion tax-cut bill, George W. Bush spent Monday trying to decide how he will spend his $300 refund check. "Maybe I'll buy some new wireless speakers," said the excited president, flipping through a Sharper Image catalog. "Or maybe I could get this massage chair." After noting the massage chair's $720 price tag, Bush said he "wouldn't rule out" passing an additional $1.9 trillion cut to get the extra $420.

Resident Of Three Years Decries Neighborhood's Recent Gentrification

CHICAGO—Bruce Smales, a three-year resident of Chicago's Wicker Park neighborhood, lashed out Monday against encroaching gentrification. "See that big Barnes & Noble on the corner? You better believe that wasn't there back in '98," said Smales, 34, a finance manager with Accenture. "This whole place is turning into Yuppieville. You can't throw a rock without hitting a couple in matching Ralph Lauren baseball caps walking a black lab." Smales then took his yellow lab for a walk.

Video Store's 'Favorites' Shelf Offers Telling Glimpse Into Manager's Psyche

ITHACA, NY—The "Favorites" shelf at King Street Video offers insights into the psyche of store manager Bruce Gannon, psychiatrists concurred Monday. "Gannon reveals much about himself with his picks," said Dr. Miles Levinson of Cornell University. "*Deliverance, A Clockwork Orange, Lolita, Blue Velvet, Eraserhead, Natural Born Killers, Caligula...* Apparently, he couldn't even find room for one film that does not contain sodomy, incest, or torture." Dr. Levinson recommended therapy and antidepressants for Gannon.

Nepotism Passed Off As Synergy

WHITEHOUSE STATION, NJ—The hiring of Adam Dwyer by Merck Pharmaceutical was described Monday by CEO James Dwyer as "tremendously synergistic." "With his impressive range of experiences, including one and a half years of bartending and four years of heavy pharmaceutical use at the University of Delaware, Adam brings a lot to the table," Dwyer said of his nephew. "We, in turn, can help Adam earn $220,000 a year as vice-president of corporate communications for the Mid-Atlantic region."

Robbie Krieger Goes 51 Minutes Without Mentioning Jim Morrison

LOS ANGELES—In his longest-such stretch since 1982, Doors guitarist Robbie Krieger went 51 minutes Monday without mentioning former bandmate Jim Morrison. "When Jim was around, anything could happen. Anything," Krieger told friend Bob Gale before unexpectedly detouring into a Morrison-free conversation about his car, a restaurant his cousin manages, and the recent L.A. mayoral election. The streak ended when, without prompting, Krieger said: "You know, in spite of his reputation, Jim was a genuinely friendly, approachable guy." Krieger then told the story of the time Morrison was arrested for indecent exposure in Miami for the 8,194th time. ✍

HOMELAND from page 175

Above: Scenes from the new nation.

rently occupy the region. U.N. officials say the West Bank site was chosen for its centralized location, opportunities for tourism, and comfortable desert climate. These factors, combined with the already diverse cultural, ethnic, and religious composition of the area, offer "a unique opportunity for many international groups to live together in peace."

"This is truly a win-win situation," U.S. Secretary of State Colin Powell said. "War-ravaged peoples from all over the world finally have a place they can feel safe. And, for the Palestinians and Israelis already there, the presence of additional ethnicities should reduce any pre-existing stresses. Arabs and Jews will enjoy exposure to a glorious, multiethnic stew, and they will, in turn, have the opportunity to lead by example, serving as role models of peaceful coexistence."

Hutu leader Kagabo Ndadaye, who between 1994 and 1996 personally oversaw the machete deaths of more than 10,000 Tutsi Rwandans, echoed the positive outlook. "The glorious Hutu are the one pure race," said Ndadaye, speaking from a Hutu settlement near Hebron while eyeing a nearby Kurdish settlement. "All inferior mongrel peoples shall be put to the blade."

Though hopes are high for Ethniklashistan—a name created by a team of linguists who combined 17 different languages' words for "sanctuary"—the establishment of the new homeland has proven rocky. Of the more than 500,000 people relocated there so far, approximately 97 percent have responded with violent resistance, swearing oaths of eternal vengeance against U.N. volunteers conducting the forced relocations.

Bloodshed also marred the "Festival Of Human Brotherhood," a weeklong, nationwide event celebrating the founding of Ethniklashistan. On Monday, 11 people were killed in a skirmish between Basques and Sikhs near Nablus. The same day, six were killed and dozens injured on the streets of Bethlehem when Somalis and Greek Cypriots exchanged gunfire and grenades.

Dozens of shifting alliances have added to the confusion and chaos. In a pre-dawn border raid Monday, Burmese Karen rebels attacked a Tamil settlement. By late afternoon, the Karens were driven back by the Tamils, who were newly armed with Israeli anti-personnel missiles smuggled into the West Bank by Zionist fundamentalists who had allied themselves—some say only as a temporary ruse—with the Tamils.

On Tuesday, guerrilla fighters made up of an uneasy Palestinian-Papuan alliance attacked an Irish Protestant church near the Golan Heights, killing 121 Irish worshippers with nerve gas before being repelled by a nearby faction of Protestant-sympathizing Zapatista rebels from the Chiapas region of Mexico.

The violence continued that evening, when the severed heads of 20 Chechens were paraded through the streets of Jericho by Azerbaijani extremists. The killings are thought to be in retaliation for rocket attacks by a band of pro-Armenian Chechen rebels, who have thus far evaded Azerbaijani attempts to flush them out of their encampments in the hills with prolonged shelling.

Alarmed by the new nation's growing pains, world leaders have launched a large-scale international-aid effort to help Ethniklashistan get on its feet. Great Britain has pledged 12,000 peacekeeping troops, vowing to "pummel with rubber bullets, tear gas, and billy clubs anyone who dares threaten the Sons of Ulster." China has pledged 40,000 soldiers to supervise the 2,000-plus Tibetan Buddhists relocated to the region. Indonesia, Cambodia, Nigeria, and Afghanistan have also sent troops.

"There is always a period of transition and upheaval in the founding of a new government," President Bush said. "That is why an international humanitarian consortium of nations, including the U.S., France, Russia, Iraq, and North Korea, has pledged $2 trillion in military aid to the new nation. This way, all Ethniklashistanis, regardless of race, color, creed, or economic background, will have equal access to the state-of-the-art ordnance they need to defend themselves and their families during this initial period of instability."

Encouraged by such aid efforts, experts are confident that a lasting peace can soon be established among the rival Ethniklashistani groups.

"When you take that many long-suffering, war-torn groups and put them in the same place, how can you *not* have peace?" asked former president Jimmy Carter, who will lead talks among the various Ethniklashistani groups. "This hatred cannot possibly last long." ✍

Product Awareness Increased With 'Advertisement'

PHILADELPHIA—Ushering in a new era of informed consumer purchasing, GlaxoSmithKline Monday unveiled an "advertisement," a paid announcement designed to educate the public on which products will best serve its needs.

"Our first advertisement, or 'ad' as we've come to call it, will soon appear in magazines across the nation," GlaxoSmithKline CEO J.P. Garnier said. "Conceived as a service to our customers, this ad employs images and words to describe the benefits of using our Aquafresh toothpaste."

The GlaxoSmithKline advertisement, provided free of charge to consumers, features a picture of Aquafresh and lists the benefits of its use: strong teeth, healthy gums, and fresh breath. It also explains how the product's patented tri-color formula helps users reach these goals.

Though similar to public-service announcements, advertisements, Garnier explained, differ in that the featured product's manufacturer pays the publication a fee to defray the cost of distribution. He predicted that ads will eventually appear in other media, from television to radio to large, free-standing signs posted next to roads.

Encouraged by the Aquafresh model, a number of major U.S. corporations, including McDonald's, Alamo, and Foot Locker, are already developing their own advertisements.

"Finally, manufacturers will have an open forum in which to compare and contrast their products with those of competing manufacturers," Pepsico vice-president Tina Grandelle said. "We're currently

New Media Format Promises Golden Age Of Informed Consumers

developing an advertisement that would compare the attributes of Pepsi to those of Coke, so that a cola drinker could decide which beverage is the best choice for them. I must say that, given all the facts, I am confident consumers will choose Pepsi."

General Motors even plans to create a entire department whose sole purpose is to be a conduit of information from the company to the consumer.

"When we proposed creating a department dedicated to generating informational advertisements for our products, our board of directors was shocked," GM CEO G. Richard Wagoner said. "Eventually, we were able to convince the board that this would be the perfect way to thank the citizens of this country for their years of loyal patronage."

Companies are already considering a number of innovative techniques to get product information to the consumer. Television advertisements may contain what are essentially short plays depicting the benefits of using the product. Print advertisements may employ striking imagery to increase visual impact. Radio advertisements may use clever slogans and songs to deliver factual information in an

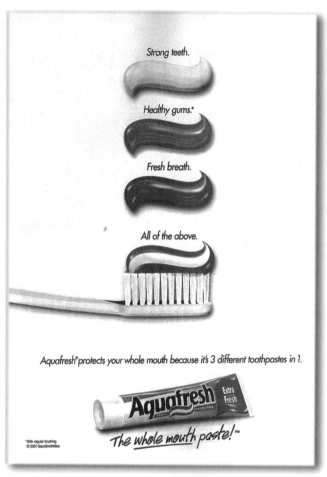

Strong teeth.

Healthy gums.*

Fresh breath.

All of the above.

Aquafresh® protects your whole mouth because it's 3 different toothpastes in 1.

*With regular brushing
© 2001 GlaxoSmithKline

Aquafresh Extra Fresh

The whole mouth paste!™

Above: The first-ever "advertisement."

easy-to-recall format.

Claire Recoy, a director of operations for Procter & Gamble's Pert shampoo, said some advertisements could even contain scientific evidence backed up with easy-to-read charts, graphs, or illustrations.

"Someone shopping for shampoo will no longer have to blindly choose see ADVERTISING page 179

WEDDING from page 175

and two breakups during their eight months of dating, Sykes, a part-time worker at Federal Express, and Pirone, a hair stylist at Supercuts, say their relationship was meant to be.

"Nobody in my family liked me going out with Maddy," Sykes said. "Everyone said she wasn't good enough for me, that she treats me like shit. But I don't care what they say: She's the love of my life and nobody can keep us apart."

Pirone agreed, saying that their families' disapproval of the relationship brought her and Sykes closer together.

"Everyone in Jerry's family said I was just dating him on the rebound

after I broke up with Mike [Harrison]," said Pirone, straightening the same wedding gown worn years earlier by her mother, who reluctantly agreed to let Madeline wear it. "So we felt like we had to see each other in secret, just like in that movie *Romeo And Juliet*, until Jerry was just like, 'Screw this, let's just get married and nobody will be able to tell us what to do.'"

Friends of the bride and groom masked their true feelings throughout the reception, peppering their conversation with comments like, "Yes, we're very happy for the both of them" and "No, really, we're very happy."

"When Jerome's high-school shop teacher, Mr. Kyzlowski, came

through the receiving line, he said it looked like Jerome had really grown up in the last few years," said Patricia Sykes, the groom's mother. "And I guess I had to agree—he technically is a man now."

Pirone's maternal grandmother, Mary Ellen O'Rourke, who after every meeting with Sykes said she "[doesn't] like that boy," was especially impressed with the wedding.

"The flowers were so beautiful," O'Rourke said. "Very pretty flowers."

"I told Madeline I was totally jealous of her," said maid of honor Roxanne David, who in March repeatedly warned Pirone that Sykes was sleeping with one of their friends. "I told her she looked so beautiful, and

that Jerry is going to make her the happiest woman on the planet. What else was I supposed to say?"

Not everyone paid lip service to the couple's prospects.

"If those two last more than a year, I'll sell my dentures," said Maria Van Kamp, 58, the harpist at the reception. "I've played a lot of weddings, and I can usually tell who's going to make it. Usually, if the groom is drunk and hitting on a bridesmaid, and the bride threatens to call off the wedding twice during the rehearsal dinner, it's a pretty good sign that they're not going the distance."

Added Van Kamp: "They make a cute couple, though." *⌀*

Though Fire, Flood, And Earthquake Beset My Path, Still Will I Get Home In Time For *The Joker's Wild*

By Bennett Vance

Rage, tempest! Blow to cleanse the Earth! Still I mock you. As God himself is my witness, wild horses shall not stay my quest to get home in time for *The Joker's Wild*.

I am a man of deepest conviction and, mark my words, I shall prevail. Send armies to intercept me! I welcome the challenge. They may kill me, but I shall not live and miss *The Joker's Wild*.

I do not pay $21.95 a month for basic-cable service so that I can miss the rich palette of knowledge and skill-testing programming offered daily by the Game Show Network, a sumptuous banquet whose main course is the peerless *Joker's Wild*. Not by half, my friend.

Let rains three men deep flood these lands. I care not. I swear I shall be home as the closing credits of the preceding program roll, and by the time the *Joker* theme fills my living room, I shall be safe and dry in my Barcalounger, sipping a Fresca, awash in every nuance of early-'70s game-show zeitgeist, from horn-driven theme music to sponsorship by Z-Brick and Jules Jurgensen, to the show-capping announcement that this has been a Jack Barry and Dan Enright production.

Neptune, send mighty tsunamis to impede my path! Knock down the highest church steeple with 40-foot waves! Drown the crops and livestock! Still will I see whether Gail from Tuscaloosa beat the returning champion, Doug from Berkeley, so many decades ago.

Were it not for this week's 39-cent soft-shell taco special at participating Taco Bell restaurants, I would be home even now, mentally preparing myself. But it matters not, for I shall not miss a second

The strength of 10 is mine, for my quest is righteous.

of *The Joker's Wild*.

Offer me no *Super Password*. Do not patronize me with *Bullseye* or *Magnificent Marble Machine*. And attempt not to pass off the children's spinoff game show *Joker! Joker! Joker!* as the genuine article. I demand the original, adult *Joker's Wild*, preferably from the Bill Cullen years. But be the host Jack Barry or Jim Peck, I shall attend faithfully to each frame of the broadcast.

Do plagues ravage the land? I may miss *Tic Tac Dough*. Has our government collapsed into civil war? Perhaps I will forgo *Match Game*. Perhaps. But though Armageddon sears the Earth, turning forests to ash and cities to heaps of skeletons, I SHALL NOT MISS *THE JOKER'S WILD*.

The strength of 10 is mine, for my quest is righteous. I may never meet the Devil face-to-face, nor defeat him by totaling $1,000 or more in the Big Spin. But should he dare cross my path, I can spit in his eye and skip away gleefully, for he has no domain over me. Mine is the Kingdom of Heaven, where knowledge is King and lady luck is Queen. ∅

---

the ONION's KritterKorner presents

Pet-Care Tips

Animals need more than just TLC to thrive. Here are some tips to help keep your pet healthy and happy for years to come:

- When going on vacation, be sure to leave cans of dog food and a can opener where your dog can easily reach them.

- Is thick pus coming out of your cat's eyes? Are its gums red or swollen? Are its ears clogged with a crumbly brown substance? Cool.

- Take your snake outside regularly. If not, no one will know you're one of those freaky snake guys.

- If your dog or cat starts wearing pointy, '50s-era women's eyeglasses, contact cartoonist Gary Larson immediately.

- Owning a colorful cockatiel or mynah bird is a great way to make you wake up one morning, slap yourself on the forehead, and say, "Holy shit! I'm gay!"

- Fish are dead when they are upside-down and motionless at the top of the mug.

- Many people consider their pets just as important a part of the family as its human members. This is psycho. Don't do this.

- If you have a pot-bellied pig, you're on your own, Mr. Individuality.

- Unless you constantly reassure your dog that he is a good dog, he will likely grow depressed and eventually hang himself.

- Once a week, comb your cat's ass hair—often matted with clumps of feces—with a special cat's-ass-hair brush.

- When choosing a pet, remember: She may be soft and cute, but *Penthouse* pet Julie Strain is extremely expensive and high-maintenance.

- Pet rabbits often benefit from a glass of white wine and light breading in a rosemary butter sauce.

- Animals should always be stroked horizontally. Never try to go across the surface of the pet.

- By blinding your dog, you may technically be able to get it into stores and restaurants.

- Your rottweiler or pit bull won't turn on you and kill you someday if you train it properly. Honest. Put it out of your mind.

- If your puppies and kittens tend to grow bigger and less cute, consider a constrictive nylon mesh suit to maintain ideal size.

- Most kittens can withstand impacts of up to 35 mph, but there's no way to be sure without extensive testing.

- Getting your kids a boa constrictor or monkey is a great way to teach them that the animal kingdom is not something that exists for their amusement, goddammit.

Sony Brings Shame To My Profession!

**The Outside Scoop
By Jackie Harvey**

The Japanese do a lot of things better than us Americans, like making cars and preparing sushi. Well, now you can add to that list **fabricating bogus movie reviews!**

It would seem that Sony Pictures couldn't find a real reviewer to say that **Tales Of The Knights** star **Heath Ledger** is a red-hot hunk, so they made one up! Why would they do that when I would have been more than happy to go on record saying that **Ledger scorches the screen**? (He does!) And, as for the movie itself, it's **a whale of a tale**, not to mention **a non-stop thrill ride!** There certainly was no need for Sony to resort to deception. It's things like this that hurt the credibility of all the **honest entertainment journalists** out there.

Is it that time already? The time for **blockbuster summer movies**? My movie-ometer just hit 110 in the shade, so you'd better believe it's time! So far, we've had some pretty hot flicks. There's **Michael Meyers** and his troll movie **Max Shreck**, in which he gets down and digital with **Cameron Diaz**. Then there's **Swordfish**, which supposedly has **Halle Berry** naked from the waist

> ## It would seem that Sony Pictures couldn't find a real reviewer to say that *Tales Of The Knights* star Heath Ledger is a red-hot hunk, so they made one up!

up! **Pearl Harbor** was a blast, with **Matt Damon** and **Kate Beckinsale** smoking up the screen with sizzling good looks and romance. Speaking of lookers, did someone say **Angelina Jolie**? Sure, her relationship with **emaciated redneck Billy Bob Thornton** is creepy, but you forget that the second she crashes onto the screen as the sexy, sultry **Tomb Robber**.

But the good times have just begun on the silver screen. Did somebody say **Apes**? As in, a whole **Planet** of them? I certainly did! And then there are the sequels. **Rush Hour 2! American Pie 2! Scary Movie 2! Jurassic Park 3!** You bet jur-assic that I'll be seeing all of those. Whew! I get exhausted just thinking about it! Look out 2000, because 2001 might just blow you away as the year with the best movies ever.

I'm still waiting for the year's summer song to touch down. Will it come from **The Backstreet Boys**? **Destiny's Child**? **Eden's Crush**? **Matchbox 20**? The suspense is killing me! I just hope it's not as suggestive as last year's "Song About Thongs" by **that little gay black man who prances around and does the cartwheels**.

The people at The WB don't seem to know how to let an audience grow. Every Friday, I would park myself in front of the TV for my weekly dose of **Tammy Mellow** and **Sara Rue** on the show **Popular**. But then The WB went and took it away! First **Grosse Pointe**, now *Popular*. It seems that every time I start to enjoy a show, **those network fatcats** yank it out from under me. If this keeps up, I'll have to rely on radio for all my entertainment.

Item! Everyone's "heiling" **The Producers**! Even me, and I haven't seen it yet! I guess it's easy to get caught up in the mad rush, particularly when the rush is about a musical comedy with **Ethan Lane** and **Ferris Bueller**! Rumor has it, none other than **Rosie O'Donnell** saw it on opening night and gave it rave reviews. Now, *that's* saying something.

Item! Actor **Steve Buscemi** was stabbed in the face and neck. I feel pretty bad about this, but I'd feel even worse if I could figure out exactly who he is. I only noticed because the newspaper article said he was with hunk-tor **Vince Vaughn** when it happened. There was a fight at a bar over a girl, and Mr. Buscemi was stabbed. Vince Vaughn, the more important of the two, was thankfully uninjured.

Also in the Celebrity Crime Beat, tough-guy actor and Little Rascal **Robert Blake** was involved in a fracas regarding his wife. Well, more of a **cold-blooded killing** than a fracas. His wife was involved in some pretty shady business, and she was shot, and Blake may have done it. But you know what? I believe that this case should be tried by the courts and not by the media. Sure, I have my opinions, see **HARVEY** page 180

NOBEL from page 175

"We've received so many articles, our review board can barely keep up," said Cathy Gapstur, editor of *The New England Journal Of Medicine*. "Yesterday alone, the mailman dropped off 27 papers on the effects of leukocyte adhesion on blood flow in microvessels."

Researchers are employing numerous strategies to increase their odds of winning the prize. Among the more popular is to submit multiple papers for publication. Another is for researchers to band together in "Nobel pools," with each participant contributing a small amount of research to a large number of studies.

"I'm working on a study of the efficacy of prescription medications in smoking cessation and whether said medications can be utilized for other chemical addictions," said Dr. Laurie Colangelo, a medical researcher at Northwestern University. "Also in my pool are doctors working on lymphatic cancer, organ cloning, and spinal-cord regeneration. We're steering clear of doing any AIDS research, because that's what won last time. What are the odds of the same subject winning twice in a row?"

With the money for the Nobel Prize in Physiology or Medicine at an all-time high, Nobel candidates from

> ## Medical and scientific journals have been deluged with submissions.

other disciplines are crossing over into medical research.

"My fight to restore the indigenous rights of Australia's aboriginal peoples was very important to me," said former Nobel Peace Prize candidate Ian Woolsey-Ganser, who recently gave up the oppressed group's cause to study genes in mice that have been shown to affect physiological rates. "But, I mean, $190 million? That's like, '*Wow.*' The aborigines can wait."

The $190 million figure represents the highest cash prize in Nobel history. The previous largest was awarded in 1987, when Nobel Prize in Economics winner Trygve Haavelmo took home $57 million for his clarification of the probability theory foundations of econometrics and analyses of simultaneous economic structures. ⌀

ADVERTISING from page 177

from rows and rows of bottles," Recoy said. "They'll be able to refer directly to the advertisements to find out which shampoos are designed to make hair stronger, silkier, bouncier, or more behaving."

Recoy added that, while the same advertisements will appear repeatedly to ensure that all consumers have a chance to see them, new advertisements will be created frequently "so that consumers are guaranteed the most up-to-the-minute data on a particular product."

Consumer-advocacy groups are hailing the creation of advertisements as a "huge step forward for consumers everywhere."

"The introduction of advertisements represents a revolutionary shift, in which product manufacturing is based on the wants and needs of the purchasers," said Dianne Lake, director of the D.C.-based Consumers Helping Others with Informed Choices Everywhere

> ## "Someone shopping for shampoo will no longer have to blindly choose from rows and rows of bottles," Recoy said.

(CHOICE). "Consumers will be able to make informed decisions about what they buy, and manufacturers will have no option but to respond with the best possible product at the best possible price. If a product does not deliver on the promises made, consumers simply will not buy that product again."

Continued Lake: "What a wonderful marketplace Americans will enjoy when all companies start providing this invaluable service." ⌀

The World War II Memorial

The planned WWII Memorial on the National Mall has sparked controversy, its critics questioning its necessity, location, and design. What do *you* think?

"I think the solution is to keep talking about this for the next 20 years. Then, when the last WWII veteran finally dies, we can just drop the whole thing."

Ronald Herr
Landscaper

"I'm not convinced what they did was so great. I made it to the end of Castle Wolfenstein in, like, two hours."

David Andujar
Auto Mechanic

"Those WWII vets are just jealous of the Vietnam vets and Holocaust survivors."

Elizabeth Oberkfell
Translator

"Isn't Tom Brokaw's plan to personally fellate every living WWII veteran thanks enough?"

Phillip Porter
Systems Analyst

"This monument ruins the symmetry of the national mall. The World War III one, though, will nicely balance the south end and lead the eye toward the reflecting pool."

Larry Hendrick
Airline Pilot

"Only by building a memorial to those who risked their lives for their country can we finally shut them up."

Dana Forsch
Social Worker

The New Di Biography

Princess Diana, who would have turned 40 on July 1, is the subject of a new biography. Among the revelations in *Diana: Story Of A Princess*:

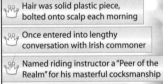
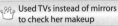

- Hair was solid plastic piece, bolted onto scalp each morning
- Once entered into lengthy conversation with Irish commoner
- Named riding instructor a "Peer of the Realm" for his masterful cocksmanship
- Used TVs instead of mirrors to check her makeup
- In 1992, beaten out by Catherine Oxenberg for role of self in TV movie *Charles And Diana: Unhappily Ever After*
- Often passed notes to other royals reading, "Do you like me? Check yes or no"
- Upon learning son William had crush on nanny, ordered the young woman drowned
- Permitted Thick Dick's Donkey-Dong Double Dildocorp to put royal crest and words "Suppliers To The Royal Family Since 1981" on all products
- Queen Mother initially objected to marriage to Charles, saying Diana "not related enough"
- Could be a bit of a snob at times

the ONION
America's Finest News Source

Herman Ulysses Zweibel *Founder*

T. Herman Zweibel *Publisher Emeritus*
J. Phineas Zweibel *Publisher*
Maxwell Prescott Zweibel *Editor-In-Chief*

FOUNDED 1871 • "TU STULTUS ES"

Your Horoscope

By Lloyd Schumner Sr.
Retired Machinist and
A.A.P.B.-Certified Astrologer

Aries: (March 21–April 19)
Your execution by lethal injection will spark endless debate on whether capital punishment in America is cool-looking enough.

Taurus: (April 20–May 20)
Don't be superstitious: The camera doesn't steal a piece of your soul every time it captures your image. Just look at all those people on the TV.

Gemini: (May 21–June 21)
The stars have decided that you, Steven P. Kreindler, wannabe Eurotrash vulture, will never get laid again.

Cancer: (June 22–July 22)
If there were a way to foretell next week without a tall dark stranger, a journey over water, or an old flame who still burns for you, we would. Sorry.

Leo: (July 23–Aug. 22)
You've always felt that your father is in Heaven watching over you, a belief that's kept you from getting a good night's sleep for 24 years.

Virgo: (Aug. 23–Sept. 22)
At the end of the day, the important thing is that you stood up to the shark and didn't run away like a sissy.

Libra: (Sept. 23–Oct. 23)
Nailing the parrot to your shoulder may keep it secure while you're climbing the rigging or sailing rough seas, but it'll also make it harder to replace.

Scorpio: (Oct. 24–Nov. 21)
You will be overjoyed next week to meet the most shameless slut the world has ever known, at long last ending your search for your real mother.

Sagittarius: (Nov. 22–Dec. 21)
You've changed, man. The stars remember when it was all about the future and your fortune, not all this other bullshit.

Capricorn: (Dec. 22–Jan. 19)
Jesus isn't likely to accept your last-minute deathbed repentance, so remind Him firmly that He doesn't make the rules.

Aquarius: (Jan. 20–Feb. 18)
You have no idea how petty your ethnic squabbles seem to people outside of the Des Moines area.

Pisces: (Feb. 19–March 20)
Your academic reputation will be ruined when the truth comes out that your dissertation's central thesis is identical to the plot of *Monkey Trouble*.

HARVEY from page 179

but I don't think this is the proper forum in which to air them. As soon as there are some hard, cold facts for me to pass along, I will.

Sharon Stone's semi-known husband got bitten by a lizard. I swear, this is true. I couldn't make something like this up if I tried.

Item! Perry Como, America's king crooner, is dead at 88. He wasn't as beloved as Ol' Blue Eyes, but he sang his way into the nation's collective heart with songs like "Chicago," "New York, New York" and other songs about cities. He also had a TV show that probably got cancelled by network fatcats. They just burn me up. They don't know a diamond from a sack of crap.

Hey, can we please keep the chatter down in theaters, folks? It seems like everyone has to throw in their two cents while they're watching movies. Unless you're **Jeffrey Lyons**, I don't want to hear it!

Well, that's all the tinseltown dirt I've got to scoop with **my golden rumor shovel**. Until next time, I'll see you the way I always do, and that is from the Outside! ∅

FLICKING MOTION from page 99

were amazed by the unusually large amounts of blood. Passersby were amazed by the unusually large amounts of blood. Passersby were amazed by the unusually large amounts of blood. Passersby were amazed by the unusually large amounts of blood. Passersby were amazed by the unusually large amounts of blood. Passersby were amazed by the unusually large amounts of blood. Passersby were amazed by the unusually large amounts of blood. Passersby were amazed by the unusually large amounts of blood. Passersby were amazed by the unusually large amounts of blood. Passersby were amazed by the unusually large amounts of blood. Passersby were amazed by the unusually large amounts of blood. Passersby were amazed by the unusually large amounts of blood. Passersby were amazed by the unusually large amounts of blood. Passersby were amazed by the unusually large amounts of blood. Passersby were amazed by the unusually large amounts of blood. Passersby were amazed by the unusually large amounts of blood. Passersby were amazed by the **see FLICKING MOTION page 196**

New Ronco Food Exposer Spoils Food Overnight

see PRODUCTWATCH page 12C

Friends Of Band Regret Going To Show

see LOCAL page 3B

Sweat Dribbling Into Stew

see LOCAL page 5B

French Routed With Longbows

see WORLD page 3A

STATshot

A look at the numbers that shape your world.

Top Skateboarding Moves
1. Grinding The Bone
2. Maxing The Card
3. The Sulk
4. 180° Piss Off Dad
5. The Study Hall Triple Skip
6. The 23 3/4 Skidoo
7. 720° Belushi To Farley Nosedrop
8. The Not A Crime
9. Gleaming The Jewel Parking Lot

---

the ONION®

VOLUME 37 ISSUE 24   AMERICA'S FINEST NEWS SOURCE™   19–25 JULY 2001

THE ENVIRONMENT

Bush Vows To Remove Toxic Petroleum From National Parks

Above: Alaska's Denali National Park, one of the many wildlife refuges temporarily closed by Bush (inset).

WASHINGTON, DC—Vowing to "restore the pristine splendor of America's natural treasures," President Bush Monday unveiled "Project: National Parks Clean-Up," an ambitious program to remove all toxic petrochemical deposits from national parks by 2004.

"Places like Yellowstone and Yosemite were once pure, unspoiled wilderness," Bush said at a White House press conference. "But over the course of the past 10 million years, we have allowed them to become polluted with toxic fossil-fuel deposits, turning a blind eye to the steady build-up of vast quantities of dangerous pollutants. It's time to end this terrible neglect."

Continued Bush: "A comprehensive survey of our parks, conducted by a team of top geologists specially commissioned by me, has discovered giant pockets of petroleum, coal, and

other 'fossil poisons' beneath an alarming 38 percent of our national parks' surface area. Though a majority of these poisons are buried under several million tons of rock strata, should they ever seep to the surface and spread into the surrounding areas, they would spell disaster for the parks' precious ecosystems."

To underscore the severity of the crisis, Bush produced a chart illustrating survey results for Yellowstone National Park, where a "staggeringly huge" toxic-petroleum deposit was discovered.

"This amount represents the equivalent of 40,000 supertankers worth of oil," said Bush, gesturing toward a line on the chart. "To put the dangers into perspective, consider this: If these 'petro-poisons' should ever spill out into the park itself, the resulting environmental disaster
see BUSH page 183

Department Of Libel: Drew Carey Killed A Guy And Paid To Cover It Up

WASHINGTON, DC—According to a report released Monday by the U.S. Department of Libel, comedian and TV star Drew Carey killed a guy back in the 1980s, then paid this other guy to keep it all hush-hush.

"I know it seems wild, but it really happened," Libel Secretary Brent Roderick told reporters at a morning press conference. "Back in, like, '85 or '86, while he was still living in Ohio, Drew Carey went apeshit one night and beat this guy to death with a golf club in the back room of some bar. For no reason at all. Then he realized that this other guy had seen it, so he paid the guy $500 not to rat him out to the cops. That's why no one knew for so long."

Roderick said the Libel Department received the information on June 20 from "a friend of a friend of the guy Carey paid off." He characterized the source as "100 percent reliable."

see LIBEL page 184

Teen Mortified After Winning Academic-Achievement Award

MARION, IN—Grover Cleveland Middle School student Jamie Ganser, 14, expressed mortification and a desire to die Monday upon learning that she had won the 2001 Eighth Grade Academic Achievement Award.

"Now the whole school is going to think I'm the biggest geek," Ganser told best friend and classmate Lacey Richards, who has a socially acceptable B-minus average. "I'm not that smart. It's just that my classes were really easy this year."

Ganser said she was "shocked" to learn that she was to be lauded for her

academic performance, as she had been careful all year to keep her level of achievement low enough to avoid attention.

"Last year, [social-studies teacher] Mrs. Knauf was so happy with my essay 'What Liberty Means To Me,' she made me get up and read it to the class," Ganser said. "I learned my lesson from that: This year, I vowed to do much worse, but it looks like I failed."

As part of her plan, Ganser answered teachers' questions only if called upon and never raised her

see TEEN page 185

Above: Jamie Ganser reluctantly poses with her award.

300 Naked Women Feared Lost In Computer Crash

ELLICOTT CITY, MD—An estimated 300 naked women, including actresses Pamela Anderson and Shannon Elizabeth, are feared lost as the result of a tragic computer crash Monday. "One minute, they were there, and the next, they were gone," said a visibly shaken Jonathan Blauvelt, 33, the Ellicott City resident whose Power Mac G4 was the site of the disaster. "To lose so many young girls in the blink of an eye like that, it's hard to comprehend. Angelina Jolie, Anna Kournikova, the chick from *Species*—it's just too much to bear." As data-recovery workers comb through the hard drive for signs of ass, Blauvelt is asking well-wishers to pray for the naked ladies' safe return.

U.S. To Slow Down Relationship With Uruguay

WASHINGTON, DC—Explaining that it is still a relatively young nation and not ready for a permanent trade partner, the U.S. announced Monday that it plans to slow down its relationship with Uruguay. "Don't get me wrong, Uruguay is great," President Bush said. "It's just that things have been moving along a little too quickly ever since we signed that bilateral tariff-reduction pact in March. They were always calling up about a treaty or an aid package and, well, it just got to be a little too much." Bush said the U.S. would love to remain "just allies" with Uruguay while pursuing relations with other nations.

Dodgers' Playoff Hopes Dashed Following Acquisition Of Belly Itcher

LOS ANGELES—Trailing the first-place Arizona Diamondbacks by three games in the National League West, the Los Angeles Dodgers dealt their own playoff chances a major blow Monday when they acquired belly itcher Shane Lesko from the Montreal Expos. "They're done for," said an unnamed NL general manager following the deal. "The Dodgers could have put themselves in terrific position for the stretch run by signing one more pitcher, but instead, they go and sign this guy." The general manager called it the worst move since the New York Mets' June 10 trade of pitcher John Franco to the Houston Astros for a glass of water.

Street-Smart Teen Dies In Library

CHICAGO—Street-smart teen Larry Witherspoon was found dead Monday at the Michigan Avenue branch of the Chicago Public Library, his urban know-how useless to him in the unfamiliar environment. "Unfortunately, the skills Larry had developed on the mean streets of Chicago's South Side did him no good in a place like this," librarian Mary Ross said. "Hypothetically, he could have located a book on library survival skills, had he known what the Dewey Decimal system was and how to use it."

Elderly Couple Dresses Up For Trip To Denny's

VERO BEACH, FL—Wishing to look nice for their evening out, Vero Beach retirees Abe and Bernice Wanamaker dressed up Monday for dinner at a local Denny's. "I think I'm going to put on my light-blue slacks before we go," said Abe, taking off the shorts he'd been wearing all afternoon while sitting in the backyard. "And the brown Hush Puppies." Bernice chose to wear her good yellow dress, which she had not worn since a March 22 trip to Lums. ∅

Plan To Straighten Out Entire Life During Weeklong Vacation Yields Mixed Results

MANCHESTER, NH—Returning to work after seven days off, Derek Olson, 31, confessed Monday that his plan to use his weeklong vacation to straighten out his life yielded mixed results.

"This was the week all the shit I'd been putting off for years—big and small—was going to get done," said Olson, a data-entry operator at A.G. Edwards & Sons. "From getting Steve and Kim a gift for their wedding two months ago to going through all those boxes I'd left unpacked since moving here in '98 to finally deciding what my future is with [girlfriend] Melanie [Stirre], it was all going to get taken care of."

"I did pay my gas bill," Olson continued, "but then I lost the envelope somewhere on the way to the mailbox, so now I have to wait for a second notice."

After using last Saturday and Sunday—the first two days of his break—to recover from "a shitstorm of a work week," Olson decided he would begin straightening up his life first thing Monday morning.

"I thought that if I didn't rest up over the weekend, I'd burn out halfway through my week off," said Olson, explaining the slow start. "Saturday night, I did write up a list of what I wanted to accomplish over the course of the coming week, but it wasn't really all that complete."

Among the goals written on the abbreviated list: a thorough cleaning of his apartment, laundry, re-ordering of checks, buying a bigger CD shelf, signing up for a T'ai Chi course, cashing in a large jar of loose change at the bank, updating his resume, looking for a new job, and "figuring out the whole Melanie thing."

Olson's plan to straighten out his life first thing Monday morning was derailed the evening prior.

"I was going to go to bed early Sunday so I could get up early Monday and start on all my projects," Olson said. "But then I realized I could go to Rocky's [Bar & Grill], where they have this really cool thing called Rocky's Sunday Night Record Jam, where this guy spins all these really cool old vinyl records, everything from Curtis Mayfield to The Damned. I normally never get to go because I have to get up at 6 a.m. Mondays, so I figured it was my big chance. But then I got a little more drunk than I'd planned."

Upon waking up Monday, a hung-over Olson decided it would be a "day of recovery" and vowed to begin first thing Tuesday. After spending most of Tuesday in his bathrobe re-reading

Above: Derek Olson stands among some of the boxes he'd hoped to unpack last week.

Harry Potter And The Chamber Of Secrets, Olson finally went to the basement that evening to begin the first of his many projects.

"I decided the first thing I was going to do was unpack all the stuff in the basement," Olson said. "When I opened the first box marked 'Magazines,' it had nothing but a bunch of socks and my electric pencil sharpener. I got so pissed off with my lack of organization, I went back upstairs and started watching TV."

Having accomplished only a few tasks Wednesday and Thursday, Olson knew he would have to "really bear down" Friday.

"I actually would've gotten a lot of stuff done Friday if the whole universe hadn't been against me," Olson said. "I took my car in to get my tires rotated, but the guy said he couldn't get to it until the following Tuesday, so I was like, 'Screw that.' I also went to Staples to pick up the computer desk I'd had on layaway for the last month, but I forgot to bring my receipt. They wouldn't give the stupid thing to me, even after arguing with the guy for almost an hour. The whole day was a colossal waste. Except I got a new belt I needed for work."

After devoting Friday night to drinking to unwind from the computer-desk episode, a once again hung-over Olson spent most of Saturday re-alphabetizing his CDs, a task he did not plan to take on during his week off but that needed to be done.

Sunday was spent fretting over the wasted week and berating himself for not going to New Orleans—a trip he'd strongly considered taking before

see VACATION page 184

I Am The Anonymous Hero Who Donated All Those Old Legwarmers To Goodwill

By Marjorie Reidel

For months, I have remained silent, desiring no recognition or acclaim for my altruism. Now, however, I feel it is time for me to step forward and admit to my magnanimous deed, only in the hope that I might inspire others to act so selflessly. Yes, I am the anonymous hero who donated all those old legwarmers to Goodwill.

It was I, motivated not by a desire for plaudits, but only by the notion that I might help those less fortunate than myself. Those poor souls who haven't the means to pay for new legwarmers and would be left to brace against the cold, their legs exposed to the harsh elements from mid-calf to ankle.

I sought no credit, no accolades, no monetary reward when I drove over to the Riverside Drive Goodwill on that April day. So that I might remain unrecognized, I stole up to the 24-hour Donation Station in the parking lot under the veil of night and stuffed the bulging JCPenney's bag full of legwarmers into the after-hours drop box. Then I drove off quickly, all the while wondering whose lives those brightly colored half-stockings would touch.

Would it be a small, shivering child, facing the bitter chill of win-

> It is time for me to step forward and admit to my magnanimous deed, only in the hope that I might inspire others to act so selflessly.

ter as she walks to school to gain an education and nobly improve her lot in life? Or an elderly widow, all alone in a small, drafty house as she struggled to cover her frail legs with a blanket that always slips to the ground? Or a promising young ballet dancer, talented enough to perform *Swan Lake* yet too impoverished to obtain the basic lower-body outfitting necessary to pursue her dreams?

I could have dropped the old legwarmers off during the day so that I might obtain a charitable-donation tax-deduction receipt—not to mention a smile of heartfelt gratitude from a Goodwill worker. But that was not why I did this deed. It was simply the right thing to do.

True, the Donation Station was right on the way home from East Towne Mall, where I'd just gone to buy new summer curtains for the girls' bedroom. Still, dropping them off required getting off at the Riverside Drive exit when I was hungry and had not yet eaten dinner.

What, you no doubt ask, drives a person to act so selflessly? How are some courageously noble while others allow their spirit to wither away in stony inaction? I cannot say, for it is something unknowable deep within the soul.

That is why, when I was cleaning out the spare room in the basement and found the bag of legwarmers in an array of early-'80s colors—teal, neon yellow, watermelon pink, and turquoise—I did not hesitate for a second before deciding to commit the whole lot to charity.

I realize I have been blessed. I have a husband and two happy, healthy children. We live in a nice subdivision on the west side of town. While not rich, we are comfortable. Some in my position might gaze down with indifference at those below them on the social lad-der. I, however, would never be so cold. I would never think to withhold legwarmers from the needy just to preserve my position of advantage.

Again, I ask for nothing in return. I have never asked for anything for the many other selfless acts I have committed over the years: the time I bought a plastic "buddy poppy" to support the VFW, the cookies I baked for the church bake sale, the day I took the time to help an elderly woman understand the Extra Value menu at McDonald's, and that rainy night I called the police on my cell phone to tell them I'd just driven by a car with a flat.

Sometimes I wonder what became of the legwarmers I so generously donated three months ago today. Whose legs are they warming? Do the wearers ever stop to wonder from whence their gift of leg warmth came? Perhaps. But it matters not. What's important is that they know somebody out there cared enough to help. Those less fortunate souls can take comfort in the knowledge that some unnamed being is looking out for them, and the world will not seem like such a harsh and uncaring place.

Yes, thanks to my selfless act, a few more people in this world will go to sleep tonight with warm calves... and hearts. ∅

BUSH from page 181

would be 40,000 times worse than the damage caused by the wreck of the Exxon Valdez."

"We cannot allow such a thing to happen," Bush said. "We must remove this oil now, before it's too late."

Under the Bush plan, 7.2 billion tons of toxic petroleum would be removed by the target date of January 2004. Unlike other federal environmental clean-up initiatives, administration officials say the plan would pay for itself, offsetting costs through the sale of petroleum byproducts produced as a result of the clean-up process.

The clean-up, EPA chief Christine Todd Whitman said, may even prove profitable, a prospect that has attracted the participation of private industry. Already, many U.S. companies have expressed interest in lending assistance, and it is hoped that these companies will carry out much, or perhaps all, of the clean-up effort.

Though "Project: National Parks Clean-Up" represents Bush's first major environmental initiative since taking office, supporters are quick to

Above: An EPA oil-removal pump begins preliminary cleaning of Kings Canyon National Park in California.

point out that he has been a longtime champion of petroleum removal.

"As governor of Texas, Bush fought tirelessly to protect the state's subterranean environment through a series of massive petrochemical-deposit clean-up projects," Secretary of the Interior Gale A. Norton said. "Under his governorship, more tons of petroleum-based subterranean environmental contaminants were removed in Texas than in all the national Superfund clean-up sites combined. The Democrats talk a good game about the importance of cleaning up the environment, but when it comes to actually eliminating the threat of enormous oil deposits lurking under the surface of our nation, no one can hold a candle to George W. Bush."

Thus far, reaction has been mixed. Some have said it is unrealistic for the president to try to remove so much petroleum so quickly. Others, such as Sen. Bob Smith (R-NH), have charged that the president is caving in to pressure from environmentalists, arguing that the government's energies would be better directed toward improving the military.

But despite such criticism, Bush stressed that the urgency of removing the oil deposits should take precedence over everything else.

"Nothing is more important than the legacy we leave future generations," Bush said. "The costs of this project pale in comparison to the importance of safeguarding our planet's ecosystem. Our primary mission must be to protect and foster our nation's most precious natural resource: oil. I mean, the environment." ∅

OPINION

The Missing Intern

Four months after her disappearance, the search continues for Chandra Levy, the 24-year-old intern who had an affair with Rep. Gary Condit (D-CA). What do *you* think?

"For years, men have been screwing women and then vanishing. But one woman does it, and there's all this hoop-de-doo."

Donald Bumbry
Systems Analyst

"Man, the Democrats sure do love those intern Jewesses."

Hal Murray
File Clerk

"I am enraged by Condit's evasiveness. Just tell us, yes or no: Did you have butt sex?"

Fred Singleton
Cashier

"While the police are at it, they should find out where *my* intern is. I asked for those copies 20 minutes ago!"

Richard Sakata
Attorney

"I've been missing for almost two years now, and it still hasn't made the news."

Jill Roenicke
Biologist

"I hope this finally shows our young people that there's no future in fucking politicians."

Diana Dempsey
Speech Pathologist

The New Planet Of The Apes

Hitting theaters July 27, *Planet Of The Apes*, Tim Burton's update of the 1968 classic, is generating major buzz. What are people saying about the new film?

- Can't resist any film with phrase "Kill them all" in trailer
- Heard new version features more footage of monkeys beating off
- Disgusted they are allowing human slave woman to speak
- Mark Wahlberg won lead role by having strongest-smelling urine
- Koko The Sign-Language Gorilla raved about film, gushing, "Drink drink apple cup now drink"
- Accurately portrays timeless problems facing time-traveling astronauts of all eras
- Animals, tits always box-office gold; movie features animals with tits
- Film carries powerful message that apes are scary

the ONION

America's Finest News Source

Herman Ulysses Zweibel *Founder*
T. Herman Zweibel *Publisher Emeritus*
J. Phineas Zweibel *Publisher*
Maxwell Prescott Zweibel *Editor-In-Chief*

FOUNDED 1871 • "TU STULTUS ES"

184

VACATION from page 182

committing to staying home and getting his life in order.

"Next year, I'm definitely going to New Orleans," Olson said. "This was stupid."

According to corporate consultant and motivational speaker Jeffrey Hatcher, trying to catch up on years of neglected goals in one week is not a good strategy.

"You have to make a conscious effort every day," Hatcher said. "You can't spend years letting things fall apart and then fix it all in seven days. It's just not possible. Perhaps if Derek had had two weeks off, he might have been able to catch up on a sizable portion of his tasks, but he won't be getting two weeks of vacation at his job for at least another three years, before which

> "Next year, I'm definitely going to New Orleans," Olson said. "This was stupid."

time he'll most certainly be fired for being so disorganized. So there's no real point in talking about it." Ø

LIBEL from page 181

Marvin Strand, Carey's attorney, vehemently denied the allegations.

"In all my years practicing law, I have never encountered a more blatant case of libel and slander," Strand said. "This is a malicious, wholly unfounded smear campaign whose sole purpose is to destroy the reputation of my client. And to think a taxpayer-funded arm of the federal government is behind it. We are definitely taking legal action."

Despite Strand's plans to file a $160 million defamation lawsuit and the absence of any hard evidence supporting the allegations, the Libel Department is sticking to its claims.

"Long story short, in the '80s, Carey's career was going nowhere. No comedy club wanted to touch him because his delivery sucked and his material was shit. And it certainly didn't help that he was so fat and unattractive—he had those dumb glasses even then," Roderick said. "Plus, he was really unhappy because he'd been kicked out of the American Nazi Party, and his relationship with [mass murderer] Richard Speck was on the rocks, and his ongoing horse-tranquilizer addiction had placed him in a pretty bizarre state of mind, to say the least. So, when you consider all of that, it's not too surprising that he snapped and lashed out violently the way he did."

Added Roderick: "They never did find the guy's arms."

If Strand follows through on his threat of legal action, it will not be the first time the Libel Department has been sued. Since its creation in 1916, the department has defended itself in court more than 4,600 times for its groundless accusations against various high-profile individuals. The department has lost every case, costing U.S. taxpayers an estimated $985 billion in damages.

Among the Libel Department's more infamous accusations: In 1919, it asserted that swashbuckling movie idol Douglas Fairbanks raped Archduke Franz Ferdinand with a Coke bottle, touching off WWI; in 1932, it alleged that the murdered infant son of famed aviator Charles Lindbergh had actually committed suicide; and in 1953, it divulged that Woolworth heiress Barbara Hutton was raised by a pack of mandrills.

Earlier this year, a New York district court judge ordered the department to pay talk-show host Rosie O'Donnell $24 million for falsely claiming that in 1998 she embarked on a Central Park rampage in which she fatally stabbed a devel-

> Roderick said the Libel Department received the information on June 20 from "a friend of a friend of the guy Carey paid off."

opmentally disabled six-year-old and a swan.

His department's losing streak notwithstanding, Roderick said he is looking forward to his day in court.

"From its founding to the present day, the Libel Department has never wavered in its commitment to its mission, and in terms of efficiency, we top all other government agencies," Roderick said. "We've done a good job and, although we have our naysayers on Capitol Hill and in Hollywood, we intend to continue our important work into the 21st century and beyond."

"Plus," Roderick continued, "I've got some unbelievable info on Julia Roberts. You'll shit your pants when you read this. She won't seem like America's sweetheart when you hear what she did to land her role in *Mystic Pizza*, believe you me." Ø

Your Horoscope

**By Lloyd Schumner Sr.
Retired Machinist and
A.A.P.B.-Certified Astrologer**

Aries: (March 21–April 19)
Forces beyond your understanding have decreed that you will have a pretty much average week.

Taurus: (April 20–May 20)
If string theory is right about the structure of our universe, then all three spatial dimensions are circular. Just like all three of *your* spatial dimensions, tubbo!

Gemini: (May 21–June 21)
You can only hope that history will recognize that you had to destroy the cream pie in order to save it in two different-sized Cool Whip containers.

Cancer: (June 22–July 22)
You should tell your lover how much you dislike the sweater she bought you. This will help ensure that she won't bury you in it next week.

Leo: (July 23–Aug. 22)
You still aren't sure what Keats meant when he called Milton "Chief of organic numbers! / Old scholar of the spheres!" after seeing a single lock of his hair.

Virgo: (Aug. 23–Sept. 22)
Ballet dancing will ruin your feet by the time you're 35, even though you've never danced and are, in fact, a line cook.

Libra: (Sept. 23–Oct. 23)
The unstoppable machinery of fate has set in motion irreversible events which shall inexorably lead to your acquisition of an unwanted nickname.

Scorpio: (Oct. 24–Nov. 21)
You will die of dehydration and malnutrition next week, shortly after hitting the snooze button for the 234,734th time.

Sagittarius: (Nov. 22–Dec. 21)
You knew your new boyfriend was high-maintenance, but you didn't think you'd have to do all the feeding and wiping yourself.

Capricorn: (Dec. 22–Jan. 19)
The tragic events of next Thursday will finally teach you that there aren't any good pranks you can pull using a kidney-dialysis machine.

Aquarius: (Jan. 20–Feb. 18)
The stars indicate that this is a good week for your love life—even in the Southern Hemisphere, where different stars are visible.

Pisces: (Feb. 19–March 20)
It turns out that a journey through the nine circles of hell is a good concept for an epic poem, but not for a restaurant.

TEEN from page 181

hand, even if she knew the answer. Though she enjoys reading, citing John Steinbeck and Ray Bradbury as two of her favorite authors, Ganser was careful only to do so at home, carrying copies of nothing more literary than *Teen People* to read in study hall.

Ganser also took pains never to take on extra-credit assignments or study too hard for tests.

"Only the biggest dorks are all into getting good grades," Ganser said. "I may get good grades, but I'm not into it. It just sort of happened by accident."

"There are lots of geeks they could've given this award to who would've totally loved it," Ganser continued. "But, no, they want to ruin *my* life. What did I do to deserve this?"

According to Grover Cleveland principal Dr. Myles Auletta, Ganser richly deserved the award.

"Besides earning straight A's, Jamie participated in band and Spanish Club, and had an excellent attendance record," Auletta said. "Jamie is a top student, but her teachers say she's not much of a leader. The committee felt this award would be exactly the confi-

dence boost she needs to get out there and really shine."

To Ganser's horror, Auletta announced the winners of the end-of-year awards over the school's P.A. system during his morning address. Unaware she would win the prize, Ganser did not even have a chance to stay home sick the day of the announcement.

"I was just sitting there during homeroom, and Mr. Auletta comes on and says, 'Congratulations to the following students…' Out of nowhere, he says my name. The whole homeroom turned and looked right at me."

Ganser said she tried to pretend she didn't hear her name announced. Her attention-deflecting efforts were foiled, however, when homeroom teacher Vicki Dresser said, "How nice for you, Jamie!" and encouraged students to "give our homeroom's very own celebrity scholar a round of applause." A handful of Ganser's classmates half-heartedly complied while Ganser blushed and paged through her algebra book.

Reviewing the full list of awardees posted on the glass window of the

school's main office, Ganser's humiliation only grew.

"Vonja Dagenhardt is that weird girl who carries all her books for the entire day with her to every class," Ganser said. "Ryan Leeven is a total know-it-all who everyone hates—his parents won't even let him celebrate Halloween. These are the people I'm forever linked to."

Reflecting on her accomplishment, Ganser said she should have worked harder to avoid such a fate.

"I knew I never should have toughed it out and gone to school all those times I was feeling sick last win-

ter," Ganser said. "Then there was the spelling bee. I couldn't decide if I'd feel stupider spelling the words right or wrong, so I just gave the right answers. Look where it got me."

Ganser said another strike against her may have been her high scores on recent end-of-year standardized tests.

"I didn't worry about doing too well, because the scores are all kept secret," Ganser said. "I scored in at least the 95th percentile on everything, but whenever anyone asked me how I did, I was like, 'I can't remember.' I thought I was safe, but obviously I wasn't." ∅

My Lady Has A Beautiful Anus

How do I love my lady's anus? Let me count the ways.

Have you seen her? Have you seen

By John Kluivert

my beautiful lady and her anus? Unless you are an ex-boyfriend, her proctologist, or an art student in that class she modeled for, you probably have not glimpsed the fairest orifice on God's green earth. For this, you have my deepest sympathies.

I would put my lady's anus up against any of the legendary anuses of the past: Helen of Troy, Joan of Arc, Marie Curie, Eleanor Roosevelt. Even Cleopatra, who, according to legend, had a team of eunuchs apply balms and liniments with silken cloths to keep her anus and inner rectum immaculate, could not stand up to my lady. (My lady needs no such fripperies to be beautiful… though I do not hesitate to lavish them on her.) Lovely as Cleopatra's anus may have been, compared to my lady's, hers is a pustulent, lesion-ravaged hole.

My lady does not like me to go on and on about her anus, but how can I resist? When I look into that one brown eye, it's like gazing into a deep, untouched lake. Sometimes, it's as if I'm gazing through a taut, puckered window into her very soul, placing myself in danger of being hypnotized by the swirls of her rectum. Her anus is like a vessel I can't seem to fill with enough love, no matter how hard I try. I am not what one would call a holy man, but when I am gently kissing my lady's fragrant anus, I am convinced that there must be a higher power out there who made this sacred aperture.

As I am very protective of my lady's anus, few have seen it. Nevertheless, I am fond of waxing rhapsodic on its beauty. This can be difficult, though, for how does one describe the beauty of a Tuscan moon? How does one tell of the glory of the cosmos? Shakespeare would have written sonnets about it. Beethoven would have discarded his "Ode To Joy" in favor of "Ode To My

Lady's Anus." And Raphael would have tried—and failed—to render its essence in oils. Lo, prodigious as these immortals' artistic gifts were, my lady's anus would have proven too elusive a muse for any of them to capture.

Yes, my lady's anus is a sight to behold. But it is not just a question of

---

> ### Shakespeare would have written sonnets about it. Beethoven would have discarded his "Ode To Joy" in favor of "Ode To My Lady's Anus."

---

looks. For all its aesthetic loveliness, the greatest thing about my lady's anus is its personality. Sometimes silly, sometimes sad; sometimes dilated, sometimes clenched, it reveals a new wrinkle every time we meet.

Whether I see it reflected in candlelight during a romantic dinner or after it has just awaken from a night's slumber, my lady's anus is still as lovely to me as the first time I saw it. My friends say I won't feel the same way about it when it's 60. I disagree. It may lose that youthful glow, but this is the kind of anus that will only ripen with age. As further assurance, I once caught a glimpse of my lady's mother's anus and, as we all know, the apple does not fall far from the tree.

People say I'm spoiling my lady's anus by buying imported, hand-woven silk toilet paper. But do you polish a diamond with sandpaper? Do you restore the Mona Lisa with a hammer? My lady's anus deserves ruby and emerald enemas. Swabs of cotton soaked in the finest champagne. Anything less would be woefully inadequate for an orifice of such sublime beauty.

And don't even get me started on her perineum. ∅

the ONION presents

Dental-Hygiene Tips

As the old saying goes, "Ignore your teeth, and they'll go away." Here are some helpful hints for keeping that smile bright and healthy for years to come:

- Maintaining an entire mouthful of 32 healthy teeth can be a daunting task. Instead, just focus on 10 or 12 of your favorites.

- Toothbrush technology has made remarkable leaps in recent years. Select a toothbrush so advanced, you have no clue how to use it.

- If, while flossing, your gums begin to bleed, give them at least six months to heal before attempting to floss again.

- Befriend a tiny African bird with whom you can develop a symbiotic relationship in which he picks fragments of food from your teeth.

- Avoid visiting dentists who received their degrees from the University of Berlin Dental School between 1932 and 1945.

- To reduce wear and tear on your teeth, stick to soft foods like pudding and frosting.

- Contrary to what today's kids think, it is not cool to have Shane MacGowan teeth.

- Remember those red tablets they used to pass out at school that, when chewed, revealed the invisible plaque on your teeth? Those were so cool.

- Brush in the morning and before bed, as well as before and after every meal. Quit your job if necessary.

- Brushing should always be done up and down, not with violent stabbing motions.

- If Toothopolis is threatened by the Cavity Creeps, immediately activate the alarm that shouts, "Cre-est!... Cre-est!"

- If you are a denture wearer, avoid soaking them in Coca-Cola overnight.

- An electric toothbrush is an excellent choice if you are such a lazy fuck that you can't even move a toothbrush up and down.

- Dentists have built an entire industry on the perception that they and they alone can provide dental care. Come on, use your common sense.

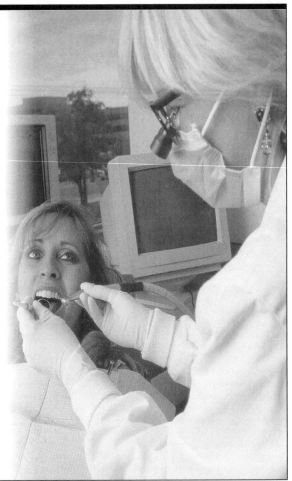

COMMUNITY VOICES

People Don't Like It When You Call Them Stupid

By Mel Turpin

Boy, you try to help people out, but sometimes they can just be so sensitive. Especially over a little thing like being called stupid.

The other day, I was depositing my paycheck at the bank, and the teller asked me, "Do you want this in checking?" Now, that's a pretty stupid question, seeing as I had closed out my savings account a month before and now only have a checking account. I couldn't believe her stupidity.

But, you know, I try to be tolerant and helpful when dealing with people who aren't all that swift. So, to give her a clue, I said, "Yeah, put it all in checking, stupid." No big speech, no insulting dissection of her dumb question. I just politely answered her and tacked on a little "hint."

Well, Little Miss Genius practically stared daggers at me! What was her problem? I mean, all I did was call her stupid. And it's not like it's even necessarily her fault she's that way. Her mother might have drank too

much when she was carrying her or something. All I was doing was pointing out that there's a problem

> ## What was her problem? I mean, all I did was call her stupid.

with her intelligence.

A similar thing happened at Pepe's a couple of weeks ago. I ordered the Beef Enchirito Deluxe Platter, and the waiter brought me a Chicken Enchirito. So, naturally, when he put it down in front of me, I gently said, "I'm sorry, but I ordered the Beef Enchirito, stupid."

The guy takes the plate back, and as he's leaving, he shoots me a nasty look. Geez, like I'm the dumbass who doesn't know a chicken from a cow! Strike two.

But even so, I try to be nice. Next time he comes to the table, I try explaining to him as nicely as possible why he's stupid. I even talk extra slow

to make sure he follows me. But does he appreciate my efforts to better him? Of course not! He tells me, "I have a lot of other tables to serve, sir," and walks off. Yeah, that would be a real tragedy, not getting waited on by this Einstein, right?

That was his third strike. As a general rule, I drop my tip to 10 percent after the first stupid move, 5 percent after the second, and on your third, you lose the whole bundle. I guess a fourth mistake means the waiter would have to tip me, but I'll never find out, because I don't give people a chance to do a fourth stupid thing. I was out of there and off to a smart restaurant.

Frankly, I don't know why I even bother trying to help these people: Every time I do, they get all huffy and defensive.

It's like the silly brouhaha that erupted when a cop pulled me over last week. It was almost 10 p.m., and I was racing to get to the Builder's Square across town before they closed so I could get the wood screws I needed for my basement shelving project. Out of nowhere, Smokey swoops down on me, apparently preferring that I get to the store after it closes.

The first sign of trouble from this

state-supported moron comes when he asks, "Do you know how fast you were going, sir?" Boy, did I ever! Ninety-three! So I say to him, "I've got a question for you, officer: If you've got a radar gun right there in your cop car, why do you have to ask? What are you, stupid?"

Next thing I know, I'm in court. I end up in front of a judge, and I think to myself, "Finally! A sensible pillar of the community who'll respond to reason!"

Well, guess what Judge Chucklehead has the gall to ask? "How do you wish to plead to the charges, Mr. Turpin?" Ye gods, was I in the Twilight Zone? What kind of question is that? I was dying to say to him, "Yeah, I think I'll plead guilty to first-degree trying to finish my shelves! May I see my loved ones one more time before you shoot me?"

But I held back, because I try to show respect to people in positions of authority, even if they don't deserve it. So, instead of responding in a condescending manner, I answered plainly, "How do I wish to plead? What do you think, stupid?"

I don't even want to get into what happened next, but suffice it to say my faith in our justice system was shaken to its core. ∅

Gore Upset That Clinton Doesn't Call Anymore

NEW YORK—Six months after leaving Washington, a despondent Al Gore expressed frustration and sadness Monday that Bill Clinton no longer calls or makes an effort to maintain their once-close friendship.

According to sources close to the former vice president, despite Gore's open invitation to "call or hang out any time," Clinton has not taken the opportunity to contact him since the duo's January departure from office.

"Just before we left D.C., [Clinton] and I sat down and talked about the eight years we'd gone through together," a sweatpants-clad Gore said. "We talked about the good times and the bad times. At the end, we hugged, and he said that even though he had no idea what the future held for him, there was one thing he did know: that we'd always be close."

"I've called him a bunch of times since then, but I've never heard back from him," said Gore, eating a Chipwich while watching TV on his living-room couch. "I guess he's been too busy traveling the world and attending $10,000-a-plate dinners in his honor."

Since January, Clinton has been extremely busy, making numerous paid speaking engagements overseas and establishing himself as a fixture on the New York high-society party circuit. He has been photographed playing billiards with Elizabeth Hurley, taking his daughter Chelsea to a U2 concert, and, most recently, paying a social call to British Prime Minister Tony Blair.

By contrast, Gore has spent the bulk of his time teaching a course at Columbia University, a non-credit seminar called "Covering National Affairs In The Information Age." According to students, the focus of the seminar has shifted recently, largely consisting of an unshaven Gore holding forth on "the forgotten former vice presidents of American history." At the conclusion of the one-hour seminar, he typically returns to his Columbia University office, where he checks his voice mail for messages before taking a leisurely stroll home, often checking his voice mail at least once more en route.

"I realize he's been busy," Gore said. "But I'm sure he could find a spare minute or two just to touch base and say hi. Or even invite me to some of these soirées he's been attending. We used to go everywhere together."

see GORE page 189

Above: Al Gore waits by the phone for a call that may never come.

Four Generations Of Americans Demand Sitcom Reparations

AMERICAN FOCUS

Left: *Hello, Larry* survivors demonstrate in front of NBC Studios in Burbank, CA.

WASHINGTON, DC—Pressure is building for the nation's TV networks to offer a formal apology and reparations to the four generations of Americans who lost millions of hours to inane sitcoms.

"We, on behalf of this nation's 215 million Telecaust victims, demand extensive reparations from the perpetrators of these heartless and falsely heartfelt programs," said Meredith Bishop, 47, president of Americans For Sitcom Reparations

see REPARATIONS page 190

Area Man An Expert On What Women Hate

HOUSTON—A self-professed expert on the fairer sex, 31-year-old Houston resident Gerald Doelpe says he knows exactly what women hate.

"Make sure you don't come on too strong tonight," Doelpe advised friend Joel Bartolo last Saturday before a first date. "Trust me, women don't like it when you come

Above: Gerald Doelpe

on too strong, kissing their hands and arms a lot on the first date. So

see MAN page 189

Judge Rolls Eyes, Upholds Naughty Baker's First-Amendment Rights

LITTLE ROCK, AR—Rolling his eyes and sighing, Judge Howard Kitna of the Arkansas Court Of Appeals upheld Sweet 'N' Nasty erotic-bakeshop owner Bill Engler's constitutional right to free expression Monday. "As there is no legal precedent for ruling against a defendant on the grounds of bad taste, I suppose I have no choice but to rule in favor of 'The Naughty Baker' and his 'Make A Wish... And Blow!' cake," Kitna said of Engler, who was arrested Apr. 7 after refusing to remove a window display featuring a penis-shaped cake with cupcake testicles and chocolate-sprinkle pubic hair. "Go ahead and display your thing."

The Backstreet Boys Or 'N Sync Release New Album

NEW YORK—*Pop*, the hotly anticipated new album from either The Backstreet Boys or 'N Sync, hit record stores Tuesday. "I'm pretty sure this is Backstreet Boys, because that's the band where The Tough One has the goatee and the beads in his hair but no blond streaks, right?" said David Blitz, manager of the Times Square Virgin Megastore where the band made a special in-store appearance Monday before thousands of screaming fans. "Whichever band this is, though, they're definitely poised to take back their crown from the other band." The new album is said to reflect either The Backstreet Boys or 'N Sync's maturing sound, with several darker tracks exploring the perils of fame.

Police Use Exact Right Amount Of Force To Subdue Suspect

CHICAGO—A pair of Chicago police officers earned accolades Monday, when they used the perfect amount of force to subdue 22-year-old robbery suspect Reggie Clifton. "Officers [Brendan] Ford and [Matt] Molloy did a terrific job, putting the suspect in a restraining headlock that was strong enough to immobilize him, yet not so strong as to accidentally cause his neck to snap," police chief Frank DeLuca said. "It should also be noted that these two exemplary officers did not open fire on the suspect when he put his hands in the air, mistakenly thinking he was reaching for a gun somewhere above his head."

Man Realizes He Shouldn't Have Told Girl On Phone He Was Taking Dump

GRANBURY, TX—Moments after ending an on-the-toilet phone conversation with a female friend, Bruce Halpern realized Monday that his candor regarding his whereabouts may have been ill-advised. "That was dumb," Halpern said to himself following the call. "I've told lots of guy friends that I was taking a dump while talking to them, but Julie seemed pretty grossed out." Halpern made a mental note to explain the echo effect in future phone calls by saying he is in the garage.

Hair Weave Shaved Off

JACKSONVILLE, NC—Choosing the popular "bald look" over a full, rich head of hair, Jacksonville resident Michael Elroy shaved off his $875 hair weave Tuesday. "I figured, hey, chicks like bald guys like Bruce Willis," Elroy told reporters following the four-minute weave removal. "Might as well go with the flow." In the past 10 years, the 41-year-old Elroy has had two tattoos removed through laser surgery, allowed three piercings to close, and twice dyed his bleached hair back to its original brown. *Ø*

Collecting All 50 State Quarters Senior's Only Reason To Remain Alive

LAKE HAVASU CITY, AZ—Lacking any other reason to continue drawing breath, retiree Raymond Pfaff, 91, clings to life so that he may collect all 50 of the U.S. state quarters, sources reported Tuesday.

The quarters, each bearing an iconic image representing its respective state, were first put into circulation in 1999, when Delaware, Pennsylvania, New Jersey, Georgia, and Connecticut were released. Five new quarters are slated for release every year until 2008.

"I've got all 13 so far, even the Rhode Island one that just came out," said Pfaff from his bed at St. Andrew's Convalescent Home in Lake Havasu City. "It has a sailboat on it because Rhode Island is the Ocean State."

Added Pfaff: "Vermont's next."

Pfaff, a former vacuum-cleaner salesman suffering from chronic emphysema and diabetes, has not let his deteriorating health keep him from his numismatic pursuit. Due to complications from diabetes, Pfaff had his left leg amputated in January, an event that coincided with the release of the New York quarter.

"Right after the operation, Dr. [William] Homsey handed me a newly minted two-bits with the Statue Of Lib-

"I've got all 13 so far," Pfaff said.

erty on it," Pfaff said. "I can't see too good anymore, but I could feel with my thumb the outline of the Empire State with proud Lady Liberty holding up her torch. As soon as they took me out of intensive care, I went straight to the official U.S. Mint state-quarter collector's board on my nightstand and stuck the coin right in the New York slot. That was the best I'd felt in a while."

According to St. Andrew's staffers, collecting the quarters has been more than a hobby for Pfaff, providing unintended "medicinal" effects.

"When Miriam, Ray's wife of 63 years, passed on in 1997, Ray fell into a pretty bad funk," day nurse Colleen Bresler said. "And it didn't help that his son and two daughters live so far away that they can only visit every other Christmas. But ever since these quarters arrived, Ray hasn't seemed quite so despondent—the suicide talk has

Above: The collector's board that keeps Raymond Pfaff (inset) alive.

almost completely stopped. They've really been a godsend for him, like a metallic version of Prozac."

Other residents of St. Andrew's say Pfaff's enthusiasm for the quarters is contagious.

"Ray and I are best friends," fellow resident Lyle Potterman said. "Some nights, we'll stay up way past 8 talking about what we think will be on upcoming states' coins. Like, for South Dakota, Ray thinks it will be Mount Rushmore, but I think it'll be the Corn Palace. I guess we'll see who's right in 2006."

The day after he was interviewed, Potterman died of an aneurysm. He was 89.

Pfaff celebrated his 91st birthday on July 13, but the date he seems most excited for is August 2007, when the quarter for his home state of Wyoming will be released.

"I wrote a letter to the Treasury, try-

ing to make sure they don't just put a picture of Old Faithful on the back," Pfaff said. "Wyoming is the Cowboy State and, by God, it should have a cowboy on it. I used to love horseback-riding. It's been so long."

In response to Pfaff's plea, the U.S. Treasury sent a form letter thanking the nonagenarian for his continued interest in American currency.

Regardless of what the image on the Wyoming quarter turns out to be, Pfaff is determined to stay alive until the Hawaii coin is released at the end of 2008. Others, however, are not so optimistic.

"I give him two more years, tops," staff physician Dr. David Reames said. "To be honest, with the condition he's in, I'd be amazed if he even made it to Mississippi."

Ronald W. Pindel, executive director of St. Andrew's, also has his doubts.

see SENIOR page 191

You Call This A Doomsday Cult?

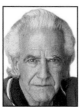

By Will Arlen

Troubled? Of course I'm troubled. But there's one thing in particular that's bothering me right now. Let me just get this out in the open. I'm very, very disappointed with this so-called doomsday cult I joined. There's so much wrong here, I barely know where to begin.

First of all, Simon, our so-called "leader," lacks the necessary charisma a man should have to lead a flock into self-annihilation. I'm not talking about a $20 haircut, either. Jim Jones, that man was nothing special to look at, but when he spoke, you believed mountains could move. When Simon speaks, there's none of that. No fire. No passion. Just a lateral lisp and a lot of "uhs" and "ums." He couldn't lead me to dinner if I was hungry.

That's another thing. Instead of a grueling schedule of meditate-work-meditate-work-work-eat-sleep, we have almost limitless free time. Sorry, Simon, but I don't think three hours a week picking up trash on our adopted stretch of highway is going to break my will. And stop handing out Snickers bars. I should be kept hungry of body but sated of spirit. Unless these things are laced with cyanide, I fail to see the point in constantly stuffing chocolate in our mouths.

And pray tell, Simon, just how are we going to have a dramatic standoff without a weapons stockpile? I've been doing some research, and do you know how many rifles the Branch Davidians had? Two hundred and twenty five. How many do we have? One. One god-damned unloaded .22 that you use to hunt squirrels. I'm sure when the BATF raids our compound, we'll be able to hold them off for at least three minutes with that thing. When we run out of

ammo, we can always turn to that mound of Roman candles you picked up in Indiana.

As long as we're clearing the air here, there's the not-so-small matter of your failure to subjugate the children with ritual sexual abuse. Kids are the future of this cult, and we can't leave them to form opinions of their own. You have to break their spirit by violating them in horrific ways. If you're not going to do it, a lot of your followers are itching to give it a try. Just say the word, and we can start getting some order around here.

You know what else? A lot of people are starting to talk about your new wife, and I can't really disagree with them. Here's a news flash, Simon: a consenting 19-year-old does not a child bride make, even if she is 24 years younger than you. Age-of-consent laws are the laws of an unjust government, not the laws of our Skyfather. You're the conduit between the Skyfather and the people—just make up some shit about how He

told you to take a 14-year-old bride. No one cares. Hell, we expect it.

And just what is our Skyfather, anyway? You've barely said a word about Him, much less made up any elaborate creation myth or Armageddon scenario. All you do is talk about The Beginning and The Great Path we're on. A path has to lead somewhere—otherwise, it's just a dirt road. Are we going to heaven? Paradise? Outer space? Is the Skyfather an alien? Are we his children? His experiment? Do we have the souls of immortals locked within us? You're really falling down on the job here.

Even our name sucks. Look at some of the greats: The Family. Heaven's Gate. Supreme Truth. Now, those are some cult names with pizazz. They're mysterious, sexy, hinting at knowledge beyond the realm of man. And you, O Great One, what do you go and name us? The Guiding Light. Christ. Didn't it ever dawn on you that *Guiding Light* is a frig-

see CULT page 191

GORE from page 187

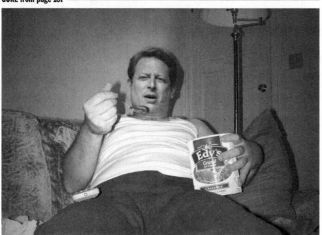

Above: A depressed Gore finishes off a large container of ice cream while watching C-SPAN.

During his eight years in the White House, Clinton faced numerous scandals and crises, including the bombing of the Chinese Embassy in Belgrade, the war in Kosovo, Whitewater, and the Monica Lewinsky sex scandal. Through it all, Gore stood resolutely by his commander-in-chief.

"I thought that over the course of those eight years, we became more than just president and vice president," Gore said. "But now it's apparent that I was wrong. He was just using me for whatever he needed, and then, when he no longer had any use for me, it was out the window with old Al. He even forgot my birthday. I'm such a fool."

Clinton's reasons for not contacting Gore have been a subject of debate within media circles. George Will has referred to the situation as "a continuation of Clinton's longtime pattern of discarding friends," while *Newsweek* contributing editor Eleanor Clift defended Clinton as "a towering figure

in American history who should be allowed to call or not call whomever he pleases."

"In these matters, it's hard to say what Clinton's intentions are," former Clinton advisor George Stephanopoulos said. "In the past, this is how he has distanced himself from people he no longer wants to be friends with—James Carville, for example. On the other hand, it could just be that he's been temporarily swept up in all the hoopla and celebrations. If that's the case, I'm sure it's only a matter of time before Al receives a call."

Whatever the reason, those close to Gore are concerned about his state in recent days.

"All he does is sit around the house and stare at that phone," wife Tipper Gore said. "All it would take is two minutes out of Bill's time, and Al would be on top of the world again. But I think we all know that's not likely to happen anytime soon. Poor Al." ∅

MAN from page 187

be careful about showering them with too much affection, because it *will* backfire."

Even though Doelpe's friends rarely see him around women, they say he is always more than willing to dispense advice on the subject of what they dislike.

"A few months ago, I was heading out to an Astros game with this girl, when Gerald suggested I change my shoes," said Tony Andruss, Doelpe's friend and college roommate. "In his experience, women really hate tennis shoes. He said that when you wear tennis shoes on a date, especially navy Converse hightops, it makes them feel like they're not special enough for you to wear nice shoes, and they probably won't be willing to go out with you again no matter how much you beg."

Continued Andruss: "One time, Gerald asked me what I was making for a girl I'd invited over for dinner. When I said I was making a handmade portabello-and-roasted-pepper pizza, he freaked out. He kept telling me how you should never have a girl over for pizza because they get insulted. He said even if you order a really nice, professionally made pizza from Domino's, they hate it."

Among other behaviors Doelpe says women hate: dominating a conversation, tickling women while they wait to go to the bathroom, ending every sentence with "I'm just kidding," not covering your mouth when you cough, comparing women's bodies to those of famous porn stars, and nicknaming women you meet at bars "Little Miss Sassy Pants."

Though Doelpe's expert opinion is generally ignored, his advice occasionally seems worthwhile.

"One time, Gerald told me that women hate it when guys play air-guitar, especially to AC/DC," friend Peter Giaza said. "Then, a few days later, I was at this bar with this cute girl, and 'You Shook Me All Night Long' came on the jukebox and I

Doelpe is currently single, calling himself a "confirmed bachelor."

---

unconsciously started air-guitaring. I thought the night went well, but she never returned any of my phone calls after that. I remember thinking maybe he was right."

Despite being such an authority on women, Doelpe is currently single, calling himself a "confirmed bachelor." Many, however, believe Doelpe's singlehood is not a choice, but the result of him not practicing what he preaches.

"He could probably actually get a date if he just did half the stuff he's always telling us to do," Andruss said. "I mean, how many times has he told me that women hate guys who have dirt under their nails? Take a look at his fingernails sometime. You could grow potatoes under there."

"Every day, Gerald seems to learn something new about what women hate," Giaza said. "He truly is a master of the don'ts and don'ts of dating." ∅

The Stem-Cell Debate

Embryonic stem-cell research, which scientists believe could hold the key to curing many diseases, is strongly opposed by pro-life advocates. What do *you* think?

Diane Backman
Legal Secretary

"As it clearly states in Leviticus, '...and the use of embryonic stem cells in biomedical research shall be forever prohibited. Thus sayeth the Lord.'"

Richard Heep
Systems Analyst

"Spare me your rationalizations. All I know is, stem-cell research kills a quasi-living four-day-old blob."

Bill Teufel
Delivery Driver

"You mean, you can actually experiment with stem cells from human embryos? Man, and all this time, I've just been throwing mine out."

Irwin Santana
Customs Officer

"*You* try looking into the eyes of a human embryo and saying, 'We need you to die for science.'You can't do it, can you? What do you mean, which side am I arguing?"

Carl Knight
Architect

"They take these stem cells from little babies. They use big, sharp knives. The babies scream, but they take their stems anyway. This makes Jesus cry."

Lori Staub
Reference Librarian

"Only the scientists would go to hell, right? Then let them find a cure for cancer and we'll keep dutifully opposing their actions."

Jordan Ponders A Comeback

Michael Jordan, mulling a return to basketball, has said he will make a decision by mid-September. What enticements has the NBA offered to lure him back?

- Secret underground Jordancave equipped with Jordanmobile, Jordancopter, and jet-powered Jordanboat
- Exemption from NBA's mandatory ball-dribbling policy
- Dancing maidens to cover his on-court path with rose petals
- His own late-night talk show, *Awkwardly Chatting With Michael Jordan*
- NBA, MLB, NFL, NHL, PGA to merge into single league so Jordan can change mind about what sport he wants to play, even mid-game
- Promise of a lucrative endorsement deal with Nike-brand sneakers
- Permission to kill a man, just for fun, before every game
- Starring role in full-length feature MCI commercial
- A lifetime supply of money

the ONION
America's Finest News Source

Herman Ulysses Zweibel *Founder*

T. Herman Zweibel *Publisher Emeritus*
J. Phineas Zweibel *Publisher*
Maxwell Prescott Zweibel *Editor-In-Chief*

FOUNDED 1871 • "TU STULTUS ES"

REPARATIONS from page 187

Above: A visitor to Los Angeles' National Center For Sitcom Reparations solemnly observes photographs in the museum's Hall Of Atrocities.

(AFSR). "For hours wasted staring at mind-numbing swill, for idiotic pap promoted as outrageous romps, for an unending parade of very special episodes, season-ending cliffhangers, and celebrity walk-on appearances, we demand justice be served at long last."

AFSR leaders are calling for each Telecaust survivor to receive a minimum of $8,900 for his or her suffering. Under the AFSR plan, an additional $350 million would go toward the creation of a memorial to time killed during the Sitcom Era and toward educational programs designed to raise awareness and help prevent future sitcom crimes.

"The big TV networks can never erase the pain they have caused," said attorney Ben Feuerstein, who is representing the American public in what is believed to be the largest class-action lawsuit ever filed. "But at the very least, they can demonstrate an ounce of regret and repentance for their crimes by compensating those who, for decades, have suffered through everything from *Gomer Pyle, U.S.M.C.* to *Herman's Head.*"

Said Tampa, FL, resident Helen Neimaier, who lost more than 20,000 hours to sitcoms from 1951 to 1998: "Every night, it was something different, yet completely the same: Mrs. Roper would mistakenly think Jack was giving Chrissie love lessons when he was actually giving her cooking lessons. Or Webster would learn an important lesson about playing with fire. But we were given nothing of substance to watch. And we would go to bed, only to begin again the next night at 8 p.m., 7 Central and Mountain."

Added Neimaier: "And, oh, the spinoffs... always, there were spinoffs."

Bishop said the AFSR is also calling for the establishment of a special air-crimes tribunal to bring "every last network executive" to justice. At last year's Burbank Trials, many major TV producers were tried and convicted, including Garry Marshall, who was executed by firing squad after 20 million witnesses identified his programs from a mid-'70s Tuesday-night line-up.

"*The Flying Nun, Just The Ten Of Us, Small Wonder*... it is all too easy to forget the crimes of the past," Bishop said. "If we are to prevent

> ## "*The Flying Nun, Just The Ten Of Us, Small Wonder*... it is all too easy to forget the crimes of the past," Bishop said.

them from happening again in the future, we must keep such atrocities fresh in our minds."

Despite the groundswell of support for reparations, network apologists are proving a vocal group, as well.

"Punishing the networks for the crimes of the past would only serve to reopen the wounds of shame they still feel," said Sean Wilheit, professor of media studies at Syracuse University. "Do you think the NBC executives responsible for *The Single Guy* are proud of what they've done? Of course not. There's no point in antagonizing these guilt-ridden, basically decent people by continuing to rub their past sins in their faces."

Bishop, however, strongly disagreed.

"We cannot, and should not, erase the scars of the episode of *Silver Spoons* where Ricky becomes a stand-up comedian," Bishop said. "In fact, we must do just the opposite and remain ever-vigilant, striving to ensure that we stop the Urkels of tomorrow before they gain power. Only by demanding full accountability can we reverse the shameful legacy of man's inanity to man." ∅

Ask A Latina Talk-Show Host

By Bonita Salinas-Vicario

Dear Latina Talk-Show Host,

My boyfriend is 34 years old, and he still doesn't know how to tell time. He's late for any plans we have together! I can't tell you how many times I've missed the beginning of a movie because I was waiting out in front of the theater. We get along great and, aside from the lateness, he's very good to me, so I'd hate to tell him that "time's up" on our relationship. Still, I'm getting seriously ticked off by his tardiness. What should I do?

—Waiting In Wilmington

Dear Waiting,

¡Hola a todos y bienvenidos al *Bonita*! Soy Bonita Salinas-Vicario. Gracias, gracias. ¡Son demasiadas amables! ¡Quiero a todas ustedes! Hoy en *Bonita*, tenemos muchos invitados muy especiales. Isabelle está aquí para maquillar a miembras de la audenca. Vamos a tener una discusión sobre la fobia en contra de declararse, y después Enrique Cordero nos enseñará cómo cocinar una cena sexy. ¡Sí, lo oyeron bien, muchachas! Enrique dice que no hay nada que sea mejor que un plato bien caliente de empanadas para animar los sentidos y arreglar la escena para una noche romántica para ti y para alguien especial. Parece interesante, ¿no? ¡Vamos a tener un gran show hoy! ¿Lo pueden sentir, muchachas? ¡Creo que sí!

Dear Latina Talk-Show Host,

Every time my husband's father comes over to our house, he arrives armed with his darned video camera. I wouldn't mind a few minutes of footage here or there, but he has the thing going constantly, even during dinner! I feel like I need to be always watching what I'm saying or doing. He says I'm just being overly self-conscious. What do you think?

—Camera Shy In Camden

Dear Camera Shy,

Nuestra primera invitada es una mujer bien dinámica, alguien que está explorando una carrera muy excitante y tiene su propio negocio aquí en Los Angeles. Sí, es muy trabajadora. ¡Soy muy orgullosa de esta mujer especial! Y es una madre de tres, también. Escribió un libro sobre su carrera como hipnoterapista—Hipnoterapia, La Salvavida. Esta es una carrera muy estimulante, y ya sé que ustedes la van a amar. ¡Yo la amo! Todas, Linda Fernández. Pues, ahorita tengo que decirlo. ¡Estás guapísima! ¿No está guapa, muchachas? Ahora, de tu

libro, averigüé que no habías tenido siempre la energía que tienes ahora, ¿verdad? Chicas, Linda pesaba mucho por varios años. Y estabas descontenta, ¿no? ¿Y piensas que es la razón que terminó tu primer matrimonio? Pero decidiste visitar a un hipnoterapista. ¡Y mira lo que pasó!

Dear Latina Talk-Show Host,

While at a friend's house, I accidentally sat on the eyeglasses he'd left sitting on the couch. Well, as you can probably guess, he now needs a new pair. I told him I was more than willing to pay for the new glasses, and he appreciated the offer, but then we decided it would be fun to ask you what we should do. Who should spring for the new spectacles: him for being careless, or me for being a klutz?

—Two Friends From Framingham

Dear Framingham,

Nuestra próxima invitada es una persona bonita. Conocí a Carmen hace un año, cuando la invitamos al show. Desde entonces, ha aumentado más de $200,000 para ayudar a los niños en Latino américa nacidos con SIDA. Dios ha bendecido a esta mujer. Pero antes de que Carmen salga, tengo un anuncio pequeño. Maria, ven acá. No estés tímida. Estás guapísima hoy. Miren su vestido bonito. Ven acá. Todas recuerdan a Maria ¿verdad? Es la directora del show, y es la mejor. Ven, Maria. Sabes de qué tiene que ver, ¿no? Pues, chicas, ¡Maria va a casarse! ¡Todas nosotras están super alegres por ti! ¡Su novio Ruben le pidió la mano anoche! ¡Enhorabuena, Maria! Estamos muy emocionados por ti, hermana. Eres demasiada amable. ¡Te amo!

Bonita Salinas-Vicario is a syndicated advice columnist whose weekly column, Ask A Latina Talk-Show Host, *appears in more than 250 newspapers nationwide.* ✍

¡Maria va a casarse! ¡Todas nosotras están super alegres por ti! ¡Su novio Ruben le pidió la mano anoche!

Your Horoscope

By Lloyd Schumner Sr.
Retired Machinist and
A.A.P.B.-Certified Astrologer

Aries: (March 21–April 19)
Behavioral scientists Robinson and Godbey once postulated that human activity is almost infinite in meaning and form. Except yours.

Taurus: (April 20–May 20)
The spider you befriend while in prison will amaze you by spinning a web reading "SOME MURDERER" above your bunk before your parole hearing.

Gemini: (May 21–June 21)
You will go bankrupt selling a set of enthusiastically narrated audio tapes designed to help you learn to relax while you sleep.

Cancer: (June 22–July 22)
Your attempts to live a life of the mind will prove less successful than your attempts to live a life of the stomach.

Leo: (July 23–Aug. 22)
Dengue, or bonebreak fever, is carried by the insect *Aedes aegypti* and occurs only in the tropics, which makes your death doubly surprising.

Virgo: (Aug. 23–Sept. 22)
You will continue to suspect that the honest, down-to-earth woman you love is faking her organic gardening.

Libra: (Sept. 23–Oct. 23)
No matter how often you administer the damn things, home pregnancy tests continue to remind you that you are male.

Scorpio: (Oct. 24–Nov. 21)
You will soon find yourself in such dire financial straits that you will not even be able to afford to pay attention.

Sagittarius: (Nov. 22–Dec. 21)
You're not the kind of person who has conversations with her dead grandmother all day, so it would be nice if she'd stop talking to you.

Capricorn: (Dec. 22–Jan. 19)
Your anxiety concerning your place in the universe is allayed when you remember that it's a cute little house on Willard Street, just off the park.

Aquarius: (Jan. 20–Feb. 18)
You will receive a letter from ex-boxer Leon Spinks, who threatens to reveal himself as your long-lost son unless he receives $9 in unmarked bills.

Pisces: (Feb. 19–March 20)
Your week will be entirely uneventful after the thing with the church fire.

SENIOR from page 188

"What Mr. Pfaff doesn't seem to realize is that assisted living costs money, and he is quickly running out of it," Pindel said. "If he wants to live another seven weeks, much less seven

---

Said Dr. David Reames: "To be honest, with the condition he's in, I'd be amazed if he even made it to Mississippi."

---

more years, he's going to have to use those state quarters to pay for his rent and medication."

But Pfaff refuses to listen to naysayers.

"The Lord will have to wait until my work here is done," he said. "When I die, I know what I want them to put on my tombstone: 'He Got All 50.'" ✍

CULT from page 189

gin' soap opera? I'm amazed you didn't name us The Bold And The Beautiful. We're the laughing stock of the entire cult world. Even the Scientologists make fun of us.

Our living quarters don't exactly inspire confidence in your leadership, either. Our compound is not what I would call a forbidding, impenetrable barrier between Us and Them. Fortified? This picket fence is constantly getting knocked over by the neighborhood dogs. I'm no Noah Webster, but I'm sure that if you look up "compound" in the dictionary, you won't find a picture of a mobile home.

Come on, let's get this cult going! Shit, my family isn't the slightest bit worried about me. My "uniform" is off the rack and doesn't match anyone else's. Our sole sources of income are selling junk at the weekend flea market and continuing to hold down our day jobs at the Pepperidge Farm outlet store. It's a goddamn travesty.

I tell you, Simon, if things don't shape up around here soon, I'm going to have to start shopping around for another cult. Because this one just ain't cutting it. ✍

191

NEWS

Gay Comptroller Tired Of Being Referred To As 'That Gay Comptroller'

see LOCAL page 7B

Steve Allen: Gone, Forgotten

see PEOPLE page 4D

The Missing Intern: Unfortunate And All, But What Does It Have To Do With Anything?

see NATION page 2A

STATshot

A look at the numbers that shape your world.

Top-Selling Fragrances

1. Elizabeth Taylor's "Overwrought"
2. N'asal D'Congestanté
3. Finnish Leather
4. Alpha Male
5. Rosie O'Donnell's "Portion"
6. Rogaine Nights
7. Some Cheap Crap For Mother's Day

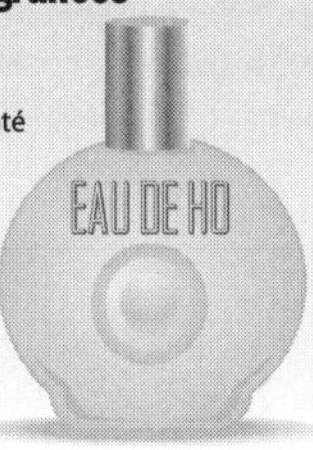

THE ONION VOLUME 37 ISSUE 26
$2.00 US $3.00 CAN

the ONION®

VOLUME 37 ISSUE 26 AMERICA'S FINEST NEWS SOURCE™ 2-8 AUGUST 2001

Fast-Food Purchase Seething With Unspoken Class Conflict

HUNTINGTON BEACH, CA—Resentment, anger, and pity were among the emotions mutually felt by Burger King employee Duane Hesketh and customer Robert Lalley during a class-conflict-laden transaction Tuesday.

According to sources, at 4:22 p.m. PST, the upper-middle-class Lalley approached the working-class Hesketh's register at the Beach Boulevard Burger King to order a meal. The two men instantly became locked in an icy showdown of mutual loathing and disrespect, each resenting the other and everything he represents. For the next seven minutes, the age-old conflict between the haves and have-nots was played out in a passive-aggressive verbal exchange that betrayed no trace of the roiling vortex of bitter hatred that lay just beneath the surface.

"May I help you?" Hesketh asked the golf-loving, SUV-driving financial planner standing before him. Without making eye contact with the mulleted cashier, Lalley replied, "Whopper Jr., large fries, and a large Diet Coke."

Hesketh, who as Lalley ordered was "thinking about how maybe I should get my G.E.D.," stared blankly at the cash register, stunning the customer with his inability to carry out the most basic instructions. As an irritated Lalley repeated his order, Hesketh made an effort to suppress his anger over being forced by economic circumstance into a life of blue-collar servility and mindless, soul-sapping repetition. He expressed this resentment by acting as if he'd failed to hear Lalley's order, asking three times, "Did you say fries with that?"

Above: Cashier Duane Hesketh and customer Robert Lalley eye each other with disgust.

The conflict deepened when Hesketh rang up the order incorrectly.

"Eighteen dollars? That can't be right," said Lalley, his weak-chinned face, conservative haircut, and business-casual attire repulsing Hesketh. The cashier's mind then wandered to

see CONFLICT page 196

Video-Game Character Wondering Why Heartless God Always Chooses 'Continue'

Left: Solid Snake lies dead on the ground once again.

ORANGEBURG, SC—Solid Snake, tactical-espionage expert and star of PlayStation's "Metal Gear Solid," questioned the nature of the universe Monday when, moments after his 11th death in two hours, a cruel God forced him to "Continue" his earthly toil and suffering.

"Is this all there is?" asked Snake, hiding in a storage locker while two masked guards searched for him in the hold of a cargo ship. "Is this why I was created? To suffer? Will I ever escape this endless loop of grueling labor followed by violent death?"

see VIDEO GAME page 195

Bush Finds Error In Fermilab Calculations

BATAVIA, IL—President Bush met with members of the Fermi National Accelerator Laboratory research team Monday to discuss a mathematical error he recently discovered in the famed laboratory's "Improved Determination Of Tau Lepton Paths From Inclusive Semileptonic *B*-Meson Decays" report.

"I'm somewhat out of my depth here," said Bush, a longtime Fermilab follower who describes himself as "something of an armchair physicist." "But it seems to me that, when reducing the perturbative uncertainty in the determination of V_{ub} from semileptonic Beta decays, one must calculate the rate of Beta events with a standard dilepton invariant mass at a subleading order in the hybrid expansion. The Fermilab folks' error, as I see it, was omitting that easily overlooked mathematical transformation and, therefore, acquiring incorrectly re-summed logarithmic corrections for the b-quark mass. Obviously, such a miscalculation will result in a precision of less than 25 percent in predicting the resulting path of the tau lepton once the

Above: Bush shows Fermilab scientists where they went wrong in their calculations.

value for any given decaying tau neutrino is determined."

The Bush correction makes it possible for scientists to further study the tau lepton, a subatomic particle

see BUSH page 196

Few Animals Harmed In Making Of Film

CULVER CITY, CA—Producers of the upcoming Sony Pictures historical epic *Genghis Khan* assured animal-rights activists Monday that "practically no animals were harmed in the making of the film.""The Humane Society and SPCA will be pleased to know that, of the 1,600-plus horses used in *Khan*'s climactic battle sequence, almost none were injured," executive producer David Shell said. "And of those, only a small handful sustained injuries that could be categorized as, you know, serious." Shell noted that the albino Siberian tiger used as the beloved pet of Genghis Khan's enemy "probably would have eventually been beheaded in nature, anyway."

Non-Alcoholic Beer Inventor Unveils New Non-Adhesive Glue

ST. LOUIS—Hot on the heels of his successful line of non-curative medicines, non-alcoholic-beer inventor Thomas O'Doul unveiled "Elmer's Slick," a glue that looks and feels like ordinary white glue but has no adhesive properties. "Say goodbye to your fingers getting all stuck together, just because you want to glue things," O'Doul said at a press conference Monday. "With Elmer's Slick, you can enjoy gluing without all the messy adhesiveness." O'Doul said he next plans to develop a flame-retardant gasoline and the world's first gelatinous construction lumber.

3822 Voted America's Favorite PIN Number

NEW YORK—Narrowly edging out 7135, 3822 is the nation's favorite personal-identification number, according to the August issue of *Money*. "Random-seeming yet easy to remember, 3822 is the 'PIN that's in' for 2001 and beyond," read a cover story revealing the results of the publication's "2001 *Money* PIN Poll." "I've never gone wrong punching in 3822," Harrisburg, PA, retiree Nancy Polk said. "Whether I'm withdrawing money for my hip medication or taking out a big chunk of my life savings for a casino trip, 3822 is the number that gets me there."

Area Love Knows Only Court-Ordered Bounds

COLUMBUS, OH—The passionate love felt by Columbus resident Jonathan Duffy for Ohio State University graduate student Danielle Graves can be stopped by no force outside the ruling of Fifth Circuit Court Judge Harlan Jameson, Duffy said Monday. "Wild horses cannot drag me away from the 100-yard perimeter I've carefully measured around her property," said Duffy, finishing a collage of photos of Graves walking to and from classes, watering her lawn, and ducking behind neighbors' houses. "No court-appointed psychiatrist can medicate away the love a man feels for his spirit bride."

Just A Stay-In-Bed Kind Of Day, Fire Department Declares

ALBANY, NY—Citing inclement weather and a general "blah" feeling among the firefighters, Albany fire chief Martin Brundle declared Monday "just a lazy, stay-in-bed kind of day." "We've been working hard all year," said Brundle, speaking from his firehouse cot. "Our men deserve a day to just lie around and watch TV, and maybe order some pizza in the afternoon." The department's outgoing answering-machine message advised citizens of the greater Albany area to "call back tomorrow." *Ø*

Out-Of-Work P.R. Exec Has Great Things To Say About Unemployment

IRVINE, CA—Calling his current jobless status "an exciting, much-needed opportunity to reassess my direction in life," former Porter Novelli public-relations executive Josh Wallace has great things to say about unemployment.

"Bringing closure to my relationship with Porter Novelli was the best thing that could have happened to me," the 36-year-old Wallace said Monday, his kitchen table piled high with classifieds sections and drafts

> ## "I've really rediscovered the simpler things in life," Wallace said.

of cover letters. "It opened up my future to any and all options. I now have the chance to reconfigure myself literally any way I dream."

Despite his excitement over his current situation, Wallace admitted he was surprised when he was laid off from Porter Novelli, where, since October 1995, he had been "helping clients meet their brand-building and reputation-management needs through creativity in thinking and execution."

"That particular move on [Porter Novelli's] part definitely was not

Above: Unemployed public-relations executive Josh Wallace enjoys his current "occupational freedom."

expected. But in the post-economic boom, the company needed to streamline operations and free up certain employees to multitask," said Wallace, who on May 15 was given three weeks' severance pay and asked to return any company-owned materials to the first-floor receptionist. "I wasn't fired so much as my job was one of the positions phased out through the outsourcing of certain activities and the restructured insourcing of others."

Eager to "reassess my career path" and "concretize my goals,"

Wallace said he is "thrilled to be off-site."

"Occupational freedom is exactly what I need at this juncture," Wallace said. "A few days of just sitting back on the couch made me see how much I needed some time to visualize exactly where I wanted to go with respect to my career."

Added Wallace: "After much serious thought, I'm confident in saying I eventually want to go back to work in public relations."

In the 10 weeks since his layoff, Wallace has sent out nearly 100 resumes, all without luck. But in spite of the lack of job prospects, Wallace's spirits are high.

"I'm completely recharged and rejuvenated," Wallace said. "When I do land my next job, I'll be going in with so much more energy than the people already at the company. There's a fresh, outsider perspective I bring to the table, thanks to my spending this time as part of the non-working world."

Unemployment, Wallace said, has enabled him to do many things he'd never found time for while working 40 hours a week.

"For one thing, I've had the opportunity to see some top-flight daytime programming I never knew existed," Wallace said. "I also went out jogging several times, and I plan to go more, now that I've discovered how great it makes me feel."

"I've really rediscovered the sim-
see UNEMPLOYMENT page 198

I Could Write A Better Rubaiyat Than That Khayyam Dipshit

By Gord Hunsacker

Down at the loading dock, me and the guys get into a lot of good-natured scraps about sports teams and movies and whatnot. Sure, it gets a little heated sometimes, but it's always in good fun. When it comes to poetry, though, there are days when I just want to haul off and punch their sorry faces.

Especially Tony. I mean, he's entitled to his opinion and all, and if he doesn't acknowledge that Keats was the greatest English poet of the 19th century, that doesn't make him evil or nothing. But when he starts mouthing off about *The Rubaiyat Of Omar Khayyam* being one of the five greatest poems ever, I want to clock him in the nuts. *The Rubaiyat Of Omar Khayyam*? A towering achievement that

> ## They should call Omar Khayyam "Ozymandias Khayyam," because when I look on his works, I despair!

stands beside the likes of *Beowulf* and *The Faerie Queen*? What the fuck is Tony smoking, and where can I get some?

I've owned one copy or another of that steaming pile of turd since I was 10 years old, and I never once got past the halfway mark. I could write a better Rubaiyat than that, and I've never been published. I swear, that thing's worse than *The Rime Of The Ancient Mariner*.

When I was a kid, I just figured it was Edward Fitzgerald's translation that was lacking. I was certain I'd learn to love the poem when a more authoritative version finally came out. But in the years that followed, none of the other translations held my attention, either. Whether it was E.H. Whinfield's so-called "definitive" version or A.J. Arberry's, one thing remained constant: *The Rubaiyat* blew.

Still not convinced that such a classic poem could be that bad, I learned Farsi so I could read it in the original text. And you know what? It still sucked! Jesus, I can't tell you how awful it was. It may actually have been worse in Farsi than in any of the English translations. They should call Omar Khayyam "Ozymandias Khayyam," because when I look on his works, I despair!

If Khayyam's Rubaiyat was all you had to go on, you'd think Islam was some stuffy, soulless religion, not the vibrant, living faith it is. Khayyam's ham-fisted quasi-narrative leaves any sensible reader flipping back and forth between quatrains to remember exactly what he said just four lines before. How in holy hell did this train wreck of a poem ever get published? Omar Khayyam Sr. must have run a publishing house or something.

Not that it's saying much, but I could kick some major Rubaiyat ass compared to that Khayyam hack. *The Rubaiyat Of Gord Hunsacker* would be, well, shit, it would be publishable, which is more than I can say for Khayyam's.

This is just off the top of my head. I'm not even calling this all that great or anything, but here's

see RUBAIYAT page 198

VIDEO GAME from page 193

Snake was then discovered by the guards and cut down in a hail of gunfire.

Snake, who has been fatally shot 2,143 times in the past six months, said he does not know why God deems it necessary for him to endlessly repeat his mission, which involves sneaking aboard a hijacked military ship and discovering who stole the walking nuclear-equipped battle tank known as Metal Gear Ray.

"Why will the Lord not grant me my final rest?" asked a reincarnated Snake, crawling underneath a lifeboat on the ship's weather deck. "Certainly there must be a greater purpose for me than to kill dozens and eventually be killed myself."

Added Snake: "As Goethe said, 'Man must strive, and in striving he must err.'"

Pitching himself over the ship's railing to avoid a trio of patrol guards, Snake pondered the notion of self-determination, wondering aloud whether he had any control over his own destiny. Before he could draw any conclusions, however, he lost his grip, falling into the sea and drowning.

"The Koran asks, 'Shall not the Lord of all the Earth do right?'" said Snake, rematerializing under the lifeboat. "But scholars have often argued whether the question is an assertion of belief or a refutation of faith in absolute goodness on the part of the Creator. As for myself, all I know is,

I'm tired of the constant pain, death, and destruction."

Snake was then shot in the head by an undetected guard, falling into a pool of his own blood before reappearing in the ship's afterdeck, where his mission began.

"I often wonder, as many video-

> ## "Why will the Lord not grant me my final rest?" asked a reincarnated Snake.

game characters do, whether God forces me to Continue to punish me for my sins," Snake said. "After all, I've deserted the American military, killed hundreds of guards, and betrayed my would-be lover, Meryl Silverburgh, by submitting to torture in the alternate ending to the first installment of 'Metal Gear Solid.' But sometimes, like when I suicidally attack dozens of armed guards with only my bare hands, it seems that God is putting me through hell merely to amuse Himself. It just doesn't make sense."

According to Rev. Paul Flessing of Yale University's Divinity School, Snake's theosophical quandary is far

Above: God, moments before determining Solid Snake's fate.

from uncommon.

"We all wrestle with the Big Questions about the will of God and one's place in Creation," Flessing said. "But the important thing is to have faith and try to find meaning in one's life—or lives, as the case may be. We must remember the trials of Job, whose faith God continually tested. It seems Snake is going through something very much like that, with this constant pattern of 'Continues.' The purpose will become clear to him in the end."

Sidling along a companionway

toward the ship's lounge, Snake considered his ultimate fate.

"What awaits me at the end of my lives' journeys?" Snake asked. "Is there a Paradise on the other side? Or will it all end in a full-motion video sequence that hints at a forthcoming sequel?"

The hallway then filled with nerve gas, fatally asphyxiating Snake.

God, also known as Orangeburg 11-year-old Brandon MacElwee, offered no comment on His greater plan for Snake, saying He was "too busy trying to get to the part with the knife-throwing Russian girl." ∅

The Missile-Defense Standoff

The U.S. and Russia are clashing over the Bush Administration's plans to develop a missile-defense system, which would defy 1972's ABM Treaty. What do *you* think?

Carl Cox
Systems Analyst

"Good for Bush. I always thought Clinton was a little weak in the pissing-off-the-Russians-over-nuclear-weapons department."

Dana Coleman
Homemaker

"Do you realize that the U.S. and Russia have held enough disarmament talks to bore the world to death 50 times over?"

Irene Schmid
Arts Administrator

"I've got a missile-defense idea: We genetically engineer a race of bird-men to fly up and defuse the missiles with their beaks. That'd be cheaper and just as effective."

Bobby Post
Landscaper

"Speaking of which, don't use the can for a while. I just violated one hell of a B.M. Treaty myself."

Bill Poulent
Cab Driver

"Gee, George, way to telegraph the sneak attack. Now they'll totally know."

Don Banks
Podiatrist

"As Kenny Rogers says, you gotta know when to hold 'em, know when to fold 'em; know when to walk away, know when to use humanity as a bargaining chip in a game of nuclear brinksmanship."

Honoring The King Of Pop

On Sept. 7, 'N Sync, Britney Spears, Destiny's Child, and other superstars will gather at Madison Square Garden for a concert paying tribute to Michael Jackson. What is planned for the event?

- Jackson to be presented with gift of Emmanuel Lewis' skeleton
- Will premiere special edition of "Thriller" video, in which Jackson's ghoul makeup is digitally replaced with his current face
- All-chimpanzee choir to shriek a cappella version of "Dirty Diana"
- Lisa Marie Presley to read 27-page statement asserting Jackson's heterosexuality
- Nose worn by Jackson on cover of *Off The Wall* to be auctioned off for charity
- Boys Choir Of Harlem to present Jackson with selves
- Lifetime-achievement award given to Jackson by *Effeminate Batshit Loonball Albino Pederast* magazine

 the ONION
America's Finest News Source

Herman Ulysses Zweibel *Founder*

T. Herman Zweibel *Publisher Emeritus*
J. Phineas Zweibel *Publisher*
Maxwell Prescott Zweibel *Editor-In-Chief*

FOUNDED 1871 • "TU STULTUS ES"

BUSH from page 193

formed by the collision of a tau neutrino and an atomic nucleus.

Bush resisted criticizing the Fermilab scientists responsible for the error, saying it was "actually quite small" and that "anyone could have made the mistake."

"High-energy physics is a complex and demanding field, and even top scientists drop a decimal point or two every now and then," Bush said. "Also, I might hasten to add that what I pointed out was more a correction of method than of mathematics. Experimental results on the Tevatron accelerator would have exposed the error in time, anyway."

Fermilab director Michael Witherell said the president was being too modest "by an order of magnitude."

"In addition to gently reminding us that even the best minds in the country are occasionally fallible, President Bush has saved his nation a few million dollars," Witherell said. "We would have made four or five runs on the particle accelerator with faulty data before figuring out what was wrong. But, thanks to Mr. Bush, we're back on track."

"It's true, I dabbled in the higher maths during my Yale days," said Bush, who spent three semesters as an assistant to Drs. Kahsa and Slaughter at Yale's renowned Sloane High-Energy Physics Lab. "But I didn't have the true gift for what Gauss called 'the musical language in which is spoken the very universe.' If I have any gift at all, it's my instinct for process and order."

Continued Bush: "As much as I enjoyed studying physics at Yale, by my junior year it became apparent that I could far better serve humanity through a career in statecraft."

While he says he is "flattered and honored" by the tau-neutrino research team's request that he review all subsequent Fermilab publications on lepton-path determination, Bush graciously declined the "signal honor."

"This sort of thing is best left to the likes of [Thomas] Becher and [Matthias] Neubert, not a dilettante such as myself," Bush said. "I just happened to have some time on the plane coming back from the European G8 summit, decided to catch up on some reading, and spotted one rather small logarithmic branching-ratio misstep in an otherwise flawless piece of scientific scholarship. Anyone could have done the same." ∅

Below: Bush circles the crucial misstep.

CONFLICT from page 193

the upcoming getting-high-after-work-in-the-parking-lot-with-Shawn-and-Joe ritual that constitutes one of the few moments of pleasure in his largely intolerable life.

"Huh?" said Hesketh, putting Lalley's middle-class Baby Boomer liberalism to the test by forcing him to realize that he deeply despises the blundering ineptitude of the uneducated.

"Christ, I've seen trained chimps respond to verbal cues better than you," the stone-faced Lalley did not say aloud. "If you were one-tenth as good at your job as you are at slouching around in baggy pants, you'd probably own the whole fucking Burger King corporation by now," he opted not to add, instead toying anxiously with his Citizen watch.

Hesketh then told Lalley that his order would have to be voided and rung up again.

"Maybe you should ask someone to help you," said Lalley, struggling to resist the overwhelming urge to grab his social inferior by the collar and smash his vacant head into the cash register until one or the other cracked open.

Eager to antagonize the despised customer, Hesketh continued to putter, spending two minutes fumbling with the "void" process before mumbling to Lalley that he would not be able to refund the money until the manager opened the register.

"I'm sort of in a hurry," said Lalley, welling with a mixture of rage and pity for the acne-riddled wage slave on the poor side of the counter.

When the error was finally corrected, Hesketh began to gather Lal-
see CONFLICT page 197

With Friends Like These...

A Room Of Jean's Own
By Jean Teasdale

Until recently, I never really believed much in the generation gap. I figured, if you're young at heart (and I like to think that my heart is 19 years old, blonde, and gorgeous!), a person's age means little. But, after getting to know my downstairs neighbors, I'm starting to see why the old fogies get a little frustrated with young people: They can be pretty "out there" sometimes!

As you may recall from my last column, three college students, Greg, Sean, and Marni, recently moved into my apartment complex. Upon meeting them, I discovered that they were Jeanketeers of the highest order—just about the biggest fans of

my column I'd ever met.

And I'm not just whistling "Dixie" here! They could recite my columns, line by line, from memory! Not just the obvious lines, either, like, "Keep smiling!" but really obscure ones: "If only I had a brain... and a 23-inch waist!" "I just love horses! They're so beautiful, and they represent freedom." "Boy, I could use a chocolate bar the size of Delaware right now!" I was floored by the depth and breadth of their "Jeanspertise"! How many columnists can claim that kind of fan devotion?

When their school term ended in May, I started to see a lot more of Greg, Sean, and Marni. (Or "The Three Jeanketeers," as I affectionately called them.) Greg and Sean worked at the same pizza place, and every night they'd bring over free leftover pizza and hang out with me as I waited for hubby Rick to return from Tacky's Tavern. Sean owned a Polaroid camera and had

this hilarious idea to snap Rick's picture the second he would come in. Of course, Rick was always tanked to the gills, and most nights he barely noticed the flashbulb as he stumbled either to the toilet or the bedroom, but Sean got some really hilarious shots of him!

As the summer wore on, Sean started taking pictures of me. They were candid shots of me doing the most ordinary things, like washing dishes, feeding my cats, grocery shopping, or dusting my Precious Moments figurines. Now, normally, I just hate getting my picture taken. (Let's just say there's a little too much of me to photograph!) But since Sean was a buddy of mine and a real card to boot, I eventually got to the point where I actually started to enjoy it.

While Sean snapped photos, he asked me tons of questions: where I was born, what my family life was like growing up, my pet peeves, etc. So one day, I decided to turn the tables on him and ask him about himself.

I laughed when he said he put out his own magazine. After all, how many magazine publishers work at pizza joints? But then he told me it wasn't a "magazine" magazine, like *People* or *Rosie*, but a "'zine": a little booklet he writes and lays out on his computer and then has printed up at Kinko's. He said he's done four issues under the name *SeanZine*, but he was thinking of changing the name to *Blossom Meadows*, which is the name of the street where our apartment complex is. I told him I thought *Blossom Meadows* sounded a lot prettier, and he smiled and said, "Jean, you sold me. *Blossom Meadows* it is." I was happy to help out. I was a little worried, since, from what I understood, the magazine business is very cutthroat. But, as a creative person myself, I understood Sean's need to express himself, and I thought, if he wants to put out his little 'zine pamphlet, more power to him.

Though the Three Jeanketeers usually came up to my place, I spent some time down in their apartment, too. At first, I felt a little strange. The place is rather, well, let's just say, *interestingly* decorated. I mean, they had a lot of cute stuffed animals, but there were some pretty odd things, too. Like—I'm not kidding—a gynecologist's examining table! They were always encouraging me to sit in it, but there was no way on Earth I was going to slip my ankles through those stirrups! Greg had no problem sitting in it, though. With his long legs and—get this—

purple hair, he was quite a sight! He'd just sit there, eating Fritos and acting like it was the most normal thing in the world! (And I thought *I* was out there!)

This other time, Greg and I made ice-cream drinks for everybody, and Sean had this crazy idea to blast Pink Floyd and watch projected scenes from old View-Master discs! We were getting pretty blotto off Pink Squirrels and Brandy Alexanders, and it was a strange sensation, looking at old fairy-tale scenes while listening to this loopy music! I'm telling you, it was the weirdest—and most fun—experience I'd had since inhaling "rush" at the old Free Wheelin' Roller Disco Rink 20 years ago!

Then, just yesterday, something bizarre happened. I still don't know what to make of it.

A pan of my infamous Four Alarm Double Mocha Chip Brownies in tow, I made my way downstairs to the Three Jeanketeers' place. But, as I approached their apartment, I could hear screaming. It was Marni! I considered making a 180 back to my abode, but my nosy nature got the best of me, and I put my ear up to the door.

I couldn't hear everything that was said, but it sounded like Marni was pretty upset at Sean. She was saying things like, "I can't believe I fell for your crap, Sean," and "God, this is so embarrassing."

Then she really let him have it. "Obviously, you led me on, and you have the nerve to deny it? What am I, stupid? How could it have meant any other thing? Oh, do not give me that look. You smug, evil prick! God, I'm sorry I ever shared a sincere, non-sarcastic thought with you! You are so immature, Sean! Go to hell!"

Yikes! Great timing to step in on a lovers' quarrel, Jean! I had no idea Sean and Marni were even involved! I started to tiptoe back upstairs when the door opened. Marni emerged, holding a box of her stuff, tears rolling down her face. She saw me and sighed.

"Oh, God, Jean, please. Not now," she said.

"I brought brownies!" I exclaimed, not really knowing what to say. But she just hurried out into the parking lot. I followed her, asking her if everything was okay. She said no, obviously not, and told me she was moving out. I was a little shocked when she threw the entire box, which contained all sorts of great stuff, including a big poster of that dreamboat *CHiPs* star Erik Estrada, into the Dumpster.

see TEASDALE page 198

CONFLICT from page 196

ley's food items as slowly as possible. The food-gathering process was further stalled when, while waiting for the fryer timer to run down, Hesketh received a cell-phone call from his ex-girlfriend. During the 90-second conversation, Lalley said he heard the words "Camaro," "the baby," "have to be in court that day," and "the other baby."

"What kind of inbred dolt wears $180 shoes to a job where he walks around in grease all day?" Lalley asked himself while watching the futureless 23-year-old stand by an empty metal rack, waiting for the Whopper Jr. to arrive from the grill area. "Especially when he barely makes minimum wage."

At no point during the seven-minute transaction did Hesketh pick up a burger and grind it into Lalley's face. Nor did he drop his pants and wipe his ass with his cap, or give in to his intense desire to set the kitchen on fire. Lalley showed equal restraint in resisting the urge to scream or repeatedly snap his fingers in front of Hesketh's uncomprehending, mouth-breathing face while yelling "Hel-*lo*? Hel-*lo*?" in a comic exaggeration of a developmentally disabled person's voice.

Despite driving both participants into near-apoplectic rage, the exchange ended without incident.

"[Lalley] finally got his food," said Huntington Beach resident Janis Monroe, who was waiting in line behind Lalley. "Then he huffed and walked out. Actually, he did say 'Thanks,' but he was being sarcastic."

After finally getting his food, Lalley retreated to the Burger King

parking lot, where he joylessly consumed the Whopper Jr. in his Ford Explorer rather than dine in the restaurant and spend another second in the presence of the doomed souls inside. Hesketh, meanwhile, retreat-

> ## "I'm sort of in a hurry," said Lalley, welling with a mixture of rage and pity for the acne-riddled wage slave on the poor side of the counter.

ed to the walk-in cooler, where he smoked a cigarette and pilfered cheese slices in a vain attempt to restore some of the dignity of which he is regularly stripped.

"This sort of situation is unavoidable when you have such a disparity in earning potential," said Dr. Art Hermann, author of *Consumer And Consumed: Class Conflict In Our Market-Driven Postindustrial Society.*

According to Hermann, such inter-class run-ins occur roughly 600 million times a day in the U.S.

"And a large portion of those 600 million incidents," Hermann said, "will be at the hand of Phillip, the arm-dragging troglodyte who bags my groceries down at the Safeway." ∅

"I'm getting rid of all the stupid crap and stupid people in my life, and I'm going to live like a normal human being again," Marni said. "I should've done it long ago." She stopped crying, looked at me for a second, and fished something from her back pocket. It was a little stapled booklet, which she slipped into my hand.

"Jean, Sean didn't want you to see this," she said. You know his 'zine, *Blossom Meadows*? Well, he did an entire issue about you. That's why he was always taking photos and asking you questions. He was actually interviewing you for his 'zine. He never told you about his little tape recorder, either."

I looked at the 'zine. On its cover was a poor photocopy of one of the pictures Sean took of me at Carlton Cards at the mall. I'm holding a darling teddy bear and smiling. "Special All-Jean Teasdale Issue! With A Cameo Appearance By Hubby Rick!" the cover read.

"I think he should have come clean with you from the beginning, but he was being his usual devious, immature, holier-than-thou self," Marni said. "He thinks he's this genius underground writer-provocateur, when he's really just an asshole with a computer who lives near Kinko's. Not that he has any money, but if I were you, I'd sue him for libel."

I was stunned by the contents of Sean's 'zine! He really did devote the entire issue to me! Many of the things I'd mentioned in our private conversations were quoted. And sprinkled throughout the 'zine were boldface "Jean Factoids": "Jean estimates she's spent over $800 on Precious Moments figurines in her life"; "Jean has always been 'a little chunky,' as she so diplomatically puts it, but did you know she put on most of that weight shortly after marrying hubby Rick?"

On top of that, Rick's drunken snapshots were all present and accounted for. And there was a little interview with Roz, my boss at Fashion Bug, in which she told Sean that I was "a good person, but she needs supervision because she gets a little distracted." Someone even drew a *Love Is* parody, with hubby Rick and me as the two little naked kids, only I was playing with my Miss Beasley doll while Rick tottered around drunk with a beer in his hand! My mind reeled!

At the back of the 'zine was an essay by Sean titled "The Tragedy Of Jean Teasdale." And, boy, was it a doozy! In it, he wrote: "During our long talks, I tried to plumb Jean's depths as best I could, but the task was almost impossible when everything that came out of her mouth was one cliché or another, distilled from something she'd heard on TV or read in *Good Housekeeping*. She seems as pro-

grammed as any robot. Meeting Jean, one is reminded of a lower-middle-class Stepford Wife. Yet, despite her ravenous desire to conform, she is perennially on the outside, lonely and condescended to when not ignored."

But wait, there's more! "Tragic as Jean may be, she's hardly unique. Anesthetized by the media and consumer culture, starved of meaningful human interaction, every day across America, millions of Jean Teasdales escape into their solipsistic inner sanctums, having long ago abandoned any hopes of greatness, instead embracing banality with something akin to fervor. What sets Jean apart from these pitiful creatures—and even this is probably inspired by her beloved confessional daytime talk shows—is her compulsive need to tell anyone and everyone who's willing to listen about her aggressively irrelevant life experiences, even at the expense of her own dignity. Clearly, her columns are a desperate cry for help."

Well, I have to admit, a lot of that essay went over my head. But I could tell it was pretty negative. When exactly did Sean observe this "Tragedy Of Jean Teasdale"? The night we made ice-cream drinks? Or maybe it was the time we went to the Junior Fair and ate elephant ears. Or the time we made Shrinky Dinks. We seemed to have a pretty good time that day, as I recall.

I couldn't understand it. How can you be nice to someone, practically worshipping the ground they walk on, and then turn right around and attack them? Then I thought, well, maybe this is a "Generation X" thing. Generation X is known for being kind of weird and offbeat. Maybe, instead of just confronting a person with their personality flaws, or just quietly tolerating them, they secretly publish a magazine complaining about them.

A few days after Marni moved out, hubby Rick asked me why I wasn't hanging out with my "freak pals" as usual. I didn't tell him about *Blossom Meadows*. I just told him that me and the Three Jeanketeers really didn't see eye-to-eye on a lot of stuff anymore, and that they were kind of immature and dull, anyway.

"Christ, Jean, I could have told you that weeks ago," Rick said. "That guy with the purple hair is queer as a $3 bill, and the other guy's just a pussy. And the girl is a ballbuster if I've ever seen one. Forget about those dumbasses."

Now, usually, Rick's advice is pretty useless, but in this instance, it made sense. I'm trying to put it behind me. Still, I couldn't resist fishing that Erik Estrada poster out of the Dumpster before the trash-removal service came. I hate to see great art go to waste! ✍

at least a passable quatrain that muses upon man's mortality: *Woe betide man for his shortness of days, Soon to be dust though frantically he prays. Envy the mountain, a million years here, A billion, too; and it evermore stays.*

You see? Now, *that's* a Rubaiyat. A couple hundred more lines like those, and you'd have a goddamn Rubaiyat you wouldn't be ashamed to tell your friends you wrote!

Now, of course, the guys down at the dock always ask me, "If you could do so much better, why don't you?" They're totally missing the point! I got a wife and kids to support! I can't just quit my job to write another Rubaiyat, no matter how much better it'd be than Omar Fucking Dipshit Khayyam's.

I just wish I could hop in a time machine and travel back to 12th Century Khorasan. I'd tell Khayyam to stick to math and astronomy, and leave the poetry to folks who have a friggin' clue. ✍

pler things in life," Wallace continued. "Who knew the pleasures to be found in just taking a walk around the city? Or walking around the mall for a few hours? Or driving down to the gas station for a sandwich? That's what I did earlier today, and it was great, absolutely great. There's lots of tremendous stuff to see at the gas station, if you just take the time to notice."

Recently, Wallace took advantage of his "freed-up schedule" by visiting his parents in Bakersfield.

"Josh just showed up in the middle of the day and surprised us," Wallace's mother Elaine said. "He kept saying something about wanting to 'touch base and make sure the whole family's all on the same page,' which I didn't really understand, but other than that it was a nice visit."

Added Elaine: "A full week was maybe a little long for him to stay, just sitting up there in his old room like that. But I wasn't going to say anything. Not when he's having such a terrible time of it." ✍

JUST FOR FUN

Your Horoscope

By Lloyd Schumner Sr.
Retired Machinist and
A.A.P.B.-Certified Astrologer

Aries: (March 21–April 19)
Your children will grow up in a world very different from the one you live in, thanks to a lucrative deal you will soon make with the Rigellians.

Taurus: (April 20–May 20)
There's a part of you that wants to go to a remote, far-off place and start eating everything in sight.

Gemini: (May 21–June 21)
You will wake up in a Calcutta flophouse between two dead Thai prostitutes, which can mean only one thing: You're now officially in a rut.

Cancer: (June 22–July 22)
Next time someone comes to your house to tell you that your husband has been shot, you should at least try to act surprised.

Leo: (July 23–Aug. 22)
Learning to love again will be hard for you: You've been burned before, and the thick scar tissue still cracks every time you move.

Virgo: (Aug. 23–Sept. 22)
You are highly prized by those around you, mostly due to your high concentrations of silver and antimony.

Libra: (Sept. 23–Oct. 23)
Confusion, a loss of self, and disorientation are your lot next week when you are dubbed into Portuguese and rereleased in Brazil.

Scorpio: (Oct. 24–Nov. 21)
The stars wish to reveal a part of your destiny, but not in a straightforward fashion. Let's just say it's bigger than a breadbox.

Sagittarius: (Nov. 22–Dec. 21)
Cupid will take aim at your heart next week, killing you with the .45 he keeps handy for major assholes.

Capricorn: (Dec. 22–Jan. 19)
You will soon have some very entertaining stories about how two species of wombats became endangered.

Aquarius: (Jan. 20–Feb. 18)
You will spend much of the next week lying around aimlessly, largely because of the lack of adenosine triphosphate in your limbs.

Pisces: (Feb. 19–March 20)
By strange coincidence, this week is the 60,000th anniversary of the invention of the hand ax, a device that figures heavily in your future.

Popeye Decries Mideast Bombings; 'Dese Bombinks Is Disgustipating,' Says Sailor Man

see WORLD page 4A

Dress Code Cracked

see OFFICE page 6C

Mall Music Store Files All Black Artists Under 'Urban'

see COMMERCE page 8B

STATshot

A look at the numbers that shape your world.

Lamest U.S. Excuses

- It was ruined in postproduction
- I thought the schoolyard accident had rendered me infertile
- There were many highly complex sociopolitical factors at work
- I thought presidents could do that
- I bought it so we could watch it together and laugh about how stupid it is

THE ONION VOLUME 37 ISSUE 27
$2.00 US $3.00 CAN

27

0 74470 94595 6

---

the ONION®

VOLUME 37 ISSUE 27   AMERICA'S FINEST NEWS SOURCE™   9–15 AUGUST 2001

Arby's Apologizes For New Beef 'N' Bacon Sandwich
'This, Regrettably, Is Just Another Sandwich'

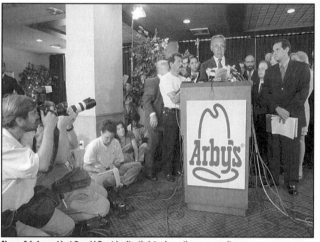

Above: Arby's president Donald Forst hesitantly introduces the new menu item.

FT. LAUDERDALE, FL—With moderate fanfare, Arby's apologetically unveiled its new Beef 'N' Bacon sandwich Monday, calling the uninspired menu addition "pretty so-so" and "more of the same."

"America, Arby's is cooking up something brand-new," said Donald Forst, president of the fast-food chain. "Just don't hold a parade or anything. This, regrettably, is just another sandwich."

The Beef 'N' Bacon, which makes its debut Aug. 15 at Arby's restaurants nationwide, features thinly sliced roast beef topped with crispy strips of bacon—a combination Forst described as "somehow lacking a truly special element."

see ARBY'S page 201

Above: Gina Von Poppel and Jason Roder.

S&M Couple Won't Stop Droning On About Their Fetishes

SANTA FE, NM—According to friends of Jason Roder and Gina Von Poppel, the sexually adventurous couple won't stop droning on about spanking, caning, ball gags, erotic photography, fetish parties, leather, rubber, PVC, latex, whips, floggers, and countless other S&M-related objects and activities.

"When Jason first told me about his and Gina's kinky sex life, I was amazed. I wanted to hear all about it," said Stan Pritchard, Roder's

see COUPLE page 202

Garage Band Actually Believes There Is A 'Terre Haute Sound'

TERRE HAUTE, IN—The members of The Weebles, a local garage band formed in 1998, actually believe there is something called the "Terre Haute Sound," sources reported Monday.

"It's great," said Weebles bassist Gary Gaspart, 22, speaking from the band's practice space in guitarist/vocalist Jonah Thompson's parents' garage. "The scene is so supportive. It's all about helping each other out, going to the other bands' shows. We're really building on the Terre Haute Sound in ways that are going to blow it up, and I mean wide."

The Terre Haute Sound is described by Gaspart as "a bit of NOFX, some revved-up psychobilly country a la Reverend Horton Heat or The Supersuckers, and some analog synthesizer thrown in just to keep it fresh." He emphasized that the definition is by no means binding, and that virtually anyone who chooses to become part of the Terre Haute Sound is welcome.

"We've got all sorts of bands in the THS," Gaspart said. "There's Cutie, who are sort of a psychedelicized version of Op Ivy with a hint of Cheap Trick-style power-pop thrown in. Then there's Spongebob Fuxx, which does grindcore ballads. And you can't forget The Vagina Splits, who are like Bratmobile but with more attitude. The Splits

Above: The Weebles' Gaspart, Murn, and Thompson.

may be girls, but they rock harder than most of the guy bands around."

"Not that there's anything wrong with the guy bands here," Gaspart added. "It's all about scene unity."

Asked which local bands would not be considered part of the Terre Haute Sound, Thompson struggled to come up with one.

"Bottom line, we all just like to rock," Thompson said. "I think that's what sets Terre Haute apart from the Danvilles and West Lafayettes of the world. That and the fact that a lot of us have the same drummer."

According to Thompson, though the Terre Haute Sound is the prod-

see BAND page 203

Slain Cop Had Only 37 Years Until Retirement

DETROIT—In a tragic twist of fate, Detroit police officer Stephen Brophy was cut down in the line of duty Monday, just 37 years before he was to retire. "Just yesterday, Stephen was talking about all the plans he and his wife had for 2038," said officer Pete Driscoll, Brophy's short-time partner, who was with the 28-year-old when he was fatally shot by an armed robber. "They were going to tour the country in an RV or maybe build a house in Maine, right after Stephen wrapped up his last four decades on the force." Added Driscoll: "His greatest wish was to see his daughter get married. Or his son if it was a boy."

Senate Votes To Add Gratuity To All Bills Of Eight Provisions Or More

WASHINGTON, DC—By a 74-20 margin, the U.S. Senate approved a resolution Monday guaranteeing lawmakers a 15 percent gratuity for all bills containing eight provisions or more. "Some of the bills around here run into the billions," U.S. Sen. Sam Brownback (R-KS) said. "This is our way of making sure we don't get stiffed." Later that day, Brownback received an $825 million gratuity on a $5.3 billion arms-appropriation bill he authored.

Richard Grieco's Star Power Inadvertently Donated To Goodwill

LOS ANGELES—Former *21 Jump Street* and *Booker* star Richard Grieco accidentally gave his star power to charity Monday, when a truck collecting for Goodwill Industries of Southern California made off with his charisma. "I just told the driver to help himself to whatever was in the garage," said the 36-year-old Grieco, star of 1991's *If Looks Could Kill*. "I had no idea my star power was in there." Grieco attempted to buy back his celebrity magnetism at the La Brea Avenue Goodwill store several hours later, only to be told that Jorge Reyes of East Los Angeles had purchased it for $4.

Elementary Schooler Clearly Just Learned To Swear

ALEXANDRIA, LA—Lakeview Elementary School first-grader Ian Schweder has clearly just taken his first steps into the world of swearing, classroom sources reported Monday. "He must've just seen a sweary movie," classmate Caitlin Lorenz said. "He always runs around the playground yelling, 'Fucky fucky shit fuck,' and dirty stuff like that." In the past two days, Schweder has composed a ribald song titled "Shit Shit Boobies," covered three sheets of notebook paper with scatological malediction, and attempted to tell a joke about "a girl who saw a boy's pussy."

That Guy From That One Show Spotted With The Girl From The Shampoo Ad

LOS ANGELES—According to Hollywood insiders, that guy who plays the doctor with the beard on that one show was spotted at this L.A. restaurant with the blonde chick who takes the shower in the airplane bathroom in that one shampoo commercial. "She was wearing this red, glittery dress," said that blonde *Extra* reporter who just had a baby. "And the guy was like, 'Hey, I'm dating the shampoo girl.'" The sighting laid to rest rumors that the guy is engaged to that girl who played the waitress in the movie about cars that came out a few weeks ago. ∅

Area Man Has No Idea Why He Wrote 'Gazebo Convo—Resolve/Tues (!?)' In Planner Six Weeks Ago

NEW LONDON, CT—Gil Woller, a marketing manager at Hartley Automated Systems, expressed bafflement Monday upon discovering the message "Gazebo Convo—resolve/Tues (!?)" in the June 22 space in his daily planner.

"I was flipping through my planner for a phone number I wrote down a while back, and this mysterious gazebo-convo-Tuesday message turned up," the 42-year-old Woller said. "I had absolutely no clue what it meant. I scanned the next several Tuesdays to see if there were any notes regarding the resolution of a gazebo convo—whatever that is—but there was nothing. I haven't been able to think about anything else since."

Woller, who has no regular contact with gazebos, either professionally or personally, said he has read the message aloud countless times, hoping that doing so might jog his memory.

"Convo... convo...," Woller said. "Conversation? Convention? Convocation? Convoy? It's got to be convention. But I haven't been at a convention since last fall, and it had nothing to do with gazebos."

Woller's confusion and dismay over the note has been exacerbated by the presence of a small, unchecked box beside it, suggesting that the task, whatever it is, remains uncompleted.

"Somewhere, a gazebo convo happened that I missed or am going to miss," Woller said. "I could kick myself, if only I knew what I need to kick myself for."

Directly adjacent to the note, in the page's margin, is a small doodle of a fish and a series of interconnected diamonds. Woller said he has carefully analyzed the drawings for clues that may help him solve the riddle.

"The fish leads me to believe that the gazebo could be near a lake or river. Or possibly a seafood restaurant," Woller said. "Or it could just be a random doodle. I don't know."

After a frustrating day in which he completed little work, Woller continued his investigation at home Monday evening.

"I asked my wife Judy if she knew anything about a gazebo," Woller said. "She said she recalled sitting in one two summers ago when we took the kids to that resort in the Poconos. But then she thought about it a little more and said it was actually more of a screened-in porch. Either way, I doubt that's got anything to do with this."

Above: Woller sits near the cryptic-note-bearing planner.

According to noted therapist Dr. Eli Wasserbaum, Woller's obsession with the cryptic gazebo-convo message is understandable.

"It is only natural that something like this would cause Gil to experience a great deal of cognitive dissonance," Wasserbaum said. "We all need to feel like the things we do in life have a purpose and aren't merely a series of empty, forgettable exercises devoid of cause or effect. But how can a person feel a sense of purpose when he doesn't even know what he did?"

Bolting awake at 4 a.m. Tuesday, Woller theorized that "Gazebo" could be the name of a business and resolved to pore over the yellow pages first thing in the morning. ∅

200

My Anti-Drug Is Alcohol

By Bobby Branch

If you're a kid growing up these days, sooner or later, someone's going to offer you drugs. "Go ahead, try some of these," they'll say. "They'll make you feel great. Come on, everybody's doing it. Don't you want to be cool?" People have told me all these things and plenty more, but I just tell them to buzz off. I tell them I don't need drugs to get high or be cool: I can do it with alcohol, my anti-drug.

The pushers who hang around the playground behind my school are always going on about the amazing high you get from drugs. But I don't see how it can compare to the pure, natural, 100 percent legal high I get from drinking alcohol. Who needs the artificial escape drugs provide when a good, stiff belt of Jim Beam or José Cuervo can put your head in the clouds while keeping your feet firmly planted on the ground?

Sure, at first, drugs may make you feel pretty good. But it's not real. Before long, you're using more and more, even as you're feeling worse and worse. Then, other things will start going wrong for you, too: Your friends won't seem to hang around you anymore, and you'll have new friends who only care about the drugs. Your grades will start to slip. Your memory will go. And your health will fade. All because of drugs.

Don't take that risk: Find something healthy, like alcohol, to take the place of drugs in your life. So, the next time you feel the urge to smoke some marijuana, try reaching for a big bottle of Bacardi instead.

The sneaky thing about drugs is how they make you feel like everything's okay when it's not. Drugs alter the way you perceive things. They change the way you behave and cause you to lose control of yourself. Who wants that? I don't know about you, but I like being in control of my actions. That's why, whenever I feel tempted to wander down the wrong road, I pour myself a nice, stiff drink, thanking my lucky stars that I've got alcohol, my personal anti-drug.

Why would anyone in their right mind want to get "stoned" or "fried"? I'd rather spend my time engaged in more constructive activities, like "wetting my whistle," "liquoring up," or "filling myself with liquid courage." You know, positive things. With alcohol, the glass is always half full. (When it isn't completely full, that is.)

Now, maybe you don't care for alcohol. That's okay. What's not okay, though, is getting hooked on an addictive, controlled substance like pot, cocaine, or heroin. Find a healthy substitute, something you can get really into, something that can be *your* anti-drug. It could be anything: Learn to play blackjack or the ponies. Explore kleptomania. Have sex with an endless parade of random strangers. Anything that makes you feel good, as long as it isn't drugs.

It's your life, and you have to learn to make your own choices. But choosing drugs? That's no choice at all.

Nothing beats the adrenaline rush that comes from knowing you're drug-free. And, if you're drug-free, you're free, period. I like that feeling, and I like myself. I'm high on life, because I'm high on alcohol, my anti-drug. ∅

ARBY'S from page 199

SAME SHIT, DIFFERENT BUN.
The Technically New Beef 'N' Bacon Sandwich®
only at Arby's

Above: A print ad for the new sandwich.

"Let us be clear: This sandwich is by no means bad," Forst said. "But we'd be lying if we said this was a great sandwich or a particularly original one. Though we have little doubt that a handful of people will love the Beef 'N' Bacon, for us to claim that we've come up with a groundbreaking new sandwich sensation would be absurd. Boasts of that measure would be foolhardy and deceptive, especially in light of the fact that Arby's has introduced much better sandwiches in the past."

"Like the Chicken Cordon Bleu sandwich," Forst said. "Now, that is an amazing sandwich. I could eat two of those right now."

Salivating at the thought of the Chicken Cordon Bleu, Forst returned to the subject at hand. "So, you know, try the new Beef-Bacon thing with an order of our delicious Cheddar Curly Fries and a Jamocha shake," he said. "If you had the fries and the shake with it, that would make for a pretty good meal."

According to Marianne Shepherd, Arby's vice-president of product development, the new sandwich was the result of a long testing process that "just didn't hit a home run this time."

"When we here in the Arby's family got to brainstorming new sandwiches, we figured a combination of Arby's delicious, hot roast beef, crispy bacon, and fresh lettuce and tomatoes, topped with a zesty pepper-jack sauce on a fluffy Kaiser bun, would be a winner," Shepherd said. "But somehow, the end result was, well, edible, obviously, or we wouldn't sell it, and possibly even savory or delectable to someone who is very hungry. But great? Certainly not. In the final analysis, our Beef 'N' Bacon sandwich is merely 'good.' But, hey, meat is meat."

Continued Forst: "I think the upshot of what we're saying is, if you love sandwiches of all kinds, then here is something moderately different that you might like to try. If, however, you are sick and tired of 'the same old sandwich,' then by all means steer clear of the Beef 'N' Bacon. Instead, maybe try the Arby's Big Montana sandwich, if you've never had one of those. Or just go to a different restaurant."

The Beef 'N' Bacon was then ceremonially 'launched' by being brought out on a domed platter and served to Forst, who took a single bite from the sandwich and promptly requested a beverage.

"We also introduce new sandwiches in the spring," said Forst, spitting out a chunk of iceberg lettuce. "Wait until then. Next spring's offering should be really exciting. A lot better than the Beef 'N' Bacon, I'm willing to bet."

Arby's efforts to develop a marketing campaign for the new sandwich have proven difficult, given the dearth of noteworthy attributes

> **Said Marianne Shepherd, Arby's vice-president of product development: "In the final analysis, our Beef 'N' Bacon sandwich is merely 'good.' But, hey, meat is meat."**

to emphasize.

"We considered the tagline 'The Sandwich Lovers' Sandwich,'" Arby's director of advertising Bill Plunkett said. "But, then, we figured that could backfire: If we overhyped it, regular customers might lose their trust in us, and first-time customers might mistakenly think it was the best Arby's had to offer and never try anything else."

The Arby's marketing team eventually settled on a billboard campaign centering on a pair of slogans, "Same Shit, Different Bun" and "Beef. Bacon. There Ya Go." Also planned is a series of TV commercials featuring blues legend B.B. King tasting the sandwich and exclaiming, "That's Food, Baby." ∅

best friend. "But around the 15th time I heard about how great it is to be tied to a chair, I was, like, 'Yeah, I know. The chair. The whip. Being straddled. Got it, thanks.'"

Roder and Von Poppel, who have been dating for almost four years, began experimenting with sadomasochism in July 1999 after buying a few S&M-related items at Santa Fe's Naughty & Nice adult video and novelty store.

"It wasn't until I began experimenting with domination and mistress role-playing that I really discovered myself sexually," Von Poppel has told dozens of people over the years. "It's so liberating to explore the threshold between pleasure and pain."

Meredith Engler, a close friend and former college roommate of Von Poppel's, said she has frequently found herself subjected to hours-long accounts of the couple's S&M exploits.

"Gina and Jason have a pretty open-minded group of friends and, at first, we all thought it was cool that they were being so frank about sex," Engler said. "That was our mistake—giving them an opening."

As Roder and Von Poppel delved deeper into sadomasochism, they began dominating nearly every party and social event with endless talk of fetishes, secret fan-

tasies, and forays into bondage and discipline.

"When Jason and Gina first told me about their 'secret,' I thought, wow, these people must have one hell of an interesting life," friend Peter Orwitz said. "I couldn't have been more wrong. How many times can a person discuss cock leashes?"

Orwitz said the only thing

Asked friend Peter Orwitz: "How many times can a person discuss cock leashes?"

---

worse than the couple's lengthy lectures on the positioning benefits of a wall-mounted restraining swing are the long-winded clarifications about the nature of sadomasochism.

"As Jason is constantly pointing out, it's not S&M that they're into: It's BD/SM, which is bondage-domination and sadomasochism,'" Orwitz said. "Apparently, there's a big difference between S&M and B&D. Just ask them. I dare you."

The couple's friends try to avoid topics that might inadvertently

lead to discussions of S&M, but the subject always manages to come up.

"It's amazing what will prompt Jason and Gina to talk about sex," Pritchard said. "We had a barbecue last weekend, and I said, 'Pass me the tongs.' So Jason and Gina exchange a knowing look and, before you know it, we're off on an hour-long discussion of how you should put your metal sex toys in the freezer for a few hours before using them."

Roder and Von Poppel have even invited friends to join them in one of their S&M adventures. Thus far, there have been no takers.

"They asked if me and my girlfriend wanted to go with them to Fetish Night at some club called The Dungeon," Pritchard said. "I guess maybe I would have been curious, except I'd already heard every last detail about Fetish Night already. I know about the transgender drag show. I know about the 'secret room' and the 'safe words.' I've heard all about the Saran Wrap woman and the rubber-tubing outfit and Metal-Cage-Around-The-Balls Guy at least five times. So I passed."

After many unsuccessful attempts to subtly communicate her irritation to Roder and Von Poppel, Engler determined that

she needed to be more direct.

"Last Friday, Gina was blathering on and on about domination, and I couldn't help but say, 'Well, you're certainly good at conversation domination,'" Engler said. "I can't help but wonder if this S&M thing is all a cover-up for their real fetish: talking to people about fetishes."

Another couple, Sara DeWitt and Ron Crandall, met them at a local bar in May.

"We all had a few drinks and ended up talking about sex almost the entire night," Crandall said. "I remember going home thinking, 'God, these people are nothing like the uptight, boring types I usually hang out with.'"

As the friendship progressed, however, DeWitt and Crandall found that every conversation with the couple eventually turned to S&M.

"The third time we hung out, I started to pick up on the pattern," DeWitt said. "Don't these people have any interests besides vibrating tit clamps? I tried to steer the conversation toward other subjects, but every time I did, they'd start right up with the S&M talk again, telling me not to be so repressed."

Added DeWitt: "For people who aren't uptight or boring, those two are pretty uptight and boring." ∅

CNN Should Be Named The Crappy News *Not*-Work

By Tom Brokaw

Cable News Network? Yeah, right. Nice try, Ted *Turd-Burglar*. Your channel should be called the Crappy News *Not*-work. Because that's what it is—crappy and not even news.

CNN is so retarded. They totally have no editorial vision. And they're always trying to act so cool. Like, "Oooh, Darth Vader is our announcer!" Whoop-de-doo. Did Darth Vader break any new developments in the Chandra Levy case? I didn't think so.

And who does CNN have for a network-defining anchor? Lou Waters? Puh-leez. Dweeb-o-*rama*. I was a better anchor than him back when I was on *The Today Show*, which is basically all *CNN Today* is, 'cause it's so stupid.

Okay, ready? This is how Lou Waters does the news: "Doyyy, I'm King Retard, and this is the Retard News. Today, the president took a

dump. I do not know what happened next, because I can't read, so I will pick my nose now. *Doyyy...* what delicious boogers! Turning now to the international scene, my butt hurts." I swear to God, that's him.

CNN acts like they're the network of record in Millennial America, just because of their award-winning Gulf War coverage. That was *so* 10 years ago, and people only watched because there was no MSNBC back then.

Oh, and check this out. This past April, I'm at the White House Correspondents Dinner, and CNN White House reporter John King starts bagging on this "Fleecing Of America" report we did. 'Cause we did this report about these pharmaceutical companies that are getting government subsidies and still charging 1,000 percent markups on pills. So he was all like, "As big a problem as I have with the major U.S. pharmaceutical companies, I found your report to be unfairly biased in favor of the consumer." *Duh.* That was the whole point, Lord Dorkenhumper! If John King is at next year's dinner, there's no way I'm going.

Speaking of John King, CNN also has Larry King, who's so old he's probably John's great-grandfather or something. Man, does Larry suck. (Or, *suck up*, that

---

"And Headline News? More like *Deadline Snooze*. How can you even call that news? It's just a bunch of headlines. That is so not news."

---

is.) I mean, *hello*? It's supposed to be a news network! Not the Blah-Blah-Blah-About-The-Power-Of-Prayer-With-Pat-Boone-and-Kenneth-Copeland Network! Or the I'm-Kissing-Marlon-Brando-On-The-Lips-Total-Stupid-Gaywad-Channel-For-Gays Network.

And Headline News? More like

Deadline Snooze. How can you even call that news? It's just a bunch of headlines. That is so not news.

Oh, my God. I totally forgot. This is totally secret. You *did not* hear this from me, okay? Maria Shriver told me that Robert Bazell said Lou Dobbs told Roger Cossack that he wants to completely make out with Greta Van Susteren. Can you believe that? Who would want to kiss her? Greta Van Susteren is so totally corroded.

And Jeff Greenfield? *Doyyy.* What is he, my science teacher? That guy is gimpier than John Hockenberry. And more boring, too. Watching cars rust is more exciting than that *Greenfield At Large* thing. Man, does that show rot. It's not just *Greenfield At Large*, though. All of CNN is bad like that. *TalkBack Live*? More like *TalkBack Dead*. Hey, Teddy T., before you start another 24-hour news network, maybe you should get some decent content first!

So, in conclusion, I would just like to say that CNN blows white-hot chunks of complete and total suckiness. ∅

Making A Midlife Career Change

It's never too late to make a career change. Here are some tips to help you get where you want to go:

- To begin your search, visit your city's employment office. They never have any jobs you'd actually want, but sometimes they have free coffee.
- If you are married and have children, it may prove difficult to change careers while maintaining financial stability. Consider moving across the country in the middle of the night and assuming a new identity.
- You were born to be an insurance claims adjuster, and the stars know it. Chase that dream.
- Switching to a brand-new field is a great way to reexperience that lost, helpless, fish-out-of-water feeling that sickened you so in adolescence.
- Why not sink your life savings into self-publishing a book of essays about your reflections on aging? There's a gold mine for ya.

- Attack your search for a new career head-on. Use a blunt, bludgeoning weapon and emit a blood-curdling shriek while charging forward.
- Know what you would be good at? Writing movies. After all, you watch a ton of them, and it's just thinking up stuff for people to say.
- It's easy to go from store greeter to grocery bagger if you just believe in yourself.
- You're never too old to go back to college. It's just that you're way too old to fit in socially in any way.
- Going from professional dancer to welder is the reverse of the traditional path. But you must do what you must do.
- Having the right mental attitude is the first step. Try not to think about how old, pathetic, and unqualified you are.

BAND from page 199

uct of many musical influences, one particular band casts the longest shadow.

"No question, the Terre Haute Sound wouldn't even exist without The Larry Byrds," Thompson said. "They were the first on the scene, and in my mind, they'll always be

> "No question, the Terre Haute Sound wouldn't even exist without The Larry Byrds," Thompson said.

the best."

"Fuck, yeah," agreed Weebles, Spongebob Fuxx, and Introversion drummer Dave Murn, 23. "Back in '92, when I was in eighth grade, I saw The Larry Byrds play an all-ages show at the Elks Lodge, and they completely blew me away. Those guys paved the way for all the Terre Haute bands to come. Without them, there is no Weebles."

The Larry Byrds, a trio of Indiana State University students, broke up in September 1994 when lead singer Elliott Greene moved to Berkeley, CA, to attend graduate school. Copies of the band's sole release, the out-of-print 1993 split single "Tempest In A Teacup," backed by The Draincloggers' cover of Mr. Mister's "Kyrie," has fetched up to $2.99 in cutout bins of Terre Haute-area record stores.

In the years since, the recorded output of Terre Haute Sound bands has been limited to three releases. Two have been compilation CDs, 1997's *Terror Haute* and 1999's *Return Of Terror Haute: A Tribute To The Larry Byrds*. The third, a 2000 eponymous release by Cutie, was printed in a limited run of 3,200 copies. All three albums were issued by Terror Haute, the local label run by Gaspart.

"There's just so much talent in this town," Gaspart said. "A few weeks ago, The Weebles and a few other Terror Haute bands went down to Evansville to do a label-showcase gig. Tons of people were coming up to us after the show, saying how amazing all of us Terre Haute bands were. They were totally going off about how distinctive and cool our sound was. This one guy said that, anyway." ∅

KNOCKED UP

Jennie Wohlpert, 17, of Lawrenceville, was knocked up Wednesday by her boyfriend, Jeff Hyatt, 18, of Waltham. Her father is Joseph Wohlpert, a doctor at Cedar County Medical Center, and her mother is Carolyn Wohlpert, a third-grade teacher at Lakeshore Elementary. Neither parent has yet been notified.

Cristina Sanchez, 22, of Lodish, was knocked up Friday by her boyfriend, Roberto Gris, 24. Miss Sanchez, a second-year student at Kane County Community College, had planned to pursue a degree in data processing and start her own bookkeeping business, neither of which she will now do.

WORLD'S FLOPPIEST from page 189

Passersby were amazed by the unusually large amounts of blood. Passersby were amazed by the unusually large amounts of blood. Passersby were amazed by the unusually large amounts of blood. Passersby were amazed by the unusually large amounts of blood. Passersby were amazed by the unusually large amounts of blood. Passersby were amazed by the unusually large amounts of blood. Passersby were amazed by the unusually large amounts of blood. Passersby were amazed by the unusually large amounts of blood. Passersby were amazed by the unusually large amounts of blood. Passersby were amazed by the unusually large amounts of blood. Passersby were amazed by the unusually large amounts of blood. Passersby were amazed by the unusually large amounts of blood. Passersby were amazed by the

unusually large amounts of blood. Passersby were amazed by the unusually large amounts of blood. Passersby were amazed by the unusually large amounts of blood. Passersby were amazed by the unusually large amounts of blood. Passersby were amazed by the unusually large amounts of blood. Passersby were amazed by the unusually large amounts of blood. Passersby were amazed by the unusually large amounts of blood. Passersby were amazed by the unusually large amounts of blood. Passersby were amazed by the unusually large amounts of blood. Passersby were amazed by the unusually large amounts of blood. Passersby were amazed by the

see WORLD'S FLOPPIEST page 213

TV Sports' Ratings Slide

Televised sports is in the midst of a decade-long ratings slump. What do *you* think of the steadily dwindling viewership?

"With all the televised sports out there—golf, NASCAR, WNBA basketball, Major League Soccer, pro beach volleyball—my total indifference can only be spread so thin."

Dan Wiggins
Bank Teller

"Maybe someone should invent a new game to reignite interest. A game where you eat snack cakes while throwing water balloons."

Ted Bevacqua
Custodian

"It seems odd that viewership is down, given all the slightly charismatic pro athletes out there."

Stephanie Nettles
Psychologist

"This is hardly surprising. That album came out nearly 20 years ago, and 'I Want A New Drug' was the only good song on it."

Dana Gossage
Homemaker

"I blame the networks. Their interstitial CGI graphics and exploding-helmet sound effects just don't pack the same entertainment punch that they used to."

Fred McReynolds
Systems Analyst

"I guess I lost interest in televised sports when I realized you didn't need to watch it to hang out in Hooters."

Carl Whitson
Drill-Press Operator

Clinton's First Week In Harlem

Last Tuesday, Bill Clinton officially moved into his new office in Harlem. How did the former president spend his first week in the neighborhood?

TUES.
- Goes on leisurely stroll around neighborhood with 25-person entourage
- Meets with Grammy-winning producer Babyface Edmonds to discuss upcoming duet

WED.
- Allocates $1 aid package to homeless guy on corner of 125th and Lenox Avenue
- Purchases and dons do-rag

THURS.
- Attempts to foster good relations with new neighbors by shaking hands on street; is unable to master several of the more complicated handshakes

FRI.
- Scans obituaries for bigger, cheaper office space

SAT.
- Assures Colin Powell neighborhood is safe
- Renames local adult bookstore "the Clinton Library"

SUN.
- Begrudgingly places framed photo of wife on desk

the ONION
America's Finest News Source

Herman Ulysses Zweibel *Founder*

T. Herman Zweibel *Publisher Emeritus*
J. Phineas Zweibel *Publisher*
Maxwell Prescott Zweibel *Editor-In-Chief*

FOUNDED 1871 • "TU STULTUS ES"

Your Horoscope

By Lloyd Schumner Sr.
Retired Machinist and
A.A.P.B.-Certified Astrologer

Aries: (March 21–April 19)
You will be forced to admit that being up to your neck in pussy is not as sexy as it sounded.

Taurus: (April 20–May 20)
The stars indicate that more Zodiac signs choose Jif than any other leading brand of peanut butter.

Gemini: (May 21–June 21)
A team of FDA physicians and researchers will soon come out with a 45-page, item-by-item recall of everything you've eaten in the past six months.

Cancer: (June 22–July 22)
Your love life will take a turn for the better when you begin to incorporate lessons gleaned from Clausewitz's *On War*.

Leo: (July 23–Aug. 22)
Your love for the classic American folk song "Goodnight Irene" will soon have the media referring to you as the Goodnight Irene Slasher.

Virgo: (Aug. 23–Sept. 22)
Just because the ambulances go by at high speeds does not mean they want to race you.

Libra: (Sept. 23–Oct. 23)
Your life will continue its pattern of long stretches of boredom punctuated by intense moments of wondering what exactly nougat is.

Scorpio: (Oct. 24–Nov. 21)
Your office romance begins to go awry when your coworkers realize that it's more of an office-furniture romance.

Sagittarius: (Nov. 22–Dec. 21)
Your date will somehow fail to be pacified when told that your tail is not, in fact, prehensile.

Capricorn: (Dec. 22–Jan. 19)
You will free up several hours in your week when you realize that there is no need for you to hold daily eating practice.

Aquarius: (Jan. 20–Feb. 18)
Saul Bellow has called modern life "an unbearable state of distraction," but you seem to enjoy it well enough.

Pisces: (Feb. 19–March 20)
Before you use the words ennui, angst, or *weltschmertz* one more time, the stars politely request that you look them up and find out what they actually mean.

KUGEL from page 116

unusually large amounts of blood. Passersby were amazed by the unusually large amounts of blood. Passersby were amazed by the unusually large amounts of blood. Passersby were amazed by the unusually large amounts of blood. Passersby were amazed by the unusually large amounts of blood. Passersby were amazed by the unusually large amounts of blood. Passersby were amazed by the unusually large amounts of blood.

I don't know *which* boatload of sailors I love!

Passersby were amazed by the unusually large amounts of blood. Passersby were amazed by the unusually large amounts of blood. Passersby were amazed by the unusually large amounts of blood. Passersby were amazed by the unusually large amounts of blood. Passersby were amazed by the unusually large amounts of blood. Passersby were amazed by the unusually large amounts of blood.

Passersby were amazed by the unusually large amounts of blood. Passersby were amazed by the unusually large amounts of blood. Passersby were amazed by the unusually large amounts of blood. Passersby were amazed by the unusually large amounts of blood. Passersby were amazed by the unusually large amounts of blood. Passersby were amazed by the unusually large amounts of blood. Passersby were amazed by the unusually large amounts of blood. Passersby were amazed by the unusually large amounts of blood. Passersby were amazed by the unusually large amounts of blood. Passersby were amazed by the unusually large amounts of blood. Passersby were amazed by the unusually large amounts of blood. Passersby were amazed by the unusually large amounts of blood. Passersby were amazed by the unusually large amounts of blood. Passersby were amazed by the unusually large amounts of blood. Passersby were amazed by the unusually large amounts of blood. Passersby were amazed by the unusually large amounts of blood. Passersby were amazed by the unusually large amounts of blood. Passersby were amazed by the unusually large amounts of blood. Passersby were amazed by the unusually large amounts of blood. Passersby were amazed by the

see KUGEL page 211

Laura Bush Noisily Devours Infant

see NATION page 6A

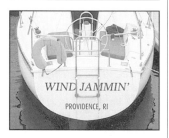

Yacht Name Conveys Owner's Easygoing Lifestyle

see LOCAL page 5C

Donut Made With Real Kreme

see FOOD page 4E

Mississippi DNR To Ban Cockfishing

see NATION page 7A

What Does Someone Have To Do To Get A Drink Around Here?

1. Blow the bartender?
2. Ferment the hops myself?
3. Take out an ad in *Thirst Weekly*?
4. Marry the Jamesons' daughter?
5. Wait until communion?
6. Ring for the night nurse?
7. Come back when you're open?

THE ONION VOLUME 37 ISSUE 28
$2.00 US $3.00 CAN

the ONION ®

VOLUME 37 ISSUE 28   AMERICA'S FINEST NEWS SOURCE ™   16–22 AUGUST 2001

Endangered Manatee Struggles To Make Self Understood To Congress

WASHINGTON, DC—Despite valiant efforts to make itself understood, an endangered West Indian manatee failed to communicate its urgent-sounding message to members of the House of Representatives Tuesday.

"Euyah, euyaaaah," said the visibly flustered 900-pound manatee, accidentally knocking over a podium with its flat, paddle-like tail. "Huuun nun. Eyah."

The manatee, one of only 3,000 left in the U.S., arrived unexpectedly in Washington after a long journey from its Florida home. It spent more than two hours bleating to House members, rolling its 10-foot-long body from side to side and waving its clawed flippers.

Democrats and Republicans were united in their confusion over the honking beast.

"Clearly, this manatee has something urgent to say, but what?" House Speaker Dennis Hastert (R-IL) said. "Something about, 'Phlupp, phlupp, phlupp,' I guess."

Many House members say the manatee's arrival in Washington was timed to coincide with Tuesday's debate of H.R. 512, a bill concerning relief of airport congestion in Florida. The bill would give the U.S. Army Corps of Engineers authority to build a seaplane base and runway on

Above: The manatee slowly works its way up the steps of the Capitol.

the Caloosahatchee River in Lee County, less than three miles from the manatee's home.

"When we were debating H.R. 512,
see MANATEE page 208

Inexorable March Of Time Brings TV's Jerry Mathers One Step Closer To Death

HOLLYWOOD, CA—The inexorable march of time, the prison into which all humankind is born, brought *Leave It To Beaver* star Jerry Mathers—and all of us—one step closer to the grave Monday.

"I saw Jerry Mathers on *Entertainment Tonight* a couple months ago," said Barry Carter, 34, of Duluth, MN. "It was weird. He still has that baby face, but he's, like, in his 50s now. I was like, 'Whoa, look at Jerry Math-
see MATHERS page 207

Left: *Leave It To Beaver* star Jerry Mathers, whose light grows dim.

> "I was like, 'Whoa, look at Jerry Mathers, he's getting up there in years,' and my wife said, 'Well, aren't we all? I guess it's true."

Retired Realtor Drawn Back In For One Last Big Score

HARRISON, OH—After 30 years in the real-estate business, Jack Parker knew what he was: retired. His time in The Life had given him more than his share of ups and downs, and the veteran RE/MAX agent was finally out of the game for good, with a little house of his own and some money socked away. Yes, Jack Parker's days of proudly serving the home-buying needs of the greater Cincinnati area were over.

At least, that's what he thought.

Last Thursday, four months after hanging up his red RE/MAX blazer, Parker was drawn back in for one

last big score. "I was out on the porch, taking a little nap, when I hear a guy walk up," Parker said. "I tell him go away, I don't want any of whatever he's selling, thank you, when a voice I never wanna hear again says he might have a job for me. And I think, oh, Christ. It's Sneaky Pete."

"Sneaky" Peter Kelp, a rattlesnake of a broker in his mid-40s who has had a hand in upwards of half of all Harrison home sales since the mid-1980s, had a job all lined up. And Parker, he knew, was the perfect guy to pull it off. All he had to do was bait the hook.

Above: Retired agent Parker stands before his last big score.

"Nice little place you got here, Jack," said Kelp, giving Parker's modest suburban split-level the once-over with what Hamilton County realty insiders call "the
see REALTOR page 208

Director Going With Unknown For Third Marriage

HOLLYWOOD, CA—James Rudolph, director of *Powerplay* and *Dead By Dawn*, announced plans Monday to go with an unknown for the role of his third wife this fall. "I'm basically looking for a young, fresh-faced newcomer, someone who can give me the same sort of effect I got from Nina in my first marriage," Rudolph told *Daily Variety*. "Daryl Hannah worked out fine for this last go-round, but this time, I want someone with no reputation or established style." Principal photography on the couple's wedding is slated to begin Oct. 21 at Huntington Beach Country Club.

Cuba To Buy Car

HAVANA—In a bid to bring its citizens greater independence, the nation of Cuba decided Tuesday to pool its resources and purchase a car. "We know of an '82 Buick Skylark in Haiti that we should be able to fix up and make usable," Cuban transportation minister Alvaro Perez Morales said. "Having a car will make it easier for our citizens to do everything from grocery shopping to commuting to work." Use of the car will be determined by lottery, with a winner chosen daily from the nation's pool of 11 million citizens.

Candidate Turns To Focus Group For Position On Rape

RICHMOND, VA—Wanting to "feel out the popular attitude before committing to a position," Virginia gubernatorial candidate Mark Earley turned to focus-group analysis Monday to determine Virginians' stance on the hot-button issue of rape. "So far, results indicate that the state's residents skew heavily toward anti-rape," Earley said. "A good 99.9 percent of Virginians say they feel strongly that the state would be a better place if rape were reduced." Earley has not yet declared whether he will adopt a hardline anti-rape stance or take a more moderate position to avoid alienating the state's estimated 35 pro-rape voters.

ESL Textbook Concentrates On Food-Preparation Vocabulary

NEW YORK—An English as a Second Language textbook focuses predominantly on food-preparation vocabulary, night-school student Eduardo Reyes reported Monday. "I must admit, I would like to learn how to say more than, 'I have diced the onions,' and, 'Did he want scrambled or over-easy?'" said a disconsolate Reyes, speaking through a translator, following his first lesson. "I had hoped to learn words for the different parts of the body so I can pursue my dream of becoming a doctor. I have instead learned much about the grilling of chickens."

Peeping Tom Tired Of Watching People Watch Television

COLORADO SPRINGS, CO—Jonathan Hargrove, a Colorado Springs-area peeping Tom, expressed exasperation Tuesday, when a fifth consecutive victim did nothing more with her evening than watch hours of television. "I thought peering in on strangers would be more, I don't know, exciting," said the 44-year-old Hargrove, speaking from his hydrangea-bush hiding place. "I guess I somehow expected other people's lives to be more sexy or interesting than mine." Hargrove did note, however, that *Big Brother 2* is "really starting to heat up." ∅

Man Alienates Friends With Self-Constructive Behavior

MILWAUKEE, WI—Turning his life around after years of aimlessness, Jay Krouse, 30, has alienated almost everyone around him with his recent upward spiral of self-constructive behavior.

"Jay used to be one of the greatest guys to hang with," longtime friend Sean McRoddy said. "He'd always be the first one out drinking at The Red Shed and the last one driving around looking for weed at 3 a.m. Now, all he wants to do is study for his LSATs so he can become an environmental lawyer. I don't mind that he wants to do something with his life, but ever since he's gotten his act together, it's just not the same."

According to McRoddy, Krouse now eschews many of the unproductive, time-killing activities he used to love.

"Jay, Teddy [Orr], and I used to go 'country cruising' all the time," McRoddy said. "When I called up Jay to do it a few weeks ago, he said he'd go but that we couldn't use his truck because he didn't want to get another DUI. This is the guy who, a few years ago, liked to say that DUIs are the small price you pay for having a good time. I'm not sure I even know Jay anymore."

Friends say Krouse's sobriety and level-headedness make him difficult to be around. One such example occurred nearly four months ago, when Krouse's friends wanted to jump Tony Hernandez's Geo Tracker over a mound of dirt. After a night

Above: Krouse enjoys a Sprite at a local bar with friends McRoddy and Orr.

of drinking only O'Doul's, Krouse refused to participate.

"If we were jumping Tony's car a year ago, Jay would have been right up front, cheering the loudest," Orr said. "But when the car got stuck, and we had to dig it out with a tire iron, Jay just stood there shaking his head. You could tell he was thinking we're idiots. Acting stupid isn't much fun when there's someone around who knows better."

Friends fear that Krouse's self-constructive habits may worsen under the influence of his new girlfriend, third-grade school teacher Pamela Tellen.

"Most of the women Jay dated in the past could keep up with us when we hit the bars," McRoddy said. "I don't think Pam even drinks. We all went out last weekend, and she wouldn't even do a Jell-O shot. [Krouse's ex-girlfriend] Kathy used to pound shots of Wild Turkey and would've kicked my ass for even suggesting a Jell-O shot. That woman was so good for Jay."

Members of Krouse's family say they don't see him as much as they did when he was "less together."

"Jay used to call me all the time," said Caroline Krouse, Jay's 34-year-old sister. "He'd sweet-talk me for a

while and then hit me up for a loan—he's quite a charmer. But I haven't heard from him in weeks. I thought he might have gone on another bender in New Orleans, so I called him. He said he'd just been really busy lately, what with trying to get back into school, getting in shape, and writing in his journal. He never even comes over to pass out on the basement sofa, lying in his own puke. Sad is what it is."

Now in his eighth month of productive, goal-oriented living, Krouse may soon be the target of an intervention. Over two-for-one Coors pitchers at Big Ed's last Wednesday, McRoddy and Orr discussed plans to kidnap Krouse, take him to a remote cabin, and rehabilitate him with a keg of beer, a carton of cigarettes, and a crate of illegal fireworks. The plans were scuttled two days later, however, when Krouse informed Orr that he and Tellen would be spending the next four weekends at a yoga/massage-therapy center in northern Minnesota.

Fearing the best, Krouse's friends cling to the hope that an act of divine intervention will bring their friend back into the fold.

"Maybe if Jay's new girlfriend got hit by a train or something, he might be so devastated, he'd start drinking and come back to us," Orr said. "But given the way he's been lately, he'd probably just find a way to turn his profound grief into a positive. Jay's got a serious appetite for construction." ∅

I've Never Been So Accurately Insulted In All My Life

By Leon Denkinger

Well, you crossed the line, that's for sure. I've been insulted before, but until today, I'd never been attacked with such appalling accuracy. I cannot believe you had the gall to unleash that torrent of utterly valid criticisms. Vicious, founded attacks like yours cut deeper than any knife.

I've had some low-down snakes spit their venom at me before, but they were usually such overdone and unwarranted insults that no one could take them seriously. But you, sir! How dare you look me in the eye and see through me to the deeply flawed person I actually am, let alone sling your poisoned barbs with such precision?

So I tell lies. Okay, you got me.

But is that any reason to call me "a dirty liar"? If that's what you think of me—and you should—at least have the decency not to rub my

> ## I cannot believe you had the gall to unleash that torrent of utterly valid criticisms.

face in the awful truth of it all. Just call me a liar, then storm out and slam the door. For the love of God, don't point out two contradictory statements I made and then ask me, in front of everybody, to somehow reconcile them. That kind of smear tactic gives me no chance to avoid being justly branded a liar. I really thought you were above that.

And my weight! The way you ripped into my weight! I mean, I've heard untoward quips about my slightly above-average girth before, but they usually take the form of grade-school-caliber "wide load" jokes that are so exaggerated that they barely draw blood.

You, on the other hand, deftly and realistically characterized my body type as "pear-shaped" and suggested that I lose "30 to 35 pounds." Furthermore, you only brought up my weight to point out my hypocrisy in judging others by their looks. You didn't cop any attitude that being fat is automatically bad, as I invariably do; you simply pointed out my double-standard, exposing me for the obese, hypocritical little toad that I am.

But the capper on the jug, the slight I shall never forget to my dying day, was when you called me immature, painting me as "an emotional infant incapable

of interacting with others in a deep or meaningful way." Again, drawing on what you have actually observed rather than *ad hominem* attacks, you used my patterns of behavior to draw a cohesive portrait of a needy, self-centered man forever wallowing in his own tiny universe of grudges and misplaced blame. You have destroyed—and impressed—me with your masterful insight into my psyche.

I mean, my God. Anyone can insult a person, but you tore me apart with an informed, well-reasoned line of argument! You sliced me to helpless ribbons, the English language your scalpel! Could I really have angered you that greatly? I'm just glad my wife and children weren't here to see my considerable faults laid bare.

How could you, sir? Why would you want to do such a thing? I know why. I bet it's because you fuck donkeys or something, you big donkey fucker. ∅

MATHERS from page 205

ers, he's getting up there in years,' and my wife said, 'Well, aren't we all?' I guess it's true. I'm not as young as I used to be, either."

Added Carter with a reflective sigh: "It makes you think."

Mathers, who recently came face-to-face with his own mortality when a worm he swallowed on *The Tonight Show*'s "Celebrity Survivor" gave him a severe stomach infection, once charmed millions as the irrepressible mischief-maker "The Beav." Yet, as sands through the hourglass, Mathers' remaining moments on Earth continue to run out, bringing the star of the short-lived '80s syndicated series *Still The Beaver* closer to the day when worms would eat not just his stomach lining, but the whole of his flesh.

"Jerry Mathers?" said Clear Lake, IA, homemaker Janet Platt, 49. "He was so adorable on *Leave It To Beaver*, the very picture of childhood innocence. But then his youthful innocence gave way—as it must for all of us—to the hard-bitten realities of adulthood and, eventually, old age. But he will live forever in my heart, as well as the hearts of millions of others, where he will always remain the quintessential American boy."

Indeed, as we all project our deepest doubts and fears onto the canvas of our earthly existence, struggling to create meaning where there is none, so too is it with TV's Jerry Mathers. The symbol of an entire culture's faith in the magic of childhood, Mathers has been the subject of myriad

rumors, all untrue. Not only was he said to have been killed in the Vietnam War, but he was also rumored to have grown up to become the legendary, death-obsessed '70s shock-rocker Alice Cooper.

But as these urban legends continue to circulate, the real Jerry Mathers remains very much alive, forging ahead day after day, as all of us must, despite the inevitable end which awaits him in the cold embrace of Death.

"I think life is a challenge," Mathers said during a recent online appearance on HealthTalk Interactive to discuss his twin battles with diabetes and dyslexia. "Every day, when you get out of bed, there's challenge after challenge. So I say, just take each one as they come. Yes, they were both challenges, but, you know, I've met other challenges in my life, and as I say, I will continue to meet and beat them!"

What more can any of us do?

Determined to maintain a positive attitude in the face of the howling void, Mathers greets each day with a brave smile. The actor, who is available for personal appearances at trade shows, never fails to sign an autograph for an admiring fan. In addition, he jogs one hour every day and has maintained a healthy diet since losing more than 40 pounds on the Jenny Craig program, for which he is now a celebrity spokesman.

He still finds regular roles in feature films, including the 1994 thriller *Sexual Malice*. And his memoir, *And Jerry Mathers As*

Above: Mathers (right) and *Beaver* co-star Tony Dow in the full bloom of youth, never to be regained.

"*The Beaver*," still in print and a strong seller since its 1998 publication, is a delightful trip down memory lane and an enjoyable book for readers of all ages. Yes, time has been kinder to TV's Jerry Mathers than to most.

Yet we can only wonder: Does Mathers dream of another sort of time? Does he dream of a Vonnegutian reverse-entropy universe

in which his smiling childhood visage recedes not into the dimness of the past, but instead moves toward a beautiful convergence, where decay becomes birth, destruction becomes growth, and all find redemption in lost innocence, regained by the reversal of our days?

Only God—and TV's "The Beav"—know for sure. ∅

someone, I think it was Karen, argued that this base would be harmful to aquatic life in the area," said Hastert, referring to an environmental report penned by Rep. Karen Thurman (D-FL) citing collisions with watercraft as a leading cause of manatee deaths. "I asked the manatee if this was what the ruckus was about, but, unfortunately, I was unable to ascertain an answer."

"Nyuuuuh," the animal groaned loudly each time the Caloosahatchee was mentioned, banging its whiskered snout on the floor for emphasis. After the manatee was provided with a microphone, it entreated the legislators in lower, more mournful tones. The manatee eventually fell silent, fixing its large, soulful eyes on House Minority Leader Richard Gephardt (D-MO).

Tuesday marked the first time a *Trichechus manatus* has attempted to speak before the nation's top legislative body. Manatees, which make their home in shallow, slow-moving rivers, estuaries, or coastal areas, are found primarily in Florida in the U.S. and rarely migrate further north

than the Carolinas.

"While I've never heard of one traveling to Washington before, manatees are migratory by nature," marine biologist Dr. Iri Yadjit said. "They can travel 35 to 40 miles a day and, I would guess, even more if a particular animal is motivated by, say, fear of extinction."

"Nyuuuuh," the animal groaned loudly each time the Caloosahatchee was mentioned.

While no one knows for certain how the manatee found its way to the U.S. Capitol, Rep. Joe Barton (R-TX) was first to spot it, just after noon.

"I was coming back from lunch, and I noticed a hulking figure slowly heaving itself up the steps of the

building," Barton said. "A few hours later, I saw it again, this time inside. From the way it was thumping its big, wrinkled head on the door to the House chambers, it was clear it wanted to get in."

According to Barton, after he and five other senators hoisted the unwieldy sea mammal over the threshold, it lumbered to the front of the House floor, pausing periodically to entreat individual representatives with loud, unintelligible lowing.

Though no manatee had ever addressed Congress before, this is not the first time an endangered species has attempted to make itself heard in Washington. In March 1999, nearly 100 St. Croix ground lizards appeared on the Senate floor during debates over regulation of timber operations in the Southeast. In February of this year, Chief Justice William Rehnquist suffered contusions when a small herd of bighorn sheep burst into the Supreme Court chambers during opening arguments of *EPA v. Western Montana Mining Company*.

Some legislators argued that the

manatee should not be permitted to address the House if it cannot speak English, but no steps were taken to physically remove the animal. Among the animal's strongest supporters was Rep. Edward Markey (D-MA), who ordered the immediate delivery of 500 pounds of edible aquatic plants and a 5,000-gallon tank "as a gift on behalf of the American people." As of press time, the manatee remains in the House chambers, where it awaits the resumption of debate on H.R. 512 at 1 p.m. Thursday.

Markey expressed confidence that no harm will come to the manatee while in Washington.

"West Indian manatees are protected under federal law by the Marine Mammal Protection Act of 1972 and the Endangered Species Act of 1973, which make it illegal to harass, hunt, capture, or kill any marine mammal," Markey said. "I don't think anyone would dare do anything that might violate these laws. Besides, the fella is so gosh-darn cute, you'd have to be pure evil to want to hurt it." Ø

sharpest gimlet eye this side of the Ohio." "I mean, it's not where you'd expect a hot Realtor to retire to, but I guess it keeps the dogs off your scent, so to speak."

Shooting Parker a telling sideways glance, Kelp added: "But it's no 1.5 acres of prime Harrison property with a 6.31 percent 30-year fixed-rate mortgage, either, you know what I mean?"

"I knew right then he was working an angle," Parker said. "He knew it hurt me to retire without that one last big score. But I wasn't about to get up out of my chaise lounge. The realty game cost me my health and a couple of perfectly good marriages. I wasn't about to go back to that. So I tell Sneaky Pete I'm retired, and that there ain't enough commission in the world, and that he can get off my property, thank you very much, and who the hell ever heard of a three bedroom/four baths on a prime piece of Hamilton County property for just $237,851, anyway? But he just smiles and throws a picture of a house in my lap."

"And, oh, man, what a house," Parker added.

Through his various realty-world connections, Kelp had been able to secure guarantees on a 3,200-square-foot one-story home on Westlake Court, an area with low property taxes and good public schools.

"Sneaky Pete says to me, 'It's the one last big score every Realtor dreams of,'" Parker said. "'The commission on this, you simply would not believe. It's a cream puff, a lead-pipe cinch in the right hands. But that's the catch: I gotta move it in 30 days, or it reverts back to the

client's estate for tax reasons. I gotta do this now, Jackie Boy, and that means I need your magic.'"

"I knew right then he was working an angle," Parker said. "He knew it hurt me to retire without that one last big score."

Parker sighed, put his head in his hands, and told Kelp to ankle it off his half-acre lot.

"I just waited," Kelp told reporters. "I knew it wouldn't be long. I left the photos and the floor plan there. And he hadn't said no."

Two nights later, Kelp received a call from Parker shortly before 3 a.m.

"Okay, damn you," Parker said. "I'm in. But we do it my way this time, with my guys. And no screwups, Kelp. I'm not letting you do me like that splanch in Walnut Hills."

Parker soon had his scheme nailed down.

"We get a guy interested, see," Parker said. "We show him pictures and tell him how lovely the place is: the all-new moldings, the built-in fireplace, the vaulted ceilings. 'They don't make 'em like this anymore,' that whole rap. Then we pick him up wherever he wants, in broad daylight. He doesn't suspect a thing. We take him right in through the front

Above: An anxious Parker cases the 3,200-square-foot joint.

door, just like we own the place, hand on his arm. Real friendly. Real friendly. We lead him around, maybe I say something about the screened-in porch or flagstone patio or some snow job like that, and I sneak behind him so I can see him but he can't see me. Then, when he walks through the French doors into the living room... blammo!"

Parker then smacked his fist into his palm to illustrate the buyer's reaction upon seeing the broad expanse of hardwood flooring leading up to the bay window with the view of Pike's Pond.

To make sure things go as smoothly as a double-glazed picture window, Parker has contacted all of his old associates from the realty game.

"It ain't gonna be easy," Parker said. "I must've cased the joint with Kelp a million times. I had two spe-

cialists drive down from Dayton with a truck full of fancy equipment to sweep the place for bugs. I got the best roofer in the business, Big Beef Manzo, checking the shingles. And, if things get down and dirty, I just call in Joe The Cleaner to have a little talk with the client. He'll clean the place up nice."

Kelp said he never had any doubt that Parker would be in on the plan. And he has no doubt about his motivation.

"Parker isn't doing it for the money," Kelp said. "He thinks he is. But I know why he's really doing it: the thrill of the sale. It's in his blood. He loves the plan, the pitch, the drama of it all. It's the only thing in his life he's ever been good at, and he knows it. It took him all of 36 hours to call me after he threw me off his acreage. Oh, he's in, all right. He's in for life." Ø

Up In Smoke

Hola, amigos. What say? I know it's been a long time since I rapped at ya, but I've had my balls to the wall lately, working an overnight shift at a convenience store.

Actually, it ain't all that bad, but I get pretty creeped out by all the cameras taping everything I do. One night, I started getting seriously hungry, so I grabbed a kippered ham stick and chowed down on that, then washed it down with a Mountain Dew. I'm telling you, that really hit the spot. The next day, though, when I showed up for work, there was a note from my manager, Mr. Dybzinski, taped to the register saying that I owed $2.21 for the food. That's all I need, having The Man watch my every move so he can bust my chops. I put the $2.21 in the drawer, then I flipped the video camera the bird. That oughta make Dybzinski

The Cruise
By Jim Anchower

think twice before he starts up with that shit again.

Also, I've been real on edge lately because I haven't smoked up for, like, five weeks. See, after my dealer went pussy and stopped selling, I've had a hard time locating any weed. I'm not even talking primo stuff here—I would have smoked the rankest ditchweed for a two-minute buzz. I guess it doesn't speak all that highly of my social circle if, between me, Wes, and Ron, we couldn't line anything up, but there ya go. That's the problem with being King Shit. The guys who follow you around can't think on their own, let alone score weed.

So, what did I do? What any reasonable man would when faced with a problem of this magnitude: I tried growing my own. Now, for whatever reason, Ron, though unable to score weed to save his life, had stashed away about a quarter-ounce of seeds he was saving for a special occasion. After spending half an hour doing everything short of sucking his pud, I was able to convince him to give me 12 seeds. He said it'd grow up to be the kindest bud I've ever smoked, and

that I'd better share when it came down to it. No problemo, I replied.

I wasn't exactly sure how to grow it, since I've never had what you'd call a green thumb. They've got ads for all kinds of growing books in *High Times*, but there was no way I could wait four weeks for the books to show up in the mail. Besides, I was pretty sure I knew at least the basics. I knew I needed dirt. Water, too. So I filled up some old soup cans with dirt and the seeds, poured in some water, and watched the magic happen.

I started out just setting them on the window sill so they could get some light. Now, you're probably thinking that was a dangerous move, putting illegal shit like that out in public view, but no one can recognize a baby pot plant. Like human babies, baby plants all look alike. After a few weeks, though, you could sort of tell what kind of plants they were, so I decided I'd better move them to a less conspicuous spot. You better believe I didn't want any hassle from the pigs. Plus, I didn't want Ron coming over trying to mooch off of me like he always does. Whenever he asked, I just told him I

hadn't gotten around to planting the seeds yet.

I looked around the house for a new spot and eventually settled on this closet. It had a bunch of crap in it, like a box of shitty old NES Nintendo games like "Duck Hunt" and "Bad Dudes," and a black-light poster of Jimi Hendrix that was waiting for a black light. I cleared that stuff out and set up shop.

From what I understood from this one *High Times* article I'd read, you need a special light to keep the plants healthy. I went out and got a light that was supposed to do the trick from a greenhouse. I think they had an idea what I was up to, because the old geezer at the register was giving me the business, asking me what I was growing. I just said strawberries, and he left it alone.

My future was riding on this project, so I did my best to do a good job: Every day, I'd turn the light on before going to work and turn it off when I got home. I also made sure the plants had plenty of water. After about three weeks, they'd gotten pretty tall. I was-

see ANCHOWER page 210

Celebrity Meltdowns

Mariah Carey, Ben Affleck, and Backstreet Boy A.J. McLean are among the celebrities to check into rehab after recent breakdowns. What do *you* think?

Fred Burtt
Cab Driver

"Mariah Carey was hospitalized for 'exhaustion,' but everyone knows what that really means: a quart of cum in her stomach."

Pete Tippet
File Clerk

"The only thing keeping me sane through all of this is Kenny Loggins' repeated assurances that he's all right, and that nobody need worry about him."

Leonard McQuarrie
Systems Analyst

"When is one of these entertainers going to be eaten alive by rats? That's a story I'll read."

Felicia Johnston
Bank Teller

"I feel for them. They suffer so much. What? 'Celebrities'? I'm sorry, I thought you said 'victims of ethnic brutality in Macedonia.'"

Angie Dykstra
Student

"Oh, my God. Is Britney Spears okay? What about Martin Lawrence? Angelina Jolie? Jennifer Lopez? Jim Carrey? P. Diddy? Nicole Kidman? Wait! Come back! I must know!"

Ed Mollo
Photographer

"Why is everybody raising a stink about these people now that they're finally entertaining?"

Headline News' Makeover

Last week, CNN Headline News unveiled its much-hyped makeover, intended to lure younger viewers. Among the changes:

- "Factoids" replaced with easier-to-understand "Factoidoids"
- Anchors help viewers understand complex stories by interjecting, "That's good," or "That's bad"
- "No-repeat Mondays": Hear the same story twice and win a Headline News Ford Explorer or other great prizes
- During slow news days, bikini-clad anchorwoman just sucks noisily on popsicle
- International stories feature helpful background info like, "This is the Dragonball Z country," or "Burritos are from here"
- CNN logo on fire
- When footage of President Bush is aired, his body digitally replaced with Halle Berry's
- Anchors renamed "NJs"
- On bottom of screen, viewer requests scroll past: "Alan Grnspan rulez! More stuff bout him cuz he's DA BOMB!!!"

the ONION

America's Finest News Source

Herman Ulysses Zweibel *Founder*

T. Herman Zweibel *Publisher Emeritus*
J. Phineas Zweibel *Publisher*
Maxwell Prescott Zweibel *Editor-In-Chief*

FOUNDED 1871 • "TU STULTUS ES"

Your Horoscope

By Lloyd Schumner Sr.
Retired Machinist and
A.A.P.B.-Certified Astrologer

Aries: (March 21–April 19)
If you put too much gasoline on the bandanna over your face, you'll get sick. Not enough and you'll be able to smell the corpses. Strike a balance.

Taurus: (April 20–May 20)
Next time you find yourself in a hostage situation, take a hostage people care about.

Gemini: (May 21–June 21)
You will be unable to cope with next Friday, mainly because our society does so little to prepare one for encounters with scary dragonflies.

Cancer: (June 22–July 22)
Your much-publicized solo circumnavigation of the Earth hits a snag when you learn that "circumnavigation" means "to go all the way around."

Leo: (July 23–Aug. 22)
Today's youths sicken you. You didn't fight a secret war against the nuclear mole people at Earth's core so they could wear baggy pants and swear.

Virgo: (Aug. 23–Sept. 22)
It will occur to you that no one in the phone book has a realistic-sounding name. Change them all, if possible.

Libra: (Sept. 23–Oct. 23)
Children are a way to achieve a kind of immortality, as recipients of their healthy young organs can extend life beyond its natural span.

Scorpio: (Oct. 24–Nov. 21)
The stars indicate, without actually saying it in as many words, that they really wish you'd be leaving pretty soon.

Sagittarius: (Nov. 22–Dec. 21)
Your attempt to reach civilization by fashioning a crude raft will astound everyone else at the office.

Capricorn: (Dec. 22–Jan. 19)
The only peace for you will be the cold, dark peace of the grave. Fortunately, there are ways to enjoy this peace before actually dying.

Aquarius: (Jan. 20–Feb. 18)
Though it's true you have a face that could stop a clock, you will soon meet someone who can throw a clock much harder than you're used to.

Pisces: (Feb. 19–March 20)
You have not learned from the history of insignificant little people who work at insurance companies and are, therefore, doomed to repeat it.

ANCHOWER from page 209

n't sure how long I was supposed to wait, but I figured I'd waited long enough.

I cut the plants down and hung them up to dry on this clothesline thing I stretched across the living room, right above the TV. Then I popped a frosty MGD and sat down to enjoy the 4 p.m. showing of *Cannonball Run II* on TNT. But while I was sitting there, I kept getting distracted by that beautiful weed, which was practically begging to be smoked. Wanting to hurry up the drying process, I put the plants in the oven and fired it up. I checked on them after 10 minutes, but they still didn't seem ready. I drank a few beers and returned to watching TV, excited by the thought of the sweet, *Cannonball Run*-enhancing bud I'd soon be enjoying.

The next thing I knew, I was awakened by the sound of my smoke alarm going off. I started to freak out, not knowing where the smoke was coming from. Then, once I figured out where it was coming from, I freaked out even more.

I ran over to the stove and turned it off as fast as I could, but it was too late.

I opened the stove, and a bunch of smoke came pouring out from the charred stalks. Thinking quickly, I sucked up as much of the smoke as I could. I think I caught a buzz off it, but it could have just been from lack of oxygen.

Man, was I pissed! From the smell of it, it was pretty good stuff, and now I was gonna have to wait another month and a half to grow more. There was no way I was going to be able to make it. On top of that, Ron came over and was totally convinced I was holding out on him because the whole apartment reeked of pot. Then he shoved me and said he wouldn't give me any more of his seeds.

As hard as I'm jonesin', though, this current dry spell ain't without its upside. Ron is pissed at me, which means I get a week or so away from him and his damn bitching. And the lack of a buzz hasn't hurt my job performance at the convenience store, for what that's worth.

Still, I'd blow a muffler for a toke off a one-hitter. I ain't an addict or nothing. I just like to have all my options open, you know what I'm saying? ∅

Cat Speed-Dials Ex-Girlfriend

see LOCAL page 7D

NASCAR Logo Slowly Creeping Across U.S.

see NATION page 3A

Obituary Skimmed

see LOCAL page 2D

Rat Race: Hoo, Boy, That Don't Look Too Good

see MOVIES page 8C

STATshot

A look at the numbers that shape your world.

What's Our Excuse For Not Visiting Historic St. Louis?
1. Arch fear
2. Their Mardi Gras stinks
3. Historic East St. Louis took all our money
4. Not Catholic
5. Last time there, forced to fill sandbags
6. Visit not mandatory, if we understand our constitutional rights
7. Thought there would always be time... were so wrong

THE ONION VOLUME 37 ISSUE 29
$2.00 US $3.00 CAN

29

0 74470 94595 6

---

the ONION®

VOLUME 37 ISSUE 29   AMERICA'S FINEST NEWS SOURCE™   23–29 AUGUST 2001

Stephen Jay Gould Speaks Out Against Science Paparazzi

CAMBRIDGE, MA—Paleontologist and author Stephen Jay Gould spoke out against the increasingly aggressive tactics of the paparazzi Tuesday, railing against "the reckless throngs of photographers that relent-

Above: Physicist Dr. Richard Kinder is mobbed by paparazzi outside his University of Chicago office.

lessly hound America's top scientists."

"The time has come to place limits on these photographers," said Gould, speaking from Harvard University, where he is a professor of geology and zoology. "They are disrupting my life, as well as those of my colleagues, my family, and my friends."

According to Gould, photographers stand poised around the clock at the entrance of virtually any facility where research is being conducted, including such science hotspots

see GOULD page 215

Bush Vows To Wipe Out Prescription-Drug Addiction Among Seniors

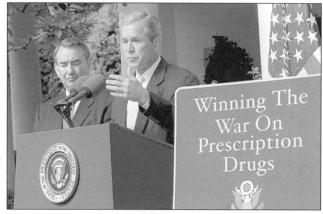

Above: President Bush unveils his plan to get seniors "off the drugs and high on life."

WASHINGTON, DC—Pledging to help "the millions of elderly Americans who can't get through the day without popping pills or shooting up insulin," President Bush announced Monday that he is committed to wiping out prescription-drug use among seniors.

"Nearly three million of our nation's senior citizens are hopelessly hooked on substances like Norvasc and Cardizem CD," Bush said. "In the past, we as a nation have enabled such addiction through the billions of dollars we give to prescription-drug programs, but this has got to stop."

To help combat the problem, Bush

is proposing stricter regulations for both doctors and pharmacists.

"Right now, drugs like Donepezil and Vasotec can be obtained with little more than a single visit to the doctor. This can no longer be allowed to go on," Bush said. "We must attack the problem at the source: the HMO-backed medical professionals who prescribe, or 'deal,' cheap prescription drugs. If we crack down on them, seniors will have a lot harder time getting their fixes."

According to a recent report by the National Institute On Drug Abuse, as many as 1,800,000 Ameri-

see BUSH page 213

Family Of Five Found Alive In Suburbs

Above: A photo of the Holsapples, taken during their years in the wilderness.

BUFFALO GROVE, IL—The Holsapple family, long feared missing or spiritually dead, was found alive in the Chicago suburbs Monday, somehow managing to survive in the hostile envi-

ronment for more than eight years.

Rescuers discovered the five-person clan after a survey plane spotted a crude signal fire the family had created in

a barbecue grill.

"Imagine my surprise when, smack-dab in the middle of nowhere, I saw these flames," pilot Tony Riggs said. "I did a second pass and was shocked to see actual human beings down there. I remember thinking to myself, 'My God, who could live in a place like that?' It's incredible to imagine they survived there for so long."

Bill Holsapple, 41, wife Meredith, 39, and son Jay disappeared in June 1993, when, two months after Jay's birth, the family of three left their Chicago apartment for parts unknown. The three were not heard from again until Monday, when they were

found in the suburban wasteland known as Buffalo Grove with two new family members, Kimberly, 4, and Jordan, 2.

To protect themselves from the elements, the Holsapples fashioned a three-bedroom, ranch-style lean-to with brick facing and white aluminum siding. During their years on the acre-and-a-half lot, the Holsapples faced many hardships, including septic-tank backups, frequent ant infestation, and the threat of rezoning to erect an industrial park across the street.

"The Holsapples were in pretty bad shape when we found them lying lifelessly

see FAMILY page 214

Bank Robbers Fail To Consider O'Reilly Factor

PITTSBURGH, PA—Would-be bank robbers Anthony Nesco, 34, and James Dumas, 36, were foiled Monday after failing to take into account the O'Reilly Factor. "Before they charged into [Fidelity Savings Bank] waving their guns, those two creeps should have thought about me and my tough-talking, straight-shooting, no-nonsense style," said Bill O'Reilly, host of Fox News Channel's *The O'Reilly Factor* and author of a best-selling book of the same name. "Normally, I take no prisoners, but I'll make an exception in the case of these two crum-bums: Lock 'em up and throw away the key, I say." O'Reilly added that it's absolutely ridiculous, the money these mollycoddled pro athletes make these days.

According To Nutritional Information, Local Man Just Had 16 Servings Of Fritos

WAUKESHA, WI—According to the nutritional information on the back of a bag of Fritos, area resident Jerry Ploeg just ate 16 servings of the popular corn chip. "Wow, I didn't realize there were so many servings in there," Ploeg said Tuesday, moments after finishing off the bag, which contained 220 grams of fat and 1,200 percent of the USRDA for sodium. "How big is a serving, anyway?" Ploeg then washed the Fritos down with five servings of Dr. Pepper.

Semiotics Department Accuses University Administration Of Anti-Semiotism

PROVIDENCE, RI—After years of budget cuts and downsizing, Brown University's Semiotics Department lashed out at school administrators Monday, accusing them of "blatant anti-semiotism." "How can such shamefully anti-semiotic acts be condoned in an enlightened society?" asked professor Don Frisch. "It deeply saddens me that in the year 2001, there are still people out there who discriminate against a group of people just because they engage in the study of signs and symbols, especially as elements of language or other systems of communication." Frisch said he is outraged that his department has been relegated to the academic ghetto.

Partygoers Drunkenly Recite 4-H Pledge

MISSOULA, MT—The 4-H pledge was drunkenly recalled Saturday, when a trio of former 4-H members recited the international youth organization's oath between swigs of beer at a house party. "I pledge my Head to clearer thinking, my Heart to greater loyalty, my Hands to larger service, and my Health to better living," shouted a heavily intoxicated Benjamin Brower, 29, who was active in 4-H from 1984 to 1986. "Holy shit, I can't believe I still remember that." The nostalgic group chant was followed by an attempt to recall what "Webelos" stands for.

Friend's Wife Encountered Twice A Year

GERMANTOWN, TN—Local resident Wayne Beller has encountered Dennis Sharp's wife 12 times during the pair's six-year friendship. "For some reason, it's always twice a year," Beller said Monday. "So far, I've run into [Sherri Sharp] once this year, when I returned Dennis' Roto-Tiller in early June. I'll probably see her again at some party around Christmastime, and that'll be it." Beller added that Sherri "seems nice enough." ⌀

Area Man Disappointed To See Short Version Of Commercial

CLEWISTON, FL—A shortened, 30-second version of a one-minute Nike commercial disappointed local bicycle mechanic Paul Hobish Tuesday.

"What the hell is that?" asked Hobish, 30, upon seeing the shorter version of the popular Nike "Freestyle" ad, in which various basketball players dribble balls in a dimly lit room. "Normally, all these guys are dribbling and dribbling and doing all these cool tricks. The thing must go on for, like, two or three minutes. It's so awesome. But this time, it was, like, 15 seconds, and it didn't even show a bunch of the best tricks."

Continued Hobish: "I've been telling all my friends how much the commercial rocks. But if they see the short version, they're going to think I don't know what I'm talking about."

Hobish, who doesn't consider himself a commercial aficionado but watches "a lot of TV," said this is not the first time a favorite spot has been disappointingly abridged.

"I used to be really into the Pentium 4 one where the Blue Man Group guys fling the paint at the wall," Hobish said. "But then they stopped running the full-length one, and it's just not the same without the whole set-up. Why do they always stop running the long versions of commercials after the first few weeks?"

Other truncated commercials have not only disappointed Hobish,

> **Said Hobish: "This time, it was, like, 15 seconds, and it didn't even show a bunch of the best tricks."**

but also caused confusion.

"During the Super Bowl, there was all this hype about the Britney Spears Pepsi ad," Hobish said. "When it came on, I thought it was pretty good. But after that one big premiere, it was always shorter, and Bob Dole would say, 'Down, boy,' to his dog, which isn't what he said in the original. I don't remember it being better or worse than, 'Down, boy,' but for some reason, they changed it."

"Maybe the first version got them in trouble," Hobish continued, "but I'm pretty sure I remember seeing the shortened one within a half-hour of the premiere, so it's not like they would've even had time to change it because of complaints."

Brett Jaglund, a creative director at Leo Burnett advertising agency, said he understands Hobish's disappointment, but stressed that cost considerations make shorter versions necessary.

"A one-minute spot that goes into

Above: Hobish reacts with displeasure to the truncated version of a favorite Nike commercial.

heavy rotation is a pricey venture," Jaglund said. "Often, a commercial will be shortened to save money. What many viewers don't realize is the level of skill and artistry required to take a perfectly realized one-minute piece and edit it down to 30 seconds without losing its essence. It's a subtle and demanding art. Yes, sometimes we have to cut out a cute thing an animated polar bear says, but it must occasionally be done for the sake of economics."

Though Hobish understands that a one-minute commercial costs significantly more to air than a 30-sec-

ond spot, he said that airing the full-length versions only during the Oscars and other major events is unfair to regular TV viewers.

"You're only going to see the long version of the Doritos ad where the sexy woman puts the Doritos in the tennis-ball machine during something big like the Super Bowl," Hobish said. "By doing this, Doritos is sending the message that they don't care about the little people who watch *King Of The Hill* or *Becker*. They only care about the Super Bowl people. That's not right." ⌀

Mary-Kate Olsen Is Dragging Ashley Down

By Kathie Kelleher
Television Viewer

Mary-Kate Olsen. I don't even know where to begin.

Can Mary-Kate really be the incomparable Ashley Olsen's twin sister? They may have the same genetic code, but Mary-Kate certainly does not have her sister's prodigious dramatic gifts. For eight years on *Full House*, the pint-sized duo shared the role of Michelle Tanner. But, despite their identical outward appearance, it was easy to tell which sister was Michelle at any given moment. I cringed whenever Mary-Kate would appear on my TV screen, her clumsy, ham-fisted portrayal of the littlest Tanner devoid of all nuance and depth. And her incompetence was laid all the more bare by her sister's mastery of the role.

The twins' post-*House* work only widened the gap. Over the course of countless children's sing-along videos, TV movies, and such sitcoms as *Two Of A Kind* and *So Little Time*, it's been made painfully obvious who's got the chops and who doesn't. Ashley is George Michael to Mary-Kate's Andrew Ridgeley. She's Daryl Hall to her sister's John Oates.

> ## Ashley is George Michael to Mary-Kate's Andrew Ridgeley. She's Daryl Hall to her sister's John Oates.

Yes, it's clear that Ashley Olsen is the one with the true talent and personality. She is the majestic airship hovering in the sky, while Mary-Kate is the oppressively heavy, rust-encrusted anchor to which that airship is cruelly tethered, preventing it from ascending high into the firmament. Ashley could be another Hepburn, another Streep, if not for the cumbersome ballast that is Mary-Kate.

Examples of Mary-Kate's incompetence are as abundant as blades of grass. Space limitations force me to restrict my examples, yet the handful I have selected are nevertheless damning:

Mary-Kate lacks charisma. That elusive quality is vital to a performer, yet Mary-Kate is almost completely devoid of it. With her vanilla features and expressionless, fish-eyed gaze, one must wonder why this singularly untalented waif was ever placed before a camera. Case in point: In 1995's "The Case Of The Sea World Adventure," from the direct-to-video children's mystery series *The Adventures Of Mary-Kate And Ashley*, Mary-Kate delivers such lively and toothsome lines as, "The pearl necklace must be in that bucket of bait... yecch!" with about as much élan as a TV agribusiness reporter delivering the day's livestock quotes. If she required guidance or inspiration, she need only have turned to Ashley, whose unmasking of the jewel thief was as suspenseful as the climax to any classic 1940s film noir. "Trenchcoat Twins," indeed.

Mary-Kate's diction is poor. Another acting skill so vital, yet so utterly lacking in Mary-Kate, is clear enunciation. Her high-pitched, reedy, mealy monotone seems oddly out of place coming from her ponderous maw. Yet, like the call of the shrike, it pierces the eardrums and inspires profound irritation. This paucity of resonance applies to her singing voice, as well, and is readily apparent in the girls' 1994 recording, "Brother For Sale." No amount of studio wizardry could conceal the cracks in her off-key, phoned-in "singing." It was clear she didn't believe in the song. Meanwhile, Ashley's hearty vocals and peerless phrasing were reminiscent of a brilliant prodigy of yesteryear, Judy Garland. Whereas Ashley sang from her diaphragm, Mary-Kate's voice seemed to emanate from a tinny transistor radio with a dying battery.

Mary-Kate is not as good-looking as Ashley. Mary-Kate's disheveled rat's-nest hairdo looks as though it has never experienced a comb or shampoo. She never seems to have a straight part, and the fussy little barrettes stuck randomly throughout her hair only accentuate its unruliness. Her wardrobe, from *To Grandmother's*

see OLSEN page 215

BUSH from page 211

cans over the age of 65 may be dependent on prescription drugs. Bush warned that the actual number of habitual users may be even higher.

"Surprising as it may be, young people are not the ones doing most of the prescription drugs," Bush said. "Seniors are responsible for a shocking 70 percent of Amiodarone abuse in this country. Nitroglycerine use among the elderly has reached similarly epidemic proportions. Because such substances are obtained legally, compounded with the clouded judgment which results from drug use, many of these addicts aren't even aware they have a problem. It's up to our government to step in and break the cycle."

Claire Lakewood, director of Partnership For A Prescription-Drug-Free America, said the cycle of abuse is hard to break if seniors don't want to be helped.

"Older Americans tend to give in to peer pressure," Lakewood said. "They just do what their doctor tells them because they want to 'be cool' or 'live,' and win their doctor's approval. They also want to fit in with all their other elderly friends, who, no doubt, are doing these prescription drugs, too."

Fortunately, prescription-drug addicts will not have to conquer their addictions alone. Bush said his plan will emphasize rehabilitation over punishment.

"Our only goal is to provide help to those in need," Bush said. "Locking up these seniors would be cruel, costly, and, in the long run, counterproductive. Treatment and counsel-

> ## "Seniors are responsible for a shocking 70 percent of Amiodarone abuse in this country," Bush said.

ing is the only real answer."

U.S. Secretary of Health and Human Services Tommy Thompson said his department is taking steps to help the drug-addicted. Outpatient treatment centers will be established at local senior centers, he said, and a 40-page booklet titled "Hugs, Not Dronabinol" will guide homebound seniors through the difficult road to clean living.

"Let's kick drugs out of our nursing homes and senior centers once and for all," Thompson said.

As part of Bush's anti-prescrip-

Above: A prescription-drug addict begs his pharmacist for a hit of Norvasc, to no avail.

tion-drug effort, a PSA campaign will soon be launched. The first such ad will feature "Sammy The Senior," a cartoon octogenarian kicking up his heels with the aid of a walker, accompanied by the slogan, "I've Got Better Things To Do Than Take Prescription Drugs!"

Hazel Tenney, a 72-year-old Tulsa, OK, resident, is among the many older Americans now questioning their drug use.

"Every day, for nearly seven years, I've taken Hydralazine to treat my high blood pressure," Tenney said. "But after hearing what President Bush said, I threw my pills away. Today, I'm feeling short of breath and dizzy, but if I can just make it through these withdrawal symptoms, with God's help, I will finally be drug-free." ∅

213

I Wish I Were Happy Like The People In The Electronics-Store Flyer

By Thelma Warner

I suppose I've never really had what you'd call a "zest for living." I've always just sort of slogged through life. Everything seems so insurmountable and complicated, and at the end of even a routine day, I feel drained. Yet I realize that there are some people for whom life is relatively carefree and gratifying. That's why I envy the people I see in the electronics-store flyer in the Sunday newspaper.

After I collect the paper from my doorstep, the first thing I look at is the Best Buy sales insert. I pore over every page, each one offering me a glimpse into a world of untold happiness. I find myself vicariously living the joyful lives of the people pictured with the various electronics products.

Take, for example, the pretty lady with the shoulder-length strawberry-blonde hair and the handsome man in the butter-yellow polo shirt, who, I assume, are husband and wife. (I call them "Katy" and "Greg.") Last week, Katy and Greg sat in front of their 36-inch JVC stereo TV with S-video and A/V inputs and digital comb filter, enjoying a still from the upcoming DVD Platinum Edition of Disney's *Snow White And The Seven Dwarfs*. The week before that, they were both seated in front of their Hewlett-Packard Pentium III Processor 1 GHz PC with 17" monitor, scanning their tropical vacation photos with a Umax 3400 42-bit flatbed scanner. In both instances, they were smiling so broadly, you'd think their faces would cleave in two.

Then there's "Kevin," the bright-eyed African-American teen who can often be found grooving to his favorite tunes on a Rio 800 128MB MP3 player or playing "NBA2K1" on his Sega Dreamcast. This week, Kevin was cruising the Internet on an 800 MHz Sony Vaio notebook computer with DVD-ROM drive while a pretty Latina girl talked to one of her doubtlessly many friends on her

> ## You cannot buy your way into Best Buy ecstasy. You must be to the manner born.

dual-mode Sprint PCS phone. Her right hand was on Kevin's shoulder, which indicated to me that he must have broken up with "Rhonda," the cute African-American girl in the midriff-baring top who just last week was snapping photos of him with an Olympus 3.3 megapixel digital camera. My brow furrowed with concern: Was there trouble in paradise? I needn't have worried, because when I turned the page, there was none other than Rhonda, beaming with pride in a trim business suit as she held a Palm m505 handheld with 65,000-color display. Not all of life's twists and turns need end in defeat and despair.

But, as much as I love my weekly Best Buy flyer, sometimes I find it too painful to peruse. It reveals to me in glossy, full-color reality what a mess my own life is, how I've wasted so much of my time on self-pity and dull care. Surely, the wheelchair-bound 6-year-old girl who appeared several weeks ago has experienced more hardship in her young life than I have in my 34 years. Yet the translucent pink Game Boy she holds in her small hands has given her profound joy. Joy that, alas, still eludes me, though I seek it always.

Surely, I am doing something wrong. But what? This past Sunday, overcome with equal measures of anguish and self-hatred, I began to crumple up the flyer. But then my eyes fixed upon the visage of a trim, distinguished, gray-haired retiree listening to a Sony compact CD audio system with stylish wood cabinetry. Though it offered only a small glimmer of hope, it put my mind at considerable ease. It was heartening to see a dynamic older man who was not afraid to try new things and, most important, was not fading from sight in a spiritual and mental freefall seemingly without end.

What accounts for the happiness of the people in the Best Buy flyer? Certainly, the no-interest financing until January 2003 must play a role. Yet the offer extends only to purchases of $399 and up, made with a qualified Best Buy credit card. Could it be the fact that Best Buy will not be undersold by its major competitors? Or that Best Buy will match a competitor's lower prices on available products of the same brand and model, plus another 10 percent of the difference, provided you produce verification of the lower price as well as your original Best Buy receipt within 30 days of purchase? Or that Best Buy boasts 41 convenient locations in the tri-state area? These enticements can only help.

I once dared ponder the purchase of one of the store's wares, a modest 1.7-cubic-foot Sanyo compact refrigerator, only $69.99 after mail-in rebate. But I chided myself for such hubris. You cannot buy your way into Best Buy ecstasy, I determined. You must be to the manner born. Such passion for all things electronic must come from within. Otherwise, I would be in that flyer myself, happily enhancing my home-theater system with a Pioneer 500-watt Dolby Digital/DTS digital receiver.

I now resign myself to going about my minor existence in my usual fumbling, furtive way, never to taint that glorious Valhalla known as Best Buy with my trifling presence. Yet I am still plagued with yearning. I have already consigned this week's flyer to the trash five times today. Nevertheless, I am irresistibly drawn to Katy and Greg. In the latest installment, they are driving in their minivan as their young son, seated in the rear, enjoys a mobile TV entertainment system with DVD player featuring remote and video-game input. Katy, in the passenger seat, peers over her shoulder at her son, her eyes gleaming with boundless affection and wonder.

So are mine, Katy. So are mine. ∅

FAMILY from page 211

on their patio furniture," paramedic Mary Gills said. "Their stomachs were bloated from years of soda and fast food, and they were all suffering from severe cultural malnutrition."

Upon discovery, the family was rushed back to civilization. Attempts to reassimilate the Holsapples into metropolitan living with a trip to the Art Institute of Chicago and dinner at a nice Peruvian restaurant were met with resistance.

"When we got to the museum, the family became quite agitated," psychologist Dr. Allan Green said. "Jay kept calling all the modern art 'weird' and Meredith said, 'If we wanted to look at art, we could just go to Deck The Walls at the mall.'"

Green feared that the family was not ready to rejoin urban life after having received little or no cultural stimuli in the suburbs for nearly a decade.

"We were going to ease them into it, perhaps with a marginally artsy movie like *Being John Malkovich*," Green said. "Then Kimberly kept complaining that she missed 'Ashley' and wanted to go home. At first, I thought we'd left one of the family members behind, but then she said Ashley was a friend. I was shocked to learn of whole tribes of suburban dwellers, people who live their entire lives there."

Upon arriving in Buffalo Grove in 1993, the Holsapples befriended the locals, called "suburbanites," and soon adopted their ways entirely, from the mode of dress to the food they eat. Meredith Holsapple described in great detail the suburban settlements called "sub-divisions" where great emphasis is placed on maintaining lawns, watching televised sports, birthing children, listening to Top 40 music, and collecting stuffed animals.

According to University of Illinois–Chicago anthropologist Dr. Arthur Cox, to survive such an emotionally, culturally, and spiritually barren place, the Holsapples were forced to "go native."

"Much like those stranded on remote islands, the Holsapple family

> ## To protect themselves from the elements, the Holsapples fashioned a three-bedroom, ranch-style lean-to.

looked to the indigenous population to learn techniques for adaptation and survival," Cox said. "Shocking as it is, one eventually becomes acclimated and then numbed to the theme restaurants, cinema multiplexes, and warehouse-sized grocery stores.

"The world is full of strange, isolated cultures, but the American suburbs are unique among these in that virtually no culture exists there," Green said. "Even the Eskimos living in the most barren, remote Arctic regions have whale-bone art and beautiful storytelling traditions. The odd part about these suburbanites is how, unlike the Eskimos and other isolated groups, they live in close proximity to places brimming with art, life, and vitality. Yet somehow, they shut all of it out. We don't know the reason for this, but I don't think anyone wants to spend enough time in the suburbs to find out." ∅

FLUBS from page 202

Passersby were amazed by the unusually large amounts of blood. Passersby were amazed by the unusually large amounts of blood. Passersby were amazed by the unusually large amounts of blood. Passersby were amazed by the unusually large amounts of blood. Passersby were amazed by the unusually large amounts of blood. Passersby were amazed by the unusually large amounts of blood. Passersby were amazed by the unusually large amounts of blood. Passersby were amazed by the unusually large amounts of blood. Passersby were amazed by the unusually large amounts of blood. Passersby were amazed by the unusually large amounts of blood. Passersby were amazed by the unusually large amounts of blood. Passersby were amazed by the unusually large amounts of blood. Passersby were amazed by the

see FLUBS page 220

GOULD from page 211

ALL GOOD WITH JANE GOODALL? CHIMPS SAY NO.

WOW! Six sizzling-hot John D. and Catherine T. MacArthur pics!

SCIENCE WORLD WEEKLY

$1.75 / CANADA $2.30   www.scienceworldweekly.com   AUGUST 20, 2001

STEPHEN HAWKING SHOCKER: "Supernovas suggest universe has small cosmological constant!"

—BROOKHAVEN EXCLUSIVE—

What are they hiding about their new method for producing electrodes using nanoscale materials obtained from hydrogen-driven metallurgical reactions?

Above: The latest issue of *Science World Weekly*.

as the Mayo Clinic, labs at MIT and Princeton, and the Center For Astrophysical Research in Antarctica. The situation has gotten so bad, Gould said, that scientists are often forced to slip in through alternate entrances, and increased security is required at any conference they attend.

"It doesn't matter if you're in the lab developing semiconductor heterostructures for high-speed optoelectronics or just going out for coffee, someone is always ready to shove a camera in your face," said Gould, who rose to science stardom in 1972 when his theory of punctuated equilibria made him a household name. "As for field studies, I may as well forget them, unless I'm prepared to bring a full team of bodyguards along with me to the dig site."

Brian Greene, whose *The Elegant Universe: Superstrings, Hidden Dimensions, And The Quest For The Ultimate Theory* spent 32 weeks atop the *New York Times* bestseller list last year, is also fed up with the media.

"Yes, I want people to read my work, but my personal life is my own business," Greene said. "Just because I'm a scientist doesn't mean I have to completely surrender my privacy. The public doesn't have the right to know everything I do every second of the day." Greene recently sued the German magazine *Stern* for publishing nude sunbathing photos of him and his girlfriend, Stanford University physicist Dr. Aileen Wang.

Members of the paparazzi say they are merely responding to public demand, providing a service to the millions of Americans who closely follow the careers of the world's top physicists, mathematicians, and botanists.

"In this country, people want to know about scientific discoveries the minute they happen," said New Haven-based freelance photographer Lance Evans. "It's only natural that the public would be interested in the personal lives of the men and women behind these discoveries."

Gould insisted that the adoring public is not the problem.

"My personal life is my own business," Greene said.

"The paparazzi are far more forceful and disruptive than they need to be," said Gould, who on Aug. 5 pleaded no-contest to a March incident in which he attacked an intrusive paparazzo with a broken graduated cylinder. "I realize they have a job to do, but there is such a thing as taking it too far."

According to Gould, paparazzi often use illegal means to secure photos for such notoriously disreputable tabloids as *Science World Weekly* and *Starz*, which bills itself as "your most trusted source for astronomy celebrity news."

Exacerbating the situation is the fact that paparazzi photos often accompany stories that are inaccurate or outright libelous.

"The tabloids make little effort to ground their stories in reality," Gould said. "A recent *Science World Weekly* story claimed I was starting a project in organic stereochemistry and conformational analysis, which is preposterous. Another tabloid recently ran a contest offering the winner a romantic evening carbon-dating fossils with me in my lab. I never agreed to any such contest."

Gould is urging lawmakers to impose stricter standards on trespassing photographers and implored the public not to purchase tabloids that print "these ill-gotten photos and

ludicrous stories."

Many science fans are torn, saying that, while their favorite researchers have a right to privacy, they still crave the latest gossip on them.

"I love Stephen Jay because he's not afraid to take on the historical genesis and broader implications of biological determinism, focusing on the question of the numerical ranking of human groups by measures of intelligence," said Tanya Bymers, 20, of Decatur, GA. "I know I shouldn't, but if I see a tabloid rag with him on the cover, I have to buy it."

Some fans felt less sympathy for celebrity scientists.

"Oh, come on, Stephen," said Trace Leefold, webmaster of www.grantwatch.com, a site that prints rumors about soon-to-be-awarded research grants. "No one put a gun to your head and forced you to enter the field of evolutionary theory. You chose that life."

Alan Heeger and Alan MacDiarmid, co-recipients of the 2000 Nobel Prize For Chemistry, said Gould and his fellow tabloid opponents are too thin-skinned. Dubbed the "Plastics Pals" for their discovery and development of conductive polymers, the researchers are among the few scientists to enjoy a good relationship with the paparazzi, arriving at meetings flanked by a phalanx of photographers.

"If it weren't for all this publicity, it's possible that far fewer people would support our work," Heeger said. "We scientists could actually be in the position of needing to scrape pennies together to complete our vitally important research."

Diehard science fan Jill Krause agreed.

"These scientists are the most important people in America," Krause said. "Our very future depends on them. They are enabling us to live longer and better, discovering the history of the planet we live on, and unraveling the mysteries of the universe. There's no way we'd ever let them work in obscurity. It's laughable." ∅

OLSEN from page 213

House We Go to *Billboard Dad*, has always been tacky and dowdy, inspired by some bizarre Schoolmarm Chic trend that exists only in her head. By contrast, Ashley is a heavenly apparition. Her strawberry-blonde mane falls in glossy ringlets, her well-scrubbed skin radiates a golden, healthy glow, and her erect bearing exudes a sylphlike grace, giving her a larger-than-life appearance despite her diminutive frame. Her fashion instincts are as unerring as Mary-Kate's are clueless.

Mary-Kate could also stand to lose a few pounds.

I say these things not to humiliate Mary-Kate. It is altogether likely that the girl possesses talent—just not in an entertainment-indus-

try capacity. Perhaps, after extensive training and a long probationary period, Mary-Kate could make a serviceable cashier, nursing-home orderly, or cafeteria worker. Or maybe she could serve as an assistant to Ashley—a star of her sister's magnitude surely needs someone to answer her fan mail, clean her trailer, and fetch her bottled water.

I fear that if Mary-Kate is not forced to relinquish her partnership with Ashley, the duo will eventually go down in a blaze of mediocrity. Their careers will become mired in a bog of formulaic sitcoms, forgettable TV movies, and mindless, mercenary merchandising peddled to the lowest common denominator. And that will be a real shame, because the girls have so much to

offer. Well, Ashley does.

Mary-Kate, please do your twin a favor: Set her free to soar like the eagle she is. Only when she is loosed of the sisterly bonds that hold her down can Ashley assume her rightful place in the pantheon of greats.

This full house must be divided, or it will not stand. ∅

see MUSTY from page 202

unusually large amounts of blood. Passersby were amazed by the unusually large amounts of blood. Passersby were amazed by the unusually large amounts of blood. Passersby were amazed by the unusually large amounts of blood. Passersby were amazed by the unusually large amounts

of blood. Passersby were amazed by the unusually large amounts of blood. Passersby were amazed by the unusually large amounts of blood.

I can't believe they're actually *paying* me to kill people!

Passersby were amazed by the unusually large amounts of blood. Passersby were amazed by the unusually large amounts of blood. Passersby were amazed by the unusually large amounts of blood.

see MUSTY page 218

215

The Clone Wars

Across the U.S. and on Capitol Hill, debate is raging on the issue of human cloning. What do *you* think?

Lisa Rossiter
Florist

"Cloning? Why? Aren't most Americans pretty much exactly alike as it is?"

Dan Preece
Truck Driver

"We really have no idea what kind of profound ramifications this could have on future generations, and on life on this planet as a whole. Let's find out."

Stewart Nicholls
Cashier

"Cloning forces us to ask some hard questions. For example, which person, the original or the clone, gets to wear the goatee and be evil?"

Danielle Yates
Student

"Can we clone a bulletproof Kurt Cobain? He was a sun that set too soon."

Bill Barron
Systems Analyst

"Anything that puts more people on the planet is okay by me."

Ken Bould
Architect

"Didn't the world learn its lesson when test-tube baby Louise grew to 60 feet tall and rampaged across London?"

The Teacher Shortage

America is suffering a severe shortage of schoolteachers. What incentives are being offered to draw more people to the profession?

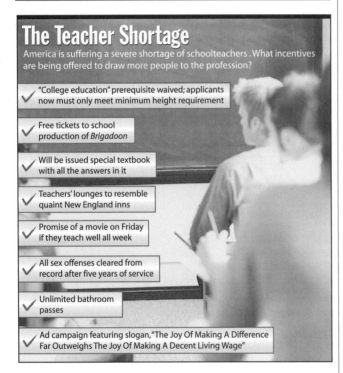

- ✓ "College education" prerequisite waived; applicants now must only meet minimum height requirement
- ✓ Free tickets to school production of *Brigadoon*
- ✓ Will be issued special textbook with all the answers in it
- ✓ Teachers' lounges to resemble quaint New England inns
- ✓ Promise of a movie on Friday if they teach well all week
- ✓ All sex offenses cleared from record after five years of service
- ✓ Unlimited bathroom passes
- ✓ Ad campaign featuring slogan, "The Joy Of Making A Difference Far Outweighs The Joy Of Making A Decent Living Wage"

the ONION

America's Finest News Source

Herman Ulysses Zweibel *Founder*

T. Herman Zweibel *Publisher Emeritus*
J. Phineas Zweibel *Publisher*
Maxwell Prescott Zweibel *Editor-In-Chief*

FOUNDED 1871 • "TU STULTUS ES"

Your Horoscope

By Lloyd Schumner Sr.
Retired Machinist and
A.A.P.B.-Certified Astrologer

Aries: (March 21–April 19)
You will finally begin to understand the events of last Thursday after studying the work of Taiwanese mathematician Shi-Shyr Roan.

Taurus: (April 20–May 20)
If jackalopes are imaginary, it raises the question of who or what has been doing your laundry all these months.

Gemini: (May 21–June 21)
You're the kind of guy who, faced with the choice of either doing the pericardiocentesis or just pronouncing the patient dead, will pronounce him dead every time.

Cancer: (June 22–July 22)
Quelling the unrest in the forest will severely limit the time you can spend with your prog-rock band this week.

Leo: (July 23–Aug. 22)
You will be shocked to discover that the police no longer reimburse citizens for shooting people.

Virgo: (Aug. 23–Sept. 22)
Next week will see you destroy a 60-foot sailboat, a 200-year-old country house, and a million-dollar racehorse, making you a legend at Harvard.

Libra: (Sept. 23–Oct. 23)
Your mother still introduces you as her son the future doctor, even though you're a woman and a dentist, and your mother's been dead for seven years.

Scorpio: (Oct. 24–Nov. 21)
Give in to progress this week. Replace that throne of skulls with a comfortable, ergonomic Aeron office chair.

Sagittarius: (Nov. 22–Dec. 21)
This is a great time for your career. Which isn't a good thing for everyone since you're a coroner, but hey.

Capricorn: (Dec. 22–Jan. 19)
Your life story is a hit in the pages of Japan's *Young Machine* magazine, but it loses something in the translation to English.

Aquarius: (Jan. 20–Feb. 18)
The stars indicate that they know very well who ate the last of the cottage cheese and would appreciate you replacing it, thank you.

Pisces: (Feb. 19–March 20)
What people don't understand is that the drinking, casual sex, and off-color jokes are the only way of coping with the pressures of video-store clerking.

PAN-FRIED from page 210

Passersby were amazed by the unusually large amounts of blood. Passersby were amazed by the unusually large amounts of blood. Passersby were amazed by the unusually large amounts of blood. Passersby were amazed by the unusually large amounts of blood. Passersby were amazed by the unusually large amounts of blood. Passersby were amazed by the unusually large amounts of blood. Passersby were amazed by the unusually large amounts of blood. Passersby were amazed by the unusually large amounts of blood. Passersby were amazed by the unusually large amounts of blood. Passersby were amazed by

see PAN-FRIED page 220

CHANGES

Cedars

Pivarnik

Hernandez

Schoepke

Frank Cedars was fired from the Quality-Plus Machine Shop after losing a hand last weekend.

Ginger Pivarnik, recently hired to work the counter at Tender's Chicken Hut, announced that she hopes to be able to take leftover chicken home some nights.

Terry Hernandez was hired Monday by the Greenwood Land O' Lakes butter-processing plant, where he will work until his death in approximately 30 years.

Ed Schoepke was promoted to shift lead at Colson's Foodmart after taking the initiative to change the mop head.

the ONION®

VOLUME 37 ISSUE 30   AMERICA'S FINEST NEWS SOURCE™   30 AUGUST–5 SEPTEMBER 2001

John Ashcroft Frolics In Secret Vault Of Winnie-The-Pooh Toys

see NATION page 4A

Teens Find This One Hilarious Store

see LOCAL page 5C

Baby Bib Loves Grandpa

see LOCAL page 2C

Diseased Pig Cured

see FOOD page 9E

STATshot

A look at the numbers that shape your world.

What Is The Weird Guy In The Coffee Shop Sketching?

1. Himself, holding broadsword, standing atop pile of dead orcs
2. Van Halen logo, 117 times
3. "Still Life With Banana-Nut Muffin And Venti Latte"
4. Klingon coffee shop
5. His boss at art-supply store being burned alive
6. Your shallow ass

THE ONION VOLUME 37 ISSUE 30
$2.00 US $3.00 CAN

Helvetica Bold Oblique Sweeps Fontys

LOS ANGELES—Helvetica Bold Oblique was the big winner at Tuesday's 73rd Annual Fonty Awards, taking home 11 statues, including those for Best Sans Serif and the highly coveted 2001 Best Font prize.

The gala event, attended by the biggest names in the publishing and graphic-design worlds, was held at the Shrine Auditorium and followed by a post-ceremony bash at the recently refurbished Linn Boyd Benton Printing House.

"A million thanks to all the wonderful folks in the font community who believed in Helvetica Bold Oblique," said an ecstatic Oliver Rudd, designer of the font, in his acceptance speech. "Without your faith in my vision, I would not be here before you tonight. I'd also like to thank Helvetica Regular designer James T. Helvetica, the giant upon whose shoulders I stand. And, of course, the designers of the Visa Card Terms & Conditions booklet, who brought my font to the forefront of the American typeface scene this year."

With its victory, Helvetica Bold Oblique takes its place in a long line of Fonty-winning Helveticas. In the awards' history, three other variations of the typeface have won Best Font: Helvetica Condensed Light in 1960, Helvetica Ultra Compressed in 1981, and Helvetica Black in 1988.

see FONTYS page 221

Above: Helvetica Bold Oblique designer Oliver Rudd accepts one of his font's 11 awards.

Above: Shoeless and shirtless Americans march arm-in-arm across the National Mall.

Nation's Shirtless, Shoeless March On Washington For Equal-Service Rights

WASHINGTON, DC—Protesting years of discriminatory treatment at the hands of America's restaurants and stores, an estimated 800,000 shirtless and shoeless citizens marched on the nation's capital Monday to demand equal-service rights.

Chanting the slogan, "No Shirt, No Shoes, No Justice," members of the nation's shirtless and shoeless communities joined together in a rare act of solidarity. Dubbed "The Million Incompletely Dressed Man March," the demonstration began on I-66 in Arlington, VA—with the barefoot participants walking on the white center line to pro-

see MARCH page 219

Recently Divorced Man Thinks Everyone Else's Relationship Is In Trouble

SCRANTON, PA—Roger Dittman, whose four-year marriage ended in June, is convinced that the romantic relationships of all his friends and acquaintances are "on the rocks."

"It's sad to say, but so many people I know are heading down the same path as me," the 31-year-old said Monday. "It's amazing how many dysfunctional relationships there are out there."

Dittman, whose divorce from Amy Dittman, 29, became final on June 6, is unusually tuned into the troubles of others.

"There's this couple I'm good friends with, Stephanie and Matt, who, on the surface, really seem to have a solid relationship," Dittman said. "They're totally inseparable, which may seem like a good thing, but they rely way too much on each other for their happiness. Wanting to spend the vast majority of your time with one person is not healthy. They're co-dependent instead of *inter*-dependent."

In addition to co-dependence, Dittman cited 15 other "warning signs" that a relationship

see DIVORCED page 220

Above: The recently divorced Dittman.

Husband Apologizing In Sleep

OGDEN, UT—For the third time in as many nights, Chuck Grimstead apologized to wife Olivia in his sleep Monday. "I'm sorry, honey, I didn't mean—hzzzzuwuh," the 43-year-old dentist muttered into his pillow at 4 a.m. "Urmmm... never do it again." Grimstead also promised to be more considerate of his wife's feelings the next time he decided to hnnrghhhh with his poker buddies.

New Robert Altman Film Released Straight To Special-Edition Director's-Cut DVD

HOLLYWOOD, CA—*Super Sunday*, the latest film from acclaimed director Robert Altman, will be released straight to special collector's-edition director's-cut DVD, *Daily Variety* reported Monday. The film, which follows the parallel stories of 14 separate Super Bowl parties in different parts of the country, is slated to hit video stores Nov. 30. "Altman buffs rejoice: This never-before-seen director's cut features 77 minutes of additional footage not included in the theatrical non-release," Criterion Collection spokesman Tim Page said.

"Also included are special commentary tracks from Altman, screenwriter Anne Rapp, and some of the film's stars, including Julianne Moore, Tim Roth, Lili Taylor, Matthew Modine, Michael Murphy, Bob Balaban, Martin Mull, Henry Gibson, Teri Garr, Jeff Goldblum, Jennifer Jason Leigh, Danny Aiello, Robert Downey Jr., Ned Beatty, and Lyle Lovett."

Trio Of Cutups Attempts To Hide Horse From Landlord

LOS ANGELES—Confusion, embarrassment, and severe cranial trauma were the order of the day Tuesday, when local numbskulls Louis Feinberg, Moses Horwitz, and Jerome Horwitz constructed a horse stall in their bathroom and attempted to hide it from landlord Theodore Healy. "Apparently, the plan was to run a cargo-hauling business from their apartment," Healy said. "But in the end, as is the case with everything these three nutballs do, their crazy scheme went awry." According to Healy, the trio attempted to mask whinnying noises coming from their bathroom by coughing, and explained the large bales of straw in their closet by saying that they were "homesick for Nebraska."

Dome-Home Sales Somehow Manage To Dip Even Lower

AUGUSTA, ME—Despite already negligible figures, sales of geodesic-dome dwellings somehow managed to drop even further in the second quarter of 2001, *Alternative Homes* magazine reported Tuesday. "Last year, I sold just one dome, to some hippie who'd inherited $80,000," Augusta dome-home-kit salesman Bruce Wyner said. "I figured, hey, it's his money." Geodesic domes are currently the worst-selling alternative dwelling in the U.S., followed closely by the yurt.

Community Rallies To Save Eyesore

HUBBARD, IA—Hubbard residents came out in force Monday to protest the planned Sept. 1 demolition of an unsightly, 1930s-era silo to make room for a halfway house and library. "This rusted, structurally unsound monstrosity is part of our shared heritage," said Save Our Silos president Ivy Case, handcuffing herself to the eyesore. "Tearing down this dilapidated, dangerous hulk would be like tearing the ugly heart out of this town." Ø

Man Has Mixed Feelings About Having Disease Named After Him

CHICOPEE, MA—In the three years since Dominic Quinn was diagnosed with a previously undetected gastrointestinal disorder, he's become a household name. Yet, for all his notoriety, the 44-year-old Chicopee claims adjuster remains ambivalent about being the Quinn behind Quinn's Disease.

"I suppose it's an honor," Quinn told reporters Monday. "I mean, how many people get something named after them? Then again, it'd be nice if I could have somehow gotten the notoriety without having to suffer from a disease."

Quinn's Disease, believed to afflict one in every two million Americans, is a non-fatal genetic disorder that impairs the parts of the brain that control alimentary and digestive functions. Symptoms include severe gastrointestinal distress, esophageal inflammation, and constipation and gaseousness. In certain cases, a narrowing of the colon and extreme impacting of the bowels can result, with the pressure becoming so great that a violent hemorrhage of blood and fecal matter occurs.

Quinn's ailment makes it necessary for him to submit to round-the-clock medical surveillance and a grueling regimen of thrice-daily enemas and anti-constipation drugs. In addition, since his March 1999 diagnosis, Quinn has undergone 11 operations to clear his large intestine of densely packed, highly toxic waste matter.

Given the choice, Quinn would prefer to derive fame from other aspects of his life, such as being a devoted father and husband and a skilled potter. Quinn is particularly proud of having spearheaded a 1987 effort to preserve and restore an 18th-century farmhouse near his home that was slated for demolition. But the public seems unanimous in its opinion that none of these accomplishments are as noteworthy as the colon-obstructing disease that bears his name.

"I heard that Lou Gehrig had a problem with ALS being named after him," Quinn said. "He was always telling his wife, 'You know, I was a completely disease-free pro ballplayer for more than a decade before I started to show even the slightest symptoms.' Boy, can I relate. Except, at least Lou Gehrig's Disease is also referred to as Amyotrophic Lateral Sclerosis. They've never even given my condition a scientific name. It's just Quinn's Disease, and that's it."

Continued Quinn: "Sometimes, I wish I'd contracted a syndrome instead of a disease. Syndromes are often given descriptive names like Carpal Tunnel Syndrome. I begged the doctors to reclassify my disease as a syndrome and call it, say, 'Anal-Blockage Syndrome,' but they refused because, technically, a syndrome is defined as a group of various symptoms that culminate in an abnormality. Mine is not an abnormality: I just can't shit properly."

Nevertheless, Quinn remains hopeful that, by giving the disease

Above: The semi-proud Quinn takes pills for his eponymous disease.

a human face, he has helped raise awareness of Quinn's Disease, increasing the likelihood of a cure.

"If my pioneering example can help one day eradicate this terrible disease, it will have all been worth it," Quinn said. "But until that day comes, I'm just Nicky Quinn, the exploding feces guy." Ø

I'm Not Afraid To Try Popular New Things

By Pete Hecker

The world is made up of two kinds of people: those who cling to the tired, old status quo and those who fearlessly embrace the new status quo. Me, I fall squarely into the latter camp. Not content to stick with the same-old same-old, I like to mix it up and put myself out there. You know, give the old heave-ho to the stodgy and staid. Say what you will about me, but no one will ever accuse me of being afraid to try popular new things.

Take movies, for example. Some folks my age might have been scared to give *American Pie 2* a chance, what with its salty language and risqué subject matter. Not me. As soon as I saw the movie's enormous opening-weekend grosses, you better believe I was second in line.

Same goes for music. I have friends who are totally out of

> **The world is made up of two kinds of people: those who cling to the tired, old status quo and those who fearlessly embrace the new status quo.**

touch with the latest music trends. How boring. Unlike them, I like to grow in my appreciation of things, to mature as an individual. That's why I recently stopped by Musicland to pick up some of today's most popular albums, like Dido's *No Angel*, the *Moulin Rouge* soundtrack, and that Wings compilation that's a big hit. I was going to get that new Melissa Etheridge album, too, but then I heard from the guy at the store that it wasn't doing so well, so I passed.

My neophilia isn't restricted to indoor activities like watching movies and listening to music. No way. I love sports and the outdoors, too. But not just boring old stuff like golf or tennis. Give me something new and trendy, like rock-climbing or bungee-jumping. Something that seems dangerous but has been successfully done by millions of people before me and made safe with rigorously tested equipment. Only when I'm living on what millions and millions of

others consider to be the edge do I feel truly alive.

But it isn't all outward, physical adventure with me. I like to think of myself as a very spiritual person, so I'm always up for an inward journey. I recently began taking yoga classes, and it has changed my life. Have you heard of yoga? It really is the latest thing. I hadn't paid much attention to it until I noticed the classes filling up at the gym where I work out. I don't know who the guy is who invented this yoga craze, but I'll bet he's really raking in the bucks.

Speaking of inward journeys, I love to try new foods. I'm a huge fan of all types of popular ethnic cuisine. I recently read in *Newsweek* that Tibetan food is making quite a splash here in the States. In fact, a new Tibetan restaurant called Himal Chuli just opened up in my town, and

see NEW THINGS page 221

MARCH from page 217

tect the soles of their feet from burning—and concluded with a rally on the National Mall in Washington.

"For decades, law-abiding Americans have been denied service in restaurants and stores, simply because of the exposedness of their skin," said Bud Hutchins, president of the National Association For The Advancement Of Shirtless People. "This is a direct attack on our civil rights, especially in the summer months when you really need to stay cool."

Waving a copy of the U.S. Constitution, Hutchins added, "Nowhere in this revered document does it say, 'But only if the guy has a shirt on.' Our Founding Fathers would be appalled to see basic service rights denied to the differently clothed."

Wiping a tear from his eye, Hutchins recalled being denied entry to a Marble Falls, TX, 7-Eleven at the age of eight. He said the store manager told him directly that he wasn't welcome in the store because of his bare torso. "I could not understand how a nation as great as America could say to me, 'You're not as good as your shirt-wearing neighbor,'" Hutchins said. "So I just sat outside the store, watching all the shirted people freely come and go with their Big Gulps and their candy bars. When something like that happens to you at such a young age, you don't soon forget it."

Standing before the shirtless, shoeless throngs, Barefoot America! director Diane Wallace said: "As

> **Waving a copy of the U.S. Constitution, Hutchins added, "Nowhere in this revered document does it say, 'But only if the guy has a shirt on.'"**

if centuries of suffering from gravel roads and hot blacktop were not enough, the powers-that-be continue to deny us restaurant seating, theater admission, and countless other niceties enjoyed by the shoed. We say, no more."

The coalition is calling for the passage of a constitutional amendment or other legislation guaranteeing "equal access to businesses and services for all citizens, regardless of one's degree of bodily coverage." If no such legislation is passed, NAASP members have threatened to retaliate with Denny's-booth sit-ins, Burger King boycotts, and a program of exercise designed to make their torsos glisten with malodorous sweat.

Despite such threats, lawmakers remain unbowed.

"Why can't these folks just put on some shirts and shoes if they

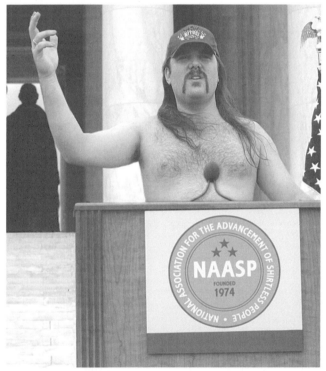

Above: NAASP president Bud Hutchins speaks at the Jefferson Memorial.

want a Whopper?" U.S. Sen. Larry Craig (R-ID) asked. "If we cave in to these demands, next year, it'll be trouserless Americans demanding equal access to Tavern On The Green. After that, the underpantsless will be calling for priority seating on airplanes. Then, people who are completely naked will want preferential treatment in college admissions. These people can

put on a full wardrobe and get treated like everybody else."

Hutchins dismissed Craig's response.

"I'm hardly surprised [Sen. Craig] ascribes to the repugnant and prejudicial notion that we have 'chosen' to be this way," Hutchins said. "Well, I've got news for you, senator: This is the way I am. I was born not wearing a shirt." ∅

Julia And Benjamin: Say Goodbye To The New Camelot!

**The Outside Scoop
By Jackie Harvey**

Item! Why is it that the best-looking couples never stay together? Megastar **Julia Roberts** and ethnically ambiguous actor **Benjamin Bratt** have pulled the plug on their three-year relationship. All accounts indicate that it's an amicable parting, but I'm sure if you scratch the surface, you'll find something unseemly. But should we scratch? I mean, on the one hand, it's my job to report the juicy Hollywood facts that matter to my loyal readers. On the other, here are two lovely people who have never done anyone any harm and are going through a difficult time. After agonizing over this for hours, I've decided that the right thing to do is let them have their privacy. When it's time for them to open up, I'm sure they will.

For the record, I don't know why Julia even bothers to use her last name anymore. She's a **Cher**, a **Madonna**, a **Roseanne**, the kind of star who doesn't need a last name like us regular folks. To me and everyone else, she's just Julia.

And from the ashes of one beautiful relationship rises another to take its place. Funnyman—and tallman—**Conan O'Brien** is getting married! No word on who the lucky lady is or where the wedding is to be held, but I have it on good authority that the invite list is a veritable who's-who of late-night talk-show hosts, past and present. **Dave**, **Jay**, **Arsenio**, **Magic**, **Chevy**, **Pat**, **Martin**, **Wil**, **Alan**... they'll all be there, because Conan knows and respects his roots. Plus, it will be a full Irish wedding, complete with bagpipes and kilts! Conan in a kilt? It's true, readers! Now, ladies, I know that some of you had your hearts set on Conan, but remember, there are still plenty of **smart, funny, handsome guys** available. (Hint, hint, hint!)

Is it just me, or does **Katie Couric**'s new hairdo look totally beautiful! Actually, I know it's not me because everyone here in the office agrees with me, so I should rephrase that: Katie Couric's new

> **For the record, I don't know why Julia even bothers to use her last name. She's a Cher, a Madonna, a Roseanne, the kind of star who doesn't need a last name like us regular folks.**

hairdo looks totally beautiful!

Item! Get your cold showers ready: The **2001 MTV Music Video Awards** show is just a week away, and we can expect to see even more of **Britney Spears** this time around! If you'll recall, at last year's show, Britney gave new meaning to the phrase "ripping your clothes off." Word is this year, she plans to lose her virginity live on-stage to her Backstreet Boyfriend, **J.C. Timberlake**! I just hope they don't block out all the good parts with **those annoying blurry pixels** you see all over TV

these days.

So, what's all the fuss about **Michael Jordan** coming back to the NBA? There's all this "will he or won't he" nonsense, and I for one say, "Air ball!" This is the sort of hype that should be reserved for the likes of **Prince William** or Hollywood royalty like **Brad Pitt** and **Courteney Cox**. Hey, Michael, you've had your day in the sun. Quit hogging the real stars' spotlight and go back to baseball or golf.

Item! The new **Star Wars** movie is called... you ready for this? **Attack Of The Clowns**! Now I *know* **George Lucas** has gone a little batty.

"Is That Your Final Contraction?" America's favorite **Regis Philbin** co-host, **Kelly Ripa**, just had a baby, and it's the cutest thing! The best part is, she had it entirely on her own, without the help of some fancy-pants doctor, fertility clinic, or **David Crosby**. That's what I like to see—good old-fashioned baby-making. Awww.

Even though **Tom Cruise** is scandalously dating his sister Penelope, **Nicole Kidman** has been holding up quite nicely after her divorce from Mr. Top Gun. I say she's not just one classy lady, she's two!

Item! What's with the super-talented songstresses going a bit nutsy lately? First, **Mariah Carey** takes off some of her clothes on MTV and gets hospitalized because of exhaustion. Then, **Whitney Houston** goes off and takes a bunch of drugs with her no-goodnik husband **Bobby Brown**. This breaks my heart to see such inspirational performers hurting so much.

I can really relate to these divas' pain. I've gone through some similarly trying times in my life. Once, after I broke up with a girlfriend, I

had a terrible time sleeping. After three nights of watching some of my favorite romantic movies, I took a cue from **John Cusack** in **Say Anything** and played a song on a boom box under her window. Only, she lived in a fourth-floor apartment, so everyone in the building heard, and I couldn't find that **Phil Collins** song from the movie on short notice at 2:30 a.m., so I had to make do with **Billy Joel's "Piano Man."** It just goes to show you that you shouldn't judge stars just because they're going through some hard times, because it could be you or me. But you probably shouldn't take cocaine, even if you are Whitney Houston, okay?

Jennifer Jason Leigh: She's always got something going on, doesn't she?

I tried that new **Red Bull** drink expecting to get wings, and I was a bit disappointed. After I drank it, I started to feel a little funny. Sort of a shortness of breath and some chest constriction. The last time I felt like that was when I had an allergic reaction to the caffeine in a cup of espresso. And I'll be darned if it didn't happen again! I suppose a trip to the **ER** is what you get for not reading the ingredients first.

Jiminy Christmas! That **Jiminy Glick** sure has the recipe for hilarity down! I would love to be a fly on the wall at one of their writers' meetings! I'd love to see where they get their ideas from.

Planet Of The Apes? It should be called Planet Of The Smash Box-Office Hit! The new **Richard Burton** film, starring **Mark Wahlberg** and newcomer **Helena Bonham Carter** (any relation to Led Zeppelin bassist John Bonham Carter? I'm looking into it!) has been mak-

see HARVEY page 222

DIVORCED from page 217

is in trouble, including stagnation, abrupt change, lack of common interests, over-compatibility, and any marked increase or decrease in sexual activity.

Often, Dittman said, relationships are the rockiest when everything seems to be going well.

"For my birthday, my husband Barry got me this wonderful, incredibly expensive present: a first-edition copy of A.A. Milne's *Winnie-The-Pooh*, my favorite book as a kid," said Jackie Peters, Dittman's sister. "I thought it was a beautiful gesture, but when I told Roger, he said Barry must be feeling guilty about something, like maybe an extramarital affair. I

told him that was ridiculous, but he just said I was probably in

> **Often, Dittman said, relationships are the rockiest when everything seems to be going well.**

denial."

Though many of Dittman's friends are grateful for his

honesty and insight, others would prefer that he mind his own business.

"If [Roger] starts another sentence with, 'Ever since my divorce...,' I'm going to throttle him," said Joanie Castona, a coworker of Dittman's at Scranton Surgical Supply. "Maybe if he weren't always offering unwanted advice and treating people so patronizingly, Amy might not have left him."

Dittman disagreed with Castona's assessment.

"Poor Joanie," Dittman said. "She must be lashing out at me because her partner Claudine is straight and afraid to tell her. I

knew this might happen to those two. See, even lesbian relationships have their problems."

For all his pessimism, Dittman saves his greatest doubts for his ex-wife and her new love interest. "That stockbroker Amy's seeing now, if that isn't a heartbreak waiting to happen, I don't know what is," Dittman said. "With both of them caught up in such busy careers, when will they find the time to be together? Then there are all those expensive dinners and weekend getaways, which can't be good for the wallet: Money squabbles are bound to drive a wedge between them eventually. Such a pity." ∅

How To Tell If You Were Adopted

Hey, Kids!

Sometimes it's hard to figure out whether "Mom" and "Dad" are your actual parents. Here are some things to look out for that mean you were adopted:

- You're not allowed to get a trampoline.
- Other family members enjoy foods that taste "yucky" to you.
- You're made to sleep in your own private room, sequestered from the rest of the family.
- Mom and Dad find occasions once or twice a year to shower you with gifts, so you won't feel so bad about being abandoned by your real parents.
- You don't remember your parents bringing you home from the hospital when you were born.
- Your parents call each other by names other than "Mommy" and "Daddy" to conceal their true identity.

- Your parents don't let you go out at night, when your real parents might try to steal you back.
- Only adopted, or "rejected," children have to brush their teeth.
- You don't have the same eye and hair color as your parents, and you're not the same height.
- Your parents sometimes go into their room and shut the door—this is to talk about whether the adoption was such a good idea.
- Your parents are not as nice to you as your friends' parents are to them.
- Your brother or sister has a nicer bicycle than you.
- You're not allowed to get a puppy, because the puppy could tell by scent.
- Once a week, Mom and Dad go to church, where they pray for a real child.

*Remember! If it turns out you were adopted, do *not* misbehave in any way, or your parents will sell you to the gypsies.

FONTYS from page 217

"The Helvetica font family is highly respected throughout the publishing world," said Bruce Chizen, president and CEO of desktop-publishing giant Adobe Systems. "Boasting an unequaled range of weights and widths, literally everybody wants to work with it."

The Fontys, awarded annually by the Academy Of Fonts & Typefaces, recognizes superior achievement in the field of typography. Winners recieve a Fonty statue, a golden "F" elegantly styled in freeform.

Awards in 41 categories, including Best Slab Serif Font (American Typewriter Medium), Best Monospaced Font (Letter Gothic Slanted), and Best International Font (Fusaka Regular), were presented during the live, three-hour CBS telecast. Technical subcategories, such as Best Transitional Serif (Apollo Roman) and Best Mathematical Symbol (Lucida Math Symbol) were presented in an untelevised ceremony last week.

"This is the one night of the year when the entire font community, from typesetters to PostScript designers, comes together to honor and celebrate its own," said Bob Helger, legendary designer of 1990 Best Font winner Utopia Italic. "You could feel the electricity in the air."

Despite the plaudits heaped on Helvetica Bold Oblique all night, some questioned the academy's choice.

"A bold as Best Font?" said Christopher Rankley, editor of *Typography Today*. "They may as well have handed the award to Chicago, for God's sake. Or, better yet, Chicago Shadow Underline."

Rankley said he was rooting for the more traditionally tooled

> ## "A bold as Best Font?" said Rankley. "They may as well have handed the award to Chicago, for God's sake."

Palatino—which snagged just one award, for Best Display Font—to take home top honors this year.

"Palatino is one of the most popular Oldstyle revivals in existence, blending classical Italian Renaissance letter forms with the crispness of line needed for 20th-century printing processes. Yet it has never won Best Font," Rankley said. "I think a lot of Palatino fans out there were thinking maybe this would be the year."

A common criticism of the Academy Of Fonts & Typefaces is that it is out of touch with the cutting edge, favoring fonts with mainstream, commercial appeal. Academy members have little awareness, detractors say, of today's more challenging fonts, such as the daring, highly ornamental Blackletter.

William Perez, a lifelong font enthusiast and editor of the 'zine *Lorem Ipsum Dolor*, is one such critic, calling the Fontys "embarrassingly conservative and tradition-bound."

"They think they're being daring when they nominate a font like Techno or Comic," Perez said. "What about totally innovative fonts like Critter, with its cute, smiling animal faces rendered into letters, or Giddyup, in which each letter is styled out of a curling lasso? These fonts don't even exist to the high-and-mighty Academy."

Perez is not the first to note that quirky, independently distributed typefaces rarely earn Fonty recognition. In the rare instances when cutting-edge fonts are nominated, they are typically relegated to the Best Decorative Font category. Such was the case with the bitstream release Eyeballs, which was nominated for Best Decorative Font but lost out to SnowCap, a long-entrenched favorite of the bagged-ice industry.

Defending his group's choices, Academy president Jack Tolleson said: "A small, independent font like Goudy Text is masterfully rendered, but it simply does not carry enough national importance to warrant nomination. We cannot justify presenting an award to a font that is barely available for viewing by the public, showing up at only a handful of renaissance fairs across the nation."

Despite such disagreements, no one objected when this year's show closed with the presentation of a Lifetime Achievement Award to Times New Roman, a proportionally spaced typeface designed in 1931 for *The London Times*. When the son of the font's deceased designer, Stanley Morrison, took the stage, the entire room rose in a standing ovation.

"Such strength of line, such firmness of contour, such economy of space," said Tolleson, his voice wavering with emotion. "I doubt there will ever be another font like Times New Roman." ∅

NEW THINGS from page 219

I'm dying to try it. Just as soon as I read glowing reviews in the Fodor's and Zagat guides and see a line of people waiting to get in, I'll be sure to queue up right along with everybody else.

I wish there were more people like me. If more people new unafraid to try popular new things, the popular things I choose to try would be even more popular, and my enjoyment of them would be that much greater. It's really true what they say: There's satiety in numbers. ∅

The OxyContin Epidemic

OxyContin, a powerful prescription painkiller whose effects have been compared to heroin's, is being abused by a soaring number of drug addicts. What do *you* think?

Rob West
Electrician

"It's been great getting my drugs at Walgreens. The pharmacists there are so much friendlier than that dickbag Zach I used get my shit from."

Barry Valtierra
Bike Messenger

"Whoa, hold on there a minute: You can get high off an acne pad?"

Dana Schwartz
Student

"You are *so* lame. They're called Oxys or O.C.'s. No one says 'OxyContin.'"

Emily Jay
Homemaker

"Didn't we learn anything from that one *Little House On The Prairie* where Albert gets hooked on morphine?"

Chris Levey
Auto Salesman

"While I am strongly opposed to drug abuse, I must applaud the entrepreneurial spirit exhibited by addicts when it comes to finding new ways to get off."

Raymond Harvey
Systems Analyst

"This is exactly why I don't want my kids hanging out with white people."

Jesse Helms' Retirement Plans

After 29 years on Capitol Hill, Sen. Jesse Helms (R-NC) recently announced he will not seek a sixth term in 2002. What are Helms' retirement plans?

- See to gettin' a water closet put in
- Finally get caught up on that stack of books he's been meaning to burn
- Retire to country plantation and devote remaining years to impregnating his slaves
- Ride lawnmower across state line to reconcile with estranged brother
- Daily watering and otherwise tending to his embryos
- Get hound dog, abuse shit out of hound dog, say it's for hound dog's own good
- Eat hisseff a big ol' cheesebugga
- Send out direct-mail "I may be retired, but that does not mean the homosexual lobby has ceased corrupting the nation's youth" letter
- Hold out trembling hand, emit ear-piercing shriek, collapse into dust

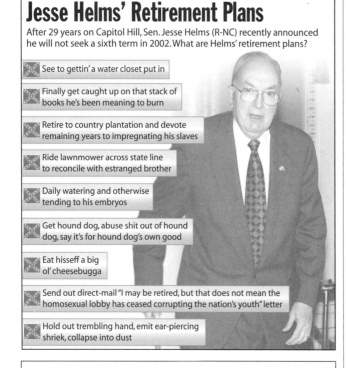

 the **ONION**

America's Finest News Source

Herman Ulysses Zweibel *Founder*

T. Herman Zweibel *Publisher Emeritus*
J. Phineas Zweibel *Publisher*
Maxwell Prescott Zweibel *Editor-In-Chief*

FOUNDED 1871 • "TU STULTUS ES"

222

Your Horoscope

By Lloyd Schumner Sr.
Retired Machinist and
A.A.P.B.-Certified Astrologer

Aries: (March 21–April 19)
You have never been successful at the game of love, but at least you've finally figured out that the rules are similar to those of Scrabble.

Taurus: (April 20–May 20)
This would be a good time to start new endeavors—far better than all previous times, which would have been utter shit.

Gemini: (May 21–June 21)
You will be endlessly pleased with your brief mention in an *Entertainment Weekly* article titled "500,000 Rising Stars Of Indie Film."

Cancer: (June 22–July 22)
You will give your love a chicken which has no bone, horrifying her as the bird flops about and clucks piteously.

Leo: (July 23–Aug. 22)
You never thought anything could ever replace sex in your life, but that was before you tried pouring yourself a nice stiff drink, putting on some music, and having sex.

Virgo: (Aug. 23–Sept. 22)
Your marriage will soon erode to the point where you'll be sorely tempted to turn him in for the reward money.

Libra: (Sept. 23–Oct. 23)
You call yourself "an avid people-watcher," but deep down you know you really only watch for the crashes.

Scorpio: (Oct. 24–Nov. 21)
Look on the bright side: If you'd done a better job designing the airliner's landing gear, Wednesday's newspaper sales would have been much lower.

Sagittarius: (Nov. 22–Dec. 21)
Stalled career got you down? Do what Sagittarius does and take a look at what Ahmad Rashad is up to these days.

Capricorn: (Dec. 22–Jan. 19)
You attempt to reconstruct the proto-language that gave rise to Nostratic and, thus, all modern tongues, but just wind up reading *The Lord Of The Rings* again.

Aquarius: (Jan. 20–Feb. 18)
You will soon rise to fame as America's greatest unromantic-inaction hero.

Pisces: (Feb. 19–March 20)
Next week, you will learn just how much polar bears hate to be teased when, while attempting to play with one at the zoo, you hurt its feelings by calling it "roly-poly."

HARVEY from page 220

ing a monkey of the competition at the box office. Being the sort of journalist I am, I went to see it, and it delivered on the action thrills and surprise ending. And the apes? I went "ape" for them! (I went "bananas," too!) This one should have just come out of the studio stamped "Oscar." Kudos to all involved!

Well, I'm out of news, unless you want to hear the boring details about my new braces or the gift I got for **Tierra and Joe's wedding**. So, in the meantime, here's a preview of some things you can look forward to in my next column: the DVD release date for **Pootie Tang**, some **Madonna** tour news, and my beef with **Hints From Heloise**. Until then, I encourage you to watch TV, go to the movies, and buy some CDs. This is Jackie Harvey, saying, "I'll see you on the Outside!" ∅

SPUDS from page 218

Passersby were amazed by the unusually large amounts of blood. Passersby were amazed by the unusually large amounts of blood. Passersby were amazed by the unusually large amounts of blood. Passersby were amazed by

Please, I beg you, let me back in the chat room.

the unusually large amounts of blood. Passersby were amazed by the unusually large amounts of blood. Passersby were amazed by the unusually large amounts of blood. Passersby were amazed by the unusually large amounts of blood. Passersby were amazed by the unusually large amounts of blood. Passersby were amazed by the

see SPUDS page 240

Cheer Introduces New Higher-Priced Cheer

see PRODUCTWATCH page 7C

Sounds Of Air Hockey Coming From Supreme Court Chambers

see WASHINGTON page 3A

Schoolchildren Watch Urinating Horse With Mounting Fear And Awe

see LOCAL page 2E

Top Jack Nicholson Sexual Positions
1. Bottom, motionless
2. Squatting on carpet with two Oscars up ass
3. Pinning Lara Flynn Boyle to mattress while falling asleep
4. Sodomizing delivery boy while eating foot-long roast-beef and avocado sub
5. Face-down in *Variety*

THE ONION VOLUME 37 ISSUE 31
$2.00 US $3.00 CAN

0 74470 94595 6   31

the ONION®

VOLUME 37 ISSUE 31   AMERICA'S FINEST NEWS SOURCE™   6–12 SEPTEMBER 2001

Plan To Get Laid At DragonCon 2001 Fails

Above: Melcher stands alone in the Dealers Hall.

CALHOUN FALLS, SC—Garry Melcher's plans to have sexual intercourse at last weekend's DragonCon 2001 were unsuccessful, the 27-year-old comic-book collector and science-fiction fan conceded Tuesday.

"I was really hoping to meet some ladies at DragonCon for a little of the old horizontal bop," said Melcher, who has been unwillingly celibate for the last 17 months. "It didn't really pan out, though."

Billed as "America's largest annual convention for fans of sci-fi, fantasy and horror, comics and art, games and computers, animation, science, music, television, and films," DragonCon 2001 was held at the Hyatt Regency in downtown Atlanta from Aug. 31 to Sept. 3. Unfortunately, not one of the convention's 20,000-plus attendees was willing to copulate with Melcher at any point during the four days of the event.

"I drove down to Atlanta with my best friend Andy [Razowsky], but I opted against sharing a hotel room with him, just in case I ended up needing a little privacy," Melcher said. "In fact, I was even thinking of going to DragonCon just by myself, to do a lone-wolf sort of thing."

According to Melcher, women in his hometown of Calhoun Falls "wouldn't know the Green Lantern from the Green Arrow." As a result, he has not had a date since former girlfriend and longtime *Illuminati: New World Order* opponent Carrie Lenz broke up with him in March 2000.

"I know a lot of girls online, but that's not really the same," Melcher said. "I needed to see some face to face."

Melcher said he was greatly looking forward to DragonCon, which offers attendees many opportunities to socialize. Events this year included three dances—the Classic Style Gothic Industrial dance on Friday, '80s New Wave on Saturday, and Electronic Body Music, Synth-Pop, and Modern Gothic-Industrial on Sunday—as well as unofficial dances and drum circles each night on the Hyatt Regency's pool deck.

"The whole week before DragonCon, people on the Internet bulletin boards were posting messages about different parties they'd be

see DRAGONCON page 225

God Finally Gives Shout-Out Back To All His Niggaz

HIP-HOP WATCH

SOUTH BRONX, NY—The Lord Almighty finally responded to nearly two decades of praise in hip-hop album liner notes Monday, when He gave a shout-out back to all His loyal niggaz.

"Right about now, I want to send a shout-out to each and every nigga who's shown Me love through the years," said the Lord, His booming voice descending from Heaven. "I got mad love for each and every one of you niggaz. Y'all real niggaz out there, you know who you are. Y'all was there for me, and it's about time I'm-a give some love back to God's true crew."

see GOD page 226

Right: Rappers Method Man and Redman give big ups to God (inset).

Tow-Truck Driver Has Great Idea For Tow-Truck Movie

Left: Tow-truck driver Beresford.

BUTTE, MT—Bob Beresford, a tow-truck driver with 11 years of experience at Central Montana Service & Salvage, announced Monday that he has a great idea for a tow-truck movie.

"I don't know why, but most people really don't have that clear a picture of what tow-trucking is all about," said the 44-year-old Beresford, standing in front of his 1995 Ford Super Duty. "They don't realize the integrity, the commitment, the strong sense of duty that go into this work. With *Towtruckin'*, I have a chance to change all that."

Towtruckin', according to Beresford, is "a classic

see TOW TRUCK page 226

Stunned Nation Mourns As French Stewart Survives Plane Crash

VIRGIN ISLANDS—Across the nation, Americans are reacting with shock and grief to the survival of *3rd Rock From The Sun* star French Stewart, who sustained only minor injuries Monday when a Beechcraft 1900D carrying him and 14 others nosed down shortly after takeoff. "Of course, I feel good for the rest of the passengers and the crew," said TV viewer Cheryl Ross of Lebanon, TN. "But, my God, French Stewart. He has so many years ahead of him." Ross added that she is "definitely going to miss" all of Stewart's TV and film appearances.

80 Percent Of U.S. Populace Now Selling Handmade Jewelry

WASHINGTON, DC—According to a Department Of Labor report released Monday, four out of five Americans derive at least a portion of their income from the sale of handmade jewelry. "In the past 10 years, the number of Americans selling or attempting to sell jewelry of their own creation has risen tenfold," Labor Department spokesman Gary Hardwick told reporters. "And, speaking of jewelry, if any reporter here has a girlfriend or wife who might like some lovely dreamcatcher earrings, I'd be happy to show them some of my designs."

Third Knocked-Over Glass Of Water Makes Man Want To Give Up

VANCOUVER, WA—A third spilled beverage in less than six hours made Dan Drayton want to give up and crawl back into bed Monday. "God, I'm pathetic," said a disconsolate Drayton, 37, following the tertiary mishap. "This is the third time. *The third time.*" Drayton then sat and stared at the puddle of water on his kitchen counter for eight minutes before getting a roll of paper towels.

Disney Still Throwing Word 'Classic' Around Like So Much Confetti

HOLLYWOOD, CA—The Walt Disney Company referred to an obscure, unacclaimed 1944 film as a "classic" prior to its home-video release Tuesday, once again treating the word as tinsel which may be draped arbitrarily upon any random object. "No home-video library is complete without the timeless Disney classic *Mairzy Doats,*" a TV commercial for the reissue said. "These four unforgettable animated vignettes, hosted by Mickey Rooney and Judy Garland, are now available for a new generation to treasure—you know, much like previous generations have done." The 45-minute video joins such previous Disney "classics" as *Melody Time, Fun & Fancy Free, Make Mine Music,* and *Tarzan.*

Friendly Note To Coworker Undergoes Eight Revisions

WILMINGTON, DE—A brief note from United Family Insurance employee Martin Schatz to a coworker regarding storage closet office supplies went through eight rewrites Monday. "I wrote it pretty quick and was about to drop it in [Al Miesner's] box when I noticed I used the word 'stapler' twice in the same line," Schatz reported after delivering the final version. "It read kind of weird, so I changed the second 'stapler' to 'it.' But then it read even worse, so I changed it back." Schatz also changed "Thanks!!!" to "Thanks..." fearing that the original punctuation was "a bit too much." ∅

Government Encroachment On Individual Liberties At All-Time High, Says Guy At Party

ANN ARBOR, MI—Individual freedom is ebbing in the U.S. due to steady government encroachment, Ann Arbor resident and camera-store employee Adam Britt told guests at a party Tuesday.

"Our way of thinking has shifted so that the individual, not corrupt private and public institutions, shoulders the blame for society's ills," Britt told fellow partygoer Jim Kass while helping himself to raw vegetables and dip. "The accused drug dealer is incarcerated without adequate due process under a mandatory-sentencing law, yet the corporate polluters get off scot-free."

Britt added that, ironically, much of this encroachment is the result of government deregulation throughout the '80s and '90s.

"Deregulation has meant the loss of accountability and obligation," said Britt, raising his voice slightly when a nearby stereo was turned up. "As constraints on corporations loosened in the early '80s, and the culture of greed intensified, individual rights took a drubbing. What's more, an American's basic right to a fair trial

Above: Adam Britt goes on and on to Jim Kass.

was undermined by skyrocketing attorney's fees and overburdened caseloads in courtrooms across the country. This meant that poorer Americans could not afford to adequately defend themselves or challenge others."

Britt was briefly interrupted by loud cheers, prompted by the sight of two burly young men carrying a full, untapped keg of Rolling Rock into the house. When the cheering died down, Britt returned to his point, noting that Americans may feel safer than ever, but that the price for such so-called "safety" may be too costly.

"Airport security areas, even in the smallest airports, resemble Iron Curtain checkpoints, yet no one ever complains about their excessiveness," Britt said. "I've seen children's Mickey Mouse suitcases inspected for bomb-making materials. People say they're willing to pay a high price to ensure their safety. But how high? Where do we draw the line?"

Turning to 23-year-old Alyssa Behrens after Kass went to the porch to "get some fresh air," Britt said that the 2000 presidential election was one of the most egregious examples of the government's disregard—and downright disdain—for the will of the people.

"The campaign had already been debased by the fact that the agendas of both major political parties were determined by corporate interests, not the voters," Britt told Behrens, whose escape plan was to finish her beer and get a refill in the kitchen. "Then Florida happened. Granted, the Democrats bear some blame for not insisting that the whole state be recounted, rather than just a few Democrat-controlled counties. But the Supreme Court's insistence that 'rule of law' must prevail even though serious doubts remained see PARTY page 228

224

Oh, Girls Are No Good At Genocide

By Alyssa Elver

I hate being a girl. It totally stinks. Boys are better at everything. In gym class, whenever we divide up into boys against girls, the boys always win. Boys are better at PlayStation and at drawing robots. Who do you think got to go to summer science camp this year? Danny Grella. A boy. Not that I wanted to go to retarded science camp anyway, but you know what I mean.

I was thinking about this even more in Social Studies class today. We learned all about what genocide is. And you know who's led, like, every single genocide ever? Yup, boys.

A lot of the girls in my class are smart, but most of them are too shy to say anything, so no one even notices they're smart. Even if they know the answer, Mrs. Culver has to call on them and ask them if they know it before they'll say it. So there's no way a girl would get up and make a big speech in

> To be good at genocide, you probably have to be really good at bossing people around. That's something girls can't do.

front of thousands of Brownshirts. She'd be way too embarrassed.

Know how many major genocides there were in the 20th century? The encyclopedia CD-ROM in the library says seven. A whole 50 or 60 million people got killed altogether. But was even one of the genocides done by a girl? Nope. Did any of the tyrannical dictator boys have a "right-hand girl" who was carrying out his orders for him? No way! There's one more thing girls are no good at.

I like to get dirty and play flag football with the boys, but none of the other girls in my class want to get their stupid clothes dirty. All they care about is going to the mall and buying stupid nail polish and purses and makeup. It's so lame. Maybe that's why girls aren't any good at overseeing the systematic mass murder of an entire race. It's too messy.

You never see a genocidal dictator wearing a dress and being all afraid he'll ruin it. He's out there in military fatigues, getting down in the mud, making sure his orders are being carried out. This boy dictator we learned about named Suharto, I bet he wasn't afraid to get a little blood splattered on his shirt. Girls hate blood. They run screaming from it.

I bet you have to know a lot about guns if you want to make a genocide. Everyone knows boys are better gun-shooters than girls. Who knows even one girl who shoots guns? Also, I bet a big part of being one of those genocidal maniacs is designing stuff, like big camps and ovens and stuff. And for that, you need to be really good at math. I suck at math. I just can't figure it out. That's because I'm a girl.

Danny Grella says girls don't have to be smart, because they just stay home and have babies. Well, my mom had babies and a career. Still, she's not the boss where she works. My dad is the boss where he works. My mom has to go in to work on Saturday if Mr. Nagel says so.

To be good at genocide, you probably have to be really good at bossing people around. That's something girls can't do. My brother Josh always gets to watch

see GENOCIDE page 227

DRAGONCON from page 223

throwing," Melcher said. "They were all like, 'Anyone can come. It's in Room 645 Sunday night. See you there!' I hadn't been to a party in a while, so I was pretty psyched."

As DragonCon approached, Melcher found himself daydreaming about some of the possible convention scenarios that might lead to sexual congress.

> "I know a lot of girls online, but that's not really the same," Melcher said. "I needed to see some face to face."

"I imagined some girl and I talking about the new Lord Of The Rings movie," Melcher said. "Then I could say, 'Oh, I have the trailer on my laptop back in my hotel room if you want to see it.' I was also thinking it'd be really cool if I was up against some girl in a trivia contest, and it came down to us battling it out neck-and-neck... I could definitely see things getting heated in a situation like that."

Added Melcher: "The crazy thing is, I did actually wind up entering a trivia contest. Unfortunately, I got knocked out on the first question. I should've known [Angel cast member] Andy Hallett's hometown was Osterville, MA."

Upon arriving at DragonCon, Melcher found himself disappointed in the dating pool, noticing a gender ratio decidedly skewed toward males.

"I guess girls aren't into dragons and superheroes as much as guys are," Melcher said. "That fact really hit me when I first walked into the main exhibition hall: Talk about a total sausage fest."

Though a distinct minority, some females were present at DragonCon.

"There was this one girl dressed up like Black Canary. She had the boots and the fishnet stockings and everything," Melcher said. "I couldn't really talk to her, though, because there was a pretty dense crowd of guys around her at all times."

Melcher's luck did not improve, even when he attended events more likely to draw females.

"Andy and I went to this Sailor Moon thing because we knew girls would be there," Melcher said. "Make no mistake—we do not like Sailor Moon. The animation totally sucks."

At the Sailor Moon symposium, Melcher finally spoke to a number of women in the target 18-to-30 age group. The women, however, were only interested in talking about Sailor Moon.

"This one girl asked me if I wrote fan fiction, and I said yes," Melcher

Above: A trio of DragonCon 2001 attendees, one of whom, significantly, is a woman.

said. "That worked pretty well until she started asking me which Sailor Scout was my favorite."

Subsequent efforts to meet women were similarly unsuccessful. Saturday evening, Melcher attended a special get-together in the Hyatt Regency's Colonel's Room. The event was populated with dozens of long-haired, middle-aged men and a handful of drunk, heavily made-up 15-year-old girls. The following night, Melcher attended a party he had heard about in an online chat room. Held in Hyatt Regency Suite 239, the party consisted of 20 people discussing comic books as They Might Be Giants' Lincoln blared on a boombox.

"It was an awesome party, but I was nervous about not knowing anyone, so I ended up drinking way too much," Melcher said. "I distinctly remember talking to this one girl who actually did inking on the last Batgirl series—right before I puked off the balcony."

"The next day, Andy had to drive the whole way home while I slept in the back seat," Melcher said. "Oh, well, I guess there's always DragonCon 2002." ∅

David-versus-Goliath story." Its hero, "Rob Relesford," is a gifted, idealistic young tow-truck driver trying to make it as an independent operator in the highly competitive world of towing and recovery. Faced with competition from Towco, a massive, multi-state towing corporation, Relesford must choose between continuing to eke out a lonely but proud existence or accepting a well-paid position on the Towco payroll. In the end, the choice is clear.

"At the end of the movie, there's a big, overturned tractor-trailer across the highway, and the hot-shot Towco guys won't move it for insurance-liability reasons," Beresford said. "Then, the hero steps forward and tows the wreck off. Not because he's a show-off, but because he has to. It's just what he does."

Beresford said he hasn't fully developed the plot of *Towtruckin'*. He has, however, worked out certain scenes, such as the one in which Relesford pulls a beautiful waitress' 1984 Sunbird off the median and gallantly refuses to accept payment.

"Rob is a real American hero," Beresford said. "He's out there with his wrecker all hours of the day and night, ready to right a tipped truck or haul a stalled vehicle to a mechanic. He's the closest thing to the cowboy we have left these days. But the point is, if something needs to be towed, by God, he'll tow it."

"To me, that's America in a nutshell," he added.

Though Beresford plans to paint Rob as something of an outlaw, he said the character's actions will always fall on the side of what's right.

"Rob would never tow away an illegally parked car unless it was impeding or inconveniencing honest citizens," Beresford said. "And he'd only tow repossessed cars of bad guys and wealthy gangsters, not poor people trying to make ends meet. Rob's like Robin Hood with a winch."

Beresford said he will likely incorporate his own personal experiences into the film.

"There's going to be this old tow-truck driver who serves as Rob's mentor and teaches him everything he knows about tow-trucking," Beresford said. "That's based on

> ## "Rob is a real American hero," Beresford said. "He's the closest thing to the cowboy we have left these days."

Red Stampfel, the guy who was boss here when I started in '89," Beresford said. "He was like the Yoda of Central Montana Service & Salvage: Boom tow, high-line towing, righting a chassis, Stampfel knew it all. He died of a heart attack in '96. In the movie version,

the guy dies, too, but Rob continues to talk to him after he dies."

Added Beresford: "Also, there'll be this girl who, at first, doesn't get why towing's so important to Rob, but eventually she comes to understand. That, of course, is like [Beresford's wife] Melanie."

Beresford is confident in his vision for *Towtruckin'*, describing it as a "can't-miss" concept. He does, however, fear that the film could be ruined by studio executives who don't fully "get it."

"There's a right way and a wrong way to do this film," Beresford said. "One of the wrong ways would definitely be to make a big deal out of the truck. Don't get me wrong, this guy'll have a nice rig, like the three-axle Ford Super Duty I drive at Central Montana. But I could see some Hollywood type putting him in a big 30-foot rollback tower with all these extra hydraulics and a crewcab and that kind of crap. That's not how it should be done. *Towtruckin'* is all about the tow trucker, not the tow truck." ∅

"All y'all niggaz, y'all be My niggaz," the Lord added.

As of press time, God has thanked nearly 7,000 of His niggaz, including those in New York's Bad Boy and Ruff Ryders posses, the No Limit soldiers and Cash Money Millionaires holdin' it down in New Orleans, Nelly and the whole St. Lunatics crew, Busta and the rest of the Flipmode Squad, His peeps from back in the day, and all the real ruffneck niggaz in lockdown. He also sent shout-outs to everybody in the Old School, as well as to Lil' Bow Wow and all the other new niggaz just coming up.

"Mad props to P. Diddy, Jay-Z, DMX, Lil' Kim, Mystikal, Eve, Ja Rule, Jadakiss, Trick Daddy, and Xzibit. And one love to Meth, RZA, GZA, Ghostface, and the rest of My real niggaz in the Wu-Tang Clan," the deity said. "These My beloved niggaz, with whom I be well-pleased."

Now nearing the 48-hour mark, the Lord's first-ever reciprocal shout-out shows little sign of slowing down. Based on estimates of the number of rappers who have thanked Him in liner notes over the past 20 years, hip-hop experts say the historic shout-out is likely to continue through early next week.

In addition to rap's current stars, God offered shout-outs to the original hip-hop heads, including such pioneers of the art form as Grandmaster Flash, Busy Bee, Melle Mel, Jazzy Jay, Kool Moe Dee, Afrika Bambaataa, DJ Red Alert, the Cold Crush Brothers, Fab 5 Freddy, Kurtis Blow, Kool Herc, and the Funky 4+1.

God also offered shout-outs to the many DJs, record labels, magazines, TV shows, and radio stations that have tirelessly supported hip-hop over the years. Among them are Def Jam, Tom-

GOD WOULD LIKE TO THANK: JUVENILE, MANNIE FRESH, BG, BIG TYMER$, HOT BOY$, LUDACRIS, MYSTIKAL, BLACK ROB, OUTKAST, NELLY AND ST. LUNATICS, FOXY BROWN, JUNIOR M.A.F.I.A., EVE, LIL' KIM, FUNKMASTER FLEX, DMX, JA RULE, MISSY ELLIOTT, BUSTA RHYMES, RAMPAGE, SPLIFF STAR, RAH DIGGA, JAY-Z, LIL' CEASE, TRICK DADDY, LIL' BOW WOW, MOBB DEEP, DR. DRE, SNOOP DOGG, NOREAGA, CAPONE, NAS, EL-P AND COMPANY FLOW, XZIBIT, M.O.P.,

AND MUCH LOVE TO: SCARFACE, PRODIGY, RAS KASS, DEL THA FUNKEE HOMOSAPIEN, HIEROGLYPHICS IMPERIUM, SOULS OF MISCHIEF, THREE 6 MAFIA, CORMEGA, BOOT CAMP CLIK, THE NEPTUNES, LL COOL J, ACEYALONE, FREESTYLE FELLOWSHIP AND PROJECT BLOWED, DILATED PEOPLES, JURASSIC 5, LATYRX, BLACKALICIOUS, Q-TIP AND A TRIBE CALLED QUEST, BONE THUGS-N-HARMONY, DIGABLE PLANETS, MC LYTE, QUEEN LATIFAH, MONIE LOVE, SPECIAL ED, KID CAPRI,

Above: A pair of shout-out tablets handed down by the Lord.

my Boy, Jive, Roc-A-Fella, *Rap Pages*, *The Source*, *Right On!*, The Box, Funkmaster Flex, Ed Lover and Dr. Dre, WBLS 107.5, KISS-FM, and Hot 97.

"For supporting the many artists who have supported Me so faithfully, I say thank you," God said. "All praise to Devante Harrell, Wanda Simmons, LaShell Thomas, and everybody else at Uptown/MCA for making this possible."

As a further sign of His love for the hip-hop community, God assured the nation's rappers that He is taking good

care of all their peers currently with Him in heaven.

"Tupac, Notorious B.I.G., Eazy-E, Scott LaRock—some of y'all niggaz are already up in this bitch," the Lord said. "For those of you who were left behind, know that the Lord has got your dead homies' backs. Faith [Evans], I promise I'm taking real good care of your Biggie. He resting in crazy peace, no doubt."

Thus far, God has not played favorites, thanking such fallen-off acts as Hammer and Vanilla Ice in the same

breath as vital artists whose careers are still going strong. The Lord has also seen fit to thank the little-known likes of Baby Tragic, DJ Phreek Malik, and Da Ill Collector—MCs so obscure that virtually no one within the hip-hop community has heard of them. All rappers, God explained, are equal in His sight, and none are too small to escape His notice.

"God sees even the smallest sparrow fall," said Dr. Cornel West, Harvard University professor of African-Amer-

see GOD page 227

ican studies and philosophy of religion. "The same is true of MCs: Whether a major superstar or a complete unknown, all rappers are His children, and He loves them all."

The sheer volume of names notwithstanding, the nation's rappers are deeply touched by God's gesture of tribute and appreciation, with many stating that they "feelin' Him."

"God is the Original," Brooklyn-based rapper Mos Def said. "The world is ruled by the wealthy and the wicked, but all respect due to the Creator who made this world and who will one day

bring justice to the wicked and righteous alike."

Despite the overwhelmingly positive response among rappers, the Lord is drawing fire in certain circles for His use of the word "nigga." On Monday's *Larry King Live*, conservative activist Rev. Calvin Butts, a longtime ally of the Lord, blasted Him for His "shocking, unexpected use of the racially loaded N-word." Some concerned parties, including decency crusader C. Delores Tucker, Sen. Orrin Hatch (R-UT), and members of the San Francisco-based What About The Children?

Foundation, are calling for a boycott of church services until God issues an apology.

Reacting to the controversy, many in the hip-hop community are rushing to the Lord's defense.

"The word 'nigga' means different things depending on how it's used and who's saying it," rap legend and Public Enemy frontman Chuck D said. "Judging from context, God obviously wasn't being derogatory. He was using 'nigga' as a blanket term of affection for all His true supporters on the rap scene. At one point, He said, 'I wanna

give a shout-out to Ad-Rock, MC Serch, and my man Dan The Automator—all y'all is real niggaz in My all-benevolent sight.' Considering the fact that Ad-Rock and Serch are Jewish, and the Automator is Asian-American, it's clear God isn't talking about race here. He's just paying respect to all those who have paid respect to Him."

"God's the ultimate playa, so naturally He's going to have some haters," rapper Ice Cube said. "But these haters need to realize that if you mess with the man upstairs, you *will* get your ass smote. True dat." Ø

COMMUNITY VOICES

Don't Run Away, I'm Not The Flesh-Eating Kind Of Zombie

In the shadows of blackest night, I lie in wait. Then, at long last, I hear that soft footstep, that clattering of hooves on the rough-hewn cobblestones of the path, sounds that can only mean one thing: a lonely traveler from the land of the living has come my way once again. From out of the dank recesses of night I emerge, my grim visage slowly taking shape in the light of the lantern, a nightmare face covered in repulsive blotches of decayed flesh, the skin peeling back to reveal the gleaming yellowish-white of my hideous skull. My half-rotted lips peel back to reveal a horrible grin as I move in clo—

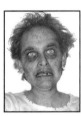

**By Solomon Grocks
Non-Flesh-Eating Zombie**

Wait! Why are you running away? No, no, don't scream like that. Wait! Come back! I promise I won't eat you! I'm not the flesh-eating kind of zombie!

I just want a little companionship. Is that too much to ask? Just because I'm an ambulant remnant of that which was once alive doesn't mean I want to eat your brains. It's just so lonely out here in the damp night, with no one to talk to, or to hold my hand, or to just go for a stroll with.

No! Don't go! I can't run that fast—my legs are just stiff and spindly splinters of desiccated skin and bones. All I can do is lurch

about in a grotesque parody of human locomotion, frantically flailing my arms in a futile effort to make you understand.

Please! Don't be frightened by my blood-curdling moan of the undead. That's just my way of say-

> ## So I'm a walking corpse! Guilty as charged! But that doesn't mean I go around eating every living person I see, does it?

ing hello. I can't make myself understood, for my vocal cords have long since turned to dust. But my friendly intentions should be clear from my past actions: I've never eaten a single living human in all my terrible years of shadowy, undead existence. Don't you think that if I were going to eat a person I would have done it by now? What is it with people these days?

Don't you understand? I have no interest in feasting on the still-warm flesh of the living. I just want to shamble slowly out of the mist with my rotting arms outstretched, staggering awkwardly toward you in a lurching limp before, finally,

emitting a blood-curdling moan of the undead and giving you a big hug! Why can't anybody understand that?

It's not like there's only one kind of zombie. Haven't you people ever heard of a zombie of the non-flesh-eating variety? The type that doesn't crave biting through a person's skull to slurp away at the soft, brainy tissue inside? So I'm a walking corpse! Guilty as charged! But that doesn't mean I go around eating every living person I see, does it? Some zombies roam the night looking to feast on human prey, and some don't. It's as simple as that. (Not that I have anything against my flesh-eating brethren; I just don't happen to be one, that's all.)

There's really no reason to fear me. I can barely move, for crying out loud. So even if I were interested in taking a huge bite out of your arm—which, I assure you, I'm not—I'd have no chance of catching you. A small, fat child can easily outrun a zombie. We only move at, like, an eighth of a mile per hour. Quarter-mile, tops. A person being chased by a zombie wouldn't even need to run. A brisk walk would do the trick just fine. People only get eaten by zombies when they're surrounded by a massive horde of them, the victim slowly encircled and grasped at, dragged down by the zombies' sheer numbers. Everybody knows that! Hello? Haven't you seen any movies? I'm all alone here!

It would be nice if, just once, somebody would think about how I

feel in this situation. Think about it: Misshapen, inhuman monster sees somebody he wants to be friends with; pretty human misinterprets his overtures of friendship; human runs away screaming their bloody fool head off; monster walks off sad and misunderstood. Come on, that's got to be the oldest cliché in the book! Do you have any idea how embarrassing that is? My whole existence is this trite, lowbrow scenario. It's only in, like, every single *Frankenstein* film ever made.

Please, please come back. I just want to, I don't know, have tea or something. I couldn't actually drink it, because it'd run down the sides of my mandible as soon as I poured it into my mouth, but it'd be so nice just to clumsily paw at the cup with my skeletal hands. We could maybe play basketball, as long as you didn't pass me the ball too fast, causing my ribcage to collapse into dust and spilling my rotting entrails onto the ground in front of me.

Or we could just sit somewhere and talk. We don't even have to sit all that close to each other, okay? If it'd make you more comfortable, I could sit a good distance away and just glare at you with my piercing, lidless eyes.

How can I go on, walking the moonlit countryside every night, endlessly searching for that which I can never have? How can I accept this piteous, eternal fate when no one, no matter how nice I act, will be my friend?

The tortures of the damned! Ø

what he wants on TV, even if I really want to watch something. I usually just let him get away with it because I don't feel like getting in a big fight about it. Unlike boys, girls just aren't bossy or stubborn enough to eradicate a race of people from the face of the Earth. It just would never happen.

Girls always want to help people. They want to take care of babies and feed them and dress them up. They don't want to throw

them into pits and cover them with dirt while they're still alive.

Girls always want to help people.

In gym class, when we divide into teams for dodgeball, the girls are always picked last. Maybe

that's what happens when a group of extremists is looking for somebody to head their regime. The Khmer Rouge picked Pol Pot because they knew he'd be good at murder and torture and all that other boy stuff. A girl probably would have planted flowers in the killing fields.

Sure, there have been a couple of evil girls, but they're never as evil as the boys. Nothing on the level of Idi Amin, this boy who

killed 300,000 Christians in Uganda during the 1970s.

All Hitler had to say was "jump" and everybody jumped. There's no way a girl could grow a mean mustache like his. Then there was Stalin. I bet no one put stupid frilly curtains up in Stalin's bedroom when he was away at summer camp and then told him they had to stay there because the old curtains were already in the garbage.

God, I wish I were a boy. Ø

The Dress-Code Crackdown

Across the U.S., high schools are banning low-rise jeans, midriff-baring tops, and other skimpy articles of clothing. What do *you* think about the fashion crackdown?

Paul Cooper
Plumber

"What I don't get is the super-low jeans where the thong straps peek out above the waistline. Why aren't those required?"

Nelson Wollersheim
Bond Trader

"Girls that young should not be wearing sexy outfits in school. I say dress them all in plaid skirts and knee-high stockings."

Lisa Hausherr
Social Worker

"I think girls who violate dress codes should be suspended and picked up from school by their mothers' boyfriends."

Tom Atack
Cashier

"The way the kids dress these days, it's becoming almost impossible to tell the sluts from the regular girls."

Michael Keller
Systems Analyst

"Thank God for Maury Povich. He's doing his part by sending all those out-of-control, too-sexy teens to boot camp."

Meredith Wakefield
Legal Secretary

"I don't know. I think some of those crotchless hot pants they sell in the JCPenney children's department are kind of cute."

The Euro Is Unveiled

Last week, Europeans got a chance to see their new currency. What are some of the euro's features?

- € Fine print explains rules, allure of soccer
- € Watermark features picture of Charles de Gaulle eating wiener schnitzel at Italian bistro
- € Coin version features secret compartment to hold hash
- € Automatically adjusts to be worth 20 percent less when spent by Americans
- € Latin motto makes vague threat to non-participating countries
- € Soothes throat, eases tension when chewed
- € Honored at Piggly Wiggly "Double Euro Wednesdays"
- € Bills to be sterilized on way out of Ireland
- € Redeemable for actual money at more than 15,000 banks across Europe

 **the ONION**
America's Finest News Source

Herman Ulysses Zweibel *Founder*

T. Herman Zweibel *Publisher Emeritus*
J. Phineas Zweibel *Publisher*
Maxwell Prescott Zweibel *Editor-In-Chief*

FOUNDED 1871 • "TU STULTUS ES"

Your Horoscope

By Lloyd Schumner Sr.
Retired Machinist and
A.A.P.B.-Certified Astrologer

Aries: (March 21–April 19)
Despite your repeated entreaties, no one seems willing to take your wife. Perhaps you should consider adding the word "please" to your request.

Taurus: (April 20–May 20)
The object of your affection seems oblivious to your romantic feelings. This is not surprising, as elephant seals have a limited capacity for empathy.

Gemini: (May 21–June 21)
Three-inch heels are coming back into style. Unfortunately for you, though, they're expected to be attached to shoes.

Cancer: (June 22–July 22)
The stars find that the time has come for you to put away childish things. Yes, that includes your three small children.

Leo: (July 23–Aug. 22)
By the time your clever ruse is exposed, you'll be safely across the Swiss border, which seems like an excessive response to substituting yogurt for sour cream in recipes.

Virgo: (Aug. 23–Sept. 22)
This would be a good week to retake control of your life. Good, certainly, but not great.

Libra: (Sept. 23–Oct. 23)
Much to your consternation, you discover that it takes more than nudity, llamas, and gin to scandalize the British consulate.

Scorpio: (Oct. 24–Nov. 21)
You will reconsider your longtime conviction that there's nothing funny about brain cancer when presented with overwhelming evidence to the contrary.

Sagittarius: (Nov. 22–Dec. 21)
You will be pleased by your appointment as Emperor Of Ice Cream, as you like ice cream and have always wanted to wield authority.

Capricorn: (Dec. 22–Jan. 19)
You will get a nose ring this week when you momentarily believe yourself to be a Brahma bull.

Aquarius: (Jan. 20–Feb. 18)
You will receive a formal letter from Johnny Cash stating, in no uncertain terms, that he is very disappointed in you.

Pisces: (Feb. 19–March 20)
Remember: Sincerity is all well and good, but your suit and haircut are what the jury sees first.

PARTY from page 224

about the accuracy of the final count was a snow job that should rank with the Dred Scott decision for pure judicial arrogance."

Jon Light, one of the party's hosts, said he was only marginally acquainted with Britt, inviting him after Britt had given him a helpful crash course in film speeds at the camera store the day before.

"He seemed like a pretty nice guy when I first met him," Light said. "But I had no idea he was one of those political guys. Actually, I didn't find out until the morning after, when I talked to [roommate] Tim [Hecht], who said he got cornered by him for almost an hour."

"I saw the guy talking to Tim for a long-ass time, but I guess I figured he was going off about snowboarding or maybe that Gorillaz CD that was playing," Light continued. "Apparently, though, he was droning on about the government's restriction of individual liberties. The only individual liberties I saw restricted last night were poor Tim's and whoever else that guy managed to corner. Christ." ∅

BLOWSY from page 218

Passersby were amazed by the unusually large amounts of blood. Passersby were amazed by the unusually large amounts of blood. Passersby were amazed by the unusually large amounts of blood. Passersby were amazed by the unusually large amounts of blood. Passersby were amazed by the unusually large amounts of blood. Passersby were amazed by the unusually large amounts of blood. Passersby were amazed by the unusually large amounts of blood. Passersby were amazed by the unusually large amounts of blood. Passersby were amazed by the unusually large amounts of blood. Passersby were amazed by the unusually large amounts of blood. Passersby were amazed by the unusually large amounts of blood. Passersby were amazed by the unusually large amounts of blood. Passersby were amazed by the unusually large amounts of blood. Passersby were amazed by the unusually large amounts of blood. Passersby were amazed by the

see BLOWSY page 238

NEWS

Sales Of *Guys Gone Wild* Video Disappointing

see ENTERTAINMENT page 4C

Johnny Cash Called In To Assess Floodwater Levels

see NATION page 2A

'Under New Management' Sign Prominently Displayed At Daycare Center

see LOCAL page 1E

STATshot

A look at the numbers that shape your world.

Top Pet-Tombstone Epitaphs

1. Fetch The Stars, Woofers
2. Flattened Too Soon
3. She Gave Her Life That Other Hamsters May Live
4. The Lease Said "No Pets"
5. Sorry I Rubbed Tuna On The Wall Socket
6. Who's In Our Hearts And Memories Forever? *Who? Who?*

PUT DOWN WITH LOVE

REX 1990-2001

the ONION®

VOLUME 37 ISSUE 32   AMERICA'S FINEST NEWS SOURCE™   13–19 SEPTEMBER 2001

Congressman Admits To Sexual Relationship

THE GRAHAM SCANDAL: DAY 62

Above: Rep. Gordon Graham (D-IL), who recently admitted to a sexual relationship with Joyce Debolt (inset), is besieged by reporters while leaving his home Monday.

WASHINGTON, DC—After months of fevered speculation and allegations in the media regarding his private life, U.S. Rep. Gordon Graham (D-IL) finally admitted Monday to having a sexual relationship with Arlington, VA, interior designer Joyce Debolt.

"I frankly don't understand this line of questioning, considering that the two of us have been seeing each other for almost a year now," said Graham, the media-dubbed "Lascivious Lawmaker," at a press conference. "But if you must know, yes, we are dating."

Pressed as to whether his use of the term "dating" implied acts of sexual intimacy—including, but not limited to, intercourse—Graham replied, after a brief pause: "Well, yes, obviously."

Graham then became visibly agitated and refused to answer any more questions on the subject, attempting to steer queries toward a discussion of energy policy. When the diversionary tactic failed, the congressman became, according to one reporter present, "ticked off" before leaving the

see CONGRESSMAN page 231

Expanding Universe Could Allow For More Than 750 Quadrillion Blockbuster Locations

Science Watch

DALLAS— The expansion of the known universe, currently growing at an estimated 80 kilometers per second per megaparsec, should eventually enable Blockbuster to open more than 750 quadrillion locations, spokespersons for the video-rental giant reported Monday.

"With more than 7,700 stores worldwide, Blockbuster is proud to be the world leader in rentable home entertainment," said chief marketing officer Joe Notarnicola, standing in front of an image of the Milky Way galaxy. "In fact, growing as we have since our IPO in August 1999, Blockbuster's market saturation on Earth will be reached in the next few years. However, our customers and stockholders will be pleased to learn of the tremendous growth opportunities made possible by the expansion of the known universe."

The 750 quadrillion stores will

see BLOCKBUSTER page 232

Eldercare Residents Long For Agonizing 'Funtime' To End

MIDDLESEX, CT— Staring at the rec-room clock Monday, Herman Oster and 23 of his fellow Eldercare Nursing Home residents waited for the day's agonizing "Funtime" to finally end.

"Not too much longer now," said Oster, 83, midway through the two-hour descent into tedium. "After we throw the big ball back and forth, there's usually

one more song, and then it's over at last."

Listed on the Eldercare Events Calendar as "Funtime with Judy," the weekly event is hosted by Judy Lyon, one of Eldercare's two recreational therapists.

"On other days, we have scheduled events like bingo or bridge or movie time," the 34-year-old Lyon

see FUNTIME page 232

Above: Eldercare residents endure another excruciating Funtime.

Bill Gates Finally Getting Into Radiohead's *Kid A*

REDMOND, WA—Eleven months after purchasing the Radiohead album, Microsoft chairman Bill Gates announced Monday that he is "finally getting into *Kid A*." "I listened to it a few times when I first got it, but it just wasn't grabbing me," Gates told *The Seattle Post-Intelligencer.* "I liked 'Morning Bell' and 'Optimistic,' but the rest just seemed like this intentionally weird mess. Then I took it out again maybe a month ago, and it finally started to sink in. Now I think I even like it better than *OK Computer.*" Gates said he still hasn't gotten around to picking up *Amnesiac.*

Hostage Negotiator Has To Admit Terrorist Has Good Point

KYRENIA, CYPRUS—Fourteen hours into tense negotiations, U.N. hostage negotiator Per Magnusson was forced to admit Monday that the Greek Cypriot hijacker of a Turkish cruise ship has a good point about Turkey's occupation of northern Cyprus. "Well, I don't approve of threatening the lives of 300 innocent civilians, but I kind of have to agree that Turkish troops have no business being in Cyprus, the only European country occu-pied by a foreign army," said Magnusson, paraphrasing a statement released by the unidentified, Uzi-toting hijacker at 5 a.m. "He's really got me there."

Manager Fails To Keep It Short Or Sweet

ADA, OH—Despite his promise, Sbarro manager Bruce Hart failed to keep his talk regarding proper straw-receptacle-refill protocol short or sweet. "He could've just said, 'Don't overstuff the straw dispenser, because it's hard to get them out when you do that,'" cashier Evan Rees said. "Instead, he spent 15 minutes going off about how much straws cost, and how customers don't like it when they have to claw at the dispenser, and how it can be unhygienic if the wrappers get torn." Rees said that Hart occasionally keeps it short or sweet, but never both at the same time.

Sacramento Columnist Really Lays Into Mass Murderer

SACRAMENTO, CA—*Sacramento Bee* colum-nist Ellen Wilpon really laid into local mass murderer Nikolay Soltys in her column Monday. "Frankly, if this creep and all the people like him were locked up and never let out, this would be a far better world," Wilpon wrote about Soltys, the Ukrainian immigrant who faces trial for the murder of seven family members. "How could we call ourselves a free or enlightened society if Soltys ever sees daylight again?" "Whoa-ho-ho!" said *Bee* reader Ed Clift upon reading Wilpon's column. "The gloves are off with Ellen and this murderer guy. Look out!"

Sci-Fi Fans Argue The Better Of Two As-Yet-Unreleased Films

TULSA, OK—Science-fiction fans Pete Carver and Matthew Wynne disagreed sharply Monday on the relative merits of *Harry Potter And The Sorcerer's Stone* and *The Fellowship Of The Ring,* neither of which hits theaters for months. "The storyboards for the Quidditch tournament I saw on this one web site look terrible," said the pro-Tolkien Carver. "There's no way that scene can be better than I've heard the Balrog one is." Wynne countered that the set design for the Great Hall of Hogwarts set "will completely blow away" that of the Mines of Moria.

Toaster-Instruction Booklet Author Enraged That Editor Betrayed His Vision

TOWSON, MD—Consolidated Concepts copywriter Ronald Leff announced Monday that his vision for the Black & Decker Electronic Toast-R-Oven™ Broiler instruction booklet was "thoroughly betrayed" in the final editing process.

"[Department head] Charlie [Standell] altered the entire thrust and focus of my operating instructions," said a seething Leff, 31, upon seeing the final edit. "I toiled over it for weeks, crafting each phrase until it was perfect, but then he just goes ahead and changes it all around for no apparent reason."

Added Leff: "The broiling directions, the safety warnings, the warranty guidelines... it's all completely different."

Consolidated Concepts, one of the nation's leading producers of consumer-goods packaging and supplementary materials, was first contracted to produce the Toast-R-Oven™ booklet in November 2000. After a series of editorial meetings were held to determine an overall direction for the work, Leff was assigned the task of writing the copy. Despite assurances that he would have full creative control over the project, Leff said the booklet's final version "barely resembled [his] last

> "The broiler directions, the safety warnings... it's all completely different."

Above: Leff holds the Black & Decker booklet his editor "thoroughly mangled."

draft."

"Look at this section here: 'Slide-Out Rack And Bake Pan.' This whole section is Charlie. None of this is mine," said Leff, pointing to a page in the "grossly compromised" work. "The heading, as I wrote it, was 'Using And Enjoying The Slide-Out Rack And Bake Pan.' I can't tell you how many drafts I went through to get the rhythm and scansion of that header just right. Then, out of nowhere, Charlie just waves his wizard wand and changes it to this clunky, graceless, 'Slide-Out Rack And Bake Pan' crap."

Standell defended the change. "A sticking point for me was the word 'enjoying,'" Standell said. "You don't really 'enjoy' a slide-out tray. I just thought 'enjoying' was off. Then, once I cut that, it became apparent to me

that you don't need any action words here at all: Just tell the reader what part of the toaster you're about to talk about, and leave it at that. This was clearly a case of 'less is more'—something that's never been Ron's strong suit. He has a real tendency to overwrite."

Leff also took exception to Standell's changes to the section warning against inserting metal implements into the toaster.

"The way I'd written that part, nobody would ever again stick a fork in a toaster," Leff said. "I wrote something truly brilliant and special. And look what Charlie changed it to."

Said Standell: "Ron had this whole long passage about how 400 Americans are killed by electrocution every year. You just don't see that sort of thing in an instruction booklet. It was way too editorializing and totally

broke voice."

Standell, Leff's supervisor for the past eight years, said he is sympathetic to Leff's objections, but insisted that the changes were for the best.

"Black & Decker's instruction manuals always have a certain gravity, a certain seriousness of purpose to them," Standell said. "Overall, Ron did a good job, but there were parts where he simply injected too much of himself rather than maintain that dry, detached, sober Black & Decker tone."

Leff said there is a "control freak" factor at work.

"Charlie makes a lot of changes that are totally arbitrary. A perfect example is my paragraph on removing and cleaning the crumb tray," Leff said. "He changed 'scrubbing pad' to 'scouring pad' purely for the sake of

see AUTHOR page 232

That Sucker Jesus Has Forgiven Me For Some Pretty Bad Sins

By Clint Hoekstra

I've done my Bible reading, and I've come up with a pretty startling conclusion about Jesus: That guy was a total sap!

In *Acts 10:43*, Peter says, "To Him all the prophets bear witness that every one who believes in Him receives forgiveness of sins through His name." In short, if you believe in Jesus and invoke His forgiveness, you'll be forgiven for whatever you do. What a sucker! That's exactly the kind of loophole I'm looking for!

Look, I never asked Jesus for eternal forgiveness. But if He's naïve enough to bestow it upon me and trust that I'm not going to take advantage, I'm certainly not going to turn Him down.

Last winter, I was driving around a little drunk. (The Rams had just made it into the playoffs, so who wouldn't be?) Anyway, I crashed into a parked car and really tore the hell out of the front fender. Nice car, too, a Lexus IS 300 Sport Sedan, the kind of car I wouldn't be able to afford if I ate nothing but shit and gravy for the next 15 years. I was starting to freak out because I didn't have insurance. Then I remembered Jesus' unending reserve of benevolence. I also recalled something from The Bible about a rich man not getting through the eye of a camel or some mumbo-jumbo. So I figured that not only would Jesus forgive me, He'd probably have wanted me to hit that car. I sped away with a dented fender and a sense of fulfillment for doing God's work.

I mean, there's an awful lot of talk about sin in the Bible, but it always comes back to the same thing: You can commit just about any sin under the sun and still get into heaven, so long as you let Jesus into your life. I figure I'm not actively keeping Him out, so He's with me all the time. What would Jesus do? Well, He probably wouldn't have fucked the first-runner-up for Miss Teen Missouri, but He sure forgave me when *I* did it.

Heck, there was that time I held up the liquor store and shot a guy, and I felt really bad about it. I'd never shot anyone before, and I thought, "Geez, what if he had a family?" I was holed up in a hotel room with a bottle of whiskey and was really close to turning myself in. But then I found the Gideon's Bible in the nightstand drawer. After going through some of the better passages, I figured the man I gut-shot wasn't fit to stand in judgment of me. As far as Jesus was concerned, I was free and clear. So I didn't turn myself in, the guy lived, and everyone was happy. Thanks, Jesus... ya big rube!

People tell me I'm a terrible person. I tell them, "Hey, I'm okay with Jesus, so I should be okay with you." Like The Bible says in *Luke 6:37*, "Judge not, and you will not be judged; condemn not, and you will not be condemned; forgive, and you will be forgiven." Why can't the Missouri Criminal Code be like that? The state of Missouri doesn't judge me, and I don't judge the state of Missouri. That's the way I like it. If Jesus wants to forgive people, who am I to argue? More importantly, who am I not to take advantage of that?

Sometimes, in my darkest hours, I imagine that Jesus is carrying me. When I was on my eight-day speed/armed-robbery binge, I could actually feel Him pick me up in his arms and carry me away from the vomit-soaked apartment. He even stopped so I could throw away the gun. Jesus is a friend, a partner, and an accomplice.

Lord, you may be a sucker, but you're a sucker for all the right reasons. Thank you, Jesus! *∅*

CONGRESSMAN from page 229

room, bringing the press conference to a halt. The reporter described the representative's expression upon leaving the press conference as "like the proverbial cat caught with the canary."

"I knew it," said Chris Matthews, host of MSNBC's *Hardball With Chris Matthews* and an outspoken critic of the legislative lothario. "They've been seen eating in restaurants together, they've been spotted in his car together, they've even been caught together in romantic getaway spots. He was clearly sleeping with her the whole time."

Debolt, from whom Graham is widely believed to have received oral sex, declined comment on the admission. Single with two children from a previous marriage, Debolt has been at the center of controversy since July 11, when allegations of her relationship with Graham first surfaced after the two of them were seen attending an AMFAR dinner-party fundraiser together.

Graham, single since his divorce from wife Sandra seven years ago, was allegedly introduced to Debolt by a "mutual friend" at a still-undetermined "social function" sometime in October 2000. It is still not known whether the two have been having sex the entire time, or if the sex only began recently.

"Well, at least it's finally out in the open," said Kewanee, IL, resident Bob Hueber, who said he voted for Graham in the last election but will never support him again.

"Still, it's still a terrible thing to hear. He came right out and admitted to everything. Imagine, a federal legislator engaging in the act of physical union. Everyone in Illinois feels very ashamed right now. Ashamed and shocked."

Doreen Salzman, a Springfield, IL, mother of four, agreed.

"A grown man, an elected federal official no less, doing God-knows-what in bed with some woman," Salzman said. "How am I supposed to explain something like this to my kids? America has truly lost its innocence."

Until Monday, Graham had refused to confirm or deny charges that he and Debolt had repeatedly engaged in sexual intercourse, insisting that his "personal life isn't anybody's business." Media experts, however, say that Graham's refusal to discuss his exploits have caused him more harm than good: The focus of months of intense media scrutiny, Graham's rumored extracurricular escapades have captivated the nation and dominated headlines, particularly in the tabloids, where the story has taken on a life of its own despite—or perhaps because of—Graham's "hush-hush" ways.

"Graham apparently thought that, by keeping his shady bedroom activities—which we now know involved naked, nude, sexy sex—under wraps, the problem would just go away," New York Post gossip columnist Cindy Adams said. "If he had nothing to hide, he could have simply said so. But, by

Above: A *National Enquirer* photo of the alleged lovers exiting a D.C. shoe store.

behaving like a guilty person, he caused himself untold damage. Now, all the sexy, naked skeletons in his sex closet are out there in the naked light of day for all to see."

Graham has refused to provide explicit details concerning the specifics of his "sexy sex-affair" with Debolt, but speculation runs rampant. Sexperts—sexual scientists who make a scholarly study of sex—say Graham and Debolt likely engaged in foreplay, including caressing and possibly tongue-kissing, leading to the removal of varied articles of clothing and, ultimately, both male and female nudity. Not long after, sexperts say, penetration of Debolt's vagina by Graham's penis probably resulted. Whether the two engaged in sex talk during their sex play is unknown, though many suggest it wouldn't be unlike the sexy congressman to do so.

"Sexually speaking, I wouldn't put anything past that guy," Adams said. "He probably has all sorts of weird sexy sex-kinks when he and his sexy sex-partner do their sexy dirty sex sex sex." *∅*

change, as though he needed to feel like he was an editor. I specifically asked Charlie about his thought process behind that one, and he couldn't even give an answer. He just said, 'I don't know, something about

> Said Leff: "He changed 'scrubbing pad' to 'scouring pad' purely for the sake of change."

"scrubbing pad" just didn't sound right.'"

"I'm not some greenhorn who needs to be reined in," Leff continued. "I wrote the instructions for the Sanyo KX-200 portable AM/FM tape player. And I co-wrote the instructions for the Amana 400 Electric Range, one of the best-selling appliances of 1999. In fact, it was the best-selling freestanding range. And I did it without Charlie's involvement at all."

Added Leff: "Maybe I'll quit Consolidated Concepts and work for an appliance company with some respect for the artistic process, like Magic Chef." Ø

said. "But on Tuesdays, I like to mix it up a little and surprise the residents. During Funtime, anything goes!"

Previous Funtime activities have included leatherworking, macrame, and waving brightly colored flags.

"I always plan something that involves everyone," said Lyon, who in 1995 received her master's degree in recreational therapy from Central Connecticut State University. "I try to provide the residents with socialization opportunities that will also improve motor function, increase relaxation, and build awareness skills."

According to Oster, the most painful Funtime activity is "Remember When?," in which Lyon asks residents questions about their lives before entering the nursing home.

"Sometimes, Judy asks us to talk about our kids, and that always hurts, because I hardly ever see them," Oster said. "I really don't like talking about it in front of the group."

John Edwards, 91, is similarly uncomfortable with "Remember When?"

"One time, Judy asked me what my first car was," Edwards said. "I had no idea. I just couldn't remember. I was so embarrassed."

Despite the depressing, non-fun nature of Funtime, many residents still feel compelled to attend.

"Whenever I see Judy in the hall, she asks if I'm going to Funtime this week," said Doris Heckel, 80. "She's so smiley, I feel bad saying no."

"If I don't go, Judy always asks me where I was," Heckel continued. "I can get away with skipping every third time or so, but if I miss two in a row, she really lets me have it."

Some residents said they attend because of the availability of food and beverages.

"The meals here are worse than the K-rations I had to choke down during the Big One, but they make up for it during Funtime by rolling out cake and coffee," said Sam Cropper, 84. "A nice piece of chocolate bundt helps ease the pain of Judy's interminable sing-alongs."

Cropper, who spends most days in his room reading the newspaper and writing letters to long-deceased friends, said he appreciates the attention paid to residents by Lyon, despite the unbearable nature of the activities she plans.

"Most of us are still adjusting to not being able to get around like we used to, so it can get pretty lonely here at Eldercare," Cropper said. "It's nice to have someone to talk to, even if it's about something dumb like what kind of flower we'd like to be."

Added Cropper: "There are many things I'd like to see and do, but since my stroke, I just haven't had the energy. Max [Franklin] has been the same way ever since he broke his hip. I guess fear of loneliness is what drives most of us to endure the distraction of Funtime." Ø

give customers unprecedented access to movie rentals, PlayStation games, the latest music releases, and much more during their diaspora into deep space.

"We have already approached NASA about the feasibility of launching Blockbuster-store payloads to the solar system's outer planets," Blockbuster CEO John F. Antioco said. "Our two-tiered franchising strategy is to have several hundred stores on the moon, Mars, the main belt asteroid Ceres, Jovian moons Io, Europa, Ganymede, and Callisto, the A and C rings of Saturn, and the Kuiper Belt asteroid KX 76 by late 2075. From there, we should be able to open a Blockbuster on every corner of this spiral arm of the Milky Way by 2500."

Blockbuster's expansion plan is being praised throughout the known business universe.

"With its aggressive approach, Blockbuster Entertainment will soon be growing at a rate approaching Hubble's Limit," said *Forbes* editor Paul Maidment, alluding to the cosmological principle which proposes that the cosmos is growing at a rate which may approach the speed of light. "Once that happens, there's no stopping this company."

"Certainly, they face challenges," Maidment continued. "If accelerations imposed by the expanding universe on the outer celestial bodies affects the structure of space-time itself, rental times and late fees will need to be adjusted accordingly. And getting the latest Hollywood hits to these stores by the release date may be problematic given the distances involved. But such logistical hurdles are hardly insurmountable when you've got the corporate might of [parent company] Viacom behind you."

Though Blockbuster officials acknowledge that their expansion plans are ambitious, they say the company is more than up to the task of saturating the entirety of physical reality.

"We're already exploring megastructures which will move our stores into the universe at the bow wave of human colonization," said Anthony Andersen, Blockbuster's newly appointed Executive Vice-President of Pan-Universal Franchising. "The first step will be establishing enormous 'generation ship' outlets—huge cylinders rotated along the long axis to simulate gravity and powered by interstellar hydrogen captured by their enormous Bussard ramjets. We'll send these to all the nearest star systems to ensure that every space traveler has access to Guaranteed-To-Be-There new releases."

Andersen also outlined plans to build artificial Blockbuster planets in space and orbit several of them around a stable G-type star, manipulating the star's magnetic field to produce jets of stellar material to serve as motive power, creating a Blockbuster solar system capable of interstellar travel.

"Currently, we're on schedule to do this around the year 25000," Andersen said. "Of course, that could happen sooner if customer interest in our new DVD section continues to climb."

Blockbuster has already begun recruiting managers for stores in the outlying reaches of the galaxy, subjecting applicants to rigorous G-force and gravity-sickness tests. Some in the scientific community, however, suspect that the hiring

Above: A computer rendering of the post-Blockbuster-expansion universe.

campaign may be premature.

"Blockbuster could conceivably hit its target if its growth and the expansion of the universe continue at their present rates," said Dr. Marina Shmakova of the California Institute For Physics and Astrophysics. "But the question they face is, Will the universe continue its expansion? Or will it one day contract into an infinitely dense, white-hot pre-cosmic protomass? These two scenarios lead to two drastically different outcomes: a creation-spanning, ever-growing, omnipotent Blockbuster hive-mind or a single, infinitely dense central location. In either case, where will consumers find the after-hours drop box?"

Despite this unanswered question and many others, Blockbuster remains optimistic.

"We won't know the outcome of this business plan for many millennia," Notarnicola said. "But whatever happens, there will be a need for a reliable provider to meet your home-entertainment needs. Blockbuster will be there to fill that massive void." Ø

True A.R. Bruthas Don't Take No Layba Day Off

**By Herbert Kornfeld
Accounts Receivable
Supervisor**

Ay yo, wassup, Gs? If y'all aksed me what paradise wuz to tha H-Dog, I'd say it be three things: customas payin' they accountz on time without me having to go all *Walkin' Tall* on they ass, a endless supply o' Nutrageous barz in tha break-room vendin' machine, an' last but not least, a seven-day work week wit' no muthafukkin' dayz off to fuck wit' mah flow.

As I've said in this space before, tha H-Dog's life be all bidness. Weekendz an' holidayz just ain't mah thang, know what I'm sayin'? When I ain't officin', it's like I get all unbalanced. Tha only good thang I can say about havin' time off is that it afford me tha opportunity to spend Q.T. wit' mah shortie, Baby Prince H. Tha Stone Col' Dopest Bizook-kizeepin' Muthafukkin' Badass Supastar Kornfeld Tha Second.

A couple Mondays ago, I be in tha Nite Rida, cruisin' ova to mah ex-bitch Agnes' crib to drop off our shortie, who I had foe tha weekend. But who answer tha door? Thass right, Agnes' old-ass mama. She all in her big-ass flowa-print housecoat, doin' that slow walk of hers. She ack like she got tha rheumatism, but I know she jus' takin' her sweet-ass time 'cause when it comes to Daddy H, she a stone-cold playa hata.

"Yo, Grandma," I say, handin' her tha shortie. "Take Baby Prince H. Tha Stone Col' Dopest Bizook-kizeepin' Mutha-fukkin' Badass Supastar Kornfeld Tha

Second. I gots bidness to attend to at Midstate."

"If you're talking about Tanner, I'll be glad to," she say. "Say, what did you do with him all weekend, Herbert? Stuff envelopes? Make coffee? Collate?"

See what I mean 'bout this bitch? A stone-col' playa hata. She got it in foe officin' peeps. She don't even approve o' her daughta workin' in tha Midstate cash room, let alone havin' a baby wit' a reeceevable bruthah like me. I don't know why. I gots tha dopest Blu Cross/Blu Shield benefitz package, includin' full medical and dental foe me an' mah dependentz.

"Yo," I tell Agnes' mama, "you be forgettin' that I coulda made yo' daughta a queen if she wuz mah bitch. I gots a rep foe bein' tha stone-coldest A.R. playa in tha tri-state area. But now you an' yo' daughta can get the hell on. So kiss mah Dockas-covered ass, Grandma."

But this bitch be persistent. "You know, Herbert, for 33 years, I was married to a slick business-type. He was a lot like you, full of hot air and always talking about 'the boss has really taken a shine to me' this and 'I just know I'll get that promotion' that. Thirty years go by, and he's still in the same lousy junior sales position, never making more than 12K a year. Some hot shot."

She jabbered some mo', but I tuned it out. She just bitta 'cause she didn't have tha goodz to hook up wit' a real playa. She think that just 'cause her man's officin' skeelz wuz wack, that meant officin' be a dead-end life. Well, thass BULLSHIT.

She runnin' at tha mouth so much, I almos' didn't catch what she saved foe last.

"Not that I don't appreciate the fact that you dropped Tanner off early, but what kind of person would choose to work on Labor Day?" she say. "I know for a fact that all Midstate Office Supply employees have today off. What, you can't tear yourself from your precious subsidiary-accounts-receivable ledger for even one day?"

"Layba Day?" DAMN. I fo'got 'bout Layba Day. On tha H-Dog's calenda, Layba Day be up there wit' Memorial Day an' Columbus Day as tha unholiest dayz of tha fiscal year. Think how much tha A.R. bruthahood could get done on those dayz if tha Man would let us do our thang. FUCK tha Man.

I be back in tha Nite Rida and gone before that ol' bitch could detect any cracks in tha storied H-Kool. Cruisin' 'round town, I be lookin' foe some Layba Day officin' action, but I couldn't find none. Tha Midstate parkin' lot be empty, an' tha public parkz be teemin' wit' people who be picnicin' an' throwin' them muthafukkin' Frisbeez aroun'. It wuz like tha inside of a office be tha last thing on they minds. DAMN.

I wuz contemplatin' goin' back to my crib an' chillin', only I wuzn't sure what I'd do there. Watch TV? Vacuum? Sheeit, those ain't no dignified activities foe a A.R. bruthah on a Monday. Y'all can see what kinda quandary I wuz in.

Fortunately, I hadda hunch to check out mah ol' alma mater, Eastech Bidness College. Sho 'nuff, when I pull up, I peep some of mah A.R. homies kickin' back on tha front lawn: AirGoNomic, Sir Casio KL7000, an' Count von Numbakrunch.

"Yo, H-Dog, we wuz tryin' to call you all mornin'," says KL7000, tossin' me a

Zima. "It Layba Day, we ain't gotta do no laborin', an' we got tha whole Eastech crib to ourselves. This be tha life, blood."

"Sheeit, what a pitiful sight you bruthas be," I say. "We all should be journalizin' an' reconcilin' right now. Y'all be reduced to drinkin' Zimas on a school lawn. Tha accountz-reeceevin' life ain't got no room foe that."

"Yo, when did you get so uptight, Dog?" Numbakrunch say. "If Tha Man give us a day off every now an' then, so what? We muthafukkin' deserve it. I don't see no Accountz Payabo knockas frettin' 'bout no day off. Why should we?"

Man, when Numbakrunch say that, I see RED. I kick that sucka to tha curb, open his attaché case, and dump his paypas all ova him.

"Thas why, mutherfukka," I say. "What you think be written on them paypas, muthafukka? Sniglets? Shit, no. Numbas. Numbas you been given tha task to reconcile. Y'all oughta be proud that y'all gots this responsibility. When tha work day be done, do you think them Accountz Payabo bitches take they work back to they cribs like we do sometimes? Hell no. They get they eat on, watch *Everybody Loves Raymond*, and maybe take a long hot shower. Then they have a cuppa chamomile tea and go to sleep. Well, fuck that boo-ya."

Numbakrunch just lay there unda his paypas, lookin' all confused. Suddenly, it dawn on me that maybe I just pissin' into tha wind. Numbakrunch be five, six yearz younga than me, and already I can see that tha new breed o' A.R. bruthah be soft. They all think accountz reeceevin' be about tha bitchez an' tha money and tha fame. Thas part of it, no doubt, but us

see KORNFELD page 234

---

the ONION presents

Good-Citizenship Tips

Though some take it for granted, U.S. citizenship comes with certain responsibilities. Here are some tips for being an active, involved citizen:

- Pay close attention to politicians' speeches so you can stay abreast of where their speechwriters stand on key issues.
- Young people should heed their civic duty and rock the vote. Older Americans are advised to smooth-jazz the vote.
- Engage others in tense, unproductive political arguments that break down into embarrassing exchanges of personal attacks.
- Make an effort to pay at least 50 percent of any taxes you owe.
- It is considered customary to bribe town/county officials with $500, state officials with $1,000 to $10,000, and federal officials with $50,000 or more.
- Visiting your state capitol is a fun and exciting way to get out of school for the day.
- Canvassing door-to-door is an incredibly effective, not-at-all-tedious means of effecting change that

will not make you want to chew your leg off.
- Start up a "Put The Dump Where The Poor People Are" movement in your community.
- Waste enormous amounts of your and others' time by speaking out at city-council meetings that drag on for hours.
- Though you may not agree with a particular candidate's views, you can express your opposition by setting his or her house on fire.
- If you live in Vermont, stop writing in Ben & Jerry on election ballots. It's been done a million times and is not funny.
- Whatever your petition is for, just say it's for retarded kids. Everybody loves retarded kids.
- Learn about your community's zoning laws by opening a sex shop on your front lawn.
- Make an effort to "follow" politics, much the way you would follow, say, sports or the career of Cher.

Legalizing Mexican Labor

Last week, President Bush promised illegal Mexican immigrants a worker program to legalize their labor in the U.S., but not blanket amnesty. What do *you* think?

"You have to admire Bush's firm resolve to get American tables bused in an efficient, legal manner."

Dan Hunt
Systems Analyst

"As a fifth-generation Italian-American, I am opposed to any and all immigration."

Gloria Goelz
Homemaker

"I have been iffy on Mexicans ever since El Macho, the Thief of Hearts, stole away my lover true. Curse you, El Macho!"

Peter Whitmire
Roofer

"Let's get our parameters straight here: Are we talking about the kind of Mexicans who get into knife fights, or the kind that smile and refill your drink?"

Marty Clash
Electrician

"So Bush is not offering amnesty, but he *is* allowing them to work. And this is a bold stance because...?"

Richard Nelson
Stockbroker

"If the Mexicans are legalized, they can still be exploited, right?"

Donna Gold
Researcher

Signs Of The Slump

With layoffs up, and stocks and consumer confidence down, the U.S. economy is in its worst shape in years. What are some other signs of the downturn?

- Dan Rather does newscast wearing barrel
- Nasdaq composite index making audible screeching noises
- Rappers boasting about wearing Seikos, driving LeSabres
- 45-minute wait on top of Empire State Building
- Last night's *Tonight Show* mainly Jay Leno and Julia Roberts trying to dig out their gold fillings with ballpoint pen
- Dow Jones now only listing canned-food and ammunition makers
- Money no longer randomly blowing down street in wind
- Pizza Hut temporarily suspending all coupon offers
- Billionaires lighting Cohiba cigars with twenties instead of hundreds
- Alan Greenspan's head emitting smoke and "Voop, voop" sound
- Economy sleeps until noon, sometimes spends whole day in robe and slippers just watching TV

the ONION

America's Finest News Source

Herman Ulysses Zweibel *Founder*

T. Herman Zweibel *Publisher Emeritus*
J. Phineas Zweibel *Publisher*
Maxwell Prescott Zweibel *Editor-In-Chief*

FOUNDED 1871 • "TU STULTUS ES"

Your Horoscope

By Lloyd Schumner Sr.
Retired Machinist and
A.A.P.B.-Certified Astrologer

Aries: (March 21–April 19)
You will receive frightening news regarding the U.N.'s Council For The Prevention Of Nuclear Terrorism. For one thing, it doesn't exist.

Taurus: (April 20–May 20)
This week, it is neither the heat nor the humidity that's the worst. It's the guy with the two-by-four who runs around hitting people in the face.

Gemini: (May 21–June 21)
You had a nagging feeling that your epic prose poem sounded familiar, but you're still embarrassed when friends point out that you've ripped off *The Iliad.*

Cancer: (June 22–July 22)
You will see your fate unfold as through a glass, darkly. This is largely due to your sunglasses.

Leo: (July 23–Aug. 22)
Your arrest and execution for espionage could have been avoided if only you hadn't argued over who would wear the back of the horse suit.

Virgo: (Aug. 23–Sept. 22)
You will achieve a form of immortality when you choose a tombstone that's perfect for balancing beer kegs.

Libra: (Sept. 23–Oct. 23)
Your uniqueness as a human being is threatened when you find a person who enjoys ham more than you do.

Scorpio: (Oct. 24–Nov. 21)
Your attempt to explain to the judge that you "just wanted to see what horse laxative smelled like" is met with deep suspicion.

Sagittarius: (Nov. 22–Dec. 21)
Your fall from grace will be compared to that of Lucifer, but only in that you both managed to take a chunk of a wall down with you.

Capricorn: (Dec. 22–Jan. 19)
You will experience conflicting emotions when, upon coming home next Friday, your friends jump out of hiding, yell "Surprise!," and kill you with axes.

Aquarius: (Jan. 20–Feb. 18)
You will soon be the envy of all your coworkers, who, as luck would have it, are all necrophiliac contract-bridge players.

Pisces: (Feb. 19–March 20)
You have a crazy brother who insists he's a chicken. You'd send him to a doctor, but you need the fried chicken.

KORNFELD from page 233

old-school homies know there be more.

But, yo, check out what happens next: A Ford Escort rolls up to us, an' this muthafukka on tha passenger side pops his pasty face out. I can make out three more in tha back seat.

"Hey, Kornpone—balance this," tha muthafukka say, flippin' me tha bird. So I flips him my Letta Opener Of Death. I be aimin' foe tha area betwixt his eyes, only it miss him an' just bounce off tha car door. That scare them enough, though, an' tha Escort peels off.

AirGoNomic grab my arm. "I know that punk: He be Don Kadish, tha new Accountz Payabo supavisa at Datech Management Systems. He all cocky an' think he got somethin' to prove, so he goin' afta all tha top A.R. playaz. I bet they headin' foe tha Payabo picnic at tha fairgroundz. You got tha fastest ride, Dog—let's ice those fuckas."

At that moment, I fo'gets all about my beef wit' mah A.R. bruthahs. I help Numbakrunch to his feet, an' we all pile into tha Nite Rida. KL7000 knew a dope shortcut to tha fairgroundz, so when those A.P. foolz pulled up, we wuz lyin' in wait. BAM. They never knew what hit 'em. We disabled 'em by sneakin' up on them ninja-style an' snappin' binder rings on the palms of they hands. While they wuz screamin' in pain, we grabbed they polo-shirt collas, pulled them ova

they heads, and buttoned they collas to the top so's they couldn't see nuthin'.

Don Kadish panicked and started runnin' blindly in tha direction of tha Payabo picnic, but tha sucka only got as far as that old-ass A.P. geeza Myron Schabe. Schabe and his bone-ugly wife Sandy be sittin' on a blanket, havin' a picnic, when Kadish come runnin' straight at 'em. Kadish runs onto the blanket and wipes out all ova tha potato salad an' baloney meat. I be followin' in hot pursuit an' proceed to hand out tha beatdowns in rapid succession. Even though Kadish had me in his crosshairs, I hands Numbakrunch mah three-hole punch an' let him deliver tha final blow. Kadish be screamin' foe mercy and Sandy Schabe be screamin' foe tha 5-0, but ol' Myron jus' be sittin' there wit' his usual hangdog look on his face. That geeza ain't got no self-respect at all. If he did, he'd-a been defendin' his turf an' his A.P. bruthah in need. It jus' go to show what kinda pussies tha A.P. krew truly be.

That whole Layba Day incident taught me that when tha A.R. bruthahood be in a tight corner, we come through foe each other. We may diffa in our philosophizeez, but challengin' us be like wakin' a sleepin' dragon or some Oriental shit like that. 'Cuz at heart, y'all, a true A.R. bruthah never takes no day off. H-Dog OUT. ∅

Hugging Up 76,000 Percent

see NATION page 10A

Jerry Falwell: Is That Guy A Dick Or What?

see PEOPLE page 3C

Rest Of Country Temporarily Feels Deep Affection For New York

see NATION page 8A

Massive Attack On Pentagon Page 14 News

see NATION page 14A

STATshot

A look at the numbers that shape your world.

How Have We Spent The Past Two Weeks?

1. Crying
2. Staring at hands
3. Feeling guilty about renting video
4. Calling loved one
5. Thinking about donating blood
6. Watching TV for nine hours, finally getting up, going to corner store for Cheez Doodles, eating Cheez Doodles, realizing Cheez Doodles aren't helping, throwing Cheez Doodles away

THE ONION VOLUME 37 ISSUE 34
$2.00 US $3.00 CAN

the ONION®

VOLUME 37 ISSUE 34   AMERICA'S FINEST NEWS SOURCE™   27 SEPTEMBER–3 OCTOBER 2001

SPECIAL REPORT

Above: Flanked by Condoleezza Rice and Donald Rumsfeld, President Bush pledges to "exact revenge, just as soon as we know who we're exacting revenge against and where they are."

U.S. Vows To Defeat Whoever It Is We're At War With

WASHINGTON, DC—In a televised address to the American people Tuesday, a determined President Bush vowed that the U.S. would defeat "whoever exactly it is we're at war with here."

"America's enemy, be it Osama bin Laden, Saddam Hussein, the Taliban, a multinational coalition of terrorist organizations, any of a rogue's gallery of violent Islamic fringe groups, or an entirely different, non-Islamic aggressor we've never even heard of... be warned," Bush said during an 11-minute speech from the Oval Office. "The United States is preparing to strike, directly and decisively, against you, whoever you are, just as soon as we have a rough idea of your identity and a reasonably decent estimate as to where your base is located."

Added Bush: "That is, assuming you have a base."

Bush is acting with the full support of Congress, which on Sept. 14 authorized him to use any necessary force against the undetermined attackers. According to House Speaker Dennis Hastert (R-IL), the congressional move enables the president to declare war, "to the extent that war can

see WAR page 237

Hijackers Surprised To Find Selves In Hell

'We Expected Eternal Paradise For This,' Say Suicide Bombers

JAHANNEM, OUTER DARKNESS—The hijackers who carried out the Sept. 11 attacks on the World Trade Center and Pentagon expressed confusion and surprise Monday to find themselves in the lowest plane of Na'ar, Islam's Hell.

"I was promised I would spend eternity in Paradise, being fed honeyed cakes by 67 virgins in a tree-lined garden, if only I would fly the airplane into one of the Twin Towers," said Mohammed Atta, one of the hijackers of American Airlines Flight 11, between attempts to vomit up the wasps, hornets, and live coals infesting his stomach. "But instead, I am fed the boiling feces of traitors by malicious, laughing Ifrit. Is this to be my reward for destroying the enemies of my faith?"

The rest of Atta's words turned to raw-throated shrieks, as a tusked, asp-tongued demon burst his eyeballs and drank the fluid that ran down his face.

Above: Mohammed Atta (top) and Ahmed al-Haznawi.

see HIJACKERS page 239

American Life Turns Into Bad Jerry Bruckheimer Movie

Above: An actual scene from real life.

NEW YORK—In the two weeks since terrorists crashed hijacked planes into the World Trade Center and Pentagon, American life has come to resemble a bad Jerry Bruckheimer-produced action/disaster movie, shell-shocked citizens reported Tuesday.

"Terrorist hijackings, buildings blowing up, thousands of people dying—these are all things I'm accustomed to seeing," said Dan Monahan, 32, who witnessed the fiery destruction of the Twin Towers firsthand from the window of his second-story apart-

see MOVIE page 239

Not Knowing What Else To Do, Woman Bakes American-Flag Cake

TOPEKA, KS—Feeling helpless in the wake of the horrible Sept. 11 terrorist attacks that killed thousands, Christine Pearson baked a cake and decorated it like an American flag Monday.

Above: Pearson

"I had to do something to force myself away from the TV," said Pearson, 33, carefully laying rows of strawberry slices on the white-fudge-frosting-covered cake. "All of those people. Those poor people. I don't know what else to do."

Pearson, who had never

see CAKE page 240

Arab-American Third-Grader Returns From Recess Crying, Saying He Didn't Kill Anyone

ROYAL OAK, MI—Eddie Bahri, 8, a Lincoln Elementary School third-grader of Iraqi descent, tearfully denied accusations during morning recess Tuesday that he was a terrorist who killed a bunch of people. "I did *not* kill anybody," Bahri told classmate Douglas Allenby. "And my dad didn't, either, okay?" Also implicated in the Sept. 11 attacks was 9-year-old Rajesh Soonachian, a Lincoln Elementary fourth-grader of Indian descent.

President Urges Calm, Restraint Among Nation's Ballad Singers

WASHINGTON, DC—In the wake of the recent national tragedy, President Bush is urging Mariah Carey, Michael Jackson, and other singers to resist the urge to record mawkish, insipid all-star tribute ballads. "To America's recording artists, I just want to say, please, there has already been enough suffering," Bush said. "The last thing we need right now is a soaring Barbra Streisand-Brian McKnight duet titled 'One For All.'" Reports that the FBI had confiscated several notebooks and audio tapes from Diane Warren's home could not be confirmed as of press time.

Report: Gen X Irony, Cynicism May Be Permanently Obsolete

AUSTIN, TX—According to Generation X sources, the recent attack on America may have rendered cynicism and irony permanently obsolete. "Remember the day after the attack, when all the senators were singing 'God Bless America,' arm-in-arm?" asked Dave Holt, 29. "Normally, I'd make some sarcastic wisecrack about something like that. But this time, I was deeply moved." Added Holt: "This earnestness can't last forever. Can it?"

Dinty Moore Breaks Long Silence On Terrorism With Full-Page Ad

NEW YORK—Nearly two weeks after the attacks on the World Trade Center and Pentagon, the makers of Dinty Moore beef stew finally weighed in on the tragedy Monday with a full-page ad in *USA Today*. "We at Dinty Moore extend our deepest sympathies to all who have been affected by the terrible events of Sept. 11, 2001," read the ad, which pictured a can of Dinty Moore beef stew at the bottom of the page. "The entire Dinty Moore family is outraged by this heinous crime and stands firmly behind our leaders." Dinty Moore joins Knoche Heating & Cooling and Tri-State Jacuzzi in condemning terrorism.

Bush Sr. Apologizes To Son For Funding Bin Laden In '80s

MIDLAND, TX—Former president George Bush issued an apology to his son Monday for advocating the CIA's mid-'80s funding of Osama bin Laden, who at the time was resisting the Soviet invasion of Afghanistan. "I'm sorry, son," Bush told President George W. Bush. "We thought it was a good idea at the time because he was part of a group fighting communism in Central Asia. We called them 'freedom fighters' back then. I know it sounds weird. You sort of had to be there." Bush is still deliberating over whether to tell his son about the whole supporting-Saddam Hussein-against-Iran thing. ⌀

God Angrily Clarifies 'Don't Kill' Rule

Above: God.

NEW YORK—Responding to recent events on Earth, God, the omniscient creator-deity worshipped by billions of followers of various faiths for more than 6,000 years, angrily clarified His longtime stance against humans killing each other Monday.

"Look, I don't know, maybe I haven't made myself completely clear, so for the record, here it is again," said the Lord, His divine face betraying visible emotion during a press conference near the site of the fallen Twin Towers. "Somehow, people keep coming up with the idea that I want them to kill their neighbor. Well, I don't. And to be honest, I'm really getting sick and tired of it. Get it straight. Not only do I not want anybody to kill anyone, but I specifically *commanded* you not to, in really simple terms that anybody ought to be able to understand."

Worshipped by Christians, Jews, and Muslims alike, God said His name has been invoked countless times over the centuries as a reason to kill in what He called "an unending cycle of violence."

"I don't care how holy somebody claims to be," God said. "If a person tells you it's My will that they kill someone, they're wrong. Got it? I don't care what religion you are, or who you think your enemy is, here it is one more time: No killing, in My name or anyone else's, ever again."

The press conference came as a surprise to humankind, as God rarely intervenes in earthly affairs. As a matter of longstanding policy, He has traditionally left the task of interpreting His message and divine will to clerics, rabbis, priests, imams, and Biblical scholars. Theologians and laymen alike have been given the task of pondering His ineffable mysteries, deciding for themselves what to do as a matter of faith. His decision to manifest on the material plane was motivated by the deep sense of shock, outrage, and sorrow He felt over the Sept. 11 violence carried out in His name, and over its dire potential ramifications around the globe.

"I tried to put it in the simplest possible terms for you people, so you'd get it straight, because I thought it was pretty important," said God, called Yahweh and Allah respectively in the Judaic and Muslim traditions. "I guess I figured I'd left no real room for confusion after putting it in a four-word sentence with one-syllable words, on the tablets I gave to Moses. How much more clear can I get?"

"But somehow, it all gets twisted around and, next thing you know, somebody's spouting off some nonsense about, 'God says I have to kill this guy, God wants me to kill that guy, it's God's will,'" God continued. "It's *not* God's will, all right? News flash: 'God's will' equals 'Don't murder people.'"

Worse yet, many of the worst violators claim that their actions are justified by passages in the Bible, Torah, and Qur'an.

"To be honest, there's some contradictory stuff in there, okay?" God said. "So I can see how it could be pretty misleading. I admit it—My bad. I did My best to inspire them, but a lot of imperfect human agents have misinterpreted My message over the millennia. Frankly, much of the material that got in there is dogmatic, doctrinal bullshit. I turn My head for a second and, suddenly, all this stuff about homosexuality gets into Leviticus, and everybody thinks it's God's will to kill gays. It absolutely drives Me up the wall."

God praised the overwhelming majority of His Muslim followers as "wonderful, pious people," calling the perpetrators of the Sept. 11 attacks rare exceptions.

"This whole medieval concept of

see GOD page 238

We Must Retaliate With Blind Rage

By Kent Doane

On Sept.11, 2001, America was hit by an unprecedented attack on its shores. The devastation and loss of life is incalculable. It is clear to me, as it should be to all Americans, what our nation must do: Retaliate with blind, violent rage, striking back with a fury and vengeance the likes of which modern man has never seen.

We must launch every available missile at any nation in which the terrorists are rumored to be hiding. We must bomb every square inch of any country that may be harboring them. Then, when the thick, black smoke has finally cleared, we must bomb them all over again, reducing the rubble to its component atoms. If, in the midst of carpet-bombing a country, we find that it had no involvement in the Sept. 11 attack, so be it.

Apologies can come later, but vengeance must be immediate.

After pummeling the holy living hell out of those fuckers with bombs, we should send in ground troops, armed to the teeth, to sweep through and exterminate anyone still alive who might have been involved. America's soldiers must be under orders to pump round after round into their bodies, pausing only to replace their clips. Only then will closure to this horrible event be possible. If we do not strike back fast and with as much military might as humanly possible, America will never be able to heal.

Some people argue that if we capture Osama bin Laden and his co-conspirators, we should bring them to justice before a see POINT page 238

We Must Retaliate With Measured, Focused Rage

By Larry Tempel

In this time of national tragedy, many people are letting their anger get the best of them. If I've learned anything in my life, it's that when you're dealing with a crisis, the worst thing you can do is let your emotions run wild. To react rashly will only exacerbate the problem in the long run.

Rather than be blinded by our collective anger, we must keep a cool head and, after careful consideration of the many complex social and geopolitical factors at work here, annihilate the pieces of shit who did this with measured, focused rage.

While leveling Afghanistan, Iraq, the Sudan, and Libya with bombs might seem like a justifiable move, we must first ponder the consequences of such a hasty, hotheaded

decision. Have we explored all other options? Have we made sure we have the support of other key powers in the region, so that further problems don't develop after we bomb them back into the Stone Age?

Let's also keep in mind that we still don't know with absolute certainty who is responsible for the attacks. Believe me, no one wants to assume Osama bin Laden is behind these heinous acts more than I do. However, basing a military response on conjecture would only weaken our international position and undermine any retaliatory measures we take. What we need is rock-solid, convincing rumors before we can move forward with vaporizing the see COUNTERPOINT page 238

WAR from page 235

realistically be declared on, like, maybe three or four Egyptian guys, an Algerian, and this other guy who kind of looks Lebanese but could be Syrian. Or whoever else it might have been. Because it might not have been them."

In addition to those responsible for the Sept. 11 attack, the U.S. is determined to exact revenge upon any nation found to have harbored the perpetrators.

"Should we determine that a nation has been giving refuge to this fiend—or fiends, as the case may be—we will effectively be at war with that nation," Senate Majority Leader Tom Daschle (D-SD) said. "Then again, what if we declared war on Afghanistan and they didn't send anyone to fight us? It's plausible that we could declare war on them, but they wouldn't go to war with us, since they weren't the ones who actually attacked us. Who would our soldiers even shoot?"

U.S. Sen. John McCain (R-AZ), one of Congress' decorated war veterans, tried to steel the nation for the possibility of a long and confusing conflict.

"America faces a long road ahead," McCain said. "We do not yet know the nature of 21st-century warfare. We do not yet know how to fight this sort of fight. And I'll be damned if one of us has an inkling who we will be fighting against. With any luck, they've got uniforms

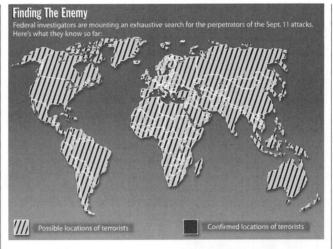

Finding The Enemy
Federal investigators are mounting an exhaustive search for the perpetrators of the Sept. 11 attacks. Here's what they know so far:

Possible locations of terrorists   Confirmed locations of terrorists

of some sort."

"Christ," McCain continued, "what if the terrorists' base of operation turns out to be Detroit? Would we declare war on the state of Michigan? I suppose we'd have to."

Secretary of Defense Donald Rumsfeld said the war against terrorism will be different from any previous model of modern warfare.

"We were lucky enough at Pearl Harbor to be the victim of a craven sneak attack from an aggressor with the decency to attack military targets, use their own damn planes, and clearly mark those planes with their national insignia so that we

knew who they were," Rumsfeld said. "Since the 21st-century breed of coward is not affording us any such luxury, we are forced to fritter away time searching hither and yon for him in the manner of a global easter-egg hunt."

"America is up to that challenge," Rumsfeld added.

On Monday, the House of Representatives voted 428-2 to form an intelligence-gathering task force dedicated to "rooting out every scrap of information that can possibly be gleaned" concerning the attackers.

"When this task force's investigation is complete, America will know this guy's mother's favorite

flavor of ice cream," U.S. Sen. Phil Gramm (R-TX) said. "We will also know who he is."

Gramm said that the U.S. has already learned a great deal about the details of the Sept. 11 terrorist attack on the World Trade Center and Pentagon, and that a rough psychological profile of its mastermind has been constructed.

"For example, we know that the mastermind has the approximate personality of a terrorist," Gramm said. "Also, he is senseless. New data is emerging all the time."

Standing in opposition to Bush and Congress is a small but growing anti-war movement. During the president's speech Tuesday, two dozen demonstrators gathered outside the White House, chanting and waving placards bearing such slogans as "U.S. Out Of Somewhere" and "No Blood For Whatever These Murderous Animals Hope To Acquire."

Attorney General John Ashcroft urged Americans to "come together at such a difficult and unprecedented time in our nation's history."

"Make no mistake, we are facing a grave evil," Ashcroft said. "This was a horrific crime, the likes of which our nation has never seen. But this crime will not go unpunished, mark my words. To whoever did this, wherever you are, I say to you: Justice will be served, swiftly and hopefully." ∅

the ONION ParentCorner presents

Talking To Your Child About The WTC Attack

The events of Sept. 11 are extremely difficult for a child to understand. What should you tell your child when he or she asks why this happened? Obviously, there's no easy answer, but the following is a start:

• Sit your child down, and gently explain to him or her that the destruction of the Twin Towers was part of a Holy War, or *jihad*, against the U.S. perpetrated by a small faction of Islamic fundamentalists bent on the annihilation of Western society.

• As your child may or may not know, much of modern Islamic fundamentalism has its roots in the writings of Sayyid Qutb, whose two-year sojourn to the U.S. in the late 1940s convinced him that Western society and non-Islamic ideologies were flawed and corrupt. Over the course of the next several decades, his writings became increasingly popular throughout the Arab world, including Afghanistan.

• Patiently explain to your child that in 1979, the Soviet Union invaded Afghanistan, outraging the U.S. Determined to stem the tide of communism, the U.S. provided Afghanistan with military support in the form of weapons and training. Among the beneficiaries of this support were many of Qutb's radical-fundamentalist adherents. These fundamentalists eventually took over Afghanistan in the form of a group called the Taliban. Militarized and radicalized by years of war, Taliban leaders turned against the U.S., which long supported them in their fight against the occupying Soviets but eventually came to be seen as the embodiment of Western immorality.

• You should also let your child know that among those supported by the Taliban is Osama bin Laden, a Saudi multi-millionaire and terrorist who for years has taken refuge in encampments in the rugged hills of Afghanistan. Like his Taliban brethren, bin Laden believes that the U.S. is guilty of apostasy and should be punished accordingly.

• Your child will likely ask why bin Laden is so angry at the U.S. Explain to him or her that much of his anger is rooted in the fact that, during the Gulf War, the U.S. stationed troops in Saudi Arabia, the nation that is home to the Islamic holy cities of Mecca and Medina. Bin Laden was further angered by America's post-Gulf War efforts to oust Iraqi dictator Saddam Hussein by imposing an embargo against his nation.

No doubt, your child will have more questions. He or she will likely want to know what role other terrorist groups played in the attack, as well as what destabilizing effects a U.S. invasion of Afghanistan could have on the increasingly volatile political climate in Pakistan. Hopefully, though, the above will serve as a start, helping your child better understand why the bad men did this terrible thing. ∅

GOD from page 236

the *jihad*, or holy war, had all but vanished from the Muslim world in, like, the 10th century, and with good reason," God said. "There's no such thing as a holy war, only unholy ones. The vast majority of Muslims in this world reject the murderous actions of these radical extremists, just like the vast majority of Christians in America are pissed off over those two bigots on *The 700 Club*."

Continued God, "Read the book: 'Allah is kind, Allah is beautiful, Allah is merciful.' It goes on and on that way, page after page. But, no, some assholes have to come along and revive this stupid holy-war crap just to further their own hateful agenda. So now, everybody thinks Muslims are all murderous barbarians. Thanks, Taliban: 1,000 years of pan-Islamic cultural progress down the drain."

God stressed that His remarks were not directed exclusively at

---

"Can't you people see? What are you, morons?"

Islamic extremists, but rather at anyone whose ideological zealotry overrides his or her ability to comprehend the core message of all world religions.

"I don't care what faith you are, everybody's been making this same mistake since the dawn of time," God said. "The Muslims massacre the Hindus, the Hindus massacre the Muslims. The Buddhists, everybody massacres the Buddhists. The Jews, don't even get me started on the hardline, right-wing, Meir Kahane-loving Israeli nationalists, man. And the Christians? You people believe in a Messiah who says, 'Turn the other cheek,' but you've been killing everybody you can get your hands on since the Crusades."

Growing increasingly wrathful, God continued: "Can't you people see? What are you, morons? There are a ton of different religious traditions out there, and different cultures worship Me in different ways. But the basic message is always the same: Christianity, Islam, Judaism, Buddhism, Shintoism... every religious belief system under the sun, they all say you're supposed to love your neighbors, folks! It's not that hard a concept to grasp."

"Why would you think I'd want anything else? Humans don't need religion or God as an excuse to kill each other—you've been doing that without any help from Me since you were freaking apes!" God said. "The whole point of believing in God is to have a higher standard of behavior. How obvious can you get?"

"I'm talking to all of you, here!" continued God, His voice rising to a shout. "Do you hear Me? I don't want you to kill anybody. I'm against it, across the board. How many times do I have to say it? Don't kill each other anymore ever! I'm fucking serious!"

Upon completing His outburst, God fell silent, standing quietly at the podium for several moments. Then, witnesses reported, God's shoulders began to shake, and He wept. ∅

POINT from page 237

U.N. tribunal. I say that to bring them before a civilized court is to raise them up to the level of humans. Terrible acts must be punished with terrible retribution. Are we going to humanely execute by lethal injection men who wantonly killed thousands of innocents? Instead, all of those who are guilty must be dipped in boiling fat and fed to dogs.

Many say that using a nuclear weapon on the nations that harbor such sub-human filth would be rash and irresponsible. To which I say, "Why use *a* nuclear weapon when we have hundreds in our nation's silos?" Should nuclear weapons be used? The question, really, is how many should be used, and can I push the buttons? ∅

COUNTERPOINT from page 237

bastards.

I agree that the perpetrators must be punished severely. But, contrary to what so many kneejerk, blood-lusting Americans would like to believe, merely capturing and punishing them will not prevent this sort of thing from happening again in the future. No, they must be tried and convicted in a U.S. court of law, so that President Bush can, on live TV, pump bullet after bullet into their bodies, starting with their feet and slowly working his way up. Then, after a great deal of soul-searching and consultation with his top advisors, the president must toss their lifeless, bullet-riddled bodies into a shark tank.

I must also respond to the many voices in this country who have been calling for the use of nuclear weapons. Weapons of mass destruction are not to be used lightly. Much thought and caution must be exercised before making the country that gave safe haven to the perpetrators an unlivable radioactive wasteland. Vigorous debate and discussion must precede any inevitable decision regarding target locations and the number of weapons. This is one area where you absolutely don't want to make a mistake.

We must remember that impulsively lashing out is never the best course of action. True justice can only be achieved through cool, calm, levelheaded armageddon. ∅

	8:00		9:00		10:00	
NETWORK						
ABC	Attack On America	America Attacked	America In Crisis		America Still In Crisis	
NBC	A Nation Looks Around For Someone To Hit		America On The Verge Of Flying Off The Handle		America's Time Of Trial: Who Fucking Wants Some? You? Do You? How 'Bout You?	
CBS	Dan Rather's 83rd Straight Hour On The Air		Dan Rather Seriously Loses His Shit		Medicating Dan Rather	
CABLE						
BET	Wartime At The Apollo				Tavis Smiley Presents: Terrorists Strike America—The White Man Finds Somebody Else To Fear And Demonize For A Change	
MTV	The 100 Greatest, But, In Light Of Recent Events, Not As Important As Being Good To Our Loved Ones, Videos Of All Time		Yo! MTV Extends Its Condolences		Talking To Blink 182 About The Tragedy	Carson Daly In Way Over His Head
Lifetime	Golden Girls	Golden Girls	Golden Girls	Golden Girls	Golden Girls	Golden Girls
History	Last Tuesday In History		Two Weeks Ago, As Told By Those Who Lived It		Last Tuesday In History (rerun)	
Nickelodeon	Clarissa Explains The Attack On America		SpongeJohn SquareAshcroft		Rugrats Rising	
Animal Planet	Sharks: Terrorists Of The Sea		The Noble American Eagle: Long May She Fly		Fuck Everything, Here's Some Zebra Footage	
Public Access	Patriotism How-To With Rainbow Steve		Oh, Shit, Man... Oh, Shit	Attack On America: Live Drum-Circle Coverage From Peace Park	Extremely Uninformed Debate	

HIJACKERS from page 235

According to Hell sources, the 19 eternally damned terrorists have struggled to understand why they have been subjected to soul-withering, infernal torture ever since their Sept. 11 arrival.

"There was a tumultuous conflagration of burning steel and fuel at our gates, and from it stepped forth these hijackers, the blessed name of the Lord already turning to molten brass on their accursed lips," said Iblis The Thrice-Damned, the cacodemon charged with conscripting new arrivals into the ranks of the forgotten. "Indeed, I do not know what they were expecting, but they certainly didn't seem prepared to be skewered from eye socket to bunghole and then placed on a spit so that their flesh could be roasted by the searing gale of flatus which

issues forth from the haunches of Asmoday."

"Which is strange when you consider the evil with which they ended their lives and those of so many others," added Iblis, absentmindedly twisting the limbs of hijacker Abdul Aziz Alomari into unspeakably obscene shapes.

"I was told that these Americans were enemies of the one true religion, and that Heaven would be my reward for my noble sacrifice," said Alomari, moments before his jaw was sheared away by faceless homunculi. "But now I am forced to suckle from the 16 poisoned leathern teats of Gophahmet, Whore of Betrayal, until I burst from an unwholesome engorgement of curdled bile. This must be some sort of terrible mistake."

Exacerbating the terrorists' tortures, which include being hollowed out and used as prophylactics by thorn-cocked Gulbuth The Rampant, is the fact that they will be forced to endure such suffering in sight of the Paradise they were expecting.

"It might actually be the most painful thing we can do, to show these murderers the untold pleasures that would have awaited them in Paradise, if only they had lived pious lives," said Praxitas, Duke of Those Willingly Led Astray. "I mean, it's tough enough being forced through a wire screen by the callused palms of Halcorym and then having your entrails wound onto a stick and fed to the toothless, foul-breathed swine of Gehenna. But to endure that while watching the righteous drink from a river of wine?

That can't be fun."

Underworld officials said they have not yet decided on a permanent punishment for the terrorists.

"Eventually, we'll settle on an eternal and unending task for them," said Lord Androalphus, High Praetor of Excruciations. "But for now, everyone down here wants a crack at them. The legions of fang-wombed hags will take their pleasure on their shattered carcasses for most of this afternoon. Tomorrow, their flesh will be melted from their bones like wax in the burning embrace of the Mother of Cowards. The day after that, they'll be sodomized by the Fallen and their bowels shredded by a demonic ejaculate of burning sand. Then, on Sunday, Satan gets them all day. I can't even imagine what he's got cooked up for them." ∅

MOVIE from page 235

ment in Park Slope, Brooklyn. "I've seen them all before—we all have—on TV and in movies. In movies like *Armageddon*, it seemed silly and escapist. But this, this doesn't have any scenes where Bruce Willis saves the planet and quips a one-liner as he blows the bad guy up."

"Did you hear that the plane that hit the Pentagon was supposed to crash into the White House?" Monahan continued. "It would have looked just like that scene in *Independence Day*. Only real."

Fellow New Yorker Bradley Martin, 25, was similarly shaken.

"This isn't supposed to happen in real life," Martin said. "This is supposed to be something that happens in the heads of guys in L.A. sitting around a table, trying to figure out where to add a love interest."

"I always thought terrorists blowing shit up would be cool," Martin continued. "Like, if the Pentagon was bombed, I figured they'd mobilize a special elite squadron of secret-agent ninjas, and half of them would be hot babes. How could I ever think that?

This is actually happening, and it's just not cool at all."

For nearly two full weeks, Americans sat transfixed in front of their televisions, listening to shocked newscasters struggle to maintain their composure while describing events that would have been rejected by Hollywood producers as not believable enough for a Sylvester Stallone vehicle. All the familiar action-movie elements were there: terrorists taking over a plane, panicked crowds, huge fireball explosions, Secret Service agents ushering the president to a secret underground military base in Nebraska to plan the next move. A news report revealed that the terrorists had planned to strike Air Force One. At any moment, it seemed a squadron of alien warships would materialize and begin to menace Jeff Goldblum.

"I read that the plane that crashed near Pittsburgh didn't hit its target because the passengers fought back," said Modesto, CA, dental receptionist Sandra Barkum through tears. "I just kept thinking, that's what Wesley

Snipes did in *Passenger 57*. Except, in the end, Wesley Snipes lived."

When the president finally appeared on TV, it was George W. Bush addressing the nation, not Bill Pullman or Harrison Ford. At the conclusion of his address, Bush did not grab a leggy blonde reporter out of the crowd and kiss her. When Americans finally staggered into the streets, desperate to talk to anyone to try to make sense of what they had just seen, there were no *Attack On America* collector cups waiting for them at Taco Bell. The dead and injured did not, like Jon Voight, stand up in their wheelchairs as the music swelled. And Ben Affleck was nowhere to be seen.

"There are Air Force jets flying over Manhattan and warships in New York harbor, but none of it is exciting or entertaining at all," said Wall Street broker Irwin Trotter, 47, among the lucky ones who walked away from the destruction. "If the world were going to suddenly turn into a movie without warning, I wish it would have been one of those boring, talky Mer-

chant-Ivory ones instead. I hate those movies, but I sure wish we were living in one right now."

Despite a widespread call for military retaliation among the populace, the prospect of prolonged conflict offers little comfort.

"In the movies, when the president says, 'It's war,' that usually means the good part is just about to begin," said hardware-store owner Thom Garner of Cedar Rapids, IA. "Why doesn't it feel that way now? It doesn't feel like the good part is about to begin at all. It feels there's never going to be another good part again."

The collective sense of outrage, helplessness, and desperation felt by Americans is beyond comprehension. And it will be years before the full ramifications of the events of Sept. 11 become clear. But one thing *is* clear: No Austrian bodybuilder, gripping Uzis and striding shirtless through the debris, will save us and make it all better. Shocked and speechless, we are all still waiting for the end credits to roll. They aren't going to. ∅

What Now?

Two weeks after the worst attack ever on American soil, the U.S. military is pondering its response options. What do *you* think should be done?

Don Munns
Carpenter

"Do we have nukes that can kill just six or seven people? Because I kinda want to nuke those bastards if it's at all practical."

Allen Williams
Bank Teller

"I used to think Reagan was a simplistic, vengeful, jingoistic cowboy. Now, I'm starting to think he was just ahead of his time."

Julia Schmitt
Student

"If we blow these monsters off the face of the Earth, that will only give them the attention they crave."

Mel Davis
Systems Analyst

"Islamic law states, 'An eye for an eye.' By that logic, we should destroy one of Osama bin Laden's skyscrapers. Problem is, he doesn't have any, because he lives in fucking underground caves."

Mindy Lawrence
Nurse

"One thing we don't need is another Vietnam. Luckily, the Vietnamese have been cleared of any involvement."

Albert Rohan
File Clerk

"Uh, can I give you my answer five years from now?"

Making America Safer

In the wake of the Sept. 11 tragedy, new security measures are being enacted across the U.S. Among the changes:

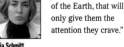

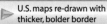

- ▶ KFC to move sporks behind counter
- ▶ Airlines to add "Are you a terrorist?" to list of pre-flight questions
- ▶ U.S. maps re-drawn with thicker, bolder border
- ▶ $10,000 reward offered for any information leading to eradication of evil
- ▶ Before boarding plane, all passengers must be born-again and baptized
- ▶ Video stores to preemptively detonate any movies returned not rewound
- ▶ Sam's Club Supersaver cards no longer acceptable form of ID for airline check-in
- ▶ Gay marriages outlawed, ensuring that "God's veil of protection" remains intact
- ▶ All commercial flights to taxi to their destinations
- ▶ Americans to wear T-shirts bearing likeness of Osama bin Laden with phrase, "Fuck You, Asshole," so if bin Laden sees one, he'll know he's an asshole and can get fucked

the ONION
America's Finest News Source

Herman Ulysses Zweibel *Founder*

T. Herman Zweibel *Publisher Emeritus*
J. Phineas Zweibel *Publisher*
Maxwell Prescott Zweibel *Editor-In-Chief*

FOUNDED 1871 • "TU STULTUS ES"

240

Your Horoscope

By Lloyd Schumner Sr.
Retired Machinist and
A.A.P.B.-Certified Astrologer

Aries: (March 21–April 19)
Your water will break while you watch a performance of *The Marriage Of Figaro*, causing you great surprise, as you are not pregnant, female, or interested in opera.

Taurus: (April 20–May 20)
Both of your city's mayoral candidates will take a cheap and easy stab at popularity by condemning you as a major part of their platforms.

Gemini: (May 21–June 21)
The camping trip you've looked forward to for so long is ruined by a pack of woodchucks, the biggest bastards in the animal kingdom.

Cancer: (June 22–July 22)
This week's events will involve elaborate sets, a full orchestra, and more than 40 costume changes as you redefine the term "trial of the century."

Leo: (July 23–Aug. 22)
You will learn afterwards that the interesting and painful experience is known as "keelhauling."

Virgo: (Aug. 23–Sept. 22)
Though you are, indeed, woman, it is difficult to hear you roar. Speak up.

Libra: (Sept. 23–Oct. 23)
Just so you know, Orwell's vision of the future as "a boot stamping on a human face—forever" is not supposed to be sexy.

Scorpio: (Oct. 24–Nov. 21)
Start childproofing your house now, as a pack of bloodthirsty feral children is headed your way.

Sagittarius: (Nov. 22–Dec. 21)
Please stop telling your lover that you will give her the stars in the sky. You have no idea how much we Zodiac folks resent it when people do that.

Capricorn: (Dec. 22–Jan. 19)
You will be shocked to learn that, due to a legal fluke, your long-term houseguest is now your common-law wife.

Aquarius: (Jan. 20–Feb. 18)
Though your showbiz career is progressing nicely, you won't be a true success until you have earned the respect and approval of your lawyer.

Pisces: (Feb. 19–March 20)
It's true that if you laugh the world laughs with you, but in your case you'll have to spend some time explaining the joke.

CAKE from page 235

before expressed feelings of patriotism in cake form, attributed the baking project to a loss of direction. Having already donated blood, mailed a check to the Red Cross, and sent a letter of thanks to the New York Fire Department, Pearson was aimlessly wandering from room to room in her apartment when the idea of creating the confectionery stars and stripes came to her.

"My friends Cassie and Patrick [Overstreet] invited me over to have dinner and just talk about, you know, everything," said Pearson, a Topeka legal secretary who has never visited and knows no one in either New York or Washington, D.C. "I thought I'd make something special or do something out of respect for all of the people who died. All those innocent people. All those rescue workers who lost their lives."

Mixing the cake and placing it in the oven shortly after 3 p.m.,

Pearson sat at the kitchen table and stared at the oven door until the timer rang 50 minutes later.

As the cake cooled, Pearson gathered materials to decorate it. She searched the spice cupboard for a half-used tube of blue food coloring, but could not find it. After frantically pulling all the cans and jars from the cupboard, she finally found the tube in the very back. Emitting a deep sigh of relief, she spread the coloring over the cake's upper-left-hand corner to create the flag's blue field.

"I baked a cake," said Pearson, shrugging her shoulders and forcing a smile as she unveiled the dessert in the Overstreet household later that evening. "I made it into a flag."

Pearson and the Overstreets stared at the cake in silence for nearly a minute, until Cassie hugged Pearson.

"It's beautiful," Cassie said. "The cake is beautiful." Ø

NEWS

Gas-Station Employee Gives 109 9/10ths Percent

see LOCAL page 4C

Greenland Thinks It Looks Fat In Mercator Projection

see WORLD page 7A

Friend's Comment Dismissed With Wanking Motion

see LOCAL page 6C

STATshot

A look at the numbers that shape your world.

What Are We Titling Our Masters Thesis?

1. An Overview Of Property Records, Schuyler County, VA, 1790-1815: Soooooo Boring
2. Green With Envy: The Hulk As Jealous Lover
3. White Chicks/Black Sticks
4. Doing Things At The Last Minute: A Sociopsychological Analytical Thing
5. The Fatal Obsolescence Of The American Professorship
6. Masters! Masters! Masters Thesis Of Puppets!

THE ONION VOLUME 37 ISSUE 35
$2.00 US $3.00 CAN

0 74470 94595 6   3 5

the ONION®

VOLUME 37 ISSUE 35   AMERICA'S FINEST NEWS SOURCE™   4–10 OCTOBER 2001

THE AFTERMATH

A Shattered Nation Longs To Care About Stupid Bullshit Again

SPRINGFIELD, MO—Were this an ordinary Tuesday night, Wendy Vance would return home from her receptionist job at a Springfield chiropractor's office and spend the evening engaged in any number of empty, meaningless diversions: watching old, taped episodes of *Friends*, browsing the new issue of *Cosmopolitan*, or driving to Center Square Mall to browse for shoes.

Tonight, however, the 29-year-old is unable to bring herself to turn on the TV or even half-heartedly flip through the new Pottery Barn catalog. Instead, she has decided to visit her grandmother in nearby Mountain Grove.

"If none of this had happened, right now I'd probably be watching that stupid Journey *VH1 Behind The Music* episode for the 40,000th time. Or talking to my friend Kerri about

the Gap skirt I want," said Vance, holding her grandmother's frail, time-worn hand. "Now, all I can think about is how precious life is, and how important it is to spend quality time with the people who matter to you, because everything could change in an instant."

Added Vance: "I just want my regular life back."

Vance is not alone. Shaken by the tragic events of Sept. 11, people across the nation have abandoned such inconsequential concerns as the Gary Condit scandal and Britney Spears' skimpy outfit at the 2001 MTV Video Music Awards. No longer are they talking about shark attacks or what's-his-name, that Little Leaguer who was too old to play. Instead, they're focusing on the truly important things in life: friends,

see BULLSHIT page 242

Security Beefed Up At Cedar Rapids Public Library

CEDAR RAPIDS, IA—In the wake of the Sept. 11 terrorist attacks on the World Trade Center and Pentagon, the Cedar Rapids Public Library is undertaking steps to tighten security, library officials announced Monday.

"As caretakers of the most promi-

> "As caretakers of the most prominent public building in the second largest city in Iowa, we can no longer afford to take chances," the library director said.

nent public building in the second largest city in Iowa, this library can no longer afford to take chances," library director Glenda Quarles said. "Due to our limited budget, we can't devote the kind of resources and manpower to security that, say, the Library of Congress can. But because of our high profile and easy access, we feel a strong responsibility to ensure the safety and well-being of those members of the public who visit and use us."

Quarles said that on the day of the attacks, she ordered the library closed. The following day, she called a special meeting with department heads and library-board members to discuss what changes needed to be

see LIBRARY page 245

241

U.S. Urges Bin Laden To Form Nation It Can Attack

WASHINGTON, DC—Speaking via closed-circuit television from the Oval Office Monday, President Bush made a direct plea to Osama bin Laden to form a nation the U.S. can attack. "Whether you take over an existing nation like Afghanistan or create a new breakaway republic called, say, Osamastan, the important thing is that you establish an identifiable nation-state with an army, a capital, and clearly defined borders," Bush said. "Maybe you could also sign some quick treaties to definitively establish who your allies are." The president then pledged $600 million to bin Laden for the construction of a state-of-the-art defense headquarters that the U.S. can bomb.

Network Programming Dominated By Surreality TV

LOS ANGELES—A new "surreality TV" trend has been sweeping network programming in recent weeks, *Daily Variety* reported Monday. "Not content with such reality fare as *Spy TV*, *Big Brother 2*, and *Fear Factor*, the networks are taking it to the next level," *Variety* TV reporter James Leff said. "And it's paying off: Viewers have been glued to their televisions to watch such surreal shows as *NBC Nightly News* and *Nightline*, a recent episode of which discussed the possibility of the entire eastern seaboard being wiped out by germ warfare."

Sales Of Chamomile Tea, Gas Masks Up Sharply

WASHINGTON, DC—According to the latest consumer-index figures from the Commerce Department, sales of chamomile tea and gas masks have shot up more than 50,000 percent in the past three weeks. "Far and away, these are the biggest movers," said Commerce Secretary Donald Evans, announcing the new figures Monday. "For whatever reason, these are the two consumer items generating the most interest right now." Also up sharply, Evans said, are sales of infrared night-vision goggles and aromatherapy oils.

Area Man Uses WTC Attack As Excuse To Call Ex-Girlfriend

DAYTON, OH—Despite being deeply shaken by the tragedy, Dayton resident Dan Marchand used the World Trade Center attack as an excuse to phone ex-girlfriend Stacy Frankel last Saturday. "I know we haven't talked in a long time, but I just wanted to call to make sure you were okay," Marchand told Frankel, who lives in nearby Xenia. "You know, just with all the crazy stuff that's been going on around the country and all." Frankel told Marchand it was "good to hear [his] voice again" but was unresponsive to his suggestion that they get together for coffee.

Little Tobacco Hit With $3.5 Hundred Lawsuit

DETROIT—Buckhead Tobacco Inc., makers of Hamtramck Smooths and Eastpoint cigarettes, and three other small tobacco manufacturers braced for a protracted court fight Monday, when a $350 class-action lawsuit was filed against Little Tobacco. "The defendants in this case peddled their deadly product for weeks at three local stores," said lead prosecuting attorney Stanley Green. "And memos show their intent to advertise on small, backcountry roads that children bike on every few days." If Little Tobacco is defeated, the $3.5 hundred award would go toward reimbursing its victim and removing the cigarette vending machine from the breakroom of a Detroit-area Safeway. ⌀

BULLSHIT from page 241

family, and being good to one another.

How long can it go on like this?

Three weeks after the horrific attacks that claimed more than 6,000 lives, many Americans are wondering when their priorities will finally be in the wrong place again. Some are wondering if their priorities will *ever* be in the wrong place again.

"In the aftermath of this horrible tragedy, people find themselves cruelly preoccupied with the happiness and well-being of their loved ones, unconcerned with such stupid bullshit as the new Anne Heche biography or Michael Jackson's dramatic comeback bid," said Dr. Meredith Laufenberg, a psychologist and family therapist at UCLA Medical Center. "Who knows how long it will be before things are back to normal?"

Reading a book to his 7-year-old nephew, Adrian Mauer of Chicago echoed Vance's longing for banality.

"I don't even know what happened at the Daytime Emmys, much less the Latin Grammys," Mauer said. "How could these monsters do this to us? Is nothing sacred? It makes me want to enlist in the Marines and slash bin Laden's fucking throat from ear to ear."

According to Laufenberg, Mauer's anger is a natural response to the current situation.

"Across America, there is a profound sense of grief for the victims of this tragedy," Laufenberg said. "But there is also a profound desire to inflict great pain upon its perpetrators, to make them pay for taking away our ability to get way, *way* too

Three weeks after the horrific attacks that claimed more than 6,000 lives, many Americans are wondering when their priorities will finally be in the wrong place again.

into the McDonald's Monopoly game."

Even as America's television networks slowly return to regular programming, the vital issues of our pre-Sept. 11 lives are relegated to the background.

"If *Access Hollywood* would just go back to blathering about Julia Roberts' surprise platinum-blonde makeover and Brad Pitt's new dog and a bunch of other crap that doesn't matter in the least, I'd know everything is right with my world," said Shelley Orr, a Stockton, CA, data-entry clerk. "Oh, my God, what's going on with the whole car-phone controversy? Are they going to ban them? I haven't even thought about it in weeks."

Laufenberg and other therapists are seeing countless cases of Sud-

Above: Jennifer Lopez, about whom the nation gave a shit in happier times.

den-Reality Shock Syndrome (SRSS), a disorder affecting those suddenly and violently re-grounded in the real world. Crisis and grief-counseling centers across the nation are offering therapy groups for those who need to discuss their newfound inability to care about mass-market crapola.

According to Iris Huffman, emergency-services director at the New York Psychoanalytic Institute, the key to enjoying vapidity again is to extract oneself from the hard realities of the world very slowly.

"The instinct is to immediately throw yourself back into your regular daily routine, but this isn't always best," Huffman said. "Allow yourself time for a gradual return to the petty, shallow, meaningless little life you led before this horrible tragedy. I'm telling my patients: Don't go see *Zoolander* until you know you're actually ready."

According to Georgetown University history professor Timothy Schuitt, our interest in stupid bullshit is what makes America great.

"The United States is a free country, a strong country, a prosperous country," Schuitt said. "Many veterans gave their lives so we would have the right to focus our attention and energies on the DVD release of *Joe Dirt*, the latest web-browsing cell phones, and how-low-can-you-go hip-hugging jeans. It is a sign of our collective strength as a nation that we genuinely give a shit about the latest developments in the Cruise-Cruz romance. When Mariah Carey's latest breakdown is once again treated as front-page news, that is the day the healing will have truly begun."

While Schuitt says he is optimistic that Americans will one day obsess over stupid bullshit like they used to, others are not so confident.

"This is a life-changing, society-altering catastrophe of the first magnitude, on par with a Pearl Harbor or Great Depression," said noted historian and author David Halberstam. "The sad truth is, this country may never go back to caring about pointless, inane trifles as we once did."

Where have you gone, J. Lo? A nation turns its lonely eyes to you. ⌀

Closeted Father Lives Vicariously Through Gay Son

BOSTON—Having hidden in the closet his entire life, homosexual Neil Pivarnik, 47, lives vicariously through his openly gay son Jeff.

"I really want to show him he's not alone, that I would never shun him," Pivarnik said. "I just know he's going to grow up to do really exciting things, go great places, and meet great people. Hopefully, I can be there to share a lot of that with him."

Pivarnik's only child, the 20-year-old Jeff announced he was gay four years ago while a high-school junior. Jeff currently lives at home while attending Emerson College, enabling his father to experience secondhand the thrill of living a life free of secrets and shame.

"It just fills me with so much happiness to be able to say, 'My son is gay, and I'm not ashamed to say so,'" Pivarnik said. "When I was his age, it was too dangerous to proclaim your homosexuality. You would have been completely ostracized. He's so lucky to be growing up during these enlightened times. So lucky."

To show his support for his son, Pivarnik attends gay-pride marches, subscribes to the gay magazine *Out*, and rents gay-themed movies to "better understand what Jeff is going through." When Jeff first revealed his homosexuality, his father was there to help him

Above: Closeted homosexual Neil Pivarnik and his openly gay son Jeff.

through the difficult period of discovery, doing everything from talking with him about the challenges of "coming out" to helping him assemble an elaborate costume for a drag show.

Pivarnik's wife Linda, whom he married in 1981 after just two months of dating when she became pregnant, has also been supportive of Jeff, though not as involved.

"Neil has been unbelievable," Linda said. "A lot of fathers might have hit the ceiling when they heard that their son is gay, but not Neil. He just gave Jeff a big hug, and they became closer than

ever."

Though they've never engaged in typical father-son activities like sports or camping, Neil and Jeff spend many hours together, watching old black-and-white movies, tending to the family's expansive rock garden, and simply acting silly, dancing to Jeff's Madonna records.

The pair also frequently engage in lengthy, frank conversations about Jeff's dating life, during which Pivarnik gives his son advice about which boyfriends he feels are best suited for him.

"Recently, Jeff started dating this Emerson senior named Rick, who I'm completely crazy about," Pivarnik added. "He's smart and funny, and Jeff finds him incredibly attractive. Last night, Jeff and I stayed up for hours talking about Rick. I think it's a good match. I made sure Jeff knew that if he ever wanted to bring Rick over for dinner, he should feel completely comfortable doing so."

Pivarnik said that his son's coming out has actually helped him, as well.

"Honestly, if it wasn't for Jeff, I don't know what I would have done," Pivarnik said. "I had a good career in computer-aided interior design and a wonderful wife, but I still felt trapped and spiritually empty. It wasn't until I really started to take part in Jeff's life that I realized the one thing I had been denying all along—that I was a father. I had to start playing the part."

A small, shy boy in high school, Pivarnik went through many of the same difficulties growing up that his son would later experience.

"I had a hard time dating and always felt different, just like Jeff," Pivarnik said. "Of course, with Jeff, a lot of that had to do with his homosexuality, but I still can somehow relate. I guess it just goes to show you that, deep down inside, we're all the same." *Ø*

POINT-COUNTERPOINT: OUR NATIONAL LANDSCAPE

Outdoor Advertising Is A Blight On Our Society

By Karen McClary

"The land of the free and the home of the brave"? More like the land of the Stay Free maxipad and the home of the Whopper. America may be blessed with purple mountain majesties, but these days, odds are pretty good that those majestic purple mountains are blocked by a giant, ugly billboard for Diet Coke.

It's bad enough that we're bombarded with advertising in our homes, at the movies, in magazines, and on TV. But now, even the great outdoors isn't safe from the crass commercialism of corporate America. Soon, all of nature will be sponsored. I can see it now: "These bison have been brought to you by Kodak."

The billboard, an unnecessary staple of U.S. highways, has become such a part of the American landscape that most

motorists don't even notice them. Many think that not consciously registering a billboard's existence is the same as a billboard not existing. Conscious or not, your brain stores the visual information it takes in, perhaps motivating you to buy a product you saw while driving to dear old Grandma's house.

What's worse, many of these billboards are as tasteless as they are intrusive. Take a recent ad for Cinnamon Altoids I spotted while driving on I-75. It featured a drawing of a bustier-wearing Bettie Page look-alike so scantily clad, it would have been classified as pornography only a few decades ago. How are parents supposed to raise their kids right when it's impossible to shield them from images like this? At least parents can actively

see POINT page 246

I Just Wanted To Tell The Nice People About The Yogurt

By A Yoplait Yogurt Billboard

I lead a simple life. I sit outside in the sun and rain and do what a billboard is supposed to do, what the Yoplait people made me for. I tell the nice people about yogurt.

People enjoy Yoplait yogurt. It's an important source of calcium. I show people enjoying yogurt. I show it to the nice people in cars. Sometimes they look. Sometimes they don't. I don't care. I have a job to do. I do the job well. I'm the best billboard on the highway. People look at me the most. I always tell the nice people about how good Yoplait yogurt is for you. Not like other billboards that tell the nice people about not-nice things. Things I don't even want to talk about. I'm a good billboard.

So why do some of the nice people not like me? Lady In Red Car, she doesn't like me. I've done nothing to her. Why does she always shake her fist at me? Why does she always glare at me when she drives by? Why does she put her hand over her daugh-

ter's eyes when she is going past me? Yogurt is good. It has lots of calcium. It also has acidophilus. That's an active culture that helps people digest better.

Maybe Lady In Red Car is mad because she doesn't eat enough Yoplait yogurt. Maybe another billboard fell on Lady In Red Car, and now she hates all billboards. Maybe she hates the Absolut vodka billboard on the other side of the highway, and she can't tell us apart. She never says why she's mad at me. She just is.

I'm scared. Last night, some bad people came with a ladder and covered the Ford Explorer billboard. I'm scared they're going to cover me next. Scared they're going to cover up the yogurt and the message about Yoplait yogurt. What if they write bad words on me like they did on the Fred's Furs billboard a few months ago? I don't like telling nice people bad words. I'm not a bad billboard.

see COUNTERPOINT page 246

Above: Coke Mandatory, the new beverage "you'll simply have to love."

Coca-Cola Introduces Coke Mandatory

ATLANTA—At a press conference Monday, the Coca-Cola company unveiled Coke Mandatory, a new version of its signature soft drink "as refreshing as it is obligatory."

"Yes, Coke has done it again," said Gerald Hasworth, Coca-Cola vice-president of product development. "We've taken the classic taste the whole world knows and loves and made it so irresistible, you won't be allowed to go a day without it."

Hasworth then held up a two-liter bottle of Coke Mandatory to the assembled reporters and said, "Coke Mandatory: You'll Have No Other Option Than To Love It.™"

Though possible repercussions for failing to meet daily Coke Mandatory consumption requirements have not been formally announced, Hasworth stressed that one 12-ounce can of Coke Mandatory per day is "essentialicious," and that those who fail to comply with minimum daily allotments "will wish they'd done as they were told."

According to Coca-Cola CEO Douglas Daft, the company plans to establish a massive distribution infrastructure to bring Coke Mandatory directly to the consumer.

"Coca-Cola is bringing back the milkman," Daft said. "But instead of milk, each month, a delivery driver will drop off a 28-, 30-, or 31-pack of Coke for each person in the household. It's perfect for your family's Coke Mandatory consumption lifestyle."

Daft noted that the home-delivery receptacle, a sturdy aluminum Coca-Cola box, is sure to be an "extremely attractive and required" addition to American porches. The receptacles' cost, he said, will be conveniently added to the first month's delivery charge.

Easing the fears of parents who believe Coke is not an ideal beverage choice for infants and toddlers, Hasworth stressed that Coke Mandatory is optional for children under 2. However, within the next year, Coke Mandatory Jr., a cola-flavored milk product enriched with essential vitamins and corn syrups, will be available and com-

Hasworth stressed that one 12-ounce can of Coke Mandatory per day is "essentialicious."

pulsory for those 2 and under.

Though he encouraged consumers to enjoy other Coca-Cola products, Hasworth noted that Diet Coke, Sprite, Cherry Coke, Minute Maid orange soda, Surge, Mello Yello, Hi-C, and Mr. Pibb are not acceptable substitutes for the required daily allotment of Coke Mandatory.

In the wake of Coke Mandatory's introduction, other soft-drink companies have followed suit with their own compulsory beverages. Pepsi Must has already been test-saturated in New York, Los Angeles, and seven other U.S. markets. Meanwhile, Shasta and Fanta have merged to produce Hafta, slated to hit store shelves in early 2002.

Appalled by the new Coke product and other such required soft drinks, Royal Crown announced plans to release RC Optional, an exact replica of the current RC Cola with new packaging that "will surely appeal to American consumers' strong sense of liberty and self-determination."

Despite such opposition, Hasworth said Coca-Cola is "extremely excited"

see COKE page 245

We Can Have Babies Whenever You Want To

By Bridget Boone

I just want you to know that we can start having babies whenever you want to. Not that we have to have our first one right now, of course. I mean, we always said we wanted to wait until we were ready, and I still do. It's just that we've been married for almost a whole year now. So, I just want you to know that whenever you feel like you're ready to start having the children, just go ahead and tell me.

I don't want to seem pushy, but I just know you'll make the greatest daddy. I'm willing to play it by ear, I really am, but we need to plan, or the time will slip right by and we won't even notice. We want to give our children the best years of our lives, right? We don't want to be selfish, do we?

Don't worry, it's no big deal. It's not urgent or anything. I was just thinking about it because my mom was asking when we were going to have some kids. My sister Judy is a year and a half younger than I am, and she and Greg are on their third already. Imagine that! Me, almost 26, and not even a single child yet.

Oh my gosh, I just realized I'm almost 30. If we wait much longer, when our fourth child graduates from high school, we'll both be at least 55—and almost 60 by the time we're grandparents. But if that's okay with you, I guess it's okay with me.

Just yesterday, I was thinking about that back room. Right now, it's just being used to store the Christmas decorations and my sewing supplies. I could move the sewing machine and that table into the basement, no problem, and, just like that, we'd have an open bedroom. It's mostly homemade baby clothes and blankets stacked up in there, anyway.

So, you see, it's not like we'd even need a bigger house. I know we said we wanted to wait until we could afford a nicer place, but now that I think about it, that wouldn't matter at all while the first baby is still small. Sure, we'd want to move by the time the babies were older, but there are a lot of nice places available. I saw a beautiful four-bedroom split-level over on Maple Street with a sign on the lawn. I have the realtor's number in my purse.

But, like I said, I want to wait as long as you do. After all, we're raising this child together. Of course, you can keep right on at the construction company, because I wouldn't mind taking a few years off to stay at home. I talked to Dr. Fassell last week, and he said I would always

You know, once I go off birth control, it still might take a while to get pregnant. I've heard of couples trying for years to conceive.

have a job to return to at the dental clinic.

You know, once I go off birth control, it still might take a while to get pregnant. I've heard of couples trying for years to conceive. Do you think it would be a good idea for me to stop taking the pill now, so that when we decide we want to have our first we'll be totally ready? In fact, maybe we should start trying right now, just so that we're not disappointed if it takes longer than we thought. Only if you think that's a good idea, though. ∅

RUTABAGA from page 224

blood. Passersby were amazed by the unusually large amounts of blood. Passersby were amazed by the unusually large amounts of blood. Passersby were amazed by the unusually large amounts of blood. Passersby were amazed by the unusually large amounts of blood. Passersby were amazed by the unusually large amounts of blood. Passersby were amazed by the unusually large amounts of blood. Passersby were amazed by the unusually large amounts of blood. Passersby were amazed by the unusually large amounts of blood. Passersby were amazed by the unusually large amounts of blood. Passersby were amazed by the

unusually large amounts of blood. Passersby were amazed by the unusually large amounts of blood. Passersby were amazed by the unusually large amounts of blood. Passersby were amazed by the unusually large amounts of blood. Passersby were amazed by the unusually large amounts of blood. Passersby were amazed by the unusually large amounts of blood. Passersby were amazed by the unusually large amounts of blood. Passersby were amazed by the unusually large amounts of blood. Passersby were amazed by

see RUTABAGA page 253

I Insist You Borrow This Terrible Book And Tell Me How Much You Liked It

By Jim Thrum

I know you love to read, and I think I have something you'll really, really dislike. I just finished this book called *Dog Days*, by J. Phillip Edward, and it changed my life. I've never read anything that so perfectly captures the shallow things I think and feel every day. You absolutely must borrow it.

I know you're a busy person, but this book is just incredible. (To me, that is.) I mean, it blew my mind. I haven't read a book this meaningful since *Catcher In The Rye* back in high school, when I stopped reading books assigned to me by people with good taste. If you just give the first few cliche-ridden pages a try, I swear you'll be so put off, you'll want to throw it away. But I won't allow that, because I'll continue to hound you about it for weeks.

Look, I have it right here, and I think it's perfect for me. It's this incredibly trite story about a man who can't connect with people, so he creates a world where he talks to his pets. Then, after a while, they start to talk back to him, only you don't know if they're actually talking to him or if it's all in his imagination. I mean, like I said, you probably will be able to put it down after the first few pages. After that, it really doesn't pick up.

I really wish you'd read it, because I've been dying to discuss it with somebody. My mind has been reeling ever since I finished it. It's like a combination of William S. Burroughs' stream-of-consciousness and J.R.R. Tolkien's fantasy sensibility. It's a little "out there," and the narrative is a total mess, but it kind of just barely makes sense once you've finished and digested it.

Yes, it is a "pointless pile of claptrap." But why would you say such a thing? That kind of cynicism is just the sort of thing this book talks about. It says that people like you mask your real feelings with sarcasm and are incapable of genuine human expression. If anyone really needs to avoid this, it's you. You won't change your tune once you get to the part about the kleptomaniac monkey in the candy store. Or the part where the protagonist tearfully confesses his failings to a cat he's dressed as his mother.

Well, okay, I'm just going to leave it here, and you can pick it up. Go ahead. I'll turn my back so you won't feel guilty or foolish. My back is turned. Do you have it? No? I can't believe you're so closed-minded! The predictable twist ending alone is worth the 572 pages you have to plod through. Actually, it's not, but it was to me.

Dog Days is so much more than an endless string of cliches with a gimmicky ending slapped on, seemingly from out of nowhere. The characters are forgettable, too, failing to leap to life off the page. Like Salty, the wizened sea captain whose life of loneliness parallels that of the nameless protagonist. Or the ghost of Eva Braun, who tempts him and tries to keep him from doing good. It's a rich tapestry of bizarre, poorly established characters, implausible plot developments, and thinly veiled autobiographical conversations that a dumb guy like me can't help but fall in love with.

Well, if you change your mind, I'd be happy to loan it to you. That is, if I haven't loaned it to someone else by then. Right now, I'm reading the new John Gray book, which you'll find every bit as bad as you expect. I'll have to get it to you when I'm done. ∅

COKE from page 244

about the prospects for Coke Mandatory.

"I think that we learned a valuable lesson back in the '80s when we released New Coke," Hasworth said. "We learned that the only way to ensure that people will consume a new product is to make it non-optional. We are confident that Coke Mandatory is so good, the American people will not be able to resist." ∅

LIBRARY from page 241

implemented to help prevent an act of violence from happening there.

The first move, Quarles said, was to upgrade the library's 11-year-old security system. The current system consists of an entrance alarm armed after closing, an anti-theft detector located in the exit aisle, and three surveillance mirrors mounted in various corners of the library. Quarles said that a new, "far more advanced system" will be installed by the end of October at a cost of $71,000.

The library also plans to hire a part-time security guard. Marlin Pendergast, 44, of Per-Mar Security, will divide his time between the library and Applegate Mall, where he patrols the food court every weekday afternoon.

"Last week, one of the commentators on TV said a very smart thing: He said that the CIA made a mistake in recent years by relying too much on technology and moving away from human counterintelligence," library-board president Mary Beth Dutler said. "That's why, while an improved security system is important, it's still vital to have an actual person there to keep an eye on things. Marlin will be able to see things a camera simply can't."

Library employees, Quarles said, are also being asked to increase their on-the-job alertness, as they are "on the front line of library security."

"I've told my staff to keep their eyes and ears open for any suspicious behavior, and to not hesitate to report it to me, no matter how trivial it may initially appear," Quarles said. "They really are our best defense."

Above: Reference librarian Joanne Paul.

Library employees are also being asked to increase their on-the-job alertness, as they are "on the front line of library security."

As an added security measure, the overnight book-depository box will be permanently sealed.

"I know this may inconvenience some of our patrons who want to return materials after hours, but we just can't take any chances," Quarles said. "Pranksters slip things like gum wrappers and lollipop sticks through the outside drop slot all the time. It doesn't take too much imagination to envision someone inserting a small bomb with a timed detonator in there. It's unthinkable, but these days we have to consider the unthinkable."

During the Sept. 12 meeting, library officials took a walk around the library, examining its current state of security. They were appalled by what they found.

"Even though they'd been up for years, no one ever really looked at the surveillance mirrors," said reference-desk librarian Joanne Paul. "But as we were walking around the place, I realized that the mirror in the corner closest to the reference section wasn't even angled correctly. I could see the tops of the shelves and part of the ceiling, but nothing else. I'd never noticed it before, but what's the use of having the mirror if you can't see people who are up to no good?"

Quarles said that the library's locks will also be changed, as key accountability has grown "a little lax" in recent years.

"There are several former employees who never surrendered their keys upon quitting, and since we unfortunately have a locksmith down the street who's willing to overlook the 'do not copy' imprint on our master set, a lot of illicit key copies are floating around out there," Quarles said. "I take the blame for that one. Well, after we get the locks changed, only senior staffers will possess keys. Absolutely no exceptions. This is the 21st century now. Things have changed."

A number of the new security measures will directly affect the public: It will now become more difficult to obtain a library card, requiring a birth certificate and two forms of photo ID. The daily children's story hour has been shortened to 20 minutes. And while the library has always officially had a no-loitering rule on the books, it will now be strictly enforced.

Cedar Rapids residents are praising the security upgrade as a necessary response to the events on the East Coast.

"Some people might consider the prospect of metal detectors and three forms of ID for library cards a bit extreme, but we're living in a whole new world," longtime resident Frank Gonitz said. "The way I figure, if you've done nothing wrong, you have nothing to hide, right?"

"I can't believe just three weeks ago, I was naïve enough to believe that a library was a safe sanctuary for quiet reading and contemplative study," said Melinda Wallach, 52. "Maybe one day, things will return to normal. But I think the lesson here is, if it can happen at the Pentagon, it can happen anywhere." ∅

245

Arming Our Pilots

The Airline Pilots Association recently proposed that pilots be allowed to carry handguns to defend their cockpits. What do *you* think?

Denise Bassett
Guidance Counselor

"Pilots need to concentrate on flying the aircraft. Arm the Sky Chefs instead."

Irfan Clarence
Comedian

"As a mediocre stand-up comic, I'm all for it...'And what's with these pilots packin' heat? Boy, you damn well *better* return your tray table to the upright and locked position, Chester!'"

Richard Barnes
Systems Analyst

"We should give the pilots unloaded guns, and then ask the media not to report that they're unloaded. Also, don't print this."

Judy Weiss
Florist

"I don't like this plan quite as much as the one with the super-robots, but I suppose it'll have to do."

Pete Hecker
Shipping Clerk

"Pilots should get sawed-off shotguns. There's no reason they shouldn't be as well-armed as our pizza-delivery drivers."

Todd Pollack
Attorney

"Armed pilots? I see. Tell me: Just how many days should I allot for a New York-to-L.A. trip on Amtrak?"

The Return Of Michael Jordan

Ending months of speculation, Michael Jordan announced last week that he is returning to the NBA. How are Americans reacting to the news?

- Feeling an overwhelming sense of loss and numbness
- Attending candlelight vigils
- Wondering if life will ever return to normal
- Hanging American flag in window
- Feeling nervous before entering a tall building
- Donating to the New York Firefighters 9-11 Disaster Relief Fund
- Still not believing something like this could ever happen

the ONION
America's Finest News Source

Herman Ulysses Zweibel *Founder*

T. Herman Zweibel *Publisher Emeritus*
J. Phineas Zweibel *Publisher*
Maxwell Prescott Zweibel *Editor-In-Chief*

FOUNDED 1871 • "TU STULTUS ES"

Your Horoscope

By Lloyd Schumner Sr.
Retired Machinist and
A.A.P.B.-Certified Astrologer

Aries: (March 21–April 19)
You will find yourself in a bizarre alternate universe where the sun is on the wrong side of the sky and everyone looks like they're sleepwalking when you get up before noon for the first time in your life.

Taurus: (April 20–May 20)
A strange mixture of worry and relief fills your heart when you are laid off from the manure-packing factory.

Gemini: (May 21–June 21)
You used to think it would be cool to drive your own giant robot, but that's before you knew they were primarily used to weld bumpers onto trucks.

Cancer: (June 22–July 22)
If the guys make fun of you for walking around in lipstick, high heels, and a silk dress, just ignore them. After all, you're a woman.

Leo: (July 23–Aug. 22)
You must stop living in the past. Any changes you make back then may alter the present irreparably.

Virgo: (Aug. 23–Sept. 22)
Now more than ever, that peace sign you carry is going to get you shot at.

Libra: (Sept. 23–Oct. 23)
Scientific engineers are currently developing a range of high-tech tools to help America's doctors in their fight against your burning, itching foot fungus.

Scorpio: (Oct. 24–Nov. 21)
These times of economic turmoil might not be good for everyone, but your personal mission is to find a way to physically surf the Dow Jones average.

Sagittarius: (Nov. 22–Dec. 21)
Though it's certainly admirable to want to stay informed, your worship of Peter Jennings is beginning to affect your ability to function in daily life.

Capricorn: (Dec. 22–Jan. 19)
You will be embarrassed to learn that there is an effective, less messy method known as "chemical" castration.

Aquarius: (Jan. 20–Feb. 18)
Financial experts know that a number of factors are to blame for the downturn, but won't be able to shake the hunch that it was all your fault somehow.

Pisces: (Feb. 19–March 20)
Someday you must learn not to run away from your problems. But not today, when your problems are all giant boars.

POINT from page 243

monitor the TV shows and movies their children watch. Not billboards.

It's bad enough that corporations are poisoning our air, water, and

What's worse, many of these billboards are as tasteless as they are intrusive.

land. But turning every mile of our nation's roads into an eyesore? That just might be the straw that breaks the camel's back. Ø

COUNTERPOINT from page 243

I'm not like the billboard down the road that tells people to listen to the mean man on the radio or shows people in their underpants. I would not like it if they came and covered me. Then, I

am only half a billboard. Then, I am sad.

Maybe one day, I will be a big billboard and cover the entire side of a

I only like telling people about yogurt like a billboard is supposed to.

building. Then, the bad people won't bother me. I will be so big that when they come, they will look at me and say, "Billboard too big to paint. We afraid. Run away!"

If they run away, I won't laugh. I don't like scaring the bad people or anybody else. I only like telling people about Yoplait yogurt and other good things like a billboard is supposed to. That is what makes billboards happy. Ø

Former High-School Bully Pulls You Over For Speeding

see LOCAL page 4C

Vin Diesel Breaks Off Tracking Collar Against Rocky Outcropping

see PEOPLE page 2D

Telemarketer Won't Take 'Fuck Off And Die' For An Answer

see LOCAL page 10C

STATshot

A look at the numbers that shape your world.

Corporations Facing Bankruptcy

1. Pandas-B-Gone
2. General Motors International Coffee
3. Omelettes By Mail
4. We Fold Anything Corp.
5. U-Trawl
6. Nike tap-shoe division
7. Free Twenties, Inc.

CLOSED

THE ONION VOLUME 37 ISSUE 36
$2.00 US $3.00 CAN

0 74470 94595 6   36

---

the ONION®

VOLUME 37 ISSUE 36   **AMERICA'S FINEST NEWS SOURCE™**   **11–17 OCTOBER 2001**

Everybody Browsing At Video Store Saying Stupid Things

CHICAGO—Video Station customer Peter Lisowitz expressed annoyance and amusement Monday, when every single person in the video store was overheard saying "the stupidest things imaginable."

"I was wandering up and down the aisles looking for something to rent," Lisowitz said. "During that time, I was privy to some of the most ridiculously idiotic comments ever uttered."

In the 20 minutes Lisowitz browsed the store before deciding to rent *Memento*, he "actually heard with [his] own two ears" customers saying that *Being John Malkovich* was really weird and made no sense, *Dead Man Walking* was depressing and went on way too long, and Frances McDormand is too ugly to be in the movies.

In addition to dismissing movies and actors Lisowitz admires, customers had high praise for those he dislikes.

"Some woman said, 'Keanu Reeves is such a great actor. He just really gets into a role. I wish he'd do a movie with Tom Cruise. That'd be an amazing pairing,'" Lisowitz said. "That's an actual quote."

see VIDEO page 250

Freedoms Curtailed In Defense Of Liberty

WASHINGTON, DC—Responding to the threats facing America's free democratic system, White House officials called upon Americans to stop exercising their democratic freedoms Monday.

"In this time of national crisis, a time when our most cherished freedoms are threatened, all Americans—not just outspoken talk-show hosts like Bill Maher—must watch what they say," White House press secretary Ari Fleischer told reporters. "Now more than ever, if we want to protect democracy for future generations, it is vital that nobody speak out about the issues of the day."

"We must all do our patriotic duty to protect our country's great ideals," Fleischer continued, "and we have to be careful about what opinions we express if we are to defend our Constitution, a sacred document behind which all Americans must stand united as one."

Fleischer's sentiments

see LIBERTY page 249

Above: Ari Fleischer urges Americans to keep their mouths shut.

Husband, Wife Have Conflicting Ideas About What Constitutes Healthy Sex Life

Above: Lisa and Craig Livorno.

KNOXVILLE, TN—Craig and Lisa Livorno, Knoxville residents who have been married for nine years, possess different ideas about what constitutes a healthy sex life.

"After almost 10 years together, we still make time for romance," said Lisa, who often equates cuddling and kissing with sex. "Barely a day goes by when we don't get a little intimate."

"My parents were so cold and stiff," Lisa continued. "Their sex life was practically nonexistent. Craig and I are the exact opposite. It's always, 'I love you, honey... Give me a goodbye kiss!'"

While Craig enjoys hugging Lisa and telling her that he loves her, he equates a healthy sex life with frequent sexual intercourse. The couple, on average, has sex once a week, which is not enough for Craig.

"Lisa and I are both to blame," said Craig, who is under the mistaken impression that his wife would also like to have sex more often. "You get caught up in your life and, before you know it, you can't even remember the last time

see SEX LIFE page 250

Dildo Manufacturers Association: Nation Must Return To Normalcy, Purchase Dildos

CINCINNATI—With sales flagging since the Sept. 11 terrorist attacks, the Dildo Manufacturers Association made an appeal to Americans' sense of patriotism Monday, urging citizens to help the U.S. economy and the nation's dildo industry by purchasing the sex toys. "Like so many industries, we have been hit hard by recent events," DMA spokesman Richard Grantham said. "But the best way we can show Osama bin Laden our resolve is for all of us to get back out there and buy dildos like we did before all of this happened." Grantham said that on Oct. 20, a 14-inch, red-white-and-blue "Star Spangled Rammer" dildo will go on sale at sex shops across the nation, with proceeds benefiting relief efforts.

Move To Houseboat Regretted By Third Day

TARPON SPRINGS, FL—Semi-retired attorney George Schulman, 62, is already expressing remorse over his move into a Suncruiser 360 houseboat last Saturday. "I thought it would be more like *MacGyver* or, you know, *Simon & Simon*. But it's just sort of boring," Schulman told reporters Monday. "The whole marina reeks of old fish, and I'm gonna kill somebody if I hear another goddamn Jimmy Buffett song blaring from that oyster bar over by the dock." Schulman went on to express regret about spending more than $400 on Hawaiian-print shirts.

Screaming Japanese Schoolgirls Overturn Greenspan's Bus

TOKYO—Federal Reserve Chairman Alan Greenspan described himself as "shaken but all right" Monday following an incident in which several thousand excited young Japanese fans mobbed and tipped over his tour bus after a speech at the Tokyo Dome. "Mr. Greenspan is at the height of his popularity in Japan right now," said Martine Engers, a publicist for the chairman, who is currently in the midst of a 41-city world tour. "And I guess we simply weren't prepared for this level of fan hysteria." Before military police restored order, thousands of frantically speculating youths drove the Nikkei average past 16,000.

Diary Lied To

GRAND JUNCTION, CO—Marnie Powell, a seventh-grader at Grand Junction Middle School, lied to her diary Monday, filling the journal with several out-and-out fabrications. "I had the best time at Jessica's party," wrote the 13-year-old honors student, recording the falsehood in purple ink. "There were tons of cool guys, and I had so much fun dancing." In actuality, the socially awkward, bespectacled Powell tentatively bobbed up and down on the perimeter of the dance floor for 30 seconds before retreating to the refreshment table for the remaining three hours of the event.

Area Grasshopper Kind Of A Thorax Man Himself

LARGE FIELD EAST OF WATER—Watching a shapely female grasshopper pass by, area grasshopper 44-3541-M told a fellow male Monday that he is "a definite thorax man." "Don't get me wrong, I love a good abdomen," 44-3541-M said. "But a nice, shiny mesothorax? Right where the wings connect? Oh, man, you can't beat that." 44-3541-M added that he'd let 97-94732-F, an attractive female praying mantis from a nearby elm tree, devour his head anytime. ∅

Formerly Evil Wrestler Realizes Error Of His Ways

PONTIAC, MI—Manzilla, the American Wrestling Federation villain reviled for inflicting countless blindside folding-chair blows and barbed-wire-bat bludgeonings upon helpless opponents, rocked the world of sports entertainment Monday by converting to the forces of good.

Witnessed by a sellout Pontiac Silverdome crowd, Manzilla's change of heart occurred almost 10 minutes into a tag-team match that paired him with Fatback against AWF pretty boy Trent Vanity and the mysterious Quasar. After Fatback knocked Quasar out of the ring, Manzilla tagged in and promptly spread a box of carpet tacks across the mat. He then grabbed Vanity and restrained him with a powerful sleeper hold.

But instead of throwing Vanity onto the dangerous tacks, Manzilla stunned the capacity crowd by falling silent, losing himself in deep thought. After nearly two full minutes of reflection, Manzilla released Vanity. The self-described Man-Monster From Beyond then picked up announcer Golden Throat's heavy chair and smashed it into Fatback's shoulder blades, sending him sprawling across the canvas and handing the match to Vanity and Quasar.

In a ringside interview after the match, Manzilla informed the world that his actions were the result of a profound personal epiphany.

Manzilla said his actions were the result of a profound personal epiphany.

"You listen to me now, people," said the 6' 7", 320-pound two-time AWF champion, speaking directly into a nearby camera. "I want to say something to all my former partners in the Coalition Of Wrong, to all my former tag-team partners, from the War Pigs to the Stink Squad, and to my now-ex-girlfriend Lustula. I have seen the light. I will no longer be a bad example to children everywhere. I thought you were my friends, but I was wrong. You thought you could control me, but *you* were wrong. And at Battle Among The Cattle, next month in the Calgary Saddledome, you'll all see just how wrong."

Manzilla was then joined by Trent Vanity, who thanked and congratulated him on his conversion amid a mixed chorus of cheers and boos

Above: Manzilla before (left) and after his conversion to the forces of good.

from the 79,000 in attendance.

Reaction among Manzilla's colleagues has been mixed.

"I, for one, welcome him out of the darkness and into the ranks of the good guys," said the Shriekin' Deacon, long regarded as the AWF's moral and spiritual leader. "Being abandoned on the steps of the San Diego Zoo's reptile house could not have been an easy beginning for young Manzilla. But he has overcome that, and now he sees the light."

"No way will I ever trust that guy," said Quasar, the self-anointed five-time Mr. Alternate Universe. "I don't care if he did save my bacon from the War Pigs: A zebra doesn't change its stripes that quick—let alone a skunk. If he truly has changed, so be it. But be warned,

Manzilla: Quasar's Virtuous Vision is upon you. If this is treachery, not just me, but my mate Bicepta and partner Vic Viking will be there."

Manzilla, sequestered in an unknown location since renouncing his evil ways, said he has adopted a new name that is better suited to his new disposition.

"The man you knew as Manzilla will use that name no more," wrote Manzilla in a letter read aloud by Golden Throat. "To all my former enemies—Big Chief Beef, Barry Hatchett, Half-Ton, Diamond Ralph, and Santa's Biggest Helper—my wrath has abated. From now on, I shall be known as Gorgeousaur, and my stunning good looks shall reflect my newfound inner peace."

The letter also made an impas-

see WRESTLER page 249

I Wish I Were Hungry

By Cal Link

Oh, man, you know what would be great right now? A big bowl of chili, swimming in tabasco, with diced onions, grated cheddar, and Saltines. Damn. I just wish I wasn't so stuffed from that big lunch, or I could dig into one of those big-time.

Or this would be even better: a full Italian dinner. Salad, lasagna, garlic breadsticks, bottomless Coke. God, if only I was hungry, that would kick ass. I'd walk into the restaurant, my stomach would start growling right as I sat down, and I'd proceed to stuff my face for a good hour or so. I'd kill to have room for something like that.

It just sucks having all this extra money in my pocket, and no food to spend it on. I stopped at the ATM yesterday afternoon, and I still have three twenties in my wallet. Worse yet, payday is tomorrow. I mean, I'm not complaining about having lots of money, but I just wish I had the stomach space to blow some of it on an all-you-can-eat Chinese buffet with General Tsao's chicken and pork fried rice. In my current state, I'd be lucky to get a fortune cookie down.

My big mistake was getting the full-blown gyro platter at the Parthenon. That always fills me to the roof. I'm usually not hungry for four or five hours after that. I guess that's what I get for overdoing it.

Oh, my God. I just remembered. The Old Towne Steakhouse is having the special this week on the 12-ounce Porterhouse. One of those, a baked potato, green beans with slivered almonds...

Curse this full belly!

Damn me for a fool, why did I have to gorge on the whole giant gyro platter? With the fries and a huge piece of baklava for dessert, no less. If I'd only had the one gyro and a drink, I might be able to eat a calzone or something now. The night ahead promises to be a grim, foodless ordeal.

I don't believe this. *Dark Angel* is on in 10 minutes, and if I can't summon up some hunger, it's going to be a less-than-total sensory experience. Just sight and sound. I mean, I could snack on some chips, but whoop-dee-doo. That's not *eating*-eating. I want to be legitimately hungry. Hungry enough for one of those big-as-your-head chicken molé burritos from Burritoville. Man, those starving peasants in other countries have it so good. They're so hungry, I bet they can eat whatever they want.

Why couldn't I have gotten up earlier today? Then I could've had that big western omelette around 9 a.m., then lunch around noon. Oh, man, my stomach is yearning to be yearning for something to eat right now!

In America, the hungry man is king! His city's downtown district is a palatial theme park of tantalizing eateries, all competing for his dollar! "Friday Night Fish Fry"? Hmmm... not today, thank you. "Serving Award-Winning Ribs And Chops For 35 Years"? Could be good, I'll make a note of it. "World's Best Peanut Butter Pie"? Eh, the line's too long. What's this? "Specializing In Moroccan And Tunisian Cuisine"? Here I choose! Fill my belly, merchant! That is the life of the American man blessed by hunger! But packed as my craw is with food, I might as well be living in Communist Russia.

Maybe if I drink a lot of seltzer, I can hurk up some gas and make room. Then, I could at least have a sandwich or something.

Damn this satiated gut! ∅

LIBERTY from page 247

echoed those of many executive-branch officials, who, in the wake of the Sept. 11 attacks, have called for broad-based limitations on civil liberties—and urged all patriotic, freedom-loving citizens to support those restrictions—in defense of the American way of life.

"We live in a land governed by plurality of opinion in an open electorate, but we are now under siege by adherents of a fundamentalist, totalitarian belief system that tolerates no dissent," Attorney General John Ashcroft said. "Our most basic American values are threatened by an enemy opposed to everything for which our flag stands. That is why I call upon all Americans to submit to wiretaps, e-mail monitoring, and racial profiling. Now is not the time to allow simplistic, romantic notions of 'civil liberties' and 'equal protection under the law' to get in the way of our battle with the enemies of freedom."

In the past, Ashcroft said, efforts by federal agencies to restrict personal freedoms were "severely hampered" by such factors as the judicial system, the Bill Of Rights, and "government by the people." Since the attacks, however, some such limitations have been waived, finally giving the CIA, FBI, Pentagon, and White House the greater powers they need to defend freedom.

U.S. Sen. John McCain (R-AZ), who advocated permitting the CIA to engage in various illegal activities during a recent *Tonight Show With Jay Leno* appearance, stressed the importance of not merely submitting to freedom-

> ## Said McCain: "Now is not the time for, 'My opinion is just as valid as yours,' and 'What are my country's leaders doing and why?' and 'I have a question, Mr. President.'"

curtailment policies, but also blindly agreeing with them.

"Now is not the time for such divisive, destructive things as dialogue and debate," McCain said. "Now is not the time for, 'My opinion is just as valid as yours,' and 'What are my country's leaders doing and why?' and 'I have a question, Mr. President.' Now is the time for one thing and one thing only: The defense of the American democratic ideal. Any and all who disagree with this directive, or who have different ideas about how it should be accomplished, should learn to shut their mouths."

As the U.S. prepares to mobilize forces against Afghanistan, the military is seeking strong limitations on the press. Defense Secretary Donald Rumsfeld said such a Constitution-flouting move would not be unprecedented, citing the suspension of *habeas corpus* in the Civil War and the order to round up 110,000 Japanese-Americans in detention camps after the bombing of Pearl Harbor.

"Remember, under the oppressive Taliban regime, people live in constant fear of an oppressive order to which all must submit," Rumsfeld said. "Under their system, it is illegal to practice a different religion or support a different political system. It is against the law for women to work or leave their homes without their faces covered. There is no freedom of speech, press, or assembly, as dissent of any kind is not tolerated. It is even forbidden to smile or laugh in public, and all who fail to unquestioningly obey are punished with reprisals of brutal violence. We must not allow such a regime to threaten our great democracy. We must stand for something better than that."

"It is therefore urgent," Rumsfeld continued, "that all Americans be quiet, stop asking questions, accept the orders of authorities, and let us get on with the important work of defending liberty, so that America can continue to be a beacon of freedom to all the world." ∅

WRESTLER from page 248

sioned plea for the hand of Princess Miss Lovelady, the AWF's most untouchable beauty. Lovelady declined comment on the matter.

AWF insiders said it's too early

> ## The letter also made an impassioned plea for the hand of Princess Miss Lovelady, the AWF's most untouchable beauty.

to know if Manzilla's spiritual reawakening is to be believed.

"If it's for real, it is the greatest turnaround in wrestling history," said longtime wrestling insider Clean Steve Borglund. "But it's hard to believe that this man is capable of good. The wrestler who single-handedly destroyed the career of Million-Dollar Bill? The fork-tongued heel who has come perilously close to race-baiting the Chocolate Tornado? The only man dastardly enough to team up with Bad Smells Smith? Something tells me we don't have the whole story here. I suppose we'll have to wait until [pay-per-view event] Halloween Havoc III to find out." ∅

Returning To Abnormal

A Room Of Jean's Own
By Jean Teasdale

When I began writing this column seven years ago, I never imagined in my wildest dreams that I'd have to address anything like the events of Sept. 11, 2001. What happened is unimaginable and unthinkable. We're all going through a really hard time right now, and I'm sure each one of us has considered our future. Will times get even harder? What is my place in all of this? How much control over our lives do we really have? All of these are important questions.

As for me, I've been thinking and feeling a lot these past few weeks, probably more than I have in my whole life put together. I've been sad, angry, mournful, contemplative, and confused. I've wondered if war will only make things worse, or if we have gone beyond the point where peace is possible. I've wanted to believe that supporting our country would keep us strong, but couldn't deny that I had serious doubts about our fate. Nor could I deny that my faith in God wavered a little. Does He disapprove of what happened? Does He even care? After a great deal of soul-searching, I finally arrived at a conclusion.

I decided to pretend that all of this never happened.

I couldn't believe how much better I felt! Why I hadn't thought of it before? I was like, "Earth to Jean! Earth to Jean, do you read? Hel-lo!" What's the point of making yourself sick with worry and doubt? That's no way to live... unless you're making reservations for a permanent stay at the funny farm!

I mean, that's what the terrorists want, right? They want us to be Gloomy Guses with frowns hanging to the ground. Well, like our president said, we shouldn't give in to these terrorists. And to that, my personal response is, "What terrorists?"

You Jeanketeers are probably wondering how it's possible to pretend that all this never happened. It's simple: Emotionally withdraw from the world! I mean, greet the world with a smile and a positive attitude, but treat everything—what's the word I want to use here?—superficially!

I think we all owe it to ourselves to retreat into our little worlds. We should bake ourselves sinful chocolate delicacies! We should coo over the 2001-edition Christmas ornaments at the Hallmark store! We should savor the latest Lillian Vernon catalog! We should daydream about making out with Patrick Swayze on an exotic Hawaiian beach as we drive to work! We should cut out pictures of mouth-watering dishes from *Martha Stewart Living* and paste them in our scrapbook! We should dress our cats in doll clothes and take pictures of them! In short, we should pursue the distractions that make our lives fulfilling and worthwhile, because life is not about getting angry over things you cannot control, but pleasing yourself.

I told this to Roz, my Fashion Bug supervisor, and she just looked at me with her mouth wide open. At first, I thought she was impressed, but all she could say was, "Jean, that's the weirdest and most irresponsible thing I've heard since all of this happened."

I wasn't fazed. I replied, "Since all of *what* happened?" Roz's mouth opened even wider, and she stormed away without a word.

Things weren't much different on the homefront. That night, hubby Rick came home from work, proudly showing me his new "When We Get Through With Them, Afghanistan's Gonna Be Af-GONE-istan" T-shirt. I said I didn't get it. He snorted, "Ain't you been around a TV the last few weeks, Jean?" I said, "Of course I have! You know I'd never go a day without my soaps!" Boy, that really knocked Rick for a loop! He slowly backed out of the living room, staring at me like I'd grown an extra leg or something!

But you know what? Roz, Rick, and all the rest of them don't bother me. After all, I can't expect the whole world to understand where I'm coming from. I realize that not everyone is a self-centered Midwestern woman with a low-paying retail job who's never been farther east than Columbus, OH. But this is what God has made me, and I think the best thing I can do right now is to not question it and just be me.

So if, like me, you're lucky enough to be in a position to be self-centered, don't feel guilty about it. Go for the gusto! (It may one day be a luxury none of us can afford.)

I'll continue to do my thing, putting up with good ol' hubby Rick, spoiling my flabby tabbies, and working at Fashion Bug. Because I think it's important that some things stay static and unchanging. It's what puts stability in our lives. And if I can do anything to cheer up even one of you Somber Sallys, it's all been worth it.

This may seem egotistical, but, for the first time in my life, I feel like I can say this with complete certainty: The world needs Jean Teasdale!

Now, if you'll pardon me, my Fingerhut catalog awaits! ∅

SEX LIFE from page 247

you had sex. We both need to make more time."

Lisa and Craig agree that they should be more adventurous in the bedroom. Each, however, assumes that the other defines "adventure" the same way.

"I'd love to push things a little further, like experiment with leather restraints and maybe even try some anal sex," Craig said. "I'd definitely be into that."

Lisa is also eager to push the envelope, having recently read a *Cosmopolitan* article titled "25 Sizzling Sex Tips To Keep Your Husband Begging For More" that suggests candles, silk sheets, and flavored condoms.

"It says, 'A woman should not be afraid to wear sexy lingerie, talk dirty sometimes, or give her man a full body massage,'" said Lisa, read-

> ## "Craig loves telling me forbidden stuff— things we'd never actually do."

ing aloud from the article while giggling nervously. "Some of the suggestions are a little out there, but a lot of it is very—how shall I say it?—intriguing."

Lisa said she believes that openness and honesty are crucial to enjoying a healthy sex life.

"So many other couples are afraid to talk about sex, but not us," Lisa said. "For example, I can say, 'George Clooney is so hot!' and Craig is totally fine with it."

In the spirit of kinkiness, Lisa said she encourages Craig to tell her his wildest fantasies and vice versa.

"I love it when Craig tells me about the crazy stuff he'd like to do," Lisa said. "It really turns me on. Once, he called me from work and said, 'I'd love for you to come by my office on your lunch break so we can do it on my desk.' I thought that was so sexy of him to say that! He loves telling me forbidden stuff like that—things we'd never actually do."

Craig, on the other hand, would like to act on some of his fantasies, a desire he erroneously assumed was implicit in telling Lisa about them.

"It would be cool, if the circumstances were right, to get together with another couple," Craig recently told Lisa. "Since we're so happy and secure, I thought a little 'swinging' might be good for us." Oblivious to her husband's seriousness, Lisa replied, "Ooh, that would be so wild! Can you imagine?"

"Sometimes, I think about rent-

ing a dirty movie," Lisa said. "You know, like an actual porno. I'm sure Craig has those kinds of filthy thoughts, too. We both like to do new things. It's what keeps a marriage interesting."

Like his wife, Craig is interested in renting pornography. Unlike his wife, however, he is also interested in videotaping themselves having sex; having Lisa "forget" to wear underwear under her skirt when they go out to dinner; penetrating Lisa doggy-style while she wears a French-maid outfit; receiving fellatio from her in an alley; having intercourse in a restaurant, movie theater, or public library; watching Lisa secretly seduce a male stranger in a bar and invite him back to a hotel room on the condition that her husband can watch; and inviting Allison, the couple's sexy 23-year-old neighbor, over for coffee, only to find out that she works as a stripper and would like to have some feedback on her act and could use a little help from Lisa getting her bra undone. ∅

VIDEO from page 247

Above: Peter Lisowitz

Adding to Lisowitz's disbelief, a college-aged male held up a *Rush Hour* box for approval from his girlfriend. She responded by saying, "Ew, I hate foreign films."

"Not only does she think, for some unfathomable reason, that the presence of Jackie Chan makes the movie 'foreign,' but she makes the blanket statement that she hates foreign films—all of them," Lisowitz said. "Yeah, you're right. Foreign films, on the whole, just aren't worth watching. Better stick to high-quality American fare like *The Waterboy* and *Tomcats*."

Added Lisowitz: "It's not like I'm some freako movie snob who only watches Fellini and Cassavetes films. I liked *Saving Private Ryan* and *Toy Story 2*. And *Meet The Parents* was pretty good. But these people are complete retards."

According to Lisowitz, when choosing a movie to rent, many customers based their decision on "shit you wouldn't believe," such as the picture on the video's box, the impressive number of copies on the store's shelf, or their memories of the trailer for the film.

"This girl goes, 'I never saw *What Women Want*, but I remember it looked really funny in the trailer. Mel Gibson shaves his legs and puts on makeup and pantyhose. And there's this scene where he catches

see VIDEO page 251

Helen Hunt looking at his crotch. We gotta get it,'" he said. "I didn't know whether to laugh or cry."

Continued Lisowitz: "Then, I hear this other guy go, 'I heard *Driven* was really good.' How? From whom? Who are your friends? Where could you possibly have obtained that information? These people were like aliens from a planet where everyone is a moron and watches bad movies."

Lisowitz said that another customer based his rental decision on a heavily manipulated, ellipses-riddled, exclamation-point-augmented quote from *Rolling Stone* film critic Peter Travers. Reading the back of the box for the critically panned *Blow*, the unidentified man told his female companion, "The guy from *Rolling Stone* says it's "full of... visual dazzle! A [wild ride] with... a bravura performance from Depp! *Blow* delivers!"

"How could anybody be swayed by that?" Lisowitz asked. "It's obvious they had to mangle the hell out of the original review to get that blurb. When have you ever read a movie review that had exclamation points?"

The stupidity, Lisowitz said, was not limited to Video Station customers. Store employees also seemed to know little about film.

"I asked the store manager if there was an anime section," Lisowitz said. "So he says to me, 'Most of the Disney stuff is in the kids section. Is there a specific cartoon I can help you find?' This is the *manager*."

Lisowitz insisted that he was not trying to eavesdrop on his fellow customers.

"I swear, I'm not a snoop—you just couldn't avoid hearing them," Lisowitz said. "The aisles were crawling with people saying things like, '*Autumn In New York* made me bawl' and 'I've seen *American Pie*, like, 25 times.' It took every ounce of strength in my body to keep me from punching that guy, like, 25 times."

Though he did not punch anyone, Lisowitz admitted to rolling his eyes several times and emitting the occasional "pfff" sound. ∅

---

the **ONION** presents

Job-Hunting Tips

Today's job market is more competitive than ever. Here are some tips to help give you the edge:

- Make sure your résumé is free of spelling and grammatical errors, grease stains, crumbs, blood splatters, and bits of hair and gristle.

- Be aggressive: Don't be afraid to call a potential employer every few hours and say, "Is there an opening yet? How 'bout now? How 'bout now? Now?"

- When waiting for a job interview and a fellow applicant is there, strike up a conversation. Then, when it's your turn to be interviewed, stand up and say, "See ya, sicko." Explain to the interviewer that he invited you to a goat-sex orgy.

- If you find the "Notable Achievements" section of your résumé lacking, consider listing the longest rat-tail you've ever grown.

- Avoid borrowing liberally from the plots of popular Tom Clancy and John LeCarré novels when describing previous job experiences.

- If you attended Harvard, Yale, or another prestigious Ivy League institution, don't bother noting this on your résumé. Or even creating a résumé at all. Just have one of the other assholes from your school get you a job.

- Be sure to pronounce résumé "REH-zoo-may," which means "a list of one's accomplishments and qualifications," and not like the word "resume," which means "to unpause Resident Evil 3."

- After providing a contact number for your "former employer at Merrill Lynch," be sure to change your answering machine to say, "Hi, this is Merrill Lynch, we're not in right now."

- If, during an interview, you sense that they have detected one or more of the falsehoods in your résumé, throw a smoke bomb on the floor and escape in the ensuing confusion.

- When a job application asks you to list "Reason You Left Previous Job," make it clear you were not at fault. Write, "Boss was total Nazi."

- Have a long history of experience in the field you're applying for and glowing recommendations. Either that, or print your résumé on really nice, heavyweight ivory paper.

- Post your résumé online. This will give it an air of authority and legitimacy that only the Internet can confer.

- Being state archery champion is impressive, indeed. But Hardee's is more interested in knowing if you're intelligent enough to avoid deep-frying your hands.

- When writing a cover letter to a prospective employer, stress that, although you used to admire their company, they totally suck now, but that if they hire you, you can help make them great again. That will definitely work.

- Don't be afraid to list "Cook County Correctional Facility" on your résumé. They could think maybe you worked there or something.

Chemical And Biological Weapons

Many Americans fear that terrorists may one day strike the U.S. with chemical and biological weapons. What do *you* think about the prospect?

Donna McKechnie
Student

"It's certainly frightening to consider, but I take comfort in the fact that it can't happen to me. It can't happen to me. It can't happen to me. It can't happen..."

Dan Desmond
Landscaper

"This is the plague The Bible done talked about."

Fran Lake
Homemaker

"Let's not take any chances—we should arrest and detain The Chemical Brothers immediately."

Christopher King
Systems Analyst

"I'm not breathing any air until I've seen somebody else breathe it first."

Jordan Ryback
Cashier

"Speaking of which, don't go in the bathroom for a while. I just dropped a toxic payload of catastrophic size in there, man."

Michael Cuyler
Contractor

"I bought a gas mask for protection. I also bought an anthrax vaccine, a safety suit, and a hermetically sealed house that I never leave."

The New *Star Trek* Series

Last week, *Enterprise* made its debut on UPN. What can viewers expect from the latest *Star Trek* installment?

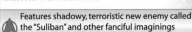

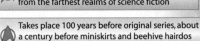

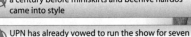

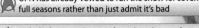

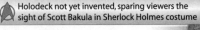

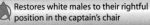

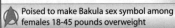

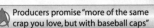

- Features shadowy, terroristic new enemy called the "Suliban" and other fanciful imaginings from the farthest realms of science fiction
- Takes place 100 years before original series, about a century before miniskirts and beehive hairdos came into style
- UPN has already vowed to run the show for seven full seasons rather than just admit it's bad
- Holodeck not yet invented, sparing viewers the sight of Scott Bakula in Sherlock Holmes costume
- Restores white males to their rightful position in the captain's chair
- Is totally unlike any previous Star Trek series because, uh, well, the guns sound kinda different
- Poised to make Bakula sex symbol among females 18-45 pounds overweight
- Producers promise "more of the same crap you love, but with baseball caps"

the ONION

America's Finest News Source

Herman Ulysses Zweibel *Founder*

T. Herman Zweibel *Publisher Emeritus*
J. Phineas Zweibel *Publisher*
Maxwell Prescott Zweibel *Editor-In-Chief*

FOUNDED 1871 • "TU STULTUS ES"

Your Horoscope

By Lloyd Schumner Sr.
Retired Machinist and
A.A.P.B.-Certified Astrologer

Aries: (March 21–April 19)
Your inability to get a cab has nothing to do with your neighborhood or skin color. It's because you live in Basco, WI, population 132.

Taurus: (April 20–May 20)
You will experience a strange kind of moral and spiritual vertigo when you find yourself sympathizing with Army recruiters for the first time in your life.

Gemini: (May 21–June 21)
Your acquisition of a state-of-the-art supercomputer will mark your entry into the elite, top rank of the world's solitaire players.

Cancer: (June 22–July 22)
You're beginning to detect strong feelings of ill will from the other people at the office. You should stop showing up every day or get a job there.

Leo: (July 23–Aug. 22)
Your best friend will finally prove to everyone's satisfaction that his crippled old grandmother could take you in a fight.

Virgo: (Aug. 23–Sept. 22)
Though they are brown and have two legs, they are kangaroos, not pants.

Libra: (Sept. 23–Oct. 23)
While reading the biography of famed designer Bill Mitchell, you learn, much to your surprise, that you are an example of planned obsolescence.

Scorpio: (Oct. 24–Nov. 21)
You will finally achieve a lifelong dream of getting on television when you jump up and down and wave while standing behind the teary, emotional reporter.

Sagittarius: (Nov. 22–Dec. 21)
In dogsledding, persistence is everything. However, you're starting to think that it would be easier to simply wait for winter.

Capricorn: (Dec. 22–Jan. 19)
After 14 long years, you will be admitted to the Baseball Hall Of Fame when you finally come up with the $11.50 admission price.

Aquarius: (Jan. 20–Feb. 18)
The stars would like to remind you that their birthday may be a ways off, but nothing on their list is exactly cheap.

Pisces: (Feb. 19–March 20)
You are starting to find yourself more and more obsessed with people who, unlike yourself, actually do things.

NODES from page 243

blood. Passersby were amazed by the unusually large amounts of blood. Passersby were amazed by the unusually large amounts of blood. Passersby were amazed by the unusually large amounts of blood. Passersby were amazed by the unusually large amounts of blood. Passersby were amazed by the unusually large amounts of blood. Passersby were amazed by the unusually large amounts of blood. Passersby were amazed by the unusually large amounts of blood. Passersby were amazed by the unusually large amounts of blood. Passersby were amazed by the unusually large amounts of blood. Passersby were amazed by the unusually large amounts of blood. Passersby were amazed by the unusually large amounts of blood. Passersby were amazed by the unusually large amounts of blood. Passersby were amazed by the unusually large amounts of blood. Passersby were amazed by the unusually large amounts of blood. Passersby were amazed by the unusually large amounts of blood. Passersby were amazed by the unusually large amounts of blood. Passersby were amazed by the

unusually large amounts of blood. Passersby were amazed by the unusually large amounts of blood. Passersby were amazed by the unusually large amounts of blood. Passersby were amazed by the unusually large amounts of blood. Passersby were amazed by the

You'll never guess what I've packed my sinus cavities with!

unusually large amounts of blood. Passersby were amazed by the unusually large amounts of blood. Passersby were amazed by the unusually large amounts of blood. Passersby were amazed by the unusually large amounts of blood. Passersby were amazed by the unusually large amounts of blood. Passersby were amazed by the unusually large amounts of blood. Passersby were amazed by the

see NODES page 259

NEWS

New 'Toastables' Offers Microwavable Pre-Toasted Bread

see PRODUCTWATCH page 8C

Rush Limbaugh's Love Affair With Sound Of Own Voice Comes To Sad End

see MEDIA page 6D

Vegetarian Opens Can Of Meatless Whup-Ass

see LOCAL page 2B

STATshot

A look at the numbers that shape your world.

Whom Are We Imagining Naked?

1. That girl who runs the juice cart
2. Wife back when we met her
3. Veteran *Washington Post* columnist David Broder
4. That chick the senator had killed
5. Teri Garr circa *Young Frankenstein*
6. The congregation

THE ONION VOLUME 37 ISSUE 37
$2.00 US $3.00 CAN

0 74470 94595 6   37

the ONION®

VOLUME 37 ISSUE 37   **AMERICA'S FINEST NEWS SOURCE**™   **18–24 OCTOBER 2001**

Bob Hope Not Told About War

TOLUCA LAKE, CA—Bob Hope's doctors and support staff have elected not to tell the 98-year-old show-business legend about the current military conflict in Afghanistan.

"Bob is a true patriot, and whenever he hears about a new war, he wants to get out there and entertain the troops," said Dr. Allan Reese, Hope's physician at Providence St. Joseph Medical Center, on Monday. "We figured between his pneumo-

see HOPE page 255

Right: Hope enjoys a bowl of ice cream.

Fourth-Graders' Button-Making-Machine Privileges Suspended Indefinitely

THOUSAND OAKS, CA—The button-making privileges of Mrs. Orlowski's fourth-grade class were suspended indefinitely Monday, when an estimated 15 students were found to have used the Harrison Elementary School button maker to create "wholly inappropriate" buttons.

"These students were trusted with school equipment, and they betrayed that trust," said teacher Karen Orlowski, 47, holding a pair of confiscated buttons reading "Suck My Ass" and "Farty Fart." "I signed this button maker out of the school supply closet so that the students could spend their lunch hour creating fun, colorful buttons for the upcoming student-council elections. Instead, I return to find this."

see BUTTONS page 256

Above: A handful of the confiscated buttons sit on Mrs. Orlowski's desk.

Walking Sports Database Scorns Walking Sci-Fi Database

Above: Moreland (left) and the object of his mockery and derision.

PASSAIC, NJ—Scott Moreland, a walking database of sports facts and figures, scorned Tim Dansby, a walking database of science-fiction anecdotes and trivia, Monday afternoon.

"God, what a friggin' geek," said Moreland, eyeing Dansby in the food court of Willowbrook Mall. "Saturday nights, I bet he gets together with his other geek buddies and whacks off to *Star Wars* on video. He's probably never even gotten laid."

Moreland, a 27-year-old bachelor who spends most Saturday nights watching ESPN and checking for injury updates on CNNSI.com, then left the food court and headed to The Fan Zone, where he browsed a rack of extra-large New York Giants jerseys.

"Back in high school, there were a bunch of guys like that in my study hall. They'd spend the entire period talking about *Alien Nation*. I swear, they knew every line from every episode by heart," said Moreland, who can recite the batting average and on-base percentage of every member of the '86 Mets. "Who needs to memorize that kind of stuff? How useless is that?"

A self-described "sports fanatic" who experiences vicarious thrills through such idols as Mike Piazza

see DATABASE page 256

Woman With Sore Throat Thinks It Might Be Anthrax

NEW YORK—Alicia Dubrow, 23, an assistant copy editor at *Shape* magazine, expressed fear Monday that her recent sore throat is the result of anthrax. "I haven't had a sore throat in, like, two years, and suddenly I get one," said Dubrow, searching WebMD for information on symptoms of the disease. "I've also sort of had a backache lately, which is weird." Dubrow, who made a mental note to watch closely for reddish-brown sores, said she dropped by the *Shape* mailroom last Friday to grab a box of rubber bands but does not recall handling any packages.

NBC To Add *Dateline: Flursday*

NEW YORK—Seeking to capitalize on the success of its nightly newsmagazine, NBC announced Monday the addition of *Dateline: Flursday* to its schedule. "Now, you can turn to *Dateline* for incisive, in-depth reporting eight nights a week," NBC News president Neal Shapiro said. "Look to NBC as the news leader—Flursdays and beyond." If the new program is successful, the network plans to add Tuednesday and Fritaturday editions.

Monkfish Wishes Monkfish Weren't All The Rage

BOOTHBAY HARBOR, ME—A local monkfish bemoaned the culinary trendiness of his species Monday. "It's nice to be the fish of the moment," said the monkfish, avoiding one of the many fishing lines littering his Gulf of Maine seabed ever since the October issue of *Gourmet* proclaimed him "the new dorade." "And, yes, my flesh is firm, sweet, low in fat, and similar to lobster. But it hardly compares to the pleasures of, say, a nice sautéed tilapia with lime." He further urged people who feel they must consume members of the Family Squatinidae to try angel sharks, which he described as "assholes."

Manager Hates To See You Go

DURHAM, NC—Twist 'N' Shout manager Dale Fontana expressed deep regret Monday over your decision to leave the mall pretzelry. "Well, you've been a good employee, no doubt about that," said Fontana, folding up your returned uniform. "It'll be tough to replace you at the register." Fontana added that, should your new career not work out, you would always be welcome back in the growing field of pretzel preparation and retail.

Amsterdam Tourist Can't Find 'Kind Bud' In Phrasebook

AMSTERDAM—While on vacation in Amsterdam Monday, Atlanta resident Brad Haines, 22, struggled to find the Dutch translation for "kind bud" in his Berlitz pocket guide. "Man, I read the entire 'food and restaurant' chapter twice," he said. "It's not in there anywhere." Haines noted that he did at least learn that Amsterdam waiters will not bring the check to the table until specifically asked.

Dad Immediately Hands Phone To Mom

SAGINAW, MI—Emotionally distant father Bill Wolk, 55, immediately handed the phone to his wife Monday upon identifying the caller as his daughter. "Oh, hello, Jessica. Hold on, I'll get your mom," said Wolk, passing Jessica off before she even asked for anyone. In the past five years, Wolk's most touching display of fatherly affection was a 1996 remark that Jessica "marched nice and straight" with her high-school band in the Rose Bowl parade. ⌀

Marital Frustrations Channeled Through Thermostat

DULUTH, MN—Continuing a decades-long pattern of displacement, Carl and Barb Kulick channeled their marital frustrations through their home's Honeywell T87 manual-control thermostat Monday.

"You should have heard Carl scream when he saw I turned the heat on today," said the understimulated, affection-starved Barb, 62. "It was chilly, and our grandson Cory was over. There's no reason for a 4-year-old boy to feel like he's freezing to death, is there? I didn't think so, but apparently, somebody around here thinks there is."

To anyone familiar with Carl's long-standing rule that the Kulick thermostat stay securely in the "off" position until November, Barb's use of it could be interpreted as an act of defiance.

"There's no need to turn it on yet," said Carl, 64, who for 20 years has strongly suspected that his wife had an affair with neighbor Phil Tewksbury in 1981. "It's a goddamn waste of money. That woman acts like we're made of money."

On numerous occasions, Barb has pointed out the illogic of tying thermostat use to a date rather than temperature. Carl, however, stands firmly by his Nov. 1 start date. As the family's sole breadwinner, working long hours at a cement-supply company, Carl said it is his right to make the rules and his duty to protect the family from Barb's "dingbat notions."

"If I didn't put my foot down, Barb would have that thing turned up to 100 all the time," Carl said. "She'd have the heat on in the middle of summer and a fan blowing it out the window."

Barb's having "no concept of the value of the dollar" is just one of Carl's many dissatisfactions with his wife. He also feels she is not as bright as him, has annoying friends, and lacks personal ambition. He has always resented her failure to bear him a son, having given birth to four girls.

Barb has complaints about Carl, as well, including his emotional inaccessibility, his refusal to include her in major household decisions, and his inability to "let loose and have fun."

"I am married to a big bump on a log," Barb said. "Other women go out dancing and get flowers. I don't even get a present on our anniversary unless I buy something for the both of us."

The thermostat is ground zero for a battle of wills all winter, with Barb silently turning the thermostat up and Carl yelling loudly as he turns it down and commands her not to "futz with it."

"I tell Barb to turn the thermostat down to 63 before she leaves the house, and she can't even remember that one thing," Carl said. "She says she forgets. That's a load of bull puckey, she forgets."

According to the couple's now-grown children, it was always easy to tell when their parents weren't getting along.

"As kids, we could tell something

Above: Carl and Barb Kulick. Left: The medium through which their mutual resentment is channeled.

was up whenever ice started forming on the windows," said Deborah Wickson, 37, the couple's eldest daughter. "Mom was always edging the thermostat up half a degree at a time. Then, Dad would come in and do the same thing in reverse. He'd even get up in the middle of the night just to double-check that he'd turned it down before going to bed."

It seems unlikely that the thermostat war will end anytime soon. In fact, the situation seems to be getting worse.

"Do you know how much the price of water has gone up in the last few years?" Carl asked. "You should see the bill. How we use so much hot water in this house, I'll never know."

With the kids gone and the house paid for, Barb said that she and Carl can afford life's little luxuries.

"I worked hard all my life, too, rais-

ing the kids. Not that Carl would notice," Barb said. "Now, I think it's time to enjoy ourselves a little bit—buy some new curtains, turn the heat up, even leave the Christmas lights on overnight instead of turning them out after the news."

While she said she would never intentionally waste energy, Barb admitted she is "forgetful sometimes" when it comes to conserving resources.

"Last winter, I baked some pies and put them out to cool on top of the deep freeze," Barb said. "Well, I must have left the oven on with nothing in it, because when Carl got home from work and found it, he came barreling down to the basement where I was doing laundry."

"His face was as red as a tomato and, boy, was he cursing up a storm," added Barb, holding back a smile. ⌀

Your Honking Has Shown Me The Error Of My Ways

By Dave Nestor

I've made plenty of mistakes in my life, believe you me. But when I do, I try to be man enough to admit it. So, I confess: I really screwed up just now when I hesitated for a split second when the light turned green. I only hope the good Lord and you, the driver of the car behind me, will forgive me. Thank you for showing me the error of my ways.

I can't believe how insensitive I was. I mean, I consider myself a pretty do-unto-others kind of guy, especially when behind the wheel. Sure, there are times when I get a little careless, especially when I'm thinking about something. That's what happened when you so helpfully honked at me. I was on my way home from work and had all sorts of stuff on my mind. I won't bore you with the gory details—just let's say it's about the big fight I'd just had with my wife regarding our daughter Ashley's upcoming surgery.

Anyway, I was sitting at the intersection, trying to figure some things out, when, all of a sudden, the light changed. (Hey, I'm not making excuses. There is no excuse for not hitting the gas the

> ## How could I have been so inconsiderate? I know what it's like to be behind someone sitting at an intersection for almost an eighth of a second.

moment a light turns green.) Out of nowhere, I hear this honking. Now, this wasn't a concerned, friendly, "Hey, I'm here, let's move it along" honk. This was one loud, long blast of the horn. This honk said, "Hey, you fucker, just who the fuck do you fucking think you are, anyway?" Only louder. Then, you followed it up with two shorter honks, as if to say "fuck" and "you!" That was the capper.

At first, unaware of my slug-gishness off the line, I was confused as to why you were honking at me so vigorously. What could I have done to upset you so much? I thought it might be my back-window sticker. I had one that said "University of Michigan Alumni Association." That was it, I thought: You went to Michigan State or Notre Dame. But then I realized that, no, that sticker was on my last car, not this one.

Then I thought you might be a Chevy driver. I drive a Ford, and Chevy drivers tend to hate Fords. But, no, you're a BMW man, so that clearly wasn't the issue.

Then, I finally realized the problem: I did not move quickly enough when the light changed! I did not act with the speed and instinct of the cheetah, potentially delaying you from making your appointed rounds. How could I have been so inconsiderate? I know what it's like to be behind someone sitting at an intersection for almost an eighth of a second. It's like they're saying to you, "I am number one, and you are behind me! I will take my own sweet time getting to my destination because I care not a whit for anyone but myself!"

How selfish I was!

Oh, if only I could do it all over again. Instead of taking my own sweet time, I would crane my neck to see exactly when the opposite light turned from green to yellow. Then, the moment it turned red, I would count, "One one-thousand... Two one-thousand," and then slam on the gas, peeling off exactly as my light turned green. That would have been the decent thing to do.

I'm sure you must be a doctor, and I prevented you from saving someone's life. Or maybe you're a dentist, and you had to do an emergency root canal on the prime minister of Japan. Or maybe you were in danger of missing the series premiere of *The Agency.* I shouldn't question your motives. All I really need to know is that wherever you were headed, you arrived .000000013 seconds later because of me.

In the end, all I can say is, "Thank you." I have truly learned my lesson. And because of my misdeed, I have decided that I cannot be trusted behind the wheel anymore. From now on, I will only walk. That's right, I am selling my car so that no one will ever risk suffering the terrible fate you did. I can only trust that this act of contrition will let me get by in life with less guilt. Please, forgive me. Please? ∅

HOPE from page 253

nia scare in August and his advanced age, it'd be best if we kept him out of the loop on the whole attacking-the-Taliban thing."

Hope, who brought USO shows overseas to American troops for more than 50 years, is currently confined to bedrest in his Toluca Lake home, where his wife Dolores and various nurses shield the comedian from the news events of the day.

"Instead of CNN and the nightly news, we've been playing tapes of NBC News broadcasts from 1976," said Lorraine DiMarco, Hope's day nurse. "He doesn't seem to notice. In fact, just this morning after the news, he scribbled down a few Jerry Ford gags for his next Christmas special."

In addition to the TV-news blockade, Hope's daily copies of *The Los Angeles Times* and *USA Today* have been replaced with old issues of *Golf Digest.*

Hope last performed for American servicemen during the Gulf War in 1991, but the show was cut short when the comedian fell and broke his hip while tap-dancing to a drastically slowed-down version of "You Light Up My Life."

Though a lack of major U.S. military conflicts over the last 10 years

has kept Hope off the performing circuit, sources say he continually updates a list of "hot new contemporary entertainers" in case world events dictate another trip overseas.

> ## "Instead of CNN and the nightly news, we've been playing tapes of NBC News broadcasts from 1976," said Lorraine DiMarco, Hope's day nurse. "He doesn't seem to notice."

Recent additions to the list include Lola Falana, Jamie Farr, Joey Heatherton, Paul Williams, and "the inimitable Charo."

"Bob has mentioned several times that he wants to bring along Perry Como and Frank Sinatra on his next tour of Europe," DiMarco said. "I don't have the heart to tell him."

In addition to his deteriorating health, Hope's handlers believe his vaudevillian brand of jokes and song-and-dance numbers may not go over well with the young servicemen of today.

"I know Bob means well, and God knows he does love doing it," said Hope's longtime publicist and friend Timothy Orenstam. "But I'm not so sure the morale of twentysomething soldiers would be helped by the sight of an incontinent old man shuffling painfully across the stage. These kids want to see rock bands like Limp Bizkit or pretty girls like Pamela Anderson, not a man born in 1903 struggling through an off-key rendition of 'Thanks For The Memories.'"

Despite efforts to shield the ailing comedian from current events, Hope has occasionally managed to glean tiny snippets of information. Communicating with low grunts and hand signals, a feeble but feisty Hope issued a press statement earlier this week condemning recent acts of terrorism.

"Ayatollah Khomeini must be brought to justice," he said. "Let's bring the Iranian hostages home." ∅

SUBMARINE from page 248

of blood. Passersby were amazed by the unusually large amounts of blood. Passersby were amazed by the unusually large amounts of blood. Passersby were amazed by the unusually large amounts of blood. Passersby were amazed by the unusually large amounts of blood. Passersby were amazed by

> ## It ain't a party unless you regret from the bottom of your heart what you did.

the unusually large amounts of blood. Passersby were amazed by the unusually large amounts of blood. Passersby were amazed by the unusually large amounts of blood. Passersby were amazed by the unusually large amounts of blood. Passersby were amazed by the unusually large amounts of blood. Passersby were amazed by the unusually large amounts of blood. Passersby were amazed by the unusually large amounts of blood. Passersby were amazed by the unusually large amounts of blood. Passersby were amazed by the

see SUBMARINE page 262

DATABASE from page 253

and Tiki Barber, Moreland said he can't understand science-fiction fans' obsession with make-believe characters like Captain Kirk and Boba Fett.

"Guys like [Dansby], they see these pretend people on TV and in the movies, and they think they're real," said Moreland, who once waited in line for three hours to get New York Knicks guard Charlie Ward's autograph at an Edison, NJ, Modell's sporting-goods store. "How sad is that, to live your life through these fictional characters from, like, *Star Trek* and stuff? It's like these sci-fi nerds can't handle the real world, so they hide in a fake one."

En route from The Fan Zone to Lidz, a mall baseball-cap shop, Moreland spotted Dansby emerging from The Astral Plane, a store specializing in fantasy games and fig-urines.

"The guy even dresses like a total

> ## "The guy even dresses like a total geek," said Moreland, who rarely leaves the house without a jersey or T-shirt displaying his team loyalties.

geek," said Moreland, who rarely leaves the house without a jersey or T-shirt displaying his team loyalties. "What does his shirt say? *Akira*? Whatever that is, I'm sure it's not cool."

Added Moreland: "The Islanders are gonna kick some major ass this year. They picked up [Alexei] Yashin from the Senators and [Chris] Osgood from the Red Wings. And Mark Parrish looks way improved from last season. Don't be surprised if we give the Flyers a serious run for their money in the Atlantic."

Watching Dansby exit The Astral Plane with a "Forgotten Realms" interactive atlas CD-ROM under his arm, Moreland questioned the science-fiction fan's enjoyment of role-playing games.

"What is that all about? Imaginary elves and shit running around doing imaginary things and winning imag-inary gold?" Moreland asked. "I mean, I could see playing D&D when you're 12 years old, but this guy's got to be at least 25. It's pathetic."

As of press time, Moreland's online ESPN.com fantasy-football team, DaJerseyJintz, was 4-1.

Dansby said he is unfazed by the contempt in which he is held by sports fans.

"Like I care what some big, fat, stupid sports fan thinks of me," said Dansby, watching Moreland exit the mall, Jason Sehorn jersey in tow. "I bet the last book that guy read was called *The Michael Jordan Story* or something. Quite a literary masterwork, I'm sure."

Dansby added that he is nearly finished with Timothy Zahn's *Dark Force Rising*, which he praised as being "in the 80th percentile of *Star Wars* novels." ∅

BUTTONS from page 253

Continued Orlowski: "Those buttons were supposed to read 'Robert K. For Treasurer' and 'Danny Carter For V.P.,' not 'Mrs. Yanofsky Has Big Boobies.' Until someone comes forward with the names of all the students involved, I am forced to punish everyone."

At approximately 1 p.m., Orlowski returned from lunch to find students hurriedly gathering the scissors and scraps of paper that littered the floor and collecting buttons in different states of completion. She said she didn't think to inspect the buttons closely until she noticed Lindsay Chao, 10, wearing a button bearing the image of Marie Curie with a beard drawn onto her face.

Chao, one of the few students willing to discuss details of the incident, said she and her classmates started out with the best of intentions.

"We were honestly making buttons for the election for, like, a long time," Chao said, offering up four "Alyssa 4 Prez!!!" buttons as proof. "But then, Amanda [Petrakis] made this one that said 'Justin Timberlake 4 President,' and it just sorta went downhill from there."

According to Chao, after the Petrakis breakthrough, the buttons began to escalate in humor value, with each student trying to top the last one. Particularly aggressive in their efforts to push the envelope, Chao said, were the boys.

"The girls were doing a lot of buttons about stuff they liked, like The Backstreet Boys and horses," Chao said. "But then the boys started doing all these mean, funny ones, like 'Student Council Sucks' and 'Mr. Cecil Is Gay.' One boy made, like, 10 different buttons calling different people gay."

Before long, the slogan-driven buttons deteriorated into more random, visually oriented ones, with students making buttons out of magazine clippings, stickers, and items found around the classroom. One button depicted the hind quarters of a rhinoceros—an image cut out of an old issue of *Ranger Rick*. Another contained a section of a math worksheet, while another contained a piece of lint.

"Nobody meant to do it," Chao said. "It's just so fun to pull down the handle and have the button drop out all made. Some kids were making them just to hear the sound."

Orlowski said neither Chao nor any other student has been willing to "rat out" all of the conspirators. Even students known to have been involved are claiming to have been in the bathroom during the incident.

"From the number of improper buttons made—I've personally seen at least 50—this was not limited to the nine kids in detention," Orlowski said. "As far as I'm concerned, everyone wearing a button not related to the student-council elections is guilty. From the look of things, that's almost everyone."

Though the students clearly acted improperly, some Harrison staffers are blaming Orlowski, citing her willingness to let the students use school equipment unsupervised.

"I wasn't sure why Karen let those kids use the button maker in the first place—it's not even pep week. But at the time, I didn't think it was my place to say anything," school secretary Millie Barthes said. "Well, I'm just thankful the machine came back in one piece."

The button-making machine, a Badge-A-Minit™ I, is kept in the main-office supply closet and is available for classroom checkout from Barthes. The school purchased the machine 14 years ago for $79, a hefty sum that, according to Barthes, clearly indicates that the machine is not a

Above: Fourth-grader Jordy Cohn proudly displays one of his creations.

toy. In May 1987, days after the school's acquisition of the button maker, Barthes made a sign that has remained taped to its base ever since: "For classroom use only! Do not waste materials! They cost $$!!"

According to school principal Dr. Richard Wagner, such incidents have unfortunately made it necessary to keep school equipment under lock and key. Wagner said that every piece of restricted equipment is the result of a specific incident of tomfoolery.

"We have to lock up the balls and playground equipment so they don't end up on the roof," Wagner said. "Kids have to go to the janitor to get bathroom supplies or we risk another Jeremy Sachs. He's also why we can no longer use the honor system for extra milk in the lunchroom. Then there's the photocopier. I'll never forget what happened with the photocopier." ∅

ATAVISTIC from page 236

Passersby were amazed by the unusually large amounts of blood. Passersby were amazed by the unusually large amounts of blood. Passersby were amazed by the unusually large amounts of blood. Passersby were amazed by the unusually large amounts of blood. Passersby were amazed by the unusually large amounts of blood. Passersby were amazed by the unusually large amounts of blood. Passersby were amazed by the unusually large amounts of blood. Passersby were amazed by the unusually large amounts of blood. Passersby were amazed by the unusually large amounts of blood. Passersby were amazed by the unusually large amounts of blood. Passersby were amazed by the unusually large amounts of blood. Passersby were amazed by the unusually large amounts

see ATAVISTIC page 262

I'm Refreshingly Naïve!

By Dolly Rettenmund

These days, nobody's shocked by anything. What would have caused the most hard-bitten vice-squad dick to blush 50 years ago has become casual conversation fodder on today's junior-high playground. Blasé, jaded indifference is the norm. People don't trust each other, always assuming the worst. Well, don't lump me with that world-weary crowd. You can keep your skepticism, mister, because I'm refreshingly naïve!

That's right, I've decided to make a clean break from the pessimistic masses and embrace the exhilarating world of guileless naïvete! My jaw-dropping ingenuousness provides a refreshing alternative to the nihilism and cynicism that rules the day.

As I was telling the transvestite junkie prostitutes I warmly invited into my home (who have since claimed squatters' rights and pawned my valuables for heroin and hormone treatments), some things are more important than being "savvy" and "streetwise."

When I give my Social Security number and credit-card information to unidentified parties over the phone, I do it without fear, liberated from the wariness and stress one normally experiences during such risky transactions. Doesn't it reaffirm your faith in humanity to know that there's at least one person out there who doesn't expect to be ripped off at every turn?

Every time my next-door neighbor asks me to deliver mysterious, wrapped bundles to an anonymous man in our town's abandoned wharf district, I don't ask why he needs a courier or what's in them. Instead, I feel flattered that he considers my services worth the $50 he gives me after each delivery. I then take that money and contribute it to an unaccredited charity. Or put it toward postage and handling for a free gift I've won in an e-mail sweepstakes.

Aren't I a breath of fresh air in this world of doubters? Call me a holy fool, a simpleton, or a sucker, but you must admit that my gullibility is like a cool breeze on an oppressively humid day.

When you're hopelessly naïve, you meet such interesting people. And your instant reaction is to befriend and trust them! For example, I recently came across a down-and-out man who needed $5 for a bus ticket to Sacramento. Not only did I give him the $5, I gave him an additional $5 to purchase a little liquid refreshment. After all, it was a hot day, and he looked parched as could be. Did I fear that he would blow the money on cheap gin? Of course not! I assumed he would run to the nearest fruit-smoothie stand and buy a delicious, healthful juice concoction with fresh-squeezed strawberries and bananas.

What's that you ask, sir? Certainly,

> ## You must admit that my gullibility is like a cool breeze on an oppressively humid day.

feel free to use my apartment to study the bank across the street with a telescope! It does have a marvelous façade, does it not? The Beaux Arts period in America was short-lived but left us with unparalleled architectural riches. You know, it's strange, I suppose, but you remind me of a young gentleman I recently met at a party, a man to whom I lent $200 for a heart transplant. I never did get his name, but he seemed earnest enough, and I presume I'll receive a check from him in short order.

I am also entirely willing to believe the claims made by the makers of the Fat Zapper, a remarkable electrode-covered girdle that melts fat and tightens muscles in just minutes. Through my rose-colored glasses, the whole world is like one of those splashy ads in the back of an old comic book in which you earn a chemistry set or 10-speed bike by selling a few seed packets or boxes of Christmas cards door-to-door.

Feel free to roll your eyes and cluck your tongue at me. But beneath that contempt, I know you are mad with envy! Your suspicious nature restricts your possibilities in life and contorts you with fear. I, on the other hand, live freely as an open port of call for every con artist and flim-flam operation that sails through. You'll never meet a bigger sap than me, but you'll never meet a more carefree one, either!

I could elaborate further, but I really should devote the next several hours to sending a chain letter to 10 of my acquaintances. The chain letter instructed me to fold a single dollar in each envelope. That way, when the chain eventually makes its way back to me, I will receive many envelopes full of cash, all for me to keep! But I must make haste, for, according to the letter, if I break the chain, all manner of misfortune will befall me, like lung cancer and eternal spinsterdom. I'm sure everything will work out in the end, though. It always does. ∅

Area Man Constantly Mentioning He Doesn't Own A Television

CHAPEL HILL, NC—Area resident Jonathan Green does not own a television, a fact he repeatedly points out to friends, family, and coworkers—as well as to his mailman, neighborhood convenience-store clerks, and the man who cleans the hallways in his apartment building.

"I, personally, would rather spend my time doing something useful than watch television," Green told a random woman Monday at the Suds 'N' Duds Laundromat, noticing the establishment's wall-mounted TV. "I don't even own one."

According to Melinda Elkins, a coworker of Green's at The Frame Job, a Chapel Hill picture-frame shop, Green steers the conversation toward television whenever possible, just so he can mention not owning one.

"A few days ago, [store manager] Annette [Haig] was saying her new contacts were bothering her," Elkins said. "The second she said that, I knew Jonathan would pounce. He was like, 'I didn't know you had contacts, Annette. Are your eyes bad? That a shame. I'm really lucky to only require reading glasses. I'm guessing it's because I don't watch TV. In fact, I don't even own one."

According to Elkins, "idiot box" is Green's favorite derogatory term for

> ## Green has lived without television since 1989, when his then-girlfriend moved out and took her set with her.

television.

"He uses that one a lot," she said. "But he's got other ones, too, like 'boob tube' and 'electronic babysitter.'"

Elkins said Green always makes sure to read the copies of *Entertainment Weekly* and *People* lying around the shop's break room, "just so he can point out all the stars and

Above: Jonathan Green, who tells as many people as possible that he is "fully weaned off the glass teat."

shows he's never heard of."

"Last week, in one of the magazines, there was a picture of Calista Flockhart," Elkins said, "and Jonathan announced, 'I have absolutely no idea who this woman is. Calista *who?* Am I supposed to have heard of her? I'm sorry, but I haven't.'"

see TELEVISION page 258

Anthrax Hits The U.S.

Cases of anthrax exposure have been confirmed in media and government offices in Florida, New York, and Washington, D.C. What do *you* think about the threat?

Thom Traylor
Bioengineer

"As the head of a biotech lab, I'm tightening security. From now on, if you want to take some anthrax spores home, put your name on the sign-out sheet by the centrifuge."

Milt Cook
Electrician

"My brother's a doctor, and he slipped me a stash of that Cipro anthrax antibiotic. That and some sweet-ass morphine."

Donna McCutcheon
English Teacher

"Hmm. Does this coffee taste a little anthraxy to you?"

Bill Lowery
Cab Driver

"Anthrax may grab more headlines, but I think we should all remember that osteoporosis remains Florida's number-one medical threat."

Richard Busse
Systems Analyst

"At times like these, I'm glad I live in a geodesic dome. Not that they're anthrax-proof or anything. They're just fun to live in."

Christine Walker
Journalist

"I'd react calmly to this news, but I'm a journalist."

Post-Sept. 11 Changes

In the wake of last month's terrorist attacks, a number of books, films, and other products have been altered or shelved. Among the changes:

- ✗ *Die Hard* altered to point where it's now a *Honeymooners* rerun
- ✗ Emeril Lagasse's catchphrase changed from "Bam!" to "Okay, there you have it. Easy now, folks. Let's all take it nice and easy."
- ✗ Frankie Goes To Hollywood's "Two Tribes" pulled from theoretical airplay
- ✗ History Channel to edit out all references to last 60 years of Middle Eastern history
- ✗ Souvenir World Trade Center ashtray forcibly removed from South Dakota woman's living room
- ✗ Upcoming *SNL: Best Of Will Ferrell* video replaces all "Bush is dumb" jokes with "Bush is a national hero we must all rally behind" jokes
- ✗ New version of Bible cuts part about walls of Jericho tumbling down
- ✗ Bomb Pops renamed U.S.A. Patriot Pops
- ✗ Images of World Trade Center collapse digitally removed from all footage of World Trade Center collapse

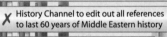

⌀ the ONION

America's Finest News Source

Herman Ulysses Zweibel *Founder*

T. Herman Zweibel *Publisher Emeritus*
J. Phineas Zweibel *Publisher*
Maxwell Prescott Zweibel *Editor-In-Chief*

FOUNDED 1871 • "TU STULTUS ES"

Your Horoscope

By Lloyd Schumner Sr.
Retired Machinist and
A.A.P.B.-Certified Astrologer

Aries: (March 21–April 19)
No force in Creation can stop you from enjoying a delicious fried-egg sandwich on your lunch break.

Taurus: (April 20–May 20)
Your life's problems will be put in proper perspective when you realize that, compared to the plague that swept Europe in the 12th century, they're still pretty bad.

Gemini: (May 21–June 21)
There must be a better way to tell your ex-husband the difficult things you need to tell him. Like, say, on the Louisiana Superdome Jumbotron.

Cancer: (June 22–July 22)
Try not to read too much into little details. It may mean nothing that your heart surgeon is named Dr. Chopsalott.

Leo: (July 23–Aug. 22)
Due to your lack of skill and experience, your new cooking show has been named *Reheating With Leo.*

Virgo: (Aug. 23–Sept. 22)
Your belief that a phone call from your mother-in-law is worse than cancer will be tested when you get both next Thursday.

Libra: (Sept. 23–Oct. 23)
The stars predict that hemlines are going to rise next season, but not nearly as much as you'd like.

Scorpio: (Oct. 24–Nov. 21)
You will soon meet the man you'll spend the rest of your life with. Shortly after that, you'll meet the man you'll *want* to spend the rest of your life with.

Sagittarius: (Nov. 22–Dec. 21)
You will find yourself enjoying a farcical, tune-filled, three-act romp that was supposed to be a meeting of the House Subcommittee on Economic Policy.

Capricorn: (Dec. 22–Jan. 19)
In a famous passage from Shakespeare, Hamlet says, "To thine own self be true." In that sense, you are a Shakespearean fuck-up.

Aquarius: (Jan. 20–Feb. 18)
You will discover incontrovertible proof that Lynn Anderson did, in fact, promise you a rose garden.

Pisces: (Feb. 19–March 20)
You will find yourself watching hour after hour of The Weather Channel next Friday, hoping to find out how the whole thing ends.

TELEVISION from page 257

Tony Gerela, who lives in the apartment directly below Green's and occasionally chats with the 37-year-old by the mailboxes, is well aware of his neighbor's disdain for television.

"About a week after I met him, we were talking, and I made some kind of *Simpsons* reference," Gerela said. "He asked me what I was talking about, and when I told him it was from a TV show, he just went off, saying how the last show he watched was some episode of *Cheers,* and even then, he could only watch for about two minutes before having to shut it off because it insulted his intelligence so terribly."

Added Gerela: "Once, I made the mistake of saying I saw something on the news, and he started in with, 'Saw the news? I don't know about you, but I *read* the news.'"

Green has lived without television since 1989, when his then-girlfriend moved out and took her set with her.

"When Claudia went, the TV went with her," Green said. "But instead of just going out and buying another one—which I certainly could have afforded, that wasn't the issue—I decided to stand up to the glass teat."

"I'm not an elitist," Green said. "It's just that I'd much rather sculpt or write in my journal or read Proust than sit there passively staring at some phosphorescent screen."

"If I need a fix of passive audio-visual stimulation, I'll go to catch a Bergman or Truffaut film down at the university," Green said. "I certainly wouldn't waste my time watching the so-called Learning Channel or, God forbid, any of the mind sewage the major networks pump out."

Continued Green: "People don't realize just how much time their TV-watching habit—or, shall I say, addiction—eats up. Four hours of television a day, over the course of a month, adds up to 120 hours. That's five entire days! Why not spend that time living your own life, instead of watching fictional people live theirs? I can't begin to tell you how happy I am not to own a television." ⌀

U.S. Postal Service Unveils New Uniforms

see NATION page 6A

Plant Dead Because Of You

see LOCAL page 8B

Gay Man Has Been Planning Halloween Costume Since July

see LOCAL page 2B

'Party-Pak' Just Cheese

see PRODUCTWATCH page 4C

STATshot

A look at the numbers that shape your world.

What Did We Forget To Ask The Doctor?

1. So is cancer, like, real serious?
2. What's the best way to contract eczema?
3. When blood comes out of your ding-ding, is that bad?
4. Can I have the fetus back as a souvenir?
5. Are Earring Tree employees allowed to do trepannings?
6. Isn't that thing on your wall a real-estate license?

THE ONION VOLUME 37 ISSUE 38
$2.00 US $3.00 CAN

0 74470 94595 6

38

The ONION®

VOLUME 37 ISSUE 38   AMERICA'S FINEST NEWS SOURCE™   25–31 OCTOBER 2001

Just Shoot Me Writer Assumes Everyone He Meets Watches *Just Shoot Me*

LOS ANGELES—Andy Kaminowitz, 31, a staff writer for the popular Thursday-night NBC sitcom *Just Shoot Me*, operates under the assumption that everyone he meets watches the show, sources revealed Monday.

"It's kind of weird how he thinks everybody should be familiar with his work," said Frank Scalia, a bartender at Dublin's, a Sunset Boulevard bar frequented by Kaminowitz. "He'll walk in, strike up a conversation with somebody, and casually bring up that he's a writer for *Just Shoot Me*. Then, he just sits back with this air of expectation, like people are going to have all these questions for him about specific episodes or whatever."

"I mean, I've seen the show once or twice, and I guess it's all right," Scalia said. "But it's not like I plan my week around it."

According to witnesses, whenever Kaminowitz meets someone unfamiliar with the program, he becomes confused and annoyed, unable to comprehend a world that contains people who are not big *Just Shoot Me* fans.

"He asked what I thought of the line, 'Man, you pretty uptight—even for a white boy,' that [guest star]

Above: Andy Kaminowitz in the *Just Shoot Me* writer's room.

Snoop Dogg said when Finch quit working for him in the episode 'Finch In The Dogg House,'" said Ellen Prior, 44, who sat next to Kaminowitz in a dental-office waiting room last Tuesday. "I told him I

see WRITER page 261

Privileged Children Of Millionaires Square Off On World Stage

WASHINGTON, DC—After nearly two weeks of heavy, sustained air strikes, President Bush made final preparations Monday for a full-scale U.S. ground assault against Osama bin Laden, the privileged, formerly hard-partying heir to a family fortune.

"Osama bin Laden is a true emblem of evil, a man responsible for the deaths of thousands of innocent Americans," Bush said. "He cannot, and will not, escape justice."

Bin Laden, son of a Saudi construction tycoon worth an estimated $5 billion at the time of his 1968 death, was not cowed by Bush's resolve.

"We will not bow to George W. Bush, the emblem of all that is evil and corrupt about America,"
said bin Laden, who frequented Beirut nightclubs as a young man, drinking heavily and fighting over women. "This is a man who spent much of his early life defiling God with his immoral ways. He will fall."

"The vile influence of the West must be driven out of the Arab world once and for all," continued bin Laden, who studied English at Oxford University in the '70s and went on to earn a degree in management and economics at King Abdul Aziz University. "And it will, for God is on our side in this righteous and holy war."

Responding to the increasingly incendiary rhetoric of bin Laden, Bush said he plans to escalate air strikes in the next five to six days.

see PRIVILEGED page 262

Above: Kristin Petrie.

Thin, Attractive Woman Accepted For Who She Is

DALLAS—In a world too often filled with hatred and intolerance toward those who are different, 23-year-old Kristin Petrie is accepted for who she is: a natural blonde with a dazzling smile and spectacular body.

"I don't know how to describe it, but Kristin has this special, magnetic quality," said Ron Angelo, Petrie's supervisor at ExecuTech, a Dallas-based headhunting firm where the willowy beauty works as a corporate recruiter. "When Kristin arrived here, she had zero recruiting experience. But did she let that stop her from landing the job? Absolutely not. Kristin is determined not to let her shortcomings keep her from succeeding. And you know what? They rarely do."

Petrie has been able to overcome numerous setbacks since joining the ExecuTech team, including fre-

see WOMAN page 263

Tom Clancy Treated Like He's Some Kind Of Terrorism Expert

WASHINGTON, DC—Tom Clancy, best-selling author of such military thrillers as *The Hunt For Red October* and *Patriot Games*, is being treated like an actual terrorism expert, having offered his opinion on *Larry King Live* and countless other TV shows since Sept. 11. "The Al Qaeda network is known to have operatives in at least 30 countries, including the U.S. and Great Britain," said Clancy, a former insurance broker and avid wearer of naval-warship baseball caps, during a recent *Nightline*. "By the way, Ted, Stephen Ambrose's *The Wild Blue* is a terrific read." Later that evening, Clancy appeared in a *Crossfire* panel on biological warfare with former CIA director John Deutch and Secretary Of State Colin Powell.

Nation's Grandmas Halt Production Of Afghan Blankets

WASHINGTON, DC—In a show of support for the U.S., the nation's grandmas announced plans Monday to stop knitting afghan blankets. "We must do our part to stand behind our country," said spokesgrandma Nettie Bennett, 87. "Even if it means my new grandson will have to sleep with a store-bought comforter, I will not make something named after a place that lets terrorists run around all willy-nilly."

Michael Jordan Not Exactly Sure What Product He Just Filmed Commercial For

LOS ANGELES—Minutes after completing a commercial shoot Monday, NBA legend Michael Jordan reported being unable to recall what product he'd endorsed. "I'm pretty sure it had something to do with phones," Jordan said. "But it wasn't MCI. It was, like, fiber-optic stuff or videoconferencing. Anyway, I talked about how you can score a slam dunk with the company and mentioned the name twice." On Friday, Jordan is slated to film a 30-second spot for Dove Bars or maybe hot dogs.

Area Man Switches To Backup Lie

AURORA, CO—At the last possible moment, area resident Gordon Kanner aborted his planned avenue of untruth, turning instead to a backup lie to explain his failure to show up at his girlfriend's sister's birthday party. "That was the closest call in my entire two years with Jessica," a relieved Kanner told reporters after the near-bust. "I was going to feed her some bullshit about how I couldn't make it to her sister's thing because I had to work. But just as I was about to, she mentions seeing my car at the Safeway. Fortunately, I was able to think fast and switch to my sick-mother lie."

Mom Uses Full Name To Refer To Bisquick Impossibly Easy Cheeseburger Pie™

HICKORY, NC—Inviting her family to dig in to dinner Monday, Donna Furness, 41, referred to the meal by its full, trademarked name. "Who's ready for some Bisquick Impossibly Easy Cheeseburger Pie™?" asked Furness while serving her loved ones the hamburger pie, made from a recipe on the side of a Bisquick box. "Just be sure to save room for dessert: We're having Smuckers Quick 'N' Nutty Jam Gems™." ∅

Downtown McDonald's Perpetually A Hairsbreadth From Complete Anarchy

OAKLAND, CA—McDonald's franchise #4793, located on the corner of 12th and Franklin in downtown Oakland, perpetually teeters on the brink of anarchy, store patrons reported Monday.

"I stopped in there this afternoon, and there's garbage all over the floor, half-dressed kids are running around throwing things, and everyone is screaming at each other," said Meredith Smith, 26. "I half-expected the National Guard to flood in."

Smith is not the only one puzzled by the restaurant's near-anarchic state.

"There's always about 15 people in the kitchen, and it still takes 20 minutes just to get your order taken," said Bill Zumbo, 33. "You just stand there and wonder, 'What is going on here? What is happening?'"

During a recent visit, despite long lines at all four registers, Zumbo spotted crew members joking around with friends, sharing cigarettes in the drive-thru area, and throwing random objects on the grill to see how well they burn. As garbage overflowed from the trash receptacles and a wide puddle of fetid, gray-brown water saturated the east-entrance floor mat, the only visible clean-up-crew member was napping in a booth.

"I sometimes go there for lunch during work, and, at first, I was kind of amused by it," Zumbo said. "It was funny how the cashier would yell back to the cook and say, 'Shut up, bitch, and get me some fries!' But then I began to question my safety. In that place, anything could happen."

Fearing everything from food poisoning to death by gunshot, Zumbo said he now walks an extra eight blocks to the McDonald's on Fairview Avenue.

With its graffiti-covered tables and restrooms unfit for human waste, the 12th and Franklin McDonald's evokes the lawlessness of the most far-flung underdeveloped banana republic. Surly single mothers toting caterwauling babies are among the restaurant's most prevalent patrons. The remaining booths are filled with an endless parade of lice-ridden vagrants, morbidly obese bachelors, and borderline illiterates with french-fry-stained pants.

The restaurant's food provides further evidence of its descent into chaos.

"When the burgers are fully

Above: Teeming hordes charge the front registers as the restaurant threatens to collapse into lawlessness.

cooked—which they rarely are—the orders are always screwed up," Danielle Costa, 36, said. "I've gotten orders with a bun and no burger, two burgers and no bun, a Filet-O-Fish crammed into an apple-pie box—you name it. And the only visible cook is bobbing his head up and down listening to music on his headphones. I can't believe there hasn't been some sort of fast-food *coup d'etat* at that place by now."

Various McDonald's district supervisors have attempted to stabilize store #4793, but all have met with failure.

"It's all about location," said McDonald's District 7 franchise owner Vanessa Ceres. "No matter how well-planned your corporate structure may be, if the customers in that area want to turn your store into a dump, there's not much you can do about it."

According to University of California–Berkeley sociology professor Richard Weber, the 12th and Franklin McDonald's will likely be overthrown and plunged into full-blown anarchy one day.

"It's only a matter of time before the employees topple the Ronald McDonald statue in the lobby and declare mob rule," Weber said. "And when that day comes, God help anyone who happens to be in the downtown area looking for a place to grab a quick bite." ∅

Now More Than Ever, Humanity Needs My *Back To The Future* Fan Fiction

By Larry Groznic

We, as a nation, have suffered. Wounded and confused, we wonder whether life will ever be the same again. But for all our pain, we can heal, if each one of us pitches in. We all have a part to play, whether donating blood, contributing to relief charities, or writing high-quality fan fiction to help a grieving nation forget its troubles for just a little while.

Such is the burden I have assumed.

Since 1997, through good times and bad, I have been there, creating rousing tales of events that did not actually take place in the official *Back To The Future* universe but could have. And now, in this time of crisis, I humbly offer these tales to the American people to help soothe their jangled nerves.

Certainly, I am neither the most

prolific nor the most acclaimed of America's many *Back To The Future* fanfic authors. But I like to think that my work is among the most heartfelt, the most human. Take my recently self-published fanfic novella *Think, McFly*, in which Marty briefly becomes trapped in 1975 Hill Valley.

Let's not dwell on, for the purposes of this brief discussion, my historically accurate portrayal of the era, right down to the TV blaring *All In The Family* (a sly allusion to the whole theme of the film series). My depiction of Marty as he discovers yet another layer of the intertwined histories of his hometown and family surely approaches the depth of Robert Zemeckis' own work. In one scene, I have Marty encounter his 7-year-old self and, along with the reader, discover why being called a "chicken" has become such a personal curse. Who else in the online fanfic-writing community has taken such a bold leap of imagination while remaining completely true to the spirit of the film

series? Can you name even one? I thought not.

But I am not here to cast aspersions on other *BTTF* fanfic authors. (Not even the wildly overrated Marion Gehl.) Now is the time for Americans to stand tall and united in the face of an ultimate evil, not to nitpick about who obviously doesn't understand what the films are even about. And it certainly isn't the time to actually dare to claim that Claudia Wells was a better Jennifer than Elisabeth Shue. But, then, it never is. (She didn't do *anything*!)

But I digress. *Back To The Future* is a timeless story of universal human experiences, like the quest for self-knowledge, overcoming adversity, and going to the school dance with your mother. It is this spirit I seek to honor and uplift through my works.

Consider my upcoming 1920s adventure, tentatively titled *Density*. In it, Marty and Doc find themselves in the year 1925, only to meet Marty's grandfather, Cyrus

McFly, operating a "speakeasy" out of a familiar-looking beverage hall in downtown Hill Valley. The naïve young Marty romances a pretty young flapper who turns out to be his own grandmother. As if that weren't enough, to ensure the proper flow of time, he must mix things up with the Hill Valley crime syndicate, led by Bart Tannen, the eventual father of Biff! Particularly deft is my passing mention of a congenital heart defect in Bart, which helps foreshadow why Biff is raised by his grandmother in the '50s.

Still hurting? The weary and dispirited among us can turn to *Biffco*, a recently completed novella that reveals more tantalizing details about the powerful alternate version of Biff that appears in the middle of *BTTF2*. I don't want to give away the ending, but let's just say that the age-old conundrum of how the elderly Biff encountered his younger self without creating a time paradox will

see FAN FICTION page 263

WRITER from page 259

wasn't sure I'd seen that one, but he just went on, saying, 'That line was mine. I didn't get script credit on that episode, but I contributed the best material during punch-up.'"

"I don't even know what 'punch-up' means," Prior added.

Kaminowitz, a *Harvard Lampoon* alumnus, has held staff-writer positions at a number of programs, including VH1's *Pop-Up Video* and The WB's *Unhappily Ever After*. After a two-year stint at *Win Ben Stein's Money*, he was hired at *Just Shoot Me* in September 2000, impressing producers with a spec script he'd written for *Suddenly Susan*. Ever since, he's held fast to the notion that people are familiar with and interested in his work on the show.

"I couldn't believe it," said Doug Hannisch, 38, a frequent customer at Dublin's, where Kaminowitz is known among regulars as "that fucking *Just Shoot Me* guy." "I once made the mistake of trying to talk to him about the game, just because I was sitting next to him when *Monday Night Football* was on. So he says to me, 'You watch TV? What did you think of this week's *JSM*? The part where Elliott and Finch were razzing Maya about the overpriced imported coffee she bought online? That was pulled straight from real life. That's based on my actual sister, I swear."

Above: A *Just Shoot Me* scene from a November 2000 episode scripted by Kaminowitz.

"I was like, 'What the hell is this guy talking about?'" Hannisch said. "I mean, '*JSM*'? Who refers to *Just Shoot Me* as '*JSM*'?"

Eventually, Kaminowitz got up and moved to another seat near Dan Carter, 41, striking up another *Just Shoot Me*-based conversation. Upon realizing that Carter was not a regu-

lar *Just Shoot Me* viewer and could not name a cast member besides David Spade, Kaminowitz let out a long, dramatic sigh.

"He looks around the bar in disbelief and says, 'Who doesn't know who Wendy Malick is? Or Laura San Giacomo?'" Carter said. "I was like, 'Sorry. Maybe I'd recognize them if I

saw their picture. The names don't really ring a bell, though.'"

According to acquaintances of the oft-incredulous sitcom writer, Kaminowitz's distorted sense of the importance of his work dates back to the early '90s, when he was a personal assistant to Ron Wolotsky, then co-executive producer of the HBO comedy series *Dream On*.

"When Andy got that job, he'd make all these passing references to 'Ron,' as if he expected us know who Ron Wolotsky was," said Melanie Myers, 32, an L.A.-area obstetrician and longtime friend of Kaminowitz's. "It's not like I walk around casually spouting Latin terms for women's reproductive organs and assume everybody's going to understand me."

Neighbor Greg Tan, who has endured numerous *Just Shoot Me* related monologues, said Kaminowitz "doesn't get out much."

"Andy puts in really long hours at the show," Tan said. "He'll generally leave his house around 9 a.m. and not get back until well after midnight. From what Andy's told me, for some reason, they make those guys work, like, 70 hours a week. Apparently, that's just common practice on sitcoms. I can't understand why: It's not like they're working to cure cancer. They're writing *Just Shoot Me*, for God's sake." Ø

261

Above: A Bush or bin Laden family oil rig stationed off the coast of either Texas or Saudi Arabia.

The president is also asking Congress for an additional $250 million, roughly the amount bin Laden inherited from his father, for operations in Afghanistan.

"Our military is strong, but it

The president is also asking Congress for an additional $250 million, roughly the amount bin Laden inherited from his father, for operations in Afghanistan.

---

needs our full backing," said Bush, speaking from his 1,600-acre ranch in Crawford, TX. "These air strikes are merely the first step in what will be a long and hard-fought war against terrorism. Each and every one of us must steel ourselves for the difficult road ahead."

According to experts, bin Laden's hatred of America and sense of mission has only come into full focus in recent years. He spent his early adulthood wandering without direction, leaving Saudi Arabia at age 34 for the Sudan, where he ran several family-financed businesses. He then lived briefly in Afghanistan before moving back to Saudi Arabia to join his father's construction company.

His spiritual awakening occurred while working on behalf of his father's construction business to rebuild several mosques in the Saudi cities of Mecca and Medina. In 1991, outraged by U.S. troops' presence in Saudi Arabia after the Gulf War, he turned to an even more extreme strain of Islam.

Bush, who spent his 30s drifting around in what he called his "nomadic" period, gained direction in 1988, when he bought the Texas Rangers with family money and built the team a new stadium in Arlington.

Speaking to the nation Monday night, Bush said the U.S. will not be defeated.

"Our fighting men are strong. They are ready for the task ahead," said Bush, displaying the same resolve he showed when he quit drinking and discovered religion at age 40, turning to his wife's Methodist faith. "We cannot lose, for our cause is just."

America's fighting forces expressed their full support for the president.

"We're gonna go in there and take out bin Laden," said Joseph Barton, a 19-year-old Army reservist from the impoverished rural village of Sissonville, WV. "This one's for W."

Barton then loaded his rifle and prepared to advance on a battalion of 18- and 19-year-old Taliban soldiers in the impoverished rural village of Qalat, Afghanistan.

According to Dr. James Cleary, a professor of political theory at Georgetown University, Bush and bin Laden exemplify how power is attained differently in the West and East.

"In America, power is the domain of the rich and well-connected," Cleary said. "In the Arab world, things are different. Over there, power is the domain of the super-rich and super-well-connected." ∅

---

the **ONION** presents

Halloween Safety Tips

Halloween, though lots of frightful fun, can also be full of potential dangers. Here are some tips to make your kids' All Saints' Eve an All "Safe" Eve:

- Pack your child's rectum with razor blades to make him/her less desirable to would-be molesters.

- Always trick-or-treat in groups of 400,000.

- Many troublemakers and dangerous people come out on Halloween night. To be safe, trick-or-treat in early March.

- Safety and self-defense go hand in hand. Be sure your child's handgun has at least a 10-round magazine and is at least .38 caliber to ensure stopping power.

- For optimum safety while trick-or-treating, be sure your child does not encounter fright-master screenwriter Kevin Williamson.

- Equip your child with a special cyanide-filled false tooth for use in case of capture.

- Be sure child closes eyes before you drill eyeholes in mask.

- Beat would-be child murderers at their own game by poisoning your kids ahead of time.

- Dress your child in an all-black costume to make him/her virtually invisible to potentially dangerous motorists.

- Tell your kids that if they see anything suspicious or scary-looking—for example, ghosts, goblins, or witches—they should run to the nearest neighbor's house and call the police.

- Pack your child's costume with safety flares.

- Before sending your children off, give their anuses a good dollop of lube. This will help prevent their tissue from tearing when they are sodomized by maniacs.

- Do not ring doorbells under any circumstances.

It's Finally The Good Life For Jim Anchower

The Cruise
By Jim Anchower

Hola, amigos. What gives? I know it's been a long time since I rapped at ya, but there's been all sorts of craziness going on. Like, first off, there's the whole situation with the terrorists. That's some pretty heavy shit. What they did, that just wasn't right. I say Bomba Osama!

Aside from that, I got a new job as a busboy at this Mexican place by the mall called California Fajita Cantina. I never thought I'd work food service again, 'cause it sucks so bad, but when you're hungry, you take what you can get. Actually, it turns out that it's a pretty sweet gig. It's just a lot of picking up plates and wiping down tables. Plus, I get two free fajitas per shift, and I'm learning a little *Español*.

Another benefit of the job is that it landed me a new weed connection. One of the dishwashers has a friend who's hooked up. So, in the past month, I've gone from having no cash and no stash to having both. Life's

funny, how nothing can be going your way, and then—boom—you're in the penthouse.

> **Another benefit of the job is that it landed me a new weed connection.**

Okay, so not everything has been perfect. Last week, my Super Nintendo finally crapped out. Man, I was pretty bummed. I never finished Earthworm Jim, and now I might never get the chance. I wish there were a good reason it died, like I spilled soda on it or something, but it just went out in the middle of a 10-hour Earthworm Jim marathon. No warning, no nothing. One minute, I'm trying to take out the crow thing, and the next, I'm staring at a screen full of static.

But you know what? I ain't all that concerned. I was thinking about getting a PlayStation 2, anyway. I got the

itch to play some of those zombie shooting games, so all I gotta do is save up some of my extra scratch. Not a lot, mind you. Thanks to all the overtime I've gotten at the restaurant, I've been living pretty large as of late.

Oh, and I lucked out and won a $100 gift certificate at Woodsmith's grocery for their 20th anniversary. It's not a free PlayStation 2, but it did free up enough cash to keep my electric from getting disconnected, and everybody knows that a PlayStation 2 without electricity is like a bong without water. And don't forget that I get those two free fajitas when I work, so between the food I won and the fajitas, I had a lot of extra money to spend on *numero uno* (that's Spanish for number one).

I ain't gonna be able to take the dinero with me, so I gotta take care of myself while I can. "Treat Jim Anchower like he's *numero uno*" is my new motto. Plus, there are all these people telling me that it's my duty as an American to spend money right now. If I say, "I can't buy a PlayStation while the gas bill is two months late," the whole country suffers.

In order to spread the money

around, I've been seeing more movies lately. I saw this one called *Jeepers Creepers*, where this thing eats dead people and chases after these two high-schoolers. That mucho sucked, so I snuck in to see *Training Day*, only I was sort of tired and fell asleep. Oh, and I saw *Rock Star*, which should've kicked ass but somehow didn't. You know what, though? Even if a movie bites the big one, it still feels good to help your country. It also feels good to catch a flick without having to get your friend who works at the theater to sneak you in because you don't have enough cash.

Got a good deal on a sub-woofer for my car, too. Now, my sweet ride positively thunders when it rolls down the street. I got a little CD player that plugs into my tape deck in the car, and I got my third Zep box set to replace the other two. Hell, I even treated Ron and Wes to burgers the other day without them asking. Why not? I'm almost rolling in it!

Yep, it's the good life from now on. I'm gonna do all I can to really make the most out of every day. "Live it to the max" is my other new motto, and I'm gonna start by getting drunk tonight. That'll be sweet. ∅

FAN FICTION from page 261

finally be answered.

These are merely one man's meager efforts, to be sure. Such fanciful tales are far less than is needed to salve the wounds of Sept. 11. But, hopefully, they're enough to assure America that better days lie ahead. Better days and even better *Back To The Future* fanfic. Specifically, my nearly completed masterwork: It's an ambitious, never-before-attempted *Back To The Future–Star Trek* crossover titled *Trek To The Future*.

Operating on the premise that Hill Valley is a suburb of San Fran-

cisco, my magnum opus takes the events of *Star Trek IV: The Voyage Home* and throws Marty, Doc, and Jennifer into the mix. While Kirk and crew stumble around the year 1986, attempting to save two humpback whales before returning to the 23rd century, Doc and Marty hover about the fringes, "helping" where necessary and borrowing Starfleet technology in myriad ingenious ways. It may well be my finest hour as a fanfic writer when Doc modifies a phaser to generate the necessary 1.21 gigawatts (I refuse to use the unscientific and meaningless

"jigowatts") of power for the DeLorean.

Trek To The Future's coda, in which Bryce McFly, the 24th-century descendant of Marty, is a skittish Starfleet Academy cadet menaced by half-Klingon Ba'Qa Tannen, will surely represent a high-water mark of American fan fiction. And the throwaway gag about Picard being descended from Principal Strickland will be masterfully rendered.

No, these humble offerings don't match the healing power of, say, an all-frills DVD box set of the trilogy (we're *still* waiting, Universal!), but

it's important that each of us does what he or she can.

Sadly, the flux-capacitor technology masterminded by Dr. Emmet Brown remains a fantasy. As such, we cannot go back in time and change the terrible events of Sept. 11. But we can draw strength by drawing close to one another and holding fast to the faith that tomorrow will be a brighter day. And also by reading my *Back To The Future* fan fiction. My next story should be up on the site as soon as my renewal money order to Dreamhost clears. ∅

WOMAN from page 259

quent error-filled reports.

"Kristin tends to be a little hard on herself when she makes mistakes, but we're always saying, 'Don't worry about it; you're doing great,'" said coworker Brett Graves, who has never verbally acknowledged Petrie's 22-inch waist or pert, C-cup breasts. "After all, we've all got our strengths and weaknesses, and it's important to live with that."

Graves was alluding to a June incident in which Petrie accidentally recommended the wrong person for a high-level position at Revlon cosmetics.

"It was very unfortunate, yes, and Kristin was extremely sorry," Angelo said. "But she wasn't to blame for it, really. I admit I gave her more than she could cope with.

The file folders she was given were too similar-looking. Thankfully, she recognized the mistake when she received a call from the Revlon people asking why she'd sent the wrong person, and she immediately set out to fix what could have been a disastrous situation. Again, I think it's part of that special quality she has that no one can put their finger on."

Continued Angelo: "Kristin was practically in tears and said that if I wanted to fire her, she'd understand. But I said that we wouldn't have hired her if we didn't think she had the goods to succeed. When dealing with people, you have to learn to take the good with the bad. We're all different, but it's those differences that make each of us special."

Like her coworkers, Petrie's friends accept her for who she is.

"Kristin can be a bit forgetful," said Leslie Barrow, Petrie's best friend since high school. "One time, she forgot to pick up Gail and bring her to her surprise birthday party. She picked up Gail's cake from the bakery but not Gail. Incredible."

"When Kristin realized her mistake," Barrow continued, "she blushed and said, 'Oops, my bad!' We had to put off the party nearly two hours as Kristin went back for Gail. But somehow, when her face went red and her long, silky blonde ponytail bobbed around as she scanned the room for our reactions, we couldn't stay mad at her. 'That's our Kristin!' we thought."

Another longtime acquaintance, Adam Streed, said he is proud to

claim Petrie as a friend, warts and all.

"I truly believe that the key to happiness is acceptance," Streed said. "I mean, ideally, everybody could stand to be a little smarter or more responsible or conscientious. But nobody's perfect, so why not focus on what's good about a person? In Kristin's case, her strong points are her warmth, friendliness, and sense of humor. I only wish more people were like her."

Streed added that he is so tolerant of Petrie, he wouldn't mind if she were to accidentally lock his keys in his car. He also reportedly wouldn't mind if, one day, she unexpectedly put her arm around his neck and French-kissed him, slowly massaging his crotch with her free hand. ∅

What's Up, Dick?

Vice-President Cheney has spent much of the past several weeks hidden from public view in a secret location, prompting rumors about his status. What do *you* think?

"Man, if something happens to him, do you realize Bush becomes the vice-president?"

Dom Delavan
Roofer

"He's probably been hiding out in a Nebraska bunker roughly 43 miles northeast of Hastings, allowing him fast access to any location in the U.S. Of course, that's just an uneducated guess."

Frank Castina
Truck Driver

"You know, Cheney reminds me a lot of my dad. Angry, humorless, dying of heart disease..."

Iris Nelson
Waitress

"The idea of a vice-president maintaining a low profile—it's just too disturbing to process."

Carla Brodson
Librarian

"Like any U.S. leader, he's where you'd expect him to be: hundreds of miles below the Earth's surface in an impregnable star chamber with top Illuminati officials, charting our fates."

Todd McKechnie
Systems Analyst

"I strongly suspect the government is pulling a *Weekend At Bernie*'s on us."

Carl Vinson
Civil Engineer

Weathering The Storm

The U.S. economy has staggered in the wake of the Sept. 11 attacks, but a few companies are thriving. Among them:

- $ Amalgamated Panic & Steel
- $ Ciproximate™, The Fat-Free Cipro Substitute
- $ Warm Fuzzy Blankets, Ltd.
- $ Post-Nuclear Bob's Canned Water 'N' Graham Cracker Emporium
- $ Mid-Nowhere Realty
- $ Flag-Slathered Shit Unlimited
- $ Emmy-Awards-Postponement Condolence Hams By Mail, Inc.
- $ Holman & Loeffler War Profiteers, L.L.C.
- $ Jack Chick Publications
- $ Guy Who Sells Pictures Of Bin Laden With Empire State Building Up His Ass, Inc.
- $ Impulse-Marriage Dating Service
- $ Lockheed Martin

the ONION
America's Finest News Source

Herman Ulysses Zweibel *Founder*
T. Herman Zweibel *Publisher Emeritus*
J. Phineas Zweibel *Publisher*
Maxwell Prescott Zweibel *Editor-In-Chief*

FOUNDED 1871 • "TU STULTUS ES"

Your Horoscope

By Lloyd Schumner Sr.
Retired Machinist and
A.A.P.B.-Certified Astrologer

Aries: (March 21–April 19)
You will meet a dark-haired stranger next week. Actually, you'll meet several, but only one of them is important for our purposes.

Taurus: (April 20–May 20)
You will thoroughly enjoy your study of world history until you realize it isn't supposed to be funny.

Gemini: (May 21–June 21)
You will be greatly relieved to learn that the Bronx Zoo rhino's newborn babies in no way resemble you.

Cancer: (June 22–July 22)
Nothing in the universe can keep you from watching your beloved Green Bay Packers, as the Venusian Space Armada will soon discover.

Leo: (July 23–Aug. 22)
You will move no one when you announce plans to embark on a hunger strike that will last until someone feeds you.

Virgo: (Aug. 23–Sept. 22)
Your psychological affliction will have no serious negative side effects, with the possible exception of a sexual obsession with Greta Van Susteren.

Libra: (Sept. 23–Oct. 23)
You might not believe it now, but dropping 1,500 feet out of a helicopter with only a parachute, compass, and knife will be the easy part of your week.

Scorpio: (Oct. 24–Nov. 21)
Years from now, strangers will stop you on the street and tell you how much they enjoyed the sight of you running from the bear that stole your clothes.

Sagittarius: (Nov. 22–Dec. 21)
You will spend the next 40 years of your life desperately preparing for the final 10.

Capricorn: (Dec. 22–Jan. 19)
You will lose one of your oldest friends in the world when you fly into a violent rage over the sight of an incorrectly used apostrophe.

Aquarius: (Jan. 20–Feb. 18)
Your long, hard journey to manhood after falling off a luxury liner and into a fishing vessel is a source of pride until you learn it was done in a Kipling novel.

Pisces: (Feb. 19–March 20)
Don't eat too many of the free corn chips at your local Mexican restaurant. That's how they get you.

SNIFTER from page 257

Passersby were amazed by the unusually large amounts of blood. Passersby were amazed by the unusually large amounts of blood. Passersby were amazed by the unusually large amounts of blood. Passersby were amazed by the unusually large amounts of blood. Passersby were amazed by the unusually large amounts of blood. Passersby were amazed by the unusually large amounts of blood. Passersby were amazed by the unusually large amounts of blood. Passersby were amazed by the unusually large amounts of blood. Passersby were amazed by the unusually large amounts of blood. Passersby were amazed by the unusually large amounts of blood. Passersby were amazed by the unusually large amounts of blood. Passersby were amazed by the unusually large amounts of blood. Passersby were amazed by the unusually large amounts of blood. Passersby were amazed by the unusually large amounts of blood. Passersby were amazed by the unusually large amounts of blood. Passersby were amazed by the unusually large amounts of blood. Passersby were amazed by the unusually large amounts of

blood. Passersby were amazed by the unusually large amounts of blood. Passersby were amazed by the unusually large amounts of blood. Passersby were amazed by

Who will lead the nation's foot fetishists into the 21st century?

the unusually large amounts of blood. Passersby were amazed by the unusually large amounts of blood. Passersby were amazed by the unusually large amounts of blood. Passersby were amazed by the unusually large amounts of blood. Passersby were amazed by the unusually large amounts of blood. Passersby were amazed by the unusually large amounts of blood. Passersby were amazed by the unusually large amounts of

see SNIFTER page 279